PRACTICAL DREAMERS

Conversations with Movie Artists

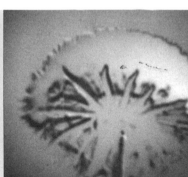

MIKE HOOLBOOM

COACH HOUSE BOOKS | TORONTO

first edition

Mike Hoolboom and Coach House Books thank the Canada Council
for the Arts for a Media Arts Dissemination grant, which supported
the creation of this book.

Practical Dreamers is published with the generous assistance of the
Canada Council for the Arts and the Ontario Arts Council. Coach
House Books also acknowledges the support of the Government of
Ontario through the Ontario Book Publishing Tax Credit Program and
the Government of Canada through the Book Publishing Industry
Development Program.

The opinions expressed herein do not necessarily reflect those of
Coach House Books.

We regret any factual errors or omissions. Should you find any, please
notify us and we will endeavour to correct them in subsequent
editions.

LIBRARY AND ARCHIVES CANADA
CATALOGUING IN PUBLICATION

Hoolboom, Michael
    Practical dreamers : conversations with movie artists /
Mike Hoolboom.

ISBN 978-1-55245-200-4 (pbk.)

    1. Motion picture producers and directors--Canada--Interviews.
2. Independent filmmakers--Canada--Interviews. 3. Experimental
films--Canada. 4. Video art--Canada. I. Title.

PN1995.9.E96H664 2008   791.43'611   C2008-902867-8

TABLE OF CONTENTS

Daniel Cockburn
Smartbomb   7

Helen Lee
Priceless   21

Deirdre Logue
Beyond the Usual Limits   35

Kent Monkman
Miss Chief   45

Nelson Henricks
Ironic Nostalgia   55

Emily Vey Duke and Cooper Battersby
I Am a Conjuror   73

Benny Nemerofsky Ramsay
The Singer   81

Shelley Niro
The Red Army Is the Strongest   91

Peter Mettler
Gambling, Gods and LSD   103

Donigan Cumming
Reality and Motive in the Documentary   111

Izabella Pruska-Oldenhof
Memos of Resistance   127

Midi Onodera
Camera Obscura for Dreams   137

John Price
Home Is a Movie   155

Daniel Barrow
After Charlie Brown and Liberace   163

Wayne Yung
My Heart the Travel Agent   169

Jayce Salloum
From Lebanon to Kelowna   185

Jeff Erbach
Soft Like Me   203

Su Rynard
After Science   211

Monique Moumblow
Doubling   221

Steve Reinke
My Rectum Is Not a Grave   231

Aleesa Cohene
Twice-Told Tales   243

Ho Tam
Season of the Boys   251

Christina Battle
Colour Processing   261

Alex MacKenzie
Blinding Light   269

Jubal Brown
Life Is Pornography   281

Paulette Phillips
Monster   293

Richard Fung
Thinking Pictures   305

INTRODUCTION

The streets are full of admirable craftsmen, but so few practical dreamers. – Man Ray

I live in a world of pictures. Once, perhaps not so long ago, the bed I sleep in, the desk I am scribbling at now, the glass in my windows – all these were pictures. They didn't come up out of the ground, these windows weren't plucked from the trees – someone thought about them once, and it's hard not to feel that the form of this thinking was in pictures. My ability to imagine this window, to create pictures, provides the frame for me to see the world. Through this frame I learn about things like: What is beautiful? Or how to behave when a car swerves into my path. Or why eating chocolate cake is better than most conversations.

Earlier this morning I was trying to understand how Thomas Jefferson could write in the American Constitution that 'all men are created equal,' even though he was a slave owner and had a long romance with one of 'his' slaves who became pregnant and had a child. To be able to refuse the evidence of your own eyes, to ignore the stirrings of your own body, and to mark a separation between a white visitor who is 'equal' and a black woman you love for years as a 'slave'; this is how pictures too often work. They are created by the powerful and beamed down (or projected, or broadcast, or printed in newspapers and billboards) to those with less power or, at least, those who lack the means of creating pictures of their own. This desk I am writing at now, the four walls of this apartment, the shape of the skyline – all these are someone else's pictures.

What would it be like if we saw movies made by individuals instead of corporations? What if there were movies made the same way as suits, custom-fitted, slimmed down for one person? Not broadcast, but narrowcast; not theatres around the world showing the same movie (the globalization of pictures) but instead a local circumstance, a movie so particular, so peculiar, it could cure night blindness or vertigo.

Welcome to the world of fringe movies, where artists from the other side of the media plantation have been busy putting queer shoulders to the wheels, or bending light to talk about First Nations rights (and making it funny at the same time), or demonstrating how a personality can be taken apart and put together again, all in the course of a ten-minute movie that might take years to make.

In this sequel to *Inside the Pleasure Dome: Fringe Film in Canada* (which sold out its first two editions), 27 Canadian artists dish about how they get it done and why it matters. The conversations are personal, up close and jargon-free, smart without smarting. The stellar cast includes Middle East maestro Jayce Salloum; queer Asian avatars Richard Fung, Midi Onodera, Ho Tam and Wayne Yung; footage recyclers Aleesa Cohene and Jubal Brown; overhead-projector king Daniel Barrow; visionary Peter Mettler; First Nations vets Kent Monkman and Shelley Niro; international art presence Paulette Phillips; and underbelly documentarian Donigan Cumming.

In the world of fringe media, the big light is lived every day by someone who looks very much like your neighbour, the person stirring up your latte, the co-worker who doesn't talk unless she's asked and asked again. It is not business or religion or hobby; there are no dreams of clutching trophies or spending vast amounts of other people's money. There are no tops and no bottoms here, no dreams of waving gold statuettes and shouting, 'I'm the king of the world,' no waiting for the applause to start, hardly a career or reputation. For the most part, these movies are a bit like reading a book with a roomful of others – everyone sees their own movie, their own way.

How much better I understood it all when I visited the old new town of Vila do Conde in Portugal, where old men are scattered across its small picturesque bridges, quietly waiting with homemade rods and buckets of lures and bait. They are fishing, and whenever I'm around, which isn't so often, everything happens very slowly – the long walk up hills disguised as streets, the perfect homemade dinner, the way fish bite on the line. The men get up early in the morning, before daybreak, and they stand there all day, sometimes only a few feet from one another, and hardly say a word. And do I even need to add that every fish they catch is hauled in and examined and then thrown back? They are unwavering in their posts, resolute in their dedication to this purposeless activity. Did I say purposeless? They have discovered, somehow, a luxury of time; they act as if they have all the time in the world, while all around them their offspring are busy getting wired and jumping into their computer time bombs, which have been created not to save time but to absorb it – like a neutron bomb of time, the computer destroys all the time that is around it, and leaves everything else intact.

The shaping of time is something fringe makers do every day. Sometimes they create movies whose only purpose is to allow their viewers to experience, for just a moment, the feeling of time that these Portugese fishermen feel. At other times they create delirious montages where pictures rush past; the point is no longer an individual picture, there is no single picture, not anymore, only a tap opening and a great rushing forward.

Mike Hoolboom

DANIEL COCKBURN
SMARTBOMB

He tells me his dreams sometimes when I run into him, which is more often than not these days. It seems we are intersecting, ready or not, but I can no more remember his dreams than my own. They are so fine I wonder why they aren't busy gracing screens across the city, though that might ruin them. The act of turning them into movies would only make them less, and so they must remain between us as a promise – a promise I can't help forgetting.

In the pages of *NOW* magazine, Cameron Bailey picked Daniel Cockburn as Toronto's best new video artist, and I can only agree. He has a rare literary talent that he serves up with visual élan, smart design sense and a playful philosophical project whose deeply lived roots are leavened throughout with humour. In fact, he's most serious when he's having fun. And even though his works appear as audio-visual feuilletons (essayistic briefs, missives from the margins), they possess an uncanny narrative order (though it is a narrativity steeped in the 20th century, not the 19th).

Here in Toronto, we are living in an age of commissions. Not Zanuck and Meyer, but Charles Street Video and Vtape. Can you imagine making art on demand? Daniel can. And when these commissioned movies arrive at last, fresh from the hard drive, there is a palpable buzz in the often home-brewed evenings, balanced by an exactly proportional degree of disappointment in the afterglow. Oh, it's only ... Except for Daniel. I don't know what it is. Perhaps the same thrill speckled rabbits get from choosing a moment to cross the road that most nearly coincides with oncoming traffic. Is it the sense that others are watching, or the more covert run of blood against blood? Whose is bigger? Faster, stronger, made to last? Not that the Canadian art scene is built on winners and losers – *au contraire*, the reigning philosophy insists that a democracy of attention be granted to anyone who asks. Is it any wonder the work often appears small and grey? But not Daniel. Not with all those borrowed movie stars swimming from the mix. And he hasn't left his Wittgenstein behind either.

The more often I see his videos, the more urgent becomes my necessity for them. Addictions are born in these oases of image. And I am not alone here. It's us now. We need these pictures, these thoughts on pictures, these new frames from which to glimpse the impossible.

Mike Hoolboom: You told me a dream once – in fact, you have narrated several, all of which I have forgotten. Am hoping you might recount again, so I can begin the task of remembering my forgetting.

Daniel Cockburn: I'm not sure if this is the dream you're thinking of, but it's the one I'm thinking of. It took the familiar shape of a horror-movie narrative; there was something terribly wrong with the world and I was the only one who knew about it. I found a MiniDV videotape in an alley and, as I picked it up, the reels started to revolve, like in *Starman* (the TV show; I never saw the movie). Jeff Bridges could hold an audiocassette to his ear, telekinetically cause the reels to turn, and hear the contents of the tape. Now the reels were turning of their own volition, and I could not see or hear what was on the tape ... but as I held it between my thumb and forefinger, watching the reels turn, I saw that the tape was slowly peeling a strip of skin off my fingers and winding it around the reels. I tried to drop the tape, but I couldn't, because my skin was inside it. I worried this process would continue until I gradually lost all of my skin to the inside of this MiniDV tape ... but some more tugging managed to snap the skin and I dropped the tape to the ground.

Later, I was with a group of people (we may have been at a restaurant, though I think that first I was in a hospital emergency room inside a mall), seated near a woman about my age whom I had never met before ... but, in familiar horror-movie-narrative fashion, I Knew That She Knew. So I leaned over to her and said, 'I think there are some terrible things happening, and that you and I are the only people who can see them.'

She responded, wide-eyed, 'Yes! Exactly! For instance ... ' and here she opened her mouth and pointed at a dark gap where two front teeth should have been. 'Look, I accidentally knocked two teeth out with my toothbrush while I was brushing my teeth this morning.'

This troubled me greatly; I knew that if teeth were so easily falling out of heads, something was amiss. She continued, 'But that's not the horrible thing. The horrible thing is that ... ' (now she points at two white teeth farther back in her mouth) '... *these* are the teeth I knocked out.' Pointing back at the dark toothless gap: '*These* teeth are still here. It's just Not Showing Up Correctly.' This, to me, was perhaps the most upsetting thing yet.

I can't remember where the dream went from there. But here's another one I had a while ago: I dreamed the existence of a 1970s TV cop show. It was about an undercover policewoman. The whole series took place with her on an ongoing undercover assignment at a summer camp for incontinent elderly people. The heroine's name was Slapper Coleco.

My dream was only about four seconds long. It was a still image, a promotional image for the TV show. The image looked like this: a woman standing in a sunlit forest, holding a gun. Beside her, text: SLAPPER COLECO, UNDERCOVER SUMMER RUBBER PANTS CAMP DETECTIVE.

MH: Do your dreams come with laugh tracks and audience applause? Mine often have closing credits (which threaten, at least occasionally, never to end – some repression of pictures seems at work, entire dreams consisting of nothing but words that appear as images of language). I am sorely tempted to offer a backseat analysis of your dreams, as they seem ripe with pictures of a threatened body in the shadow of videotape, specifically digital video. Video and the body have been a duet since the beginning, when black-and-white portapacks were too heavy to carry around easily, and artists' studio practice refocused art matters onto the body, the videotaped body. You often appear in your own work, a fact I thought initially unlikely, perhaps because you appear to lack some necessary fundament of narcissism, but of course I don't know you so well. As your work slowly gains a public life, how have you begun to reimagine your body, which has been pried loose from its physical moorings and now exists (in always younger, presumably 'better' versions) independently of you, as an image?

DC: I can't think of any dream I had that included laugh tracks or audience applause, or any indication of a studio audience. That's so TV; my dreams are cinema!

To your question of body: I have a group of media-making friends who meet irregularly, and we sometimes set each other challenges ('obstructions' in the Jorgen Leth/Lars von Trier

Rocket Man

model). A few years ago, we were speculating as to how each of us would deal with the parameters of a certain project, and one of the group said to me, 'Well, we know your movie won't have anything to do with sex!' This sentiment was laughingly echoed by everybody, including me.

That is to say, I have made it a habit of ignoring the body's presence in my life and in my motion pictures. To my mind, my body has been a mere conveyance for the life of my mind. You may disagree, since as a viewer you see only the result, not the intent, but my position as maker means I can see only the intent, never the result. (Once enough time has passed since the making of a video, the trueness of that statement fades to grey; I can look at *Rocket Man* and at the very least think it interesting that I am/was that fellow with blond tips and a beard.)

You mention that 'Video and the body have been a duet since the beginning,' but I wasn't around in any meaningful consumptive/productive sense for that beginning. I've come to video (via Super 8, 16mm and linear video editing) more or less as a 'user' in the Microsoft™ sense. The tools I know are the ones software companies deem worthy to provide, based on some sort of überdemographic knowledge they have of me whether or not I've ever filled out any survey (for the record, I'm pretty sure I haven't).

Digital video scares the crap out of me, moreso than film by a long shot. *The Other Shoe* was a not-very-veiled plea for the virtues of film over those of digitalia; *Metronome* alludes to the physical experience of life in a digital age; the/my body is presented as a thing stuck living out the mental loops of its controlling brain. Governor Schwarzenegger is condemned to the seven circles of digital hell in *WEAKEND*, and I think *Continuity* is the most explicit statement of digiphobia I've yet made. Tasman Richardson asked me after its first screening whether the scene in which I burned my hand with a cigarette was real; in

answer, I showed him the scar, reaping and revelling in the perceived benefits of full macho I-sacrifice-myself-for-my-artdom. He was glad it was so, and made the pertinent point that up until that moment there had been ambiguity about whether I was 'merely' portraying a character or existing as myself in the time of the video. But at that self-immolative moment, the two merged into one; scripted or not, That Guy Onscreen was really burning himself, the pain was real and fiction blew out the window.

Four Addenda:
1. But I feel sorry for that guy who was me, though any apology is futile since it was my fault that I made him do that.
2. Since Tasman had to ask whether the burning was real, the moment must not have been fully realized.
3. Jubal Brown fully believed that I had burned myself but asked whether the preceding nerve-steeling swig of gin was actually water; in fact, it was straight gin, but I suppressed my wincing reaction so I wouldn't seem like a wimp. The effect of my steely self-control apparently made me seem like a wimp for drinking 'fake' liquor.
4. A few days after shooting that scene, I realized how stupid it had been, since the mark on my hand was just getting worse and worse, and maybe I'd actually have a scar ... which would make me more like the scripted character than I would care to be.

Similarly (so similar, in fact, that it's probably redundant): in (repeatedly) shooting the final shot of *Stupid Coalescing Becomers.*, in which I unfall upward out of frame, I hurt my knees and they ached for days afterward. I never remember this fact when I watch or think about this video now. That guy onscreen has a lot to do with me, but he doesn't have much to do with right-now me at all.

Continuity

Certainly I harbour a fear of film, insofar as I harbour a fear of anything that purports to represent the real but whose representation is not 100 percent infallible/unquestionable (i.e., everything). But digital video seems to offer the most seemingly perfect representation while also translating it through the longest and most cryptic series of incomprehensible procedures. I remember reading a *Film Comment* article about the impending release of *Fight Club* that said, in effect, 'with the arrival of this movie, film is no longer an index of physical reality.' An exciting turning point, to be sure, and also one I keep wanting to persuade myself we haven't passed. Whatever you say about it, a film frame is an object that bears the physical imprint of reality. A videotape is an object that bears an analogically encoded imprint of reality. This is still somehow acceptable to me – but once you get into digital video, and the tape object is merely a carrier for various file formats, for language that humans will never be able to comprehend (though they may have invented it), it seems somehow heretical that we should think the image and sound that spew out the other end of this tape/computer actually embody a connection to reality. Bearing a resemblance and embodying a connection are two different things.

I make things that, without the benefit of decoding devices I can never hope to comprehend, would be unintelligible to anyone, including myself – things that, without the benefit of said devices, would cease to exist, even though their rectangular plastic-and-code containers might live for ages.

Writing all this, I am extremely dissatisfied with my expression of it; my thoughts have been translated from various states and media into this final digital output via text via fingers. And, of course, to say it is untruthful because the number of links in this chain surpasses some reverse quota would be silly. Nevertheless, I am frustrated at the chain of translations that makes the seeming truth seem to recede.

So here's something else. You asked earlier, 'How have you begun to reimagine your body, which has been pried loose from its physical moorings and now exists (in always younger, presumably better versions) independently of you, as an image?' I recently visited the dentist and was told one of my wisdom teeth is rotated 90 degrees sideways, assuming it's 'showing up correctly.' It should be taken out but it's sitting right on top of a nerve, so the operation could possibly result in losing some sensation in my lower mouth. And I wondered what it would be like if I were to have my mouth go slack/disfigured, denormalizing my face and voice. Would I still continue to use my face and voice in my videos?

I realized it would feel difficult to do so without some acknowledgement of that face's/voice's abnormality. And this made me realize that I therefore must currently be using my physical audiovisual persona as some 'normal' or 'normative' manifestation – a body and voice via which I can express all of my concerns that don't really have specifically to do with body and voice. Were my actual body to undergo some change, I would feel uncomfortable about using it as an idealized vehicle – which is ridiculous, since it implies that I consider my current (youthful white guy) body-state not only normative but idealized. I don't think I have reimagined my body at all, in an actual sense, but my encounter with my inability to reimagine it has at least exposed some of my own hypocrisy to itself.

MH: Your attentions lie with models of subjectivity and cognition, using yourself as model. What stops this from being only narcissism? There are terrifying cruelties enacted around us daily, the AIDS pandemic continues to ravage large parts of the world, genocide continues in Indonesia – what does it mean to make video art in the midst of these punishing realities? Is it only a more rarefied form of escapism?

DC: I don't think art has to change the world, only the people in it. And escape can be a form of change, provided the escapees return to the world after their stint abroad or inside, and provided said stint is a fruitful one. I think video art that speaks not one explicit word to the problems of the world is as defensible as an equally 'escapist' conversation. Political discourse is necessary, but if every verbal exchange were graded against a quota of explicitly political content, there would be a sore limitation on the number of possible dreams – to say nothing of the number of implicitly political dreams.

How it's positioned is the greater difficulty/problem. My videos certainly have a narcissistic core – and, worse!, it's the narcissism of a well-off, white North American male – but your phrase 'using [my]self as model' is key. If I examine myself closely and rigorously and honestly enough, it will be useful not only to me for my own reasons but to others for their own reasons. I'll be satisfied if people glean from my videos not 'This is what Daniel Cockburn is like' but 'This is what a particular well-off white North American male in the early 21st century is (or was) like.' I don't mean that I am submitting myself as a representative sample, a normative or ideal or 'model' citizen for time-capsule posterity (though this is a problematic subconscious tendency of my work I mentioned earlier); I mean that I am offering myself in my work as a self-expressing locus of various external tendencies at this point in time and space. My environment in large part has made me what I am, and from my work the audience may extrapolate various thoughts about that environment.

All of this, however, assumes people actually see the work. Current presentation modes ensure that my videos are seen only by a very specific slice of the population. Work away at work that will be seen by precious few? I can do nothing else, and few is infinitely better than none. To somehow preach the gospel of alternative dream-styles to the uninitiated and uninterested majority would, perhaps, if I really believe in all of the above, be less of a sellout. And anyway, I have not yet given up the ghost of narrative feature filmmaking.

MH: Doesn't your work rely on an audience already hipped to art recodings, savvy in the ways of stolen pictures, drunk and drunk again on deconstructive cocktails? Isn't this insular insider art, and isn't this the forever instance of Canadian art scenes? Hosting government-appointed screenings for the faithful, an audience of like-minded makers, where consensus is everywhere and who can even remember what you saw in the blizzard of the too many shows on offer? Politically, at least, this seems (the situation, I mean, not your work in particular) to be a large step backwards.

DC: I would like to think my work doesn't require that the audience be hip, savvy and/or drunk on art and deconstruction. Or, to put it another way, I think anyone even slightly schooled in our current mass media should already be sufficiently hip, savvy and drunk. Personal video diaries, amateur (read: non-Hollywood) narrative filmmaking, rejigging of iconic images and sounds – anybody with internet access should be familiar with these and other previously non-mainstream modes of making and receiving. And even if you don't have a broadband connection, as long as you've been watching some movies or television in the last decade, you're fully attuned to postmodern intertextuality (the contemporary version of which is certainly toothless, far from the critical weapon it was originally meant to be, but nevertheless it's a popularized form). The consuming majority accepts intertextuality in Michael Bay's *The Island*, video diaries on *Jackass* and cultural appropriation on fenslerfilm.com, so there's no reason they shouldn't accept like-minded fringe media.

Yet we know they don't. Audiences for fringe work are composed almost exclusively of fringe makers and people otherwise closely affiliated with the arts sector – and the latter set, I suspect, rarely exceeds the bounds of the former. This is at first encouraging (you get more applause from friends than you do from strangers), but eventually demoralizing. Where are the people who don't give a rat's ass about 'art,' who just want to see something good? They don't come and, frankly, I don't expect them to.

At this point, a greater obstacle than form or content might be modes of presentation. People will accept most anything if it's in a music video or on some crazy website; when they pay money to sit down and look at a screen, they expect to see movies. The parameters of what constitutes a 'movie' are broadening, but they're not yet wide open. So artists are left showing videos to each other in rec rooms that we rent with arts-council money.

This problem could be eliminated by revoking the funding, in the same way that a lot of bad art could be eliminated by dispensing with production grants. But both those tactics solve only the superficial problems. Ceasing production grants won't cause more good art (though it might up the good:bad ratio). Nor will ceasing exhibition funding cause the general public to seek out fringe work. We're in a holding pattern right now; nothing wrong with that, but the fuel doesn't last forever. What at first seems encouragement becomes lack of criticality; the community is so small and interconnected that I think people are terrified to express honest opinions of bad work – how, then, are artists supposed to get better?

Is the solution for video art and fringe film to enter the market – not the art or educational market, but the popular market? Sure, the popular market will not necessarily support the most worthy work; even in our current system, artists struggle to achieve a standardized level of compensation for their work. Every impulse I have with regards to this situation feels more capitalist than I thought I was. I'm not convinced that that is always awful. I'm not convinced, you may say, of much.

In summary (working backwards): my art is made for and shown in an insular insider art scene, but it is not insular insider art.

MH: Why can't artists produce work that conforms to more generally accepted media portals: the feature film or 50-minute television documentary? Why all this work on the signifier, on skewing the form, changing the way we show pictures or listen to sounds? Does it really make new experiences possible? I used to think so, but that would mean that fringe devotees would be exemplars of virtue, their happiness organs bigged up on all those hours of difficult light. But fringe media is hardly a guarantor of a better life, so why bother?

DC: Refusing to make your work accessible is not a sin, though doing so for no reason other than elitism or spite is plain silly, and I think that refusing in your creative process to acknowledge and incorporate the existence of your audience is at least a mortal error. Certain types of experience cannot be transmitted in the feature-film or 50-minute-TV-doc format, just as certain types of experiences that those formats transmit so well are anathema to short-film or non-narrative work. Not all art has to be free, unfettered newness, but the spectrum of available art absolutely has to be an arena of possibility, otherwise what's the point? Form can be founded on a moral foundation, but that doesn't mean form will necessarily generate morality in the receiver. This is how communication works, and we have to take what we can get (and give what we hope can be gotten).

My experiences of fringe transcendence are pleasures like no other I know. Why shouldn't new pleasure be a worthwhile offering? Our happiness organs do get bigged up on light-bending – it's just on a very narrow spectrum of happiness. This is a problem if you mistake light-happiness for world-happiness, which is certainly the case for some of us who get a

Subterranea Gargantua (Prelude)

certain horizon-broadening from fringe work and then seek out a repeat of that same, lovely, immensifying feeling at screening after screening, rather than going out looking for it in a world whose horizons have supposedly just been broadened. Every pleasure carries within it the seeds of addiction.

However deluded or realistic our motives, we who are familiar with experimental form and work are prepared to wade through the shit for the good stuff. The general public isn't, nor should they be. If a chef friend took me to a tapas restaurant that she highly recommended, and we ordered 20 dishes, two of which were mind-blowingly succulent, 14 of which were passable and four of which were repugnant, would I not be justified in refusing to return (especially if I knew the menu was entirely changed twice daily)? The festival-programming or curated-screening format works for those of us who are already in the thick of things, but hoping that people open up to new ideas on the basis of an assorted appetizer platter is at best naive – and thinking that the appetizer platter is the only kind of meal there is is dangerous self-limitation at the individual and the community level.

A previously typed aside that no longer feels integrated but that I cannot quite bring myself to delete: the MuchMusic Video Awards just named 50 Cent 'the year's best video artist.' Video art obviously has a very different meaning for most people than it does for us. Not to say we're right and they're wrong, but the phrase's current majority definition obscures the existence of the type of work we're talking about. The only other 'video art' reference in the public canon I can think of is David Thewlis's portrayal of 'Knox Herrington, the video artist' in the Coen Brothers' *The Big Lebowski* – itself only half-public, but an underground cult thing of the above-mentioned order that I would love to see some experimental work attain (and anyway, you haven't seen that movie, or at least you hadn't when Mike Bullard asked you about it, so maybe you're the problem here) – which more or

less reaffirms the general cliché stereotype of video art=high pretension.

I feel my answers are growing increasingly committed to absolute diplomacy; my eyes are sliding farther apart from one another and soon I'll have one over each ear, resolutely seeing both sides of everything. Which will be great, except that I won't be able to see where I came from or where I'm heading.

MH: What kinds of experiences can't be relayed through mainstream portals? And what is it in your biography (real or simulated), or your work, that can't be dished up in familiar audiovisual formattings?

DC: The image-propagation world is growing; it's increasingly the world in which we communicate with one another and experience imagination. The more often pictures replace the world we live in, the more we accept dominant forms as a fundamental syntax. As advertising, feature films, TV, news, video games and the worldwide web converge, we need to remember that, for example, while moving images may not be the ideal way to convey foreign policy news, moving images that borrow specifically from advertising or video game forms can only limit such conveyance even further.

We can use images to explore alternate ways of transmitting and receiving – oh, but what ways are they? That was your question, wasn't it? I'll answer by first seemingly avoiding it for a little while longer.

Images are becoming less and less precious, and their connection to our world increasingly superficial and misleading (and this goes back to my greater fear of DV than of film). I think this leads us to regard our own lives as less precious.

Tarkovsky said, 'I think that what a person normally goes to the cinema for is time,' and he wasn't just talking about art-house audiences. All films offer an experience of time segments that have been elongated or compressed into a singular experience (otherwise why not just have a relationship with time on the street outside the ticket booth?). The current trend is one of speed and diversion; these have their uses, but at this point the fringe is where I have to go to find the alternative.

There is one place you can find plenty of static shots, and that is TV advertising. We have learned that slowness can be appreciated, but only briefly; slownesses thus follow one another with great rapidity, as refreshing as ice cubes shooting out of a volcano.

Gus van Sant's recent work (and he, I suppose, is on the fringe of the mainstream) is exemplary of current success in this regard; watching *Gerry* or *Elephant*, one becomes reacquainted with the pleasures of long-form attentiveness summoned forth by a slow-moving object, and I'd like to think I carry the taste for this pleasure outside with me afterwards. I'm convinced we'd be better off were the world at large (me included) more attuned to such things; longer attention span means greater capability of complex thought, means greater empowerment (and awareness on which to found your choice as to what to do with your power). I've made stabs at this kind of pleasure with *The Other Shoe* and *The Impostor (hello goodbye)*, placing single takes in a multiframe context, which I hope will point out their purity while distracting from and, sadly, destroying it. Not that I am fixated on slowness and the long-take aesthetic, or that I think we need to become a society of humanoid glaciers; *Metronome* and *Stupid Coalescing Becomers.* both seek to foreground time awareness via other means (rhythm and reversal).

You also mention my 'work on the signifier, on skewing the form, changing the way we show pictures or listen to sound.' I hope that in my appropriation I manage to express my relation to the current way in which I receive pictures and sounds, thus providing a model for my own thought, which can form a model for the viewer's. I can't imagine this would have as much chance of success on, for example, television, where in the first place image appropriation is illegal and, secondly, it would be subsumed into the background noise, becoming indistinguishable from its original sources. My appropriation videos are preplanned and highly controlled channel-surfing, as indeed is any montage; in this sense their pleasure is the same as the pleasure of narrative film. The other pleasure, though, is that of being taken on a guided surf through the media we've already consumed; this will hopefully spread the desire to reorder the contents of one's own brain to arrive at one's own conclusions.

If I still haven't answered some of your questions, prod further, prodfessor.

MH: I've always wanted to make a movie in paralyzing slow motion so that afterwards, after watching someone get off a chair for half an hour, or drink a glass of milk for ten minutes, one could leave the theatre and everything would appear strangely sped up. But of course these effects don't last; these perceptual oases are temporary effects, the crack cocaine of the picture world, soon requiring another hit to keep the senses from reorienting. How to deal with our present deluge of too many pictures? Why bother producing when there's already too much, knowing that whatever you do will so very quickly become subsumed in the evening news, the morning headline, the restless chatter of celebrity?

DC: If by 'these effects don't last,' you mean they don't last forever, then I agree. But I also agree that they're temporary, and anything that's temporary does last, just not infinitely. And just because something isn't infinite doesn't mean it's not worthwhile – the pyramids have lasted quite a while, and they're likely to last a long while longer, but they are definitely not going to last.

I was about 13 when I saw *Midnight Cowboy*, and today, the one thing that stands out for me is not any of its famous lines or images, but a small speck of time in which Jon Voight defends his cowboy attire to Dustin Hoffman. 'Why do you have to make fun of my clothes?' he says. 'I like these clothes and I like the way I look in them. I feel good about myself when I wear them.' I was a teenager with an intellectual-superiority complex living in a small town, and this moment forced me ever so subtly, but consciously, to reconsider my sense of being better than a lot of people around me on the sole basis of personal taste. And that moment of consciousness is one I have returned to (or have had returned to me) over the years, up to and including even now, whenever associations conspire to re-uncover it.

Things get subsumed, but, as I mentioned, they leave residue, and that layer of intra-cranial grime can certainly last, and even occasionally contain seeds.

MH: Daniel, as usual, you put it so well. Grime that contains seeds, or as Jonas Mekas once asked, 'Where are we, the underground?' It's too much for anyone to bear, to carry the burden of representation for all pictures, all the time. Pictures, we imagine them (don't we?) as something evanescent, made of light, as light as air, and yet sometimes they're heavier than lead. And just as opaque.

I would like to shift focus and speak about a couple of your movies. Can you talk about *Stupid Coalescing Becomers.* (2:31 min, 2004)? It is a backwards time fantasy, a home movie redressed as science fiction. Would you briefly describe the movie and tell me how it came about?

DC: *Stupid Coalescing Becomers.* is a three-minute video with continuous voice-over. The images are fairly standard backwards footage: a cigarette burns from ash to fullness, a hammer-wielding hand smashes glass shards into light bulbs, etc. The voice-over is a moral diatribe against the 'stupid coalescing becomers' who think they can avoid acknowledging the cause-and-effect workings of the world by temporarily (but ultimately futilely, in the narrator's opinion) reversing time for themselves. The narrator's identity is ambiguous; even at the end, when a human body falls reversedly up and out of the frame, it's uncertain (unless you know me) as to whether this body is the

WEEKEND

narrator's or whether it belongs to one of the Becomers.

A few years ago, I met up with Jeremy Rigsby (artistic director of the Media City Festival in Windsor, Ontario) at the opening night of Toronto's Images Festival. I asked him at one point whether he had seen a Super 8 film called *Smartbomb* (the filmmaker's name did and does escape me, though it might have been Marnie Parrell), and he said there were too many experimental films called *Smartbomb*, and someone should make a film called the opposite of *Smartbomb*. 'Stupid ... Flowers?' was the tentative first title suggestion, but we gradually came to the conclusion that the opposite of an exploder would be a coalescing becomer. We both agreed that someone should make a film or video called *Stupid Coalescing Becomers.*, and I thought it would be lovely and hilarious if I could present him with a vhs tape containing said movie before he went home at festival's end. So I made the movie that weekend (adding the period to the end of the title for greater assertive effect, the three-word phrase having taken on a definite insulting third-person tendency) and gave him the vhs tape on closing night when I said goodbye. He got a good laugh out of it (my handing him the tape, that is), which was the sum of my original intent, to please someone and myself not with the movie itself, but simply with the fact of its existence.

Then, of course, I hemmed and hawed about it for a year and a half, vaguely thinking about re-editing, re-recording some voice-over ... I can't remember if I made any cosmetic changes before mastering it and taking it off my hard drive, but I probably didn't.

The backwardness seemed a natural concept with that title as the starting point; I think I was leery of the fact that I'd already seen several experimental videos that year alone that took backwards footage as their main selling point: Saki Satomi's *M. Station Backward*; Eno-Liis Semper's *FF/REV*. I hadn't (and haven't) seen Jeroen Offerman's *Stairway at St. Paul's*, but I'd heard plenty about it, where he learned 'Stairway to Heaven' backwards and sang it while people strolled past. Most of the ones I'd seen were good, but taken together it seemed like artists were in need of a new hook, and here I was making another backwards movie. So I think the voice-over grew out of a tendency to chastise them and myself for using a device that, let's face it, has been around long before that guy backwards-sang 'What a Wonderful World' on *America's Funniest People* back in the '80s. And, it occurs to me, my above description of the Becomers as beings who 'think they can avoid acknowledging the cause-and-effect workings of the world by temporarily (but ultimately futilely, in the narrator's opinion) reversing time for themselves' fits with your previous and implied definition of video artists/audiences as wilful self-oblivionizers.

MH: In the future, not only an iPod, but iDrives in iCars. iMovies already exist (you claim you make them yourself), and iJournalism we already see too much of. Now, let's see. Your *WEEKEND* (7:15 min, 2003) project turned Governor Arnold Schwarzenegger into a reflexive digital philosopher. Can you write about how this project began, how restrictions (prohibitions, taboos) can provide freedom, and why the governor is a particular apt figure (or is he?) for the new role into which you've cast him.

DC: How it began is the easiest question. Media-art collective famefame curated a program called *Attack of the Clones* for the Tranz Tech Media Art Biennial 2003 in Toronto. The call for submissions requested videos whose sole audio/video source was *The 6th Day*, a Roger Spottiswoode–directed Hollywood sci-fi film whose star is Arnold Schwarzenegger and whose subject is cloning. The idea was, of course, that all videos in the program would have the same DNA, so to speak – all clones of the original 35mm opus.

I want to answer the question of how restrictions (or, rather, let's call them parameters) can provide freedom. It makes me think of the Lars von Trier/Jorgen Leth film *The Five Obstructions*, in which von Trier gives Leth a series of assignments consisting of parameters to which Leth must adhere in remaking his own short film *The Perfect Human*. Leth breaks the rules in the second assignment and von Trier punishes him by making the next assignment devoid of parameters: absolute freedom. Leth retreats to his hotel room, where he laments, 'This is the worst one yet.'

We always have restrictions, more and less visible, when we make anything. You can't make a video that lasts longer than the life of the universe; you can't have a projection screen bigger than Ontario; you can't render explicit something you're too frightened to admit. It's simply a useful exercise to start out with a more-defined-than-usual parameter set. In the case of *WEEKEND*, my remix of *The 6th Day*, I was very excited about the project – until I finally watched the film and was so underwhelmed by its content and images that I felt sullenly noncommittal. The best I could come up with was a series of digital gimmicks to perpetrate upon Arnold, which would be fun but hardly seemed enough to hang a video on. So I felt I needed to give them some context and use (and also expiate my moral twinges at playing with Arnold so cruelly, doing to Arnold what I usually do to myself) by giving Arnold the epilogue in which he criticizes the proceedings.

By splicing together words, or parts of words, I have him speak a new text: 'You think you are a media artist because you control me with a piece of software? This is terrible. This is not natural,' and so on.

You know, I saw footage of Ronald Reagan's funeral, or at least memorial service, and Schwarzenegger was there, and he made the sign of the cross, but I could swear he made it backwards: up-down-right-left instead of up-down-left-right. Mirror images of religious iconography do not often portend well, at least in my experience (of watching horror movies and other less interesting movies in which characters played by people like Arnold Schwarzenegger fight demons). It also occurs to me that perhaps the explanation is simple: the image itself was flipped mirrorwise for some purely pragmatic reason known only to the networks. Which itself is cause for alarm in ways I hope I've already expressed at length in this interview.

MH: We were both invited a couple of years ago to produce a short video as a reaction to the life and work of the late Canadian video artist Colin Campbell. One of the curiosities of this commission was that Colin had long been surrounded by über talents from the art world, but Lisa Steele, the woman who commissioned the project through Vtape, a distribution organization co-founded by Colin and Lisa, amongst others, approached only artists who didn't know Colin well. She always has an eye for outreach, and it was from this missionary position that the work advanced. I felt ambivalent about the results, particularly because Colin was dead, so there was no way he could defend or represent himself (why do I imagine defence and representation are the same?). To add this insult to his untimely death: a badly made piece of video art struck in his name. I was confused by your movie, *The Impostor (hello goodbye)* (8:48 min, 2003), when I first saw it: it was so archly ironic and spoke incessantly about death, but in an almost cartoon fashion, without any feeling at all, though there is much mention of tears. When I saw it I thought it was an image of an image of grieving. But now that I've soaked in it awhile and screened it more often, it's becoming clearer. I've crossed some threshold of your intention and am happier for it. I'm wondering if you can talk about its making and your thoughts about Colin.

DC: I hadn't realized that *The Colin Campbell Sessions* were such an outreach project. (Nor am I sure which video you're referring to as 'a bad piece of video art struck in his name' – all of them,

perhaps? Including your own?) Are you sure none of the artists involved knew Colin? I was under the impression that at least you had known him; you've certainly done well to foster this impression in eyes mine and public with your own Colin video and with much allusive talk and activity since. But maybe you aren't counting yourself.

Anyhow, it's funny if you are right about that, because my entire video is a response to my (mis?-)apprehension that everyone else in the program had been intimately familiar with and influenced by the man and his work, whereas I had virtually no knowledge of either. I thought it had been assumed that I, like everyone else, was a Colin-friend and Colin-ophile, and I felt I'd be a fraud if I accepted and took the money and got the glory – but then I figured that to come clean about this in the video would be even braver than declining the invitation altogether.

So, of course, my 'coming clean' is a little cryptic, and I've substituted a fictional dream about my fictionally dead father for my real misgivings about Colin. This is partly because saying exactly and artlessly what you mean is generally, well, artless, and partly because (I must come clean here!) I was afraid of saying what I meant.

Even as artifice-woven as it is, at its premiere I was very afraid that in so exposing my own ignorance and fraudulence amidst an audience of Colin's friends, advocates and aficionados, I was about to pour salt in their wounds and incur their wrath ('Who is this nobody who made us think he was somebody and then rubbed it in our faces after we'd already given him recognition?').

But the reception was warm, so either they didn't get it – which would likely be a combination of their inattentiveness and my intent-obscuring crypticism – or I had managed to extrapolate from my feelings about my non-feelings about Colin a less specific and more resonant experience. I don't know how much I can agree with you that it's unemotional. Certainly it's inexpressive facially and vocally, as I usually am in my videos (I try to know my limitations), and you also call it 'cartoonish,' which reminds me that most of my videos (including this one) evoke audience laughter, which I get such a quick taste for that I forget the surprise and conflict I felt on first hearing it.

Alex Glenfield's music is the emotional anchor of the movie (Tarkovsky said that electronic music at its ideal could 'be like someone breathing'). I think anybody who finds *The Impostor* entirely arch or comical is focusing so much on the text that the music is not allowed to get under the skin. Alex composed and recorded it a couple of years before I was invited to make the video, and he first played me the CD while I was formulating the concept. I thought it would be appropriate for *The Impostor*, with its waxing/waning, loop-like structure, and when he told me the title and the sonic ingredients, I knew it was doubly perfect. He'd been thinking, he told me, about Morse code and its use as a means for soldiers to send messages to their allies during wartime. Would anyone ever have formulated a message for his enemy?, he wondered, a proposal that sounds melancholy and humane to my ears, and so he made this piece of music that is the phrase *For my enemy* in Morse code, repeated and superposed at various pitches. (There is also, he later told me, a second Morse code phrase in the piece, but no one has yet been able to decipher it, and he refuses to tell.)

It seemed fitting, since the character in the video has an adverse relationship to his late father (who is also himself) – an antagonism born of disassociation, of one party's ignorance and the other's absence. If the video is resonant, it's because of his attempt to throw a connective rope over this chasm, even as a third aspect of himself scissors the rope into little bits. And this is a pretty good expression of the way I feel, or don't, about Colin.

By this I mean Colin is an influence at second remove; I understand his work by having heard people talk about it, by having seen work made in its shadow. So my work is the shadow of a shadow, a second-generation copy at best. For me, in the context of video art, Colin is like, for instance, Orson Welles (and I mean the Welles of *Chimes at Midnight* and *It's All True!*, not the Welles who made *Citizen Kane* and *Touch of Evil* and the other few that I actually have seen), or like all the Godard or Snow that I know enough about to pretend I've seen if the conversation doesn't get too specific.

And if we stand on the shoulders of those who come before us, then I'm standing on someone who's standing on Colin's shoulders, and I've gotten to this height to no credit of my own (no self-aggrandizing, this – by 'height' I only mean the point at which everybody now is at, as a result of everything made up until now).

And I want to build on what I'm standing on, not just fritter away my vantage point from atop the dead, yet it feels that to do so I have to wrest attention away from them, toward myself (because attention is a finite resource). I don't know if they are my enemy – I doubt it, in fact, for they have given me so much – but quite often I feel I am theirs (or maybe *rival* is a more accurate, less stinging though also less evocative term than *enemy*).

At any rate, I feel a need to justify or defend myself – even if only to myself, to make me happy. And as you imply, defence equals representation, so I can at least represent myself. That's *The Impostor*, and Colin, and me.

I am, of course, wondering what was the threshold of my intention that you crossed, and where you found yourself.

MH: I met Colin only twice, and he lit me up like a fuse before disappearing again into that swarm of adoring and remarkable friends that I am slowly getting to know as I continue this project of portraiture, chasing his echoes. When we glanced off one another, he seemed a formidable figure from the past of a medium I had embraced only recently. He was able to make magic when video meant black and white and bad sound and no editing, so his practice provides, just as you suggest, the necessary sediment, the firmament, on which we are having this discussion.

You make a gesture toward this ur-time with your tape, which is made in a single shot (no edits), as a performance for camera, a first-person funeral oration for your dead father. You deliver this monologue in a manner Colin would have relished, brimful with irony. But irony is very low on my pleasure register; the joys of camp and kitsch have proven elusive – I am either not large or not small enough to appreciate them. The music you mention, I must confess, has breezed past four or five times now with hardly a notice, not that music requires notice to be effective, but I am fixated, as usual, on your performing presence. In this movie you play a self-conscious fairy-taler who narrates a dreamed deathbed visitation with dear old Dad and then hyperbolizes a moment of response at the funeral. Your inheritance, you insist, relies on the volume of tears you can wring from your audience. This is all recounted in such a studied fashion that the first few times I watched I felt nothing but far away. Is this the theatre that old Brecht had in mind? The alienation effect, the ability to study the scene in front of you without the mess of identification. The truth is, I still don't find it moving, but as George Lucas once said, hitting a cat on the head with a hammer is emotionally stirring for audiences, and anyone can do that. I once felt Colin's passing deserved more, but no longer. I don't believe your movie needs to reach past itself to provide emotional transport for strangers. Nor to provide a stage for our emotions, or to demonstrate how emotions are made (oh look, they're crying, no wonder I feel sad). Instead, your movie offers the more vicarious pleasures of the meta-verse: not emotions, but emotions that are about emotions. And this is familiar ground to me. All of my dreams take place in bookshops and cinemas. I know it must have been different for previous generations, perhaps for someone like Colin, who could dream of something like primary experiences, actual encounters, instead of reading about them in a book inside a dream. And then, of course, there are the generations who came before Colin, some born before the unconscious was invented. What hope for these brave men and women who were left no apparatus to dream with?

DC: I'll begin with a technicality: it is true that *The Impostor* is made in a single shot, but it's not entirely true that it is without edits. There is one not-quite-hidden but not-usually-noticed dissolve that enables me to present an 18-minute take as a nine-minute (hopefully invisible) split-screen. (I feel uncomfortable saying this, as if I were Hitchcock letting the dead mother out of the bag just because it seemed a fitting thing to do in the middle of a chat with some decent fellow down at the press club.)

I always run into this problem of doing things I know are alienating not because of any really marvellous reasons that Brecht might have had, but because that's the approach I identify with. The alienating tactic isn't alienating to me, not at all; it's the expression of how I feel about the material.

Hal Hartley described himself as a scientist carrying out an experiment, telling the audience what's going to happen before it happens, making them recognize that the movie they're watching is just a shred of film passing past a light bulb. His aim is not to destroy their emotional experience – quite the opposite. When this experiment succeeds, it creates a kind of magic – not only are we involved and invested, in spite of ourselves, in things we know to be untrue, but we are aware that this is the case, that we have this desire. In his view, this bald-faced suspension of disbelief is a fuller goal than the conventional one of total immersion, which he calls 'emotional effect as opposed to emotional involvement.'

I read this in an interview years ago; looking at it again now, it seems I internalized it enough that I applied its method to an artifact composed of its own method's metaphorical ingredients: *The Impostor*'s introductory remarks give away the ending, the lab scientist foregrounds the film strip's passing and both onscreen figures reveal their identities' shared artifice.

MH: What a terrific answer – even your sidesteppings are terrific. I hope you are not feeling that my intention is to keep you spinning round the centrifuge until all your features flatten into some grotesque, uniform, two-dimensional space. The grotesque is best appreciated in three dimensions, don't you think?

DC: In Borges' 'Funes the Memorious,' the narrator has a conversation with a man incapable of forgetting anything, and expresses his anxiety thus: 'I thought that each of my words (that each of my movements) would persist in his implacable memory; I was benumbed by the fear of multiplying useless gestures.' I know this interview is creeping along, and it's because of the anxiety I feel in committing words to a likely life beyond my control. This anxiety manifests as half-compulsion to make the words right, half-reticence to make them at all.

So for now I'll keep putting it off by resurrecting the words of others, throwing zombie texts up in front of myself as a front line of defence. Atom Egoyan wrote, in the foreword to your *Fringe Film in Canada* book: '[I]s the traditional grammar of cinema a direct expression of how we dream? Do we dream in multi-angle coverage, with static masters, close-ups, tracking shots, and pans? Do we never cross the magical axis, except when we wake out of our sleep in terror? Is this why the language of early cinema came so quickly – because we've been playing it inside our heads forever?'

I heard him espousing this theory in a radio interview a few years before I read it (and, I imagine, before he wrote it), and when I first heard him (paraphrasing himself before his time?), I thought, 'How wonderful, how true.' But now I'm more inclined to think it's something a film director would say and a film student would believe. It certainly has the ring of aphoristic truth to it, and it still pleases me, but I'm more compelled to believe that Egoyan's connection is backwards. The contemporary language of dreams is indeed the language of cinema, not the other way around; the language inside our heads has come to us because we've been playing it to ourselves incessantly for the last hundred years.

We dream about our apparatus, or at least in its language. Maybe the pre-cinema people were tied to other machines and languages, maybe they dreamed more words than we do. The dreams of the even older past are still around, but I don't think they're compatible with our dreams. Our dreams are noisy and addictive, and I think they drown out the old ones.

My friend had a dream once in which he opened a book, read it in its entirety, closed it and awoke. Now, that's what I call a dream! But of course it's still using the language of an apparatus, just an older one. I wish I dreamed more about bookstores. Borges dreamed about texts (and about dreams, ad infinitum), and he put the 'words' outside the parentheses, the 'movements' inside. His words were the primary experience, his body the secondary, but what else could be expected of a dreamer whose apparatus was the library?

The hope for those brave gone people, as you mentioned earlier, might be that they need not fear the multiplication of their gestures, useless or otherwise. (They may well have not even understood this fear, except dimly, abstractly, as a literary or pre-literary fantasy.) They can rest in peace – if silence, invisibility and stillness amount to peace. Though if they do, then I wonder what hope for us.

MH: Are stories a way to 'kill' time, a way to foreshorten the drift I feel settling in as each day trips past, heedless, joining all the other small habits of all the other small days in that pool of forgetting I insist on calling myself?

DC: Stories are a way to reacquaint ourselves with time, which can also mean reacquainting ourselves with mortality. I saw *Broken Flowers* a few weeks ago, and I can't say I thought it was thoroughly great, but there were a couple of minutes during which I knew I was going to die. I write it now and it just feels like words, almost like a lie, but for that brief time it was a new understanding, intense and acceptable. I knew it was new, and I also knew it would probably leave me soon, and it did.

The Impostor (hello goodbye)

The fact that I have absolutely no recollection which part of the movie's 'story' (in the sense of 'plot') brought this on shows, I think, that it was not a purely plot-based epiphany, but rather one enabled by some temporal experience.

MH: Take heart, we are nearing the end. But not before you scribble a few words about *Metronome* (10:40 min, 2002), your breakout hit. I remember when James Benning released *American Dreams*, the Hoberman review in the *Village Voice* asked: *avant-garde MVP?* And something of that shadow hung over *Metronome*; it was just so smart and hurting and funny. If I'm remembering correctly, it was yet another commission, and features yourself, of course, the last beating heart of the video fringe. Or the first one. What might be curious, for the singularity trackers, those in search of an artist's interiority, is that this movie, which so flamboyantly and elegantly demonstrated your own, is largely made up of other people's pictures. Do you see what I see?

DC: Yes, I suppose I do.

But to agree feels a little too close to an admission of defeat, or at least defeatism, taking the stance that all worthwhile images have already been made, so there's nothing left to do but shift them around like puzzle pieces. The famefame group seem to occupy this position (or, at least, they seem to profess to occupy it). The extreme aggression of their reorganization is an attempt to annihilate received pictures and, hopefully, reveal something behind. I think the project is a good one, but I can't agree with its despairing impulse. If I thought there were no more new images left to be made and/or found, I doubt I would be very interested in looking at them or working with them – or, at least, I would no longer be able to convince myself that doing so had more to do with joy than addiction.

It is very true, though, that the invention of imagery is not my strong suit. The images I shoot myself (or get friends to shoot for me) are usually illustrative of ideas but not seductive in their own right (this is a discredit not to my friends' shooting skills, but rather to my imagistic imagination). The pictures are there to support the narrative throughline, and I'm capable of making them do that undistractingly, while also ensuring that they don't look crappy, but I have made relatively few shots I find really aesthetically pleasing. The single widescreen shot of *The Impostor*; portions of *The Other Shoe*'s black-and-white 16mm slowfall; certain compositions in *Doctor Virtuous*, *You Are In A Maze* and *Stupid Coalescing Becomers*. – not much else really springs to mind.

Metronome is all about a mind formed by the images of others, so it's only fitting that it be comprised in large part of pictures from outside. But I'm less interested in that nowadays, maybe

every night,
the man heard
his upstairs neighbour

hit the floor.

The Other Shoe

because I've done a couple of post-production-heavy remix projects and I feel like I want to get my hands on the world again. Maybe because I've seen so much remixing and puzzle-piecing even in the three years since I made *Metronome* that I feel that confining ourselves to existing images is a deader end than trying to make new ones. And maybe because I know this is something I need to practice, to get better at, because I've always known that thinking in pictures can go farther when it's combined with invention, aesthetic and otherwise.

I'm a singularity tracker too. I understand they used to be called auteurists.

Metronome's conceptual starting point is my attempt to keep a steady beat for an extended period of time. It's a 'day in the life' movie, from breakfast to bedtime, with me pounding my own chest at 144 beats per minute in sync with a constant table-drumming on the soundtrack. A just-as-insistent voice-over makes a fairly deterministic and despairing relation between meter/order/loops and the experience of repetitive thought patterns.

The monologue acknowledges its debt to other monologue-based movies I've seen (repeatedly, in many cases), and goes on from there to speculate on how two decades of moviegoing has insinuated certain aesthetic and ideological beats into the polyrhythm that is my psyche. Footage from narrative feature films (primarily Hollywood, with a focus on science fiction and its love-hate relationship with order) is intercut with the me-footage; both sets of images are for the most part illustrations of the internal monologue. I could also say it begins with a Wittgenstein aphorism via Steve Reich: 'How small a thought it takes to fill a whole life!' – in a way, that says it all (how could it not?).

MH: My previous question still waits answering: how is it possible to arrive at something like auteur moments via quotation? How do you manage to express your subjectivity through others' pictures?

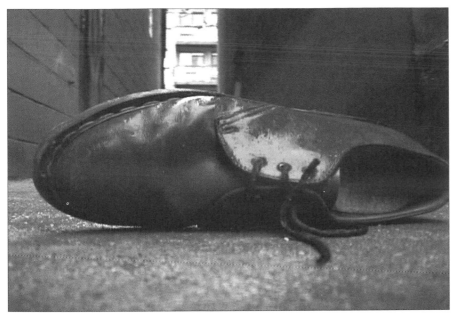
The Other Shoe

there are plenty of such image-makers, neither I nor anybody else knows about them. I don't see how it would be possible to learn from such an example; if the task is to be invisible, where do you find pictures of your role models?

I understand 'subjectivity' to mean a singularity through which the world is passing in a particular way, in a particular order, 'a piece of the world through which the world looks at itself,' as Italo Calvino described his Mr. Palomar describing himself. And since a subjectivity can't take a picture of itself, it can only take a picture of the world. I suppose the goal in self-expression is to take enough pictures of the world that the viewer undergoes an analogue of the self's experience. And if that world the self is taking pictures of is already full of other people's pictures, then so be it.

DC: I hadn't realized you asked that. If I were limited further – e.g., if I were unable to write and perform voice-over – then personal expression would be harder for me to achieve – though didn't I say in talking about one of my remix movies that I liked restrictions, parameters, limitations? So strange that this conversation, which has taken months, is going to be compiled into a single something that will take minutes to read. Contradictions and redundancies I would have never noticed, separated by weeks, will arrive on top of one another.

At any rate, I do have all these other tools at my disposal, to say nothing of montage. In *Metronome*, you could say that the appropriated footage is like a POV shot, and the footage of me is a reaction shot. My voice-over, in connecting the two, fulfills the function that would in classical cinema be fulfilled by my eyeline. This might in fact be more subjective, since it's a shot-reverse-shot alternation motivated by the mind's eye rather than the retina's (of course, saying this assumes some primal connection between language and subjectivity).

Your question implies an equation of picture ownership with subjectivity ownership. I want to agree with that equation, but I'm not sure it holds water. Pictures are part of the world now. It's ridiculous to lay claim to them, and it's ridiculous to say others have already legitimately done so. Yet we do every day. Our careers as filmmakers or video artists depend on our ability to put our names on packages of pictures. You or I or anyone might espouse the belief in an open-source model of image accessibility (though, for the record, I currently don't), but that speaks only to the control-related aspect of ownership. Unless you cease associating your name with the works you make, cease reaping the benefits of the attention those works garner and allow yourself to recede into anonymity and obscurity, you're claiming some ownership of images. Ego is another aspect of ownership, and I think very few image-makers are willing to forfeit the opportunity to propagate their ego across space and time. If

Daniel Cockburn's Videos and Films

Doctor Virtuous   5:30 min 1999
Rocket Man   5 min 2000
monopedal Joy   1:20 min, 2001
The Other Shoe   5:10 min 2001
IdeaL   2:18 min 2002
You Are In A Maze Of Twisty Little
   Passages, All Different   9:11 min 2002
Metronome   10:40 min 2002
i hate video   8 min 2002
PSYCHO / 28 x 2   3 min 2002
Subterranea Gargantua (prelude)   3 min 2002
WEAKEND   7:15 min 2003
The Impostor (hello goodbye)   8:48 min 2003
Denominations   1 min 2003
Audit   3 min 2003
Figure vs. Ground   7 min 2004 (with Emily Vey Duke)
Nocturnal Doubling   4:07 min 2004
Chicken/Egg: The Williams Equation   1 min 2004
Continuity   21:58 min 2004
Stupid Coalescing Becomers.   2:31 min 2004
Brother Tongue/Langue Fraternelle   15:43 min 2006

Single-channel works distributed by Vtape.

Daniel Cockburn lives in Toronto. He is currently at work on a feature-length video (working title *You Are Here*). In 2009 he will be a filmmaker-in-residence at the DAAD Artists-in-Berlin Program. For information on his videos, films and writing, visit www.zeroFunction.com.

HELEN LEE

PRICELESS

She was supposed to be far too famous to be in a book like this. *Helen Lee!* She should have eaten up the director's fortnight at Cannes, then produced her crossover hit, before retreating back into a first-person cinema that hurts to look at, the way you turn your eyes from certain kinds of beauty. But there are some dreams that only someone else's money can buy.

Like Jeff Erbach, who appears elsewhere in this volume, Helen can't just pick up a camera and go wandering out into the streets in search of the good light and a face that looks back. Instead, she needs a script and a director of photography and a crew to realize the pictures that are lying inside her. These capital-intensive efforts mean that picture-making is a slow and sometimes cumbersome affair, and one that involves waiting and organizing and turning yourself into a personal bureaucrat. She has handled all that on a small scale in her work to date and produced a suite of glowing promissory notes that elegantly lend stories to a post-colonial condition. She is one of the smartest filmmakers I've ever met, rousing herself out of a temporary haze of shoe stores and insider food jokes to lay down incisive and unsettling critiques. The pictures that have already arrived and the pictures that are in the midst of being born, they cut to the quick. They are somehow always unexpected, as if one were ambushed by a cool beauty, the steady throb of minor-key glamour, the raw intelligence that bursts out of the background details.

MH: Helen, I am just back in Toronto from Windsor's Media City Festival, a gathering of fringe moviemakers bent under a rigorous light. Landscapes rules, okay? Silent movies are better than sound. It was a stern demonstration of a cinema that remains abstract, first-person, sometimes lyric, reflexive to a fault, an examination of the apparatus and of the act of the seeing itself. And, of course, it was helmed by white males. Everywhere I looked there were more white males, like me. And I found this distressing, that this 'genre' had been commandeered, once again, without anyone saying a word, by more white males. As if dominance in the dominant genres weren't enough. Of course, we were all crouched behind our marginal attitudes, our First World poverties, and whenever I brought up the fact that this festival was dedicated to staging a white aesthetic, people looked at me as if I'd swallowed all the blue pills and not the red ones like I was supposed to. Have racial politics taken a giant step backwards over the past decade? Has the constant bludgeoning of the neo-con right won out, after all, and allowed, even in the grottos of the fringe, a white male supremacy to rule again?

HL: To announce that cinema itself, at root and centre, is a white male enclave seems to be stating the obvious – and people don't like to hear it, not then and not now: *how boring, oh do we have to bring that up again, get over it already.* To have the same sentiments reinscribed in what's assumed to be a more progressive, now-rehabilitated environment of indie experimental makers, well, it's a bit galling, isn't it (as if we expected better from our peers than the more commercial arena of feature films)? What being male and white (gay or straight) endows is, of course, not a natural aptitude or in-born talent for cinema, but rather a feeling of enfranchisement, that yes, I'm able to go out and make movies as if it's my right. Thank god there are some women, and increasingly more and more, who believe they are equally entitled. I don't think anyone was ever happy with the term *people of colour*, but we created that space for ourselves, pried it open, carved it out, squatted it and made our own uses of it. So, Mike, now you're back in Windsor and it's feeling so old-school again; that's a bit demoralizing. I did love that scrutiny, the precise and passionate attention to cinema itself. The revitalizing gestures of reflexivity were part of a time when I discovered cinema in the mid-'80s, and were part of the sea change that occurred a few years later, where social and political matters went hand in hand with aesthetic considerations, making the work all the more strong, pressing and provocative. I'd hate to think of a backwards movement, or even a lateral one – more of a coexistence, perhaps, whether one likes to acknowledge others or not.

MH: Could you speak about your relation to the avant-garde? Do you believe this is a historical consideration, something that used to exist, for instance, in Russia during the 1920s, but not any longer? When *Sally's Beauty Spot* came out, it really lit up imaginations around the globe, in its own small, avant way, of course. It seemed part of a generational agon around issues of racial representation that remains ongoing. But your work represented part of a new frontier of visibility and intelligence, a new way to address racial politics, perhaps, a new kind of aspiration and a new sort of pleasure. I don't need you to mull over whether you were more avant than the next liberation theorist, but I'm hoping you can describe something of this heady time.

HL: There is certainly that avant-garde you speak of, which includes *Battleship Potemkin*, Dziga Vertov, Kuleshov, et al., that we learned about in our cinema studies classes. Of course it's inspirational but historically circumscribed and reified – possibly exactly what the avant-garde is exactly not about. It's become a genre in itself. It has an 'experimental look,' a 'music-video feel' – you know what I'm talking about. I was exposed to art and artmaking early (my parents, particularly my mother, believed in art) and started to view the world aesthetically, at the same time as sensing my own foreignness in early '70s immigrant Canadian culture. My grade school coincided with the era of Trudeau's multiculturalism as official government policy colliding with the changeover to the metric system and visits to Ontario Place ... It all seemed extremely modern and shiny! Finding words for a racialized identity, and then moving toward cinematic expression, was altogether organic with the artistic and intellectual goals of my education, which culminated then. I was in New York in 1989 at an astonishingly vibrant time for critical and cultural studies, learning from groundbreaking figures like Homi

Bhabha, Mick Taussig and Faye Ginsburg. My illustrious teachers at NYU and the Whitney were wondrous, and we students were tadpoles in a very deep pond. At the same time, nobody was saying anything exactly about my experience in the Asian American world, the way I'd like to see it – which is more sideways and askance – in the critically challenging way that was exciting me at the time. In that sense, criticism and theory (Stuart Hall, ideas of Third Cinema) came slightly before the watershed moments and prepared the way. But very quickly, they arrived hand in hand (Trinh T. Minh-ha, Sankofa and Black Audio Film Collective), inseparable and stronger for it. The most compelling artwork, for me, is almost always socially engaged.

MH: In his seminal 1991 essay 'Yellow Peril: Reconsidered,' Paul Wong writes, 'In general, few Asians venture into the field of contemporary art practice. Those who do, make fully assimilated Eurocentric work or choose to work in traditional forms or commercial art areas.' How did you get hooked on movies, and how did you avoid (or did you?) the Eurocentric banalities Wong warns against?

HL: Doesn't everybody love movies? I had a steady diet of '70s kids' TV shows and California sitcoms, graduated to watching black-and-white oldies and Duran Duran music videos, before becoming thoroughly semioticized through years of film theory. Seriously, that's the narrative. And ringing through my head was hearing about Kathryn Bigelow and how she had to 'unlearn' everything she was taught in the Whitney program in order to make her Hollywood films. That said, I've hardly watched any television over the past 20 years, and narrative filmmaking is still an unending puzzle for me. Writing a script is such a mind-crunch, especially when you want to engage in genre but not be entirely subsumed by it (those reflexive experiments hardly ever really work, do they?). I had an early interest in meta-narratives, especially those with a feminist perspective (Chantal Akerman), even when these perspectives are not obvious (like in the fearless films of Claire Denis). In the 15 years since Paul's essay, the ground has definitely shifted and there are certainly more Asian artists in the sphere. To lapse into arguments of Eurocentricism even seems quaintly outdated, glad to say – everything's become so much more decentralized, and it's widely acknowledged that some of the best cinema comes from other parts of the world. Korea has also been 'discovered' for cineastes and lionized at international festivals and popular in art-house circuits. But there is always Hollywood as some kind of global standard, and the obsession of box-office statistics as daily news. The making of feature films, especially in English, will always be circumscribed by this context, between the American behemoth and European felines. Which is why Canadian cinema fares so poorly on the screens, even (or, should I say, especially) on our own.

MH: There is an abiding stress placed on women around the question of balancing a 'work/artist's' life with duties of family

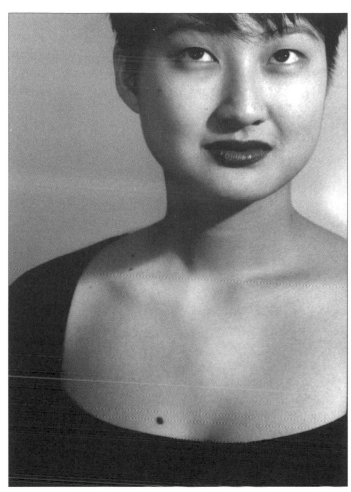

Sally's Beauty Spot

and home. A friend of mine complained that since she had a child she was no longer taken seriously as an artist, at least not in Toronto. As someone recently hitched, with two kids as part of the deal, could you comment on the continuing joys and pleasures of balancing a world of self-made pictures with everyday demands of those near and dear?

HL: Haven't been able to learn that trick yet, Mike. That uneasy, if not downright ill-fitting, match of artistic aspiration with motherhood. Perhaps they are equally vital creative endeavours? We all know about Jane Campion's work after becoming a mother – whatever happened to that edge and visual incisiveness, her adroit direction – and I say this as someone who was her biggest fan. Something about focus, I imagine (no pun intended), and the intense burning passion and extremely hard work that attends both filmmaking and raising children. I know that to pursue film properly, everything (and I mean everything) has to go by the wayside, including personal relationships. Men can put family on the backburner as they go into production, but it's harder for women, who usually carry the domestic burden on their shoulders, to ignore the laundry, kitchen mess and hungry children. Some of the most successful filmmakers have extremely supportive spouses (i.e., wives), though I don't know many women directors with kids who have been able to muster the same support.

Even the dance of development, when financing is in limbo and endless meetings with various people you want on board your as-yet-unrealized project, combined with creative uncertainty and constant script changes, can be overcome only by 110 percent energy plus luck, and that can be a bit difficult when you have to be home by five for the kids. The domestic juggle alone is exhausting, never mind adding the more-than-full-time occupation of being a filmmaker. Right now I don't feel like a filmmaker anymore. Though, believe me, I am craving to make those cuts, add the sound, recut to make it work, rescreen, cut again – that completely obsessive activity so ingrained it feels like part of the DNA. Maybe when the children get older it will be easier, more in the realm of possibility. Or, in the interim, scale down the projects into mini-movies, little video projects. Somehow I'll try. But right now I have to go and make dinner.

MH: What a thrill it was for me to watch *Sally's Beauty Spot* (12 min, 1990) again, though I'm guessing if you made it today it would be quicker, slicker, its surface a smooth sheen. Which makes me wonder: is there a pitch and speed that 'belongs' to each time of making, and do movies both express and reflect that attention? Does the flow of pictured events, even in narratives, provide models of time that we watch so they can inhabit us, so we can inhabit them?

HL: That's so funny. When I see *SBS,* all I see is how rough, even primitive, it is. It was shot on a hand-cranked, non-reflex Bolex camera I bought at a country auction, with those 100-foot 16mm rolls, no sound, and we had practically nothing in the way of lights. I think we shot the whole thing in our pyjamas. We'd all roll out of bed and I'd wake up Sally: 'C'mon, we gotta go shoot now.' One thing I was preoccupied with, besides the ideas of the film, was the rhythm and pacing, because it was originally done for an undergrad editing class when I was enrolled at New York University's graduate cinema studies program. I took it as an extra course because I wanted to learn some filmmaking while studying theory; everyone in the class had to edit something, anything, like found footage, but I thought I'd just shoot some of my own footage to cut together for the exercise. I cut the work print on a Steenbeck, with magnetic sound. I think there's a fundamental difference of time and duration between film and video. It's a much faster and more expedient process cutting in video, of course – cleaner, even sterile. Pushing buttons allows you to cut more impulsively, try dozens of variations, and in the process become confused with all the minuscule variations. With film – and stop me if I sound nostalgic – you are forced to think things through more, to respond more to a physiological impulse, because the cut is physical. The feeling of ribbons of celluloid running through your fingers, or threading through the machine, creates a different sense of time and timing. When you're fine-cutting, you can tweak it to the frame, see those individual frames literally pass before your eyes. It's a feeling like being inside the text, and being part of its texture – you don't get that same

feeling with video, which offers a feeling of gliding mastery, manipulation and digital dexterity. Despite its anachronistic status, in some ways I think film-cutting is a more conceptually sound process; the construction of the film can be more holistically achieved. You can have all these trims of different shots and selects sitting in your bin and then an idea strikes. Some happy little accidents can happen while editing, as you're putting one shot next to another. The physical proximity and handling of the footage is what we miss when working in video.

MH: Your movie is, among other things, a very intimate exploration of your sister's body. The beauty spot of the title is a mole just above her breast, which she is constantly scrubbing and picking at; we watch her putting her shirt on over and over again, rouging her lips, kissing a couple of handsomes. Why did you cast your sister for this role? Was the 'issue' of her beauty spot already a point of discussion between the two of you? Did you ever ask her to do anything she refused? *Sally's Beauty Spot* is redolent with pictures of Asian skin: the disrobing of Suzie Wong ('Take that dress off!'), for instance. There is a delight in looking expressed throughout the movie, accompanied, of course, by theoretical hat pins, an erotics of attention that lingers despite the quick-witted montage. Can you comment?

HL: My sister Sally is now seven months pregnant and I feel her pregnancy in a wholly different way than from when, say, other relatives or friends were pregnant. Obviously it's because of the relationship I have with her body, our bodies, over time, as sisters close in age (she's two years younger) growing up. Koreans have a term called *skinship,* which means the feelings of closeness and tenderness engendered from literally touching the skin, or say a couple on their first date and one of them accidentally brushes by the other's arm or something. It's not so much sexual as it is sensuous. I think feelings of absorption, feeling subsumed, and otherwise giving yourself over to the other, is part of it. My sister and I are unusually close. When boyfriends weren't around (and sometimes when they were), we were still each other's significant other. (I guess that's all changed now since we both got married this year.) Just after completing the film, I showed it to a fellow Canadian studying in New York, David Weaver (who was at Columbia and also became a filmmaker), and he mentioned pretty much the same thing, the 'erotics of attention' you speak of. And for the first time it struck me how sexualized my sister's body was in the film! I was so preoccupied with the concepts of the film that the idea never even occurred to me. Although it is a sexualization that comes from a self-possessed self-actualization rather than objectification, I'd argue. Biographically speaking, I don't think Sally had any complex whatsoever about the mole on her breast, and I had only a vague awareness of its existence even – it was just a rather convenient cathexis. One of my academic highlights was being able to do an independent study with Homi Bhabha through the Whitney Program, a kind of one-on-one seminar with him when he was a guest professor at

Princeton in 1992. Since he was one of the inspirations of the film, I showed it to him. He commented on the mole on her breast as a kind of Barthesian punctum, the peripheral detail that is so telling. My sister, no slouch in theory herself, immediately ripostes, 'Hey, no way, the punctum is the stretch marks.'

MH: You make ample use of clips from *The World of Suzie Wong* by Richard Quine (starring Nancy Kwan and William Holden). We see Sally watching this movie; as she takes cues for her own life, she offers us a model of picture reception. She is the first audience, and we watch the movie over her shoulder. Or at least part of it. Why was it important to insert the viewer into the frame? How did you come to choose this movie, and how does it function within your film? And how does the complicated exchange of looks 'work' in your movie?

HL: It was important to assert Sally as an active and interested viewer who took pleasure in the images of Suzie, a stereotypical 'dragon lady' and 'hooker with a heart of gold.' Although *The World of Suzie Wong* is addled with clichés, it was one of the few attractive mass-media images – one of the few images whatsoever – for young girls like us growing up in North American suburbs in the '70s, and this old 1960 film seemed to be on TV all the time. She looks smashing in a cheongsam; her sassy attitude and flagrant sexuality was part of the hook (and even more so if she had actually spoken with the British accent Nancy Kwan must have had, since she was raised in England – how interesting would that have been). So Sally's viewing provokes a discussion about how we find pleasure in things that are supposedly 'bad' for us, in reputably racist images such as Suzie Wong. It upends the rather simplistic argument that only 'positive' images are good for us, for the so-called model minority citizens that Asian Americans are purported to be. But then I wondered: isn't it just another kind of simplistic reflex to position Sally as a viewer in front of the film? And then I realized that film is fundamentally full of simple gestures, basic human responses and behaviours. Sally is no longer ignored or invisible but, rather, becomes a 'reading against the grain' kind of viewer. Because that's the only way to look at old films or old pop songs – otherwise we revert to nostalgia and sentiment. We have to invent a new historicity to make it relevant to us, how we live now.

MH: One of the voices in the soundtrack says, 'Skin as the key signifier of cultural and racial difference in the stereotype is the most visible of fetishes, recognized as common knowledge in a range of cultural, political, historical discourses, and it plays a part in the racial drama that is enacted every day in colonial societies.' Do you still believe this to be true? It is rare to hear statements like this made in movies made today. Why do you imagine that is?

HL: Yes, it does sound rather totalizing, doesn't it? Especially for most of us who don't see the world in that way, despite the dialects of north/south, white/black (or brown or yellow), master/slave – because history can't be ignored. But probably class and economics penetrates all this. I mean, practically anyone will work with anyone and put prejudices aside if the money is right. That's probably too crude or jaded. I think in cities like Toronto or New York you'll find both race-identified clusters and also a cosmopolitanism that tends to elide or mask the conflicts – but they're there, especially in terms of class (as other places such as Los Angeles and the Paris suburbs have found), or obviously in terms of religion (London, the Middle East), and the perceived threat of difference. Everyone likes to believe there's progress and tolerance, and that education and assimilation are working. But the issue of race remains. It may be parodied in Hollywood, or commodified and niche-marketed, but it's still an 'issue.' It's not often talked about as 'skin' per se, because that would be so wrong and retrograde, wouldn't it? French films that take up race with a heavy skin factor at play, like *La Haine* and some of the earlier films by Claire Denis (who I immensely admire), seem to be made under the ghost of Frantz Fanon and the spectre of Otherness, like it's an inescapable legacy. No matter how far away from a post-colonial environment we think we may be, we're always confronting the Other and, in turn, ourselves.

MH: *My Niagara* (40 min, 1992) opens with home movies taken in Japan. Where are these from? How do they escape the aura of cliché and redundancy that clings to all home movies (which all seem to be made by the same cameraperson, showing the same family, doing the same things)?

HL: We shot those 'home movies' on Super 8 Kodachrome, then transferred to 16mm, a beautiful process that renders supersaturated colour and grain you can almost touch. It exemplifies the difference between digital and analog, with all of its scratches and hiccups – a much more 'human' look. In a sense we wanted to remake that cliché. I saw the opening sequence as a fantasy, a childhood nostalgia for the main character, Julie Kumagai, whose mother is an idealized, untouchable figure, long-dead. I don't know all that many Asians, especially Asians like me who immigrated to Canada in the late '60s or '70s, who took those kinds of pictures – we were caught in snap cameras or Polaroids. But it was different for Japanese-Canadian/American communities who had been here one or two generations – some of them made those beguiling pictures. I couldn't resist, at the end of the home-movie footage, to steal some thriller genre music (from a 1948 Nicholas Ray film called *They Live by Night*) to undercut its sweet nostalgia, a foreshadowing of Julie's sullen, introspective character.

MH: The clothesline at night with its ghost-like sheets, the snake-like green hose glimpsed in moonlight – you've rendered suburbia as a mythical place of beauty and terror. You grew up there, didn't you?

My Niagara

HL: And I have tremendous nostalgia for it, despite having desperately wanted to escape it, especially at the time of *My Niagara,* because I was living in Toronto without my family. My parents and siblings had moved to California and then Vancouver (though my sister subsequently moved back), leaving me immediate-family-less in my hometown. The situation gave me time to mull over my childhood and upbringing. We shot the film in Etobicoke, in the house that Kerri Sakamoto (the co-writer) grew up in. It was different than Scarborough, where I was raised – a little denser, not as spaced out – but also the same. The safety, the ennui and also the repressions lie beneath a pretty and peaceful exterior. The cinematographer, Ali Kazimi, had an idea to shoot these day-for-night shots that would bring a spark to the silhouettes and evoke loneliness. Now that my existence has been completely urban and downtown the past 20 years, I think I look back too fondly on it, even now with all the big-box retailers. Of course, I could never live there again.

MH: Throughout *My Niagara* there is an eye for lingering details. The impulse to stop and admire the shape of a plant takes one outside narrative requirements that are fundamentally paranoid – in this sense, that every gesture, no matter how small, has significance, and that these significances 'add up' to a closing denouement, the *aha!* moment. Your movie presents these nomadic attentions as asides, and these two movements of the film seem in opposition. Can you comment?

HL: That's so astutely observed, Mike. Because again it was an unconscious process at the time. All I know was I was extremely concerned about these little details, and when we were shooting, the crew members (who were much more experienced than me) referred to these shots as 'cutaways' and seemed to relax and not care so much about these short set-ups without actors. But to me they were just as important as the dramatic sequences! In fact,

there were more of these asides than what ended up in the film, because, exactly as you say, they were hard to reconcile with the story and tended to hold up the film's narrative momentum. In that way I felt the narrative had won out over the anti-narrative impulse I was exploring at that time. Those experiments fascinated me, those films by Sally Potter, Patricia Gruben and Chantal Akerman. I thought the film was a 'failure' not to fulfill these puncturing effects, these quiet moments outside the story proper that still had something to say. There were similar sound cues in the film: sounds of water dripping, sprinklers, that kind of thing. I think that's what gives the film its enigmatic character, this sense of estrangement from a typical narrative film, because there's something else at work. The film ends with Julie serving two bowls of rice for herself and her father, and it's shot at waist level. There was never a full shot that included her head, or a close-up of her face that would 'tell us what she's thinking.' It was exactly her gesture that was important, the same daily, never-changing, never-questioning gesture of duty and obeisance that ruled her life.

MH: *My Niagara* is set at the waterworks, part of Toronto's small cache of mythic architecture. It is the setting for the climax of Ondaatje's *In the Skin of a Lion* and the subject of Rick Hancox's *Waterworx (A Clear Day and No Memories),* among other cultural stargazings. What is your fascination with this place?

HL: I originally attended a site-specific show of installation artworks at the Harris Filtration Plant, not knowing its place in the lore of Toronto cultural geography. It was revelatory because the Beaches was an entirely new neighbourhood for me, and felt both part of contemporary Toronto but also outside of it. The place has mythic dimensions and a certain haunting quality. Before the filtration plant was built, the grounds served as a sanitorium for lepers and tuberculosis patients at the turn of the century. This bucolic and barren environment with its functional industrial complex filtering drinking water from the adjacent lake was very inspiring. Since water was always the metaphor at work as this piece slowly seeped from our brains (mine and Kerri's), it made perfect sense for Julie to work at this water filtration plant. It all seemed possible, though it was a big scale-up from *Beauty Spot'*s shooting-in-our-loft-one-weekend, that's for sure. It's become a really popular location and all sorts of commercials and music videos shoot there now.

MH: Each of the characters lives a double life because of their ethnicity. He's Korean trying to escape the Japan he grew up in, while she longs for the Japan she's never seen (and hopes to find in him). This double vision that troubles the transparency of representation is typical for makers of fringe movies, which feature a disproportionate number of first-generation transplants. Their (our) parents grant us an irresistible sense of another world, even as we are busy growing up in this one. Your movie articulates this double vision, both content-wise and in its stylings and vagrant attentions. Can you elaborate on this theme and why it is important for you?

HL: At that time, in the late '80s and early '90s, there was so much critical theorization around otherness and alterity, post-colonialism, Third cinema, oppositionality, marginality, fringe films ... it nearly busted my brain! Here I was in cinema classes studying Wittgenstein and the Frankfurt School and continental philosophy – and I thought I was supposed to be studying film! (At the time, cinema studies was concerned about its position in the humanities and institutionalizing itself in the academy.) It was so much more pleasurable and productive, I thought, to try to apply these interesting ideas to making films. So I was extraordinarily preoccupied by these themes; they were there first for me, preceding the filmmaking apparatus and production skills I learned in conjunction with the making of these films. These projects were, at first, a critical enquiry or investigation, and then a film proper – as if I were making films instead of writing essays. Making *My Niagara* was so much about the way its characters were seared by marginality, but we didn't want to portray only that. Their ethnicity and backgrounds were a given (race wasn't 'the story,' so to speak), so that we could contemplate something else about them, their particular foibles and self-projections. I was also obsessed with tracing a kind of subjective cinema, and how to shoot a film that let subjects speak from a naturally empowered position, not as objects of sociological or anthropological interest. Which is still why I am asked, when someone finds out that I'm a filmmaker, 'What kind of films do you make – documentaries?' Because if I'm an Asian woman, then it's about sociology first and films second. The challenge is trying to bring a cinematic structure to this 'double vision,' as it's so aptly called, wherever that doubling or tripling may take place – on the level of aesthetics (experimental films), gender (feminist films) or race and ethnicity (films by 'people of colour'). Don't you love that line in Miranda July's film where Tracy Wright's curator asks about an artist, 'Is she ... of colour?' It's such a knowing comment about the contemporary artistic cultural environment, isn't it, along with its jaded, aren't-we-all-past-that posture. Well no, we aren't.

MH: Can you comment on the figure of the father? He is a box maker, able to make containers (which are empty – it's as if only those at home here in the new world can fill the containers, while he is able to provide the frame, the shape of experience). When his daughter Julie expresses her admiration and accepts one of his handmades as a gift, she provides a bridge between old and new worlds.

HL: It is that little gesture of offering and acceptance that provides the tiniest suggestion of where Julie's gone as a character. Otherwise, she's someone who's changed very little throughout the course of the film, as tied up as she is in the trauma of her mother's disappearance in her childhood. That may have been a problem for some audiences, that she didn't change or transform, as is ordinarily expected. We want our main characters to advance themselves, to learn something, etc. Her mother's spirit still haunts and disables her. Her relationship with her father is a kind of inverse – it's so everyday, but their exchanges are stilted. The father is the classic Nisei (second-generation) character, which is to say, though he was born in Canada, speaks only English and likely spent some of his childhood in the internment camps during World War II, he is still identified by mainstream Canada as a Japanese man. But again, that wasn't 'the story.' That's how Kerri and I approached the script – we weren't stuck with announcing the character's ethnicity or racial background all the time. We wanted those histories to be already absorbed by the characters; it's a part of who they were, and it wasn't our job or theirs to explain it all the time. In some ways the father is a vacant figure, or rather evacuated from Julie's life (which is fairly solitary anyway), so they are in that sense two solitudes living in one household. He can express so little, except by giving his daughter one of his empty boxes. The running theme through most of my films is, ironically, the absent mother. It started with *My Niagara* and then continues through the other shorts and even my feature film. I can't really account for this repeated pattern of maternal loss, except to say the figure of the mother is also a symbol of the motherland, the repository for all the cultural longings, memories and projections that remain unfulfilled.

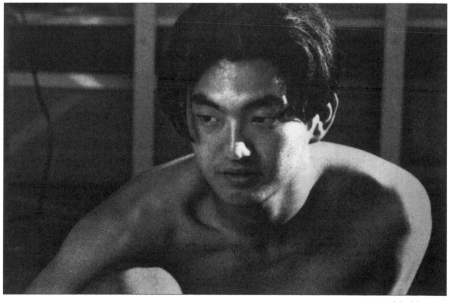

MH: *Prey* (26 min, 1995) is a self-assured drama about Il Bae (or Eileen), who works in the family's convenience store and falls in with a young drifter. The move revels in the beauty of its stars, the hunky Adam Beach and beauty queen Sandra Oh. While their onscreen chemistry and acting chops raise them well above the level of eye candy, do you worry that their fine looks present an ideal the rest of us will never manage, and that this frustration will further the cycle of beauty debt and pharmaceutical potions that has extended the reach of capital into every moment of the consuming body?

HL: Sandra and Adam are hardly beauties of the typical sort, but they inherently have stories to tell, a lived-in experience that makes us want to know them. I'd be dishonest if I said they weren't cast for cheekbones, but more than the physiognomy, there's a steady gaze that holds your eyes. And most of all, the two had a chemistry that busted archetypes and memories of staid, objectified characterizations. So I don't think the film presents them as idealized figures in any way. (In fact, Sandra wondered why she had to look so grungy, but it was all in character to say that Il Bae got woken up in the morning with an emergency and stayed that way all day.)

MH: Could you elaborate on the title, *Prey*? This is a movie where every character seems both predator and prey.

HL: When we were in production we had another working title, *Automatic*, but that seemed didactic and cold, while *Prey* already sets up a kind of narrative in the title and has a metaphoric dimension. I don't remember exactly where the title came from – probably from Cameron (Bailey, my partner at the time), he's really good with titles. In any case, it's not meant to be literally interpreted. Although there is that section in the film where Il Bae sits down with her grandmother, Halmoni, to watch a

nature documentary on TV. This is shortly after the surprise encounter with her semi-naked, now banished Native lover in the same room. Avoiding the obvious, Halmoni remarks on a lion devouring its prey, correlating it with Korean survival, not without nationalistic pride. But then she's completely oblivious to calling this Native stranger a 'foreigner.' Who is foreign, native or other here? The immigrant still trumps the Native on Canadian soil, both economically and socially. In terms of enfranchisement, visibility and power, it is still, ironically, immigrant lives that have advantages over Aboriginal people. And it's a sorry state, isn't it, to be comparing and contrasting oppressions, but these differentials in history, and educational and social opportunities, must be taken into account. Factor in the privileges of whiteness and class, and there's a minefield of difference at play. There are no 'white people' in *Prey* (save the pawnshop owner) who act as a 'base' from which people of colour are positioned as being different. And that's the one thing that's common in all of my films: we are the 'base.'

MH: Among other matters, *Prey* relates a story of young love (whose desire makes prey of each other). Does love occur only where there is something missing – a deficiency that needs to be smoothed through touch and language? Despite their wounds, both Il Bae and Noel appear to be trying on roles, posing with guns and lovers, sometimes shopkeeper or juvenile delinquent or dutiful family member. How do the pictures that surround them, that they are busy occupying, help or hurt them in coming together? Please forgive this dangerously naive question, but might your movie also suggest that ethnicity itself can be a pose or position?

HL: There is a certain amount of positioning that occurs as soon as you place a non-white character onscreen. You automatically do the mental calculus from your position as a viewer – it depends where you're placed or how you place yourself as a spectator, how you can thus read the character. An insider can have 'special knowledge' or assumptions about the character, which means less explaining is needed, or a different approach. We already know that backstory. Can the same be said of, say, gay characters in a movie? You can go only so far with that logic. Because then we're relying on generic stereotypes, even as we play with and manipulate them. Il Bae and Noel were entirely independent creations, but they are constantly flirting with each other on that edge of race, ethnicity and gendered expectations around desire. The challenge was to frame it in a dramatic story that seduced you and shook up your expectations.

MH: Il Bae has lost her mother, Noel his sister, and Il Bae's father has lost both his wife and homeland. Is the displaced place of the

Prey

Prey

immigrant always one of loss? Is every gain measured by what must be left behind? Is that why you conjure this geometry of loss?

HL: I do think the immigration story is suffused by loss, and not only the gain of a new life in a new country. Somehow there's a conflation of mother and culture in my films; this yearning for cultural connection is symbolized by the lost mother. The relationship between Noel's loss of his sister and Il Bae's loss of her mother, tenuously linked in the story, is also a linchpin for their connection – not that they should be defined by negatives, however. They've both known sadness in their lives, that much is shared. And how does one calculate loss, particularly a concrete one such as a family member? I can imagine that one feels that loss in the body, like the perpetual pain of a phantom limb. If you leave your homeland, the loss can be as profound as the gain. I think of my aunt, who my father sponsored to Canada in the early '80s. I don't think she stayed six months, not even two changes of season (maybe it was winter; that would drive anybody away), before returning to Korea. Of course, it was because she was in love with a man from her hometown, who she eventually married. But the connection to the homeland can remain forever compelling. Look at all of Canada's immigrants who return 'home' on a regular basis, to the point of buying land with the expectation of retiring there. So where is home, really? In the most positive light, it's like having two homes, which isn't a bad deal at all. But you need economic flexibility for this. Or, conversely, economic burden – for all the people who make monthly remittances to their parents or relatives – another familiar immigrant duty.

MH: If shorts mattered in this country (or any other country, for that matter), *Prey* might have become Canada's *Do the Right Thing*. Does the marginal status of shorts trouble you, or does it provide more freedom (no one is looking, so you can do what you want)?

HL: *Do the Right Thing* was a watershed film for its time, a no-holds-barred provocation on cultural politics that seemed to define that era. It was extremely influential for a whole generation of indie filmmakers, of colour and not, who felt like they needed to address these issues, if not as head-on as Spike Lee did, at least in a way that was culturally responsible and, moreover, culturally relevant. It was very 'new' for its time, very exciting. As for the short-film format, I remember attending the Clermont Ferrand Short Film Festival in France with *Prey* and realizing, hey, shorts are not marginal here in Europe at all; they make them in 35mm and they're shown before features in theatres and bought for television. Canada and the U.S. have caught up somewhat, but the status of the short filmmaker is still zip. In Europe, you can be a short filmmaker forever, and not necessarily have to 'graduate' to making feature films – it's a viable format. But I didn't start off making films with the ambition of making features. Shorts were very much my world, having worked at DEC Films in Toronto and Women Make Movies in New York; the arena of non-theatrical film and video for the educational market was/is mainly short films. To me, they weren't marginal at all, and I made short films with that attitude. Every frame, every scene and every minute had importance. The fact that it was under 45 minutes and would never show in a film theatre or be known to general audiences, that had no bearing. And then my purview widened some more, as I went beyond my own intellectual and aesthetic pursuits to realize there's a whole world out there who didn't even know what a short film is. I was, maybe, wilfully naive about it.

MH: Do you feel responsible to your 'community' to represent their loves and lives? Is there a notable gap that your movies embrace and do these omissions (the movies that haven't been made yet) create pressures to make accessible, positive pictures?

HL: I definitely felt/feel like part of a community, albeit one that has shifted and splintered over the years. I'm acutely aware of my filmmaking peers who are women, who after some promising short films had children or got married or moved on to other work. It's the men who remain, actually. Most, if not all, of my filmmaking colleagues now are men. But the pressure is all mine, the pressure to produce, to make films that are good and that matter. I think if one were pressured to make accessible, positive pictures, that'd be like some kind of Disney film or after-school special. Given that I was raised on that kind of suburban-fed media fare, it wouldn't be too far off for me to make that kind of work. But if you mean community-minded films or videos,

Prey

in a number of video formats (1-chip and 3-chip MiniDV, Beta SP), then transferred to 35mm film. We shot it over an eight-day period and somehow the small five-person crew I originally planned ballooned to 15 – although we were still quick and mobile enough to grab shots in markets, on the streets, by the Han River (there are no filming permits to speak of in Korea). There was enough of a narrative impulse, enough of a kind of story musculature, to permit these 'abstractions,' as you say. I was aware that the fish-out-of-water and search-for-roots story was familiar enough to take other liberties, and I let these scenes slacken into something else. Yes, there was definitely a sense of the closer she got, the further she was, and that her search was less about finding her mother than about losing herself. I think it's a self-obliteration story.

well, social responsibility can only go so far. So many other things (European art cinema, experimental film, semiotics, etc.) have demented my brain. The desire to reach many people, though, without compromising too much the kind of work you want to bring out there, that's another trick. And film distribution – well, that's another game altogether.

MH: *Subrosa* (22 min, 2000) is a pop-coloured monodrama about a 20-something orphan, newly landed in Seoul to look for her mother. This quest narrative ends with little resolution: the city turns into an increasingly blurred and abstract backdrop as she uncovers few clues. Why this story that refuses storytelling, these arrested moments shirking any sense of closure?

HL: I never feel like my films are at all autobiographical, but the desperation and futility of the protagonist was something I felt while making *Subrosa*. The film originated as a kind of prequel for the feature film I was developing at the time, called *Priceless* (which was never made), which dealt with the same character five years on, still living in Seoul, still engaged in a fruitless search for her mother, among other trials. I'd been enamoured with Korea for a number of years. It's the place of my birth and, at the time, a country I knew very little about. So of course it had a huge place in my imagination. For immigrants, there are two contradictory impulses about your home country: one is to negate or ignore it, and the other is to romanticize it and puff it up. I did the latter. I had wanted to make a film in Korea for a number of years, but had a hard time finding the right shape for it – it is indeed a kind of inchoate, all-consuming feeling you're trying to hammer out into script form, which was a difficult task for me. But, oddly, the script for *Subrosa* came out in a couple of days. I was in the throes of a personal crisis, a breakup that I was taking very badly, and the film came out of my wallowing. It was shot

MH: The lead is often lensed in extreme close-up, whether taking in her first impressions of the city, talking on the phone or checking out floral arrangements. The camera proximity centres the action and grants the viewer an anchor. We are always seeing with her, alongside her. But is the closeness also a kind of deception, because we don't find out so much about her? Like her lost mother, she is close and far at the same time. We discover little about her in a strict biographical factoid manner – perhaps there is another level of knowing that arrives before that, and that is finally more powerful and more cinematic?

HL: Again, I wanted our knowledge of this character to be organic and not psychological. You may be detecting a kind of anti-psychological refusal of character, at least in the Western sense, where we enunciate all the time who we are, our tastes, our status, our opinions, our sense of ourselves in every way: what we like to eat, where we went to school, our favourite authors. This is a conception of individualism that is wholly Western. We know very little about this Subrosa character. She wears a red coat. She speaks English in an off-accent – although, in fact, she speaks very little. There's a diaristic feeling to the film. The close-ups you mention are part of an exploration of subjectivity that had been obsessing me for some time. But those decisions also came along with tiny, hand-held cameras that allowed us to fit into tight spaces and produce tight frames. There's something about seeing someone so large onscreen, getting to know an eyelash or a mole; sometimes that says enough about the character, because that's all she's willing to tell you. The danger, especially dangerous for Asian characters, is to end up being called 'inscrutable,' because then you're finished. The viewer doesn't have an entry point and it's game over. There's that fine line between enigmatic and unknowable, a line that many art cinemas graze against, that may be compounded by ethnic or cultural differences that further frustrate or intrigue the viewer, depending on who s/he is. As the main character plunges deeper into an unknown Seoul, she loses herself even more. When she plunges into the river and emerges, she arrives at a zero point. As if she's been born again.

MH: She is the visitor, the seeker, and is corralled into a bar where she has a nearly wordless sex encounter with the handsome barkeep. You deliver this extimacy in a single, red-tinted medium shot, but I'm wondering if you could elaborate on the question of onscreen sex. It so rarely approaches the boredom and disgust, the rawness and emotional accelerations, of 'real' sex – is it possible? Pictures have allowed the surrogate experience (as if we were there ...) of so many things, does sex lie beyond the image's capacity?

HL: She, the main character, is deliberately unnamed. When she asks to see her adoption files, to find out her 'real' name, she is denied access. She goes into this search with nothing but her body and her wits, and a small sense of history. The fact that she unwittingly mimics her mother's past, travelling to the army-base town, visiting the brothel for information, and then has passionless sex with a stranger – well, it's more than ironic. I want to cry for her. The red-tinted shot is alluded to early in the film when she checks into a *yeogwan* (small motel) where she pulls on the overhead light, fluorescent white and then red. All the love motels have it – the red light that's supposed to be sexy or discreet or something. It's pretty lurid, that's for sure. And it's the same red light under which she has sex. It seemed very appropriate. As for capturing 'real sex' on film, I'm not sure what to think of all those 'non-simulated' sex-cinema experiments by Catherine Breillat, Leos Carax and the other French filmmakers, or the American one by John Cameron Mitchell (and future blogspots or reality TV cable shows – just the thought itself ... I'd rather not), except that you invariably feel a bit like a voyeur. But I know in my films the

sex acts are more signifier than signified – it's about much more than the act itself, and I think most filmmakers would tell you that. But sometimes, like for the aforementioned filmmakers, the act itself is what's important. I think cinema acts as a kind of 'condenser' for all sorts of things, including sex. And the fact that the emotional and physical components, inextricably linked in most forms of sex (even when they are 'unemotional' or 'empty' experiences – the lack still means something), exceed the limits of cinema's capture – is that a bad thing? Cinema is many a marvellous thing, and functions from mirror to mimesis to metaphor, but it's not life. Yes, at times cinema can be realer than life itself, but sometimes woefully not.

MH: One of my enduring frustrations is the coverage of 'independent' media. Cover after cover, month after month, there are stories that take readers behind the scenes, the making of this month's big flash.

But there is a story much larger than any of this that is seldom told. Many of these folks will never appear in any kind of magazine again, because after their 15 minutes is over, they will hit a wall of impossible funding they won't be able to climb over. I've yet to speak with a feature maker who hasn't been cast into the wilderness, wondering if she would ever make another movie, unable to raise interest or money in her new project(s), no matter how successful or heralded her past efforts. You have gone through this experience in trying to make *Priceless*, and I wonder if you could take me through the frustrating steps that have led to the current impasse. And I can't help but wonder whether questions of ethnicity and gender exacerbate these problems.

HL: As you said, regardless of gender and ethnicity, every filmmaker has had these problems. But perhaps it's best to think about these not as 'problems' per se, but just a natural, inevitable part of the process of filmmaking. And the process can be soul-destroying. Most of my peers from my 20s have fallen away to other professions outside of film, adjacent to filmmaking (such as teaching) or steady-paying gigs (jobs in TV). The irrefutable, practical aspects of making a living and feeding yourself come to the fore, never mind taking care of a family. It's okay to starve for your art in your youth, but few of us have the means and heart and single-minded devotion that independent cinema demands. At the end of every project, you're left with a blank slate, returned to zero. You might have garnered some good reviews, sure, and attended some festivals, and made the rounds of university classes or had the occasional speaking or guest-teaching gig, but in terms of continued sustenance it's a hard trick, isn't it?

I worked four years on a film that was never made. We garnered continual interest, and

Subrosa

attended every selected market from CineMart in Rotterdam to Independent Feature Film Market in New York to International Film Financing Conference in San Francisco, to Pusan. Is this in any way sane or normal? No, of course not, it's potentially self-destructive to put so much of yourself in a project and have it fail. It's like starting a small business that goes bankrupt before it even opens. And then there's the whole psychic, emotional and intellectual investment that seems all for naught. A colossal waste of time and energy. But then you think, hey, maybe it was good practice to write 30 drafts with four different script editors (because, as Toni Morrison says, there's no such thing as writing, only rewriting) and to continually defend its reshaping, even though it still wasn't good enough in the end. I think there's an alchemical aspect to filmmaking, outside of logic and reason, akin to karma, that works in your favour and tips you toward a green light, or not. Sometimes it's your time and sometimes it's not. Most people can't wait it out.

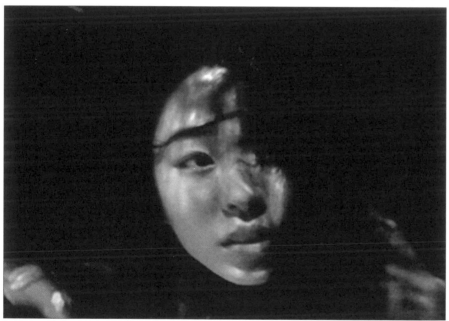

Subrosa

Priceless was a culmination of all the ideas I had explored in my short films about ethnicity and being an outsider, about cultural displacement and estrangements. But it would be set in a new location for me, Korea, before the plot moves it back to Canada. It was a fish-out-of-water tale, with some thriller/crime elements (starting with an immigration scam that turns into an inadvertent child-kidnapping case), but it was an essentially personal story. It's now five years dead. At the time I thought the funding structure disintegrated and my relationship with producers along with it, but now I realize the opposite is true. Canadian international co-productions with countries other than England or France or Germany (where deals are made in the lingua franca of English) were fairly rare, and the Canadian producers simply felt threatened by the prospect of working hand in hand with a Korean production company who didn't speak their language but would have equal say. This was shortly after the IMF collapse of

the Korean economy in 1997, mind you. The irony is that now, with Korean cinema being so hot, it seems like the time is ripe for this kind of film to happen. But back then it was wild, unexplored territory. And, simply put, Canadian producers are a cautious lot, with a lot of tethers choked to the purse strings. It's the whole oxymoron of the term *independent*, which often means dependency on a lot of things, including funding sources tied to deadlines, policies, quotas, etc. It was altogether a demoralizing professional experience.

When *Priceless* collapsed, co-producer Anita Lee approached me about making *The Art of Woo*. It would be done very quickly, and ultra-low budget.

MH: Could you continue with your story about *The Art of Woo* (90 min, 2004)? The version I (badly) remember is that you had a treasure-island deadline: if you finish a new script in six weeks, we'll get you the money to put it onscreen. Was your turn toward romantic comedy a move away from the heaviness and difficulties of the *Priceless* years? Could you describe your favourite moment of the shoot?

HL: The fact that it was a romantic comedy was definitely interesting, because it was so different and out of my usual sphere of reference. And yes, the lightness was very appealing. I remember I had to rush out and watch all these classic romantic comedies to study the genre and understand the structure of these stories better, to see how we could add our own twists of gender and ethnicity into the mix. The first draft was written very quickly, in about two weeks. We rushed it off to the Canadian Film Centre's Feature Film Project, to make a deadline. The program offers 100 percent financing for a low-budget film, and that budget is $500,000. From the beginning it was an ambitious plan, because the script isn't truly a low-budget kind of movie – tons of locations, characters, lots of art department and costume requirements. We worked with Peter O'Brian, the then-executive producer of the FFP, and he was extremely supportive and found the themes of mistaken identity and masquerade intriguing. We had a scheduling conflict with the intended female lead (Sandra Oh, whose HBO series was unexpectedly renewed for another season), and the production schedule was fixed (FFP had to spend Telefilm money before the next fiscal year), so we undertook a casting call for a new lead. We eventually cast Sook Yin Lee, who took time off from her VJ duties at MuchMusic and even did a crash acting course with Jacqueline McClintock in Montreal. It was a harried, intense time. The upshot was that it was less than a year from project conception to premiere at TIFF the following year – pretty remarkable in itself.

I've always loved the soundtrack stage of making a film. One of the highlights was working with Ron Sexsmith (who won a Genie for his original song contribution) and Kurt Swinghammer, who both wrote the film's score. And it was fun to include members of Toronto's artistic community (Michael Snow and Suzy Lake were very gracious in lending their artwork) and incorporate familiar locales (the Power Plant, University of Toronto, Archive Gallery Inc. opened their facilities to us). What was not particularly fun was to be so rushed in the shooting (20 days), with limited resources in time, equipment, manpower, etc. It felt that we shot just barely enough to cover the script, not enough to attain performances and coverage from the angles we really wanted. But then every filmmaker at almost every budget level would tell you that. Filmmaking is an art of compromise.

MH: Alessa Woo is a social climber forced to choose between love and money, represented by two suitors, the playboy *avec* mansion and the Native artist who has just moved in next door. She is also a self-made picture, posing as an Asian heiress and living beyond her means. What was your interest in this picture within a picture, and why this traditional division in matters of love?

HL: Alessa is not exactly a likeable character, is she? We found that question coming up – her glibness, seeming superficiality and mercenary ways – how could the audience ever sympathize with her? For some reason I never cared about it. Or rather, I think we can see through her 'character' – the pose she puts on for people, the airs she takes on. The film was, in some ways, meant to be a confection, a froth to be enjoyed and consumed. I had hoped to insert my usual interests in gender and race along the way – the class distinctions, social anxieties and cultural displacements of her character. We were aware of trying to do a take on classical romantic comedy, albeit with these twists. At first we conceived it as a run-and-gun kind of shoot, given the parameters of time and budget. After meeting with the cinematographer, we thought, why not try to make it more classical? I'm not sure that was a good decision in the end, because we weren't playing with the beautiful sheen and expanse of 35mm, where you can revel visually in the image, but were shooting digital video that was transferred to film. So the film has another kind of look, blown out sometimes, with intense and saturated colour. As for the splits in her personality, the picture within the picture you mention, we were trying to convert a late-'50s/early-'60s bebop Cinderella escapade in the present-day art scene of Toronto. But because the lead was a person of colour, why not give her a happy ending? She (and we) deserve it.

MH: Some notable performers insist they never read reviews, good or bad, because those opinions only get in the way. Writing about movies has become distinctly more shopping-oriented in the past couple of decades; the marketplace is filled with stars and thumbs that say simply: buy this picture. Or don't. Has this dumbing down affected the way movies are made? How did you feel about your *Woo* reviews, or did you read them at all?

HL: I think everyone has expectations around their first feature film, but in my case this was diluted by the fact that *Woo* was made and *Priceless*, that stillborn child of a movie, wasn't. When the film was released domestically, it was slashed by critics, who, while they've never loved Canadian films in general, seemed to take a particular disliking to *Woo*. To be honest, I took a masochistic interest in reading the reviews, quite possibly because I worked as a critic (music writer for *NOW* magazine) before I became a filmmaker, and I can sometimes similarly distance myself from my work. Or possibly because I think you can also learn something from your reviews, that even if you don't care for that critic's taste, it's still part of a public response. It's amazing how things are received and read in ways that you never expected or intended. I tend to wallow anyway, to mull over and consternate to no productive end. It's all part of having an obsessive character, a trait common to all filmmakers, I think, because filmmaking is, if nothing else, a completely obsessive activity. I read movie reviews like everybody else, to find out if a film is good and deserving of my time: do I want to go out (to the theatre, to the video store) and sit down and watch this movie for two hours? Only recently have I turned off films if I don't like them, because like some folks I'm also afflicted with a completion complex and feel I should watch until the end to know whether it really was good or not. But as time creeps on, and minutes become scarcer, I just switch the thing off, and sometimes even walk out of the theatre.

Overall, though, apart from a few exceptional critics (A. O. Scott, Jonathan Rosenbaum, Jim Hoberman), there aren't nearly as many consistently interesting people writing in film as there are in music. While the aesthetic and ideological underpinnings of serious cinema are ripe for intellectual consideration, it is, oddly enough, in music that you can find truly stellar writing about the art form. I think it's partly because writing or criticism is such a projection itself, that what's on the film screen somewhat limits the scope and scheme of the writing about it, whereas music is a complete abstraction that invites the full play of your imaginative powers. Yes, you can seize on the music's genre, history, artist's oeuvre, lyrics and other concrete things, but often that is the least interesting aspect of reading a well-written review. Often the delirious devotion and exuberance of the fan comes through in a review that perfectly encapsulates, in words, what moves you about the music. Film writing is often completely passionless.

MH: Every artist I know makes dazzling things on occasion, and then years might follow that are filled with variations on the same theme, or the minor chords, placeholders, the marked time between new ideas or bold expressions. *The Art of Woo* feels like one of those movies. How strange that it should be your longest work (not to mention that smooth Dolby sound and 35mm image). The smallest has become the largest: does this seem similarly disproportionate to you?

HL: Oh god, I just hope it's not my last. I haven't made a film in such a long time. I've had a burgeoning personal life that I can't complain about (though I do), relocating to a new country, learning another language (my forgotten mother tongue), taking on responsibilities of motherhood. All the emotional investment and time that I put into films is diverted elsewhere. As for the small/large thing, I don't regard *Woo* as either large or small, but one and the same. Because I had that odd view, years ago, that the short film was/is important. It feels so vital at the time, almost like a compulsion, otherwise why would you put up with all the bother and hardship that it takes to cobble together a film? And *Woo*, despite or probably because of its weaknesses, was truly a learning experience. Sometimes, I agree, you need to 'feed' yourself, to simply live life. And then your work takes a different shape, seizes other concerns that reflect this broadening horizon. I can sense this shift happening, because now I live in a context completely foreign to my Canadian upbringing. It's been a huge adjustment; being in Seoul still makes me feel like an outsider, only with different layers of estrangements and feelings of foreignness. As for what will happen to my filmmaking, yes, that would be nice, to think of it as a breather.

Helen Lee was born in Seoul, Korea, and raised in Toronto, Canada. She is a graduate of the University of Toronto, New York University, Whitney Independent Study Program and the Canadian Film Centre. www.helenleefilm.com.

Helen Lee's Films and Videos

Sally's Beauty Spot   12 min 1990
My Niagara   40 min 1992
To Sir with Love   3 min 1992 (with Shu Lea Cheang)
M. Nourbese Philip   3:30 min 1995
Prey   26 min 1995
Subrosa   22 min 2000
Star   3 min 2001
The Art of Woo   95 min 2001
Cleaving   2002 (video installation)
Hers at Last   18 min 2008

Distributed by Women Make Movies, Canadian Filmmakers Distribution Centre.

DEIRDRE LOGUE
BEYOND THE USUAL LIMITS

ovies have been designed from the very beginning to promote the beauty spots of our lives, the high-impact thrill of a face. But there is another kind of beauty that is unafraid to lose the mask of youth. It is the beauty of witness, of a person who has returned from the frontier. What a gift this is, to be able to look into a face that has seen too much. This is our pass-key to the labyrinth, to be granted admission to the very brink of what can be seen or imagined. This face, this look, carries it all, if we could learn to read it. These faces are a testament: *I was there and didn't look away. I saw what it was. And now I give you the gift of this face that has looked.*

In 1969, videotape was a single ribbon of black-and-white tape that lasted half an hour, and if you edited it, you had to cut the damn thing with a razor blade, which would produce a large glitch smack in the middle of the image. So, mostly, nobody cut: you rolled the tape and when you stopped the camera the tape was finished. It was standard fare in those early days to make tapes that ran the full length of a reel, which meant shots lasting 30 minutes of what they used to call 'real time.' Look at John painting his body green, look at Vito talking and talking and singing and talking some more. Thirty minutes of real time in black and white. Sony hadn't figured out how to turn the world into colour yet, and the microphone was a little pimple moulded into the body of the camera, a crappy little thing situated for maximum camera-noise delivery – and forget about adding music or anything later. What you see and hear in these tapes was what happened lo-fi style, what the camera was staring at for half an hour, and I don't believe attention spans were any longer or shorter than they are now, so it's hard to vouch for how many people saw them – probably not a lot more than are watching Deirdre's movies. There is a line, a lineage. The way these early video thoughts are transmitted doesn't require a direct hit; it's all up in the air now, it's part of the weather; you breathe it in, you breathe it out, and sometimes it takes root, sometimes the seeds fall and it all comes up again as bad copies or déjà art vu. But Deirdre doesn't have to worry about that. Sure, her chops are express-delivered from these earliest moments of video art, but she's found a way to live it, and that means when the work is finally ready it arrives hard and clean and hurting, the way art is supposed to be. She's not much for 30-minute shots, though; she reserves her punishments for herself, so instead of dishing the long take, she slices it all up into pieces and then joins the data files in the computer until these so many moments are one movie and then she calls it *Enlightened Nonsense* and then, five years later, *Why Always Instead of Just Sometimes.*

The artist performs in each of her movies. This work is too important to be left to others. She never leaves the stage of the frame, and hardly speaks – she lets her body do the talking. She shows, demonstrating the cost of living in a body. She offers us the trial of ideas and their execution, her skin appearing as a book, written over and over, and without end.

MH: You often appear as the subject of your movies, and the camera accompaniment seems to bring with it a particular pressure that manifests as punishment. The camera doesn't glance or graze; instead, it seems to push its look toward you, like the wind, an unseen force that compels you to act, even if these actions are painful. There's a question in that wind and I'm looking for it now. Could you comment about this duet of bodies, yours and the camera's?

DL: On the implications of there being two (of us).

My arm is a branch, the camera in my hand a leaf, photosynthesizing.

There is my body – me, and then a warm 'something' inside the camera that I allow myself to believe in and relate to when I record things. It is another somebody, but it's small, only part human, and it can be turned on and off, which I like to do often. I am prone to talking to it in simple terms. I often ask it for things, negotiating the probability of success or failure, looking into the lens for feedback, critiquing my image and sharing with it my insecurities. We often commiserate, expressing a shared sorrow and trying our shared best to put on a good face.

Despite our closeness, I feel the camera can sometimes be very quick to judge. In fact, I've recorded lots of things I felt the camera simply didn't like.

I think the creation of an anthropomorphic relationship with the camera is essential to working with your self as subject. The camera is always there, held easily in the hand, just an arm's length away, waiting for you to make something of the moment. To act. This perceived need from the camera and its consistent proximity makes for a very intimate yet demanding experience. I almost always feel like I'm being watched. And it is precisely this intimacy mixed with expectation and antagonism that makes it personal for me. It's really just the two of us.

If the camera had no carnality, who but me alone would be left?

MH: Curious, I always felt the camera was an equal-opportunity looker. It never turns away or refuses its subject: *no, please, not that, it's too much.* Every bit of gore and terror and banality is rendered in the same glass stare. But you have embraced this stare in a new suite of videos entitled *Why Always Instead of Just Sometimes* (33 min, 2005). After the party's over and everyone's gone home, the two of you are left together, quiet conspirators, conjuring something that may be fit for public consumption (for strangers) later, but certainly not now. Now, it's just the two of you in a series of encounters that are intimate but not confessional. Can you talk about how your relation to the camera has changed (from film to video, from something that has to be wound up to something that is ready all the time, not to mention the recording of sound)? Why do you always shoot with your face so very close to the lens, as if you were pressing your face into its face, the two of you locked in a forever kiss?

DL: One of the things that seems very different for me between using film and video is the device.

When I use a film camera, I make a big to-do about loading the film into it – this part always scares me, actually. Once it's loaded, I feel like it's then a matter of using the material within it, like paint in a tube. Even when I am throwing the camera around, being a bit cavalier about it, the emulsion inside feels precious to me, like it has a special purpose and life of its own. I have never felt this with video.

The way I work with a film camera incorporates my not being able to see myself, not being centred in the frame, unsure of the exposure, just not 100 percent in control of the potential image. I have to try and trust it and allow that my 'mistakes' are a part of what I do. I depend on the film and the camera to record my image, but on its own terms.

I am aware of and a bit embarrassed by my attraction to self-referencing devices and my current infatuation with video cameras. A video camera feels to me more like a mirror than a

Why Always Instead of Just Sometimes (Per Se)

mirror. With a mirror, once you step away, your image leaves with you. With a video camera, your presence or absence is caught quickly like a fish on a hook. I have never felt this with film.

As soon as I take it out and plug it in, the video camera starts feeding on me and I let it. I can see myself in the little screen and I'm surprised. I like to get as close as I can to the lens so I can see everything, even if it's ugly. I like to see how I look up close, how I could look different, older, maybe younger, if I shift just so and the camera just hums along, taking whatever I give it, listening to me breathing as I wonder what to do about everything and it never tires, and I indulge myself and I am ashamed.

MH: Shame – could you tell me more about that? Is it produced in the moment of encounter, because of something you do, or fail to do? Or does it only come later, when you revisit a moment?

When you do something again? Isn't there something about a life with cameras that means doing something again? Doesn't having a camera around mean it never happens for the first time, only over and over? Isn't there already something compulsive, looping, eternal or interminable about the act of a camera's reproduction, which is already shameful?

DL: A life with cameras is a life of moments captured and moments missed.

Moments are times when my wetware is on.

And then it's here, the moment and the body and the camera and the knowledge and the desire, it's all ready to go. And then it comes, the shame that comes with even thinking for a second that anyone would ever be interested in you or what you think.

And then it comes, the self-doubt, the feeling of worthlessness, inadequacy and ineptitude and the shamefulness inherent in a desire to expose your imperfect, all-messed-up, uncertain, poorly defined, needy self to another.

MH: Another question: much of your work carries echoes of the earliest moments of video art. I'm thinking of folks like Vito Acconci or Ulrike Rosenbach, when time was real and tapes were unedited. Solo performances for camera. Do you feel you are part of this line of makers? Some of these artists were also part of a gesture sometimes named Body Art, using the artist's body as a material to conjure experience or ideas. Your work fits rather easily into this niche, so I wonder: are their bodies also your body? Are you not only recalling their bodies in some of your work, but inhabiting them, or allowing them to inhabit you? Is this how tradition works, and when it reappears, does it turn the present into a ghost? Does it turn the body – your body, for instance – into a haunted house, a ghost chamber, a grieving vehicle?

DL: Early conceptual art, body art, performance, happenings, have had a significant impact on my work. It was actually this kind of work and only this kind of work (for a long time anyway) that attracted me to an art practice. I remember recognizing an immediate, distinct and terrifying difference between this work, these artists and the rest. I remember seeing the works and being shocked – face flushed, mouth dry – by the flesh, the confrontational voice, the dangerous ideas, the deception, the duration, the moments of exposure, courage, irreverence and the humility of it all.

I like to think that any similarities between what I do and this body of practices means carrying on in a tradition. This happens out of admiration, because I believe it's important work to make and recalling their bodies brings information for my own.

I love the idea of having one's body haunted by the ghosts of dead performance/body artists from the '60s and '70s. It would be a very raw, introspective, sad and complex life, full of smoking, coffee, art openings and profound misunderstandings. (Wait a second ... this sounds very familiar.)

In anticipation of your next question: I would be the bastard child of Sophie Calle and Bas Jan Ader (he would still go missing at sea). My babysitter: Yves Klein. My first teen crush: Hanna Wilke. My first love: Jenny Holzer. My first and last couple crush: Marina and Ulay. Smoking buddy: Vito Acconci. Arts school dream team: Chris Burden, Bruce Nauman. Crazy lady next door who would tell me things only she could tell: Carolee Schneemann. Cameraman: Bill Viola. Funeral director: Orlan. And music by Laurie Anderson.

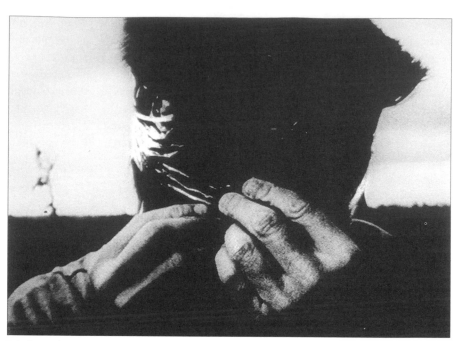

Enlightened Nonsense (Tape)

MH: There are so many ways of looking, and the camera, one of our machines of looking, makes certain kinds of looking visible. It shows us a view, it presents us with a scene, but it also shows us the way a scene is looked at. One of the 'scenes' you turn to over and over has something to do with the unwatchable, with what cannot be shown or said. In *Per Se*, the opening movement of your new *Why Always Instead of Just Sometimes*, you appear in front of the camera insisting that there are things that can't be shared, that there's a line between the visible and the invisible that the camera redraws. On the other hand, mainstream cameras are busy giving us the illusion that we, the audience, have the best seat in the house – that we are seeing everything, and from an optimal position. Your camera, however, is trained on twilight moments when the thing itself cannot be shown; it sometimes looks 'off-screen' to a place outside representation. This look is also a refusal; your camera look is sometimes a way of saying *no, this much but no more.*

The camera look seems to hurt you, wound you; it seems that other looks have arrived before this one and left their scars, and now the camera has returned to pick at them. And behind the camera is the weight of 'us,' the unseen viewers, ready to receive confession, the artist's palette of sufferings large and small. What does a 'wounded sight' mean for you? When you bandage yourself or draw stitches all over your body in *Enlightened Nonsense* (22 min, 2000), are you re-marking the wounds that are already there, that you want above all to escape from, even as you can't help showing them?

DL: Sight and language are located in two of our most visible and most articulate wounds, the eye and the mouth. These are not simply openings in the body where certain things can occur – they are opened and closed with intention. (My nephew, when he doesn't want to accept a situation or, more specifically, hear what

you are saying to him, he turns his head ever so slightly and simply closes his eyes. They remain closed until the situation changes.)

There are many different ways in which I deal with the concept of 'wounds' in my work. Most often, these wounds are specific to my experience – they are my psychic wounds, given a physical representation or a chance to speak. They are made visible not simply to prove they exist, but so we (artist and audience) can determine their dimensions, contemplate their origins, examine their characteristics. So, for example, in applying bandages to my hand in *Why Always*, we assume that a wound is being covered even though none is seen. After ten or 20 or 30 bandages have been applied, we know this is about something larger, not simply a cut or a scrape, but something more substantial. This is some kind of wound that a million bandages could never fix. It is also in the urgency of the application of the bandages and in the excessive number of them that we sense the need in the individual to cover, to protect, to expedite healing, to stop the bleeding.

I believe my moments of disclosure occur not in the public recognition of the wound but in my response to them. This is what I let you see: my fighting with them, my talking to them, my trying to understand them – this is the work I make. Artist and audience discover together and simultaneously both the visible and the invisible wound.

And cameras, like the eye and the mouth, are opened with intention and closed when they have seen enough, for the moment anyway.

MH: *Per Se* is the opening salvo of your new movie, *Why Always*. In it you talk to the camera and remark that there are many things you could say, might even want to say, but can't. Instead, these words, this preface. Once again you make a line between what is allowed and what is not allowed; you alert us to the off-screen space of your life and its onscreen symptom of demonstration. Is it out of a sense of decorum, privacy, embarrassment, that these facts are pointed to but then omitted? If we were to know more about you, more details about your life, would that diminish your work, make it less 'artful' somehow? I remember interviewing a filmmaker who was pregnant and making a movie about pregnancy, but who didn't want to mention her own condition, as if that would render her making impulse impure. Do you share that feeling?

DL: *Per Se* is the disclaimer warning viewers of the confusion made possible in a space where fact and fiction collide. *Per Se* is about the subject of subjectivity and the difficulty of accessing language. I wanted to give the audience a sense – in preparation for understanding the work to follow – of how making images about oneself feels uneasy and how the act of articulation can render one suddenly uncertain about the truth.

I want to speak – and am in fact speaking – but in *Per Se*, I have presented my statements as precarious. Not so precarious as to be unbelievable, but just enough to be suspect. I should be able to say that I know who I am, but I can't, not exactly. I can say that I know something of who I am – but there are still so many questions, can I really say for sure?

MH: Both your major projects, *Enlightened Nonsense* and *Why Always Instead of Just Sometimes*, are works made in parts (or sections, chapters), and in their insistent focus on the body it is difficult not to imagine them as Frankenstein bodies, stitched together out of parts composed and decomposed. It's difficult to think that you would begin with anything like a master narrative (who knows what the body will produce in advance?), so I'm wondering if you could describe the process of assembly, the afterthoughts that bring all these parts together?

DL: For me it's an accumulative process. I have chosen to work in this way – in parts that accumulate toward a larger, more articulate part (a whole?) – because I believe that I am a composite of fragments. When I am falling apart, I feel it literally, pieces of me separating out, bricks coming loose. When I am together, I feel it too, all parts close, tight, all parts touching. I have never felt like an entity.

In both *Enlightened Nonsense* and *Why Always Instead of Just Sometimes*, I started with a basic premise within which all works are produced. There is no beginning, but there is a beginning of the act of making. Once that has begun, all works relate back to the first act in some way. So it really is a series of actions or events for the camera, falling loosely into an overarching theme.

The body could be considered that overarching theme, but more specifically, it would be the body's failure, weakness, betrayal and ultimately its instability – physically, emotionally and metaphorically. I do not work from or with a master narrative unless one would allow that master narrative to be me.

With both works, I set out with the explicit intention to produce a series of ten to 12 shorts within a particular theme. I then determine an order in which they will function conceptually and formally together. They are interrelated and so pose an interesting challenge – it's like lining up ten stormy skies. Each may appear similar, but each sky produces a different storm.

I do not edit the works either. I might make changes to affect their speed or colour or make additions, but little if anything is taken away from what is captured. I show everything that comes out of the process of shooting that particular part as 'complete.' Like in *Eclipse*, where I'm cracking my jaw: the piece is one continuous shot, with the black 'spot' added to respond to the brightest part of the image.

This 'blackness' starts to creep into the image like bad thoughts sometimes creep into a perfectly good day and spoil it entirely. This blackness takes over, eating up all of the light. It

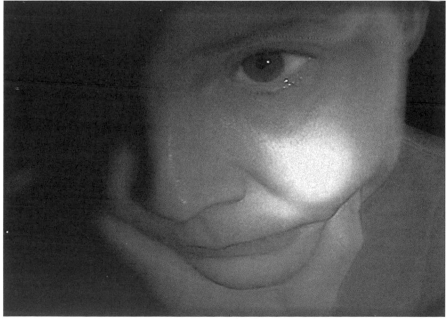

Why Always Instead of Just Sometimes (Eclipse)

then narrows in on the area of my face I am preoccupied with: my jaw and cheek, where the cracking comes from. It then grows as if feeding off the energy of my obsession, to obliterate me, erase me, consume me, like obsessions sometimes do.

As for Frankenstein, there are many works that refer directly to the idea of a Frankenstein body. There are stitches, illness and doctors and the study of my physiology. There are cracks and bandages and reconstruction and transformation. The idea of being a monster, well, that's there too, always.

MH: You run a series of three very short home-movie fragments in *Why Always*: one shows a boy popping a wheelie and falling, another shows a pair of tricycles colliding, another a trio of girls dancing. Each loop has superimposed titles that begin: 'When I was 38 years old ... ' Where are these loops from? Why have you chosen these in particular and why these titles?

DL: The tricyclists and the *Wheelie* popper are from an amazing film from the '60s on toy safety. The audio clip 'that beauty right there' from *That Beauty* is also from this film. The *Worry* loop is myself at a Christmas party, I was around seven or eight, I would think; the dervish in the foreground is my sister Glynis, and the two in the back are my cousins Judy and Suzie.

The toy-safety film is terrifying. It is narrated by a football or maybe baseball star, a handsome, commanding sort in a monogrammed jacket. It's educational, made for young adults and their parents, and proceeds throughout to identify a long list of toys you (foolish you) thought were safe, but (gasp) are child-killers. And it's not the most obvious toys either, and maybe that's why it's fascinating to me. It's a bit of a game: they sort of ask you, as an audience, to guess which toy is the worst. And it's never the science kit with its saltpetre and acids and glass – it's always the teddy bear. In fact, in *That Beauty* I have grabbed the audio from a scene where the narrator shows us a plastic eye he has just removed from a teddy bear's face – the eye has a three-inch spike on the back, and the camera zooms in on the offending spike and the narrator says, 'like that beauty right there,' as if he is describing a prize leech.

This found film footage has an everyday, commonplace, innocent aspect to it combined with something deeply sinister, unpredictable and life-threatening. So, kids, watch out next time you hold that plain, normal, loving teddy bear too close to your face! Total blindness is just a kiss away. And it keeps going. Kids keep trying things, wrong things, and crashing and falling and rubbing their elbows and wiping their eyes; toddlers are holding throat-size blocks up to their not-so-tiny mouths ... It's mayhem! And it is from here that I retrieved my crashing cyclists. Maybe it's obvious, but I was looking for cycles and accidents and more specifically for both happening at the same time.

Worry, which shows the girls dancing, is more a reflection on my own history. When I see old home movies of myself, I can see myself performing, like in *Sleep Study* (from *Enlightened Nonsense*), hungry for the lens of a camera, serious about its presence, anxious to make an impression. I can also see the worry evolve and grow and take up residence in me. Like a virus, it spread throughout my childhood and remains a constant for me in adulthood.

The texts are a reflection for me on my failings. While I am busy repeating my mistakes, going round in circles, crashing into the same old walls, I am missing things, and forgetting, and subsequently failing to do (new) things.

And around it goes. And then I start to worry that there's not enough time, that I've missed my chance, and my chest gets tight, and it's harder to breathe, and around it goes.

MH: I think the audience fave of *Why Always* is the section where you crawl between the mattress and the box spring. Can you talk about why you shot this, and why you never show us what you find on 'the other side.' Why does the camera remain in a single, fixed position throughout?

DL: First, let me say that I think the bed is the only place where we are able to be really 'in ourselves,' alone or with another, whether in sleep or in sex. I love my bed and yet each night I have to be either convinced or coerced to go to it. I love my bed once I'm in it, but until then I am estranged from this place where we are 'in ourselves' to such an extent. I'm not a good sleeper.

The *Beyond the Usual Limits* series, of which there are three in *Why Always*, is a group of works based on a few concepts that sort of coexist to 'inform' me as I work. One is the concept of disappearance, i.e., disappearance between the mattress and box spring, a hand disappearing under a hundred band-aids, an ear or a face into blackness, a person into a space, a space into a person.

By exploring this desire for disappearance, I am able to see exactly what I'm trying to hide (from me and from you), which I couldn't have identified before trying (if that makes any sense). As an example, am I trying to hide my ear by painting it black? No. I am trying to make my ear disappear so I don't hear what I don't want to hear. I see the 'disappearing' ear as shutting out, a sealing off of the entry point of language. Sometimes I am tired of hearing, but really I'm tired of listening.

So, in the case of the work where I enter and crawl into the bed, I am performing a disappearance. I am 'hiding' in a very intimate setting, inside a very intimate object. Look around your house ... there are few places 'all of you' can disappear into

Why Always Instead of Just Sometimes (Wheelie)

(fridge too cold, furnace too hot). The bed was the only object I could find that was meant to fit me (albeit the other way round) and also had meaning. So it was here, in the bedroom, wearing a T-shirt and underwear, that I proposed to myself that I 'try' to disappear. After a scraping and splintering attempt at the laundry hamper, I settled on and subsequently into the object best suited to fit 'me' formally and conceptually.

Another is the concept of silencing the body's constant hum. I feel/hear this weird noise in me I can't really quiet. And some of that noise is the body's crying out for food and sex and water and comfort and sleep and all those 'normal' almost conversational noises. But then there's this other white noise, and it's a mean, buzzing sort of annoying noise. Some call this noise anxiety. It's this one that I try to silence. I shut it off at the ear with black paint, smother it in soft cloth, pinch it between two heavy thick buffers. I look for ways to dominate it, even if just for a moment.

And finally there is the idea of testing my strength, both physically and emotionally. I started to explore this in 1997 when I began *Enlightened Nonsense*. I choose small feats for myself, ones that can't be so hard as to be impossible for me, yet they must challenge my physical ability and carry some emotional weight. Despite a certain 'accomplishment' communicated in the piece with the mattress and box spring, that shit is really hard. It is physically very intense. The box spring is not meant for the body – its wooden slats are bare and sharp and hard. And if you add the weight of the mattress on your back (80 to 100 pounds, I know, I called Sleep Country) to the weight of your own physicality (150 pounds) and then try and slide (push, shove, drag) your almost-naked self along this hard, sharp object over a six-foot span (plus your own length, which must be put in first and extracted later), it is painful and exhausting. There is no air, and it's hot. Your shirt really rides up and your ribs get scraped, and your knees get rubbed raw and your elbows get sore. (A real crowd-pleaser.) And then, as suddenly as it started, you are out on the carpet on the other side, sweating, injured and red-faced, and a winner in the psychic Olympics of your own weird little life.

MH: In the *Eclipse* section of *Why Always*, you appear in night-vision mode, your face very close to the camera, cracking your jaw. After a short time, you interrupt your solo camera performance because 'somebody,' you say, is coming around, and you put the camera away. It makes us feel that we are witness to something private, but also that there is something shameful at work here. A curious dichotomy, that you would hide this activity from 'somebody' and yet display the results to anonymous audiences. Is this dichotomy another 'crack' you are exploring?

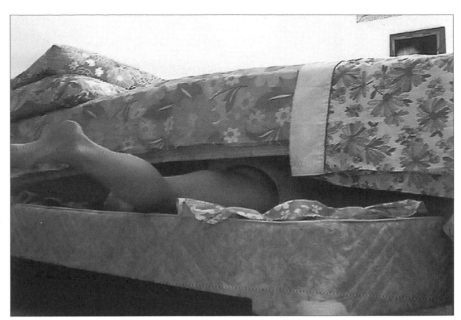

Why Always Instead of Just Sometimes (Beyond the Usual Limits Part 1)

DL: I like to explore the subtle differences between intimacy and privacy. When does something become private, what lines get crossed to make privacy occur, what measures do we use to determine it, can something be intimate and private and still be public? Is there some sort of universal way to determine privacy? Like, two or more witnesses to an event or action = public?

In *Eclipse*, you are witnessing something I would call semi-private. I'm in my house and there is another person there somewhere, but I've found a little moment and I'm just doing what I'm doing in that chunk of semi-private time and space. I'm in the act, so to speak, when I hear the footsteps of someone coming too close for me to maintain my intimacy with the camera. This relationship that I play out with the camera is something I don't want people to see. It's like a secret recipe; you can eat the cake but not know how I made it so special. So even though it's something private, made for a public, only the making is the private part. And yes, it's a curious dichotomy, but a necessary one.

This crack I am exploring is like a fault line that runs the length of my earth; each day it gets a little bigger, a little longer, threatening each day to open me up and swallow me whole.

MH: In *Blue*, you use a split-screen to show yourself blowing up a bag, and then allowing it to deflate or exhale (inside yourself), again and again. The same action appears on both screens, though it's not identical footage. Why the two screens? And why is this section shot on film and tinted blue? Is the breath meditation another way of composing the frame, a meditation on artistic self-reliance, a tautology?

DL: *Blue* is one of my favourite sections in *Why Always*. I shot it in PixelVision in an edit suite at the Centre for Art Tapes. (I hardwired the camera right into the Avid so that it was acting as a lens and always kicking around on standby.)

I love these cameras for their neither-film-nor-video aesthetic and for their 'either/or' response to light. It's like making a work with photosensitive blocks of ripe cheese. These cameras are also perpetually broken; mine is, in fact, broken (which, as you have probably already figured out, is something I relate to), and most people who own one have had a variety of experiences with them being broken in some way, at least once, if not forever. (Why, Mr. Fisher Price, why?)

Like in *Repair*, I have the same image relating to itself. In *Blue*, it's the same image mirrored and delayed in such a way as to create the sense that they are feeding off one another. We have two images, codependent and coexisting – creating a third.

There are lots of references here, including ones to hyperventilation, anxiety and subsequently hysteria, but it's also a formal work based on the concept of exchange. Start with one, make it two and make them share.

And it's as if through this sharing and the asynchronous formal element that the image calmed right down. It surprised me in that way. A work that felt anxious in the making now feels so zen. The sound, an electrical static, increasing in intensity as the bags fill, becomes more organic than antagonistic (as was the initial intention).

Blue is the colour of blood that has been through the body and is on its return to the heart and lungs. When I made *Blue* (and *Suckling*), I was also falling very deeply in love. I was experiencing an amazing and sudden symbiosis. I was falling in love with someone and myself through the eyes of another. Everything became flesh and blood, breath and body, you and I and all that we are or could together become. *Blue* is sending and receiving, a passing of something essential between two bodies and a touching of each other's insides.

MH: As the son of immigrant parents, I was granted a double vision: the world as picture arrived through the usual scrim of childhood confusion, but also through the experience of faraway places and devastations that I could find no evidence for but sensed lurking beneath everything. This unsettled look provided the basis for my interest in fringe media, where both the way and the what of retelling is up for grabs, new contents demanding new forms, because notions of the 'natural' or 'transparent reality' were never available to me. I wonder if you could talk about your work in relation to queer culture, or being queer – is it easily or uneasily located in the large queer nexus of media work here in Toronto? I also sense in your work this double vision at work, which is related to the sometimes discomfiting, paranormal queering of experience.

DL: I am always curious if audiences see anything with a capital Q in the work. Not much has been discussed about the works,

never mind from this particular point of departure. I think if it was pursued, much of my psychosexual and psychosocial experiences could easily be located in the works – many of the underlying themes are linked to issues of gender and sexuality.

As a cultural producer, I believe that my queerness and my artistic production are intrinsically linked. Outside of this, the degree of queerness in my work varies depending on the context within which the work is presented. The idea of a double vision, or a queering of more universal experiences, is certainly a part of my subject matter. In the works there is lots of duality and doubling and codependent, relational images suggesting some duality of experience as well.

Am I part of a queer nexus? I think Toronto is overflowing with queer production, but I feel that useful discourse on the subject of queer, experimental media is absent. I've often wondered, can you be queer and an artist at the same time, or do you have to choose between one or the other? I suspect the latter.

Why Always Instead of Just Sometimes (Repair)

MH: Why do you feel you have to make a choice between being queer and being an artist here in Toronto? Isn't the media-arts scene suffused with queer sensibilities, and isn't there something about queer performative stylings that underlies many places/works/nights out? Do you feel your work lands into that circle of folks that you see when you go out? The folks who showed up at the Gladstone Hotel for the premiere of *Why Always*, for instance, do they make it worthwhile? Or is that only another obstacle?

DL: It embarrasses me a little to say what I'm about to say, but here goes.

I really don't feel like the Toronto arts community – straight or queer, media or visual – has expressed that much interest in my work since I moved here permanently in 1995. This is also true for the larger Canadian media and in particular the visual arts community. I have had my works shown in queer festivals (very few straight ones) and had a few individual works curated into shows (very few straight ones) and have even had solo shows at two relatively large artist-run centres, but overall I feel my work has had little attention. This is not to suggest it should receive more attention necessarily either (see, here's the rub). And I'm embarrassed to say this because ... (in my darker hours I wonder) why should it?

Does everyone feel this way or is it my fragile ego?

I try not to think about your question, because to feel somehow underappreciated as an artist in such a powerful and supportive arts community (by comparison to many) feels ungrateful, self-centred and myopic. I'm sure many would see me as one of the lucky ones, and I probably am. But I think feeling under-recognized as an artist plagues a great many 'queer media artists' (see, now I'm one of 'them'), and it's not because the community – queer or otherwise – is unsupportive. I'm not sure

Why Always Instead of Just Sometimes (That Beauty)

why this is exactly. I wonder this in response to your question – if there is so much queer work out there, and 'we' have created such a strong and unified presence as cultural producers, why would anyone feel isolated within this?

But I do.

Is there too much work or too little, too many exhibition opportunities or not enough? I say more of everything, but most importantly, I think many 'queer media artists' – as artists of significance – are grossly underrepresented in the majority of our public institutions, if not all. There is a conspicuous absence of 'queer media artists' – as artists of significance – in the press and in publications, and there is little representation of 'queer media artists' – as artists of significance – in most commercial settings. We don't talk enough about 'queer media art' as 'art,' we talk about it as queer. And I guess that's why I get scared and feel like I have to choose. Because

I choose to make art first, I guess I feel like an artist first and queer second.

Am I horrible?

I want to also suggest that people, for the most part, find the film and video work I make hard. It's about things that are not really easy to program or take responsibility for programming. It's difficult work, and I think it makes it difficult to contextualize, talk about, recognize or even see. I often feel like it's the subject matter of my work that keeps me on the outside of the in crowd.

Am I a freak?

And, of course, each and every person who came to see *Why Always* at the Gladstone made a difference, made it worthwhile. I fought tears throughout the experience, and not because I was (like so many in Toronto) 'exhausted' and not because I was relieved or overwhelmed by my own accomplishment. I felt the moment speeding past me, I couldn't catch it, keep it, hold it or make sense of it. I cried when it was over because it was personal and it was gone. And it is rare.

Am I too sensitive?

It's also important to acknowledge my own kind of refusal to be absorbed into a larger, more present and perhaps more active, queer cultural community. I am often invited to make things for events or screenings or programs, and I say no. I say no because I really can't make work that way. My process is very introspective and it takes time, and even when the work is done, I am reticent to exhibit it and I can't make stuff for fun. Even if sometimes I wish I could, making things for fun in order to be part of it all is something I resist.

Am I mean?

MH: You have been active in Canada's fringe media communities for the past couple of decades, working for the Media City Festival in Windsor, running the Images Festival and the Canadian Filmmakers Distribution Centre before moving on to Vtape. The small pictures made and disseminated in these places, aren't they simply reaching the usual suspects, isn't 'community' just another name for an insular incrowd already hip to fringe pictures? Does the failure of fringe media to sustain wider audiences mark a failure in the project of alternative work? And can this failure be located in the work (who could watch that?) or the delivery systems?

DL: I ask myself this question daily. I wake up and wonder, 'What can I do to ensure that art made with film and video is seen by as many people as possible?' Unfortunately, I go to bed every night asking myself, 'I wonder if you really can make over $1,500 a day stuffing envelopes from home?'

I believe experimental film and video is the most important kind of 'media.' I believe in its aesthetic innovation and its capacity to change us. Despite numerous outstanding bills at Blockbuster video stores all over Toronto, I have little patience for commercial productions. Works that operate deliberately outside of the mainstream are one of the few things I feel I can talk to and about. I love them. They are my people.

I have been a part of a large community of dedicated individuals trying to make sure that audiences are complex, that the works are represented well, that the works are paid for and have a life beyond the cultural closet. I think 'we' – you and I and our 'community' – are more savvy to fringe media than we all were 15 years ago, but this to me does not signal its failure, it signals its ability to function, at least on some of us.

The fact that this kind of work (my work and yours) lacks a substantial and sustainable audience is not the failure of the projects, the practitioners or the organizations charged with the task of dissemination. I believe this is a result of social ignorance and cultural apathy, for which I blame the performing arts.

And yes, you, my community, are my first and often my only audience.

Deirdre Logue's film, video and installation work focuses on self-presentational discourse, the body as material, confessional autobiography and the passage of 'real' time. Recent solo exhibitions of her work have taken place at the 2006 Images Festival – where she won both Best Installation and Best of the Festival – the Berlin International Film Festival, Beyond/In Western New York, Art Star in Ottawa and Articule in Montreal. She was a founding member of Media City in Windsor, the executive director of the Images Festival, the executive director of the Canadian Filmmakers Distribution Centre, is currently the development director at Vtape and lives in Toronto. www.deirdrelogue.com

Deirdre Logue's Media Work

Enlightened Nonsense: 10 short performance films
 22 min 2000
Untitled Human #1: Ride   8 min 2002
That Beauty   2 min 2003
Prototypes 1–6   15 min 2005 (film projection performance)
Why Always Instead of Just Sometimes: 12 short film and videos
 33 min 2003–2005

Distributed by Vtape.

KENT MONKMAN
MISS CHIEF

He walks me past his main-street shopfront window, and a table filled with thoughts that float in paper piles across the flat-screen monitors and Post-It Notes and coffee cups. This must be the office. Beyond it a hulking canvas fills the wall, a concatenated rush of colour, smoothed and controlled and bursting from its new canvas home. It is so fresh and perfect and newly made that I want to step into it and away from it at the same time. Kent's painting is all bigged up now, revealing epic encounters filled with the mythic beauty of North America at a moment when contact between two cultures was first made. It is a primal scene of sorts, which he returns to over and over again, in his paintings and performances and movies. When he started producing these first-person testimonies, First Nations movies were rare, so perhaps it comes as little surprise that he would want to start again, or reimagine beginnings, or, at least, the beginnings of pictures. Let me take you to the other side, let me stand behind the camera, the canvas, let me do the talking. Using his trickster spirit (Miss Chief Eagle Testickle, who else?), he walks back into the ghosts of those First Nations folks who first laid eyes on European settlers. He tells the story while he slides the myth under the door – he can't help remembering, even as he pushes his audiences forward into imagined futures.

What lies beyond the canvas is a postage-stamp kitchen and bedroom – of course, it's all here, his living and working and sleeping and thinking. There's no need to draw a line between his looking and his painting and his movies any longer, it's all flowing from one end of the room to the other. He has the appetite for work, and each day he gets on up to the large canvas and starts in on one of the small figures caught in an eternal embrace (loving, hoping, escaping – no one stands aloof in judgment). When I stand in front of it, I am also one of these figures, caught inside that looming scape, because this painting, like Kent's movies, is always opening toward its viewer.

Each of his movies is filled with visual delights and a lyric gaze that settles into the body, again and again. The body is a symptom of historical displacement, pushed from the land it belongs on, cheated in treaties, then redrawn through white stories and pictures (it must be the master race that turns genocide into the western, or whose systemic deceit wraps itself in the camouflage of 'Indian givers'). Kent's movies offer a corrective, and he doesn't mind sexing it up along the way, taking time for a laugh or three, a mother's overbearing charm, a street boy's lightning glimpses of a city's underside. If the national anthem could be cracked and opened, this song would rise in its stead, lovely and haunted and funny and sad and wondering what took us all so long to come check it out.

MH: You are a painter and performance artist as well as a media artist. Did you enter into art via painting?

KM: It was something I developed an interest in and pursued because I was encouraged as a kid. It's one of those things that defines your identity. I became the artist in the family – it was a way of entertaining myself and exploring my imagination. There was never any question in my mind I would do anything else, only how I would go about it. My brother is a year older and he went to Sheridan College to study illustration, and I followed in his footsteps. It was a practical way of engaging my artistic talents. How did one become a professional artist and make a living? I didn't know. Very quickly after college, I realized I didn't want to be an illustrator. Instead I started painting. To pay the rent I did storyboard drawings for TV commercials. I would pick up a few gigs and then go travelling for a few months. Or work one or two days a week, then have the rest of my time to develop my paintings.

I started painting with oils and dropped it five years later because it was too toxic. The turpentines and fumes were toxic and the contact with my skin was affecting my circulation. I knew I would be doing this for the rest of my life, so the sooner I made the transition to acrylics, the better. It was a tough transition because I was approaching the first few acrylic paintings as though they were oil paintings, and they didn't come off. I needed to find a way of working that capitalized on what acrylic does naturally. I've spent the last 15 years moving paint around, exploring what it can do.

I've always been a studio painter, drawing inspiration from the figure primarily, and then my subject matter drifted away into more organic shapes, shapes abstracted from nature, microscopic imagery, wildflowers, that kind of thing. But the figure kept creeping back in.

One of the last series I did uses Cree syllabics, and figures were buried below layers of text. The figures were quite simple, and the overall effect is somewhat abstract. Each painting shows a different Christian hymn. Cree syllabics were developed by Reverend James Evans, an Anglican missionary who was trying to convert Aboriginal people. There are different stories about how the syllabics originated; some credit Evans with inventing them, others feel he was taught how to use them by Cree informants. Because Cree and Ojibwa words are so long, the translation of the Bible or Christian hymns became unwieldy. Evans used glyphs that convey sounds instead of letters, and Cree people picked it up very quickly.

I was interested in how Aboriginal sexuality has been colonized, and the Cree hymns became the vehicle to explore this in my work.

With the influence of Christianity, there was a reduction of varied sexual expression in Aboriginal communities: polygamy and homosexuality became taboo. Of course, there were also the residential schools, where many Aboriginal people were victimized by sexual predators. I was interested in the direct impact Christianity was having on our communities, but also in the complexities and conflict in this relationship. Christianity was introduced to my Cree family several generations ago, and to them it did not seem antithetical to being Cree. Yet there is a dark side to this relationship between Christianity and Aboriginal peoples that has been very oppressive.

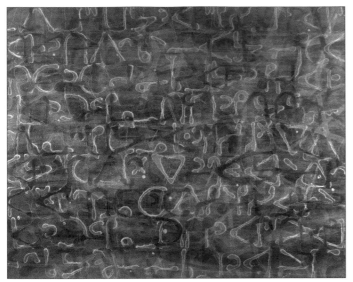

Nearer My God to Thee (painting)

After doing those paintings, I felt I had reduced my palette, in terms of the formal aspects of painting. I was dealing with large themes, but because I was using a highly personal style, I was not communicating very well with the average person. I started thinking more in depth about the identity of the ghostly figures. The bodies hidden beneath these Cree syllabics were based on photographs of men wrestling, and emblematized the idea of an eroticized struggle. I wanted to identify who those figures were, and to speak more directly about sexuality and the influence of Christianity in our communities. I had to locate those figures in a real space, and this led me to the landscape; the site of the conflict between Europeans and Aboriginals has been the land. Exploration of landscape required me to look more critically at art history and particularly the Group of Seven.

MH: The Group of Seven formed in the 1920s, travelling, painting and exhibiting together. These Canadian icons, familiar to every school kid, eschewed the studio, mostly painting Impressionist-influenced landscapes in the open air.

KM: I started using their paintings in my work to challenge what these paintings represent, and as their work is so graphic, it adapted easily to the way I was painting at the time. Then the struggling or wrestling men became cowboys and Indians. That was the launching point to start looking at cowboy and Indian images again.

In the 19th century, Euro-Americans were projecting their imagination and ideologies onto the North American landscape. These paintings are manifestos of the European presence, justifying their invasion and discovery of a promised land. My work with Cree syllabics was an exploration of the impact of Christian ideology on Aboriginal peoples, and the same theme was expressed in the pastoral scenes of these paintings, where God himself appears to be present in the clouds.

The mid-19th-century Hudson River school, which included Thomas Cole and Albert Bierstadt, painted the sublime in nature, transplanting biblical scenes onto the North American landscape. The Garden of Eden, the expulsion and manifest destiny are all thrust onto North American land. They produced paintings of heroic settlers taking possession of their promised land at the expense of the darker, uncivilized aspect of humanity, 'the savage.'

MH: It's strange to think that painting was a popular art in the mid-19th century, that some of the Hudson River folks were major celebrities, causing hundreds to line up and pay to see a single large canvas. Many were also founders of the Metropolitan Museum of Art in New York.

KM: Judeo-Christian understanding places the centre of the universe in the Middle East – that's where attention always seems to be focused in the mainstream media. But if you don't believe in that way of seeing the world, if you don't have those roots, the centre of the universe lies elsewhere – like here in North America, where Aboriginal histories go back many thousands of years. My work is about presenting another perspective; I've been going back and reclaiming the landscape from these European paintings, inserting lost narratives, the histories that have been obliterated and the absent mythologies.

I also began looking at North American painters from the 19th century as individuals, with their own egos and ambitions, in order to challenge the authority of their work. That's where my persona Miss Chief Eagle Testickle came from – she emerged as an egomaniac who could upstage them and insert herself in her own work, just as they did. Painter George Catlin (1796–1872), for instance, was a grand showman. To exhibit his paintings, he assembled a travelling gallery that included dancing Aboriginals and a menagerie of bears. He was something of a ringmaster.

Edward Curtis (1868–1952) was a filmmaker and photographer renowned for his contrivance. His pictures have greater

Group of Seven Inches

documentary authority than paintings, but it was well-known that he exercised a heavy hand in their production. For instance, he routinely asked subjects to don ceremonial clothing to perform household chores. Both he and Catlin travelled all over North America with the belief that the red man was dying. They felt it was their moral duty to document this race before it vanished. Catlin published several books that broke down Aboriginal traits, or characteristics, before and after European contact. There is such contempt in that document. The implication was that Aboriginal people were beautiful and became ugly, they were virtuous and became libidinous. It's a gross simplification of how he perceived Aboriginal cultures to be contaminated or spoiled by European influence, as opposed to cultures that could adapt and change. His conclusions were clear: if Aboriginal people no longer lived in a pure state, they ceased to exist. Paul Kane (1810–1871) lamented about similar obstacles for finding Aboriginal subjects in Toronto. He insisted he couldn't find any appropriate or authentic subject matter because Natives were already wearing European clothes. I borrowed text from Kane and Catlin for my film *Group of Seven Inches* (7.5 min, 2005). In it, I performed a simple reversal, making the white man the subject of these texts, demonstrating the absurdity of reducing an entire race to these maxims.

The European male will live forever in my pictures as living monuments of a noble race.

I have procured authentic examples of their costumes for the amusement and instruction of future ages.

It has become my life's work to make a record of them before they are obliterated completely.

I never romanticize my subjects. I paint each sitter with profound feelings for his individuality.

[intertitle excerpts from *Group of Seven Inches*]

Group of Seven Inches

The definitive moment for this film was an opportunity to do a weekend residency at the McMichael Gallery in 2004. It is a large gallery in a beautiful rural setting in Kleinburg, one of the last bastions designed to protect and promote the Group of Seven. There was a period when the museum became increasingly progressive and moved away from a strict focus on the Group. They started acquiring contemporary work, but during the Mike Harris (former right-wing premier of Ontario) government, the McMichaels regained curatorial control of the museum. Robert McMichael managed to extend his reach posthumously, hiring a lawyer who now sits on the board, ensuring that programming doesn't extend beyond a celebration of the Group of Seven. The

gallery then began to deaccession work by contemporary artists, some of them Aboriginal.

I had been invited to be an artist in residence, a modest program that would grant me access for a weekend. This program is one of the few loopholes that doesn't require board approval, and this exception provided an opportunity for subversion. When I went to the gallery for a walk-through, I arrived knowing that work from a couple of friends of mine (Mary Anne Barkhouse and Michael Belmore) had been dismantled and put beside the dumpster. When I entered the First Nations gallery, there was an Edward Curtis film being screened as an authoritative document on First Peoples. There was no mention of who he was, or any historical context provided; his film was showing amidst the totem poles and masks gathered in the room. In response, I thought I would do a performance with the Miss Chief persona – she had appeared in some paintings, now it was time to bring her to life. I wanted to explore power relations, specifically the ability of an artist to manipulate his subject – an exploration of the relationship between artist and model.

The performance, *The Taxonomy of the European Male*, happened in the Founder's Lounge at the gallery, and the film *Group of Seven Inches* became the cinematic version. It was shot later that day during regular gallery hours. It was made guerrilla-style, and this was so liberating for me as a filmmaker. I had always felt that the conventional filmmaking process never really suited me. In earlier work like *Blood River* (2000), I tried to squeeze myself into a box that just didn't fit, and it wasn't where I wanted to go anyway. I never saw myself pursuing a career as a writer/director in Hollywood. *Group of Seven Inches* was a great experiment in breaking away from all of that; I had enough money to buy the film stock and that was enough. Jody Shapiro and Gisèle Gordon, who I've worked with since 1996, were my two main collaborators. Jody had worked with Guy Maddin and brought insights into his methods as my cinematographer. We would shoot without sync sound, using two or three Super 8 cameras at the same time. It wasn't scripted, but we knew what each scene would basically contain.

Miss Chief rides on a horse through the gates of the McMichael Gallery, where she spots two European males running through the woods in loincloths and moccasins. She seduces them into Tom Thomson's shack, where she plies them with alcohol and gets them to model for her painting, and then she has her way with them. In the end, she dresses them up in authentic European clothing so they can perform in her travelling gallery, the same way Catlin's gallery toured Europe.

We shot in painter Tom Thomson's shack, which had been removed from its original location and rebuilt – plank by plank – on the gallery grounds and dressed with period props to make it look like an authentic studio. There are small glass windows for viewers – it appears like a diorama, and that's what I loved about it. There were eight of us in that little shack with the late August sun bearing down – it must have been over 40 degrees. The scene descended into chaos at one point because while Miss Chief is pouring booze over the two boys and licking their nipples, Maxime (one of the European males) spotted two kids at the window and then their horrified parents pulling them away. That sent Max over the edge and he began laughing uncontrollably; the energy in the room descended into the hysteria that we caught on film. We didn't really know how it was going to go, but it just went that way. Then we stopped filming, all a little naturally high, and packed everything up and drove away. As we were driving home, my co-director Gisèle said we forgot to shoot the scene where we dressed the boys up as Europeans. That was part of the live performance, but we forgot to shoot it because we got so carried away. And because we had to work during regular gallery hours while there were two weddings taking place, we had to vie for space outside the shack. But it worked out better in the end because we shot the final scene the next day in my studio, using my paintings as the background. The movie was very experimental, but the energy is there.

MH: It is beautifully shot in black and white, complete with piano music and intertitles, like an old silent movie.

KM: I was inspired by silent-era films, the Edward Curtis film and Guy Maddin's films, and I wanted to make what looked like a period film. It followed the same gesture as my paintings, playing with the authority of period idioms and narratives by reproducing them from a different point of view. My partner, Dustin Peters (also one of the European males), composed the music.

Shooting Geronimo (11 min, 2007) was more carefully constructed at script stage, but we used the same liberated approach when we shot it. We found a location called Docville one hour east of Toronto, where Doc has a western set on his farm that he rents out for films, parties or weddings. It has a general store, a saloon and a sheriff's office. It's pretty minimal, and you can only shoot in one direction because there's a busy road next to it, but that didn't bother me.

MH: It features an Edward Curtis–like filmmaker using a wind-up camera to film cowboy and Indian dramas on a stage with a beautiful painted backdrop. I'm guessing you painted the landscape?

KM: Yes, I wanted to paint Monument Valley as it appeared in the John Ford westerns. I located the actual rock formation in *The Searchers* (1956), one of the most racist films ever made. The backdrop is part of the film's reclamation, taking those landscapes to tell the other side of the story.

I was also interested in retracing a history of performance in Aboriginal cultures. In *Shooting Geronimo*, the filmmaker wants his Native subjects to show him an authentic dance. That idea came from the Edward Curtis film called *Land of the Headhunters* that I saw at the McMichael Gallery. The performers in the film told their children and grandchildren that Curtis wanted to capture authentic ceremonial dancing, but these ceremonial dances were not for European eyes, and they undermined him and changed the dances for the film. In *Shooting Geronimo*'s first dance scene, what is supposed to be a Ghost Dance turns into a balletic pas de deux. It was choreographed by my friend Michael Greyeyes, a trained ballet dancer and choreographer. The second dance shows Miss Chief's intervention. She appears as a

Shooting Geronimo

Shooting Geronimo

KM: I wanted to get inside the minds of people who created pictures of Aboriginals a long time ago, and the power they had to shape the way audiences saw their subjects, both then and now. Catlin, Kane and Curtis had so much influence on how Aboriginal people were portrayed. If you trace the Hollywood western back, it's all derived from their images. Returning to that moment of inspiration or creativity is a way of intercepting it and moving it forward in another direction. You can't change history, but you can get people to think again about what happened back then, and hopefully they will see the present in a different light.

MH: How did your first movie, *A Nation Is Coming* (24 min, 1996), begin?

mysterious force, a trickster character, and after she tumbles into frame, the boys perform a mix of capoeira and breakdancing.

MH: The film director, who is always running onto the stage to show his Native actors how to act more Native (fiercer, more 'savage'), is shot and killed by accident. The two actors quickly make another short where his corpse thanks them, via intertitles, for helping him, and assures them (and the audience) that he was shot by a white man. In the final scene, Miss Chief leads his corpse spirit away on a horse.

KM: As Miss Chief's character in this film is that of a spirit or trickster, perhaps the motivation behind all of her mischief-making on the filmmaker's set is simply to find a cute partner to join her on the other side. The original script was written in 2003 without a role for her, as she didn't make her debut as a performer until after the film had been scripted. As the writing evolved, I realized that the film would be more interesting if there was a mischief maker, a supernatural element, representing Aboriginal philosophy. Actually, it was just another star vehicle for Miss Chief.

Shooting Geronimo was carefully scripted and storyboarded. We had two, sometimes three, cameras shooting at the same time, so we got a lot of extra footage, which is proving useful to us now in creating a two-channel version. We weren't recording live sound, and we worked with available light, so we moved quickly. We found a great location, and the backdrop and stage were planned well in advance. We had only two days, but were able to accomplish a lot.

MH: Both *Group of Seven Inches* and *Shooting Geronimo* are about making pictures – paintings in the first instance, movies in the second.

KM: *A Nation Is Coming* started as an idea for a dance video installation I proposed to the Banff Centre for the Arts. It was my first collaboration with Michael Greyeyes and an opportunity to take advantage of Banff's professional television studio and high-end facilities. It started small, but once we got there, it took on a life of its own, and we wanted to make something that could be a video in its own right.

MH: A series of intertitles narrate prophecies that punctuate the action, including this one that lends your movie its title:

> The whole world is coming
> A nation is coming, a nation is coming
> The Eagle has brought
> The message to the tribe
> The Father says so, the Father says so.
> [Lakota, Ghost Dance Song]

Another says: 'You shall live in square grey houses in a barren land and beside those square grey houses you shall starve. Drinks Water as quoted by Black Elk.' This cautionary prophecy contains an uncanny juxtaposition of having little (starving) amidst plenty (houses). Where is it from?

KM: This was at the end of the 19th century, the end of the freedom that Plains Indian people had enjoyed for thousands of years. They were dying from smallpox, being hunted down and killed by the U.S. army. It was probably the most desperate time for Native American people. The prophet Wovoka began the Ghost Dance religion to provide a ray of hope, forecasting that the world would be restored and that they weren't all going to die.

I was interested in Aboriginal prophecies because at the time we were making the film, there was a pervasive millennial angst, which derives again from a Christian viewpoint. But prophecies from Ojibwa culture and other nations say we are living in the time of the seventh fire, a time of renewal.

MH: Does each fire represent a generation?

KM: Yes, and when Aboriginal people talk about the seventh fire, they're also reflecting on the future. Every decision you make for your community also affects the seventh generation. This prophecy reminds us to take care of our future. Our film counteracts the bleak fears of the millennium, looking to Aboriginal prophecy for inspiration to interpret where we are and where we're going.

MH: Landscape scenarios are set against a dancing figure who is rapturously lit, sometimes with flowing abstractions projected around him. He is introduced freezing in the snow, but then comes 'back to life.' The tape plays out this dichotomy between an interior space and landscape, alternating wide shots and close-ups. Could you elaborate further on this division?

KM: We used the epic landscapes of Banff as a backdrop for historical narratives. There's a scene in which Michael's character is lying frozen in the snow that is inspired by the photographs from the massacre of Big Foot and his band at Wounded Knee. Men, women and children were slaughtered and left frozen in the snow. The Ghost Dance religion was born out of that time. Banff had expansive vistas, and we dug into history for inspiration.

MH: With its beautifully choreographed set pieces, the tape revels in the beauty of its co-creator and male lead, Michael Greyeyes, who appears in various states of undress throughout. This ritual of memory is also (or first of all?) erotic, an exposition of the body, a history that comes up out of the experience of the body.

KM: If it's erotic it's because Michael is a stunningly beautiful man, but it wasn't intended to be. I wanted him to look like a Ghost Dancer. I was studying archival photos of men with body makeup, painted with clay. I wanted his character to have the feel of a time traveller.

MH: Are the movements of the dancer related to 'traditional' choreographies? Can you talk about the relation between traditions of movement that carry spiritual significance and present-day interpretations: is it like rewriting lines from the Quran? Or more like how Shakespeare cops a riff from histories of Ancient Rome to write *Antony and Cleopatra*?

KM: Michael was at a very interesting time in his career. He'd been a professional dancer with the National Ballet, then started exploring powwow dancing. His repertoire as a choreographer and dancer was an unusual mix of these different traditions. He did some preliminary work before arriving, but most of the choreography was developed while we were in Banff, actually in the studio. Our film provided a good opportunity to draw upon his different influences and an interesting way of bringing Native philosophy alive.

Incorporating influences is rooted in the same understanding that Aboriginal people had to be innovative to adapt and survive. The attempts of George Catlin to freeze Aboriginal people into a time capsule is counter to the philosophy I was taught by my Cree family, which was to move toward the future and not be afraid of taking something and making it your own. Whether you play the piano or make paintings, adapting influences from other cultures is a very empowered way of thinking about who you are. A lot of my work deconstructs received ideas about Aboriginal people: for instance, the notion that it is a negative thing that our culture has changed.

An iconic sculpture, *The End of the Trail*, was created by James Earle Fraser in the late 19th century depicting a dying Indian on a horse. It's an image of death, and was created to commemorate what was believed to be a dying race. Endlessly reproduced, it still

A Nation Is Coming

holds a great deal of power, particularly in the United States. The effect is that you're always reminded that the Native American race is supposed to be departed, or impotent. As this sculpture is the tombstone that others attempted to impose on us, I refute this image in my work.

MH: Were you surprised at the positive reception *A Nation Is Coming* received?

KM: Yes, it was much bigger than we thought it would be. Sara Diamond, then head of the Media and Visual Arts Program at the Banff Centre, was very supportive. She sent the tape out to festivals, and it ended up at Sundance. From that point, I started thinking that filmmaking is something I could pursue further. At that time, there was very little dramatic filmmaking coming from Aboriginal communities. I'd heard that Shelley Niro had made a dramatic film, but I'd never really seen much coming out of Aboriginal communities, aside from some docs by Alanis Obomsawin or Loretta Todd. Audiences were interested, even hungry, for this material. And I couldn't help thinking about the many stories from our communities that we hadn't even started to talk about. I was a bit overwhelmed by the weight of what lay ahead of us, and at

Blood River

the same time I felt completely liberated because it had never been done. Faced with that magnitude, I became seduced by one of the many possibilities: dramatic film. The Sundance Institute had just started their Native Screenwriters Lab, which I was invited to attend. It was a question of being at the right place at the right time. It felt that things were really opening up for Aboriginal filmmaking when I started work on *Blood River* (23 min, 2000).

MH: In *Blood River,* you tell the story of a teenage girl uncovering her Ojibwa roots. The traditionally staged drama moments of Rose and her hectoring, trying-too-hard mother are juxtaposed with kinetic, street-life montages of her brother Clayton, a street hustler who turns tricks and is eventually gay-bashed. Why these two very different approaches?

KM: It's a common story. My sister was adopted into our family, and I watched her go through a similar experience trying to locate her birth mother. My grandmother kept foster children, and these kids came and went in a large foster home. Aboriginal communities are home to a lot of lost boys and girls.

The idea was to make these two worlds as different cinematically as possible, but I was going to bring brother and sister together at the end of the film. The sister's world is a 16mm TV sitcom, plastic, perfect world: detached, predictable, static. This contrasts with the slow-shutter-speed digital video showing the underbelly life of foster kids who end up on the street. These scenes have an experimental, dreamlike quality. At that time, it was technically challenging to marry the MiniDV footage with the 16mm. We couldn't find anyone who had done it, but we wound up transferring it to 16mm and cutting the film negatives together. It's easy to do this now, but at the time it was a technical nightmare with time-code problems.

MH: Can you talk about the depiction of violence in the movies? Do you feel that violent movies lead to a more aggressive, less tolerant society? Do we live in the reality of these pictures? Does onscreen violence make off-screen violence more prevalent, or more 'normal'?

KM: Clayton, the street kid and hustler, gets gay-bashed. These scenes show the vulnerability of children who are at risk, without protection. I wanted his sister to experience his world through her dreams, as if she's psychically connected. She doesn't even know she has a brother until the end of the film, but she finds him in her nightmares. You often read about twins who feel each other's phantom pains at great distances. I tried to convey their blood connection by marrying the danger of his world with her dream life.

I'm not interested in showing actual violence. If it's not handled well, overt displays of violence diminish the experience, and I felt it was unnecessary for this movie. I tried instead to find a way to create an emotional impact.

MH: Reports of a deadly airborne virus usher in *Future Nation* (16:27 min, 2005), while young queers party on. There is a tension between these fin-de-siècle youth, who feel that every moment is their last and life is a picture. The shirtless bartender, the young romantique with the just-so hair, the throwaway farewells and pickup lines, the swarm of tops and bottoms: all this has been done and seen before. Your future fantasia, like the genre of science fiction itself, looks like a rehearsal of the past. I wonder if you could talk about pictures produced by 'subcultures.' Whether we meet punks, drag queens, bears or femmes, they all arrive in a uniform of personality. Somehow their deepest desire, their most personal inflection, is a strict repetition of what others have experienced. And these are the folks who are opting out of the mainstream hallucination.

KM: Originally I wanted a kid on the reserve to reflect on his former life, before some kind of devastating event occurred – in this case a biological disaster. He would fall in love with a boy, and this would occur on a reserve where he would have to grapple with his sexuality in a context that wasn't urban. I filed the idea away until Big Soul Productions approached me. They had worked with a federal agency called Human Resources Development Canada to produce short films in a program that trained Aboriginal youth to use cameras and make stories. They were also pitching a television series called *Moccasin Flats*, which came through, and then funding arrived to make another short in Toronto. They asked if I could do a story about a gay kid, because after working with Aboriginal teenagers, they felt homophobia was an issue that needed to be dealt with. This was already a big part of my work, knowing how homophobic our communities had become as a result of Christianity. It used to be different – there had been a respect for people with different sexualities – but the Church has changed the way we think about our own people. I pitched this idea to them and imagined it executed in flashback – images of the city's destruction would arrive via television or on his computer – but the producers said, 'Let's show all the plague's effects.' All of a sudden the film became a more ambitious production, though in the end budget restrictions made creating the look and feel of this world more challenging.

Si je t'aime (painting)

There were a series of travelling scenes between the reserve and the city, with four or five characters in an SUV. Needing to save time and money, we decided to shoot in a studio and light it to suggest movement, but it wasn't convincing. The scenes just didn't work. As a result, while we were in the edit room, I rewrote the whole film. It was a real struggle, and took time, but finally I went back and looked at the original idea and reframed it that way, as a more personal, diaristic film.

I was thinking about the story of an Aboriginal kid who comes to the city to find his freedom. As a gay man, I've seen that play itself out many times. You see small-town kids land on Church Street and assume a new identity. It's a way of gaining acceptance. I think that's what kids do at that age, they gravitate toward a group where they can feel safe and belong. Often they have come from homophobic environments, so when they arrive here, they assume one of the available types.

In *Future Nation*, you see this kid falling into an urban gay world of drag queens and leather, but I knew the story of the two boys would still be unusual. I've never seen a film about an Aboriginal boy from a reserve having a drag-queen boyfriend, and this twist would add a new and important layer. The film also shows a cowboy type who is topped by an Aboriginal drag-queen dominatrix. I play with these types, shifting the balance of power. The film contains many recognizable elements that make it accessible, but at the same time there's something new in its incarnation.

MH: The end of your movie is beautiful and curious. In traditional comedic fashion, it's all going to work out – the lovers are reunited, the family will have enough food to survive – but then you refuse to wrap it up with a bow. In a throwaway closing speech, delivered in voice-over, the boy lead announces that times have changed and his great love has moved away. Just like that. Was it necessary to refuse the closure that narrative seems to require, the way a dinner wants cutlery?

KM: This was a chapter in his life that he reflects on; it wasn't The End, only a memory. I wanted to imply that there is something outside the movie, where the audience lives.

MH: Do you have a specific audience in mind when you're working on a movie?

KM: My primary audience for both paintings and films is Aboriginal, they are my community. That's who the stories are about. An Aboriginal audience will be the first to understand what I'm doing, but the work is open enough so that others can enter it. I would like to reach as wide an audience as possible. That's one thing I learned through painting. When I felt I was failing to engage and communicate, I adopted idioms that would allow me to open further. It's so important for these alternate perspectives to be out there – I'd be failing if I couldn't reach a wide audience.

Kent Monkman is an artist of Cree ancestry who works with a variety of mediums, including painting, film/video, performance and installation. He has had solo exhibitions at the Art Gallery of Hamilton and the Museum of Contemporary Canadian Art in Toronto. He has participated in various international group exhibitions, including 'We come in peace ... ': Histories of the Americas at the Musée d'art contemporain de Montreal and The American West at Compton Verney, in Warwickshire, England. Monkman has created site-specific performances at the McMichael Canadian Art Collection, Compton Verney and the Royal Ontario Museum, and has also made Super 8 versions of these performances that he calls Colonial Art Space Interventions. His award-winning short film and video works have been screened at various national and international festivals, including the 2006 and 2008 Berlinale and the 2007 Toronto International Film Festival. His work is represented in the collections of the National Gallery of Canada, Montreal Museum of Fine Arts, the National Museum of the American Indian (Smithsonian), Museum London, the Mackenzie Art Gallery, the Woodland Cultural Centre, the Indian Art Centre and the Canada Council Art Bank.

Kent Monkman's Films and Videos

A Nation Is Coming   24 min 1996 (with Michael Greyeyes)
Blood River   23 min 2000
Future Nation   16:27 min 2005
Group of Seven Inches   7:35 min 2005 (with Gisèle Gordon)
Robin's Hood   5:53 min 2007 (with Gisèle Gordon)
Shooting Geronimo   11 min 2007 (and two-channel installation)

Distributed by Vtape.

NELSON HENRICKS
IRONIC NOSTALGIA

There is something old and sad and wise in his expression, and then he bounds up from the chair and squeezes out another bon mot on his way to the fridge and I have to pinch myself in reminder that he is still young. In his face, which erupts in sudden and unexpected delights, I can feel some deep acceptance of limits; it is a face that has glimpsed its own frontier, it has combed the furthest reaches of itself before settling into a more comfortable posture. But the gravity of his speaking carries this understanding of limits, and it is a knowledge that he brings into one videotape after another, though in truth he is a kind of filmmaker in disguise, with his careful framing and his raw-to-the-skin feeling for the surfaces of pictures. He was inclined from the beginning toward the cinema, but played out his aspirations in the low-cost realm of video, at a time when extreme technical limitations led many to an artless style. But he has been steadfast in his pursuit of beauty, the compulsions and lists, the mad detours and taxonomies – they would still be fine and sharp and well-cared-for if they were beautiful, wouldn't they? Yes, they would. Nelson is a prairie boy living in Montreal, a single-channel maestro locked up in galleries, queer-eyed in a straight world. These displacements, enacted with a painstaking precision and meticulous attention to detail, continue to mark his work.

There are some painters who rush out into the landscape and settle their tools in front of a tree or a mountain or a running body of water. Nelson is not amongst their number. He is a studio artist. He is busy building models; he is out in the world and then he takes that experience back into the studio and changes its scale. He blows it up so large we have to walk around it and let it slowly enter us, or else he reduces it in scale, shrinks a terrible tragedy down to a few enigmatic images, caught in a series of variations, until the heartbreak becomes clear enough. He builds models for living and seeing and thinking and then sets them loose, imagining that the audience will be as intelligent as his makings. Yes, he believes in utopia, after all.

MH: Artists often play with the means of expression, the way a message or story is told. For the uninitiated, this often makes the work bewildering and confusing. Why is it necessary to alter the shaping of pictures?

NH: If I understand the question correctly, I believe you are asking why artists' work looks so much different than what we see in mainstream media. My initial response was going to be that artists' work is part of a larger constellation of alternative uses of film and video media, so it isn't all that extraordinary. When we think of image production in the broadest possible terms – amateur video and filmmaking, home movies, surveillance videos, webcams, film and video outside of the occident, pornography, etc. – we see that the majority of moving images produced globally are not what we usually think of as the mainstream (though the mainstream is unquestionably dominant). Most

people underestimate the breadth of possible uses of media. Artists are simply engaged in a conscious exploration of the alternatives.

But are all artists wilfully exploring? A commitment to experimentation and what used to be called the avant-garde has certainly guided my work. But beyond this, I think it is much easier for people to make the work they make than it is for them to follow conventions. The work of most artists is guided by an interest in representational systems other than Hollywood cinema and network television, and it refers to a broader spectrum of human activities than can usually be contained within conventional forms.

When I was in a band, we started doing cover versions, but soon realized it was easier to make original material. I remember the singer saying, 'It's easier to write and play our own songs, because no one can tell when you make a mistake.' You immediately abandon questions of technique ('Can I play this perfectly?') and move on to something more enabling ('Can I play *something*?'). Perhaps this is all a question of intellectual styles. Some people naturally gravitate toward imitation and technical mastery, and they would call me a lazy guitarist because I can't play 'Stairway to Heaven.' Yet I have written a few songs. Was it more work? I don't know.

MH: We are all familiar with the virtues of the small moment, narrowcast not broadcast. But where is the political efficacy in this range of fringe media? Isn't it only too easy to ignore these wilful obscurities, which may be found only in specialist houses playing to in crowds? Or is it, instead, supposed to rely on the 'universal' values of great art: transcendence, the truth in materials, consciousness, time and memory? At a moment when the lies of mainstream, corporate-owned media are more transparent than ever, how is fringe media working to enter the breaches of representation?

NH: Well, I don't think fringe work is politically efficacious. Most of it was never meant to be. Someone (I forget who) said that politics should not be used as a measure of the worth of something. Bad art can have good political effects, but does that make it better art?

Deleuze and Guattari wrote about rhizomatic structures as a way of combatting fascism. The current historical moment is probably a good time to again consider ways of eliminating fascism. Their argument was that fields of decentralized modules (like a potato plant) were the best way of destabilizing monolithic, centralized structures (like trees). But it's not enough simply to make a bunch of rhizomes. The key is to connect them. When linked, rhizomatic structures can have political potential.

Perhaps the queer festivals of the '80s and '90s are a good example of this. Make a queer movie, and so what? But get a hundred people to make queer movies, show them all together and call it a festival, and suddenly you have something that has some political weight. So if we want to make fringe work political, maybe we need to think about creating links.

I choose to understand politics as activities that have social effects. Usually, I am depressed that my work is so useless, politically speaking. But if I think in terms of social effects, perhaps my production has encouraged other people to make bewildering and confusing work (and I believe it has). If one thinks rhizomatically, this probably has some net political effect.

I saw a 76-year-old woman do a puppet show a few days ago. She was a Holocaust survivor, and the show was about her experiences in the camps when she was 15. I was literally speechless afterwards. The people I was with – video artists, performance artists and experimental musicians – were all mute. There was a question-and-answer session and no one in the audience could say a word. I would be hard-pressed to explain why this was so powerful (in political and other ways), but it had something to do with the immense humanness of this person. There weren't more than 25 people in the audience. Was that old woman's testimony useless because she wasn't on TV? Was it any less politically efficacious? Was her puppet show good art? I am not sure I can answer these questions, but I know that what I experienced that night made all the difference in the world. It was like the difference between life and death.

MH: Video art began in the mid-1960s with the advent of portable video recording; finally, the apparatus could be taken out of corporate broadcast centres and put into the hands of individuals. In the literature of this time, there is much talk about a hoped-for utopia of representation, that these tools would make possible a genuine democracy of what could be shown. Television by the people, for the people. And, on the other hand, personal expressions that lay far from the strictures of ratings and advertisers could also be celebrated. But the liberation of production was not accompanied by a liberation of exhibition: the portals remain as closed today as they were then. Another utopia has come and gone. How do you see the ongoing disconnect between production and exhibition? Do you feel that most artists' work simply shows to other artists, and that this in-crowd insularity is creating a body of work whose means and messages lie further and further from any who don't already know the secret handshake, possess the decoder ring, speak the riddle?

NH: Video, as a medium, has been always dogged by a certain between-ness: *between* television, cinema and art, but never completely *of* them. I think people had already begun to realize that video's utopian potential – in terms of broadcast television anyway – was pretty much nil by the mid-'70s. People (myself included) continued to explore this terrain up into the current decade, but with limited success. And let's not forget that other utopias have disappeared as well. People don't even pretend that television has the possibility to educate anymore. It's nearly impossible for anything difficult to survive in the current televisual ecology. And don't get me wrong: I love television. But I just don't go there with the same expectations I do when I enter the cinema or an art gallery. Perhaps this is why I feel my work func-

tions best at festivals or in galleries. Over the past five years, I have begun to feel more strongly that the gallery is where my work belongs. I am an artist and I make art. Festivals, unless they are dedicated to art or experimental work, tend to provide a distorted context for the work. They set up the wrong kind of expectations about how the work should be seen, how it functions, what it should do.

As a videomaker, I feel the potential for audience is great, and my most satisfying experiences have occurred outside of the usual venues. In Atlanta, my work was shown in a public park, and a few teenagers really responded strongly to it. They simply weren't an audience I ever imagined having. Another time, I was working with ten 'at-risk' kids in an alternative school, and we made a tape collaboratively. When it was done, we presented it to the entire school. The students were so enthusiastic that we watched the tape three times in a row. They cheered when it was over. So I believe the audience is out there. Somewhere.

As a person who comes from a working-class background, I was very conscious of the rift between the general public and art from the outset. One of my friends said to me while I was in art school, 'Don't forget that you are making work for us too.' And I suppose those words have stayed with me. This is primarily a problem of educating the general public. But I think there are ways for people who have no education in art or experimental film to enter my work. I have employed narrative and tropes derived from popular culture to facilitate this. I don't think every artist needs to do this, but some of us do. This is a niche I am happy to inhabit because I adore pop culture. And art. I am a pop artist!

I think we underestimate the value of our own production if we don't admit that it is a specialist discourse on some level. You couldn't expect to understand everything a doctor says without some education. Some aspects of medical practice are extremely specialized and can take years of education to understand. There is an assumption, by both artists and the general public, that art is transparent and requires no special expertise. It's the same kind of thinking that lets people say things like, 'My kid could do that!' when they are standing in front of a Jackson Pollock. Not all aspects of medicine, physics or even hairstyling are accessible to everyone. And the same is true of art.

There is a subtext to your questioning that seems to assume a natural and interlocking relationship between visibility, popularity and success (financial, cultural and political). I am not sure we can assume this is so. Three years ago, three of the most successful artists in contemporary music worldwide were Canadian: Céline Dion, Alanis Morissette and Shania Twain. (And let's not forget Avril Lavigne and Nelly Furtado!) Now, I ask you, is this the best Canadian cultural product, musically or otherwise? I realize this is going to sound like a loser's argument, but it seems to me there is a hazard in making work that is too accessible, too popular. And that hazard, I suppose, is that you are going to start making kitsch, making entertainment.

Between the most popular bit of television fluff and the most impenetrable chestnut of experimental film, there is a vast spectrum of work. For myself, a healthy cultural ecology supports both fluff and chestnuts, and everything between them. Our society is increasingly inclined toward entertainment, so it falls to artists to do something else: to provoke, to educate.

MH: The advent of digital video is realizing the utopian hope of the '60s: that 'everyone' can do it. Soon, video/cellphone at the ready, 'everyone' will. But who will watch all this stuff? There is more artists' media work being made this year than in all the previous years put together, but the rise in audiences is not commensurate. Is such a proliferation of personal expression such a good thing when it leads to increasing disappointments and dashed dreams? Will we ever get over the sense of having come 'too late,' after all the important events, discoveries, inventions, have already occurred?

NH: Teaching video at a university level gives me the impression that production and dissemination will probably occur much differently in this century than it did in the last. The emerging generation conceives these issues within an entirely different framework. One of my students posts his work on a website as soon as he finishes it. Some say broadcast television as we knew it is on the verge of collapse. The new model of web distribution for television, film and video favours small, specialized audiences (recall the rhizomatic structure I mentioned earlier). Clearly, we are entering another utopian paradigm, one dependent upon storage space, bandwidth and data flow. Time will tell whether it is viable or not. We may need to rethink our notion of what an audience is and how it interacts with work.

The transition from analog to digital has been a long and painful process, and the question of distribution is hopefully the closing bracket on this slow and expensive arc. The shift has had both positive and negative repercussions. I marvel at the fact that the post-production facilities on my laptop are vastly superior to what was available in 1986 at EMMEDIA, the artist-run centre where I first started making work. Paradoxically, I am dogged by the feeling that making video is much less interesting now that it's so much easier to do. I would have killed to have personal, unlimited access to these kinds of tools 20 years ago. Now that I have it all here at home, it seems very ordinary. I feel that is reflected in a lot of the work being produced today, which seems very banal. That probably sounds snobbish, but there you go.

MH: The first person to rub two stones together produced an unthinkable fire, then everyone did it so no one notices anymore. The first couple of generations of video art are filled with utopian and originary gestures large and small that mapped out the field. Our generation, on the other hand, seems condemned to montage, recutting and reshaping moments that often already exist (either as found footage or modelled in other lives/works). Everything's been done, and who would know better? Our generation learned all about it in 'art school.' The major strokes have been laid down, the outlines and arguments constructed – it's

been left to us to fill in the colours, fuss with the borders. We are the generation of ornamentation, made helpless by privilege and precedent. Gatekeepers between the analog world of presence and a digital microverse of mirrors.

NH: The epoch we are living in now is incredibly unique. I can't think of another historical period when there was such a glut of images and information. Certainly the invention of the printing press and the first wide proliferation of books must have been a similar moment. Perhaps moving away from authorship and toward filling in colours and fussing with borders, as you say, is the only suitable response. This, I feel, is the crux of what Barthes was saying when he described the 'death of the author.' When I was working on *Satellite*, I was very satisfied to be working with found footage. It felt responsible: reduce, recycle, reuse! As artists, we are working in an unprecedented historical moment: one would think this alone would allow us enormous possibilities to create something original, and I think it has.

I remember walking into a group exhibition in Rome in the summer of 2004 and seeing so much poorly installed, conceived and constructed video work that for two weeks afterwards I was convinced the only option left for me was to move on to another medium. Most of the time I still feel this way. Every video I have made since *Planetarium* feels like my last one. And with my newest project, I feel I have made a decisive (if self-sabotaging) break from single-channel work. It's sad for me to think I may have to abandon video, because it is the medium that best suits my voice. I still have things to say with video (in fact, I have two projects that need to be finished). But the sheer glut of bad production, coupled with a lack of critical and curatorial standards necessary to contextualize it, leaves me increasingly wary of going any further.

In private, I wonder: am I an anachronism? Is my failure to love this glut of badly crafted, ill-conceived work just a failure to keep up with the times? I think we all need to ask ourselves these questions. Has the medium reached its endgame in the same manner that painting and sculpture did, and is now poised to be absorbed within a new multimedia hybrid? Or is this a paradigm shift that merits serious critical attention? Diplomatically, I feel I should say it's the latter, but in my heart, I am almost sure the former has prevailed. I don't feel I need to defend video. But I can't imagine myself becoming one of those people who gleefully shouts, 'The emperor still has his clothes!' when clearly he does not. Being a deluded fool is a fate more terrible than working with an admittedly anachronistic medium.

MH: *Satellite* (6 min, 2004) looks like it's made entirely of '50s industrial playthings culled from the Prelinger Archives. Prelinger has taken his block-long stock-footage library and put it online, an open-source dream available to anyone with a download button. Do you feel your movie is one possible arrangement of an infinite series? Or does it signal, more ominously, an exhaustion of imagination where there is nothing left to discover?

NH: I am embarrassed to say it, but *Satellite* was built in old-school fashion. I happened upon a guy selling educational films. The first one I bought was called *Hearing and the Ears*. I bought several more in the next months, took them back to my studio and watched them one at a time. The films I didn't think were useful I exchanged for others. When I felt I had enough material to work with, I reshot the films off the wall of my studio and built the rough cut. Eventually I had professional film transfers made. Still, there wasn't enough footage. I found another person selling 16mm films and repeated this process a second time. All in all, *Satellite* is built with elements from eight or nine films, though I viewed many more. Lack of immediacy (among other things) is one of the reasons *Satellite* took nearly two years to complete.

Even though five versions of *Satellite* exist, the arrangement never really changes. This is largely due to the text, which is (kind of) carefully ordered. As the images are linked to the text in specific ways, I don't think they would be easy to shuffle. I suppose my interest in using these images was due to their generic, 'archetypal' quality. In my work I often tend to use pictures as ideograms. In montage theory, Sergei Eisenstein compares film editing to Japanese ideograms. He theorized that montage produces meaning in the same way. In Japanese, the symbols 'child + mouth = scream,' 'knife + heart = sorrow,' 'door + ear = listen' and so on. So I guess what I am trying to say in a pretentious and overly complex way is that I use images as symbols. Still, there is a nuance to Eisenstein's idea that is interesting, namely that meaning is produced in an interval between two images, rather than by the images themselves. These educational films produced that 'ideogrammatic' effect abundantly. A friend commented that the images in *Satellite* look like things I could have shot. Maybe watching educational films in junior high and high school influenced my camera aesthetic. I was also interested in notions of the scientific and objective truth, which was another level of appeal these images contain: they seem to represent a world of absolutes that the text attempts to undermine.

MH: 'You are everything you hate. Intelligence is insanity by consensus.' These titles occur in rapid-fire succession over the pictures, provocative throwaway lines (unrelated, unattached) in this throwaway world. 'Stare at something until it is meaningless. Ambiguity is obsolete.' Everything is visible but no longer means anything. Isn't that also part of the message you're conveying? Even your catchphrase, 'Hangover Without Pleasure,' evokes a party you weren't invited to, perhaps the original place where these pictures were made. All you can feel, all you can deliver to the audience, are the after-effects, the reaction shot. 'The characters are trapped in the same story.' Are you, the author, condemned to rewrite the same book, or is the audience condemned to watch the same movie?

NH: Yes, the aphorisms were trying to tap into an ephemeral style of language that is prevalent these days: advertising buzz phrases; mottos you can tattoo on your arm, write on a T-shirt or spray-paint on a wall; slogans for political parties; names of bands, films, magazines or products. The kind of language that is prevalent in urban environments. I was also very interested in paradoxes and nonsense. I suppose I wanted the aphorisms to be disposable, but, at the same time, to stick in your throat. There is something disturbing, off-kilter or just baffling about these phrases that is hard to dismiss.

'Everything is visible but no longer means anything.' I think perhaps meaning is where we make it. The brain has a fantastic capacity for creating sense out of random information. I was trying to set up a space where the production of meaning was problematized. People have described *Satellite* alternately as political, bleak and funny. Or my favourite: ironic nostalgia, which simultaneously sounds like an aphorism from *Satellite* and a good capsule description of my work generally.

CONSUME OR LOSE

Satellite

MH: There are a long and curious set of superimposed titles that close out *Planetarium* (21 min, 2001). Titles like 'Essen Ich Koln NR.' Can you talk about how these texts were generated and what they mean? Their scrambled rearrangements recalled for me Joyce Wieland's *Reason over Passion* or some of Hollis Frampton's work. Do you find moments of your fringe movie viewing sneaking into your work, especially because as a teacher you likely see some things again and again? Do Harold Bloom's well-known formulations around anxiety of influence concern you (all texts are created out of existing texts, and 'break-throughs' occur within a generational tension between canonized forebears and the present), or has all that been left behind?

NH: I was sitting around in my studio killing time, waiting for someone, and I started doing anagrams of my name. I'm interested in games and unproductive uses of time. Most of the phrases come from sitting around making up anagrams. 'McKinley Morganfield' is Muddy Waters' original name. 'Merc Montclair' is a reference to a song by Captain Beefheart called 'When Big Joan Sets Up.' 'Uh turqoise scarf 'n uh sleeve rolled up over uh Merc Montclair.' (He's referring to a car, a Mercury Montclair.) I listened to Beefheart exclusively during the editing of *Planetarium*. I was interested in how he uses nonsense to create really wonderful meanings.

This interest in nonsense fuelled the writing/collecting of the *Satellite* aphorisms, which were originally to be included in *Planetarium*. Most were removed because they made the tape impossibly dense. A few are still there: NO REVOLUTION and YOU KNOW YOU ARE WRONG, for example. It is about names and naming, and forms a kind of credit sequence. It leads the viewer through a field of nonsense until it arrives at my name and the end of the tape simultaneously.

Perhaps my use of the word *nonsense* is misleading. I am not trying to absolve people from searching for sense in the work, but I am raising the bar considerably higher than what the general public is accustomed to. It's a broader, more diffused sense, and people have to work harder to order an experience. In the Occident, and particularly in the mainstream media, all information is totalized to make some kind of meaning. And as a people, we are very frightened when we encounter things that don't make sense or, rather, that aren't groomed to make sense by a boardroom full of power brokers. I believe there are a whole lot of things I encounter on a daily basis that don't make sense. I am buying hothouse tomatoes in my grocery, while on the radio the American president announces the commencement of the bombing of Baghdad. What kind of sense can I make of that? The fact is it does make sense, but one that is hard to contain or totalize within speech. We feel the sense of it intuitively, somewhere beyond the limits of language. And this is one place where art can actually perform rather well. It is perhaps the only thing we have: this ability to speak in a way that doesn't fix meaning into these little iron-hard pellets of ideology. Okay, now I am slipping into a rant. Can you hear my fist pounding on the desk all the way in Toronto?

I hadn't really thought of Wieland or Frampton, though I love their work very much. Any plagiarism/citation was unconscious. I can't say I am aware of Bloom's ideas, though generally I would agree with that hypothesis. It sounds like an apt description of my process (though that is probably a damning confession to make). I quote/borrow/steal very liberally in my work, usually taking for granted that in the process of translation, the theft will become invisible. For example, the soundtrack of *Window/Fenêtre* is meant to be a combination of the bands Tortoise with Cypress Hill, but because I lack the skill to do this well, I end up with 'Nelson Henricks.' I have always felt that style is something artificial: my videos are very diverse, stylistically speaking, and I have tended to jump from one aesthetic to another. What is original is the content – the writing and the ideas – which provides a lot of consistency from one work to another.

MH: The anagram/nonsense titles appear over an image (of you? a friend?) spraying shaving cream over his body in reverse motion, mostly in such close-up splendour it's difficult to know what we might be looking at. Apart from its ambiguous beauty, why this picture to end everything? (I was going to ask: why did you leave this as the last image in the corpse's eye, which would have to resuscitated by forensics?)

Planetarium

NH: That's me with the shaving cream. My earliest works were performance-based; many were concerned with constructing aliens out of the human body. 'Become an alien.' I also wanted *Planetarium* to look cheap, aesthetically speaking. 'Plastic' was the guiding material theme. And because the tape was a comedy, a slapstick style of abject humour prevailed.

Like the nonsense texts that accompany these images, it is very difficult for me to talk precisely about what this sequence means. I proceeded intuitively, sensing if something was right or wrong, whether it worked or not, whether it was boring or interesting, and building things accordingly. It's like cooking spaghetti: if you throw it at the wall and it sticks, it's done. If it falls to the floor, it's not. Everything in *Planetarium* is the stuff that, for one reason or another, stuck to the wall. I do remember very vividly that we had leftover shaving cream in the bathroom and deciding to shoot this scene was very spontaneous. My partner Pierre did the camera work. My hope – my very sincere and honest hope – is that my work is capable of articulating something, of making a sense that is beyond the limits of language. This makes it a bit frustrating to talk about. I can explain what I was thinking about or why I did things, but I can't always discuss what something means.

I suppose another guiding principle throughout *Planetarium* was to give the viewer unrecognizable images and have them slowly become recognizable. So there is this alien body running backwards, and at some point it becomes apparent that it's a guy spraying shaving cream on himself. And there is the text running backwards and slowly becoming recognizable as anagrams of my name. I liked the feeling that the tape was running backwards toward the beginning (rather than ending), which is why the tape ends 'Nelson Henricks a video by PLANETARIUM.' This idea of reversibility, that the tape can be played forward or backwards, is also present in *Window* and *Crush*.

I don't really know why I wanted to leave people with this image. I suppose the idea of reversibility made it the logical end sequence (that and the music, which refers back to the opening credit sequence). It's also a signature to the work, in which I am presented in a somewhat ridiculous position while taking credit for the work. And it's funny. It's like a pie in the face. I wanted to end on something upbeat, after so much death and destruction.

MH: *Time Passes* (6:30 min, 1998) is made of exquisitely rendered time-lapse shots inside and outside your apartment, punctuated by intertitles. It is a portrait of a place, and a writer's solitude. 'They write in order to disappear.' It is a portrait of something that can't be pictured; the act of writing remains an invisible activity, even if you can watch pen move on paper. What led you to want to show the unshowable? The opening and closing phrases are the same – does this suggest that living and writing arrive in circles, that we are condemned to repeat ourselves? Or is it simply that our display modes are acts of repetition, because we are forced to accommodate already existing forms (in language or clothing) in order to make sense? In this sense, writing is always an act of rewriting.

NH: I was looking for a third work to flesh out the *Window* trilogy. I was toying around with some ideas on paper that dealt with silence. For many years, I had been interested in making a work about an empty house. What is it like when no one is there? (This impulse winds its way through *Murderer's Song, Conspiracy of Lies* and *Comédie*, which all feature architectural spaces devoid of people.) Sometime during the early '90s, I read Virginia Woolf's *To the Lighthouse*. The middle section is a 30-page description of an abandoned house falling into decrepitude. This was really enabling for me, because I could see (through Woolf) how it could be done: how you could make something about nothing, but keep it dynamic and exhilarating.

I had borrowed a Super 8 camera from Yudi Sewraj and Monique Moumblow with an intervelometer function: it allowed the camera to expose one frame automatically every few seconds, depending on where you set the frequency dial. It was December 1997. I had a couple of spare rolls to burn (and no ideas, having just finished *Crush* that month). The film cartridges had already been opened and I wasn't sure if they'd been used or not. I was reluctant to put a lot of work into a shoot and then have it all come back unusable, so I devised a low-effort method of burning the film: I set up the camera on a tripod looking out my window and pointed it at the horizon visible from our living room.

I have never liked shooting. In fact, I hate it. And so I was walking around all that day, shopping, talking to people, having lunch, and I kept thinking, 'I am shooting! This is great!' But other things were rolling through my head too: the trilogy, Virginia Woolf, writing and time. I realized I had finally found a way to make my video about an empty house. I came home and over the next week hammered out the script that would become *Time Passes* (which is also the name of that central chapter of *To the Lighthouse*, which I found so inspiring).

The opening and closing sections, then, are about an empty house. I edited this together as a rough cut and realized it didn't make much of a video on its own. I had a beginning and end but no middle. So I added the section about writing, which was cannibalized from two other works in progress. Aside from the reference to Woolf, my interest in writing sprang from an interest in superimposing two different time scales that make up human experience: the time of the mind and the time of the body. The time of the body is slow: the time it takes for a scar to heal, the time it takes to age and mature. The time of the mind is lightning-quick, mercurial. So I suppose what I wanted to do was start and end in this slower, organic time of the body and then take the viewer into this space of the mind: that protracted temporal envelope where it is just you and the words, locked in the here and now. I felt that writing represented that friction between the two time spaces well: those moments when the thoughts are coming fast and your hand just isn't quick enough to get it all down. And of course the character in the text is writing to escape the body.

These weren't things I was engaging in consciously. My interpretation, sitting here at my desk in 2006, is that the tape was about these momentary epiphanies: moments of intense awareness bracketed by what Woolf herself referred to as 'cotton wool' moments (those times when we are less conscious, less aware). But this is one interpretation among many. One of my professors in film school told us we should never trust what the director says about the work. They can only tell you what was intended, but not what they achieved.

MH: 'History is everything that happened to me before I was born.' *Shimmer* (7 min, 1995) is a tape about memory, and I wonder if you could recount it to me now from your memory of it. Would it concern you if only a single picture survived, if an

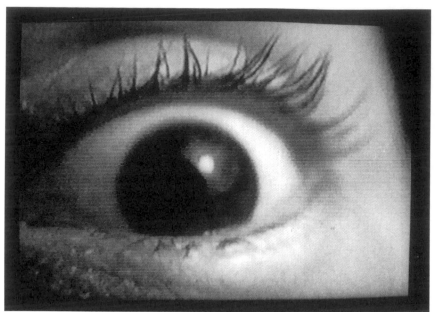

Time Passes

entire audience left the theatre after seeing it and a poll was run and a week later just one picture remained? Your memory brief refuses storytelling, and while it is ostensibly 'about' your parents, they hardly appear – there are no home movies or recountings, just a few pictures that quickly fall out of frame. Instead, we see stylized, dramatized moments that stage instants of recall: there is a toy train, a camera panning a bedspread (like a descending plane), a hand holding a cup to a wall. Why these moments? Why so much refusal and restraint?

NH: Recount the tape from memory? Do you mean recall the whole tape, word for word, shot by shot? I am sure I could. I have a very good auditory memory. I can play the soundtrack of the video in my head right now. If I wrote it down, I could fill in the images later. This is essentially how I have worked for many years: sound first, picture second. All of my early work is built that way, and *Shimmer* is no exception.

'Would it concern you if only a single picture survived ... ?' That's a good question. Of course I'd be concerned. I would want the audience to remember all of it! But the reality is, they probably do remember only one image, one phrase. And that's if you are lucky! I think we can't really count that as a failure. What I remember from the whole corpus of all the film and video I have experienced probably comes down to just a few moments. Jeanne Moreau leaving Marcello Mastroianni's book launch in *La Notte* and aimlessly wandering the streets of Milan. Things like that. It's not the images or the text that are memorable, but the sensations they evoke. For example, the sense that, at that precise moment, Jeanne Moreau just decided to walk out of the narrative flow of that film. It's amazing to me because I remember all the times I have attempted to do that in my life.

Shimmer stands at the end of my autobiographical work, and in many ways it is a summation of all those impulses. It is a rallying of all the techniques and tools I had developed in my early

work, deployed in one concise statement. It was the first time I really felt in control of the medium, that things weren't just occurring accidentally. On one hand, the restraint you speak of was due to material concerns. I was incredibly poor, I could afford to buy only so much film, so retakes were impossible. But there were other impulses at work as well.

I was very impressed by the work of two Irish artists/authors: James Coleman and Samuel Beckett. I had seen an incredible film installation by Coleman called *Box*, in which shots of two boxers fighting are intercut with black leader. Every cut to black left strong retinal retentions: ghost images of the two fighters remained for a few seconds after the image cut. So the idea of using long passages of black in *Shimmer* came from there. I was interested in retinal effect, which is much stronger in the film version, as a physiological analog for memory. I liked also how the film interacted with the eye physically. The conceit in *Shimmer* was to work with a film theatre in a site-specific manner: the cinema as the inside of someone's head and the screen as mental imagery that flashes before the mind's eye. At one point, I wanted to present *Shimmer* as an installation in an actual cinema. I wish I'd had the courage to do this, as it is probably the way the piece should be shown. So that's why many of the images appear as they do: a colour field, an out-of-focus image, a flash, a simple image. It was about making the architectural space of the cinema analogous to mental space: a theatre inside the dome of the skull.

The one image I will carry with me from *Shimmer* is the glass against the wall. That image alludes to the sources of the work. When I was moving out of my first Montreal apartment in 1993, I had intended to do a performance once it was empty. I would light each room with a different-coloured light bulb and lead the audience from room to room. I wouldn't have any props: only a waterglass, which I would hold to the wall and listen through. In each room, I would recount a story of a previous occupant of the apartment (the building was over a hundred years old). Anyway, somehow the process of moving *and* doing a performance (ah, youth!) were a bit too ambitious, so the project was scrapped. The script I wrote became the basis for *Shimmer*, and the image of listening to the wall with a glass was the only element that remained from this aborted work. The other images I will carry with me forever are the blue and yellow screens. These colours were the poles of *Shimmer*. When you are on the prairies, and the setting sun hits the horizon, all the light is golden, and all the shadows go purple-blue. I don't really know of any other place in Canada where you can see this. It's a really a prairie thing.

Anyway, James Coleman and poverty had some influence on the restraint in the images. Beckett was responsible for the spartan text. I was reading his later texts, *Worstward Ho, Stirrings Still* and *Ill Seen, Ill Said*, and I was really impressed by the economy of language. Up until this point, I was under the impression that good writing should be evidently so, with gymnastic uses of adjectives and punctuation, the kind of writing that draws attention to itself. Beckett seemed to be the reverse of that.

Shimmer opens with an ominous dedication: 'For Mom and Dad.' In a way, the tape was first conceived of as a gift for my parents. Then it became a way of saying, 'Thanks. I love you.' Then it became an apology. Heavy-hearted was I in the sound booth, doing the voice-over paragraph by paragraph. On the final section, I cried on the first take (à la Michael Jackson). I thought this was brilliant. Laurel Woodcock and Nikki Forrest (who were operating the tape) said, 'Um, we don't really think that's working. Maybe we should edit the text.' And so we did right there. It helped enormously. It opened up something that was very closed and personal into something that had the possibility of speaking to a public beyond my parents. So, hopefully, it is more about memory and the place of family in defining identity than it is about the relationship I have with my parents and my homeland, per se.

From the perspective of 2006, it's easy for me to find fault with *Shimmer*. It is too personal and precious for my taste, and verges dangerously close to being maudlin. There are images I don't think work as well as they should, particularly the ending, and this undermines the strength of the overall work. Still, it was a big breakthrough. I was able to resolve my autobiographical impulses, which was very liberating for me. It gave me a lot more options as a writer. I also gained a great sense of how to organize a time-based composition, and this had a great impact on everything that came afterwards, especially *Crush*.

MH: *Crush* (12 min, 1997) is a movie made in close-up, gathering moments of flesh (a torso turning, a hand clenching) in a monologue about changing shape, 'becoming animal,' dissolving the self. 'When I become animal I will dissolve, become anonymous, interchangeable with any other member of my species.' Is this a critical take on gay male gym-clone culture, where a steady diet of workouts, aimed at the same muscular ideal, has produced bodies that appear alike? Is this a harbinger of the body's globalization? 'Becoming animal' is a term I hazily recall from Deleuze and Guattari, who were inveighing against genital-oriented hierarchies and sexual pleasures, insisting that revolt against hegemonic capital needs to begin with one's own body. Do these social pressures and shared ideals form the crush of the title?

NH: In some ways, *Crush* was a response to the cult of the perfect body that is emblematic of mainstream queer culture. But questions of body image are also a concern for heterosexual men and women, and they also engage in these practices. Gay men have just invested in it in a more conscious manner. In fact, gays have articulated a variety of modified bodies as fetish objects (I am thinking about bears and growers as well). I suppose we are pioneers in that regard. Meanwhile, alteration of the body occurs in more underground and subversive ways too. I was interested in all the axes that extend from that discourse of body modification – tattooing, subcutaneous implants, voluntary amputation – basically, everything that Research brought to the fore in the book *Modern Primitives*. The character in *Crush* is interested in an extreme form of body modification that will allow him to become an animal. It is more about efficiency than aesthetics. He wants to become an aquatic creature: a seal, or a fish, or a sperm, something that swims in a school. Moving from human to seal to fish, or from man to sperm, evolution runs in reverse.

Crush is part of a cycle of works about animals that include *Emission* and a chapboook, *The Pig's Tale*. About two years after I'd finished *Emission*, I had come to feel that the tape was a complete failure. Out of anger, frustration, or perhaps in a sudden moment of clarity, I scribbled out a short text that said everything I'd failed to say in *Emission*: a kind of postscript. At a certain point, I planned on making this into a second tape and tacking it on the end of *Emission*. This short text became the basis for *Crush*.

I had done a lot of research for *Emission* around this idea of the half-animal/half-human. It's a powerful archetype, and it appears often in mythology and contemporary pop culture. *Emission* situated human consciousness on a trajectory between machines and animals. *Crush* was a crystallization of those impulses regarding one half of the spectrum: where does human begin and animal end?

The title, alas, is a bit of a red herring. I liked the sonority of the word and I liked its paradoxical meaning. On one hand it means being 'in love,' and, on the other, being destroyed; the destructive power of love and a love of destruction. In some ways, this encapsulates the protagonist's journey: he is following this

Crush

desire, but there is something destructive about it. I didn't really want to resolve his dilemma at the end. I wanted the spectator to choose between either of two possibilities: either he succeeds and swims happily away or he has entered into a world of delusions. The title echoes that duality. There is also the sense of compression and refinement contained in the word *crush* (coal being crushed into a diamond) and this fit well also. So the title isn't meant to direct your reading that specifically. It is more like an odour than a signpost. Not long after *Crush* came out, a feature film and several pop albums of the same name were released, so I have certain misgivings about the title. But it is definitely better than the original name, *Brotherhood*, which was scrapped for obvious reasons.

In my reading of Deleuze and Guattari, what captured my imagination was the dissolution of ego boundaries, the idea of becoming multiple. So perhaps another *crush* is invoked: the crush of bodies in a crowd. It's about becoming a fish or a school of fish (or sperm). On a related topic, I had also heard about a phenomenon called 'the rapture of the deep.' Deep-sea divers, the ones who go down very deep, sometimes experience a sensation of no longer being capable of determining where their body ends and the water begins. Here is another unresolved duality: is this transcendental or a destructive loss of self?

Incidentally, *Crush* is probably the work that is most indebted to experimental film. The shots of the lemons at the end were a very conscious nod to Hollis Frampton. Marie Menken inspired the flowers. Even the knife sequence was a quote from Buñuel and Dali.

MH: *Window/Fenêtre* (3 min, 1997) features a rapid-fire oscillation of seasons, entirely constrained by the views outside your window: a nearby tree blooming and icing over as the year turns. Punctuated by titles, this year-long vigil offers a meditation on knowing (how do we know what we know?) through theme and variations (same window, different look, or a variation on a look). The title prepped me for an ambient experience; instead, there is a compressed, every-moment-counts feeling, as if a mind is rapidly recalling (in reverie? nervously flicking through the moments?). Can you talk about how you structured this movie and the inspirations behind it?

NH: I started shooting *Window* in the winter of 1996. I had just bought my first video camera and for some reason felt compelled to film out my front window. I really loved the arrangement of the dark bare branches that slashed across the frame. It always reminded me of a Japanese watercolour. For both *Crush* and *Window,* I was living with a camera. It changed the way I shot. I don't think I would have engaged in this kind of structuralist exercise if I didn't have that camera sitting on my desk every day.

By the end of 1996, I had traversed the seasons in Montreal. I vaguely thought about using the footage for an installation, but an opportunity arose that dictated otherwise. PRIM and La Bande Video (video production centres from Montreal and Quebec,

respectively) were initiating a project called Neige sur Neige – the title translates to Snow on Snow and is an obvious nod to Malevich's painting *White on White.* Videos on the subject of snow would be produced through PRIM using their new Avid. I had never edited non-linear before and was eager to try out this technology. So I pieced together a proposal for the project. I did several demo versions of the tape on a Hi8 edit system. The text was a paragraph I'd written for something else. I honed it down to a haiku, and then ran the English and French texts forward and backwards over each other to beat the dual-language problem of subtitling.

It had been a while since I had completed *Shimmer,* and *Crush* was far from being over. I felt I needed a hit single to maintain visibility for my work. I took Holland-Dozier-Holland as my inspiration. Armed with the footage and the rough demos, Monique Moumblow and I edited *Window* in two eight-hour sessions. A week or two later, Martin and I worked out the soundtrack in about the same amount of time. At this time, I was under the influence of hip-hop and Chicago post-rock: De La Soul and Cypress Hill (who were using big booming bass beats) and Tortoise (noisy ambiance of the first album). All throughout the editing, I had Carole King's 'winter, spring, summer or fall' running through my head. My partner Pierre had a copy of *Tapestry* that I listened to a couple times. I did some impromptu scratching that we edited together for the credits.

Every tape seems to have a particular screening that marks it and becomes memorable. The idea behind the Neige sur Neige project was to project the finished works on snow onto a wall of snow. The Quebec people had sculpted a massive television set made of ice on St-Denis, just facing the cathedral that is integrated into the UQAM campus. It was here that *Window* was premiered. It was very, very cold. We drank vodka to keep us warm. Between the cold and the alcohol, I didn't get the feeling anyone was really watching the tape. But while it was screening and you could hear my voice counting backwards, the church bells started to chime the hour (nine o'clock). It was a great moment.

MH: Nelson, your early work continues to overwhelm me. It is so unexpected, succinct, fragmented, unabashedly beautiful and playful, terse and cinematic, it provides a terrifying basis from which to proceed, as if you'd written all your hits at a too-young age, ensuring you would have to play them even when they trot you out in a wheelchair. I'm wondering if you could describe the three-part structure of *Emission* (12 min, 1994), how you gathered material and shaped it. Were there particular circumstances that led to its making?

NH: It's funny that you can be so enthusiastic about a tape like *Emission,* which I count among my least successful works. It was my first Montreal production, based on a script I wrote in Alberta, and I have always regarded it as a transitional work. Transplanting my practice to the East was difficult. I had to build a new crew, find locations in an unfamiliar city and work with a new video production centre, where the costs were higher than what I was accustomed to in Calgary. As a consequence, I didn't always feel in control of the project. Though I had a production assistant, I also had to do a lot of the production work in French, a language I could barely speak. As *Emission* is a video preoccupied with semiotics, working in Montreal gave me an opportunity to explore those avenues in ways I couldn't have done in Calgary. But otherwise, it presented a series of challenges on all fronts, many of which hampered my ability to obtain effective results.

Emission was based on three performances I did in Calgary in the late '80s. I was an active performance artist from 1985 to 1991, and there was a strong interplay between my live work and the videos during this period. Performance allowed me to create in a spontaneous manner.

Emission

Video became a method of archiving the best of the live experiments. *Emission* was also inspired by a carpet commercial – 'CRAZY CRAZY CARPET FACTORY WAREHOUSE FACTORY OUTLET' – with lots of text rolls and images flying up at the screen. It was intended to be like one very long, dense television commercial (in six different languages) for sex, illness, gender, language, communications technology, animals, werewolves and evolution. Ideas that, for some reason or another, I felt were complementary.

When the time came to finalize the script in Montreal, I wanted to go into detail about the connections between these themes. So I started to do research, and the script got longer. And longer. At a certain point, I discarded the idea of credits altogether, opting instead for a bibliography. The tape became impossibly baroque. I would get into conversations at parties where someone could mention almost any topic and I would say, 'Oh, my tape is about that.' I was getting a lot of raised eyebrows. Then one day, I realized I wasn't actually smart enough to write the script I had devised. It was too complicated. And so I radically cut back the structure to what it is today: 12 texts in three languages in a three-act structure.

I had moved to Montreal to study cinema at Concordia. Initially I was in film studies, but then I moved to film production. The 16mm footage was all shot during my second year at film school. My first film, *Silent Film*, was incorporated whole into *Emission*. Only one image from the performances ended up making it into the video: the newspaper dress. The other tableaux, though theatrically flavoured, were all developed for the tape or resulted from improvisations.

Emission is a mixed bag of stuff: newly minted film work and original video material were combined with texts I had written for performances five years earlier. This, coupled with scripting troubles and transplanting my practice from one city to another, accounts for many of the tape's weaknesses. This is not to say it

hasn't had a certain amount of success. It has been shown a lot, and some people seem to genuinely like it. But, for me, its weak points outnumber its strengths. Sitting here today, it occurs to me that the project had probably gone stale on me, and I was suffering from a kind of writer's block. Throughout the '90s, I often felt I was one project behind. When I was working on *Conspiracy of Lies*, I really wanted to be making *Emission*. When I was making *Emission*, I really wanted to be working on *Shimmer*. This lag continued up until *Time Passes*.

The perceived failure that was *Emission* was ultimately productive. I channelled it into more resolved works. As I said earlier, *Crush* was an attempt to correct the errors of *Emission*. *Emission* tried to take on too many themes. Focusing on just one, as I was able to do in *Crush*, allowed me to obtain better results. Over the years, I have come to assume that the reason people like *Emission* is the same reason I dislike it: it is incoherent. This has led me to feel that incoherence is its chief strength, and I have tried to emulate this in certain works. *Planetarium* was a conscious attempt to create something looser and open-ended like *Emission*, and *Satellite* was probably the closest I ever got to realizing that 'CRAZY CRAZY CARPET' tape. Failure can be generative, if you try to learn from it. This fall, I will extricate *Silent Film* from *Emission* and show it as it was conceived: as a stand-alone piece without sound. I feel good about this. It feels like a restoration of sorts.

MH: *Comédie* (6 min, 1994) is a philosophical psychodrama, a contradiction in terms, I know, because psychodramas are generally wordless, exactly about the entry into language, but having arrived there, the author remains a spectral figure in your movie. He is never seen, though he features prominently in the voice-over. He is captivated by a station in the metro, speculating that there are patterns in the tiles, that he is surrounded by secret alphabets if only he had the eyes to uncover them. At last he realizes the tile spacings represent tones, and when he puts

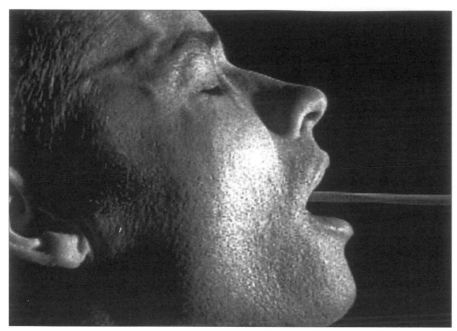
Emission

them through a music program at home, we hear an amateur version of 'MacArthur Park' sung while the credits roll. Is this movie a one-liner, or is there something more going on? It is so beautifully shot and carefully composed, its progressions avowedly cinematic at a moment in video art when those who cared about the image were (mostly) busy making films, and those who cared about other things (like content, for instance) were busy making video. This is a ridiculously reductive schema, of course, but your early work, with its universalist themes, its looming black and whites, its use of silence and dark spaces, the time lapse and quick edits, all seems to belong to a world of film.

NH: Well, *Comédie* is a bit of a one-liner. Or a two-liner. As I mentioned previously, I was studying film at Concordia University. I'd already been through one year-end screening with *Silent Film*, a work people admired for the lighting more than anything else. I wanted my second film to be a real crowd-pleaser, something funny but tough. And that's where *Comédie* came from. I remember the idea came to me very suddenly and I wrote it all down on a cafeteria napkin. Of course, this must be a false memory: cafeteria napkins are notoriously difficult to write on. But I choose to believe the essence of the story, which is basically that the tape came to me fully formed, in one lump.

Comédie is indeed a very cinematic work. It continues what I was doing with camera movement in *Conspiracy of Lies*, and refines it through Eisenstein's ideas about montage aesthetics. I can't remember if I'd already seen Frampton's *Nostalgia* or Godard's *Deux ou trois choses que je sais d'elle*, but it seems likely. Ultimately *Comédie* was finished as a film, with a neg cut, an answer print and everything, but I didn't like it. *Shimmer* was released and distributed in a 16mm version, but the print of *Comédie* lacked subtitles, and there were colour-timing problems as well. Because they could only print my black-and-

white film on colour stock, the images would turn blue during the dissolves. So *Comédie* has only ever been available as a video.

In spite of *Comédie*'s cinematic pedigree, it has stronger allegiances to video. Robert Morin and Lorraine Dufour's *The Thief Lives in Hell* was a template, an archetypal video about the social reality of living in Montreal, and *Comédie* was, above all else, a kind of homage to my new home and all the architectural sites that fascinated me. I was also reacting to Steve Reinke's work. I had met Steve around this time and organized an exhibition of his work at a gallery here. So if *Comédie* bears a resemblance to *Squeezing Sorrow from an Ashtray* from *The Hundred Videos*, it's probably not accidental.

The text came from autobiographical sources, but I was definitely writing with other people's voices in mind. I wanted C. K. Cousins to do the English voice, because I liked his delivery. There was a fellow student at Concordia I wanted to do the French voice-over. He was a young guy with a working-class accent that reminded me a lot of Robert Morin's voice. But on the day of the recording, he couldn't make it, so the duty fell to my partner, Pierre Beaudoin. Pierre was terribly ill, but he came through in an emergency. His voice sounds dreamy and disembodied because he was delirious with fever. He has a clearer accent – more of a Radio-Canada voice than working-class – but he did a great job. This was the first of many contributions Pierre made to my work.

In the end, *Comédie* did work very well at the year-end screening. People laughed, which is the result I wanted. It was easy for me to make. It has a simple structure and is one of the few pieces I didn't write the music for. It was supposed to be a trilogy but the middle section got cut. Which is why it maybe seems a bit ... partial.

So is it a film or a video? At the time, I felt pretty adamant that I was putting film in the camera and videos were coming out. My fellows at Concordia were mostly producing conventional narrative work, so my stuff looked very arty by comparison. I was convinced *Comédie* and *Silent Film* (and later *Shimmer*) were videos masquerading as films. Looking at it now, I can see that perhaps the reverse is true. I don't know. That's why I am such a bad defender of inherent characteristics for either film or video.

MH: *Conspiracy of Lies* (12 min, 1992) begins with this line: 'I found some papers in a shoebox when I was walking to work today.' What follows are, presumably, writings contained in the shoeboxes, which range from lists ('Things that would probably bring me happiness') to diary entries. Here's the description you wrote that appears in distribution catalogues: '*Conspiracy of Lies* speaks of the alienation of minorities, consumer culture, urban isolation and the fine balance between mental order and chaos. The tape begins with my voice recounting the story of the discovery of a series of diary entries and lists written by an anonymous author. When I found the texts, I assumed the author to be a white, gay man, like myself. Through the use of 12 narrators of different race, gender, religion and sexual orientation, I attempted to destabilize my own subjectivity and challenge my pre-existing assumptions regarding difference. The tape begins and ends with two texts written by myself. This, I hope, helps to render the boundary between myself and the anonymous author more fluid, thereby questioning the 'authority' of authorship.'

This work recalls (amongst others) Sophie Calle's *The Address Book*, which similarly turns around a found street object. Calle interviewed everyone in the book and published the results in the French newspaper *Liberation* in the summer of 1983. The owner of the book returned to Paris and found that his missing property had been turned into a very public artwork. I wonder if you might lend further comment on the relation between these two works, and your very different treatments. The visuals that accompany these voice-overs are blue-toned, low-resolution tracking shots (usually), moving over supermarket shelves, emptied diners, bars and dance clubs. Why these pictures with that text? What does the title of the work refer to? And why do you have an interest in taking apart your own identity, or anyone else's?

NH: There are definitely marked similarities between *Conspiracy* and the work of Sophie Calle, whose practice I became aware of long after I'd finished the tape. I enjoy her work very much, though I sense she is more concerned with investigating the dividing line between private and public space. I can't really say this was among my chief preoccupations when it came to making *Conspiracy*, though the tape obviously implicates itself in the ethical problems related to privacy and what happens when we introduce intensely private things into a public arena.

My concerns emerged from dynamics in my own practice that needed to be resolved. As I mentioned earlier, I was actively engaged in performance art from 1986 to 1991. My work was autobiographical in nature, text-based and anecdotal. At the time, I felt I could best speak about my own experience. I didn't trust myself with material that lay beyond my own subjectivity. My first video (after the eight tapes made while still a student at the Alberta College of Art and Design) was called *The White Studio Tapes* (1987). Like *Emission*, it was based on performance work. My second tape, *Legend* (1988), was created as a video installation and was also autobiographical in nature. Dreading accusations of narcissism, I decided to try to take on two projects that looked outside myself. The first, *Murderer's Song* (1991), was about a childhood friend I'd lost touch with for 15 years, who ended up shooting and killing an RCMP officer on the outskirts of Calgary. It was derived entirely from newspaper accounts of the story, cut up and reassembled à la William S. Burroughs. The second was *Conspiracy of Lies*. Both were based on found text. Though they bear no real aesthetic similarities, they were deeply related in their attempt to engage subject matter that was beyond my experience.

The story of the discovery of the texts is true. Some people think it is fictional, but it isn't. As I said in the quote above, when I read the texts, I made a lot of assumptions about the author. I don't think I was capable of articulating it in this way at the time (or even in the didactic text you quoted, which seems awfully rigid), but I guess I was interested in the space of projection that exists between the self and the other. I felt that by filtering the words of the author through many people, many voices, some essence of that person would emerge, something that exists outside the space of projection. I don't think the piece is an attempt to break down identity per se. It's about destabilizing the position and privilege of the reader. This is another distinction between Calle and *Conspiracy*. She is engaged in a kind of detective work. I never really wanted to find the author in such a specific way.

The bulk of the tape is made up of found lists and diary entries. There are two texts written by myself: the introduction, obviously, and the last monologue. The title, *Conspiracy of Lies*, is the last line we hear in the tape. The closing text is one of the most overwrought, pretentious and self-pitying things I have ever written. I felt that if I had put the author on display to his or her disadvantage for so many minutes, it was only fair that I expose something embarrassing about myself, to achieve some balance. So I suppose if we want to know what the title means, we need to go back to that text. It seems to be about the necessary illusions we maintain to continue our existences. This seemed appropriate to the subject matter of the tape. It was a real improvement on the working title, *Shadow Song*.

Conspiracy of Lies

Conspiracy was conceived in late 1990 or early 1991. Like *Comédie*, it came to me fully formed, in one lump. I remember someone asked me what I was working on one day, and I said, 'Well, the tape will open like this ... ' and I described it from start to finish. I had the whole video in my head. Making it was like taking a dictation. I never once doubted or questioned what I had to do. As with many of my works, the soundtrack came first. It was produced for a radio show in Calgary. I did the shooting and the final video edit during a residency at the Banff Centre during the summer of 1991. Many of the images in *Conspiracy* came from the text: the Off Centre Eatery, mentioned by the author, other locations that were chosen in relation to the author's goals (go to more movies, visit art galleries) or activities (I worked at an Italian restaurant). I added a few generic locations that fit with the notion of routine or the difficulty of negotiating social space, an idea that impregnates the found texts pretty heavily.

The treatment of the images is another question entirely. I deeply wanted *Conspiracy* to be a beautiful video. I felt that the facilities at Banff would allow me to do this. But in those days, artists had access only to 3/4-inch gear, not BetaCam. Still, I had a good camera, so I was sure I could get beautiful images once the footage was dumped onto Beta and put into slow motion. When the process was complete, I realized the video footage was full of jumps and jitters, which hadn't been visible when it was running at full speed. I was very angry. In frustration, I refilmed all the slow-motion footage off a monitor. It was like taking a beautiful, tightly rendered drawing and then scribbling all over it. Still, the final result is intriguing, and it is probably better than what I originally intended.

In the end, *Conspiracy* wasn't that successful in evading auto-biography. After the first screening, people came up to me and said, 'That video is about you!' which I found more funny than frustrating. It was the first of my tapes to show outside Canada, though initially it didn't do very well. Because of my move to Montreal, I don't think it really started showing until 1992 or 1993. I feel it still holds up rather well. Many people feel that it is my best tape, and that I haven't made a good one since then.

MH: Does the reaction to your work figure in your making? How do you contend with your audiences? As your 'popularity' as a video artist (this is admittedly a slight proposition) grows, has your making become more self-conscious, and how has this affected your work? You also teach – does having to convert motion pictures into explanations and digestible comprehensions help or hinder your practice?

NH: That's an interesting question. Really, I would like to think that on some level I am not all that concerned with audience, but this has been a recurring theme in many of my responses, so I can't deny this. The idea of audience has had greater and lesser relevance from tape to tape. Certainly *Comédie* was made with a specific audience in mind. *Shimmer* was made for my parents. *Window* was conceived for a specific context. *Handy Man* was, to

a certain extent, conceived for queer audiences. When I am making the work, I'm engaged in a dialogue with my peers, whoever I perceive that to be at a given time. Other tapes weren't really affected by these questions. They were just things I was working on, and I didn't consider the public beyond the fact that I wanted to make something that was satisfying to watch. So perhaps my sense of audience contracts and expands. When I'm in the edit suite, I am really just thinking about one person, one viewer. The works are literary in that sense. The relationship between the work and the audience is like that between a reader and a book. It's intimate.

My popularity, fame or notoriety for me as an artist is difficult for me to quantify. I feel a certain degree of entitlement because I have been committed to making work for 20 years, so some recognition is not exactly unexpected. But I don't imagine for a minute that there is a throng of people waiting for my next tape. For this reason, I haven't tended to be overly self-conscious from work to work. Perhaps this is a minor benefit of limited success: you don't really have to obsess about these things. This is one thing that makes me sad about independent film and video, and visual art in general. There is a very low level of discourse around the work. I would like to go on a site like allmusic.com and see all my tapes rated and reviewed, but that is never going to happen. Every video seems to have its own career, and it can take years for a director to get a sense of whether a tape 'worked' or not. Some tapes show everywhere in one or two years and never show again. Others show one or two times a year for many years. And other tapes surprise you by doing things you would never expect.

In order to teach, you need to learn. Much of what I have learned as a teacher has benefitted my work in some way. It has probably deformed my practice as well. Again, it's difficult for me to quantify. I tend to feel that teaching has little bearing on my practice as an artist, but it has an enormous effect on me as a writer, a curator and a person who is called upon to speak about screen-based art in various contexts (juries, panels and so on). Teaching gives you a perspective on how young artists see video fitting into their practices. Beyond this, teaching forces you to return to those fundamental questions and to articulate a conscious response to them. Why make art? What does art do that nothing else can? Hopefully, when you have answers to these questions (at least provisional ones), you can move on to other things. It's like peeling an onion: you never get to the centre.

MH: *Map of the City* (21 min, 2-screen installation, 2006) presents itself as an inventory of fragments – neon signs, maps, bookshelves, the feet of statues, the faces of statues, graffiti tags are juxtaposed with or interrupted by titles that interrogate them, trying to make meaning of all this. Many titles are written in the second person, to 'you' – is that because this is the viewer's journey?

NH: I have used this style of direct-address writing since my first videos and performances. It's something I probably borrowed from Laurie Anderson and have since made my own. I like how the second-person pronoun involves the listener. I suppose this also gets back to what I was saying earlier about audience and a certain literary quality that the works aspire to. Really, I am narrating to just one person: that is my ideal audience. This became apparent when I began translating the works into French. Translators would always write *vous*, as in the plural *you guys* or *you people* – the audience as a mass. But for me, *you* has always meant *tu* – singular and informal. Describing the narrative as the 'viewer's journey' is a good way of putting it. I want people to feel that what I am describing is happening to them.

MH: Are you concerned that the singular attention of a black-box (cinema) audience will be missing when you present your work in galleries (the white box), that viewers will arrive 'in the middle' and leave after just a few minutes (a length of time that is already greater than most spend watching any piece of art)?

NH: If people decide to take a peek and walk away, I have to accept it. It is part of the conditions of working with the gallery as a site. *Map* was built from a series of short episodes, so you can jump in at any moment and have an experience. And I am surprised at how patient installation audiences can be. In pieces like *Fuzzy Face* (2001) or *Happy Hour* (2003), which are unedited performances that clock in at 30 minutes and 20 minutes respectively, people did sit through the entire loop, which astonished me. That said, *Map* does have a narrative arc of sorts: it is a video with a beginning, middle and end, so people who duck in and out will definitely miss something. It's always a compromise.

Working with gallery space has allowed me to do things that can't be done in a cinema. Both *Fuzzy Face* and *Happy Hour* were unedited duration performances. They emerged out of the same performative impulse that fuelled *Planetarium* and were a return to tapes like *Emission* and *The White Studio Tapes*, which were also performance based. I deeply admired the bravery of a lot of '70s video: people like Colin Campbell, Lisa Steele, as well as Americans like Bruce Nauman. They would do these long, boring works that were almost aggressive in their refusal to entertain. I adore these works, and I wanted to do something in the same spirit. *Planetarium* was supposed to be about twice as long as it is now, but I knew people wouldn't stand for it. You just can't make long work anymore and have people sit through it (let alone distribute it). Our sense of pacing is different than it was in the '70s, so working in a gallery permitted me to explore those impulses. I was grateful to have that option.

The gallery context also allowed me to work with multiple screens, which is something I can't adequately explore in a theatrical setting. I know there is a history of expanded cinema extending from people like Abel Gance through Warhol and up into the late '60s/early '70s, but I feel freer to do that type of work in a gallery. The ability to edit spatially was something that slowly evolved in my work. *Handy Man* (in its installation form) was a triple-screen piece, as was *Happy Hour*. *Satellite* was a double-screen piece that ran synchronously, as does *Map of the City*. The ability to edit both linearly and laterally is very exciting to me. The two pieces I am working on now (one about Africa and another about singing and music) will both use multiple screens.

MH: You adapted some of your text from the Bible and the Gospel of Thomas, uncommon sources in a media arts scene that is largely godless. Why these texts?

NH: Actually Gary Hill used the Gospel of Thomas as the basis for *Disturbance (Among the Jars)*. In the end, I don't think I used much of the Gospel, partly because I knew Hill had already been there. There are just four lines that made it into the final edit. The majority of the text is from the book of Ecclesiastes: this appears onscreen whenever you see small objects on coloured backgrounds.

The decision to work with the Bible was difficult. I usually do my own writing. I had used found text before, but referring to the Bible as 'found text' is an impossible understatement. You can't. It has too much weight to it, but this weight is paradoxically what attracted me to it.

There are two stories I need to tell you in order to explain my decision to use Ecclesiastes and the Gospel of Thomas. As you know, *Map* was conceived during a six-month residency in Italy. One evening I was with a friend in Viterbo, a small city just north of Rome. It was a cold evening and we were walking by a wall. You could see the Renaissance wall built on the medieval wall built on the Roman wall built on the Etruscan wall. My friend ran his hand over the Etruscan block at street level and he said, 'One day, someone put that rock there.' Not long after, I was in Pisa, looking at a museum filled with Madonnas. Many women, all

Emission

holding babies. It was that pre-Renaissance Byzantine style, which is more iconographic than representational. I looked at virgin after virgin. Suddenly it occurred to me that these images emerged from matriarchal pagan cults that predate Christianity, and that this narrative, this history, was still embedded in these images. Many women were represented here: a woman of the 13th century was standing in for Mary, who was herself standing in for a Roman or Etruscan goddess. Suddenly I could sense the textual depth in these paintings. These images were the sum of something much greater than they appeared to be.

The words from Ecclesiastes and the Gospel attracted me because they also had this kind of textual depth. And there was no way I could write it. One day, several thousand years ago, someone wrote this down. And we are reading it today. These texts come from Greek philosophy and from Hebrew cultures that are much older than Christianity. So all that history is there, though superficially – what we are left with is the Bible.

I was astonished when I read Ecclesiastes, especially the translation I found, which uses *meaningless* in lieu of *vanity*. 'Meaningless. Everything is meaningless.' You don't expect the Bible to say something like that. It's not supposed to be bleak and existentialist. It's supposed to be dogmatic and crystal-clear. I would define myself as an atheist, and I have a general antipathy toward Christianity because it has been grafted to a right-wing political agenda I disagree with. The Bush administration has a lot to answer for. Yet, as a discourse, I believe the spiritual has enormous value, and perhaps people of my generation and political background (or myself anyway) have been too quick to dismiss it. Reclaiming this as a lefty queer was very empowering. It was like saying, 'Look! The Bible is very contradictory and vague and even kind of bleak and existentialist!' It's a slap in the face to all those people carrying 1 *Corinthians 6:9* placards at anti-queer rallies. My interest in engaging with religion as a discourse also emerges from my experience in Africa in the summer of 2002 and 2003. My partner and I were in Senegal for ten weeks. It was amazing to me to see a culture that is organized around a spiritual paradigm rather than a scientific one. I had read so much about modernism and its connection to the scientific paradigm, but I don't think I really understood what that meant until I spent time in Africa. *Satellite* was definitely a response to that experience: destabilizing the scientific. And so is *Map of the City*, in its own way. It's an attempt to reconsider the spiritual as a discourse that is several thousand years old, and to recuperate it.

In the end, I am not sure the text is immediately recognizable as 'biblical.' Most people I have shown it to assume I wrote it, but I am sure people who know their Bible will spot it immediately. I rewrote the passage a bit (which was also a bit daunting), changing some punctuation and making certain passages less gender-specific. But otherwise, it is unchanged. I am also afraid it will scare people off or alienate them from the work. Again, it was a hard decision to make, but I needed to follow this impulse to its conclusion.

MH: This installation refuses (for want of a better word) 'the real,' or some documentary trace, some engagement with the outside. Everything is reduced to simulation and model, all experience is levelled out (granted the same amount of time, presented without context) – design elements of an overarching consciousness belonging to the narrator/author. Everything is airtight, controlled and above all clean: this is a very hygienic display; there is scarcely a sign that any of this has been lived. You write 'Millions of images, each crying for attention,' and certainly your animation technique delivers a steady flow, but these pictures are all interchangeable – there is no punctum, no place in any of these pictures to 'look back,' to hurt or touch the viewer. Why this sealed simulation of exchange, the impossibility of the Other?

NH: I find it a bit depressing that you feel there is a lack of engagement with the outside in this work. In my practice, there are two streams: one that is more outward-looking (*Conspiracy, Comédie*, the *Window* trilogy) and others that are more inward-looking (*Shimmer, Crush, Planetarium*). I usually alternate between one style and the other, though occasionally both appear in the same tape. *Map of the City* is inward-looking, like *Shimmer*, trying to reproduce the texture of mental space and built from a documentary approach. I lived with my camera and took thousands of photos for months on end. Though the small objects are definitely staged (more on that later), other sequences emerged from reactions to certain places: museums, people's apartments, cinemas, hospitals, as well as the streets of Montreal and Rome. These images were born from a lot of wandering and a high degree of responsiveness to my surroundings. I hoped some sense that these images emerged from lived experience would be apparent in the work.

That said, I do know that from very early on I wanted *Map* to feel cold. Because I knew the subject matter (and material) I was dealing with was emotionally charged, I felt I needed to counterbalance it with a more reserved approach. This really dictated a lot of decisions I made musically. I went back and raided the soundtracks for *Planetarium* and *Time Passes*, as well as generating a lot of new sounds that had a neutral emotional register. I was thinking about clicks and beeps: bank machines, alarm clocks, slide projectors and roulette wheels. So perhaps this antiseptic quality that you sense is linked to certain aspirations I had for the work not only in terms of mood, but how it would ultimately be displayed.

The twin poles of *Map of the City* are the book and the building. The building as book, the book as building. I was thinking about places like Giotto's Cappella degli Scrovegni, a chapel that is like an immersive, three-dimensional book. This is typical of many basilicas and chapels, where the Bible is presented spatially. So, on one hand, *Map* is like a book (which you can infer from the double-screen format, which looks like facing pages), but meant to be projected large enough on the walls of the gallery to surround the viewer. It was conceived as a design element in relation to architecture, like paintings or mosaics in chapels and basilicas. And its graphic quality refers back to books and page design. The possibility for exchange is perhaps simulated, but not any less so than it is with a book. Or architecture. It requires an active reader.

As for the ability of the images to 'look back,' to 'hurt or touch the viewer,' I am not really sure that was my primary aspiration. Again, I was trying to create a work that had a certain emotional neutrality. In any case, this type of response is deeply subjective, and will shift from one person to another. For example, the small objects are things I have been collecting since I was a kid. The green turtle was on my sixth-birthday cake. Other objects have very specific meanings that obviously won't be apparent to anyone but my family and me. They are a physical manifestation of my memory. I wanted to use these objects because I liked them as a texture and I felt that, at the very least, they would communicate a sense of the repository, an accumulation of data. I was worried they wouldn't act as memory triggers for other spectators. Yet people connect with very obscure things. A woman came up to me after a screening and asked, 'Do you know so-and-so?' because she had seen an image he had made that was incorporated into one of these sequences. And again, this amazed me because the photos are up for four frames each – less than a sixth of a second. But she recognized this image and had a very specific experience. So that was encouraging for me. It seemed to signal that, yes, these images, these objects, could work in the way I hoped they would.

There are images in the tape that have teeth for me. Hadrian's face. Certain drawings. My mom in that crazy fur-lined coat. So perhaps punctum is in the eye of the beholder.

MH: You've raised the spectre of experimentalism, a notion I once imagined every artist embraced. There are few rewards for invention – to produce something incomprehensible, illegible, hated and ignored, what could be the point of that? Part of the problem is that only received forms are intelligible, but surely part of the rub in new shapings is allowing new contents to issue. Do you feel that your work has been engaged with bringing new contents to the screen? Do you feel that being queer puts you 'outside' somehow, lends you a productive vantage from which to view the onslaught of mainstream medias?

NH: Stephen Merritt from the Magnetic Fields pop group says he likes only two kinds of music: pop and experimental. And this pretty much sums up my ethos. I actually enjoy experimental work, and I assume there must be other people out there who like things that are incomprehensible, illegible, hateful and ignorable. I get a definite frisson from discovery. I am awed by the ability to think outside of conventions, so I try to emulate that in my work. Even though we have dispensed with the avant-garde in this postmodern age, I am still part of that tradition. Whether I have managed to bring new content to the screen is not a question I feel I am in a good position to answer. My voice as an author is original, but the content? Perhaps that is for others to say.

As for how queerness fits into that equation, I have a lot of strange and arcane theories about that. When asked why Canadians are so funny, comedian Mike Myers said something like, 'When Americans watch television, they are watching television. But when Canadians watch television, they are watching American television.' This little interval, this space of reflexivity, is crucial. Perhaps we queers participate in society with the same built-in distantiation. We see everything that transpires in the straight world from a distance: as artifice, as a performance. So authenticity and 'the real,' in both perceptual and ideological terms, have to be parsed in more complex ways. I know that instability and removal have infected my vision in other ways as well, whether it was my knowledge of being colour-blind from an early age or my experiences with drugs when I was a teenager. The outside world has always been provisional. Being queer has compounded that sense.

Nelson Henricks' Videos and Media Art

Visa   3:30 min 1985
New York   4:30 min 1985
Enola Gay   2 min 1985
Rain   5:20 min 1986
Dream   5:40 min 1986
Industry   3:30 min 1986
Stupid Video   2:40 min 1986
Dance   3 min 1986
Salomé   3:20 min 1986
Untitled   1 min 1986
The White Studio Tapes   15 min 1987
Legend   28 min 1988
Murderer's Song   27 min 1991
Conspiracy of Lies   12 min 1992
Comédie   7 min 1994
Emission   12 min 1994
Shimmer   7 min 1995
Harvey K., 69   2:06 min 1995 (with Steve Reinke)
Travaux Publics   20 min 1995 (with Pierre Beaudoin)
Crush   12 min 1997
Window/Fenêtre   3 min 1997
Time Passes   6:30 min 1998
Handy Man   3 min 1999
E for Excel   1 min 1999
Planetarium   21 min 2001
The My Heart... series
   My Heart the Optometrist   1 min 2001
   My Heart the Philosopher   1:30 min 2001
   My Heart the Bureaucrat   1:30 min 2001 (with David Clark)
   My Heart the Devil   1:10 min 2002 (with Nikki Forrest)
   My Heart the Interior Decorator   1:50 min 2006
Fuzzy Face   30 min 2001
Happy Hour   20 min 2002
Substance   2003
Satellite   10 min 2004
Map of the City   21 min 2006
Sénégal/Québec: Echanges?   18:30 min 2006
Untitled (Score)   7 min 2007 (with Jackie Gallant)
Failure   7 min 2007
Countdown   :30 min 2007

Distributed by Vtape, Video Data Bank and Vidéographe.

Nelson Henricks was born in Bow Island, Alberta, and is a graduate of the Alberta College of Art (1986). He moved to Montreal in 1991, where he received a BFA from Concordia University (1994). A musician, writer, curator and artist, he is best known for his work in video, which has been exhibited worldwide. Henricks was the recipient of the Bell Canada Award in Video Art (2002) and the Board of Govenors' Alumni Award of Excellence from the Alberta College of Art and Design (2005). www.nelsonhenricks.com

EMILY VEY DUKE &
COOPER BATTERSBY
I AM A CONJUROR

s there nothing they won't say in front of one another? Is there no terrible infatuation, no secret longing they cannot share, instantly, as soon as it occurs to either one of them? The foundational vaults of repression that are at the very root of togetherness have been left behind by this dynamic duo whose ongoing domestic adventures provide a glimpse of what couples might look like in the next century. While they wait for the rest of us to catch up, they keep busy taking their funny, damaged, word-smart incarnations out for a walk in video after video. *Being Fucked Up* (2000), for instance, opens with our heroine huffing crack, singing a song about a perfect nature world, before a cartoon drawing says via voice balloon, 'Her soft breast. The sweet, warm milk. Her arms around me. I will punish her for making me wait!' More songs and drawings follow before it concludes with a series of questions they answer by violently shaking their heads yes or no. Do we need to know more? These bittersweet episodic tapes might be the latest pop epistle from a shoegazer outfit from Portland, deadpanning their way through another MTV day about getting through their 20s one habit at a time. Instead they have turned to the sometimes rarefied zone of video art and laid their claim, recasting themselves as backwards-talking scientists lounging in the bath.

Emily: We hated the idea of betterment, which was used on us like a club – ironic in a solar system whose fundamental principals of design are entropy and decay.

Cooper: So after years of failing to change the things we hated, we decided to change ourselves.

Emily: And now we are conjurors. We can bring anything into existence.

In their apartment (their world), animals know everything, while humans destroy all they touch. Emily will sing in a multi-tracked a cappella (if you can't count on yourself for accompaniment, then who?) while Cooper makes the pictures sing, gathering time-lapsed moments from surveillance cameras on the internet (cameras are a last resort, he says). Teenaged boys, daddy's porn ('I hate pornography. It has colonized my orgasm. But here I am, enacting it again'), dope, threesomes, fame – they swing through it with quick epithets in short, scorching scenes.

MH: There is a myth of how you and Cooper met and fell in together. Could you tell that story?

EVD: Okay. When I met Cooper I had been at the Nova Scotia School for Art and Design for a few years. He had moved out east from Kelowna, British Columbia. I was an intensely bitter 21-year-old. I told Cooper when we met that I thought it was rude of him to crack jokes because some people were so unhappy that they found jokes painfully alienating. I found jokes painfully alienating.

I had seen him a couple of times before. Once he was hitch-hiking on the side of the highway and I begged my mom to stop and pick him up. The second time we were on the bus together and I farted, and two really tough girls were on the bus too, and one of them said, 'Oh gross! Who farted?' That was horrible.

We finally met at the Khyber, which used to be a booze can by night and shitty gallery by day. It was great. I gave Cooper an invite to a show I was having there, and he recognized the style of it, because I had been doing public poster projects in the same style. He told me he made posters too, and when he described them I was blown away. I had been wondering who had made those posters for so long.

He also told me in the course of this conversation that he was leaving Halifax to go on a hitchhiking trip for a year in three weeks.

He handed me a little card (photocopied on construction paper) that said, 'Let's Dance,' which had a picture of Emmanuel Lewis verso (made by Sandy Plotnikoff, Cooper's best friend from Kelowna). I didn't drink and I hated my physicality, so dancing was not my favourite activity. We danced briefly and awkwardly, and then I leaned over to him and said, 'Look. I think you're really cute and interesting and I probably wouldn't say this if you weren't leaving.' Then I turned on my nervous heel and walked away, thinking, 'He'll follow me if he likes me too.' He didn't, and I took the next bus home. I went up to my bedroom and made a poster in what I knew he would recognize as my style. It said, 'Wish you said' spray-painted on it through a specially made stencil. The next morning I got up and put them all over downtown Halifax (which took about ten minutes).

Cooper saw them and made a response poster. He had been collecting love letters between teenagers for a couple of years, and he put one up next to each one of my 'Wish you said' posters. It was the most fucking ridiculously romantic thing ever.

So then we went hitchhiking across the U.S. together. Cooper was really mean and kind of humiliated me, but I stayed with him. And then I kind of humiliated him, but he stayed with me. Sometimes the unforgivable ought to be forgiven.

MH: You work and live together, and your art seems to come out of your living. Is there a strict delineation of duties (I write the songs, you sing them; I press the buttons, you work the camera ...)?

EVD: No. Yes. Yes and no. It's certainly organic, but there are also things we know I will do (like answering email and writing applications and insisting on expressive emotionality in life and work) and things we know Cooper will do (like hooking up the free cable and reading software manuals and, I am ashamed to say, dealing with our finances). We don't talk a lot about it, nothing is rigid, but we have different strengths and weaknesses.

Okay, I'm not answering any more of these tonight. I'm too tired and I have to shower. But that was fucking awesome. Maybe I'll just take them one or two at a time. These aren't questions I can just toss off an answer to. Oh, I'm reading a really amazing book that Shary Boyle sent me called *Carrington* (a life of Dora Carrington). She was sort of peripheral to the Bloomsbury Group. She was also very fucked up and amazing ... She *seems* like a peripheral figure – like people I've known who are amazing artists, but not spotlight seekers – or simultaneously spotlight seekers and shunners. People, I think, like me. Not that I'm peripheral to anything that a book will be written about. Which could be my answer to your question: 'Is it painful to be working in a medium where even if you did something show-stopping and perfect, you couldn't be famous because no one notices?'

MH: Do you think that most artists have in them two or three (sometimes it's more – a limited number anyways) of perfect, necessary things (videos, paintings, books), while the rest is simply placeholders, the work you do while waiting for something else to occur?

EVD: Yes, I do think this. I also think, more terrifyingly, that we may *only* have one or two perfect things that may get wrung out early – the product of an unrecoverable lack of self-consciousness that we continually move away from. Then sometimes I don't. Sometimes I think I'm just treading water. I also think it's essential to continue making work (for me, that means to write), even when it feels like I'm dead and making only dead boxes of dry dead death. I think Stephen King reiterated the adage about the muse needing to know where to find you in his book *On Writing*, something about having to spend a good deal of time at one's desk.

One of the really painful changes the last few years have brought is a new sense that I have to make new work because it's my job. It's expected of me by some infinitesimal (possibly fantasized) public. I think many 'professional' artists and writers experience this. It's probably one of the reasons that we all make, or are tempted to make, work about the trials of making work. That's what our stupid, smarmy tape *The Fine Arts* is about. It's certainly why we make the things that you've described as 'placeholders.'

I could say something here about the accelerated pace of life in the 20th and 21st centuries putting pressure on artists to produce more faster, but I've always been suspicious of the idea that people experienced the world differently in the past. Artists have been driven to madness over the quality and quantity of their work for all of recorded history.

MH: When I was in film school, I found myself surrounded by a group of singularly inarticulate students – language had refused them, and they were looking for another way to say *I*. Your work, by contrast, is very literary, beautifully written and performed. Can you talk about the relation of reading/writing and making video?

EVD: As a child I learned to be deeply ashamed of the fact that I didn't love anything (nature, bicycles, computers, chess) more than I loved talking. I felt incurious about 'the way things work.' Because of that lack of curiosity about things other than human intercourse, social and sexual, I despised myself, in large part because it left me vulnerable to being hurt by others – all of whom from time to time would prefer to play soccer or read a handbook of some kind rather than talk about our 'relationship.' It left me 'needy,' which is in my opinion the most pejorative descriptor in the English language.

I have been able to achieve a modicum of self-love through my intense curiosity about language. I love words. I love *The Elements of Style* by Strunk and White. I love the Merriam-Webster Word of the Day. If I could have only one book in the world, it would be a really excellent dictionary. *The Complete Oxford*. Many volumes. Etymological.

Right now I am working on a project of writing a series of plot synopses. I love the words, yes, but that's a poet's minefield. I've always been short on plot. This project is about packing the humanity – the identification and emotional immediacy I always strive for – into a form that is both more conventional and more challenging than my autobiographical default. Autobiography is like a reflex for me. It's beginning to feel too self-indulgent and precious. It's time to try something new. But then, is that drive (to 'grow' or 'progress' as a maker) even more self-indulgent? The reader doesn't care if I'm being formally redundant. Or do they? Who is the reader? I'm meandering.

MH: Steve Reinke has been a teacher for you in two cities now. Can you talk about what he's meant for your work? Is it necessary to kill the father? How would you kill Steve?

EVD: Steve's work is too coy, clever and sadistic. Sometimes he lacks the perfectionism necessary to make the tapes stand out from the sea of mediocrity that is contemporary film/video. That is how I kill him.

Rapt and Happy

I also kill him by loving him and wanting to protect instead of exceed him. And yes, he is me and Cooper's beloved dad, and every animal we kill we drag back to him for his approval.

MH: Is it important to know tradition, what's been done in the field and other fields, in order to make your own work? Do you suffer from 'anxieties of influence'?

EVD: I think (and this is so obvious it barely merits writing) that it is both a blessing and a curse. It can be crippling to know what's already been done. If I had known the fucking banquet of backwards delights being brewed up at roughly the same time as *I Am a Conjuror* and *Attention Public*, we probably wouldn't have made them. However, seeing truly excellent artists like Miranda July and Eija-Liisa Ahtila inspires me to press on, to make works that are not the shit I usually see at festivals and screenings.

MH: Can you talk about talking backwards? It's a structuring mechanism you use in several of your tapes, all of which feature you and Cooper. Why backwards?

EVD: Nobody wants to hear this, but it truly is just a device to compensate for the fact that we are terrible actors. After we used it the first time, we of course started to question what meanings and connotations it held and how we could potentially exploit them. It worked, so we stuck with it.

MH: Do you ever feel that you've shown too much? When you're smoking crack in *Being Fucked Up*, or dancing naked, or describing your threesome livings, or socking Cooper in the face. How do you give yourself permission to show and share these moments?

EVD: I feel that others think I've shown too much. For me, it's like my certification to be fucked up in life. Sometimes I feel that it's a professional liability, but I cling to it as a badge, as a line-marker. I will not be totally obedient to the conventions of public and private. Honestly, my very sick fantasy is that if I make my private self public I can be absolved for my manifold sins.

MH: Is art an indulgence, a luxury, an extra? People are starving in the world, AIDS is rampant, wars are brewing, Palestinians are being slaughtered by Israeli teenagers dressed up as soldiers, the American empire continues to pillage. What does making art mean in the face of this?

EVD: This may be my biggest concern as an artist. I think about it constantly and have no answer. It's been thrown into high relief by the fact that my little brother Peter has just returned from a

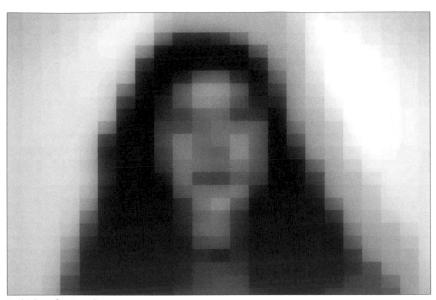
Bad Ideas for Paradise

year doing aid work in Sierra Leone. Another project I'm working on right now is a collaboration with him based on the fucking astonishing journal he wrote while he was there. He's so pragmatic about it, and I know that he feels (as I did about my Khyber 'art' job) that while the work might be noble in some sort of Platonic Ideal sense, the reality is pretty mundane and ineffectual.

Part of the way I've been thinking about this: the greatest pain I've ever experienced is the pain of romantic rejection. This pain was great enough to hospitalize me for over a month after a youthful (but serious) suicide attempt. It was also my impetus to 'find my voice' and make art.

I thought that anyone who didn't share my suffering was either an idiot or in denial. It was all very clear: women were destined to live a life of intolerable psychic agony because our romantic impulse was unmatched by men. Men fear entrapment; women fear abandonment. I was certain of these truths in the way that only a person with extraordinarily narrow experience can be certain.

There was no room in my model for the suffering felt by child-soldiers who were forced to rape their own mothers and then kill them and the rest of their families, for slaughtered or exiled activists, for people who had their lips and limbs hacked off with an axe, for people who watched their houses and families swept away by weather, for people who endured torture, for people who watched everyone they loved, everyone who accepted them, die of AIDS. Those things were too important to have any relevance to me, if that makes sense. When I saw artworks that took as their subject the great injustices of the world, I thought something like 'Oh, issues art. Bo-ring. Who *cares* about people being disappeared in Chile? Nobody really cares about that. Why don't they make work about what they really care about, like how much it hurts to be rejected.'

My pain, which felt uncontrollable and huge, is petty. My art, which I made with the great urgency I felt about expressing that pain, about reaching out, is petty. And yet that isn't the end of me speaking. That isn't the end of my voice. Maybe it should be, but for whatever ridiculous reasons, it isn't.

MH: What is the compulsion to keep working? Isn't what you've made enough? Does there have to be more? Should there be more?

EVD: Maybe we make more because we think eventually we will make something that helps. Or because of capitalism. Or because we think we'll get famous. Or because it's the only thing we believe in about ourselves.

MH: Video is a medium that has nothing essential in it. Reel to reel, ?-inch, High 8, one-chip digital, three-chip digital, Beta-cam – it's always giving way to the new so quickly. Do you worry what you make won't be showable in any way in a few decades?

EVD: No. I think if the work is strong enough that people continue to want to see it, it will continue to be remastered. If it languishes on the shelf, it's because people no longer find it interesting. I hope our works don't get remastered just because some place like Video Out gets a Canada Council grant to create a climate-controlled archive where every tape in their library will exist for perpetuity etched on special diamond chips that you can plug into your personal entertainment videophone day-planner goggles. That would be depressing. Nobody would ever choose to plug *Being Fucked Up* into their goggles! They could be watching the female-ejaculation Olympics or the new reality TV show about psychopaths where the winning psychopath gets out of jail but has to have cameras embedded in his eyeballs so we can be with him (or her – that would be really good; a child would be really good too) when he goes on his next rape-and-murder spree.

MH: Why did you move to Chicago?

EVD: To go to graduate school, and because Steve asked us to. Chicago was totally irrelevant to us before we went there. It's possible that in seven years of being together, Cooper and I had never ever said the word *Chicago* to one another. Still, R Kelly is from there – you know, the one whose lawyer said, 'The bank of R Kelly is now closed' when Kelly was faced with yet another statutory rape charge, this one involving Kelly urinating on a 14-year-old girl. Still, the Ignition Remix was *the* song that summer, with lyrics like 'Girl I'm feelin what you're feelin, no more hopin' and wishin'. I'm about to take my key and stick it in the ignition.' The record label told Kelly he couldn't say 'your ignition' because it was too suggestive.

When we went to Chicago, Cooper and I were both like, 'Chicago, whatever.' But when we got there it took about ten seconds before we were like, 'Holy shit. Chicago! I've heard of O'Hare airport before and now I just flew into it! It's like being famous!'

The proximity to fame – famous people and places, famous architecture and public art and bridges and stuff – is one of the most interesting things about going to the U.S. Even if I was in Fucktown, Ohio, or Suckyberg, Kansas, I felt like everything I looked at was famous – the way a waitress put a glass down on the table, the big flaccid families scarfing down big flaccid food. Maybe I'm just describing the experience of the exotic, but the way in which America is exotic to Canadians has something to do with the proximity to – and hence the possibility of – fame. That would be the worst part of it. The constant, vague pressure to do more, be better, be prettier, be ready to pounce when the opportunity comes. It's bad enough here, where it's a pipe dream most people outgrow as soon as they're old enough to distinguish between us (reasonable, earnest, frumpy) and them (grandiose, boorish, fabulous).

MH: Why did you move away from Chicago?

EVD: Because we were scrambling for money and it looked like a hard year ahead. Then I got the Khyber Art Gallery job, which offered security and a perverse symmetry to my life: returning to the centre on its tenth birthday, which coincided with the tenth anniversary of Cooper and I meeting and falling in love there. And because I never, ever felt at home in the U.S. I always felt like a spectator, like the people I was meeting and becoming friends with would only be part of my life for a short time. As soon as I got back to Canada, that feeling went away and the opposite took its place: 'These are the people I will be seeing at art events in Canada for the rest of my life, and I love them. Grudges will wax and wane, slights and sex will scald and be forgotten. We're home.'

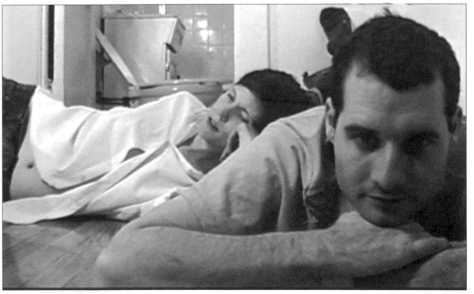

I Am a Conjuror

MH: Is it difficult to look at yourself in your own work? Of course you're both very young, but the tapes are a record of your aging, amongst other things. Is it hard looking at yourself as a thing made of pixels?

EVD: To answer this question I have to explain something complicated. Actually, it's not that complicated – it's just been described so often and misunderstood so completely that I need to be precise. The way it's usually talked about centres on the word *objectification*. I remember hearing that word as a teenage girl and thinking, 'That makes no sense. Objectification! What on earth could that mean? I don't feel like an object, like a table or a car!' I guess my understanding was too literal. When I was in university it shifted from being a totally foreign, irritating concept to being the perfect word to describe how I had felt all my life. It was about women being objects to look at and desire, not functional objects. Not objects like skill saws. Objects like flowers. Objects like antiques. Objects like children. It wasn't that women (or children) weren't understood as having interiority either – interiority was on display too. Our insides also had to be desirable. Because we were there to be evaluated, and the thing that determined my rank was how much desire and tenderness I could evoke. And that was incredibly painful for me, because I knew that my insides were not desirable and would not evoke tenderness. I was bad and a liar and self-interested. And my outside wasn't desirable either, not until I became an anorexic fashion plate doing cumbersome, soul-crushing drag. But in my formative years I was a little fatty, and inside I am still a fatty.

Becoming thin on the outside was an act of feminist terrorism for me. I know now that it was a bad strategy, that it failed to bring me the results I wanted, but rage was my impetus. I wanted to pay 'men' back for subjecting me to their painful evaluation (and especially for communicating to me that I failed to meet their standards of beauty and goodness). I thought I could do that by making myself desirable and then rejecting them. It didn't work.

It's harder for me to stay away from the camera than it is for me to perform, because there has never been a moment of my life, not for as long as I can remember, that I haven't been imagining someone was watching. One of my first memories of this is when I was about eight years old. We were at my grandparents' cottage in St. Margaret's Bay, and I was off by myself in a field full of wildflowers. It was a perfect summer day. I remember throwing my hands up and spinning around and around until I fell down, thinking, 'If only someone was watching me right now, then I would be happy. I'm sure I look beautiful now. I'm sure I look innocent and good.'

MH: Is showing work part of its making (its completion)? Could you make work and not show it?

EVD: I don't know if I would describe showing the work as a part of the process of making it. It's the reason I make work, to create mutual human feeling.

As for the question of whether I would keep making stuff if I couldn't show it or had taken some kind of vow against showing it, I'm not certain. People often talk about the concept of 'creativity' in art. They say things like, 'So you're an artist? You must be very creative,' or 'My daughter has a really good art teacher. She really brings out the students' creativity.' I've always been baffled by this term. I remember having what was called a 'creativity test' when I was in Grade 6. I thought, 'Oh good. I like art and I write poems – I should be good at this.' We had to take out a piece of paper and a pencil, and the teacher said, 'Okay, now I want you to make a line in any direction. Any direction at all.' I made a diagonal line toward the upper left corner of the page. I waited for the next instruction. My teacher said, 'All right, that's it. Keep your pencils right where they are. I see we only have one creative student in this class!' She pointed at a boy whose pencil was suspended in the air above his page.

Making my work has absolutely nothing to do with that kind of creativity, which is for computer programmers and physicists. My work is about communication. If the work no longer had the possibility of an audience, I would stop making art with that aim. I would definitely stop making videos. But I think I would start to use my 'creativity' more, because it would be fun and useful to solve problems and invent diversions for myself.

MH: Was it ever difficult to think of yourself as an artist? What did your parents think?

When I was about 11 I asked my mom if she would be upset if I was gay. She told me no, that she would love me just as much if I was gay, but that she would worry that my life would be harder. I wish she had had the same foresight about my decision to be an artist. Instead she just encouraged me to follow my interest in art and writing.

We have artists in my family, so it was never a very big deal for me to think of myself that way. It didn't seem to denote any special status – my uncle had been an artist all my life, and he was still living in a drafty garage and doing occasional stints as a cook. He was, however, incredibly cool – probably the coolest person I knew – and I was totally preoccupied with being cool, especially after I graduated from high school.

MH: Do people fall in love with you after seeing your work? Is art the prelude to love (or is love the prelude to art)?

EVD: People don't fall in love with me, but it does make some people see me as more powerful and desirable than I really am. I'm certain that it makes other people write me off completely, either before or after they've met me, but those people are much less likely to approach. It's a strange thing about being an artist (or a performer, a writer – or maybe just a human). We mostly hear the positive things people have to say about our performance in the world.

If I am completely honest, however, I have to confess that my drive to make work is essentially the same as my drive to make people fall in love with me. I have a kind of emotional disorder that makes me want everyone in the world to be in love with me. It's a very destructive part of my personality (destructive to myself and to others), and I use my moral energies to fight it back.

MH: Your work is very accessible, but it's not TV or feature films. Why don't you make work that formats into available accessible genre formats in order to reach a larger audience?

EVD: This is a question I ask myself again and again. The answer isn't straightforward, it's kind of like saying, 'You're a Canadian proctologist, but they need a lot of urologists in India. Why don't you become an Indian urologist?' I work in video art, an incredibly (and rightfully) obscure world where the bar is low. I don't like watching most video art. If I had a big library of video art tapes (which I do) and a TV/VCR (which I do), I would watch TV. I wouldn't watch the art videos. In fact, I'm half-watching TV right now. *King of the Hill.* And the reception is absolutely awful.

Bad Ideas for Paradise

So why do I stay in this world? For a few reasons. The first and most significant is that I am simply not talented enough to work in television. I couldn't, for instance, write for a situation comedy. My humorous insights are few and far between.

The second is that my parents totally discouraged me from my first passion, which was acting. From the age of four until I was in my early teens, I was dead set on being a Broadway star. As a little girl I collected soundtracks from musicals: *My Fair Lady, Oklahoma!, The Sound of Music, South Pacific* and so on. *Fame* was my favourite TV show. Danny Amatullo was one of my last true sexual passions. I wanted to go to school at the Fame school. Then one night, when I had been sent to my room for being bad in some way or another, I heard my parents talking about me downstairs. I snuck to the top of the steps so I could listen to them, and I heard my mother say something like, 'Jim, I'm just so worried

about what Emily is going to do with her life! She's so set on this acting and singing thing, but I really don't think her voice is that good! And she's so terrible at math.' I went into my room and cried, and then I made up some math questions and brought the answers down to show them. But that's an extreme example. Mostly they just subtly communicated to me that it wasn't feasible. My mom said things like, 'Do you know how many little girls want to be stars on Broadway, Emily?' Also, I was never given a speaking part in any of our elementary school musicals. They always went to the perfect blond popular girls, especially Christy and Karen MacDonald, the identical twins with blond ringlets whose mother made them drink whole milk because they were so thin. I was a fat little social pariah, and my music teacher, who cast the musicals, found me repugnant. In Grade 3 I boycotted. I auditioned, and when the list was posted on the music room door, I fought my fat little way to the front only to discover that I had been cast as an extra in the tea-party scene. I was absolutely devastated. I think that's when I gave up on the idea of being a famous performer in the mainstream media. Maybe if I had grown up in New York or L.A. it would have been different, but I think the only real change would have been in scale – I would still have been a fat little pariah, but Christy and Karen would have had their own sitcoms.

Finally, I think film and television are nothing more than the poisonous tentacles of the free market, configuring our desire in perverted and devastating ways.

MH: Can you talk about the role of animals in your work?

EVD: Animals, like children, are a repository for all our fantasies about innocence and simplicity. Animals can be forgiven for things that we would despise a human for. Imagine how irritating it would be if Cooper and I had performed the dialogue between the otter and the muskrat in *Curious About Existence*, where one of them quotes Nietzsche to the other. It would seem insufferably pretentious. Put the same words into the mouths of animals (or children) and it's funny and charming.

MH: Are drugs good for creativity?

EVD: The term *drugs* describes a vast territory, but I'll assume you're referring here to illicit or recreational drugs. Certain illicit drugs may be good for creativity, but addiction is unquestionably not.

I'm more interested right now in the effect that selective serotonin reuptake inhibitors and other neuro-active 'mood brighteners' have on creativity. I'm talking about drugs like Paxil, Prozac, Wellbutrin and Selexa. These drugs fascinate me. They are prescribed very widely, in large part because they are thought to be non-addictive (although when people stop taking these drugs cold-turkey, they describe horrible withdrawal symptoms), and they have complex and poorly understood effects on personality.

I've been on Selexa for about two and a half years, and I spend a lot of time thinking about which changes in my life and my work are attributable to the drug. For instance, I have felt a loss of urgency around making and exhibiting my work over that period of time. Is this a side effect of the drug or just an effect of getting older? Also during that span of time I became an alcoholic. My alcoholism was never particularly distressing for me. I didn't feel the guilt I used to feel after drinking. I regretted the stupid things I did while drunk, but I eventually resolved that problem by only drinking at home. I finally stopped when other drugs re-emerged as a problem, and I recognized that alcohol was a gateway drug. Once I decided to stop drinking, I noticed something for the first time: I had been working so hard at achieving oblivion that I had essentially missed a year of my life. Did I become an alcoholic because the drug freed me from remorse or because I had a dreadful artist-run-centre job and a houseguest who wouldn't leave?

It's such a terrible cliché, but I can't help but wonder if suffering is a crucial part of my practice as an artist. I mean, it's not like I don't suffer since I started taking antidepressants. I still suffer, but much less. I used to feel such intense despair that I became hysterical. I don't become hysterical anymore. Maybe I was more interesting when my moods were more extreme. Maybe I had to feel those things to be able to write about them with passion. I have little interest in describing my emotional landscape now. I'm inclined instead to write about other people or natural phenomena. Worse, I fear that I wouldn't like to consume my newer work, the work I've made while I've been on Selexa, as much as I would like to consume the work that came before.

Cooper Battersby and Emily Vey Duke have been working collaboratively since June 1994. Their work has been broadcast and exhibited around the world. Duke and Battersby are currently teaching at Syracuse University in Central New York. They are represented by Jessica Bradley Art and Projects in Toronto. www.dukeandbattersby.com

Emily Vey Duke and Cooper Battersby's Videos

Rapt and Happy   17 min 1998
My Heart the Lumberjack   13 sec 2000
Being Fucked Up   10 min 2000
The Fine Arts   3 min 2001
Bad Ideas for Paradise   20 min 2001
Perfect Nature World   3:30 min 2002
   (collaboration with Shary Boyle)
Curious About Existence   11 min 2003
The New Freedom Founders   26 min 2005
Songs of Praise for the Heart Beyond Cure   15 min 2006

Distributed by Video Data Bank, Video Out, Vtape and Jessica Bradley Art and Projects.

BENNY NEMEROFSKY RAMSAY
THE SINGER

He's the funniest, most charming human you've ever met, and he looks at you with eyes that never seem to stop opening, as if he is always looking into the very deepest part of you, the part where two cells once united to form the beginning of every desire you would ever call your own. That's how far it goes. But the depth is not terrifying, because he carries you in a swoon of stories, and when he lays them down like a red carpet, you know you are the most special and beloved person in the universe.

And then the next moment he doesn't know you at all. What was your name again?

Benny is a changeling. He doesn't switch his address – he gets up on a plane and changes continents; he learns a new language and a new way of thinking in that language. Perhaps he is on the run from his legions of lovers. Perhaps he is moving toward them.

His work is smoothed and buffed and polished, like something that came out of the candy factory at MTV, only there is a heartbreak he reserves for the camera. Lights, camera ... and the action is always from the heart. He doesn't see the point in making movies where he doesn't appear in every frame; this self, too long left behind, can at last find a stage here, and provide an image of hope for everyone else who thought they could never, *oh no not me, surely you don't want me.*

His small-screen star turns have provided him a chance to sing of love and loss. And he is drawn to the popular form, to the overplayed radio hiccups of the transnational pop kingdom. You might write a thousand songs in your life, but in the kingdom there is room for only one, again and again. He has dedicated himself to this moment, to the picture of love as it appears in the mouth of a teenage daydream frothing it up over a sea of guitars. When we meet I say, 'Benny!' but it carries an association with eggs he can't abide. He was going to launch a proper singing career as Nemerofsky, then decided to retreat back into his frequent flyer points. No doubt he is saving Ramsay for some future incarnation.

MH: One night over dinner you recounted your television debut at a precociously young age, and described a funny serious encounter with a TV camera. Could you go over it again for those who couldn't make it that evening? In relation to this, there is an old notion dating back to Augustine (I think) that speaks of a 'calling,' often heard as a voice. A calling is one's always vocation announced at some precarious moment, or heard in whispers through the inner monologue. Is making art your calling?

BNR: I like the idea of a calling, of whispers that surface in the cacophony of voices that inhabit my mind. I like thinking about, listening to and producing voices in general, so the idea that we exist in an envelope of voices is very appealing to me. But while I think I probably produce art in response to callings, I don't think art is my calling.

I can be a very in-one-ear-out-the-other kind of person, I am terribly forgetful at times. But sometimes experiences or emotions choose to occupy my mind, they repeat, they refuse to leave. I think I am looking for meaning in my life, so when these matters adhere, they become symbols of – or hints at – meaning. This creates a kind of itch, or a rush of excitement, a need to interact with and embody this meaning and give it more tangible form. Just last night at a concert I heard a sound that reminded me of an idea I have had for many years, an idea that rarely changes shape in my mind, but has never taken form as an artwork. I don't think it will leave until I make something with it. I wrote its name on my hand in the concert. The ink is already fading from my skin, but I know the idea will keep calling.

But of course the bigger question for me is whether or not I am expressing these ideas in the right form. I can't think of non-art forms to express these questions, desires, itches, but I sometimes wonder if I am being lazy, if there is another way. I might have locked myself into art-making as my métier and can no longer see outside its boundaries. This skepticism and ambivalence makes it hard for me to attach to the idea that art-making is my calling. I'm just not convinced.

I wonder if there are any answers in the story I recounted about my first encounter with a video camera. The work I am known for always involves me in front of a video camera, singing, performing emotions, multiplying, seeming generally desirous and regretful. For a few years I have been incubating a concept for a video that uses old footage from an aerobics television show my mother was a part of in the 1980s. She was a backup 'dancer' for a host who spoke to the camera, telling viewers all sorts of '80s things about health and bodies. My mother sometimes spoke, but mostly just looked great in turquoise leotards and pink legwarmers and headbands. In my research, I went through my mother's collection of VHS cassettes of the show. One episode was devoted to returning to fitness after pregnancy. All the show's performers introduced their children on camera one by one, transmitting the idea that even after having children they were able to maintain fit, tight bodies. The camera pans from mother to mother, each one naming her children and telling the audience something about each child's character.

I'm sitting with mother and sister on the floor of the very white aerobics studio. We've been arranged by someone so that we form little family clusters. My sister is sitting in between my mother's legs, and I'm somehow a bit behind my mother, maybe on my knees. Something unnatural. My mother says my name and that I am ten years old, an artist, and that I sing in a choir. The host of the show says, 'Good for you.' My mother introduces my sister, saying she wants to be an aerobics instructor when she grows up. The host says, 'Well, she's come to the right place.' It's all supposed to be humorously light, but it's very staged and rehearsed. My mother has already come up with a script in her mind that she follows.

I am wearing a blue golf shirt with thin, hot pink stripes across it. I haven't had braces yet, so my teeth are bucky and crooked and stick out from under my top lip. I don't say anything, but one can see I am obsessed with the camera's gaze. There is an excruciating moment when I perform laughter, acting amused by my mother's comment about my sister's aerobics future. I look into the camera as though I am sharing this joke with the audience. My body sways forward as part of my performance of laughter; there is something exaggerated about the gesture, and yet not over-the-top enough for it to be comical. I don't remember experiencing this moment, but watching it now I am stunned at this image of myself. I can't tell if it is a true window into how uncomfortable I felt in my body, how the idea of 'natural' behaviour had already been stolen from me at that age, always being pelted with comments on how I was inappropriately effeminate, identifying with all the wrong characters in the media. Or instead, as a regular television consumer, does it show how I inhabit the idea of how one acts on television? It's probably both. I think I was always in a stage of performance as a child, always searching for the elusive, acceptable way of behaving, and the explicitness of the television stage intensified this feeling of performativity for me.

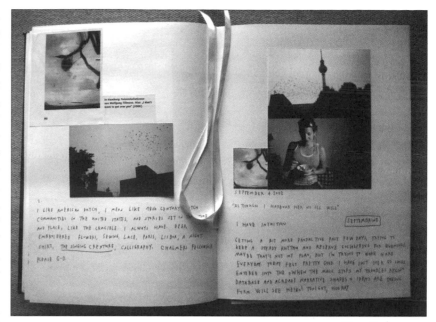

Diary, Berlin, 2002

What I find particularly strange about this 20-second clip of television is that in describing what I think is going on for me in that moment, I find myself using the same language I use to describe my current art practice. I have a body of videos in which I try on appropriate behaviours, I perform myself, I seek out what is natural for me in a public, 'televised' way. There is a terrifying seed of my art practice in this moment in the 1980s. In a way this makes it harder to negate the idea of having a 'calling.'

MH: Your body is an image and onto it you have secured other pictures, deciding on the perpetual marriage of the tattoo. Could you talk about your tattoos?

BNR: I have three tattoos, in fact. On the inside of my left arm is the outline of the Hebrew letter Beth, pronounced *Beys* in Yiddish. I had it done in 1997 at a time when my ethnic identity as a Jew was very important to me. I was studying Yiddish, my grandfather had just died and I was planning a first, genealogically motivated trip through Europe. When I returned from the trip I had a faint, almost invisible blue-green line added just underneath the letterform. It was meant to represent my struggles with fear in some physical form, as a reminder. On my right arm is a tattoo from 1999: it is a single line that begins on the inside of my wrist and spirals about 15 times around my arm, ending in the crevasse of my armpit. At one point, on the inside of my forearm, the line splits into two for a few inches and then closes again, making a small frame around what was once an important scar that was beginning to fade when the tattoo was made, acting as a marker of the scar that would soon disappear. Both tattoos were done in Toronto.

On my side is a deer that was tattooed in 2002, in Lucerne, Switzerland, coincidentally while I was travelling with a man I was falling in love with, but who was unavailable to me. It is a jumping deer, a design that, by chance, this man had found for me. I had been developing an affinity for deer over the years – I identified with their ambiguous gender, their simultaneous strength and grace, their benignity. I had begun collecting deer figurines and objects. The deer jumps along the side of my waist. From the front, one can only see the deer's hind legs kicking back. Its body stretches across my side. It's not too big, and is carefully placed to be a bit elusive.

I've done something rather clever with my tattoos. It wasn't meant to be clever, but as time goes by, it is working out this way. All the tattoos, save the pale blue-green line, are in white ink, giving them an almost invisible, secret effect. They are rarely seen, only noticed by chance if the light is right. Both the Hebrew letter and the deer are on rather hidden parts of my body, and the spiral is only viewable from the underside of my arm; otherwise it is obscured by my arm hair. Only on sunny, sleeveless days do people sometimes notice it. Even I, looking in the mirror in the morning, rarely see them.

The images emerge from my body – there is something almost natural about them. As my sense of identity changes over time, I'm glad the tattoos are subtle. A few years ago my interest in my Jewish identity began to shift and my interest in Hebrew letters waned. Similarly, this past year has seen my fondness for deer gradually fade. My body and gender and sexuality have been changing form, and deer don't seem to capture the spirit of my identity anymore. And so my tattoos become markers of past selves, as they do for so many people. In my case, I am reminded of these moments and selves by chance, when someone asks to see my tattoos, or accidentally, when naked. In fact, looking at my deer now, I realize I haven't set eyes on it for many months. That's a long way of saying their permanence is very light, something that comes and goes, like memories. I hadn't anticipated this quality when I first had them made, although in choosing white ink I was attracted to the ghostly possibilities of tattoos.

I met a man in Paris this summer who had a tattoo on his lower back, reaching down almost over his buttocks. The tattoo was made up of a single phrase of text, 'Real Men Take It in the Ass.' The script was decorative and used various typefaces that were extremely contemporary, in the moment – '*tendence,*' as they say in France. I remarked later to a mutual friend that I couldn't imagine getting a tattoo that was so dramatic and such a reflection of a particular cultural moment on such an important, provocative part of the body. My friend commented that the tattooed man lived largely, without undue concern for the future. Not sloppily or ill-considered, but fearlessly and fully in the moment.

MH: You seem a bit of a changeling to me, hairful and hairless, a Berliner, then an honorary Parisian, then back to Toronto, a nomadic cultural worker skipping from residency to gig to homes that seem always temporary. How does your relation to your shifting appearance, and the restless erotic quest to which it's attached, line up with your media work, which, while it shifts with each screening, has something permanent and indelible about it.

BNR: As a teenager I attached myself to superhero comics, one of the few gender-appropriate activities that interested me. I was singularly interested in metamorph characters: werewolves, shape-shifters, people with bodies made of materials that could transform into different selves. Looking back, I'm convinced this was some articulation of teenage queerness, fantasizing about changing into another body because my current incarnation was unacceptable.

There is definitely a sense of trying on various identities in my work, multiple selves within a single frame, embodying images and texts from the culture around me, becoming a host body for diverse media messages. But there is also something about seeking the truth within myself, using these performances as ways of finding something real inside me. It's hard to articulate. Whereas my childhood fantasies of metamorphosis were about escaping the unacceptable body, my videos are about performing different characters as a way of digging for the truth about myself.

Similarly, I try on different representations of love and romantic ideals. These acts are also about encountering messages from the media sources around me – critiquing them, perhaps – but also trying to feel my way through them. I think this is why my performances read as simultaneously ironic and earnest. I suppose I could simply say I live my life this way too. I change my appearance, I change the city I live in, I try on versions of myself in hopes of getting closer to the truth. Or, more accurately, the truths, because there are so many.

MH: You are a diary-keeper, and unlike most, your journals (from the glimpses you've so generously permitted) are beautiful works of art, tremendously personal, but fastidiously organized, often granting equal weight to picture and text. Could you talk about when you began making journals, and the relationship between text and image in these pages? And what about the relation between these journals and your artwork?

BNR: It's nice to reflect on my history of diary-writing, because I've gone through many different phases and have settled into what feels like a very focused state right now.

I began diary-writing in a serious way when I was 17. I had seen Merchant Ivory's exquisite film interpretation of E. M. Forster's *Maurice* that year and was inspired by the title character's turn toward diary-writing as a way to process and cope with his emerging homosexuality, feeling he had no other outlet of expression. Because I often carried sensations from films beyond the actual viewing experience, I wound up identifying with and enacting this particular gesture in my own life. My first diary risked an elaboration of very private thoughts, mostly about my sexuality.

Diary-writing came and went for a few years, but became a central part of the way I lived in my mid-20s. At one point my diary-writing reached a fevered pitch – I had about five diaries happening simultaneously, devoted to different themes: daily life, erotic fantasies, dreams, food I was eating. Diary-keeping really became a practice, and different periods of my life are marked by different diary dimensions, from little pocket-sized books to larger-than-life sketchbooks. It's true that I went through many years of creating illustrated diaries, books in which the bottom half of the page was reserved for writing, and the upper

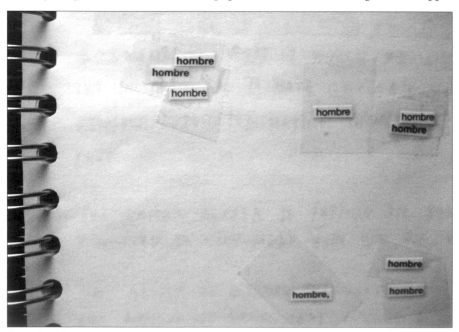

Diary, Barcelona, 2002

half for photographs, little collages and drawings. I went through an artmaking phase in which I recreated elements from my diaries in large-scale works on paper, but I never took this very far.

Lately, images have disappeared from my diaries. Little by little the spaces left for images were being left empty, and so I started filling full pages with writing. I've stopped using sketchbooks and now use smaller, portable diaries. I made a pact with myself that by the time I turned 30 I wanted to have a more developed handwriting style. I often printed in my journals, having perfected a style of printing, always finding my handwriting sloppy and sophomoric. But printing took too long. I had been reading Anaïs Nin's strategy of what she called 'white heat' writing – diary entries written as soon after a sexual experience as possible, in an attempt to capture some essence of the experience. I needed a satisfying writing style that could happen fast and passionately. I spent a lot of time pushing my hand, trying different papers and pens, and by the time I found a handwriting style that satisfied me, I had let go of images altogether. I sometimes draw maps of cities or relationships in my diaries, but they are mostly devoted exclusively to writing.

MH: Could you tell the story of Art Fag 2000 and how you carried off the laurels attached to this heady tag? That standing-room-only event at Toronto's Images Festival featured your video debut, and everyone was obviously impressed by how much work you had put into your piece.

BNR: Art Fag 2000 was such a strange phenomenon. I don't think about it much anymore, but, *sans doute*, it changed the direction of my life. I had been little by little insinuating myself into arty, faggy spaces in Toronto, going to galleries and art parties. I was drawing and printmaking, trying to figure out what kind of work I wanted to be doing, what kind of contribution I wanted to make to the creative world I was so stimulated by. My work was very earnest, but also decidedly amateur. I was pushing myself through different media and ideas I had missed out on by not going to art school. Anyway, I reached a point where people started to know who I was without anyone having much sense of what I did.

RM Vaughan and Roy Mitchell were curating a crazy event called *The Search for Art Fag 2000* for the Images Festival, and I was selected as one of ten contestants. It was a funny, beauty-pageant-cum-talent-show; each contestant was expected to dress up, make a short Super 8 film to support their candidacy and answer skill-testing questions related to art at a much-hyped event that closed the festival.

My boyfriend at the time, Guntar Kravis, an artist and photographer and general aesthete, worked with me on the film, a kind of over-the-top day in the life of an art fag. It featured me flitting about town, eating breakfast modelled after a Wolfgang Tillmans still life, communing with my inner Cindy Sherman, flirting with John Greyson, getting fashion tips from Karma Clarke-Davis and gorging myself on free food at a gallery opening in lieu of dinner. The film was a hit and I won the competition and thus the title Art Fag 2000, against such local greats as Will Munro, Keith Cole and Andrew Harwood.

I don't know what I expected Art Fag to mean – in the moment it was just fun and I was able to rewrite adolescent narratives of always losing popularity contests. But pockets of the art community – and to a smaller degree the community at large – were titillated by this event and title, and I found myself receiving unexpected attentions. Strangers called out, 'Art Fag 2000!' as I passed by on my yellow bicycle, and local and national newspapers began doing little profiles on me. The timing was ideal: I was in a very productive creative state at that time, working on a photo series, an exhibition of drawings, a dance piece at a local festival and my first video, so there was plenty of art activity to promote. 'There's no rust on my crown,' I quipped in one newspaper after listing my multidisciplinary activities at the time.

But aside from this 15 minutes of local fame, two other important things happened connected to my tenure as Art Fag 2000. Kelly O'Brien and Scott Beveridge, filmmakers and curators of a program for Toronto's Splice This! Super-8 Film Festival, saw my Art Fag film and invited me to produce a short work for a curated program of local filmmakers. The result of this commission was *Je Changerais d'Avis*, the video that began a new narrative in my life creatively and professionally. Vtape founders Lisa Steele and Kim Tomczak were in the audience and approached me immediately after the screening and asked to meet with me. They championed the video, initiating international distribution for my work. This video is also special to me because in it I established all the core themes that would guide my practice for the next five years: interpreting love images, emotional performance, multiplicity and translation of texts into different languages.

My Art Fag title led to another life-changing experience. At the time I was making regular trips to Berlin, having fallen under its spell during my first visit in 1997. In the summer of 2000, I went for three weeks. As my Air Transat flight landed in Schoenefeld Airport and I stood in the aisle waiting to deplane, a woman came up to me and asked, 'Excuse me, but are you Art Fag 2000?' I was dumbstruck to be asked this question in Europe. It was Laurie Young, a Canadian contemporary dancer living in Berlin, a member of the Sasha Waltz company. Her sister was a Toronto filmmaker and had spotted me at the airport before I went through security, and told Laurie about the event. We exchanged numbers and agreed to meet during my stay to get to know each other better. During those three weeks I spent much time with Laurie, who introduced me to many artists and dancers in the city. We stayed in close touch upon my return to Toronto, and in less than a year I was her roommate in Berlin. I know that my fantasy of moving to Berlin couldn't have been realized without Laurie's support, and in its own strange way I can thank Art Fag 2000 for making it happen.

MH: In *Je Changerais d'Avis* (4 min, 2000), you sing a love song, or a song about a once-love, which is simultaneously translated

Je Changerais d'Avis

into English, German, American Sign Language and even weather reports. How did you choose the song and why all the translations? Your six-screen address is reminiscent, at least superficially, of the info-channels that show traffic/weather/late-breaking events and a news ticker, but you dish some powerful emotions in the course of this four-minute song. And more than that, at the end of the song, just at the right moment, you cry. This is so lovely, but at the same time constrained, as your picture is inside all these digital frames within frames (your headshot appears in four images at once, variously colourised) – it's hard not to escape the feeling that you are performing your emotions, that this is theatre, that some moment of intimacy has been mined for its calculated effect on the viewer.

BNR: This was really my first video art piece. I came to this process very naive about what was relevant or contemporary, so my answers are very much after-the-fact, as though the apple of knowledge was bitten much later. I had no intentions of exhibiting it beyond the screening it was commissioned for; it was made as a love poem to a single person. No other video would be produced this way, with this purity of thought and intention.

Two disparate emotions came together to produce the idea for *Je Changerais d'Avis.* I was in a troubled, fragile relationship with a man I was very much in love with, and was having difficulties expressing my unhappiness to him. A friend had heard the Françoise Hardy song and played it for me. (It was actually written by Ennio Morricone as *Se Telefonando* a year earlier in 1963 and recorded in Italian by Mina with lyrics that tell a very different story.) I remember not fully understanding the French, but responding immediately to the mounting emotions of the song and the few lines I could make out – 'I would leave my friends for you,' 'I wouldn't ask any questions if you would just take me by the hand.' I was fascinated by the desperation of the emotion being transmitted, and I identified very much with the sentiment.

Meanwhile I had become interested in CP24, a Toronto-based hyperinformation channel that divided the television screen into different smaller frames, each offering various informations. The station sought to give the viewer all the news anyone could need: live images of current traffic conditions, a week's worth of weather forecasts, a local news broadcast and stock numbers running tickertape style along the bottom, with entertainment and sports headlines fading in and out like subtitles. This everything-at-once aesthetic strategy fascinated me – it seemed very of-the-moment. Though despite the station's goal of transmitting all the news simultaneously I found that, paradoxically, this overload left me confused and unable to absorb any information.

The piece of music and this television format met in my mind. I wanted to filter a performance of the song through this format as a kind of test: I'm singing this desperate song in French, translated into English and German; an expressive, almost dancing sign-language interpreter is enacting the text and the song's rhythm; the song is further reflected in a weather forecast and a webcam. Maybe now this unnameable emotion can somehow be transmitted. Or maybe it is futile.

As for my performance, the question of authenticity often comes up. There is a moment between two verses when I sigh and roll my eyes in exasperation that always triggers laughter in an audience. In the final verse of the song, the sign-language interpreter and I become increasingly agitated. Breathing loudly, I look around, my forehead breaking into wrinkles as the interpreter throws her hair and arms around pleadingly. Here the audience usually quiets, in sharp contrast to the outburst of giggles that happened moments before. The performance – whether interpreted as comical, heartbreaking, outlandish or unnerving – seems to transmit something real for the audience.

I sang the song five times to the camera, at first melodically but eventually in a more spoken, broken, plaintive voice. While five performances might seem to dilute and 'de-authenticize' the emotions, instead they distilled them. I became comfortable and at ease, and let the feelings embody me. I knew I was making a video, but I did not yet have a sense of an 'audience.' Sure, I turned the emotions on to match the text I was singing, but I didn't break down and become unable to complete the song, overwhelmed by tears. But as I recall, my emotions were always very close to the surface at that time; my feelings for my boyfriend were the epicentre of my emotional identity. When I look at the video now, I see the flicker of genuine emotions and wonder if I'll ever feel that way for anyone again.

MH: I'm wondering about received forms, the shapes that already exist. The songs you inhabit are like going to live in someone else's house for a while – there are certain inevitable restrictions, flows of movement and desire each house makes possible. Will you feel my love if I make it look like Madonna's version? If I disguise myself as a radio jingle, will you love me then? That's what I wondered when I watched your *Live to Tell* (6 min, 2002). I marvelled at your ability to convert this too-well-known song into your song. The other remarkable thing is how you've staged it. You appear in a series of frames that seem an echo of the enclosure of the song itself, or the thwarted love that inspired it. You perform a series of everyday gestures, mostly cleaning an empty room, pausing every now and then to throw a leg up in a gesture toward dance. You are like the proverbial washerwoman discovered at the record company who can really sing. And out of this drudge of the everyday, the monologue of our lives, there is something that underlies every waking moment, and pierces it, and flows out of it. This wound is your singing; you open your mouth and out it comes, all of this unexpected emotion, and delivered so beautifully. Each of these 16 boxes shows you, singing in gathered and regathered arrangements of yourself, a chorus that amplifies and counterpoints your voice to stunning effect.

BNR: I heard the Madonna song for the first time again as an adult at a party. I was very struck by the text and had a choral arrangement made. Why the surveillance cameras? I used to have another answer to that question and then I had a screening in Stuttgart where it was raised again, and the Mexican video artist Ximena Cuevas whispered to me afterward, 'It's because of the impossibility of privacy.' That's my official answer now. It is about looking for a witness and settling for anything, even a surveillance camera. I had been to the Albright-Knox Museum, where small security systems are visible on each floor. Guards sit before an array of monitors that show multiple views of the gallery, creating beautiful patterns of people moving. I had 16 different performances to do, choreographed exactly against the already-recorded music. Most gestures are in unison. They all raise their arms up together at the same pace and that creates an

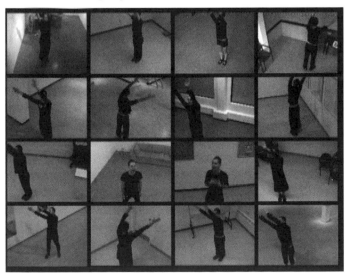

Live To Tell

overall effect. Or maybe they're all doing the same thing but facing different directions, or patterns are created where eight are doing this and eight are doing that. The choreography was based on who's singing and who's not, as the song begins with a solo voice that becomes a duet, later still quartet, octet, and finally all 16 voices sing together. Further variations ensue.

In Berlin I saw a large building off Alexanderplatz that was under construction. It hosted a public art project entitled Project Blinkenlights, where the artist put a single, identical light in each window. Using computer programming it became like a giant LCD screen, creating forms out of moments of light. It was a sensation for nearly a year in Berlin – Kylie Minogue featured a similar concept in one of her videos.

I saw a piece by the French choreographer Jerome Bel called *The Show Must Go On*, where he used everyday expressions and club dancing and ersatz '80s jazz movements with great irony, losing the earnestness that characterizes so much contemporary dance. This influenced my choreography in *Live to Tell*. It's very unvirtuosic. I lift one arm to shoulder height, then the other, then I bring them back down. Or I put both hands in the air as if I'm praying to God, and then I bring them down. But if you do it 16 times, which appear all at once on 16 frames, it creates a sad choreography. I was absorbing different moments that spoke to me: the surveillance cameras in the museum, the Madonna song, the Jerome Bel choreography, the illuminated building at Alexanderplatz – that all became *Live to Tell*.

MH: *I Am a Boyband* (5 min, 2002) features a performance of a John Dowland song where you sing all four parts. Can you talk about how this tune found you?

BNR: The song is from 1597. John Dowland was a major Elizabethan composer who published books of songs, airs and lute music. The song that I sing, 'Come again sweet love doth now invite' is from the *First Book of Songs*, and is one of his best known works. I kept all the words and harmonies, and worked with electronic musician Taylor Savvy, a Canadian living in Berlin. He gave it a boy-bandish treatment that left the meter intact. At the end of the song, the accompaniment stops and the four voices sing a cappella; you can hear how much this version retains Dowland's original form.

There are four characters in the original song, appearing one at a time. Each singer expresses a different moment in the arc of the love narrative. It begins with a character requesting that the beloved return so that they can enjoy each other again. He's the one that has a normal outfit, a blue T-shirt and jeans, and my normal hair. The other three are much more costumed. He's the most confident because he is still in a state of 'Just come back and let's have fun.' The second singer repeats the request, but this time wants the beloved to return in order to end his suffering. 'I sit, I sigh, I weep, I faint, I die in deadly pain, and endless misery.' I'm wearing a sporty Adidas top and really tight jeans and a mini wig. I was living in Berlin and was really into the sport fetishism that I first noticed in the gay scene there. He's usually everyone's favourite because he's sweet and shy.

The third singer is very affected by the lover's moods. 'When you smile it is spring, when you frown it's the winters of my woes.' There is a move from pleading with the beloved to an acknowledgment he isn't coming back. The third man was supposed to be the tough one. He has sunglasses and a cut-off T-shirt and makes punching moves. That was me being butch. It's hysterical for me to watch, because I see how much I can't pass.

The fourth guy has given up. He sings only about himself, not even referring to the beloved. 'All the night my sleeps are full of dreams. My eyes are full of streams, my heart takes no delight.' Seeing others only underscores how unhappy he is – he has been assigned storms of misery while others are granted its fruits and joys. This swooning romantic in his silken shirt is lonely and bitter. Even when the other boys step up and do their moves, he just looks on with a disdainful rejection. And then, all together,

I Am a Boyband

they sing the last phrase, which is now addressed to Cupid, to love itself. 'Gentle love, Thou canst not pierce his heart, for I that do approve. By sighs and tears more hot than are thy shafts, did tempt while he for triumphs laughs.' The beloved is not touched/pierced by love, and there is also a sense that he is laughing triumphantly at the singer's misery.

MH: *Lyric* (2 hours, 5-monitor installation, 2004) was your first venture into post-cinema reception, breaking with the monoform of beginning, middle and end into a scatter of viewing possibilities. It is at once home movie, song cycle and virtuosic pop manifesto. How did it begin?

BNR: It began on Berlin's Hagenauerstrasse in my first summer there in 2001. That was the street I was living on. I was in so much grief, I had moved to another continent. And I had that very typical experience in which I felt that every song on the radio, even the most common and banal, was speaking directly to me. We are supposed to be media-savvy sophisticates, but we're still busy filling the airwaves with hetero-normative monogamous impossibilities. Whether blaring out of cars, or drawling from the phone when you're put on hold, these oppressive love narratives keep following us. I had received a letter from my ex-boyfriend in Berlin and couldn't think how to reply. Every attempt was a disorganized explosion of grief that could never be sent to anybody. The pressure to respond occurred while I felt surrounded by these banal pop lyrics. At one point I had the idea to send him lines from individual pop songs, but in the end I sent him a letter that simply said, 'Life sucks without you.' Actually, it was very poetic. I wrote it very small on a large piece of paper. I rolled it up and put it in a glass bottle I had found. In Germany, you can buy packages at the post office that are used for sending bottles of wine. It was my message in a bottle.

I began actively collecting single lines from love songs that were meaningful to me even if they were ridiculous, like 'I will die without you,' because that was what I felt. This is too painful, I can't go on. I had never experienced anything like that before.

Usually when I talk about *Lyric*'s beginning, I say that the iPod came out in the same year. The first ads for iPods promised a thousand songs in your pocket, which is considered a small number today. In fact, there is no iPod that has so few. But at the time I was struck that songs were measured as quantities as opposed to style or quality. In my research, I had come across stories of epic singers in Russia, Asia and Armenia who would sing an entire culture's history at events like weddings. There were families of singers, where roles passed from generation to generation. Somehow all these interests came together. I wanted to create an epic love song composed of 1,000 lines from pop songs. I arranged these into hybrid, Dadaist songs, grafting together similar lines until they morphed into new themes. I performed these lines over the course of a day in my grandmother's house, singing through a few themes, then going into the kitchen and looking into the fridge, washing the dishes and then singing another theme. I wanted to show the ubiquity of love and grief, and consuming music, perhaps. I chose my grandmother's house because it is a place of love and longing for me. I used a lens that created a strange dollhouse effect where I'm very close to the camera but if I move away a sense of miniature furniture evolves. It became a strangely private world with a pervasive sense of isolation.

Most of the sections of *Lyric* are arranged by lines that correspond to a theme like 'I will love you forever.' There is one section that moves from 'I call you' to 'I am calling out your name.' It becomes a section where I collected a hundred first names from songs and sang them alphabetically. I can still sing it off by heart, because I've now turned this segment into a live performance.

MH: Can you sing the A, B and C's?

BNR: Right now? [sings] *Aaron, oh Aaron/ Alice/ Anastasia/ Angie, Angie/ Anna/ Ariel/ Barbara Ann/ Ben/ B-B-B-Benny/ Billie Jean/ Billy/ B-Bobbie Bobbie McGee/ Candy, Candy, Candy/ Caroline/ Cecelia/ Chiquitita* ... That's ABC. Each name is sung as it is heard in its original, which makes for a lot of fast changes. In the live version I sing with a video projection beside me showing the words as a sort of subtitle, which is important for a non-English audience. The audience usually laughs in recognition of some of the songs, marvelling at the endurance required to move through different key signatures and moods.

MH: You present *Lyric* as a five-monitor installation, each showing you in different rooms of your grandmother's house, singing with the iPod. Was it always going to be an installation?

BNR: No. It was originally conceived as a single-looped projection. Its first presentation at New Langton Arts in San Francisco in 2003 was a projection in a room. The audience could enter and exit. I left that first exhibition feeling anticlimaxed about a year's work becoming this single projection. There was something wrong because audiences didn't spend much time with it. As some passages last as long as 20 minutes in a single room, there was no clear sense that different themes or rooms emerge. Lisa Steele and I looked at it and examined different possibilities. She came up with the idea of viewing stations, which I then translated into five monitors, each with its own headsets. Each shows the same DVD but begins at a different point. It's timed so there's always a different room on each monitor. It's subtitled, so without listening to everything you can see that different themes are being explored. Sometimes people take the headphones off and just watch it silently, building sentences with the subtitles from monitor to monitor.

MH: You mentioned coming to an impasse in your work and not knowing what to do next. Could you elaborate?

BNR: I had an exhibition at the PlugIn ICA in Winnipeg in 2004. It was a survey exhibition of my video work to date – it had only been four years, so there wasn't a lot. But I had *Je Changerais d'Avis* on a monitor and a looped projection of *I Am a Boyband* in one room and a looped projection of *Live to Tell* in another. And then *Lyric*, in its full five-channel glory, was in the centre of the gallery with a bookwork. It was a luxurious experience seeing all the major pieces of the last four years, all at once, in the best conditions I could ever imagine. Everything looked and sounded gorgeous. I left feeling I no longer had anything more to contribute to this particular creative strategy. It was a completed body of work, which at the time, almost two years ago, was very exciting and empowering. Okay, so what's next? The last two years have been a period of vague experimentation. I have tried a few things and produced a few other little videos, but have found it a challenge to discover what the next move is.

I had spent time singing other people's work, reinterpreting existing pop music with the goal of analyzing – perhaps critiquing – its language of love. What about my own text and identity? Not Benny pretending to be the different faces of a boyband or making fun of the way love is sung about, but Benny's words, tunes and melodies. I felt that the next logical step for me was to become some sort of art-pop singer. Following that line I produced two songs, one with Andrew Zealley and another on my own, rearranging an existing piece of music. But as far as I'm concerned, they were not successful creative undertakings. For one of the songs, I produced a video at the Banff Centre, but as I was attaching the final credits I decided to abandon the project.

MH: I don't think it's unusual what's happening to you right now, though the degree of self-awareness you bring is singular. When I started making films, I was surrounded by folks making their early movies which were beautiful and powerful. I was busy floundering, trying on styles, seeing what might fit. Is this me? Meanwhile, all around me masterpieces were trotted out by the kilo. But after five or ten years, I watched as one after another ran out of steam, exactly as you describe. That initial burn left them and they began making their in-between things, the sidesteps and shelf-fillers, the minor versions of what they'd already done, or what someone else had already done. Years have passed in this state, and most have made inevitable decisions about families and security and jobs, and all these necessary human things that lessen the chance we will ever climb up out of the trough.

BNR: When I felt the burn, I thought it would never end. Lately I've been asking myself whether or not I'm an artist. I've had a certain amount of success and have been living as an artist, but I've started to look at the work I've made not as art, but evidence of the way I was, which happened to be called art, or was shown in art venues. The videos have come to feel more like by-products of my living, evidentiary traces. If I can claim to be anything right now, it's that I'm a diarist.

MH: You're in almost every frame of your movies.

BNR: It's not because I'm some great actor, but there's a feeling I'm chasing and it's my feeling, I suppose. My entire art practice is about controlling the way in which audiences encounter my image. Though perhaps the work has less to do with creating an emotional impression than figuring out a way to stop performing. When I was a teenager, people would say things like, 'Just be yourself.' It was such a conundrum. Being myself was a state I feel I lost long ago. In my early 20s I started actively trying to honour all the parts of myself that I felt had been abused and stigmatized, giving them space to re-emerge. Video became a tool in that project.

I've become increasingly interested in the term *interpreter*. It's a word often used in French to describe many different kinds of professions: singers, musicians and dancers – perhaps even actors abide by it. Within contemporary language translation circles, there has been much discussion about dropping the term *translator* and using the word *interpreter* to acknowledge the fact that texts can't be translated literally, word for word. It's always an interpretation. In my video work, I reinhabit songs and texts, so the word *interpreter* also applies. Lately I've been jamming on that word to help envision new creative directions.

Benny Nemerofsky Ramsay's Videos

White   4 min 1998
Je Changerais d'Avis   4 min 2000
Forever Young   5 min 2001
I Am a Boyband   5:10 min 2002
Live to Tell   6 min 2002
Audition Tape   8 min 2003
Lyric   2 hrs 2004 (5-monitor installation)
Subtitled   2 min 2004
Together at Last   6 min 2004 (with Cooper Battersby)
Patriotic   4 min 2005 (with Pascal Lièvre)
Uropop   1.5 min 2006

Distributed by Jessica Bradley Art and Projects, Netherlands Media Art Institute, Vidéographe and Vtape.

Benny Nemerofsky Ramsay is a Montreal-born artist, diarist and aspiring bon vivant. His video work has screened in gallery and festival contexts internationally. He divides himself between Canada and Europe. www.nemerofsky.ca

SHELLEY NIRO

THE RED ARMY IS THE STRONGEST

I get off the bus in Brantford and stumble into a billiard bar that still has flecks of blood and sawdust and a hover of flies milling in a far corner. For those used to the two-dimensional space of a screen, directions can be confusing. A bottled blond with yesterday's hangover tells me I have to turn up the hill, so I do, walking past the beautiful perched houses and hopes and driveways, past the cemetery on the other side of the road, where the dead lie peacefully at the bottom of this journey, until I get on up to Shelley's house, with its bright, welcoming face. She already has her smile on, and I'm sniffed all over by her dog, and then we sit for coffee. We talk over an open laptop that is filled with words that might one day race from the mouths of actors on big screens around the world.

If ever there was an artist who could make feature dreams come true and not lose a moment of her artful heart, it is Shelley. She laughs and talks and drinks another cup of coffee and laughs some more. For someone as politically hip as she is, laughter is a necessary balm, and she brings it along in her astute, ambitious work. In order to be serious, it's necessary to keep laughing – otherwise why go on? She walks me to the back of the house, where a large glassed-in room overlooks a green world, and the good light spills over paint and easels and canvas. It is a room dedicated to light and looking. She has lived in this light all her life, and brought it, along with her good humour, her easy way with people (she is not going to make movies about a wall, or a piece of sky, or a tree – she needs people around her, singing and talking and living) and her keen storytelling chops into a first-person cinema.

While she is still too young to be an elder, she is one of the first to articulate a First Nations media practice (*pioneer* is a word only she can refuse), providing an example for so many others across the country. There is such a large gap, so much that remains to be said and shown and shown again. Shelley has not been afraid to put her work up into the infinite stretch of this absence, this loss, the how many pictures that should have arrived by now from Canada's Native communities. How wonderful and how strange, then, that her sounds and pictures should have come from such a personal place. It is hardly surprising that they are charged with a political imperative, but what is unexpected is the good humour, and her insistent gathering of voices and communities, using her practice to stage a collective expression. Somehow, the many folks gathered in her movies are already a reflection of her audience, as if the audience itself has been catapaulted onscreen, lifted onto the image, laughing in celebration.

MH: Do you come from a family of artists?

SN: We drew all the time. It was something to do. That was pretty normal on the reserve, there were a lot of drawers around. We were free to draw whatever we wanted, but as far as imagination goes, maybe we'd draw the Beatles covers again. [*laughs*]

MH: But drawing wasn't enough? It didn't show enough?

SN: I wanted to take part in the real world, the contemporary world. Having a camera (and later film) allowed me to reach out in a different way. I wanted to see whether I could make an image out there. There was a lot of satisfaction pursuing that.

MH: Did you feel that drawing was old-fashioned?

SN: Drawing builds a subject one line at a time. It's very elegant, but for me it wasn't fast enough. That's why I liked sculpture; because you can bend materials, it's much more physical. I've drawn all these years, but I'm still not satisfied. I don't consider myself a drawer yet, it's still at the 'Look, Ma!' stage.

MH: Most photographers won't show everything they make, and some feel their work is like sketching, trying things on for size. Much of what they do is practice and preparation.

SN: I feel that way a lot with my photography. When you're trying to do something creative, you know you want to do something, but what is it? You keep creating, and maybe one out of ten projects really arrives. You look at it and know it came from a real place, no matter how quickly or slowly it was made. Creating means being in search; whether it's for subject matter or a certain colour, there's something you're trying to find.

MH: Do you think of yourself as an artist? Or a filmmaker?

SN: I'm an artist. Is it strange to call myself that? Yes. I didn't say I was an artist until I was past 40. It's a big responsibility, announcing a willingness to take on what society gives you. You're ready to be a voice for those without a voice. It's a vocation. I didn't take art in high school because I didn't want to do what, for me at least, looked very fashionable. I didn't really know what the context of my work was going to be; I didn't have a handle on any of that until I was in my 30s. It took that long to be clear about the issues I felt were missing in a lot of Indian art at the time. Back in the 1980s, there were only a small number of women making work – it was a male-dominated scene. Once I established for myself that there was a narrow visioning of how Indian women could be shown, then I was outside the box – I could go anywhere with that in mind.

MH: Did you see a lot of the work that was being made and shown at that time?

SN: I tried to keep up with what was happening. There were a few people doing political work and that became something else I had to rethink. I didn't want to jump on the bandwagon of politicizing my work because it was expected. Sometimes I find it a little too easy to take up the cause and let that guide the work. It has to come from an authentic place.

MH: Did you feel part of a community of makers?

SN: Very much. The work was really beautiful, and stimulating, and I was so grateful to be able to see Indian art. This was mostly off the reserve, in museum settings, and I was getting a lot of information from magazines. I've watched Native art grow a lot, even during my lifetime – there are so many more artists now.

MH: When you were in your 20s, you never had the feeling that you were getting behind, or 'Why aren't I producing more?'

SN: No, I'm going to live forever! [laughs] I didn't want to start making art to make art. I would make stuff and give it away or throw it away. It was a period of practice and brushstrokes and composition, trying to get a figure right. Drawing a figure is forever my challenge. If you learn any kind of art history, they're always putting Michelangelo and da Vinci in your face, and then you look at your own drawings and think, *Oh my God.* You weigh yourself against the masters because you have no one else to compare with. Later you mature a bit and think, *Well, they had their time.* You see there are different things you can do. From 1987 to 1990, I went to the Ontario College of Art, still stuck on painting, drawing and sculpture. I should have taken some experimental stuff, but I wanted to get the basics right. I had to make the toes and the head in the same proportion. I took courses with Carol Laing in feminist theory and that was important for me. I was interested in women's studies and the feminine voice.

One day Carol came over to my house for supper and brought Anna Gronau with her, and I said, 'Hey, you're a filmmaker, let's make a film!' We started in earnest when I left school, and finally made *It Starts with a Whisper*. We started in 1991, when Native filmmaking was very small. If you went to festivals, it was always the same five filmmakers you ran into. The way Indian women were portrayed in films was pretty narrow. We were stereotyped as older, stoic, silent types, always in the background. The story was never our story. If they were younger, they were losers and victims. I wanted to see more Indian women onscreen, and not only beautiful Indian women with long hair blowing in the wind, because that's all there was. Audiences, whether Native or non-Native, are comfortable with stereotypes. If you're put in front of something you're not sure of, you don't want to see it. It's ridiculous, or it's not part of what I'm about. Fortunately, audiences liked the women in our film. It made people happy to see that something else was coming along.

MH: Was *It Starts with a Whisper* (25 min, 1993) always going to be a story film with actors and dialogue?

SN: People like narrative, and if it's a story they've never heard, and it's a good enough story, they'll see it through to the end. But if it gets too far out, they won't really care.

MH: You didn't want to make a movie that was more like a painting in motion? Something non-narrative, for instance.

SN: I didn't know movies could be made another way. At the time it was, 'Hey, look, people are moving!' [laughs] But no matter what kind of film you watched, there weren't too many with real Indian people. You see actors play roles again and again, and it's a treasure because you get to see them age before your eyes. I wanted to start making films for that reason. Film captures someone's body and puts it into frame, and as time goes on you can still see them. If you're lucky enough to make a film and put people into it that you like, that's a treasure.

It Starts with a Whisper was made exclusively for the celebration that was taking place in America and parts of Europe in

It Starts with a Whisper

recognition of the 500th anniversary of the discovery of America. Countless exhibitions and festivities were scheduled. Native artists responded to these events as anti-events and created work to show the impact on Native people that Columbus had by setting foot on the shores of North America. I didn't want to make something that would have a year-long shelf life and felt a film would be the most effective way to make a statement.

The story begins with a young girl named Shanna (combination of my name and Anna's). She carries the knowledge of many people's sufferings. Her collective memory stops her from becoming a productive and happy adult. She spends her time walking along the shores of the Grand River communicating with the spirits of ancestors who used to live along a particular spot on the river. The Tutelo Indians were given a small piece of land by the Six Nations when they were escaping the Indian Wars out west in the 1800s. The remaining Tutelos were absorbed into the Iroquois Confederacy. Their songs and ceremonies are still alive in the Iroquois ceremonies. Shanna can feel their presence when she comes to Tutelo Heights, just outside of Brantford. She carries this burden, but doesn't know how to process her feelings.

One day after work, Shanna is picked up by her three aunts. One of them has won a honeymoon suite in Niagara Falls. Her aunts are trying to make every occasion fun. Shanna can't relate to their desire to laugh; she is stuck in her own vision of the world. She has survivor guilt, though she doesn't know it and perhaps doesn't even know what it is. But she gets in the car and goes with them. In the car they compulsively offer her food. They are trying to nourish her and get her out of the trench she has built for herself. They laugh constantly and see jokes in everything. They are insensitive to Shanna's feelings and don't have a clue what she is going through. They keep the mood light and festive.

Shanna keeps rejecting their offerings and sees them as 'not quite with it.' When they finally get to Niagara Falls, Shanna runs away from them and goes to the Falls themselves. Here, she is again surrounded by spirits from the past. The most powerful source of energy overwhelms her. In a dreamlike state, she is visited by a prophet in the form of Elijah Harper. He understands her predicament and reassures her that she is not going crazy. She complains about the people around her. He listens and leaves her with a charge to be happy. He lets her know she is on the right path, reminds her not to forget about ancestors and people who have passed on, and that it's her turn to live her life. She takes his words to heart and returns to her aunts. She is now ready to participate with them. They get dressed in traditional New Year's wear. They are here to celebrate the coming of the future. With fireworks in the background, they sing their song, eat their cake and pour a cup of tea as a symbolic gesture to good health. A poem by Pauline Johnson makes it to the table as the women's voice always being there.

MH: Can you talk about the scenes with Elijah Harper?

SN: He's part of a line of ancestral voices. It's important to acknowledge spaces that are already occupied and lived in by these spirits. It goes back to having ancestors talk to you, having the confidence to let someone give you advice. In those scenes she is anguished and conflicted. Elijah tells her to live her life and get on with it. I'm sure everyone has their own particular brand of ancestral meetings.

MH: There's so much life in your film. Despite the cumbersome production equipment of 16mm moviemaking, the portrayals are never stiff or airless. How could you manage after waiting all those hours for the lights to get set up and the marks made and the camera rehearsals done and redone?

SN: I wanted to work with my sisters and make it a family experience, something we could watch in our old age and celebrate that quintessential joy of creating something together. But, as it was our first film, we didn't appreciate the amount of time and energy needed to do this. Two of my sisters had small babies at home, so they came to the set on time but were in a real rush to get home. By the end of the week, we were all exhausted. They also didn't understand you have to stick to the script. My sister Bunny kept improvising lines and reactions in the film. I think these are the best parts – they came unexpectedly and are the funniest. Her reaction to Shanna and me in the back seat still makes me laugh.

It takes place in a hotel with a heart-shaped bed, and there's a song they sing that goes, 'I'm pretty, I'm pretty, I'm pretty mad at you.' It's a song directed at anti-colonialism, the loss of language and history that goes back to residential schools. It even goes further back than that. But residential schools were effective in their duty to destroy the Indian in the child. Taken away from their families, these children had the fear of God put into them, had their Native language knocked out of them and generally became generations of dysfunctional members of society. No longer able to relate to their communities, they often came back as outsiders. With no recourse, they would go to the urban areas and not fit in there as well. Watching documentaries in which these broken people share their experiences is often shattering to the spirit. It will take a few more generations of community rebuilding and acknowledgement of what occurred and how it affected every Native person in the country. But you can't keep the spirit down – the spirit is going to survive, and then you have to put a big shiny dress on and start singing.

It Starts with a Whisper

MH: Why Niagara Falls?

SN: It became a symbol. The Falls start at the mouth of the Grand River in Elmira in a small pond. The pond trickles down into the Grand, then into Lake Erie, which goes into Niagara Falls. The giant hydroelectric power plants all begin in a small pond. That's why we called the film *It Starts with a Whisper*.

MH: Did you and Anna sit at a table and write the script together?

SN: Yes, we did. But like I said, I was very young and naive. Now I don't think I could do that again. We worked on the script for a long time. I had worked with my sisters before and knew I wanted to work with them again. But it was a lot harder than I thought. I made a photo-graphic series with them called *Mohawks in Beehives* the year before. It was created in 1991 after the Oka crisis, just as the Gulf War was beginning to happen. During the summer of Oka, reports were broadcast live, every minute of the day. So, the story goes that the mayor of Oka wanted to expand a golf course onto sacred Indian burial grounds, so the Native population blocked off the roads. Then a police officer was killed and it turned into an armed standoff. I wasn't there, but it affected everyone in the country. You couldn't pick up the paper without reading another article about it. It showed the poverty of Native communities and how their issues wouldn't be recognized, and there was a lot of negative reporting. This is costing us $10 million a day, soldiers are costing so much a day, and it's coming out of taxes paid for by average Canadians. As if the average couldn't be Aboriginal.

After Oka there was a dramatic rise in army enrollment: what's that all about? You see that in the newspaper and wonder why. Of course, you know the reason why. The country needed something to focus on collectively. Prime Minister Mulroney needed to look like he was doing his job. How to fight this feeling of having no control: what can I do as an individual? I asked my sisters if they wanted to be in this photo project where we would dress up in beehive hairdos for the day and try to have some fun, turning our identities as Native women into something positive.

MH: Why beehives?

SN: The hairstyle known as a beehive is pretty glamorous. It makes you taller than you are. It's like when you meet a bear in the forest: don't run, make yourself look bigger than the bear. Maybe that's the real purpose of a beehive – it's a feminist survival technique. And it's funny. [*laughs*] It seemed like a funny thing to do at the time. We went downtown in our beehives and our dangly earrings, lipstick, tight sweaters and just kind of harassed people on the street. [*laughs*] 'If they want extra fries,

It Starts with a Whisper

give it to them.' When there's four of you, it's okay; if there's one of you, you're crazy.

MH: Are your sisters also artists?

SN: They make corn-husk dolls. They do a lot of craft and bead-work.

MH: The work you're doing doesn't seem unusual for them to participate in? They're not all accountants?

SN: I wish they were. They're crazier than I am.

MH: When the film was finished, were you happy with its reception?

SN: I had no expectations. Anna said we could take it to festivals, and that there was a possibility of selling it to television, but I didn't know anything about that. I had no idea. My idea is that we'd make it and show it on New Year's Eve, because the 500th anniversary of Columbus setting foot on North America was in 1992. I wanted to show the film over midnight, so we'd enter 1993 and the beginning of a new millennium. The film relooks at the effects of Columbus and how colonialism has destroyed Native North America. It was intended to mark a starting point – after this, things would get better.

For the premiere screening on New Year's Eve, we approached a nursing home on the reserve and asked if they would be interested in us sharing it with the community of Six Nations. They said that would be great. There was one stipulation: you have to be out by 8 PM. [*laughs*] It showed at the Woodland Cultural Centre the following May. I go to most of the screenings. People are interested and they want to know: what was that all about? It has mostly shown at North American festivals.

MH: Did you start thinking of yourself as a filmmaker?

SN: Not really. But I liked the whole process of making movies, the writing, being on set. It's like sculpture, it's very physical, but you need a lot of money and you have to depend on other people to bend it the way you need to bend it. Sometimes they don't quite understand how I am seeing things: I'd like it to be a little longer here, a little shorter there. That's when it gets frustrating, with all those knobs sitting in front of you. Sometimes you have to give somebody space to do what they do.

MH: That takes a lot of trust.

SN: Yes, it does. But if you don't give people that trust, then you'll never be surprised.

MH: Where did you make *Overweight with Crooked Teeth* (5 min, 1997)?

Overweight with Crooked Teeth

SN: I did that at the University of Western Ontario. When I was finishing my MFA. I'm trying to be a professional. [*laughs*] It's about security. If I'm in a position where I have to work, I'll be in a better position to teach. After I finished I was so burnt out I couldn't pick up a book for a long time. They had a video-editing suite that I wanted to learn how to use, but it was hard because the technology is always changing. I'm constantly on a learning curve. I don't know when to stop.

Michael Doxtater is my brother. He wrote a poem in 1979 called 'Overweight with Crooked Teeth,' which stayed with me for a long time. It talks about guns, germ warfare and Darwin's theory of evolution, but it has a funny spin. Native people are put in a box so quickly – we're the result of the past. The poem felt strong to me, short but strong. I wanted to adapt it, taking it a line

at a time. We didn't have any money. Would I have done it differently if I had a budget? I don't know.

MH: The first shot shows your brother walking down a long road, before peering directly into the camera. Then a title appears: 'What were you expecting anyway?' Who is the 'you' addressed to?

SN: The general viewer. Who are you expecting? A noble savage? I probably had a non-Native audience in mind.

MH: You take up a suite of Native stereotypes (the noble savage, Sitting Bull). Why was it important to name and show these types?

SN: These are the types we are shown all the time. If you see a Native in a film, you expect to see them this way. We're making fun of the stereotypes. Michael's dressed up as Chief Joseph of the Nez Perce, saying, 'The earth and I are one!' and then he takes his bag of chips and throws it into the landscape. Again, we're playing with expectations. The stereotype says we are the caretakers of Turtle Island, the earth – I wish it were true.

MH: The next year you made *Honey Moccasin* (49 min, 1998), another very ambitious film that gathers many people and performances. What was the beginning of the movie for you?

SN: It began with ideas about AIDS and the 50th anniversary of the Second World War, which my father served in. I thought of the suffering people were going through because of AIDS and how much homophobia was related to the disease. On a personal note, my husband had gone through chemo and needed blood transfusions. Years later, he had to be tested for AIDS because blood supplies weren't being checked at that time. So it hit home in a roundabout way. The media hype about the upcoming 50th anniversary provided a collision of people suffering, from past and present. On the one hand, my dad has seen a lot of grief, but he could be so homophobic. Many people of his generation saw it that way. This became a convenient scapegoat for him. I would think to myself, *Dad, you're kind of smart – why do you have to be so dumb?*

At that time as well, I had done some research on the Berdash societies in traditional communities. These were people who held a place of respect and served as medicine people in these communities. They brought a lot of joy and benefited the community as a whole. Often they were men who dressed like women. They were accepted as women. And because children

Honey Moccasin

were a treasure, these medicine people committed themselves to the children of the group – usually they didn't have their own. I thought this was a beautiful and intelligent way to include diversity. I was also thinking about the impact colonization had on Native societies. After the European priests arrived and saw how these people were given a respected place in society, they were discriminated against and seen as witches and sorceresses and had their status erased. This is a topic that has to be addressed. How to produce societies that are not so stiff and exclusive? Traditional communities operated for millennia using their own justice systems.

Some thoughts about sentencing circles were also a part of it. If someone commits a crime, instead of taking them to court, everyone from the community would sit in a circle with this person and decide what would be done. There are so many things happening in that film. Every film feels like it's the last one, so I have to get everything in there.

The 50th anniversary of World War II ending was a marker in time. The world has gone through these wars, and democracy is supposed to be an ideal that was fought for and cherished. Meanwhile, Native people have had so much taken away. Every time a Native language disappears, we lose a lot of information about the environment, ecology and natural medicines. Science is 'discovering' things already known, which have been kept in these disappearing languages as part of the earth. It's important to try to keep that history alive or activated. There's a reason why so

many Native communities are in dire straits, and it's up to us to figure out how to help.

MH: How did the Second World War change your father?

SN: He was 18 when he enlisted and he came out when he was 23. He was there for the whole war. It was pretty horrifying for him. He told us some things, but not so much. He loved being a soldier, and Veterans Day parades. He is really proud to be a veteran. My father was pretty crazy. We'd be in the car with him, and if someone was driving badly he'd jump out of the car and shout at them, 'You don't know how to drive!' [*laughs*] He blasted anybody and everybody.

MH: *Honey Moccasin*'s title sequence is very beautiful: each name looks embroidered and is lit by a hand holding a match. Why this detailed attention to something that is often considered a frill, an accessory?

SN: The titles were all sewn by hand using beads. You can hear Billy Merasty, the bead thief, sneaking around and finally knocking some beads over. Whoops. People who do craft or beadwork are holding on to a culture and making it better. There was a period when craft was looked upon as tourist-trade stuff; it was almost a shameful thing to do, selling out your culture. There was a time in this country when Indian people weren't hired, so they had to sell whatever they had on the side of the street, and I wanted to pay homage to that genre of artmaking.

MH: It also relates to the central narrative event, the theft of beads from the community. It's a very canny device that allows you to float from newscasts to bars and homes. The story feels more like a frame that allows a community to gather.

SN: The bead theft points to other things that have been stolen – it gets back to the stereotyping of Native people. I didn't want to set up a bad non-Native versus the good Native. I thought we could play both parts. I wanted there to be a balance between the whole society. Sometimes people get a little offended because there are no non-Native people in the film. But when you're in a community, there are some bad people there too. When I showed the film in New York, someone asked, 'Why is the bad guy also gay?' And someone else jumped up and said, 'Why not?' And I thought *yes, that's it, why not?*

The beads represent a lot of things that were taken. We had languages taken away from us, histories erased – even people's names disappeared. Government workers were sent to reserves; they would line up everybody to take down their names. So this family here gets a blanket and a pound of cheese, and your name is ... The agents didn't care what the names were, they often gave families their own names. The bead thefts acknowledge those vanishing acts. As long as you have the capacity to think, you have to say *yes, this is gone, but from this point on I will own it instead of remaining a victim.* What are we going to do? You need a starting point. We now have an opportunity to make something new, and if it's done by caring for your community and family, it has to work. We have no place to go but up.

MH: Much of the movie takes place at the Smokin' Moccasin Café, which hosts movies, performance art, bands and fashion shows, a real gathering of First Nations empowerments. It feels like an idealized site of community, where every watcher is also a maker. Could such a place exist only in the movies?

SN: I wanted a place where you could be expressive, and have beauty on the screen. To host singing women from different generations, for example. It has a cave-like feeling, a womb environment. We used Veteran's Hall on the reserve; behind the stage you can still see photographs of veterans. People who were doing the set asked if we should take those pictures down. But I said no, just leave them there. It was the 50th anniversary of the war – taking them down would have been sacrilegious.

MH: The Smokin' Moccasin is contrasted with another café that offers karaoke and health food, jumping on trends to rustle up business that isn't coming. The owner of the failing café, also the bead thief, is always checking out the Smokin' Moccasin, the way business folks might go slumming to see what artists are up to, so they can bring it back to a corporate culture and make it work.

SN: We wanted the other bar to be tacky and goofy. We shot that in a storefront on Colborne Street in Brantford, but everything else is shot on the reserve. I try to shoot as much as I can on the reserve. There's a relaxed comfort being in the environment we're supposed to be portraying.

MH: Florene Belmore sings/talks 'You give me fever' in a smoking teepee costume, while slides of colonizers arriving in the new world are projected onto her. Did you adapt this performance for the movie or did it already exist?

SN: It was my idea to have the face look out from the teepee. In the story, Florene's a film student doing artsy things in the city, then she comes home and performs in front of her audience on her mother's stage. I asked her to be in my film and she said okay.

The lyrics to 'Fever' are pretty deadly. I had been listening to a lot of love songs, which have designs on you, they make you want to go to war. I think you could write a thesis about love songs. The obsessive-compulsive character, the way they protect your heart while taking away your spirit. The lyrics are really something.

I asked Jeff Thomas to put photos together for the slide presentation on the teepee, because he was working at the National Archives in Ottawa. The royalties were too high for some of the pictures I wanted, but he found powerful things, many of them showing residential schools. One image shows three nuns holding three little babies. That is so *Damien*. There are pictures of soldiers with Indians, and the song relates to these meetings and the illnesses that the Europeans passed on to us.

MH: The movie has a mosaic, cabaret style, with a variety of performances hung together on a narrative skeleton. How did you find your performers?

SN: When I finished the script, I sent it to Tantoo Cardinal and Billy Merasty and asked if they would be interested. I thought if they said no, then I don't have to worry about it anymore. [*laughs*] But they said yes, so I had to find money.

This is the second film I did, and it required money from the arts councils and a lot of other places. If I had had just a little bit more knowledge I wouldn't have done it this way. I would have held the money and shot it all at once, but instead I did it in chunks, two minutes here, five minutes there. It was shot over a couple of years.

MH: It has the feeling of something living and moving. I think shooting piece by piece turned out to be a great advantage.

SN: It was about finding real people for the film and putting as many of them as I could in front of the camera, so that 25 years from now they can look at it and say, 'There I am.' Maybe it's not a filmmaking process, but for me it's a little documentary of what's going on at the time.

MH: In *Sky Woman with Us* (7 min, 2002), we watch for a long time as a woman daubs a man's face with water. This movie opens with a study of this landscape of faces. Is all of our personality stuck in the trap of our faces? Would it have been the same if you'd concentrated on their elbows or knees? Why this emphasis, this endless return, to the face?

SN: This was an experimental, make-work project originally done with two other directors: Jody Hill and Ken Davis. We each put in $500 and had about a week. The other two projects took a couple of days each to shoot, and mine took one day. We all worked with the same two actors and it was up to us what we were going to do with them. We were going to make seven-minute shorts, and put them together to make a 21-minute movie in the end. I wanted to do something without sync sound that would be very emotional. Usually I'm arm's-length emotional, but this time I really wanted to go for it. Sky Woman is an Iroquois creation myth about a woman who lives in the sky. She is part of a society that has never known illness until her husband gets sick, and then they don't know what to do. He tells her to go to the tree of life, where people have been forbidden to go, and take a drink of water for him. She leaves him then, and that's when you see a doorway with fruit hanging off it. This tree falls over and leaves a big gap in the ground, which is our sky, and she ends up falling through it. As she falls, she grabs on to tobacco and strawberry plants, which become her medicine.

MH: Did you want to leave the movie wordless because of the mythical nature of the story?

SN: The film translates their faces into a quest for some kind of relief. She's the caring woman and he's the man who needs her care. I wanted to see how capable people were of expressing these feelings. They were so great, I wondered why they didn't become real actors! Sheila Pohkiak is a filmmaker living in Ottawa; Chris White is a good-looking guy who is also an ironworker.

MH: She is expelled from this space and arrives in a freezing-cold city wearing only a silver dress. A man wraps a blanket around her. Why this park scene?

SN: It's about homeless people and how we regard them. There are shelters for them, so we don't have to think about it. It's always someone else's problem. But when we remember the legends and the suffering they describe, and how that translates into modern times, I think we need to be more compassionate instead of thinking: *Our legends say ... our teachings say ...* You can have all this knowledge in your head, but do we really extend ourselves? Or are we only pretending that we're compassionate? That's what Sky Woman is about.

MH: In *The Shirt* (5:55 min, 2003), dreamy landscape pans lead to a woman in a shirt, a living intertitle. A succession of shirts read:

> My ancestors were annihilated, exterminated, murdered
> and massacred.
> They were lied to, tried and deceived.
> Attempts were made to assimilate, colonize and displace
> them.
> And all's I get is this shirt.

In the midst of this outrage is humour. Is that important in order to keep a perspective, in order to find a way to go on? Is it difficult to bring up questions of Native displacement and genocide, because audiences don't want to hear about it anymore? I'm thinking of a parallel, perhaps, with AIDS narratives: many audiences feel, *Enough already, we've seen that. More feel-bad movies, I can't anymore.* How do you overcome that?

SN: I really like humour, though it's not always easy. It's something you have to work at, but I want the work to be digestible, not mean-spirited. I want it to be a satisfying experience no matter who you are. Sometimes humour has to be the bottom line. And often movies need to contain a surprise, people have to think, *Oh, I didn't see that coming.* You have to talk about the

difficult things, and perhaps they're thinking, *Yes, yes, I know that.* But then if you give them something unexpected, that is amazing. I'm so aware of the audience being diverse; I think work needs to be presented so that many can see it.

MH: Do you feel the short movie is a viable form? Real filmmakers make features, don't they?

SN: I think shorts are more challenging than features, because of their time restrictions. You have to surprise your audience at the end of it, leave people holding their breath. It's a magic trick – you really do have to pull that rabbit out of the hat. I have a lot of respect for short films, they're like little paintings. You can't take your audience for granted.

MH: Why is there a new woman wearing the shirt at the end of the tape?

SN: There's a Native woman wearing a shirt with a series of indictments and then the statement *And all's I get is this shirt.* The shirt represents health care, dental care, the treaties that were signed, all the accommodations put into place by governments. As time goes on, those things are no longer there. Because of Indian Affairs and bad bureaucracy, a lot of money has been stolen. That's what *The Shirt* is about: you think you have something, but you have nothing. So the woman in the film loses her shirt, while someone else now wears it, they get the benefits now.

MH: Can you tell me about *Tree* (5 min, 2006)?

SN: It was commissioned by Roberto Ariganello, who was the director of the Liaison of Independent Filmmakers of Toronto. He wanted to know if I would make a new film for the New Directors Series LIFT was hosting. He said I could use any camera and a small crew for a day, so how can you say no to that? I said I'd like to have a 35mm camera with black-and-white film, and came up with a storyline.

MH: A Native woman is the only person left in the city. She walks from a lake to an abandoned cityscape and cries. The experience is wordless; she is rendered 'speechless' (and there is no one to tell the story to). Do our most important experiences lie outside language?

SN: I wanted her to be a spirit or presence: she's Mother Earth visiting her home. She rises out of the ocean and sees the destruction of the city. I was also thinking of the Keep America Beautiful campaign with Iron Eyes Cody, the Native man who walks through the landscape. Did you ever see that? He walks along shores and roads and sees garbage everywhere, and cries one tear. It was a beautiful commercial that came out in the 1970s, and I thought, if we have to be known for something, let it be for keeping America beautiful. *Tree* is an extension of that idea, and goes on to show a scene from Vegas, and the Caledonia protests. These protests started at the end of February 2006. A land development was stopped as a result of protestors from the Six Nations Reserve. This land claim is based on a tract of land given to the Six Nations after the American Revolution in 1776. The Iroquois were allies to Britain, so we had to leave the Mohawk Valley in New York State and begin life on the Grand River. Six Nations was given six miles on both sides of the river from the source to the mouth. I don't know how long this river is, but it is quite a bit of property. Today, the Six Nations lives on a land base of approximately ten miles by ten miles. The big question is where did our land go and how come people keep building subdivisions on it? It goes on and on.

The film also includes a shot of the memorial dome in Hiroshima, and a fire at a paint factory up the road from here. The Native woman encounters these moments and, horrified, turns into a tree. It's about nature's response, which is occurring now with global warming, for instance. At the end, she has this great look on her face, I love that part, where her eyes are so intense. It's about humanity and the environment.

MH: Her walking somehow brings the lake into the city. Do you feel the old opposition between city and country are still at work? Is nature the only way to be natural? Can't a computer program, or the spread of something like YouTube, also be considered part of nature? Is human nature also nature, or are we something apart?

SN: There's a lot of death in nature. We must be designed to be self-destructive. We can't stop ourselves. What do you do? Decide not to have kids, stop using electricity? Remember when the power went out about three years ago? That's such a sign of the times. I went to the grocery store and they were only taking cash, so we had to buy our ice cream and potato chips with cash. [*laughs*] You can talk about these things and get really depressed.

MH: Do you paint or write every day?

SN: When I'm working on something, I can write every day. I wish I could paint every day. I like writing – it's like visiting with people.

MH: *Suite: INDIAN* (57 min, 2005) is a long episodic work with secret threads holding it together. Can you talk about it?

SN: I was inspired by Akira Kurosawa's *Dreams*, which also has six stories and narrates the history of Japan. It begins with a young boy who sees the sun shining, even though it's raining. Whenever this happens, he's cautioned, he can't leave the house because the fox and wolf will get mad. The next episode is about cherry blossoms in Hiroshima.

I also wanted my movie to contain loosely connected episodes that would narrate Native experience. There are six stories, each

Suite: INDIAN

with its own title. It begins by looking at artisans on the reserve, then moves into another story about a young girl who has everything. She's smart and beautiful and talented. Finally she's challenged by Sitting Bull: *You have so much, but what are you going to do with it?* He gives her a gauntlet, which she puts under her pillow. She sleeps, then it's up to her to pick up the gauntlet. The next episode shows a flirty little love story between a boy and a girl on a park bench. Then there's a strange story about an older couple. The husband doesn't talk to the wife, who tries to get his attention. In the end, her life continues the way it was. After that, there's a story called *Home* about how a homeless girl spends her day. It shows the people she shares her life with.

Then the tape gets really wacky, moving into a dance piece with Santee Smith, who is an excellent dancer, she's won all kinds of awards. She starts out dancing by herself, representing the spirit of Native existence. She lies down on the ground, covered by flowers, and experiences a kind of rebirth. When she wakes up, she has a partner with her. He tries to follow her dance and finally catches up with her.

The last piece is called *The Red Army Is the Strongest*. The Red Army Choir was the propaganda choir of old Russia. The czar's troops had no weapons, food or supplies – nothing. The only thing the czar could send to his troops was this choir. I use that song as the finale, because of the play on the words *Red Choir*.

MH: Watching your tape was like walking through a city that you had carefully made, with its abrupt juxtapositions and hidden connections. The emphasis on movement (from the hands of the artisans to the dancer's hands), for instance, and your beautiful use of colour. Every frame is bursting with colour, and as usual it's shot very beautifully. Sometimes I feel I am watching small moving paintings, that what is 'important' is not so much what someone is saying or doing, but the beautiful juxtaposition of a bright red and a glowing orange. Am I being too reductive? Of course your movie contains political messages, and an abundance of good humour, but there is a painterly side as well. Often political work can leave these painterly sensibilities aside: there's no time for beauty anymore, thank you very much, we've got important things to say. Can you talk about how you work to reconcile this old dichotomy?

SN: I like the way film uses so many art forms. I like the way you can build a set with objects, giving the viewer a chance to roam the background as the story unfolds. I'm interested in the creativity of the environment and how it has been manipulated to give the character personality. Also, I like a set when it is trimmed down to nothing. This gives me a place to start and try to work my way through the layering of the perspectives the filmmaker is enfolding for me, the viewer. I get captivated by the three-dimensional aspects of the path that is being opened before my eyes. The costuming and the placements of props. Sometimes I do this consciously, but most times unconsciously. Composition is always a tricky device. What is being said with the angle and how much of the character is being exposed and what the purpose serves with angle, cropping, placement. There are so many decisions to make. I believe the soundtrack has to be considered as much as the dialogue. After the film is finished, I find myself saying, 'If only I had thought of this then.' I see film as a frame and it's up to me to put what I want into it: picture, object, sound, text. Being a painter/photographer makes me want the film canvas to be brimming with emotion and positiveness. I want the viewer to have a good time and to react to the images that are put in front of them. I love music. Making films is as close to composing music as I will ever get. Melodies, harmonies, contrapuntal themes, leitmotifs can be incorporated to make the story interesting and complex. These are themes you can always build on and drive yourself crazy with. A never-ending desire, something that will keep the brain motivated to the end.

I am just finishing a two-minute dance piece with Santee Smith. The title is *rechargin'*. I am showing this at the OBORO gallery in Montreal for my exhibit *Almost Fallen*.

Shelley Niro is a band member of the Six Nations, Bay of Quinte Mohawk, Turtle Clan. Niro received her MFA from the University of Western Ontario and graduated from the Ontario College of Art. Shelley likes to create visual art that tingles and shakes the senses.

Shelley Niro's Films and Videos

It Starts with a Whisper   28 min 1993
Overweight with Crooked Teeth   5 min 1997
Honey Moccasin   49 min 1998
Sky Woman with Us   7 min 2002
The Shirt   5:55 min 2003
Suite: INDIAN   57 min 2005
Tree   5 min 2006
rechargin'   2:49 min 2007

Distributed by Vtape and Canadian Filmmakers Distribution Centre

PETER METTLER
GAMBLING, GODS AND LSD

At first, it didn't seem like Peter belonged in my world, the place of small cinemas, easily ignored and trampled underfoot. There is something large in his making – these are big dreams for the big screen, and they take up space and time. He will never be one of those who runs eight or nine short hopefuls out of the basement laboratory in a year. He has flirted with dramatic features and performed the devil's dance that accompanies every hope that wants to be shared with too many. But he has found his real home in the documentary, where he is best able to exercise his first and most formidable talent: Peter lives in a force field of slow motion. Speaking to him is a rare pleasure: there is time to search for the right word, to feel the full impress of an argument, to savour a witticism, a view. The time bombs of the personal computer and the automobile hold off for a moment, and sometimes a moment is all you need.

In his first-person travelogue *Eastern Avenue* (1985), he conjures a suite of portraits of friends and intimates, but most remarkable is a single two-minute shot of the artist himself. A self-conscious grin, a rapt stare, a bored wandering – somehow he gathers so much of living in this simple shot. He doesn't try to keep us up on the high wire every moment; he knows the ascent is where the real juice is, the walk toward the door, the anticipation, the journey – call it what you like, he's already on the way.

I would be remiss if I didn't mention his remarkable skills behind the camera. He sure can take us home. While tens of thousands are busy handling picture machines, there are only a handful who are able to live alongside them. Peter uses his camera the way wild Oscar used language – in order to lift every situation, embracing the mask and the years that have gone into the making of the mask. His is always – and this is the hardest thing of all to know – at the right distance from his subject. His cinema makes us more human.

MH: Edward Said describes travelling as an act of abandonment, of abandoning yourself, even though you're the one leaving.

PM: Islamics say that while you're travelling, your soul travels behind you, an experience analogous to jet lag, which is heightened by film festivalling, when you change environments on a weekly basis. Even though your soul hasn't yet arrived, you're already moving on to the next place. Your senses aren't aligned with the environment, and the further away you travel, the longer it takes for your body to acclimatize. When I arrive at extreme places like India or Indonesia, I'm shielded from events, presented with my expectations (agreeably or in contrast).

MH: Your travel in *Gambling, Gods and LSD* (180 min, 2002) begins at home and spirals out, setting out to destroy, or at least realign, notions of what home is.

PM: There was a set list of questions I asked everyone who appeared in the film, including 'What is your sense of home?'

This question was also pertinent to myself. Home is where you are, being comfortable with yourself. It means not constructing experience through projection, but perceiving what's in your presence and allowing it to speak. This is paradoxical because every encounter triggers memory, but there are degrees of disarming and receptivity as you attempt new discoveries. Travel doesn't free you from a birthplace; events point back to you, because you're still the person who decides when to push the camera trigger, as much as you try to empty yourself out. Each response has a history.

The first time I went to a foreign place was Morocco, where my sensibility changed, along with my tempo and thinking. I was 18 years old and thought I would never be the same again, but, sure enough, I returned to Toronto and old cycles of thought and perception returned. But a new filter of experience ran over them. One of the happiest times in my life was spent in Bali – the natural environment, the integration of creativity in the culture, the warm assurance of the people – and it gave me a feeling of integration with other humans. When I came back to North America, I had a very peaceful demeanour and laughed a lot. People made fun of me. I went to a festival in Athens that hosted a sophistication of thought and cynicism where being Bali Peter didn't seem to fit – it was too much of a contradiction. But in the end, maybe home is just where all your practical matters work out easiest.

MH: How did you begin organizing the film?

PM: I laid out four concrete themes to put in my back pocket as I went out into the world to shoot: transcendence, the denial of death, our relationship to nature and the illusion of safety. These broad themes were never mentioned but remained my organizing principles as I explored four different cultures: Toronto, Las Vegas, Switzerland around the Zurich region and southern India. The film was making itself while I acted as a medium. I was the person carrying the camera and sound equipment, letting these events occur as they do when one goes on a trip. I didn't want to script the film, but to follow its unfolding. Film in this way is a process of living and catching things along the way.

MH: The first person we meet in *Gambling, Gods and LSD* is John Paul Young, who lives here in Toronto.

PM: He was living with his parents in a house very close to the neighbourhood where I grew up as a child. The river where he took me on our walk was downstream from a place I'd run away to as a child. One of my early memories was leaving the shelter of our suburban family home and striking out on my bicycle past familiar borders, wondering how vast the world must be geographically and experientially, though I was just a couple of miles from home. It wasn't the reason I interviewed John Paul, but this coincidence, this departure from home, laid a foundation for the film. Home is your habits and experience, and travel can offer the illusion of leaving that behind. But ultimately you have

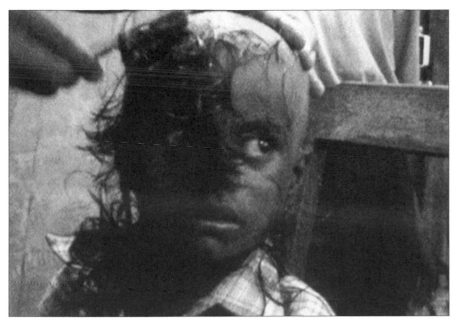

Gambling, Gods and LSD

experience that lasted six weeks in all. I went there with two people, a camera assistant and sound recordist, because it's hard to move around on your own. The film travels were made over a period of two years, though shooting wasn't continuous.

Many scenes in the film occurred spontaneously, like the boy running at the end of the film. We were travelling on a boat and I saw him calling out to us. The camera was in a good position, so I got down and started rolling. I didn't know where he was running or where the boat was going, I just responded to the moment. His run ended up referring to the early scene in the film where I describe running away from home to another river (the John Paul scene), longing for something outside the familiar. That's why it's the last shot in the film.

to return; otherwise, you're in a constant process of running away from yourself. Addiction follows the same process: denial, avoidance and escape. Our society is filled with things to distract us, to take us away from ourselves. The mainstream offers temporary pleasures that don't ultimately satisfy. Our neediness is taken advantage of as we are sold more and more temporary gratifications that seem only to enhance the need further.

John Paul had found God, which isn't explored deeply in the film, though it's touched upon. He's the first encounter in the film's journey, but almost all of the people I meet along the way speak about similar issues: what catches them? What do they use to find meaning, to give them a sense of self and importance and belief? Everyone I met reflected my own concerns and processes. I was using the film medium in the way that someone else might use a drug or the pursuit of science – everyone has their method of anchoring. Sometimes the anchor is an escape, sometimes a way to be focused more in the present.

You understand your understanding of other people, not necessarily the people themselves. It seems impossible to leave your own experience entirely, so how will you ever know if you're sharing perceptions? As you get older, the world gets more mysterious – you think you've got it sussed around 30 and then you fall in love. Again.

MH: Were you often alone while gathering the pictures?

PM: Shooting began in Toronto, where I live and have my gear. I travelled to Las Vegas and the surrounding desert for three months, living in a camper. Sometimes I quickly taught acquaintances how to use the audio recorder so I would have another sound perspective. In those three months I was constantly shooting, though not necessarily every day. Later I travelled to Switzerland, which was similar to Toronto because I had a base there. India, like Las Vegas, was a very concentrated and transitory

MH: What is the relation between John Paul and the man who crutches his way toward you in India?

PM: We met him in Hampi, a former kingdom with a lot of ancient architecture; today, people live in the ruins of this empire. Our Indian trip had been intense and agitated, full of stimulation, which made me want something quiet and meditative, so we wound up in Hampi. We went the day before and sat around watching people playing in the water and cleaning their clothes and sweeping up debris – local village life – when a man appeared dragging his body down toward the water to bathe. He could use his arms but not his legs; he had a bundle of clothes and a towel he would throw in front of him, then drag himself toward it, and this went on a long time before he got to the water and started bathing. I was taken by him because it's rare to see an invalid in our streets engaged in an activity along with everyone else. He was integrated in that small society, doing his own thing. I said to my friend I'd really like to film him, but I don't think I could because it seems like voyeurism. She said no, he wouldn't mind.

The next day we came back and I was shooting the temple area when he suddenly appeared in front of me and started dragging himself toward the camera. I kept the camera running and filmed as he approached. It was like a meeting of different worlds through a mechanical instrument. He was as curious about us as I was about him, and it didn't feel at all intrusive or sensational. He was coming to say hello. While some find this scene difficult to watch, I felt it was important to have him in the film because he's another human showing an experience fundamental to us all. He shouldn't be separated because of his disability and his potentially disturbing appearance, but accepted as one of us. The voice-over used to say something about the difference between looking for something and just looking, where observer and observed are equal. This voice-over occurred a couple of minutes before his appearance, and I took it out. It drew attention to poverty versus wealth, ability and disability, and I didn't want to highlight that. I wanted this person to look at the audience and feel a connection, but saying 'You're equal' takes it in a different direction.

MH: Unlike most of the other people in the film, he never speaks. Does that matter?

PM: It's a different kind of engagement. Language wasn't something we could share, but that was part of what was profound about the encounter. How do you engage with someone you can't speak with? It's a prime example of understanding your understanding; in his case, it's likely that I have no idea what he's really perceiving. While editing, I had an experience that underlined this. Martin Schaub was one of Switzerland's main intellectual film critics for years, an aesthete, eloquent and well-read, and he'd become one of my best friends. He had sinusitis and the bacteria went into his brain and was starting to cause serious problems, so they had to operate quickly. They cut out part of his skull and cleaned the infected area of his brain. I visited him a couple of times in the hospital. His head was circular, but there was a corner missing – the bulge of his brain was draped in skin. He sat, obviously occupying a reality different from the one we'd shared, but he recognized me and could still speak English. He spoke out loud as if in a dream, in apparently incoherent strings of associations, not knowing who he was or where. I asked if there was anything I could bring him when I came back, and he said, 'Yes, it doesn't matter what colour, but please bring me a gypsy.' He kissed me on the lips and I asked him, 'A gypsy?' I think

Gambling, Gods and LSD

he'd always wanted to travel and live like that. We had shared so much understanding over the years, then after the bacteria I experienced him as such an altered person. A couple of months later I saw him back in his home. The tubes had destroyed his swallowing mechanism and he had to be cared for all the time. He was more coherent, and the thing that disturbed him most was the year he couldn't recall, how he'd become disabled. One day last year he didn't wake up, he died in his sleep.

MH: Churches are sacred sites, but now some function only as tourist destinations, no longer used for service. Your movie also turns you into a church pilgrim. Why did you go?

PM: I was told that God had made an appearance in the airport district of Toronto when 4,000 people began laughing hysterically and fell to the ground in an ecstatic stupor. It happened in a church housed in a metal warehouse-type building, which announced it as the fire of God. The church was right beside the Constellation Hotel, which I knew as a child, having dreamt about one day visiting its futuristic-looking top-floor lounge. I was exploring the airport district, and this became another thread of the film. Catching the fire spread around the world: people fly into Toronto for a few days and stay at the hotel and experience God and take the fire back to wherever they're from.

I had to talk to the pastor and explain that the film would juxtapose his church against other faiths, and he accepted that. We put up signs saying *If you don't want to be filmed, stay away from the camera*, and also made announcements. Although they were going through something very personal, people welcomed us – there were only two in a room of thousands who said no. They were busy embracing ecstasy and invited newcomers to adopt that enthusiasm. You actually do get a giddy, high feeling. Over the course of several hours, the room brewed up contagious waves of quiet, hysterical laughter in anticipation of the climax of the night. They played rambling rock-gospel music, and while we were shooting, it actually helped me move through the space. I was very energized and felt quite welcome to do anything.

The pastor had one stipulation: he wanted to see the film before giving the final okay. This was the only subject in the film who asked, and I was a bit worried, but they loved it. Of course, some in attendance were going through the motions, self-consciously enacting rapture, as opposed to the genuine trance I'd seen in Bali. But the desire is genuine; it's still a release even if you're play-acting. It reminded me a lot of the techno-rave-ecstasy experience. There was the same relinquishing of self, and group belonging. It's a comfort and release to forget our problems, triggered in the rave by music and drugs, in the stock market by making money, or while making films and discovering something beautiful. We all seek the same experience in different ways. We are radically different but fundamentally the same in our drives and motives and what we're looking for.

India offers a different perspective, full of representations of gods and Ganeshas and Krishnas. One man named Shiva tells a story in voice-over as you watch a pilgrimage ceremony. They fast and bathe in a particular way, preparing in a ritualized manner that culminates when they stand in front of a particular carving or image of a god. When they arrive, they close their eyes, looking at the god within themselves. The deity is a trigger to look at the god within. They have an interesting term in India, *darshan* – looking at a deity – which is also applied to someone like Amma, the hugging saint you see in the film. This witnessing of the divine is also called *darshan*. When I was shooting in India, I became preoccupied with *darshan* as I looked at life around me: the invalid crawling toward the camera, for instance, looking at god and self-applied to everything.

If you're shooting on the street here in the West, people look away or leave the frame. In India, people stare right down the barrel of the lens, and once again I thought of *darshan*. Are they looking into that moment of recording as they look at a temple deity? I'd always thought recording film had something of a holy quality to it, in part because of the cost of recording a moment that's going to be frozen and memorialized, available for review. That holiness is more profound in film than video, because you can't shoot so much.

MH: The church ecstatics propel you out into the desert, where the film slows down to look – really look – at the snakes and rocks and petroglyphs, and my favourite moment, where you stop on the road and watch the rain on the windshield. These shots convey an equivalence of energy, perception and movement.

PM: I tried to respond, not impose. Each environment dictated visual interpretations, strained through my experience. If you're moving a camera around frenetically in the desert, you won't see much – you need slowness to appreciate the details. The desert shows what the past might have been, what the future may be. The walls reveal thousands of years of sedimentary deposit and erosion, and fossils and Native American traces are still there. I was in deserts in Utah and Nevada, and ventured to a site once used for nuclear testing, filled with radioactive warnings, but wondered if I was risking my health to get an image of empty ground.

Las Vegas was interesting because it was constructed in the middle of the desert, a virtual city that refabricates marketable world sites (Venice, Egypt) as a backdrop to gambling. Here is another way of finding escape, meaning and epiphany. I shot a lot of gambling footage, and one person in particular who was paying his way through college by card-counting poker. He always played with headphones running Nine Inch Nails so he wouldn't get distracted. The truest version of *Gambling, Gods* is eight hours long and would include these scenes, but because of agreements and money that allowed the film to be made, I had to leave out scenes that I love but that didn't fit into the three-hour

composition. I didn't want to shorten everything down to get it all in, because I felt scenes were already too short. There's still a question of whether I should make an eight-hour movie that would better reflect the actual journey.

MH: There's a quietly funny scene in Vegas where a woman in red leather is strapped into an orgasmatron and you ask her about her favourite recipes.

PM: That scene was delicate to edit, because Dante is fairly outrageous and the situation is quite sexist. Dante rang up a woman to model his sex chair, and I wanted to disarm the situation by drawing out her humanity. In the orgasmatron, she tells me that her favourite thing is talking to her parents and cooking lasagna. Her speaking allows viewers to look deeper into the people of the situation.

I did a lot of research before leaving, which functioned as a subconscious tuning. The research gave me antennae, but if encounters naturally arose in the process of exploration and it felt intuitively correct, I would go down that road. When I went to Las Vegas, I knew the sociologist Kate Hausbeck, whose main study was the sex trade, and she led me to new people, like Dante, the man who makes the sexual chair. Ideas grew through association. The dust in the desert foreshadows the dynamiting of the Las Vegas hotel and the remains of a loved one. All these moments narrate the idea of impermanence. We believe in the illusions of our construction, but they eventually become dust.

For instance, I was interested in the wife of Maurice Strong, a Canadian industrialist who bought land for water export, a practice she opposed. She wanted to set up a spiritual retreat instead. She said I should stay with a filmmaker who had worked a lot in Tibet, and he took me to a poker game where I met Jose, and that's who I eventually filmed. I had no idea he was keeping the bones of his wife in a scarf. He brought it to the table as I let him direct the scene, and it unfolded the way he wanted. I can't put a schematic on it (first thought equals best thought) – it's informed observation, not forced exposition. Its logic is mysterious, but the journey had its own structure, which it became the film's task to reveal.

MH: The Switzerland section has an establishing-shot sequence that contrasts the clean and the unclean. You say in voice-over that you are going back to the perfect world of your parents. What do you mean by that?

PM: Switzerland has achieved a kind of utopia of urban planning, with its fine public education, beautiful landscapes and transportation systems, but at the same time there is an underside that can't abide these rules – the heroin culture, for instance. The opening sequence points toward the fact of decay, death and shit, natural cycles that are pervasive no matter what the system.

I had always been interested in the heroin scene in Switzerland and met Roger Greminger and Christine while editing.

Gambling, Gods and LSD

When I was 17, I went to school in Switzerland for a year and was compelled to stick my thumb out on the road and see where I wound up. Someone took me to an old monastery that had become a rehab centre for heroin addicts. I connected with the priest who ran it, took a lot of photographs, then went back to Ryerson Polytechnical Institute in Toronto to learn filmmaking. I'd been interested in what draws people to heroin, what kind of people they are. Heroin is the darkest, most taboo drug. People consider heroin users fucked-up criminals, but my experience was that they were some of the most sensitive and compassionate people I'd ever encountered. What desire is heroin fulfilling? In Switzerland it's easy to get on the streets, and for a time Yugoslavia sold drugs to buy arms for the war, and these arms (in part) were made by Swiss companies down the road from Needle Park. This seemed to fit the web I was following for Gambling, Gods. When I met Roger and Christine, I was struck by their warmth and compassion for each other, despite the fact they were deep into this addiction and Roger was in a wheelchair with a spinal infection and she was taking care of him. There was a beautiful love, even though they were really toxic for each other.

We had a sit-down conversation with the camera rolling, which I'd done with a number of people. It was talk- and information-oriented, and then I asked Roger if there was something he'd like to show me about his life in Zurich, and he took me to a clothing depot where he used to sleep. There was no great strategy behind that. In all the interviews I had a core of ideas, but what tended to happen was a process of discovery that led us toward meaningful places. Often I would spend a day or two with these people, talking until it went into a realm more pertinent to the film. I had to say a lot about myself – they wanted to know who I was and feel a level of trust before they would talk about what was personal and important to them. I would often pause for a long time. When you ask a number of questions, the interview form feels familiar, and then it would arrive at a point where I

would pause for an uncomfortably long time, and that's usually where it got interesting. They would start to talk, and the real preoccupations of the person would come out in a voluntary way. There was a set of questions I asked at the end of each interview, a simple list of questions to which you could answer yes or no or elaborate. These became a mantra throughout the process, though few ended up in the film. One of the installation works I did included a collection of these questions, but I didn't adhere to that schematic while editing.

The film's three hours may seem a long time, but many-layered conversations are shrunk to a few essential matters, and people are left only a few minutes to talk. In almost every case, the person interviewed had far more to say in the assembly stage of the film. With Roger and Christine, the edit focused on why they were attracted to heroin. Roger said he might have meditated for many years and arrived at the same place. They were quitting at that point, talking about addiction as if it were the past, but it was a very recent past. As it turned out, they both managed to quit – Roger's had a couple of lapses, but it's essentially gone. It had been an experience of peace that was very comforting for nearly 20 years. I asked Christine if it was an answer for something she was searching for. She said no, it stopped the need to search. They both insisted heroin was a temporary fix that pulls you into a dependent way of life. You need money, and then the fix only takes away your peace. Every day is captured by getting this drug inside you – it's a horror. But at the same time, she saw aspects of herself before addiction she didn't like and didn't want to return to. Going through this extreme experience taught her a lot about herself, and she was fortunate enough to pull out of it and use what she learned to continue. I was concerned that they would be comfortable in their presentation, so I showed them different stages of the editing for their feedback, secretly hoping that having announced their quitting in public would provide an incentive. I don't know how much the film influenced them in the end, but I think it may have helped.

It's always difficult to watch yourself on film, knowing a few sentences represent your entire experience – you understand the innuendo of every muscle twitch and eye flutter. It's like listening to your voice on tape: it's unbearable at first, there's always a process of becoming familiar with looking at yourself. My task was to put this drug story into the context of their personalities, so it was no longer 'drug addicts talk about heroin,' but 'This is Roger and Christine, and they took heroin.' I tried to do that with everyone.

MH: Christine says, 'Well, it's so … ' and then later, 'Somehow, it's so … ' and those are her last words – she never manages to finish the sentence. In a normal documentary, these unfinished thoughts and long pauses would never be shown. Why did you leave them in?

PM: For me, that's one of the most beautiful moments in the film: it points to dimensions of mystery we can't find the words for. After Christine, you hear the rain and see something very banal, a circling pan out of a window again and again, and that's something I found more and more beautiful during the film's making, looking at everyday things that had no obvious sensation or meaning, yet feeling the profundity of being there.

MH: Can you tell me about the title?

PM: I'd been researching different kinds of peak experiences, addictions and escapes, and drew a large page of identifiers. I put words together and came up with *gambling, gods* and LSD. The title stuck until it was finished, though I tried to abandon it – the film has an LSD logic in terms of time and observation.

MH: It's called a trip.

PM: Albert Hoffman invented LSD in Switzerland, but in the film he ended up talking about childhood. His discovery remained a suggestion as opposed to an explored subject. The sense of wonder of childhood he describes is revived by the drug he contends is an important tool for the expansion of consciousness. He felt Timothy Leary was both overly flamboyant and overly simplified, and the resultant publicity made further medical research impossible. Before he found LSD, he researched the colours of flowers and their function. He approached chemistry in a wondrous and artistic way; he's published a couple of books that don't seem to come from a scientist, but from a mystic. I finally met him at the premiere screening in Nyon. Sitting beside him was very interesting because he emoted a lot – he moaned when he enjoyed passages. He thought of LSD as a triggering or revisitation of childhood states – there is something familiar about it, but it's an unconscious visit by something forgotten.

MH: Why is it forgotten?

PM: We use our brains to structure events, to analyze and define – in other words, to cut. We're forever processing thoughts, preoccupied with getting things done and taking little time to appreciate the way clouds are floating overhead or to listen to a piece of music profoundly. We forget we can do that. Different belief structures and systems can engage people in similar processes of focusing.

MH: How is this stillness the same as being at the all-night raves you show in the film?

PM: The ecstatic induces high adrenaline and exalted epiphanies, whereas meditative, inward peace involves slowing things down, taking distractions away – yet they bring you into a state and focus that is also epiphanic. One is active and requires taking something – drugs, dancing or worship – it's going to blow me out the top of a volcano. It adheres to triggers. Religion is similar to drugs; a belief structure can be a substance as well, similar to sports or dancing, which structure altered social states. The other method requires putting it all away and finding clarity within. Silence.

MH: The Swiss scientist speaks about death on a molecular level, as an exchange of energy. But he also says he will live on in his children. Is your filmmaking a way of cheating death, of holding on to a present that is always slipping away? For someone so concerned about the present, you spend a lot of time condemned to pictures made some time ago – it's been seven years between films, and a lot of that time was in the edit room.

PM: Film is a paradox, using a medium to see into the present, which immediately becomes a recording of the past for future viewers. I want to create a cinema experience that includes a self-reflection in the audience no longer holding on to my journey, but bringing viewers into the present. That presentness is a state that can remain an accompaniment when leaving the theatre.

It's a challenge to keep that improvisational energy while editing, when it's natural for your mind to create compositional structures. How do you clear the mind and play your instrument? Editing often induces trance, so you go further in, then step out and ask what does this mean? This was different than *The Top of His Head* or *Picture of Light*, which had more thematic unfoldings. *Gambling, Gods* works much more by association – that's why I can still watch it, it doesn't add up neatly.

There was a lot of material, and we didn't know how long the film was allowed to be. Reviewing, logging and assembling the material took a year. We tried not to editorialize, and kept chronologies intact. The logistics of editing in Switzerland took a lot of time, and we didn't have enough money to finish an hour-and-a-half film, though we had an assembly of 55 hours. Then we worked on a five-hour cut to show the television people and distributors to allow us to get enough money to finish the film. That was the second year. Then we began to cut toward a three-hour cinema film.

It begins with proposal writing. With *Gambling, Gods* I was very honest about describing the film as an exploratory process, and while I didn't know what would be in the finished film, I knew the themes and provided possible scenarios. People trusted me based on my previous work, especially *Picture of Light*, which had a similar approach but a much narrower subject. The managing and producing side was so overwhelming that I don't know if I would ever do it again. Essentially, you're setting up a platform to work intuitively, but building the platform takes up 90 percent of your energy and requires at every turn an explanation of why you're doing it and what it will be in the end. It's exhausting not falling into the trap of giving a false proposition. The five-hour demo required them to drive a long way to our edit room in the countryside and they were riveted. They said okay on the spot – I'd never had that happen before. Luckily it won prizes. ARTE was the main TV participant, and that is one of their rewards. If the film gains notoriety, it encourages them to work that way again.

One of my interests is to bring artistic processes and themes more often found in experimental film to a wider audience. You need industrial structures to get your film shown, but I'm still not sure it's the right way. In the end, you lose power over the work and it becomes part of the machine, but we're opening in 200 theatres in Paris and there's a DVD that's widely available, and that wouldn't have happened any other way.

MH: How did you know the film was over?

PM: We had edited for so long, knowing there were a number of configurations that would work. I went out for a walk on September 10, reviewing the whole experience, flashing through the years and components, and remembering John Paul Young at the bridge at the beginning of the film. What you don't see in the film was his challenge that I ask God to make an appearance. When I told him I couldn't think in those terms, he said, 'You have to pray.' This kind of filmmaking is my prayer, but how do I know it's finished? I felt I needed a sign, and the next day was the infamous September 11. I was scanning through the film on the Avid, getting an overview, looking for spots I might want to change or react to, and stopped on a rooftop scene in Bombay. A Muslim man prays and then the camera tilts up to the sky where an airplane flies into the distance. That's the last shot I touched. Then I put all the different timelines together on the Avid, and the moment I was finished the phone rang and a friend of mine said, 'You won't believe what just happened in New York City.' We began sticking wires into the TV to get a signal and finally saw a jet going into the World Trade Center. I watched the film later that night through the filter of that news, seeing traces and anticipations of that event. Belief systems and the conflicts they provoke, prevalent images of airplane travel and imploding buildings, civilization at a boiling point where something has to break. That was a sign. The timing was uncanny.

Peter Mettler's Films

Reverie   20 min 1976
Poison Ivy   20 min 1978
Home Movie   15 min 1979
Lancalot Freely   20 min 1980
Gregory   25 min 1981
Scissere   88 min 1982
Eastern Avenue   58 min 1985
The Top of His Head   110 min 1989
Tectonic Plates   106 min 1992
Picture of Light   83 min 1994
Balifilm   28 min 1996
Gambling, Gods and LSD   180 min 2002

Available from Grimthorpe Film, 91 Brunswick Avenue, Toronto, Ontario M5S 2L8 (grimfilm@ca.inter.net).

Peter Mettler's films have garnered many prizes and been the focus of several retrospectives internationally. A book on his work entitled *Making the Invisible Visible* was published in 1995 and another entitled *Of This Place and Elsewhere, The Films and Photography of Peter Mettler* was published in 2006 by the Toronto International Film Festival.

DONIGAN CUMMING
REALITY AND MOTIVE
IN THE DOCUMENTARY

What I like to do most is curl up in a chair and listen while some outrageously smartbomb personality inveighs against the latest incursion by the American empire. I want to hear Robert Fisk tell us all about the Israeli cluster-bombing of Lebanon, or Seymour Hersh dishing about the CIA's secret torture prisons in Afghanistan. I like my politics clean and far away, so I can be filled with outrage and then get on with my day. Donigan Cumming doesn't share my sympathies. He enacts his politics with a camera that can't get close enough. I am surprised he hasn't invested in those microcams that surgeons use to illuminate hidden cavities and organs and blood flows. Instead, he holds his camera right up into his subject's face: *Here, go ahead, what do you think about this?* And he's not shrinking away behind some facade of neutrality: forget about it, these faces pressed up close to the camera glass talk right back to him and tell him what a soft-headed know-nothing he is. Or else he is muttering to himself in a manic whisper, part of an interior/exterior monologue that runs through so much of his work.

What does he see?

He is drawn to an invisible underclass: the old drinkers, the rooming-house recluses and gap-toothed smokers. He is undertaking a kind of urban ethnography, but he does it up close and personal; he's the one racing to the hospital to get required medications, or offering another concerned question. He is part of this sad, broken picture, and he never stoops to pity or easy-chair emotions that come from far away. He works on the front line of a class war, and his tapes are part of the cost and scar and symptom of that war. How many more friends will have to be buried? In this kind of cinema, in this kind of living: until death do us part.

MH: Donigan, for years you practised the esteemed and virtuous art of photography. You were collected, shown in museums; you seemed to maintain that most elusive of Canadian expressions: a career in art. And then you decided to begin producing in the most ignored, left behind and generally despised medium of art: video. What led you to make such a decision? What is it that can't be shown in a single frame, in an instant?

DC: If we were doing this onstage, I'd thank you for your generous review of my 'career in art,' then suggest we get down to business. To go back, I've never been particularly enthralled with the single photographic image. In fact, my photo installation/video project *Reality and Motive in Documentary Photography* was all about unveiling the conceits and visual hooks used to create the icons of the documentary tradition.

MH: I must admit I have been astonished on more than one occasion at what photographers are 'allowed' to show in art galleries. Snapshots from foreign countries? No problem. Gig journalism in war-torn places? Step right up. Anonymous atrocities, intimacies of strangers exposed: sure, why not. Somehow the binding questions of race, imperialism, representation, transparency, point of view – in fact, the bulk of critical thinking that has gone on for the past century – seem to have passed much of this work by. As if photographers exist in some more 'innocent' stage of picture-making.

DC: Well, you've touched on a number of issues that drove me to make *Reality and Motive in Documentary Photography*, though the counter-inspiration was not only what people now see as the pornography of misery. I was also offended by what was called 'concerned photography,' which seemed to carry on with reformist ideas from the 1930s, as though depiction in a signature photographic style could give people back their 'humanity.' I conceived *Reality and Motive in Documentary Photography* as an elaborate experiment in making social-documentary photographs. This resulted in an exhibition, which was shown in progress at various places in Canada, and in its final form in New York, Paris and other cities, beginning in 1986. This project was also the making of a community that has been central to my work in video. In *Reality and Motive in Documentary Photography*, the malleability of certain stereotypical conditions, such as motherhood or old age, and the authority of social-documentary style, were combined in a kind of photographic laboratory. An important strategy was repetition, showing that things could be done again and again. The same strategies, laced with sentimentality, made up the soundtrack of the third part of that piece. So, from the beginning, I was interested in time-based media – sound, but also the time-based activity of the spectator, who is asked to look at episodic sequences of images and to try to put some kind of narrative or social construction on them. I suppose the difference between the photographic frame and the video passage comes out when you compare *Lying Quiet* (book and photographic grid) and *Fountain* (video). I made the book first, using the video material I had shot for 18 videotapes. The grabs were latent in this material – images I found by applying a fairly rigorous editing system, then looking at the results and building a visual sequence. *Fountain*, which enters this sequence somewhere in the middle, represents those source video passages in the order of the book, bringing back the thickness of the recording experience – flow, rhythm and sound. I don't think of my work as evolving from the still to the cinematic image. I go back and forth.

By the way, I've never thought of video as the most ignored, left behind or despised of media. I can be despised in any medium, even encaustic.

MH: I saw *Fountain* (22 min, 2005) for the first time in Nyon, before the panel where only those without anything to say were able to speak at length, and it was the first time I came all the way around on your work. It is a monstrous video, a quickly paced theme song of despair and decay, not 'over the top' but 'under the bottom.' It seems you've cut together scenes from all your work, and more besides, that show human beings in states of despair and distress, drunk and out of control and dying; mostly what we watch are no-income drinkers dying in front of our faces. And you really pour it on in this tape, like a card sharp with all the aces, trumping your own trick. At first I thought no, this is exactly the kind of sound-bite exploitation that TV specializes in. Run into the lower east side (Vancouver, for instance), snatch a few pictures of the lowlife, then move right on. But you are so relentlessly close, for one thing – your camera rubbed up to their bellies, their faces, their vomit – that it's clear you are part of the scene, not to mention that you talk with them (not 'over' them in the all-knowing voice-over manner). And also: after some minutes (I wasn't counting, sorry, no time to look at the watch, not with all that despair blown up big), I got over my initial repulsion and saw some measure of compassion – a curious kind of compassion, spoken as you lean into their addictions, their almost-at-the-end-of-the-rope directives, their sorrows – but somehow you produce the subjects, they arrive, they are really there, and you are really there, and they are more than just montage objects or picture trophies from the other side, but as alive as I am, or moreso, howling and whimpering and mewling into the lens.

DC: Your response is strong medicine – a bit shocking to me. As I read it, there are two aspects to the initial reaction, repulsion. First, that there was a plan to extract and string together all the harshest bits of my work – to go down to the bottom, as you say. This resulted in scenes of almost unbearable 'despair and distress.' Second, that the work was reminding you of reality TV's exploitation. That those impressions eventually shifted into a recognition that I was part of the scene, showing some manner of 'curious' compassion, was naturally gratifying, and I suppose I could answer simply by saying you took the trip I intended. Repulsion to Compassion – end of story, except that there is no story, because there's no plot. The beginning of the tape (this applies to all my tapes) is crucial. Starting, as I said, in the middle-of-the-book sequence was a choice to start with the conversation with Dave, in which all the rules of engagement are displayed, in which I suggest I might be an exploitative monster, awakening concerns in Dave that he might get caught for doing something wrong, which was, in fact, trying to help a sick neighbour. I'm there in the picture, Dave's there, Duchamp's *Fountain* is there – we're all cornered.

Fountain is difficult to watch, because it's a display of the whole conundrum. Reflexivity is also displayed – reflexivity as just another luxury. Perhaps operating under video's founding delusion (of which we the 'despised' have long been disabused) that video work could find larger audiences, I had some hopes for tapes like *Erratic Angel* and *if only I*. But I know better now, having been exposed to the machinations of ARTE, the NFB, etc. So I know who's watching *Fountain* – we are, the filmmakers are – and I want to provoke that audience. Some people respond negatively to the unevenness of my exchange with Dave, to an apparent display of power relations in the making of the tape. It makes them feel uncomfortable that they are participating in this theatre of 'exploitation.' Possibly it reminds them of their

watching and making habits. *Fountain* is, in a way, a special case – certainly less accessible, possibly more self-conscious than other tapes. I am cornered and I am angry. If we want to talk about tapes that are hard to watch, I guess *My Dinner with Weegee* would be a good place to start, especially since the subject, Marty Corbin, had his own point of view on the end product.

MH: But wait, before we go feasting with Marty and Weegee, I need to ask for some elaboration first. What do you mean when you say reflexivity is 'just another luxury'? Do you mean real people are dying while artists are busy navel-gazing into their apparatus? Is this why you want to provoke artists (who too often use their work not so that they can take up the task of looking, of encounter, but instead for covering up, of replacing or displacing – much work is simply another form of distraction or visual noise). And what about the title, *Fountain*? You just mentioned Duchamp's *Fountain*, the most famous toilet in the world because it was found and signed and named as art. Are the people in your *Fountain* also found objects? And, of course, I am including you in this question: are you also found, foundered, foundering?

DC: What a thicket. No, I don't mean that 'real people are dying while artists are busy navel-gazing into their apparatus.' I don't divide the world in that way. There's a lot of senseless distraction, narcissistic eye candy, that's not worth bothering with, so let's not go there. Who are we talking to? Humans are self-absorbed, but paradoxically gregarious, with fits of mystifying altruism. I don't condemn reverie – it's important. And displacement may mean psychic survival. I mean that even a fine idea like reflexivity in film and video work is shaped by our own interests as creators. Most people don't want to pursue the implications. Reflexivity becomes a marketing strategy. We see a lot of reflexivity lite. I'm trying to follow this problem to the bitter end. It's a matter of bringing a few viewers with me, people who are aware of the absurdity of their position. The title, *Fountain*, is a barbed tease. Your interpretation is okay and plays to the title's aggressive side. It's also an art-history joke, the sort that Lenny Bruce might make just before shooting up on his toilet.

MH: In *My Dinner with Weegee* (36:26 min, 2001), we see you with an older friend, Marty, who is in very bad shape. Years of drinking too much (and continuing to drink) have made him a physical wreck, which you demonstrate in scene after scene. His hands shake, his underwear is soiled, he can hardly walk anymore. Your depiction is merciless and unflattering in the extreme – presumably that was clear to Marty before he agreed to appear in the tape. Did it became an issue after he saw it? You wrote that he 'had his own point of view on the end product.'

DC: Well, first of all, when I started working on this tape, nothing was clear to either of us about the direction it would take. This is a typical situation for me. It was enough that I was drawn to Marty because of our linked pasts. The radicals of Marty's

My Dinner with Weegee

generation had been actively engaged with the issues of my generation in a way that seemed unique. I wanted to explore that connection, in part because I didn't feel the same continuity between my generation and the ones that have followed. There seems to be more amnesia now and less sense of history. Of course, I don't blame anyone for dismissing the struggles of the past. The record of my generation is, on the whole, pretty appalling: former '60s radicals now happily wallowing in a trough of greed, set in the middle of an expanding sea of concrete. Talking to Marty allowed both of us to consider other possibilities.

When we started, Marty was sober and I was the serious acolyte. This benign set of circumstances shattered when Marty slid into a period of depression and drinking. It's not my habit to break things off when confused or surprised, so I just kept shooting and tried to grapple with developments as they twisted around me. The Marty I started with had virtually disappeared. He would return in the blue-tinged footage I shot just a couple of months before he died, when he had been forced back to sobriety by his health problems and a threatening doctor. By that point, I had the kind of footage you describe, very rough and sad. I began to worry about Marty's response to the stuff I had accumulated. So when things settled down and Marty was sober, I rough-cut the worst of it into about an hour of material and screened it for Marty and my friend Colin. They both watched without much comment. When it was over, Marty surprised me. He simply said, 'That's a cautionary tale.' I pointed out to him that I wanted to use it – possibly all of it. Then I asked him if he'd release it. He said yes and signed and that was it. We didn't talk about it again. I finished the tape.

I think Marty saw this tape as his last radical act. He didn't want to be remembered as an approximate figure. It was a gamble. I think he won the clash between his heroic Dr. Jekyll and his anarchic Mr. Hyde. Marty felt, as I do, that any system that forgets to be nervous about its own certainties is headed for

deep shit and, further, that the rough descriptive elements in this tape actually soften the underlying nightmare – the bleak absurdity of any life.

MH: You speak with Marty about Dave Dellinger (Marty's former roommate), who was part of the Chicago Seven. Who were they and why are they important in this tape as an icon of lost ideals?

DC: The Chicago Seven were '60s radicals charged with conspiracy, inciting to riot and so forth, because of the anti-war protests mounted in Chicago during the 1968 Democratic Convention. The arrests led to a show trial. This episode represented to many the courage of convictions carried to the bitter end. Marty had been closely associated with the most senior member of the Seven, Dave Dellinger. We agreed that Dellinger was the only honest and truly dedicated pacifist of the Chicago Seven. The others had very mixed agendas, as their subsequent histories showed.

MH: You concoct an elaborate scenario with Marty to take him to the hospital and try to get him admitted to the emergency ward. Are the two of you rehearsing, playing with moments of his decline, instead of allowing them to swallow you?

DC: I never thought of this scene as concocted. Actually, you could look at this episode as an outbreak of realism in the tape. This is a very clear exposition of how the social actor prepares to interact within the current state of socialized medicine. Marty, Colin and I were aware of the problem of getting him admitted for detox. There is limited patience, or sympathy, for alcoholics who have not exhibited a convincing desire to stop drinking. Marty was known to the authorities as a repeat offender and backslider. So we felt they had to be tricked into admitting him. That's why we 'rehearsed' in the car. It's interesting that you see this as a game that forestalls the realities of his decline. To me, it's the older, or terminally ill, person's way of asserting that they are in fact still alive, not ready to be written off. They're trying to get better or, at least, feel better. For someone in Marty's situation, it's not the end game.

MH: You are also a 'character' in this tape, and you talk about being put on trial for refusing the draft to fight in Vietnam and being sentenced to five years in prison, and then coming to Canada as a result. You also talk about years of drinking and a mentor who cruelly refused you, emphasizing the shared pasts of you and Marty. But you have wound up in very different places. You are a successful artist, and so have earned the right to move between the straight world of acceptance and career, and the alcoholic miseries of Marty and Colin and their friends. Isn't there resentment and tension as a result? This is never raised as an issue in the tape and I wonder why.

DC: On the tape, Marty and I are talking quickly and finishing each other's sentences. This introduces certain confusions that I kept in the final edit because they are true to the experience of talking about key episodes in a person's life – the stories that get told again and again, in shorter and shorter bursts. Marty and I had had that conversation before. So the facts get a bit telegraphic. The story Marty and I both knew is that I resisted the Vietnam war by refusing the draft. I came to Canada because I thought that all the in-country official options for protesting the war were suspect and fed the beast. I rejected conscientious-objector status for that reason, and I rejected going to prison. On tape, Marty is commenting that I could be liable to five years' imprisonment for refusing the draft. That was true, but I left the country without getting caught, so it didn't happen to me.

In the stream-of-consciousness section, when I muse about drinking and a lost older mentor, I wanted to mix aspects of my past with the present of the video. In my lost years, after coming to Canada, I had some experience with alcohol abuse. That's when I met Colin, and we talk about this in *Erratic Angel*. I got out of it and he didn't. Or he stayed in too long. Is there tension and resentment as a result? Yes, and Colin's outburst in *My Dinner with Weegee*, when he accuses Marty of philosophizing and drinking himself to death, is a symptom of that resentment. Across the board, Colin likes to remind me that he's a hard-body and I'm soft. He knows that a whiff of resentment plays really well within the context of this kind of filmmaking. At the same time, the reason he still works with me is that he likes to debate these points. He has long ago used up the listening ear of the social services – in the making of the tape, the fact that I'm still listening can be good for Colin. The dissemination of the tape works for him sometimes, and sometimes backfires. But even the backfiring has some appeal. He told me recently that his nurses resented some of the things he said in *Erratic Angel*. He told me that on tape. Being able to say that shows he's still standing. In *if only I*, Colleen used the opportunity of the tape to tell her story as she wanted it told. All of the people I work with use the medium in that way, but they do so in a charged atmosphere. They know that I have the final edit – in a way, that ups the ante, because they challenge me to keep things in.

MH: Most of your tapes have a central 'character' who is brought into focus, his or her portrait rendered, as you hold the camera up. In *if only I* (35 min, 2000), the motor is Colleen, a woman who speaks with you very frankly about leaving her husband and children for a heroin addict, stripping, drinking, drug abuse and her suicide attempt. Were these stories you had heard many times before? In your answer above, you suggest that the tape was her idea – did she have suggestions about what she wanted to talk about and how she should appear onscreen?

DC: To start with, to set the record straight, Colleen says she left a husband who was cheating on her with a woman he was supposed to be helping in AA. The rest of your summary is about right. At the point in time that forms part of the tape, yes, I had heard the story before, because this wasn't the first take. I had also heard versions of it from Colin. But more significantly, Colleen had told these stories many times before, and was accustomed to telling them, whether at AA meetings or to social workers involved with her case. When I ask her on tape if she will feel comfortable starting her story from the beginning of her life (as she says, her 'wretched' life), she responds, 'Well, I guess I will be comfortable doing it,' then raises her eyebrows conspiratorially. The tape was first proposed by Colin. When Colleen was thrown out of her halfway house, Colin brought her straight to my door. He wanted the story recorded as it was unfolding. So the tape was, in a sense, their idea, inasmuch as they formed a unit at that moment. Colleen did not make the kinds of suggestions you've listed, though it's important to remember that we worked by permission and by appointment. After the initial crisis, when I followed Colleen and Colin back to Marty's apartment and recorded what was going on, I made arrangements to see them in advance. It's obvious on the tape when I am interviewing Colleen by pre-arrangement. That said, it was a developing situation and I saw them every day over a few weeks.

MH: Colleen has been taken in by Colin, a recovering drug addict who is still in rough shape. He bristles (strangely, perversely) at your suggestion that because the two of them are sleeping together, his motives are not entirely altruistic. He is alternately

if only I

defensive and hostile toward you. He insists, 'The pictures don't ever match the words in this culture.' Can you comment on this exchange between the two of you?

DC: Actually, that's not what I suggest. My question is whether sleeping together has changed the nature of their relationship. It's Colin who goes to the issue of exploitation, not me. I'm interested in whether they have a romantic relationship. He tears my 'neophyte ... sophomoric ... romantic' head off. Colleen is more open to the idea, even though this is the very period when he is pushing himself on her. She is evidently quite fond of him, at least at that moment. What's important here is that I'm teasing Colin, baiting him, because I know he will rise up with his street-life, hardball-player identity and put me in my middle-class place. Since that frequently happens off-camera, I thought it should happen on-camera, so I sparked the discussion. As for the pictures not matching the words, Colin's hopes for the tape are tied up in this statement, which continues, 'That's why we're doing this.'

MH: What does Colin mean when he says, 'She's not even a human being right now. And neither am I. And neither are you'?

DC: He means that Colleen's lost all her legal rights and social entitlements. They're feeling like cornered rats. But the system that has done that to Colleen is not human either, and he's tossing me into that system. In fact, he's just warming up.

MH: Some of Colleen's saddest moments are reserved for sexual memories. After her mother is taken away to a state hospital for the insane, her father forces her to have sex with him. She recounts an incest survivors' group where she was able to look round the room and see at what age the abuse had occurred, because something in the face gets stuck there. Can you see that in her? Is that quality of seeing something the camera can assist? Once Colleen has identified this quality of seeing, can it be learned? (Via the camera, for instance, and alongside it, perhaps other kinds of seeing? Is this also part of your project of portraiture?) She then describes sex with Colin, which is once again complicated by power and bad timing.

DC: Colleen is referring to a psychological hypothesis that appeals to her because it gives her, or gave her, a feeling of maturity and superior knowledge in the moment. She smiles about it. It's not clear how seriously she takes it herself. If one were going to apply it literally to Colleen, when would you fix the date? As she tells it, there was violence in that house from Day 1. The story of the older sister is intriguing. She is mentioned only in passing as having suffered the father's 'possessiveness.' What caused the mother's breakdown? It's all very

confusing, even in Colleen's mind. What I see in Colleen is a life-long desire for security, complicated by a desire to be onstage, to be admired. The camera certainly allowed her that.

MH: Aren't you simply a voyeur of these tragedies, able to walk in and out of these desperate lives whenever it becomes too much? Isn't there a profound difference in economic circumstances between you and your subjects? Don't their addictions make them particularly susceptible to the imbalanced power relations any act of filmmaking entails?

DC: In one short burst, you've raised four different power relations. I think they need to be separated before they can be answered. First, the psychological power of the voyeur. Second, economic disparity. Third, the power of the well over the sick. Fourth, the power of the documentarian over the subject. These are loaded questions, peppered with assumptions.

First, voyeurism is taking sexual pleasure from watching people who don't know they're being watched. Masturbation generally follows. This is not my practice. Nor is it the practice of people who watch the tapes, at least to my knowledge. If you're asking if I take vicarious pleasure in the misfortunes of others, the answer is no.

Second, Colin and I have substantially different economic statuses. That is undeniable. He comes from a middle-class background, as do I, but he hasn't stayed there. The underlying question is whether I engage in a relationship with Colin with a view to profit. One could argue that I have, in the sense that sociologists profit from the existence of different social and economic classes, giving them interesting disparities to study. The real question that you have not asked is whether I am using Colin and giving nothing in return. Maybe we should talk about that in light of *Erratic Angel*. In the case of *if only I*, I was asked into a crisis situation and stuck with it until Colleen was safely moved into her own apartment and had her civil rights restored. The happy

if only I

ending is not part of the tape, because letting the audience off the hook is not what my work is about and, in any case, only shores up the power structure. All's well that ends well. The poor will always be with us. That kind of thing.

Third, at the time I made the tape, Colin and Colleen were in recovery. Their addiction is not really at issue in the tape, unless you count their addiction to nicotine. Colleen was susceptible to a documentary treatment and desirous of one, because she was in very bad trouble with the health and social systems that she needed, and felt victimized. At the same time, she takes responsibility for her situation right from the beginning, which is a way of taking control of her life.

Fourth, the nut of this question. As you say, any act of filmmaking entails imbalanced power relations. So why throw up this extra ammunition, such as voyeurism, profit-making, manipulating the sick? I have to wonder why these accusations are tossed around so liberally, even as the documentary dance continues. Isn't the question simply: why make films about people nobody wants to see onscreen or pays attention to when they see them on the street? Looking at other lives, especially the lives of people in crisis, makes us uncomfortable. Why shouldn't we be uncomfortable? I certainly am. Would it be enough to say that, yes, I wish it were better for Colin, and many other people I've known throughout the years. But it isn't, and I do what I can to represent what's happening to many people in our society, without imposing feel-good narratives. In short, I try to make the pictures match the words.

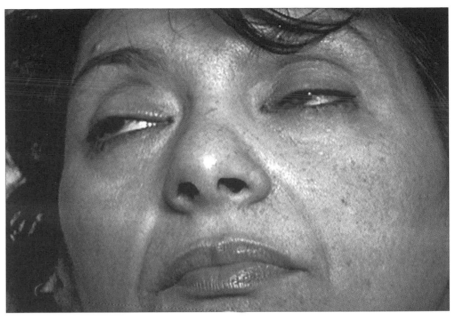
After Brenda

MH: *After Brenda* (41 min, 1997) follows 50-year-old Pierre Lamarche, who falls in love with Brenda after finding her wallet in a trash can. They wind up together, but after she charges him with rape he is put in jail. After he gets out, he is beset with fantasies that Brenda is part of a prostitution ring and is madly servicing clients next door. At first it's hard to know who or what to believe, but it eventually becomes clear that Pierre is suffering from terrible delusions and that he has abused the woman he professes to love. What was it that drew you close to him, and why did you want to tell this story of obsessive love?

DC: I met Pierre by chance at Nelson Coombs' apartment. Nelson was one of my long-time models. Nelson had given Pierre shelter because he had lost his apartment while in jail over Christmas. Pierre had a broken-hearted story and I liked it. It fit very well into the plan I had to move from genre to genre. Making a romance after an elegy (*A Prayer for Nettie*) and a ribald wake (*Cut the Parrot*) seemed just right. The self-absorption and excess of obsessive love is perfect screen material – I'm hardly the first to have that insight. I asked Pierre to let me tape him telling the whole story. He was very enthusiastic; in fact, he claimed the role of 'producer.' I met Brenda, Pierre's on-again-off-again girlfriend, at Nelson's apartment. The other characters, except Colin, were part of Nelson's circle of friends. As recounted in the tape, Mina was at the point of moving in with Nelson. Pierre's qualities as a very self-conscious performer and his passion for storytelling made him a perfect subject.

MH: Brenda's story is crosscut with Colin recounting the beginnings of his cocaine/alcohol addiction and how you found him recovering from a binge and told him his friend had died. What role does Colin play in the movie?

DC: Colin's story runs in counterpoint to Pierre's. Both characters are single-minded and isolated – Colin obviously living alone – and both have stories to tell. Colin is an absurd injection into what appears to be a normal storytelling event, as embodied by Pierre. Crosscutting their soliloquies allows Colin-the-character to comment on the confessions and conflicts taking place in another room. Colin, in some respects, represents my feelings about the charisma and false promise of storytelling.

MH: What are these feelings and why do you have them?

DC: Narrative, as the modern world frames and enjoys it, is a poor way of getting at, or delivering, the facts. At root, narrative is not interested in the truth. The narrative forms we favour are products of a revenge culture, organizing material to suit circumstances and ambitions in the present. The result is mythology and propaganda. In *After Brenda*, there are two intertwining streams of narrative: Colin's delivery is philosophical, verging on mystical; Pierre claims to be dealing with reality, the raw facts. Neither tale, in the end, coheres as trustworthy.

MH: In *Karaoke* (3 min, 1998), you begin with a typically tight close-up on a man's face while a religious folk tune plays, expressing happiness that Jesus has been born. The man looks barely alive, his eyes are mostly shut, though when you pan down to his untended feet (is he in a hospital?), his foot is tapping along to the song, which then begins playing backwards. Who is this man and why is the tape called *Karaoke*, when he never utters a word, nor do you?

DC: The man in the bed is Nelson Coombs. He isn't as sick as he looks – he was actually at home recovering from a bout of the flu, being tended by Mina. In terms of domestic arrangements, this is the follow-up to *After Brenda*. Nelson has taken my advice and gotten a larger apartment in the same building. Mina is living with him. On the day *Karaoke* was shot, Mina's girlfriend was visiting. She had brought a cassette tape of her sister singing a mix of songs, mostly Inuktitut covers of Western and pop

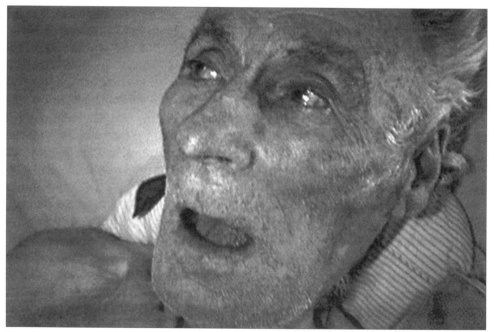

Karaoke

spirituals. One tune in particular caught their fancy. They were playing it and singing along, thus the title, *Karaoke*. Nelson was lying propped up in bed listening. I asked them to sit beside him and sing the song again. The tape starts with the cassette being loaded and a tight shot of Nelson's head as he licks his lips. The movement of his tongue is slightly accentuated in the edit with some slow motion. I panned over Nelson's recumbent body, from his head to his toes, which were tapping in time to the music. Reversing the tape introduced a musical variation, something you can't do with speech.

The confined repetitive camera movement of this tape and the monumental scale of the figure really interested me. I made five more works in this vein, for gallery and theatrical projection, called *Moving Stills*. The series title refers to the emotional weight of the content, as well as the mobility of a figure constrained by

the framing of a photographic portrait. In installation, *Moving Stills I* consists of *Karaoke*, *Four Storeys* (Colleen) and *Petit Jésus* (Pierre). This is a very emotional grouping; *Karaoke* is by far the jolliest of the three. The tapes play simultaneously, usually in a row, with the soundtracks alternating – that is, two silent, one audible. The heads are as large as the space will allow.

The camera can make Hitler dance. We know that, yet we don't believe it. In *Karaoke*, the horror of a deathwatch is pure illusion. The transgression is a set-up, which turns on the spectator when the camera gets down to the feet. Nelson is not dead! He is tapping his toes! Then we go back to the grizzled face, and the deathwatch starts over, to a happy tune.

MH: Could you describe the circumstances that led you to make *Petit Jésus* (3:02 min, 1999)? What is the text the man recites? It's incredible: he delivers it with such eloquence and feeling, in a single take, even pausing at 'the right moment' to break down and cry. Why are you looking at him in such an extreme close-up, filling the frame with his face?

DC: Pierre showed me a poem he'd written in jail. There were two versions, the original in French, the other translated by Pierre into English. He liked to recite them over music from the movie *Once Upon a Time in the West*. We taped both language versions over the course of one afternoon in his apartment; only the French version worked. Pierre knew the poems pretty well by heart, but needed some prompting. I fastened the poems to his bedside table and he referred to them by the dimmed light from the camera. This work was conceived within a series of portraits entitled *Moving Stills*. All of these works are extreme close-ups.

MH: Pierre looks very intoxicated while singing his beautiful song – absolutely caught up in the emotion of it, but also terribly alone. Was he drinking because he was always drinking? Or perhaps he was nervous, or unsure of how he would appear?

DC: At that time in his life, Pierre was using alcohol for all kinds of reasons – he speaks of 'solace' in *After Brenda*. For his recitation in *Petit Jésus*, he felt he needed to drink to get into the mood, like Rimbaud, Burroughs, Coleridge, et al.; he wanted a drug to disorder his brain. He was not nervous about his performance or appearance on-camera. He had seen *After Brenda*, so he knew what he looked like on-camera in high emotion and weeping. This was the effect we sought on that long winter afternoon.

MH: In the description of *A Short Lesson* (1:18 min, 2000), you write, 'The euphoria of genius and why we try to make pictures.' Could you elaborate?

DC: Marty Corbin tells a story about James Agee's genius and alcoholism, which reminded me of Robert Lowell's line in the poem 'The Drinker' – 'no voice outsings the serpent's flawed, euphoric hiss.' This is one part of the lesson; the other is borrowed from the butler's speech in Preston Sturges's *Sullivan's Travels*, as he comments on Sullivan's desire to make a socially concerned film, dismissing it as a conceit of the privileged.

MH: Do you feel your moviemaking is a conceit of the privileged? Or their viewing?

DC: As you've said yourself, it's rare that our films will be seen outside the artists' circle, shown to a more general audience. So the butler is right: socially concerned films may address unjust conditions, but they do not alter them directly and predictably. What they sometimes do is make the privileged more aware of their privileges. This information can be used in two ways: to justify more gated communities and/or to redistribute wealth.

MH: Could you talk about how you made *Wrap* (3:03 min, 2000), and how you structured this single headshot that runs in and out of sync.

DC: *Wrap* is a gift from an early video card that promised more than it delivered. The card claimed it could capture a video stream. It would try, and then screw up as the card and computer overloaded and finally crashed. The decay path was mesmerizing. The visuals would disappear completely into white screen, but the audio stubbornly faltered along in swan song. I saved the sound track and then redid the visuals on a better system sometime later. The repetition represents the layers of storytelling, building to the reflexive climax when I suggest we bring in more light for another take.

MH: Could you recount *Wrap*'s story and what compelled you to tape it? It sounds like a fragment from a much larger narrative: how did he end up in jail, what were the conditions like, how did he get involved in this revolt? Did you ever want to tell this larger story? Why stick to this moment instead?

DC: The story Gordie tells is about an incident in prison when he tries to stand up to a new bullying inmate and gets stabbed. It is a fragment: I like the tape's compactness. These issues – violence and racism in prisons – are regularly addressed by inmate advocates, who have myriad examples. This condensed version seemed effective to me because Gordie does not come off a hero, just a guy who wants to get through his sentence as peacefully as possible and, especially, without being killed. The sense of an inner community in the prison comes through clearly: 'the

guards must have seen something.' It's fascinating, because on the outside we think of prison experience as constant surveillance. Here is a case of acute vulnerability because the guards weren't watching. Why was Gordie in prison? He had done the thing drug dealers aren't supposed to do: he had gotten into his own product and lost control of his business, with the usual episodes of assault, concealed weapons and so forth. Because the viewers don't know this, they don't try Gordie twice. They just listen to his account. The distortions and repetitions reinstate the surveillance, turning Gordie into a fish in a fishbowl. The audience sees him and hears him through a breakdown in the technical process that mirrors breakdowns in the social and judicial systems.

MH: Much of *Culture* (17:04 min, 2002) finds you rooting around in Nelson Coombs' apartment, searching through moulding food and mementoes for a chequebook. What is the relation between you and Nelson Coombs, who is glimpsed briefly, and movingly, in the hospital before his death, and then later, as a fragment of a hand, unwriting his name? Why did you name this piece *Culture*? At one point you find a stack of photographs in a drawer – did you take these pictures?

DC: I met Nelson on the street in 1983 when I was working on *Reality and Motive in Documentary Photography*. He was pulling a child's wagon full of tomatoes, very pleased with the deal he'd gotten at the market. When I asked to photograph him in his apartment, he laughed and said okay. Nelson was then in his early 60s. He'd grown up in Newfoundland and moved west as a young man. He'd worked all over Canada. He liked a bargain and I began supplying him with pictures for his friends and covering special occasions at his place, like Christmas and birthday parties. He loved to decorate his apartment, and I got into the routine of visiting him and photographing the changes and whatever was going on. Nelson also enjoyed being photographed. He had a circle of like-minded friends. Even so, in the beginning I was shy and hesitant about shooting. I learned my lesson on the day I was visiting without a camera and watched a small, neat man in a suit open his attaché case near a window. The case was empty, except for a half-eaten pork chop covered in cling wrap. A shaft of sunlight caught the plastic, making it sparkle and glow. Time stopped; the man reached into the case and began to eat.

Nelson carried a sort of funny white magic. Joyce, his wife, and Princess, the dog, liked the camera too. Joyce was always laughing; the dog was very clever. Nelson and Joyce frequently appeared in my work, including *A Prayer for Nettie*, in which Joyce both appears and is grieved for by Nelson. They are all gone now: Princess, Joyce and Nelson. When Joyce died, Nelson made a tombstone for her on a piece of slate, and we continued to visit her grave every spring. Nelson died in 2001, about a year after I taped the episodes that you see in *Culture*. They were spectacular people and I miss them. I also regret the circumstances that surrounded Nelson's death. I feel I betrayed him by not being there at the very end. My mother always advised me to see people through and she was right. The summer Nelson died I was out of town. I had been visiting him regularly in the hospital; I was worn out, physically and mentally, and going through a period of almost being afraid to go near illness. I tried to keep it all going by phone between his people in Newfoundland and the hospital. Nelson had been sick before and he was tough. I was counting on us both recovering. All too late – I was wrong about 'time enough.'

I called the tape *Culture* because it seems to illustrate all the dictionary definitions of the word, including our propensity to archive. Most of the photographs are mine.

MH: Could you elaborate on what you mean by 'models'? Besides Nelson and his circle, how did you find these 'models'? How do you work together? Are they paid? Do they come to openings? Could you talk about how the video work is different from the photo work you did with the same people? What would a 'modelling' session look like?

DC: The community that became *Reality and Motive in Documentary Photography* was formed by my trolling the streets, reviving old social contacts, expanding the circle, mixing together the known and the unknown. I needed to find people who were photogenic, had a sense of theatre and could play to what I then wanted to make, which was the facsimile of a socio-economic community. The models were paid and they released their work on the spot. Some wanted copies of the images – that's what you see in *Culture*. It's a complicated story, because it truly is case by case. I've kept up with many people for over 20 years; I saw some people only once. I don't think many of the original models saw their images in art galleries, especially since so little of *Reality and Motive in Documentary Photography* was shown in Montreal. However, many of the models saw *The Stage*, which was a 250-image installation and book. In fact, they purchased the book for themselves and their friends.

Some of the people I photographed have continued to appear in the videos, but the dynamic is different and their roles have changed. Colin was a very small figure in my photographic work; obviously, *that* has changed. Gerry Harvey has worked with me from the beginning.

A modelling session: actually, Bruno Carrière made a film about this, entitled *A Session with Nettie*. The way I am working with Nettie on-camera is pretty typical of my approach. I worked by appointment, and would shoot a set number of rolls. The video is different because the involvement is more intense and personal on both sides. The projects are considerably longer, involving a schedule, which both sides have to keep. I start out with an idea, but developments in the lives of the people I work with, and in my own life, frequently change the direction of the project. Ironically, while the tapes involve more planning, they're much more open to accident.

MH: Could you write about your relationship with your older brother Julien and the influence he had in your artmaking?

DC: A complex question for me, which I was unable to address photographically, although Julien appeared in my pictures. My relationship with Julien is not all that my work is about, but it informs its reflexivity. This comes out in *Cut the Parrot*, and constitutes major themes in *Locke's Way* and *Voice: off*. My older brother Julien, my parents' first child, was probably brain-damaged at birth. The cause of his developmental difficulties has never fully been determined. His condition, his position in the family, and his circle of friends have a sweeping influence on his four 'normal' siblings. I'll stick to the influence on me. The fact of Julien made me extremely sensitive to the tenuousness of being normal or well; my father's strokes at the end of his life reinforced this lesson. It struck me early and often how easy it is to walk around with the most outrageous overconfidence about one's grip on things – our bodies, our thoughts, our circumstances. The effect that Julien has on others has also coloured my world view. I am frequently suspicious or cynical about people who claim to feel others' pain. At the same time, I know something about the discomfort and fear of the body and mind failing. I intend the work to be a site where people can exchange their feelings about these things, without trying to rein them in through 'correctness' or dominance. To sum up, what life with Julien has offered is an edgy sense that life is arbitrary – that arbitrariness, not continuity, is the norm. I vacillate between these feelings, in a steady state of dissonance.

MH: In *Locke's Way* (21 min, 2003), you shuttle back and forth between a typed hospital report about Julien's early years on one floor and a cache of your family photographs. You deliver a breathless live narration throughout, searching through these pictures for clues, moving between image and text. What are you searching for exactly? Why is the entire movie made in a single shot? And how have you wound up in the role of family detective – how did you come into possession of these pictures? Did you choreograph the trips up and down the stairs, the pictures you would select after each descent, and your accompanying voice-over?

DC: In *Locke's Way*, my role is as a character in my own life. Using photographs and other documents, my character is seeking confirmation of a certain person's existence and condition. The photographs I rummage through, and narrate, are inadequate, sometimes treacherously inaccurate. The clash between the facts as presented in the pictures and the memories evoked by the pictures pushes everything into a grey area of conflict between evidence and hearsay.

What is really wrong with this person? Is there anything wrong at all? He looks very normal, at least as a child. As he ages in the photographs, he begins to look more damaged. But maybe there's nothing wrong with him at all. So many people have said this and that – all confusing, all reflecting their various agendas.

The visual material for the video comes from my own archive of family photographs and documents. I brought these things home after my mother died. The video begins with a photograph I took of my mother on her deathbed. All the photographs are of my family and friends, including Julien's circle in institutions and group homes.

The video is a single shot – a record of a performance – because my character needed to be pushed to the outer limits to capture the headlong drive and immediacy of grappling with this elusive material. I planned the performance roughly, and then did it several times over the course of an afternoon, not stopping to rest. I wanted to reach a state of physical exhaustion, to sweat, breathe heavily and appear to suffer. The stairs between office (text/medical history) and basement (pictures/family memories) wore me into a frazzle. At one point, the dog grew concerned and joined in. She was very encouraging, which I rewarded by stepping on her tail. The order and shape of the thing was developed extemporaneously over several repetitions, as I forced my character (I almost said *myself*) to go faster and faster, to open up to the material. The performance-enhancing drug was adrenalin. I chose the best take.

MH: *Voice: off* (39 min, 2003) has a duet structure, moving back and forth between your examination of photos and moments related to Gerry Harvey's life and the brain damage that marked it. Over and over these photos are scrutinized to find the turning point, the moment, here in this place, this is where it must have changed. This is why it went so badly. But instead the evidence accumulates without a story to put it all together; there is no primal scene to return to, after all. You remark, 'This just goes on and on ... You can't put your finger on it, you keep moving past it.' Does the still photograph, with its hold-in-your-hand object-hood, always promise a fullness, an accounting, which it fails to deliver? You have devoted a lot of your life to making pictures – how does it make you feel as you comb through them, sorting them in different orders? Does it help you to remember, even if there are only fragments?

DC: When I began working toward this video, I was in a particularly frustrated state of mind. I was angry with the whole idea of storytelling, especially narratives designed to deliver life experience and satisfying endings. I was verging on them myself, with *if only I*, and the facts – Colleen's death so soon after she 'got her life back' – made me unhappy, and not a little bitter. Gerry's life was not going to be wrapped around a spine of brilliant tape. I'm talking here about my own method: shooting into, and around, a half-imagined scenario until five to ten minutes of great material flows into the camera, that moment when everything seems

right – reaction time, rhythm, mind, body, situation – the camera takes on a separate life, like a small, curious animal in your hand. Around that unique piece of tape, you assemble your video, sequencing, balancing, trying to build out from, or against, the rhythm with all the other pieces you've accumulated.

To that point, *Cut the Parrot* had been my most successful assault on order – an absurd Ionesco roll in the aisles, sparked by Albert's untimely demise. But this time I was too angry – part of me wanted to make an unwatchable video, while the other part, the dogged artist, kept on arranging and rearranging things until it was finished. The dark side may have carried the day. There are comedic aspects to *Voice: off*, but it withholds the permission to laugh that opened up *Cut the Parrot*.

As for the photograph, yes, it promises, beckons and teases, but finally the photograph is mute. It holds out; as you say, 'it fails to deliver.' My anti-documentary work (*Reality and Motive; The Stage*) is built on photographic phantoms. Considering what you say, it seems the spine of *Voice: off* is the non-story of photographic evidence. I think the rest of the tape picks up on photography's episodic nature.

MH: You insist on returning to a burn mark Gerry's cigarette left on a carpet six years ago, in an apartment since abandoned. Workers are busy jackhammering the premises into oblivion, so viewers can barely hear you pronounce, 'Heart attack,' as if this life has come and gone struggling against the indifference that is busy converting his rooms into something unrecognizable. Why did you go back there?

DC: The cigarette burn in the linoleum floor is a direct reference to *Cut the Parrot*, in which much was made of the mark as the site of Albert's death. It was his last cigarette burn, made when he collapsed on the floor with a lit cigarette in his hand. Over six years, I watched over it, checked on it, as new tenants moved into

Fountain

Albert's apartment. I never told anyone that it marked the site of Albert's death. It put me in mind of Robertson Davies' *Fifth Business*; I felt like the keeper of the stone. When Gerry and I started to work on *Voice: off*, we did a lot of visiting. Gerry was just recovering the use of his legs, so we drove around, looking up all our old friends. There's a section of the tape when I report on a typical outing. When we got to Albert's old apartment house and found Bea, we learned that the place was being renovated. Actually, the whole place was sinking. The jackhammer you hear is breaking up the foundation. Albert's apartment was in the basement, so the tile was doomed. Bea and I went back and shot it for the last time. I suppose I should have torn it out with my bare hands, but the documentarian prevailed over the Duchampian. The eternal conflict. It leaves me with regret.

MH: Albert's friend makes this comment about the carpet burn as you both stand watch over it: 'We not only see a burn, we see Albert with his finger clutching a cigarette, slowly burning away.' This benediction might also be offered about *Cut the Parrot* (40 min, 1996). Who makes this statement, why are the two of you there, and what does the title mean?

DC: First let me clarify the circumstances around this comment. There are two people, Jeff and Elizabeth, in the shot. They are sitting on the floor beside a bed in Albert's old apartment – now Elizabeth's – looking at a burn mark on a linoleum floor tile. The mark was left by Albert's last cigarette when he collapsed on the floor after his fatal heart attack. We are there to offer up a prayer for Albert. The mood is both sombre and goofy. A cat suddenly appears from under the bed and winds around Jeff's leg, past the ashtray and cigarette butts that have been scattered around the burn. As an improvised psalm, both characters speak the benediction and response.

The title is an artifact of a scene that did not survive the edit. As these things go, I was very attached to it: a scene of Gerry talking to a caged parrot. I sought advice about this scene. It was generally agreed that it had to go. Miserably, I blurted out, 'I'll have to cut the parrot.' The words hung in the air, somehow invested with importance. I think something similar happened when Ionesco found his title for *The Bald Soprano*. I like the title because it is insistent and somewhat brutal, refers to nothing, yet infects everything that follows with absurdity.

MH: In the first of a series of performative close-ups you deliver to camera, you say the police asked you to come and identify the body of your friend Albert Smith. At the station, you are handed two Polaroids and confirm it's Albert, but then insist on seeing the body. Why?

DC: Curiosity, dread, affection – the usual mixture of motives that draw the living to peer over the edge of a coffin. In this case, I really needed to say goodbye, which required seeing Albert in whatever state.

MH: Begun with Albert's death, *Cut the Parrot* veers sharply into the lives of Susan (who you ask to sing 'Que Sera Sera') and Gerry. Why these interrupting intervals, and how do they contribute to the gathering storm of mourning the tape presents?

DC: *Cut the Parrot* is a kind of Irish wake. The characters all knew Albert. They are speaking as people do at funerals and memorial services, which are sites of reminiscence, sentimentality, gossip and humour. Digressions and cacophony are normal, possibly just heightened because of the characters in Albert's circle and my relationship with them. The long exchange with Susan is particularly significant. The idea was to talk about Albert, a longtime friend of Susan and Jimmy, her partner. Albert had introduced me to them in 1984 and Susan ended up playing a leading part as Betty, the deluded Elvis fan in *Reality and Motive in Documentary Photography, Part 3*. In addition to modelling, the part of Betty required Susan to 'speak to Elvis,' sing his songs and improvise dialogue about her obsession with Jimmy. Working with Susan was a revelatory experience for me, very difficult at first. I was entering new territory by asking people to bring their memories and raw emotions to the work. At first I found Susan very cautious and easily upset by strangers and new situations. Until she got to know me, it was difficult to get around her haze of defences. But eventually, her empathy for Betty flooded to the surface. She became very open to the material and readily slipped into whatever fragments of Betty I asked her to consider. What made Susan's performances so affecting was her innocent desire to please. Her trust was exhilarating, but at the same time a burden. I felt I had more power than I needed. The tables turned and I became the nervous one.

This role reversal is re-enacted during our exchange in *Cut the Parrot*. I probe, I manipulate Susan, then suddenly she turns the tables, starts flirting with me, while asking pointed questions about my marriage and giving me advice. The long unbroken take and use of the camera really heighten the intimacy of the scene; Susan is looking into my face, not into the camera. By the time I made *Cut the Parrot*, I'd known Susan and Jimmy for over ten years, keeping up the relationship with irregular visits. They were part of this troupe of actors who simply accepted my presence, never caring about what I was doing. For them, and in a way for me, the pleasure and suspense of our working together was all in the moment. Susan has given me a lot. I've paid back, as best I could.

MH: There are two scenes in particular I hope you could comment on: in the first, two men sing 'What a Friend We Have in Jesus,' while you lens a crotch close-up of one of the naked singers, who is casually and persistently masturbating. In another scene, this same man (Gerry) recounts events following the death of his mother; one of her friends paid for the funeral, but when Gerry is contacted to contribute he flatly refuses. At the end of this scene, which concentrates on the speaker's mouth, you walk around his body, revealing that he's naked. Why did you stage his nudity in this way, and what is the relation between this story and the one you tell earlier about Albert's death?

DC: Gerry wasn't actually masturbating. His hand is just twitching nervously between his legs as he sits on the table. If he were dressed, you might see him as simply nervous or tapping along with the song. Of course, he's naked. The prurient confusion that this scene causes in the viewer is a good Brechtian distancer. The other singer is me. I wanted Gerry to sing something for Albert, and this was a hymn both of us had been taught as children. Neither of us is particularly religious. Gerry's story about funeral expenses seems entirely appropriate, in a skewed kind of way. It's a tale of cunning within the social welfare system in which the neighbour's foolish intervention snares her in the funeral industry and is properly punished. It goes well with Gerry's other story of power relations overturned, in which the landlord is stunned to learn that his jani-

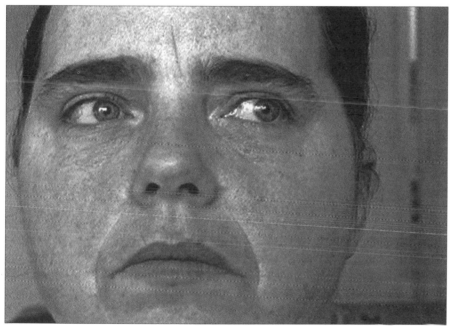

Cut the Parrot

tor has been accepting sex for rent. Gerry and Albert were old lovers and practiced pirates. Why is he laid out? He is mimicking Albert on the slab, talking from beyond the grave; he is nude because nudity is a symbol for truth.

MH: *Erratic Angel* (50 min, 1998) is a moving portrait of your friend Colin, who, as your note for the movie describes, 'looks back on a life of drug and alcohol abuse.' He is becoming involved with Colleen (never seen in this movie), who will become the subject of your *if only I* two years later, and he rails against a medical system that is based on drugs. He is alternately self-deprecating and angry, a voluble and articulate speaker, making the most of his video pulpit. The closeness between the two of you is palpable. Had you discussed the prospect of a tape for a long time before it began?

DC: I didn't plan to make a portrait of Colin; the idea grew out the difficulties of shooting something else – pretty typical of my approach. I started the tape with a Victorian comedy, *Three Men in a Boat*, as inspiration. Colin had played an anonymous part in *After Brenda*. I wanted to use him, along with Pierre and Gerry, to make a tape involving three male characters. The scene of the three of them lying under a Salvation Army blanket in bed was part of the original idea. After I'd brought them to Colin's apartment to shoot these scenes – they had not met each other before – I got a lot of static from Colin about 'bug-infested strangers' intruding on his life and screwing up his recovery program. Clearly I wasn't going to pull off the three-man thing again. But Colin had begun to take the lead as a character, so it was easy to change direction and let him take centre stage. I say 'character' because Colin, throughout the tape, was very aware that he was playing a version of himself. You can see this when he breaks out of character in the middle of a rant to politely greet a neighbour. Colin was also very aware that the video could become, as you say, a pulpit, and this idea was being reinforced by the nurses running his recovery program. Having noticed his articulate intelligence, they had decided that Colin might be a very effective advertisement for their 'groundbreaking' mental-health outreach program. Colin was a prize and they went through a period of courting him for their own movie, bringing in a professional documentary filmmaker and working Colin up to their idea in all the usual manners: they 'did lunch,' they gave him special attention. Off to the side, I was curious about all this, and wondered how Colin would digest the two opposing camps. The nurses knew I was working with Colin, but they pretty much dismissed me as an amateur, albeit a friendly one. Colin, on his own initiative, even showed their filmmaker *After Brenda*. He wasn't impressed and was critical of my shaky camera. Colin began to tease me with this professional's critique. Still, as far as Colin was concerned, we were both contenders. In the end, the official project fell through.

Perhaps Colin's sense of being a subject contributed to the polish on the film. *Erratic Angel*, as you've noted, was almost TV material. My Canadian distributor, Cinéma Libre Studio, came very close to selling it, but the TV people ultimately decided the video was 'too social.' Colin was convinced that the evil nurses had scuttled distribution from behind the scenes. Maybe he was right. The downside of spending time with Colin is that his world view begins to make very vivid sense.

MH: Your camera work in this tape is markedly different than in other work, filled with smoothly joined pans that wander from the subject, investigating moments of a room, or spinning in space, before moving back to rejoin Colin. Why these camera stylings here and nowhere else?

DC: That's a striking observation, because I've always used a Steadicam; liquid shooting has always appealed to me. Of course, it's a bit addictive, and I indulged myself in *Erratic Angel*, though it seemed very appropriate to the material at that time. It calmed the shooting – kept it patient – in the face of Colin's ferocious energy. I still like the feel of a flowing shot, and continue to accumulate this kind of material, but I've become stricter with it in the edit. The same rule applies to slow motion and zoom: tread carefully and remain parsimonious.

MH: Colleen manages to play a central character in the tape, though her presence is withheld. Was this a deliberate strategy on your part, or did you feel that would pull focus away from Colin too much?

DC: I was certainly apprehensive about introducing Colleen into the tape, except through Colin's comments. She was at that time in a psychiatric ward. I had not actually met her. Unseen, she came across as a very powerful element in Colin's life, another reference point, like the nurses. In fact, conflict with the nurses over their treatment of Colleen and their insinuations about Colin's interest are significant motors of the tape. Logistical problems aside, I felt that bringing Colleen into our exchange, on-camera, as something other than a phantom obsession, would distract Colin and take the video in another direction, one that I was not yet able to contemplate, or control.

MH: Do you feel that your videos function as social protest, advocacy work for a marginal, largely unseen underclass? Do you feel that the political efficacy of your work would be enhanced if you had larger budgets, if you were able to 'deliver your subjects' in a more polished manner, giving you access to large windows of dissemination? Would your work matter more if it were more widely seen? Do you feel that you are part of a lineage of 'social protest' image-makers (like the photographer who first took pictures of the Bowery in New York at the turn of the century, exposing decrepit housing conditions there), or that your work exists in argument with this lineage?

DC: These are four large questions – quite a mouthful. The first thing I would say is that trying to combine these functions – advocacy, propaganda and self-promotion – within the framework of an 'exposé' is what has gone terribly wrong with the lineage of Jacob Riis and other social reformers. So, starting with your last question, I would say that I have tried, first, to make people think a bit harder about the Faustian pact made by every social artist and, second, to find a way of working that matches the complexity of a social project. Now, what is that social project? That's your first question, which I would answer, yes. I do think – and I've had enough feedback to believe – that the tapes do

function in the way you describe, though I insist that the subjects do not form a cohesive group that can be labelled 'marginal, largely unseen, underclass.' In fact, I think the work has not found broad distribution for that very reason: because it represents individuals whose stories don't boil down to a statistical roux, because it features people in the complexity of their circumstances, including both positive and negative traits (people don't clean up before I drop by, and so forth). The glib line *too much information* comes to mind, because the tapes, whether by real or surreal devices, plunge deep into the day-to-day existence of the people I work with. Their statements are digressive, sometimes tedious; their situations are often irremediable, and the solutions are not obvious; within the limits of my audience and myself, I keep that stuff in. Documentarians who want to sell you on their subjects throw that stuff out or, worse, they soften its effects in ways that actually distance the audience from the subjects and from their own subject positions. If I started doing that, trying to make the work more saleable, more palatable, it would matter a lot less. I wouldn't be doing a key part of my job, which is critical practice, and I wouldn't be reflecting the lives of the people I work with, and finally, I wouldn't be inserting anything of myself into the mix. The basic formula of my work is that the material has to carry the seeds of its own critical destruction. It is not a transparent window into otherness. When people watch the tapes, I hope – I believe – that they are conscious of themselves watching, reacting, being turned off, being turned on. The strategies are twofold: I 'go too far' by seeking to provoke, even offend, defensive sensibilities; I show my hand. Actually, getting back to where we started, Riis did that too, which is why many people today find his approach 'incorrect.'

MH: Could you elaborate a little on your last remarks – what do you mean by 'showing your hand'? How did Riis show his hand and how do you do it? Why is it important for you to be in your own work? And why is it important that people are 'conscious of themselves watching'? Is your work intended to lead to social change and action? If it fails to do so, does the work fail?

DC: Damn it, Mike. I thought I answered the questions. Hard questions. We see Riis in his shots when the magnesium flash holder pokes into the frame, or when his arrangements of the figures seem mannered, or when the flash startles the posed figure – Riis had an aggressive artlessness, a smash-and-grab technique for getting his pictures. Weegee had many of the same moves. So do I, when I attach microphones to Joyce's breathing apparatus, or drape wires around Nelson's apartment, or include my off-camera directions in the tape. I never want the audience to forget that they are looking through a medium that has its own agenda. At the same time, I want people to get so engaged with what's going on that they come close to forgetting, so that a small visual or aural shock affects them deeply, makes them realize they are watching. People who are conscious of themselves watching are more implicated in what they are seeing.

Their own agency is heightened, and not as a promissory note – 'I must write a cheque to the United Way when I get home' – but in the moment. They are actually engaging with the people onscreen and, sometimes, to my exclusion. That is, they start to become advocates for people they've never met, would likely try to avoid meeting (outside a theatre), and tell me to leave Colleen or Pierre alone. To put it another way, audiences don't look at the tapes and dream of a better life for the Colleens and Pierres of this world. The tapes are too personal and provocative for that; the audiences come out fighting – sometimes they try to shoot the messenger. I think that anger can be sticky, as an *aide-mémoire*, so maybe some of the righteousness lingers and is transformed into action outside the theatre. I don't know. I don't follow people home.

Social action: what can that mean? Possibly it means that people who have gone through some kind of trauma or break-down, or who work in the social or medical services, or who are simply sick of social ills being papered over, are able to respond to the work. I'm gratified when people who self-identify as I've just described tell me that the tapes have touched something in them, or told a truth they think needs telling, or helped them in some other way. That's social action on a small scale, and if the tapes have met with any success at all, it's because they reach audiences in that way. So for the resistant, social action may be acted out in the theatre as a form of anger. For those who feel empathy – not a bad word – with the subjects, myself included, social action may be the creation of community, again, possibly just in the theatre, but hopefully further afield. I can't measure this, but I could not do this work in a vacuum, so I guess, by the standards you have set (does the work lead to social change and action?), I have to call it a success. Certainly it has changed me.

I have to question your question, because I'm not sure what you would count as a positive outcome. Earlier we exchanged thoughts about reaching larger audiences by improving the production values of the tapes. A good example of a mainstream film that reached lots of people is *Bowling for Columbine*. Many of us had a laugh at the expense of Charlton Heston; today, the NRA is bigger than ever, and there are still school shootings. Is this work a success? When a work preaches to the choir, is that a success? My conceit is that the tapes I make split the choir, disturb its complacency. That's important, unless you just want people to say *Amen*. In the end, you can only communicate with people who think, as you do, that art is important and worth discussing.

MH: In the 'traditional' fine arts, it's easier to see that artists are busy making pictures. Or trying to. In the worlds of film and video 'art,' it is harder to see what those pictures are, in part because of their ostensible subject matter. These moving pictures are always and necessarily 'about' something, even if it's an object someone laid down on a strip of emulsion and exposed to light in the darkroom. There is always a referent, a path running back into a world of 'real time.' I think you're engaged in the genre of home movies (a genre that would include Mike Snow's *Wavelength*, Joyce Wieland's *Watersark* and *Rat Life and Diet in North America* and Steve Reinke's *Afternoon*, to name only a few), but instead of the tried-and-truisms of most home manufactures (with their endless vacation shots and Christmas presents), they show what happens when that movie ends. When the dream of a certain kind of home, safety and comfort come to an end. They are produced for a largely middle-class milieu, but they don't come from that place; these are home movies of a class war that is raging largely unseen and unheard, especially in this country, this prideful multicultural paradise of Canada. Your movies insistently tell us: this is also home.

DC: I like this definition of the home movie, though I would be wary of clear-cut distinctions between the conventional home movie and mine. I'd rather say that dreams of safety and comfort are hollow across the board and should be read for that hollowness, their desperate appeal to the ideal cutting across all classes, all rebellions. As members of a media-addicted society, we need mediations that access the fear and anxiety within ourselves, so that we don't hold them against others whose failures, as Erving Goffman puts it, are more spectacular than ours. Earlier in this interview, I said that 'any system that forgets to be nervous about its own certainties is headed for deep shit.' Analysis has to be willing, rigorous, repetitive, continuous, ravenous for correction. It's easy to lose sight of that necessity under pressure – we need constant reminders. That's the point of splitting the choir. Down with pride.

Donigan Cumming's Videos

A Prayer for Nettie   33 min 1995
Cut the Parrot   40 min 1996
After Brenda   41 min 1997
Karaoke   3 min 1998
Erratic Angel   50 min 1998
Shelter   3:22 min 1999
Petit Jésus   3:02 min 1999
Trip   2:11 min 1999
Four Storeys   2:04 min 1999
Untitled (Colin's room)   4:33 min 1999
A Short Lesson   1:18 min 2000
Docu-Duster   3:03 min 2000
Wrap   3:03 min 2000
if only I   35 min 2000
My Dinner with Weegee   36:26 min 2001
Culture   17:04 min 2002
Locke's Way   21 min 2003
Cold Harbor   3 min 2003
Voice: off   39 min 2003
Controlled Disturbance   6 hours 2005 (DVD box set of 18 videos)
Fountain   22 min 2005
3   3:45 min 2007

Distributed by Video Data Bank and Vidéographe.

Donigan Cumming is a visual artist whose work integrates video, sound, text and photography. *Moving Pictures* (2005), organized by MOCCA in Toronto, surveyed Cumming's diverse and challenging practice: monumental photographs and multimedia collages, *Prologue and Epilogue*; video projections and a bookwork, *Lying Quiet*. A DVD collection of 18 video works, *Donigan Cumming: Controlled Disturbance*, is distributed by Vidéographe and Video Data Bank. www.donigancumming.com

IZABELLA PRUSKA-OLDENHOF
MEMOS OF RESISTANCE

When I first saw one of Izabella's movies, a great sense of relief washed over me. The movie was beautiful and flickering – perhaps it was *Light Magic*, which she made by laying many small items right onto the surface of the film and then giving them a pulse of illumination, a flashlight glance, so we can watch their outlines, their direct impressions. There is no lens or looking at in this making; this is a rubbing, an imprint of the thing itself, one after another. Beautiful. And it was so old-school. It might have been a movie made 20 years back, when all around me folks were busy messing with emulsion, cooking up new solutions in their kitchens, using every kind of print stock in every kind of condition, stretching out the possible ranges of colours and textures, because sometimes you don't want to use the paint as it comes right out of the can – there's a kind of blue you remember from waking up as a four-year-old and you need to have that blue right up in front of you again. That's when the factory settings won't do, the presets and push buttons aren't bringing it home, so you throw away the manuals and every notion of how it's supposed to be done, because you need to get down to something they're never going to write manuals about. It's a lonely, lo-fi world, and here is a new person taking it on, and doing it so damn well. The fact she was young meant the fringe wouldn't wither and fade, after all – there were others who would come after and carry the fire their own way.

She's young and serious and gets up onstage and tells us all about it without a whit of hesitation. She explains the moods and sensations that attached themselves to her and wouldn't let go until she spent some serious time in the dark with an array of gathered forget-me-nots waiting for their turn to be laid onto the plastic and exposed with a small light searching in the dark. The small light, she has a feel for it – she can strain her entire history through this small light and make it live again. Her material leanings would feel a lot more familiar if we were in painting land or sculpture world, but it exists in the movies too, and she's worked hard enough that it's already become a necessity. She has passed into the darkness where that childhood shade of blue is waiting once again, and this time she will be able to share it, to throw it up in front of a projector's flicker with all the conviction of her knowing and seeing and hoping. The injunction still holds: revel in your time.

IPO: I don't know how I ended up in film, because I was supposed to be a musician – I guess it happened by chance. My parents began my initiation into music when I was three or four – actually, now that I think about it, even earlier, when I was in my mother's womb. She sang every day (classical music at school during the day and popular music at night) until nearly one month before my birth. My parents told me an interesting story, although I don't know whether I should believe them, that when I was born I did not cry like other infants but made *la ... la ... la* sounds. Apparently, every time I made those sounds, the nurses in the hospital would say, 'Oh, that's the singer's daughter.' My parents were both classically trained musicians who performed popular music in Poland. During the Communist regime, you could make a decent living doing that. Popular music from the West wasn't played on the radio, so people had to listen to forbidden stations or find someone who had smuggled tapes from abroad. Bands that had access to music from the West got most of the gigs, and my parents' ingenuity in transcribing Western music ensured numerous contracts. I travelled with them when I was little, from about three to six years old. We lived in the city of Wałbrzych in Lower Silesia, a very industrial part of Poland, with over 40 coal mines in that region alone. Most of my family were either miners or worked in industries related to coal mines. But my father refused to follow the coal-trodden path of his ancestors; he wanted to be a musician.

I have a very vivid memory from when I was about six years old, roughly 1980. I remember watching news on our black-and-white television and seeing Lech Wałesa jumping up on the fence of the Gdansk Shipyard announcing the beginning of a strike and the Solidarity movement. The miners in my city struck almost at the same time, and my father said we had to flee because the situation in Poland was not going to get any better. My father tried escaping on several occasions, until he finally got a contract in Switzerland in 1982, and then he sent an invitation for my mother and me to join him. The Polish government refused to let me go with my mother because they knew we wouldn't come back. My mother decided to go without me, not realizing she would not come back, leaving pretty much everything behind. When she arrived, friends in Switzerland assured her it would be easy for me to join them; unfortunately, this did not happen, because the Swiss government did not permit any more immigration. So my parents had to emigrate again in 1985 from Switzerland to Canada. I finally joined them in 1986, four years after their departure from Poland.

Incidentally, I have met several other Polish people in Canada who share similar experiences of being separated from their parents for several years in the '80s and their parents having to immigrate several times before settling in Canada. This four-year period was an eternity in my child's mind. I was only eight when they left. I lived with my grandparents and had moved to a tiny city outside of Kraków, in Upper Silesia. This period of separation from my parents was also a pause in music, four years of silence. This is when my attention began to shift from the auditory world of my parents to the world of vision and immersion in the WWII recollections of my grandparents. During this time I focused my attention primarily on drawing. I am convinced that this visual inkling was always present in me but was pushed aside by the overwhelming presence of music in my early life. I think my uncle, an amateur painter and sculptor who delivered coal to people's homes to make a living, ignited part of my visual world. Our home was adorned with his paintings. My parents also have visual-art abilities, but never brought them to fruition. I used to ask them to draw pictures for me when I was very little. I loved watching images unfold on paper under their hands – I thought it was magical. When I arrived in Canada, I was very eager at first to get back to music. However, trying to learn English quickly prevented me from spending enough time with instruments. My parents were heartbroken when I told them I didn't want to continue.

In my third year at Ryerson University, I discovered experimental film. R. Bruce Elder came back from his sabbatical leave and I enrolled in his experimental film processes course. He showed Ed Emshwiller's dance films and also a lot of Stan Brakhage's work. This was also the time when Elder was working on his book *The Films of Stan Brakhage in the American Tradition of Ezra Pound, Gertrude Stein and Charles Olson*, and that year I also began to work for him as a research assistant on the book and as an assistant on his film *A Man Whose Life Was Full of Woe Was Surprised by Joy*. For the next two years I shared his addiction to Brakhage, and I must admit it still has not subsided. I remember watching TV and wondering when the film was going to start. Because it lacked the dynamism of Brakhage's work, it seemed like it wasn't moving! Before this I didn't even know the experimental work existed. I think this is usual, that people come across it by chance. Bruce's course was that chance or 'open sesame' for me, to use Brakhage's words.

MH: Stan Brakhage is a permanent referral service in the avant film scene, and certainly when talk turns toward movies that are 'abstract' and handmade, like yours. But I heard Stan back off the A word more than once, insisting that his movies were documentaries of the perceptual process, the inner workings of the bloodstream and cranial/eye relations in the active act of seeing. He said they embodied some very specific life experience, wrested up out of the body, where memory can be replayed not as story but as a collision of colours and shapes our kindergarten eyes insist on calling abstract. I wonder how you feel about this.

IPO: Stan Brakhage certainly figures very prominently in cinema in general, if not in the history of 20th-century art. He was able to connect art to the bigger questions of life, sex and death by creating films as documents of the lived bodily experience of their maker and therefore transcended surface issues such as politics. There have been others, notably the Surrealists, who, via their collages, tried to send into disarray and transcend the linearity of time. But the artists who made the biggest impact on Brakhage were poets, as Elder asserts in *The Films of Stan Brakhage in the American Tradition of Ezra Pound, Gertrude Stein and Charles Olson*. And chief amongst his poetic influences was Gertrude Stein, whose poetry embodied the notion of the 'continuous present.' Perhaps the most telling example of this idea of time, and the one Brakhage often

used during his guest lectures and artist talks in Toronto, was Stein's 'Rose' poem: 'A rose is a rose is a rose ... ' and so it goes in a circular form. When reading this poem out loud in its circular formation, without any punctuation separating the words, the resonance of the words might throw the reader into a state akin to a creative trance where time ceases to exist, allowing your senses and mind to wander, transforming sounds into new constellations and meanings. For example: rising, resurrection, arousal, hence birth, sex and death, if you slur the words just so slightly. This kind of raw experience that lies concealed deep within the body and the unconscious, which is perpetually kept in check by the conscious ordering of the mind, was exactly what Brakhage was trying to capture and inscribe in his work. Furthermore, this experience is also an opening or a bridge toward something bigger than just us, something that at once grounds us in our mortal, carnal being but at the same time connects us with the 'Other.'

All of us experienced this raw thinking and being when we were infants, because our feeble minds could not put our senses and drives into order. Preschool children still retain this kind of freedom, and it is always interesting to show them films that induce visceral experience. Interestingly, they, moreso than adults, respond to these works in an open manner. In this sense, Brakhage's films are not abstract but are the true documents of our lived being in the world. This reminds me of the time I showed one of my photogram films, *Light Magic*, to my friend's little daughter, who was two at the time. She connected immediately with the work, and right after the film finished she insisted on seeing it again. I rewound the film and played it again and again. I don't think anyone has ever responded so genuinely to my work as little Luka did. It is interesting to consider why we so seldom open ourselves to aesthetic experience and feel unembarrassed to express our genuine feelings and opinions, be they good or bad. But this brings us to another place, that of

Song of the Firefly

foreclosure from ourselves and from 'other(s),' the level of reason and social codes.

In terms of my own films, I find them extremely difficult to talk about in part because I'm still in the very beginning stages of my work as a filmmaker. To keep on making, I had to give up this struggle to understand. Sometimes I pick up hints from my films, which seem to surface involuntarily. It is like trying to get a glimpse of yourself after someone has asked you to look at yourself, but not being able to find any reflective surfaces.

On a purely formal level, my images are unlike the painted films of Stan Brakhage, yet I would argue that, like Brakhage's films, they are about something more than the sheer representational content of the film. Content is only a vehicle or a door onto something other, the experience of life itself. However, Brakhage's painted films right away throw you into the pulse of raw experience, while my films don't. I have been trying to figure out for some time why I have not decided to fully part with representation.

The closest I have been able to arrive at as an answer was in *Image and Identity*, another one of Bruce Elder's monumental writings. In this book he goes back to the history of early Canadian settlers from Europe who were not used to the rigid climate. Struck with the horrifying vastness of this country – so unlike what they were used to in Europe – they tried to tame it by clearing the dense and impenetrable forests and slicing up the land with their farms. This idea of taming the vastness of space has migrated onto the canvases and celluloid of our Canadian artists, who insist on holding on to representational forms in their work and filling space with these forms. Consider, for example, painters such as Tom Thomson, Paterson Ewen and Jack Chambers, but most importantly filmmakers such as Michael Snow, Ellie Epp, Bruce Elder, Richard Kerr, Gariné Torossian, Carl Brown, and the list goes on: their works always keeps one foot in representation while the other slips into abstraction. Likewise, my own films have this playful tendency of back and forth, or ebb and tide, of representation and abstraction. This shifting momentarily loosens the grip of your conscious ordering of the world, allowing body and mind to unite.

Perhaps another piece to my own puzzle is my Polish roots. After all, I lived in that country until I was 12 years old, and I would not be surprised if it had inscribed itself into me by then. Poland has a very interesting history of abstract art. Władysław Strzeminski and Katarzyna Korbo introduced Poland to Constructivist art, including Rayonism, which they both studied in Russia with Constructivists such as Wassily Kandinsky and Kasimir Malevich. I discovered very recently the tradition of Polish abstract art and avant-garde filmmaking, which was forbidden during Communist times. Two years ago Bruce Elder introduced me to Wiesław Michalak. Wiesław and I have spent many hours talking about Polish art and filmmaking, and I was amazed that all this time I was making films that echoed Polish avant-garde films, in particular their preoccupation with light and abstraction. Interestingly, in 1930 Franciszka and Stefan Themerson made a

photogram film titled *Apteka* (*Pharmacy* in English). The subject matter of this film, just like in my own photogram films, was light. Four years after I began doing my first photogram tests, I found out that my fellow countrymen also made such films 70 years prior. One really has to wonder how these old and new roots work on the individual who becomes a vehicle for the manifestation of forces beyond conscious apprehension.

MH: In the catalogue for Canadian Filmmakers Distribution Centre, you write that *Light Magic* (3 min, 2001) was one of the 15 films commissioned by the Liaison of Independent Filmmakers of Toronto (a local film co-operative that makes equipment accessible to members at discount rates) on the occasion of its 20th anniversary. The subject and the aesthetic of this film are a response to the theme Self and Celluloid: The Future. Why are you interested in the materiality of film? Many artists have worked on the material signifier – do you feel there is much more to uncover?

IPO: I created it in part to ease my corporeal disengagement. After working with 20-layered, frame-by-frame visual collages on the computer for *Vibrant Marvels* (22 min, 2000), the constant sitting created a void in me, and a necessity to pursue another kind of making where I would be fully engaged. Sebastjan Henrickson runs a small boutique lab for artists called Niagara Custom Lab, and we work together on all my films. I approached Sebastjan and said I wanted to do some tests with photograms. He gave me some print stock, which I brought into my bathroom, and I gathered glass objects, feathers and some plants, first holding them up to light to see if they were slightly transparent or translucent. Then I would place them on the film, emulsion side up, and flash it with my still-camera flash. To my surprise, these tests worked out and I decided I wanted to work that way. There's an intimate contact between film emulsion and object, while the light is the intermediary in the copulation and birthing process of the photogram image. Our eyes usually look only at the surface – we don't have time to pick up an object and look through it – and we seldom reflect on the beauty of something as insignificant as a fly's wing. In our world there is less and less engagement of our bodies with the physicality and materiality of our world. My husband's cousin is a furniture maker, and the imprint of his body is left on the shape of everything he makes. As technology advances, our bodies become more disengaged. Those who champion the idea of the post-human world ask: why do we need these deteriorating bodies? The minute we come into this life, we're dying, and yet there's something so marvellous about our bodies. There's a false utopian promise that our skin colour and gender can be left behind if we lose our material bodies, but how is this helping? You want to create a space where people have compassion and accept you for who you are. What grounds us in humanity are our bodily experiences, the experience of bodily pleasure as well as physical pain, and understanding what that pleasure or pain might feel like in another person, i.e., being able to empathize, care and love the other. When we get rid of our bodies, how are we going to be empathetic human beings?

Just as I weave my body into my films, the presence of my body will be communicated and experienced by the audience by means of the same 'sense' that initially guided me and gave rise to this work (its form and content). At the same time, the body of the audience is prompted toward new connections that will join with their previous experiences. One can also think of it in terms of energy: an artist takes energy from the world, which is subsequently discharged into the work and eventually transferred to the audience. Charles Olson and Andrzej Pawlowski viewed art in this way, as a transfer of energy. One thing is certain: the body is always present – we can't just leave it behind, nor would we want to.

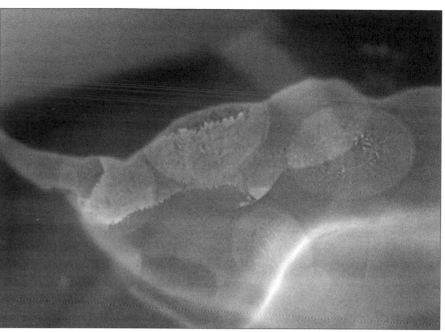

fugitive l(i)ght

MH: How did you structure the film?

IPO: When I go into a dark space, I can barely see anything, and I work with my hands, by touch, arranging these things blindly, giving myself and this project to chance. The initial rhythm is made by touching. When the footage came back, I saw the underlying rhythms that I could respond to and reshape. Making a film while being practically blind, I guess this must be every filmmaker's nightmare – how can I make a film without being able to see? Incredible things happen when you abandon intention.

I see the recent closures of commercial labs as a possibly positive turn for experimental filmmakers. I'm shocked that I am saying this, but one has to try to make the best of even the most dire situations. These closures and the film industry's dispensing of equipment is a sign that commercial cinema is moving away from celluloid, thus leaving it as an open territory to explore and reinvent by those eager filmmakers who will breathe new life into it. I think and hope there will always be labs around, and filmmakers have been doing a good job using their kitchens and bathrooms. One day perhaps we won't be able to make prints, but then it will be more like painting – each film will be an original.

MH: *fugitive l(i)ght* (9 min, 2005) is a movie based on American Loïe Fuller. Can you talk about how you intersected with her, and how her work and interests have informed your own? Do you feel it is always necessary to go back in order to go on?

IPO: Loïe Fuller was a Chicago-based actress often cast in comedic roles, who wanted to be a dancer. However, in the 1890s this required her to be graceful and slender; her biographers described her as chubby. In 1892 she appeared in New York in a play called *Doctor Quack*. In one of the scenes she enacted the

experience of undergoing a hypnotic trance induced by Dr. Quack. This is when she performed for the first time her famous serpentine dance in a voluminous silk skirt with coloured incandescent lights spilling all over her undulating skirt. Fuller was the first person to introduce coloured electric light onstage. She also often worked with large crews of light technicians who projected colour lights and various animal and plant shapes on her dresses. Her performance in *Doctor Quack* transformed her into an overnight sensation, and her serpentine dance was immediately replicated by others, not only in the United States but also in Europe. One year after her New York performance, she travelled to the Folies Bergère in Paris where she discovered that someone had already been doing her dance. Fuller's whole life and career as the inventor of the serpentine dance is woven with her numerous imitators, who would even take on parts of her name. This is why the artists who adored her and deemed her their muse, namely the Symbolists, Italian Futurists and Art Nouveau artists, named her La Loïe (the Loïe).

Her dance anticipated the abstract or absolute cinema that arrived 30 years later; the origins of films by Walter Ruttman, Hans Richter and Oskar Fischinger were already being experienced by Parisian audiences onstage at the Folies Bergère in the 1890s. Fuller continued to develop the design of her costume, as well as the stage and light designs, after her initial serpentine performance in New York. She also obtained patents for everything she developed for her dance. Her skirt was transformed into a dress and expanded to hundreds of yards in length, to which she attached long wands that acted as extensions of her limbs which permitted her to move larger volumes of fabric. Furthermore, she developed a glass platform on which she danced. Underneath this platform were housed coloured lights, illuminating her from below, while mirrors behind her further dispersed her image. She became quite skilled in her dance and was able to create shapes that suggested images of flowers, snakes, butterflies, birds, etc. Symbolist poets loved the suggestive quality of her performances. Fuller took the skirt dance, then popular on the burlesque stage, where women unveiled their bodies to the male spectators, and subverted this dance by making the female body disappear into a voluminous dress and transform into other shapes. Her performances were about the flux or tension of the transformation of the human body – on the one hand, into sheer pulses of energy when dispersing her body and dematerializing into rays of light, and on another, into constantly morphing representational shapes (snakes, butterflies, lilies, pansies, bats).

Fuller, along with the Symbolist poets such as Arthur Rimbaud and Stéphane Mallarmé, were the pre-postmodernists, who already in the late-19th century, challenged the unity of the subject and authority of the author. Therefore, it was no surprise that Loïe Fuller figured as an enigmatic and somewhat paradoxical persona on- and offstage. Her life bore a significant resemblance to her performances in its quality of (dis)appearance, because much of her work has been obscured by imitators like Annabelle Whitford Moore and Chrissie Sheridan, who were filmed by Thomas Edison. Most of the surviving film documentation of serpentine dances show Annabelle. Apparently, Edison approached Fuller and asked if she would like to be filmed. She agreed. Edison thought that he filmed her, but Fuller later claimed in one of her interviews that she sent her sister instead, although she didn't have a sister. Some scholars believe another imitator by the name of Chrissie Sheridan is actually Loïe Fuller. There is a mystery as to whether we actually ever see Fuller on film. Kathy Elder was terrific in helping me trace Fuller's archives to the New York Public Library. This archive had a film sequence shot in 1908 of Fuller's performance in *Salome*, but the woman who performs the dance doesn't look like her at all. This is quite fascinating and frustrating at the same time. One of the dancers in my film is supposed to be Chrissie Sheridan, although I think this is actually Loïe Fuller. But who knows?

MH: *her carnal longings* (8:30 min, 2003) begins with what looks like close-ups of skin, and a cascading colony of abstract fronds – as if the skin were regarding itself, taking apart the eye-centred stability of perception and remaking the entire body as an aperture of sight. It is a love story of him and her related through bodily close-ups, but they are bodies seen in isolation, as someone might see their lover sleeping. The film is in hyper-motion with its colliding frames and quick editing, in stark contrast to bodies that are no longer moving. Why this division? It's as if the act of seeing paralyzes the body, rendering it incapable of movement. Or is it the act of filmmaking that paralyzes the body?

IPO: This was my MA thesis project. It is a love film, not only between me and my partner, but also me and my friends. I didn't ask these bodies to move – they posed and then I set them into motion using emulsion lifts to make the surface dance. I was thinking about film as a body, the emulsion as a skin. I contacted Brett Kashmere, who was working on Richard Kerr's *Collage d'Hollywood*, a film made using emulsion lifts. I asked him how to do it and he sent me a wonderful list of recipes. I tried various chemicals, but I don't like using them because I used to work as a lab technician and became oversensitized to chemicals. But one of the methods involved boiling film. I was using polyester stock so the sprockets don't break; the only thing that moves is the emulsion. I bought a large stainless-steel cooking pot and stirred in all the bodies and cooked them like meat. There was something very cannibalistic about this process. I thought, 'These are all the people I love, what am I doing?' I cooked it for about 15 minutes and pulled out the bodies and started playing with the

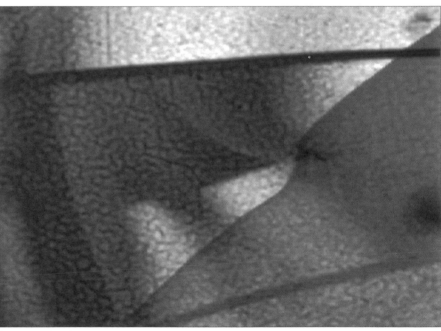
her carnal longings

flesh of film by moving it with my fingers. Pushing and pulling at the emulsion, slowly creating a wrinkled flesh. This film is very much about dissolving the differences between bodies. It is about reconnecting with our primal love, the love between child and mother, or child and world. I call and she comes, her nipple is in my mouth and I'm filled with milk. You see the head of a penis turning into a nipple, labia morph into eyelids. The human body carries echoes of itself, which I pursued, giving into this plastic play of editing without intentionally thinking about it.

Some people felt quite uncomfortable after seeing this film, in particular people related or emotionally connected to the bodies in the film. This is important to me. Making people uncomfortable is good, as it brings us back in to ourselves, the discomfort prompts questions. I'm becoming more and more interested in that.

MH: It's also a utopian gesture, remaking a community of friends through the emulsion.

IPO: Absolutely. It is a gesture that points toward the very foundation of our human being, our flesh and its vulnerability as a means of communion, communication and community with(in) the world we inhabit. In this film I'm working with the perishability of human flesh and film, the questioning of human flesh (the post-human) and the continued and threatened existence of film; these recent questions are inseparable.

MH: Do you think fringe movies could reach a much wider audience?

IPO: Absolutely. But when people are inundated with popular conventional forms, experimental filmmakers are disregarded, especially those who embrace the aesthetic of the amateur, because the general public has been fed the beautiful, clean image. They regard experimental film as beginners' cinema, produced by those who can't make it in the commercial world. I doubt that 'amateur' filmmakers – lovers of filmmaking in Brakhage's terms – ever wanted their films to be placed next to commercially consumable blockbusters, far from it. What concerns me more is that experimental cinema still doesn't have a clear place in the fine arts either, at least not in Canadian public museums or galleries. Neither the National Gallery of Canada nor the Art Gallery of Ontario collects or even screens experimental films on a regular basis. This is very sad and disappointing, especially for someone who is relatively new to this art form. I wonder if these and other fine-art institutions will attempt to preserve the memory of whatever will be left of the celluloid-based Canadian heritage several decades from now?

It is therefore certainly not a big surprise to me that the general public doesn't know what to do with experimental film. On the other hand, the public does not seem to have much patience or interest in fine art either. I wonder if this doesn't begin with an educational system that places little value on art. This might be endemic to the capitalist system in general, which dispenses with everything it cannot exchange and make profit on. Therefore the public, with its daily diet of consumable entertainment, cannot digest experimental cinema and spits it out. On another hand, I don't know if experimental film is meant to be digested. I think reaction and jolts are what it is after.

MH: Would you make your work available on the internet?

IPO: The Canadian public is paying for these works, so it shouldn't be denied access. Once film or any other artwork is completed, it no longer belongs to the maker but to the world. Having it on the internet means it's not put away or hidden somewhere. It is obviously not an ideal form, and issues of translation from one medium to another are always a problem, just as they are with languages. Who knows, there might be some poten-

tially incredible filmmakers out there, but because they've never been exposed to it they're just spinning their wheels. At the same time I'm very conscious of the medium I work with. Part of this comes from working with Mike Snow. He is sensitive to how each medium wants to manifest itself and how it shapes the artwork. I would obviously want to emphasize that celluloid-based films need to be experienced as celluloid projected on a screen. *Song of the Firefly* doesn't translate well to video because it needs a dark space and a projector that lights up your eyes, but I would not deny anybody the viewing of this work because they had no access to a 35mm projector. Even I don't have access to a 35mm projector and have seen it projected as a film only a handful of times.

MH: Over and over again you raise the spectre of the body, the ghost of the body, which is waiting before light ever strikes emulsion, to be resurrected, to be borne, not only on this plastic material, but also in that off-screen space that is a maker's living before the first camera is ever wound. A friend of mine has written two out of a projected three-book serial, the only three books, he insists, he will ever write. When I asked him about the third one, he says he is waiting until he has enough experience before beginning. He says he is interested only in doing things, and meeting people, that will make him wait. Waiting is the most important thing now; it will unburden him of the habits of his personality, his imagined needs, and will deliver him, or so he is convinced, to his body.

Isn't waiting always a central concern of the body, which is forever changing speeds? The quick hurt of a burn, for instance, is very different from the way a chill can enter the body, slowly, over the course of a morning, or the way a long illness can waste you over years. Some pleasures can arrive too quickly and dull too easily, while others take more time. How does this changing time of the body relate to the medium of film, which is always forward-moving, hurtling into the projector gate 24 frames per second, driving toward its own end? You write about the visceral experience of making a movie, and how there is pleasure attached to the pains of becoming a body, but in the cinema, bodies no longer exist. We watch in the dark, inert, bodiless; we are a life support for eyes and ears, that's all. How to reconcile this notion of the body in film's exhibition with the re-embodiment you are conjuring with your work? Or is the body only a spectre whose presence is endlessly deferred, only appearing 'later,' 'afterwards,' when all the lights are closed and everyone has gone home?

IPO: I am very sorry my responses are taking so long, and I really feel bad about making you wait. You are very kind to put such a positive spin on waiting for my responses, but waiting is for the most part not a very pleasant process. When I was very young, I experienced the ambivalent emotions that are inseparable from the process of waiting: the torment of being separated from my parents and waiting to see them again, and then the pain of being separated from my grandparents to be happily reunited with my parents, and again painfully waiting to see my grandparents, etc. Every life begins with waiting, which at first is pleasurable but soon enough becomes unbearable as we painfully force ourselves into this world. Only when our life ceases does waiting end.

I don't see our bodies – or waiting, for that matter – as 'always' aiming forward at the future. For example, we carry within us our past as well; some of it is concealed from us in the unconscious and some makes its way to our consciousness, most often when we dream. For many people, waiting is also a path toward an eventual unveiling or the backward movement toward their past. When we dream, time ceases to be ordered according to past, present and future, giving us a profound feeling of the present. I already remarked on Gertrude Stein's writing a 'continuous present' and how Stan Brakhage also tried to engender this sense of time with his films. One could argue, therefore, that experimental cinema, just like some avant-garde poetry, through its disintegration of narrative's temporal progression, has the unique ability to disengage the forward thrust toward the end, despite the fact that the projector motor runs forward and the film strip will eventually end, unless it is a loop. Experimental cinema, just like dreams, rely on devices that are similar to poetry's metaphor and metonymy, which permit the viewer a more dynamic and embodied engagement by connecting ideas and experiences while continuously shuffling between the past and present. Experimental cinema and psychoanalysis both play in the dark and refuse to follow the illuminated path. Freud used to call psychoanalysis an 'imaginary walk,' drawing our attention toward the (in)visible sides of our being.

A quote from Stan Brakhage's *Metaphors on Vision* might be helpful here. He writes: 'The artist is one who leaps that fence at night, scatters his seeds among the cabbages, hybrid seeds inspired by both the garden and wit's-end forest where only fools and madmen wander ... Realize the garden as you will – the growing is mostly underground. Whatever daily care you may give it – all is planted only by moonlight. However you remember it – everything in it originates elsewhere.'

Now this idea of 'elsewhere' I think is of tremendous importance. It helps to dislocate the mastery of the maker over the work by pointing out that the seeds of these creations have their origin 'elsewhere,' i.e., not in the conscious intent of the maker but in the 'wit's-end forest,' the unconscious past working on the maker and directing her/him like an 'instrument.' The humbling experience of being an 'instrument' depends on the ability of the maker to be attuned to one's bodily prompting and intuition, in order to follow the path and create the work. Often when I am in the middle of collecting materials for a film, I ask myself where is this going, and yet it always leads toward somewhere, a revelation. A part of me is revealed to me.

I think it is important to address the current and rather trendy rhetoric of disembodied audience, or as you stated, 'the life support for eyes and ears.' All one has to do is show aggression or a sexual act and the audience becomes very embodied – some might become aroused or hit the streets with revolution.

This happens quite often: all you have to do is show Brakhage's *The Act of Seeing with One's Own Eyes*, or Georges Franju's *Blood of the Beast*, or Carolee Schneemann's *Fuses*, or Bruce Elder's *Crack, Brutal Grief*. However, works like this are unfortunately not seen often enough, and I must agree that the audience is usually inundated with content that certainly reduces the amount of whole-body participation. It is interesting to observe that several filmmakers – for example, Carolee Schneemann and Bruce Elder – have continued to present the human body onscreen and they have taken quite a bit of heat from the public for it. I fully agree with them that it is very important, especially today, to show people our humanness and everything that comes with it, the good and the bad. My films have never really gone as far as theirs to push the buttons of public taste. But one of my films did leave some people with rather mixed feelings: *Vibrant Marvels*. This was the hybrid film I completed in 2000, and it incorporated various images of nude and clothed bodies, dancing, moving, swimming, etc. Perhaps the body that irked people most was the nude body of my pregnant friend. I received lots of criticism for this film because people just did not know what to do with this strange body-dance-lyrical film, they did not know how or where to slot it. Too many bodies, and not the right bodies perhaps, or not presented in the 'appropriate' way or context. It was certainly a tremendous learning experience for me, one that unfortunately did not start on a happy note, but I also had supporters who encouraged me to continue. So here I am.

Back to the disembodied views on the audience, I take the position of phenomenologists such as Maurice Merleau-Ponty that we are not just eyes and ears. As long as we have bodies, they will always work as a 'communion' of senses, motor functions, emotions and cognition (memories and conscious thought). But this problem with disembodiment certainly extends toward the whole technologically optimistic Western culture and its faith in progress. I have been quite amazed that artists like Stelarc have such a tremendous sway and popularity in both art and academic circles. After all, what this guy is really saying is get rid of this fleshy mess because all you really need is your mind – the rest is unimportant and, in fact, curtails its possibilities by being enslaved by flesh and limited by its longevity.

MH: Yes, but the body as imagined by the cinema remains a picture, and don't we become pictures while watching? Don't our bodies become moments in a montage of the capitalist decoupage that isolates moments of the body for resale (toothpaste is for teeth, shampoo for hair ...)? To further the illusion of cinema's shuddering continuities, the body is cropped and cropped again, cut away into moments. Vito Acconci, a recent in-town visitor, said vision was about mastery and control, and what site more readily reproduces this than the cinema? He maintained that change in his life has been made possible by the close-up, when vision is blurred and indistinct, when the rest of his senses re-engage, when he is no longer an objective onlooker but part of

my I's

I completely agree that there is a tremendous difference between the mainstream cinema and fringe or experimental cinema in the way they depict the human body and how they employ or explore vision. One might also wonder whether this difference is dependent on distance, which in turn guarantees the difference or otherness, if you will. The close-up of Acconci, or numerous other media artists, is precisely about annihilating that distance where our eyes are permitted to dwell on the object in the distance for a long time, wanting to possess. The close-up also disarms the mastery and control of vision that always needs a slave, the object that guarantees its position of mastery. Carolee Schneemann, with her *Fuses* (1964), diffused that distance with another form of vision, the desirous feminine gaze, which does not separate subject from object, or the spectator from the experience on the screen, but instead fuses and confuses lovers in the act of lovemaking, and the spectator in the emotion of the two lovers and their bodies and the spectator's body. In other words, it refuses distance and difference, and through her use of extreme close-ups, out-of-focus shots, scratched-up, painted and baked footage, she attains the refuse, the mess, and not the 'ideal' of the dominant capitalist mode of seeing.

This form of embodied seeing, whether it is attained by using close-ups, single-frame animation, performative camera work or surrealist montage, has punctuated the history of experimental cinema. So has the body, and not always in its beautiful form but in the sick, the traumatized, the dismembered, the ugly, the underbelly of society. Most importantly, the body in experimental film is always presented as a real lived body in direct opposition to the 'ideal' of the capitalist system, which is a non-body or no-body. Rather than thinking of the experimental cinema, the underground or fringe as 'asocial' in terms of being the circle of its exclusive (elitist, specialized) members, one should think of it as 'asocial' in terms of resistance to the current 'social' system and what is considered as the 'ideal' in this system's capitalist economy. These 'elitists,' these 'specialists,' are not closing their circle to others but instead call out to them with their works: *Come and join in.* Now, is that 'elitist' or 'specialist' or just another tag concocted by the system itself and put around the necks of revolutionary people to act as bait and distract others from joining in? These are rather common camouflage tactics of the machine. The social function of these 'transfers of energy' (from world to artist, and from artist to artwork, and artwork to spectator, and to the world again) is precisely 'asocial,' the resistance to the dominance of the system by jolting people with surges of energy that will awaken the repressed areas of our existence (the repressed memories that reside in our unconscious, the memories repressed by the 'social' order) while simultaneously redirecting

the mess, the front line of his life. My question is about the difference between fringe and mainstream cinema in its depictions of the body. I believe their common theatrical frame renders both experiences equivalent, though the social body is articulated in mass cinema as a unified chorus, and in the fringe as a diaspora of opinion. (Convulsive) beauty in the eyes of beholders. But the fringe is a notoriously asocial space, geek kingdom, home to specialists and fellow practitioners, elitist to the core. What, then, is the social function of these 'transfers of energy'? How can new combinations of pictures and sounds affect the way we interact with one another?

IPO: I have to disagree with your statement about our lived bodies becoming picture elements that are sucked into the centrifuge of the capitalist economy while watching a movie. If that were the case, there would be no space for resistance. I think that this disembodied body-in-fragments, without agency, is the 'ideal' of the capitalist program, but one that fortunately has not been fully realized, thanks to the efforts of many revolutionaries, students, disadvantaged workers, artists and theorists who have resisted it for over a century now and continuously aim to ground people in the embodied human dimension of our existence that comes with both pleasure and pain.

I agree that cinema is a powerful place where the body of the spectator can momentarily disarm and open itself to the world of fantasy, but it can also be a tremendous place of mobilization of the masses that might potentially lead to revolutionary manoeuvres. I attended a cinema like that when I was a little girl in Poland. This cinema was in a church where they showed us movies about Jesus Christ or *Quo Vadis* by Henryk Sienkiewicz. Our identification with the victims of injustice onscreen, and in particular the son of God, was very effective in mobilizing the masses to overthrow the regime.

people's attention to their bodies and those around them. Because ultimately, if revolt is to happen, then somebody will have to start it, and you will need movements of many somebodies to accomplish it. Therefore, if we choose the 'asocial' as the space of resistance, it is because it is the only place that permits us the free play of new combinations or constellations of images and sounds, unregulated by the social ordering of the system. Only then can we have the possibility of redirecting people's attention toward one another in empathy, love and understanding rather than the indifference and competitive strife of alienated people in the competitive market. This 'transfer of energy' is like a thread that runs through our bodies and binds us with one another and the world we inhabit. Without this energy, there is no movement, there can be no revolt and therefore no resistance.

Izabella Pruska-Oldenhof is a Toronto-based experimental filmmaker. She is a graduate of the Media Arts Program at Ryerson University (BAA) and the Communication and Culture Program at York University (MA). Her works have been screened internationally and have received several awards. Izabella is the co-founder and an active member of the successful Toronto-based experimental-film collective the Loop Collective. She is currently completing her Ph.D. in Communication and Culture at York University while teaching at the School of Image Arts at Ryerson University.

Izabella Pruska-Oldenhof's Media Work

Homoiomereia   15 min 1996
my I's   10 min 1997
Vibrant Marvels   22 min 2000
Light Magic   3 min 2001
Song of the Firefly   4:30 min 2002
Body of Water/Body of Light   4 min 2003
Scintillating Flesh   4:30 min 2003
her carnal longings   8:30 min 2003
sea-ing   1 min 2004
fugitive l(i)ght   9 min 2005
Pulsions   9:30 min 2007
Echo   9 min 2007
The Garden of Earthly Delights   8 min 2008

Distributed by Canadian Filmmakers Distribution Centre and, in France, Collectif Jeune Cinéma.

MIDI ONODERA
CAMERA OBSCURA FOR DREAMS

I met her at the Funnel, Toronto's avant hope and movie theatre and sometime equipment co-op. She was in charge of the gear, and was the first person I knew whose hair colour came from a bottle, the first woman I knew who was romantically attached to another woman – all those facts arrived together somehow (yes, it was a long time ago). Because I tried as hard as possible to imagine that no one else existed in the world, we didn't speak much, but she was a reliable presence, at once equipment geek and hipster, adding a rare edge of glam to a dowdy east-end haunt notable for its mirthless, uptight gatherings. So it was doubly remarkable when she left behind the narrow-gauge formalisms that were the unspoken code for correct practice and produced *Ten Cents a Dance (Parallax)*, a movie that combined the structuralist motives of a previous generation with queer sexual mores. In my years of weekly treks to the difficult light, I never imagined that these movies would be shown anywhere else, certainly not anything made here in Toronto – who would be interested? But Midi's movie had a life outside clubhouse vanities, and she would go right on creating a unique, first-person cinema in the long years after the Funnel shrunk to a small spot and then vanished entirely.

Midi has dedicated herself to opening doors that look like walls to most people, movie after movie, decade after decade. She has tasted the forbidden fruit of dramatic features, celebrated the work of other artists in her own making, created a movie a day for an entire year for internet/cellphone perusal. While she is rarely in front of the camera, the surface tension and framings belong entirely to her; the light appears onscreen like a fingerprint. To live differently, and to make of that living a picture that can be held up to the light and shared. Not a dream but a necessity. She has the knack of being able to show even small familiar things in an unexpected fashion. She approaches the picture with a long-distance look, getting hold of some bit of seeing technology, some prosthesis for the eye, and only once she's found a way to use it that is all her own does she brings a picture into focus. It can take time, it can happen all at once. She is making haste slowly.

MH: Midi, I wonder if you could tell me about your beginnings in film. Were they an important part of your growing up? Did you enter the fray in order to change the kind of pictures that surrounded you, or to enter into that starlight? Perhaps all art begins with emulation, and variations on received wisdoms become one's practice. But did you feel yourself in the early days of your witnessing to be outside the mainstream flow, or was the seduction intact?

MO: I started making films in high school through a film studies class. The class mainly consisted of criticism and film theory, but at the end of the semester we had a choice of making a film or writing an essay. Naturally, I chose to make a film. With Super 8 cameras courtesy of the Toronto Board of Education, I embarked on my first film, *Reality-Illusion*. Although I knew very little about the technical aspects of filmmaking, I remember reading various how-to books and bugging my teacher for tips. The seven-minute film was 'experimental.' Although I had a vague premise of the 'teenage outsider,' destruction, violence, etc., there was no clear storyline. I recall that the main character wore a long black cape and a gas mask and carried a scythe. The costume came in particularly handy since I just asked various friends to fill the role (counting on those who were skipping classes or on a smoke break). Highlights of the film included a few scenes in a Jewish cemetery, a single-frame animation scene with styrofoam wig head and pyrotechnics (using the family barbecue). Unfortunately, the Board of Education did not have any splicers, and since I, of course, needed to edit my film, I set up a system using a razor blade to cut the film after measuring off the footage with a handmade 24fps ruler. I joined the film using scotch tape and then punched the sprocket holes out using a straight pin.

Immediately, I loved the hands-on aspect of filmmaking, holding the footage up to the light and selecting my shots. It was all very primitive but fun and incredibly rewarding. My second film was a kind of homage to Robert Wiene's *The Cabinet of Dr. Caligari* (1919). I loved the hyperdramatic expressionistic look of the film, the exaggerated acting and otherworldliness of it all. My version, *Contemplation*, was a short abstract study in teenage suicide. The 'actors' wore black tights and white bathing caps with white paint-stick face makeup. By the time I graduated from high school, I had made three films. After that, there was no looking back.

Naturally, I gravitated toward an arts education and, although it broke my parents' hearts (they had dreams of their daughter as a successful doctor or lawyer), I decided to go to the Ontario College of Art. At that time, in the late '70s, there were very few Asian students at OCA, let alone of Japanese descent. I recall two other Asian students in my class, both determined to pursue a career in graphic design. I too was influenced by the commercial tide and had aspirations to become a fashion designer. I knew nothing of contemporary experimental film and never imagined I could actually survive as an independent filmmaker.

Gradually, through my film-studies classes at the college, my knowledge of cinema increased, as did my filmography. The main stumbling block I faced in those days was the technology. It was a challenge to successfully create what I saw in my mind and realize it in film. Feminism was the buzz word of the day, but somehow most of the male film and video (technical) instructors hadn't heard it. Luckily, my parents gave me a Super 8 camera for my 17th birthday and this gave me tremendous freedom. Gradually I purchased my own Super 8 editor and splicer, and guided by my dog-eared copy of *Independent Filmmaking* by Lenny Lipton, I eventually worked through the mechanics of Super 8 filmmaking. Throughout OCA, I continued to make films, alongside painting and photography. By the time I graduated, I had made 11 more films. All of the work was shot in Super 8, and with the exception of one film, remained in the Super 8 format. I learned how to optically print film because I wanted to include subtitles in a piece I was working on, and eventually I started to use the optical printer to manipulate the Super 8 original and blow it up to 16mm.

There is no question that in the 1980s the worlds of film and video were universes apart, and from the beginning I fell into the film camp. Although I was exposed to many video artists' work, I always felt visual explorations in video were limiting and the technology overly complicated. I love the romance of sitting in a dark theatre and falling into the world of film: the flickering of the projector light, the mechanical hum coming from the back of the room, the magic unfolding onscreen. Even the technical language of film seems to be more lyrical than video: the legend of MOS – 'mit out sound' or 'without sound' spoken in a German accent – answer prints, reversal film stock, etc. Compared with the clinical and sometimes sexualized language of video: female-to-male connectors, 'lesbian' connectors, etc.

As far as the mainstream aspects of cinema, I never felt I wanted to make a Hollywood-type drama. I was so drawn to the work of avant-garde filmmakers such as Joyce Wieland, Maya Deren, Man Ray, Dali and especially Kenneth Anger, that I didn't even go to the regular movie theatre very much while I was at school. Perhaps it was my punk, feminist, Japanese background that made me feel like I could have a voice in experimental film. I could express myself on my terms rather than conform to mainstream expectations of cinematic representation. But even within the haven of experimental film, there were remnants of the 1970s presence of structuralism – the endless viewings of work by Stan Brakhage, Michael Snow, Hollis Frampton. I tried to like the work, really I did. It just never touched me.

MH: When I met you in the early 1980s, you had been hired to be the equipment guide and technical director at the Funnel, a now-defunct fringe-movie showcase that aspired to vertical integration. There were twice-weekly screenings, equipment for hire on the cheap (for members, at least) and a modest distribution program. What drew you to the Funnel and why did you stay there?

MO: Although I graduated from art school in 1983, my exposure to the Funnel began around 1980. At the time, experimental filmmaker Ross McLaren was one of my teachers. Besides showing various classic and current experimental film works, he tried to expose us to the world beyond school. This, of course, included a field trip to the Funnel. Located in the industrial edge of King Street East, the Funnel was *the* centre for exhibition, distribution and production of experimental/artist-based films. I believe filmmaker Anna Gronau was the director around that time. To me, the Funnel was the centre of the universe. It was the coolest place in the city and somewhere you could go and immerse yourself in experimental film. I recall thinking it would be amazing to show my films there, never mind that it was a small theatre (100 seats?), away from the rest of the Queen Street art scene, and freezing in the winter and boiling in the summer. I recall seeing Kenneth Anger and Ondine as a student, which was on par with meeting the Sex Pistols.

I got my wish and did indeed show many of my early works at the Funnel, first through student shows and later as a practising artist. My first non-student screening took place in 1982 in a series called *Formal Film by Women* curated by Anna Gronau. That particular evening included a film by Joyce Wieland, another one of my role models. I couldn't have been more thrilled. I recall speaking with Joyce after the screening and was touched by her warmth and generosity. Later, I got to know Joyce a bit better as I worked on restoring some of her old film prints.

When I look back on the early '80s now, I realize that many of the screenings I had took place within a feminist context. Some of my early exhibitions (photography and text pieces) and screenings were part of the International Women's Day conferences, and benefits for various lesbian and feminist publications. There seemed to be so much going on within the feminist community and in the world of experimental film.

Being an artist-run centre, the Funnel was on a tight budget and couldn't afford to hire new staff unless it was through a government-sponsored program. But, as a recent grad, I knew I wanted to work there and start my life as an artist. Through a program called Futures, I was hired as the equipment coordinator and paid the grand sum of $150 per week. Needless to say, I was barely able to survive, living mostly on Jamaican beef patties, popcorn and soup. My job consisted of checking all the equipment, keeping it in running order, orienting members on all the equipment at the Funnel, organizing workshops and assisting with the biweekly screenings. It was one of the best jobs I've ever had. I worked first under the leadership of filmmaker and Funnel director Michaelle McLean and, with the great help and patience of Villem Teder, a fellow filmmaker, Funnel member and techno-wiz, learnt how to solder, make seamless reel changes and load the ancient 16mm Frezzolini camera. I worked during the day at my job and then would stay on late into the night working on my own films, using the equipment free of charge. During my years at the Funnel from 1984 to 1986, I met and hopefully assisted probably every artist who was working in film in Toronto at that time.

MH: Going twice a week to the Funnel, hardly managing to say a word (like church, silently raising eyes up to the light), I held the preposterous belief that watching these difficult movies would imbue the viewer (magically, like fairy dust) with a high moral intelligence. Nothing in the organization bore this out, though I was undeterred by examples; I imagined these fringe movies were nothing less than the thin edge of a social revolution that would one day empty out the other theatres. Did you imagine (was it only me?) that these movies possessed a larger social/political purpose? Would 'changing the image' mean that life outside the image would also – must also – change?

MO: Briefly, before I got the job at the Funnel, my brother got me a job working in a custom colour photography lab just a few steps away. It was my first real taste of working in a 'corporation.' I put myself through school working as a cook at various restaurants in the city but had never worked in a company per se. I hated my job. I was the minimum-wage low-life hired to collect people's orders, check and package them for pickup or shipping. Nine to five, 30 minutes for lunch. My boss was a single mom who seemed to be searching endlessly for a Cabbage Patch doll for her daughter. She had nothing but contempt for those around her and made my short time there miserable. After work I would go over to the Funnel and hang out, my oasis of normalcy. I tell you this story because it influenced my concept of 'changing the world.' I realized that the mainstream – those clamouring for Cabbage Patch dolls and commuting from the burbs – was not an audience I had any hope of reaching. I didn't believe that anything like 'experimental' film could ever change their daily lives. My audience seemed grounded in those regulars who attended Funnel screenings.

The '80s was an exciting time. I felt the rawness and tension of the feminist movement, the debates around women-only events and spaces, the constant conflicts about pornography and censorship; the dying flames of the punk movement, its commercial morphing into new wave; the rapid growth of lesbian and gay culture through the beginnings of lesbian and gay film festivals; the embryonic development of 'multiculturalism.' But these events and communities were completely separate from each other, and any kind of crossover was usually viewed with suspicion. How could I love punk and call myself a feminist? The gay and lesbian movement at that time was predominantly white; issues of race hardly ever entered into discussions of equality and the reverse was the same for various ethnic communities.

Art, film, personal practice was the glue that held my life together. Without it, I think I would have gone mad. In some ways I never felt I could truthfully be myself in any of the politically charged communities, except at the Funnel. At first I believed I had found my home, a community of like-minded people. But in the end, the utopian world I thought I had found didn't really exist. It's difficult to explain: it's not that I faced distinct and direct racism, homophobia or sexism. It's just that there was this undercurrent of tension, this off-kilter feeling that I was intruding, that I didn't really belong.

As I gained more exposure to the growing number of films being made by women, my confidence grew and I felt more and more that I could embrace what naturally came to me – storytelling. This discovery was completely empowering. Finally, with the rise of 'new narrative,' I saw that stories could be created outside a Hollywood framework. To this day, when I think of some of the early films by Chantal Akerman, Chris Marker, Valie Export and some of the New York underground scene, I can still see shadows of their influence in my current work.

But as much as I found these works energizing and provocative, I think they helped to create a kind of creative divide amongst the Funnel membership. As some of the women embraced this infusion of narrative, some of the men resisted this 'trend,' staunchly defended structuralism and tried to preserve their perceived role as dominant 'experimental filmmakers' in the city. For me, this aesthetic/political/theoretical split finally took its toll when I started to make *The Displaced View.*

Michaelle McLean was one of my producers for the film and, besides the obvious route of arts council funding, we decided we needed to source alternative methods of funding. One of our first thoughts was having the Funnel sponsor the film so we could collect donations in exchange for a charitable receipt (since the Funnel was a registered charity). Michaelle presented our proposal to the board, who rejected it on the grounds that my film was not 'experimental.'

I guess, to go back to your original question about 'changing the image' and its possible impact on 'changing life outside the image,' well, from my experiences, I did see change occur within the genre of experimental film: changes that took place on the screen, in terms of feminist content, representation, narrative exploration, etc. Off-screen, in life, those changes were also present. More women were making films, learning the technical foundations of production, developing their own voices. But naturally there was resistance to change. The rejection and labelling of my film as 'not experimental' seemed incredibly narrow-minded and rooted in a dying aesthetic. I did not subscribe to the idea that 'experimental' film had to be 'difficult' or 'obscure.' I was interested in exploring the technical aspects of film as they related to the content. I saw that different genres were all part of the same family. It was the exploration and employment of different techniques and styles, the dismantling of cinematic stereotypes and construction of a unique world, that had the ability to transform a work from 'traditional' to 'avant-garde,' from mediocre to amazing. I saw the label 'experimental' as something created by the old boys' network. Something so prescribed that it sometimes became mind-numbingly painful to watch. So rigid in form and technique that it was turning in on itself.

Looking back at the Funnel, I clearly recall that in all my years going to screenings, working the job, hanging out, I met only one other Asian-Canadian filmmaker, Keith Lock. But although he kindly loaned us his 16mm moviola, he was rarely around. I don't recall ever meeting another Asian-Canadian woman or, come to think of it, anyone of colour. As far as lesbian 'experimental' filmmakers at the time, there was Barbara Hammer. It's not that I needed role models, but there was so much of myself I felt I had to keep under wraps. That's not to say I thought the lesbian/gay communities and the Asian-Canadian communities would be more welcoming. On the contrary, those communities had – and in some ways still have – expectations about work produced by 'their artists.'

MH: The first story I heard about famed New York underground legend Jack Smith in relation to the Funnel was that he had been invited to show *Flaming Creatures,* a movie many of us were eager to see, and which had been banned by the provincial censor board years ago. The story goes that he had showed up at Customs with a print of *Flaming Creatures* attached to his wrist with jewel-encrusted handcuffs. The jewels were dime-store glass, of course, and when he refused to open the case, Customs refused him entry. Perhaps this was another one of the apocryphal stories that circulated around someone who seemed both smaller and larger than life. The Funnel paid for another flight that brought him into town for a week-long performance in 1984. There are two indelible moments for me. On opening night, about an hour after the announced start time, with Jack still shuffling around tweaking the position of the furniture and disappearing backstage for long stretches and very occasionally putting on a record, Phil Hoffman turned me to and said, 'I think this is it.' We were all waiting for it to start, but this waiting was the play itself. The second moment occurred three nights later. There were only four or five in the theatre, and I had come a bit late, only to find Jack at the door, crying because there were so few. That was so touching and raw and beautiful. You made a movie of these events called *A Performance by Jack Smith* (5 min, 1984–92). Given his notorious difficulties with people, I'm surprised you were able to film at all. Can you describe your interactions with the maestro and how the movie came to light?

MO: Jack Smith. My memory might not be that good, but I've never heard the jewel-encrusted handcuff story. The truth is far less colourful. You are right, Jack was originally invited to screen *Flaming Creatures*. This was to be the first screening of the classic film in Canada. We were all terribly excited and, like school-children anticipating the final bell on the last day of school before summer holidays, we all waited for his arrival. I recall that for some reason then Funnel director David McIntosh and I were playing endless card games, after regular Funnel hours, waiting to hear that Jack had arrived. I guess because none of us had access to a car, no one met him at the airport. The clock kept ticking and we kept waiting. Yes, his plane had arrived, but he wasn't on it. David reached him at home in New York. He had missed his flight and was in the middle of getting rid of all the hard angles in his apartment, a major plastering job. After David spoke to him (at length), it turned out that Jack didn't want to bring *Flaming Creatures* up to Canada – he was afraid of crossing the border with the film. Finally he agreed to come and do a series of performance nights. David arranged for another ticket and we took up our second night of waiting.

When Jack arrived, it was my job to arrange any technical requirements he had for the performance. I had been used to dealing with all kinds of equipment requests, but wasn't prepared to find a chaise longue. Thankfully, David took care of that, but in the end we had to purchase it since it went through a lot of wear and tear during the week. Your description of the performance is fairly accurate. Overall, the performance grew over the week and involved not only Jack but other Funnel members and

fans who participated in sewing various brassieres – some perched on ladders, others floating around the stage. The audiences were never full and most people wandered in and out, like yourself, unsure what to make of it all. I worked most of the week in the projection booth, occasionally putting on a record that Jack had brought with him, and, I suppose, other technical things, which were minimal at best. As a kind of off-stage performance component, there were several Funnel members rushing around taking photos and shooting film. I admit, I was one of them. But instead of being at the front of the stage, I set my Super 8 camera up in the booth, shooting time-lapse.

For me, the whole thing was a bit of a letdown. At that time in my life I hadn't seen very much performance art and didn't feel I understood the language well enough to critique it. Meeting Jack, on the other hand, was absurdly fun. He was rather a quiet guy, with tremendous energy that he always seemed to keep in reserve. There is no doubt he was slightly paranoid (although I can see that some of it was justified) and he was a master at creating something out of nothing.

Later, after the week-long adventure was over, I heard that Jack had absconded with all the photos and film footage shot by the other Funnel members. Later still, I heard that Jack exhibited the work and called it his own. The only reason my footage remained a secret was because he never knew I was also filming. I had the footage stored away for years, more as a personal record of the event than anything. But after Jack died, I thought it was time to share it with others. The footage was shot in 1984 and finally released as *A Performance by Jack Smith* in 1992.

Jack touched so many people that week in Toronto that I am sure that there are a million different stories. It would be interesting to hear what other people at that time experienced. There are probably still hidden treasures, like photographs and audio recordings of that time.

MH: *Ten Cents a Dance (Parallax)* (30 min, 1985) remains a touchstone fringe movie on many counts. Its frank sexuality was especially striking in a climate where the provincial censor board was actively banning movies and shutting down art spaces. Could you describe the film's making – were all three sections made at the same time?

MO: I received my first Ontario Arts Council grant for *Ten Cents a Dance (Parallax)*. I think I got $2,000, which was not a lot even back in 1984. It was, however, a vote of confidence from a jury of peers and money that I would never dream of having otherwise. The film was originally proposed as a vehicle to deal with issues of communication. I wanted to try and illustrate the idea that communication between two people, regardless of sexual orientation, contains unspoken truths and underlying meanings. The grant application conjured images of a blocked writer sitting in front of typewriter, the persistent hum of the electric typewriter taunting the artist. Now that I think about it, the proposal was probably pretty weak, so I am thankful for the small grant.

I recall that early on I wanted to make the film as a double-screen projection. I was quite influenced by Andy Warhol's *Chelsea Girls* (1966), *Forty Deuce* by Paul Morrissey (1982) and John Massey's three-projector installation *As the Hammer Strikes (A Partial Illustration)* (1984). Massey's work especially impressed me, since I was the equipment coordinator at the Funnel and I assisted him with the premiere of this work. He had specially built three 16mm projectors that ran in sync. I remember that there was a main power switch for the set-up that reminded me of a Frankenstein movie. It was extremely loud when it ran and John was very tense during the entire presentation, because if there was a break in the film, then all three film prints had to be checked to ensure they were back in sync. We talked about how he constructed the whole thing, how expensive it was, etc. To save on money, I decided I would build a dual-projection system from second-hand machines sold off at government auctions. But I guess I am digressing.

How did I make it? Hmmm. As I said, I wanted to comment on 'unspoken' or 'between the lines' communication. I really have no clear recollection how I actually progressed from shots of typewriters and 'communication tools' (my original thought) to one-night stands and sexual encounters. But when I hit upon it, it struck me that the situation of a one-night stand personified the difficulties of communication.

I knew I wanted to shoot in 16mm with two cameras. I had never really done any work with 'actors' and didn't have a clue about directing in a conventional sense. I decided that, instead of using real actors, I was pretty much at the mercy of people I knew or friends of friends. I worked out of the place where I was living at the time and decided to shoot over a few weekends. Everyone worked either for free or a few hundred dollars. We had great food and beer. But like directing 'actors,' scriptwriting was beyond me. I decided I would choose 'characters' who had a dramatic flair about them and just ask them to play themselves. There would be three scenes, although I didn't really know what they would be.

The first pair I decided on were acquaintances: two women who had a kind of S/M relationship that manifested itself as a twisted mother/daughter bond with a codependent addiction to Buckley's cough syrup. I was almost terrified of them and their eccentricities, but very much wanted them to be in the film. That first shooting day, I remember they asked to have two white sheets erected in front of the cameras, which were side by side. Relying completely on their improv talent (so I hoped), I put up the sheets, told them they had ten minutes (roughly a 400-foot roll of film) and started shooting. As the minutes dragged on and I saw the money I had spent on the day waste away, I kept hoping the sheets would drop revealing something, anything, other than a white sheet. After what seemed like hours, we heard the film run out of the cameras, but the sheets never dropped. The women were completely stoned on cough syrup and who knows what else, so they thought their performance was amazing. As I worked with the rest of the crew to wrap up for the day, I just felt sick. I had wasted two rolls of film, didn't have even the

beginnings of a film and thought I would never be able to direct people on-camera.

After a few weeks of moping around, trying to figure out where to go next, I decided on a few things. 1. I would really have to take more of an active roll in conceiving, shaping and directing the scenes. 2. There could be no more costly mistakes or else I would never make the film. I had already gone through my contingency, and I could afford only six more rolls of film and that was it. (As it was, David McIntosh helped me to secure a deal with the old original PFA lab. He called the owner of the company for me and asked if I could get a discount on processing. He got me 50 percent off! I was thrilled.) 3. I would have three scenes: a gay, a lesbian and a straight encounter, each of them involved in either a sexual encounter or negotiating a one-night stand.

As I continued to struggle with the actual content, I came across ads for phone sex in the relatively new free Toronto weekly, *NOW* magazine, but all the phone numbers were based in the U.S. I decided to cast Ross McLaren, my old OCA experimental film teacher, and through David I met artist Wendy Coad. One night we all got together and, with the help of Ross's credit card, made a collect call to one of the phone-sex places in Buffalo. We recorded the conversation, Ross on one line, Wendy and I, barely containing our laughter, on the extension. After the brief ten-minute call was over, I gave the tape to Wendy to memorize. This was the script. A week or two later, we shot the scene. One camera was downstairs in the basement and the other was upstairs. I operated the camera focused on Wendy downstairs while David Bennell shot Ross upstairs. We rehearsed a number of times – it had to be perfect. Both Wendy and Ross were terrific, each of them adding little touches as we reworked the scene. Finally, as the day was turning into evening, we shot.

For the lesbian scene, I searched high and low for someone to play the roles, but couldn't find the right people. The script was derived from an actual dinner conversation/improv I had with my girlfriend at the time. I recorded the 'Japanese restaurant' soundtrack at a real Japanese restaurant while I was on a date with another woman. Finally, desperate to cast the roles, I asked Anna Gronau to help me out. Surprisingly, Anna agreed. Again, over a weekend, we rehearsed and drank sake until we felt we could do it perfectly. The whole thing was much harder than I had anticipated. The timing was critical since we had to sum it all up before the film ran out of the camera. The cameras, like the doomed sheet scene, were side by side. David B was setting them up and he called me over to look though the lens. He had overlapped the frames slightly – it was perfect, parallax!

The final scene was done with the grateful participation of David MacIntosh and John Goodwin. Inspired by the 1985 St. Catharines public washroom bust, which had occurred a few months prior to our filming, we shot the film at the Funnel. The St. Catharines raid had a tremendous impact. Not only on that community, but nationwide since the men who had been arrested for public washroom sex had their names published in the national newspaper. As a result, one of the men committed

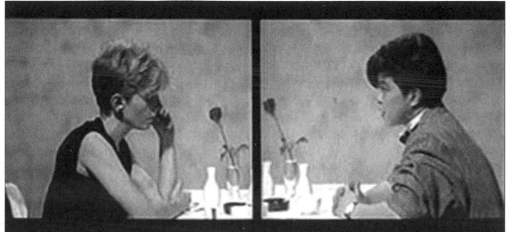

Ten Cents a Dance (Parallax)

extent of the disease. Now, 25 years later and over 25 million deaths and counting, there is no question that if I made the same film today, safe sex would be automatically included in the film.

MH: Finally, I wonder if you would talk about the reaction you had when presenting the movie, particularly the 'riot' during the Frameline Festival at the Roxie Theater in San Francisco.

MO: This is a major question. *Ten Cents* was made at a time when lesbian and gay film festivals were still finding their way. They were dealing with issues of representation, definitions of what makes a film 'lesbian' or 'gay,' and issues of including or excluding work done by marginalized filmmakers within the community (i.e., most films made around that time were made by white men). Super 8 seemed to be the cheap format of choice for the economically struggling dyke, and there were very few works being made by queers of colour.

The riot you speak of took place during the 1986 San Francisco Lesbian and Gay Film Festival. *Ten Cents* was programmed in two separate short-film evenings. The first screening that took place was called *Four from the Commonwealth*. As odd as it sounds today, my film, representing the commonwealth of Canada, was shown with other short films from New Zealand, Australia and Britain. This screening took place without incident.

Because of the perceived lack of lesbian works in that year's festival, the film was also programmed in an evening called *Lesbian Shorts*. I did not attend the festival, but was told afterwards by the festival director, Michael Lumpkin, that my film caused a riot to break out in the audience.

The reasons for the audience reaction were mainly focused on the issue or definition of what makes a film a 'lesbian film.' Does the maker of the work need to be a lesbian? Does the subject matter she chooses to explore have to be a 'lesbian-specific' subject? Can a lesbian portray other sexualities in a film and still make a 'lesbian film'? These questions, combined with the lack of lesbian-oriented work in the festival, and the ongoing tensions between the gay and lesbian communities, all contributed to this reaction.

Although I had screened *Ten Cents* at other mainstream festivals, San Francisco was one of the first lesbian and gay festivals to pick it up. I had no control over how it was programmed and didn't have a clue about the brewing anger from the local S.F. lesbian community. I knew the film was controversial from the beginning, but had no idea it would be a match on the firewood.

I remember talking to Anna at length about the growing number of film festivals that were specifically lesbian and gay or women's film festivals. I hated the idea that my work would only

suicide. We chose the Funnel since it was free and the men's washroom was so rundown we doubted anyone would notice if we carved a glory hole between the stalls. Once again, it was all shot in one take. (A few days after we shot in the washroom, there were metal plates covering our glory holes! In a building where nothing ever seemed to get fixed, it was astonishing.)

The situation of a one-night stand ideally personifies the difficulties of communication, as well as generating mixed emotions, risk, excitement. Overall, I had the sense that certain sexual activities were at the time very foreign to a film audience. The first scene was at my instigation. I thought most lesbians had had the experience of being approached by a straight woman who was curious, but I had yet to see this negotiation take place on the screen. Similarly, the third scene of the film involved phone sex, a relatively unexplored topic.

MH: Did you feel it was important to be in the movie yourself?

MO: It happened more by default, and it was only afterwards, when critics started writing about the film, that it became an issue of representation of an Asian-Canadian woman and a mixed-race relationship.

MH: The toilet-cubicle sex scene, filmed from above, is a riff on the surveillance cameras Ontario police had been using. Did the question of safe sex come up at all? Do you feel responsible to the queer community in terms of producing pictures that represent 'healthy' sexual practices?

MO: In 1985, in Toronto, the issue of safe sex was just beginning to make an impact on the community. In places like San Francisco, where there was a large gay community, safe sex was a very hot topic, and this is where some of the initial negative reaction centred.

Back in 1985, four years after the U.S. Centers for Disease Control published its famous report describing the deaths of five gay men in L.A. from a rare form of pneumonia, there was panic in the gay and lesbian communities. People just didn't know the be accepted and shown within (what I saw as) these social ghettos. Yes, I am a lesbian, a woman, of colour, etc., but I just didn't and still don't subscribe to this programming agenda. I see my work as extending beyond these classifications. I want the work to be seen by as many different people as possible within an independent context. For me it's about finding the connections between marginalized groups, drawing people from differing backgrounds together, not separating them further and isolating them. It's about breaking down the walls that separate us, not creating them.

As far as S.F. goes, what the 'riot' did for the community was to open up a dialogue with the festival's board of directors and the lesbian and gay communities in the city. I don't know if it caused the festival organizers/programmers to become more sensitive to work produced by lesbians and women of colour, but I think it opened their eyes to a number of debates and issues. Sometimes I wish these discussions would take place more in the different

The Displaced View

community-oriented festivals today. We, both as makers and audience members, have become far too complacent in our expectations and definitions of what a particular film should do or represent.

MH: In an essay called 'Centre the Margins,' Richard Fung talks about the absence of gay Asians on movie screens and cites your *The Displaced View* (52 min, 1988) as a notable exception. He goes on to write: 'In my own video work in the area, I have seen the most important task as the representation of gay and lesbian Asians as subjects, both on the screen and especially as the viewer. I believe that it is imperative to start with a clear idea about audience. This in turn shapes the content of the piece.' Do you feel the same? Do you begin your work with a clear idea of the audience and the political arena your work is entering into? Do you feel the responsibility implied in Richard's remarks about his

own work, and does it similarly shape the form and content of your work?

MO: Ideas for *The Displaced View* developed while I was in art school. One of my teachers was Morris Wolfe, who taught a number of classes in film criticism and theory. He was extremely encouraging, and through his screenings and commentary I saw films from around the globe that embraced a kind of cultural specificity and delicacy I wanted to convey in my own work. Morris encouraged me to look into my history, my cultural and familial relationship with the Japanese-Canadian community. I wrote a personal-history piece narrating the conflicting views of three generations of Japanese-Canadians based mostly on my family history. This piece was later published in *Fuse* magazine and was the beginning of *The Displaced View*.

When I began work on the film, I decided immediately that my primary audience would be the Japanese-Canadian communities. Within that community, my priority viewer would be the Issei, first-generation JCs. I felt that this generation, my grandmother's, was dying out, and it was important for me to convey their story in their language. I felt that the gay and lesbian audience would not be interested in the work since it did not deal directly with issues of sexuality.

In Richard's paper, he talks about the importance and scarcity of films and videos that represent lesbian and gay Asians. With *The Displaced View*, I never saw my audience as lesbian and gay Asians. Perhaps this was due to the fact that back in the 1980s I had met only one other Japanese-Canadian lesbian. I was not active within the JC community, which was predominantly heterosexual, while the lesbian communities in Toronto I had come across were predominantly white.

Politically, I did not realize the terrain I would be travelling would be so charged. Naively, I believed my work was more culturally charged than politically. Although I realized that my film would be the third made in Canada by a JC about the internment, I honestly thought I was storytelling, not making a political statement. (The first film was made by Jesse Nishihata, *Watari Dori: A Bird of Passage*, back in 1972; the second film was *Clouds* (1985), by Fumiko Kiyooka and Scott Haynes).

My motivations have never been solely politically driven. I am not a documentary filmmaker; I am interested in stories, the construction of identity, memory, personal history. I am not a political activist, though I do inject my personal political views into the work. But just because I don't personally impose a political framework does not mean that others (audiences, funders, etc.) follow suit.

Like the San Francisco Lesbian and Gay Film Festival audience reaction, audiences in marginalized communities have enormous expectations about work produced by artists who they believe represent their communities. In 1988, when *The Displaced View* was launched, it was invited to a few lesbian and gay film festivals, based on my reputation with *Ten Cents a Dance*. For the most part, I think lesbian and gay audiences were disappointed. It was not the sexually charged follow-up to *Ten Cents* that people expected. In fact, the lesbian content is minor, some would argue non-existent. Most lesbian and gay audiences didn't even consider it to be a 'lesbian film,' nor one that was suitable for that specific audience. On the other hand, within the mainstream festival world, the film got substantial play at international film festivals to mixed audiences – straight, gay, mixed races, etc. As far as Asian-specific festivals, there were far fewer back in those days, but overall I recall a positive reaction, although for the most part it was classified as a documentary – but that's another issue.

If I were naturally a more socially driven person, I might feel more political responsibility for my work. Perhaps if I had to rely more on my subjects to tell a story, as in documentary practice, I would feel the community pressure more intensely. But my favourite way of working is in solitude. I want to shape the work according to the material, the shot, the sound, the rhythm of the sequence, not around political motivations.

MH: In *The Displaced View*, you take up the issue of Japanese internment during the Second World War via a portrait of your born-in-Japan grandmother. In voice-over you say, 'You only talk about what you want and don't remember the bad.' She is very reluctant to speak about what happened to her, so your historical/reclamation project circles around its subject, looking for a way forward. Was her reticence frustrating for you?

MO: By the sound of your question, it appears you're viewing the film as a documentary. In fact, it's a construction, a collection of truths or stories that have been assembled into a structure describing three generations of Japanese-Canadian women. Although all the stories and details in the film are true, they didn't all happen to my family or a real family. I hired someone to conduct audio interviews across Canada with women from three generations (Issei, Nisei, Sansei) and got them to share their wartime stories with the Sansei generation. I did so for several reasons: I needed to collect stories to build on, rather than simply rely on my family's history. Many JC families had never told their children or grandchildren about their experiences, so it became an oral history project, something each family could build on as a personal archive. The reluctance to discuss this history was of course locked in the horror, disenfranchisement and demoralization caused by the internment. Naturally, I started with my parents and grandmother's stories, but they were so different I started to wonder how to tell such conflicting truths and whether these differences existed only within my own family. When I played those audio interviews, I heard the same shock and dismay from the Sansei women. I felt their sense of a lost culture and an almost forgotten history. It was therefore critical

for me to tell as many stories as I could, making a screen family rather than relying on the truth of one or two memories.

So when you mention the grandmother character (played in the film by my own grandmother, who was already in her late 90s when we shot), I have to smile. She was actually reading a translated script. I wrote the script based on some of her experiences and the experiences of others, and then my translator, Tomoko Makabe, created the Japanese text, and together we worked with her on her performance. There is one moment in the film when she suddenly goes off the script and starts to question her memory of the events – it was so spontaneous and in character that I left it in.

All the scripted voice-overs are archetypes. They represent three generations of conflicting thoughts and stories, three different voices with varying degrees of 'ethnicity,' colouring the viewer's impressions. For this reason, the tone and text of the voices was very important. For instance, the voice that represents the mom character is not my mother at all, but someone I hired to perform the role. I needed a voice that was more heavily accented with Japanese, and although my mother attempted her best Japanese accent, she unfortunately did not get the role, although she does appear in the film visually.

MH: During the Second World War, in a political gesture that echoed the Americans, the Canadian government rounded up its own citizens, those of Japanese descent, and without trial or recourse of any kind, forcibly removed them from their homes and put them into camps. How did you find about the internment?

MO: I think almost every child explores the books that rest on the shelves of their childhood home. For me, it was a book called *A Child in Prison Camp* by Shizuye Takashima (1971) that first made me aware of the internment. The book, a rarity of sorts, was full of watercolour paintings by the artist/author; the story told of her time spent in one of the B.C. camps from the age of 11 to 14. I don't believe I actually read the book from cover to cover, but the paintings drew me in and kept bringing me closer to imagining my parents when they were younger.

MH: Why does your grandmother say she has no regrets coming to Canada, even though she was taken from her home and put in a camp?

MO: My grandmother came to Canada in the 1920s and, like many others who arrived back then, life was most difficult back in their homelands. War, poverty, hunger and little hope of a future led these people to the 'land paved with gold.' America and Canada were the new frontier, just as they still are today for some people. I imagine that before WW II, many immigrants did not expect to be treated kindly by their adopted country. But for whatever reason, they could not return to their place of birth and instead learned to live with intolerance and discrimination.

Most people of my grandmother's generation developed a strong sense of pride for their new homeland. But as the generations get further away from that first generation of New Canadians, we find it difficult to believe life could have been worse in their birth country.

MH: Were there a lot of other voices speaking out about internment when you were making your film?

MO: Although the issue of redress was one that had been brought up in a personal lawsuit against the federal government as early as 1969, it wasn't until the 1980s that the community actively and vocally started negotiations with the government. I didn't have much to do with the many community meetings and discussions that were taking place – most of the talk centred on compensation and political work, but I was interested in the personal stories. It wasn't until I approached Multiculturalism Canada under the Secretary of State for production funding in 1985 that I was exposed to the political nature of my film. The project was initially rejected due to a funding freeze, then. as I continued to inquire about the possibilities of future funding, I was told by the office that any proposal dealing with Japanese-Canadian history was perceived politically and that, since the Japanese-Canadian community was currently in negotiations with the government, any support of my project would be perceived as support for the entire community and that the federal government was not prepared to do so at this time. Finally after a continued battle with Multiculturalism Canada, I received funding for the film in 1987, shortly before the government announced that they had reached a settlement with the Japanese-Canadian community.

MH: Could you elaborate on this statement you make in the film in voice-over: 'To fight for my sexuality, I ended up protecting my culture.' Did you feel you were 'coming out as Japanese woman' with this movie?

MO: Up until the making of this film I had pretty much ignored my 'Japaneseness.' As an adult I didn't have any Asian friends, nor was I involved in any Japanese-Canadian community activities. Up until that point, I was concentrating on honing my craft and skill as an artist filmmaker. I felt that the JC community in general, and my parents' generation in particular, was conservative and rather narrow-minded. Because I had already made *Ten Cents a Dance*, I felt my radical views and lifestyle would not be accepted. To answer this question properly, one could write an entire book on homophobia within cultural/ethnic minority communities. But, in short, I felt I didn't belong in what I perceived as the Japanese-Canadian community. Most of my Sansei (third-generation) peers had been encouraged by their parents (in part because of their wartime experiences) to become doctors, lawyers, accountants and business people. There were very few artists in the JC communities across Canada period, never mind a lesbian artist/filmmaker.

Originally, I had no intention of even mentioning my sexuality in the film. I wanted to concentrate on my 'Japanese' side and felt that it might alienate the JC communities I was trying to reach. But the more I worked on the script and tried to make some sense of what had happened to my parents and grandparents, I could only compare it to my struggle for equality and recognition as a lesbian. Once I made this connection, I could more clearly picture the struggle that went on for the Japanese-Canadian and -American communities. I felt that one line suddenly refocused the film in a different way and brought together these different yet similar struggles against discrimination and prejudice.

MH: There are many evocations of 'Japan' in your film, from the drummers to rice makers to Japanese landscapes. The central image of the country that endured for me were the shots of you sitting on a train, with the window admitting moments of passing landscape – the outside looks like a movie passing by on the other side of the glass, remote and untouchable. Could you talk about your choices of how to create a picture of Japan and Japanese culture?

MH: The film was shot entirely in Canada. I didn't go to Japan to shoot any of it. I used images that were familiar from my childhood or that I thought illustrated a cross-generational bond. The images of mochi-making or rice pounding were recreations from my youth (I actually shot them in the gymnasium of the church I went to as a child). The scenes with the Japanese dancing, tea ceremony, shrine raising, etc., were all shot at the Powell Street Festival, the annual mid-summer celebration of Asian-Canadian arts, history and culture in Vancouver. These images of 'Japanese-Canadian culture' are different from images of Japan; these images are a fabrication of 'Japaneseness.' They are traces of an old Japan that no longer exists in the contemporary world. The 'Japanese' elements in my film are more reminiscent of a Japan that my grandmother's generation left when they came to Canada. Like most immigrant communities, this kind of attachment or recollection of their past lives and memories is like a generational marker captured in aspic. These markers become cultural touchstones for the preceding generations, until these memories, traditions and rituals are replaced by a new wave of immigrants and their children.

MH: You make a lovely and radical choice by refusing to translate your grandmother's Japanese voice-over. Can you talk about this decision?

MO: I made *The Displaced View* primarily for the Issei generation. Since most of that generation continued to speak Japanese long after their arrival to Canada, translation was part of the project from the very beginning. I had noticed, like many immigrants, that the Japanese language my grandmother's generation spoke was beginning to disappear as that generation died. Like their memories of Japan and Japanese culture, their language was also trapped in time. Some of the words and slang of their day simply weren't used in modern Japanese. I knew that once that generation had gone, all traces of their language would die with them. I wanted to try and preserve it, but at the same time I was aware that some of my audience would be like me, Sansei, unable to speak or understand Japanese. So I decided to use language as an element that would play a dual purpose: to directly address and privilege the Japanese-speaking audience, and to place the non-Japanese-speaking audience in my position – someone who does not understand the language. The latter point was taken further in my decision not to have an English translation. I wanted the non-Japanese-speaking audience to experience the Japanese language the way I did as a child, without direct translation. To this day, my relationship to the Japanese language rests on my memories of listening to my grandmother speak Japanese. I listened to the intonation of her voice, the rhythm of her sentences. I watched her gestures, her eyes, to find clues about the meaning of her words.

But even the decision not to translate the Japanese into English became a political one. This film was sold to almost every public educational broadcaster across the country with the exception of the Knowledge Network, ironically located in British Columbia – the province where most of the Japanese-Canadian community lived before WW II. Although I had a verbal phone agreement that they were going to purchase the film, the deal was suddenly stopped when a more senior executive found out there was untranslated Japanese dialogue and subtitles. At a face-to-face meeting, I was told that audiences wouldn't be able to understand the film, but when I offered to translate the film into English, the producer I was dealing with stumbled and stuttered, and it became clear there was another agenda at play.

MH: Because the number of queer Asian indie media makers remains modest, I'm wondering if you find yourself pulled into arguments of personal expression versus community hopes?

MO: Yes, the number of queer Asian filmmakers/videomakers is still relatively small, and yet the numbers have steadily increased over the years. The responsibility that one feels is of course personal and depends very much on the scale and form of the work. For instance, the bulk of my work has been 'experimental,' which gets viewed by very few people. However, when I did my theatrical feature, *Skin Deep*, starting in 1988 and finishing in 1995 (a seven-year nightmare), I was directly faced with a number of community pressures. In this case, it was from the transgendered communities, since one of my main characters was a FTM transsexual. Marginalized groups have a political responsibility to demand that characters drawn from their communities are fully developed, three-dimensional entities; they

have a right and perhaps an obligation to speak out about representation. But in the end, it's the decision of the artist and what they believe is important to the story that ends up onscreen. But, within a feature-film context, there are so many compromises that are finance-dependent, outside the director's control. The main reason it took me seven years to make that film was funding, or lack of it. Not that my budget was high by first-feature standards; it was just not something that interested distributors. This film was conceived before *The Crying Game* (1992) and way before *Boys Don't Cry* (1999) and, as a result, most distributors didn't see that there was an audience for the film. I remember I had one meeting with a distributor who really thought that k.d. lang should be cast as the transgendered character, for no other reason than she was a known lesbian, not that that made any sense. But I think if the deal were truly predicated on hiring k.d. lang and I would have received all my money for the film, I might have done it.

MH: Was your decision to make the dramatic feature *Skin Deep* (85 min, 1995) based in part on hopes of reaching wider audiences, or even making a living? Did it feel like a departure or an extension of concerns already raised in previous work?

MO: After making *The Displaced View* in 1988, I did want to reach a wider audience, but on my terms. I also wanted to explore a more conventional narrative structure and try my hand at writing scripts. Back in 1987–88, multicultural monies were pouring guiltily from the federal and provincial governments; one of the windfalls from this was an internship for 'people from various multicultural communities' made possible by the CBC and a production company called Toronto Talkies Inc., primarily run by Paul DeSilva. I was accepted into this internship, and along with a handful of others, I was taught how to write a TV half-hour. The end result of this internship was a possibility that one's screenplay would actually be made into a 30-minute one-off for

The Displaced View

national television. I was lucky and my script *Then/Now* was produced. The story itself was a rather straightforward father/daughter tale: father has a flower business and wants his daughter to take over, but she plans to become a writer, how to tell Dad? Oh yes, and the daughter is gay. Deepa Mehta was originally booked to direct but unfortunately had to drop out, and instead Richard Flowers, an assistant director I had worked with previously in my career as a camera assistant, took on the role. It was great to observe the process of a commercial production from the perspective of a writer and of course I imagined how I would direct the scenes myself. Everything went fine, except when an upper executive at the CBC read the script, realized it contained a lesbian kiss during prime-time TV and demanded it be censored. The battle was a hard one and Paul really fought for the kiss, but, in the end, it was cut, left to rot on the cutting-room floor.

From this experience and after writing a second TV drama called *Heartbreak Hoteru* for a B.C. production company back in 1990, I decided I wanted to take what I had learned about mainstream screenwriting and try my hand at a dramatic feature. Looking back on the experience now, I can see why it took me so long to produce. Although getting top grants from all the arts councils was not a problem, getting viable commercial support was impossible – I was nobody to them. While I had gained a reputation in the film art/festival scene, I had no commercial directing credits, nor had I even worked with actors! After working seven long years on the feature, there was no way I was looking at a future in that world. Making a living as a commercial director was just not in the cards for me.

MH: *Skin Deep*'s Alex Koyama is a film director interested in making a movie about tattooing, skin pictures that provide a nexus of pleasure and pain, control and abandon. Alex says to her lover/assistant (work and play are another duality that are deliberately mixed here), 'You let go completely. It's not you anymore.' This confusion/obliteration of identity is emblematized by Chris Black, a young, pre-op transsexual (a woman presenting herself as a man), and by Penny, a woman playing a man playing a woman. Penny is experience while Chris is innocence, though a quickly overwhelmed and dangerous innocence. What drew you to these themes, and why did you choose a dramatic form to realize them?

MO: (as excerpted from an arts council application, circa 1990) My interest in the area of gender identity began ten years ago when I had the unique opportunity to correspond with a young woman who had cross-lived as a man but who was being medically treated as a lesbian. While cross-living as a man, this particular woman was involved in a 'heterosexual' relationship with another woman. However, due to a set of circumstances, she was forced into proving her 'manhood.' Desperately seeking to preserve her relationship with the young woman, she committed murder and removed the genitalia of the male victim, which she proceeded to 'crazy-glue' to her own body. She was found innocent for reasons of insanity and confined to a psychiatric institution.

Over the years her story remained with me and, due to my own interest in the lesbian community, I began to question whether this woman had gender dysphoria (was uncomfortable with her socially and culturally assigned gender role) or had difficulties accepting her sexual orientation. As a non-medical observer, it is impossible for me to guess. However, from this initial incident my curiosity regarding the relationship between sexual orientation and gender role identity began.

In terms of exploring themes of gender and racial identity, I wanted to use a 'dramatic' structure in order to attempt change within the conventional film form. In other words, I wanted to place marginalized characters into a conventional cinematic framework and see if I could subvert an audience's sense of these characters. Again, you must remember that the conventional mainstream film framework I am talking about was pre–Quentin Tarantino, pre–*Crying Game* and pre–*Boys Don't Cry*. So much of what was happening to mainstream cinema in the early '90s had a direct impact on how marginalized characters were represented. So much of what I wanted to explore in *Skin Deep* became standard film fare by the time my film was released.

MH: The myth of the breakout feature continues to haunt the filmmaking imaginary. I wonder if you might offer your reflections on those who are looking for their moment on the big screen. Has the glass (lead?) ceiling that keeps men helming lucrative TV gigs and monied features in this country changed greatly in the decade since the release of your film?

MO: Making *Skin Deep* and then my weak attempts to try and break into the mainstream film and TV industry as a director showed me a side of the industry I had only previously experienced during my years as a camera assistant or through war stories from other women. Sadly, the war stories were true. There is no question that a glass ceiling exists and most likely continues to exist for women and especially women of colour. In North American productions, men are still looked at as authority figures and given the benefit of the doubt in terms of the diverse subjects they are allowed to explore. Women are relegated to soft women's dramas, soaps, emotionally driven stories. Very rarely do women directors get the opportunity to do action movies. If you're a woman or a man of colour, for that matter, you are somehow led down the path to make films that reflect your cultural/ethnic background. One only has to think of Mina Shum, Clement Virgo or Deepa Mehta to get the idea. It's much more difficult for these filmmakers to break out of what the public expects from them in terms of community representation and subject matter. Being Japanese-Canadian, the public's expectations on me become focused on wartime stories, stories about the internment, about being a JC woman, etc. I think there is a double glass ceiling for filmmakers of colour: one imposed by the industry and another by public expectation.

Now, in 2006, the endless landscape of reality TV shows makes it very difficult for all dramatic directors. Canadian TV drama, which used to be the bread and butter for many writers, directors, actors, etc., is almost non-existent. As far as feature filmmaking goes, that's another story. No matter where you are in the world, making a feature film is hard. You have to be prepared for a lot of meetings, compromises, disappointments, delays and disasters. And in the end, if you survive, it may not be with the film you had intended to make in the first place. In some ways I felt that after making *Skin Deep*. It was too soul-draining to think of continuing on that path.

MH: In *Alphagirls* (3 × 15 min, 2002), you work with a trio of performance artists: Kinga Araya walks the neighbourhood with a third leg, Louise Lilifeld repeatedly immerses herself in water, stares or flogs herself, while Tanya Mars does a more conventional filmic turn, talking about her dog Woofie, which leads to a *My Dinner with André* conversation about cloning. This trilogy is collected on an interactive DVD for gallery display or home use. Why is that?

MO: While developing *Alphagirls* back in 2000, the DVD format was just hitting the consumer market. There were very few interactive DVDs being produced by the mainstream and nothing I could find produced by artists. The format and all its possibilities were hardly explored; it was used mainly as a distribution tool for releasing Hollywood movies, including directors' commentaries and production stills.

To quote myself from the *Alphagirls* website: *Alphagirls* continues my exploration of non-linear narrative structure working within the boundaries of recorded performance. I chose to deal with performance art as the basis of the DVD project in order to shift traditional concepts of live performance and audience interplay. Conventionally, performance art lasts for the length of the performance. Film or video of the performance is considered documentation of the artwork and not the artwork itself. *Alphagirls* shifts this concept of an appointed time and space performance and forges a kind of cyber-link between audience and performer.

From an aesthetic and stylistic standpoint, I am interested in utilizing the most appropriate and complementary technical practices that enrich the visual impact/relationship to the viewer. With *Alphagirls*, I have combined the high-end technology of the DVD format with simple digital toy recording devices such as the Tyco toy camera and the Trendmasters digital camera. The premise of *Alphagirls* centres on advancing technologies in relationship to a feminist framework. The three performances are as diverse in their subject matter as they are in the execution. Tanya Mars's piece, *My Dinner with Woofie*, is a seemingly simple commentary on cloning; Kinga Araya's *Grounded (III)* focuses on a bodily manifestation of female identity in a public space; and Louise

Liliefeldt's *Quarter After* is an intense portrayal of the physical and psychological nature of work/labour. Through this diversity, *Alphagirls* highlights the possibilities of interactive performance art through the digital frontier of DVD.

MH: Interactivity was a great watchword of the '90s, promising a liberated viewer the chance to finally become her own director. But one rarely encounters interactive work these days – what has become of these hopes?

MO: Yes, buzzwords, interactivity. Hmmm. I'm afraid I am a product of my times. I love technology, and my gaming obsession comes into play a bit around my own work. When the DVD format was introduced, I was excited by the possibilities and wanted a new way to approach audiences. In fact, I even went to the New Media Lab at the Canadian Film Centre and dove into the whole 'interactive' thing. What I discovered was that, for the most part, the world of film and video are rather separate from web-based interactive works. Often the people who are the best at coding and the technical side of online work or interactive projects do not have an arts background. There is no motion-picture history for many new media producers to fall back on, so content can become overshadowed by technology.

In the case of interactive DVDs, I think the reason there are so few works done in this format is because the technical specifications are so limiting. DVDs must be authored to conform to standards so they are playable on all computers and DVD players. This can be very frustrating to an artist trying to push the limits of the format. When I got the disk for *Alphagirls* authored, I went to the best commercial house in the city and to this day my disk was the most complicated job they have had. I could go into a lot of boring technical information, but let's just say the format didn't quite live up to what it promised.

I still believe artists have not even touched the surface of possibilities for interactive work. It is a new field with constantly shifting parameters, and one really has to understand the tools before one can produce meaningful work. On some levels, I don't think *Alphagirls* was terribly successful because, in the end, too much was left open to the user. I couldn't figure out a way to direct the interactivity of the work. But I did learn an enormous amount about the format and interactivity. I think that in some ways the piece worked better in a controlled gallery environment than as an 'at-home' experience.

MH: Can you describe how you used interactivity to enhance each of these performers?

MO: The interactivity for each performance is slightly different. Each of the artists were given a set of parameters to work with, such as:
- Each artist had to work with a different low-tech visual format (a toy camera of some kind)
- Each artist was limited to 15 minutes of visual time

- Each artist could work with up to five different audio tracks
- Each artist could access up to four subtitle/title/pop-up menus

From these parameters I worked with each artist independently and, using their previous work as a basis, we co-created performances that would exist in the DVD realm. Tanya Mars's work was developed from her ongoing interest in storytelling. Her performance, which deals with the subject of animal or pet cloning, was based on the movie *My Dinner with André*. We decided her piece would break down the 15-minute time restriction into two video and audio tracks, each approximately eight minutes in length. On one track Tanya was having a discussion about cloning her dog, Woofie, with her friend David. On the other track, David is talking to Woofie about Tanya's desire to have him cloned. The performance

"Funny girl", she said in that way of her's.

The Basement Girl

can be viewed as two separate scenes or can be switched between both audio and video possibilities. Ideally, I would want the viewer to watch both tracks as an entire piece and then switch between the two. Further, each track contains two flashbacks of sorts that reflect or comment on the primary viewing track.

In Kinga Araya's piece, *Grounded (III)*, she wanted to play with language and movement in different parts of the city. We used five different tracks, each approximately three minutes long. In each of the tracks, Kinga navigates her way through a different part of the city with three legs. On the audio tracks she speaks either Polish, Italian, English, French or gibberish. As the viewer manipulates the audio, the story or voice-over continues to progress in these different languages. From a visual standpoint, Kinga's location is constantly shifting as one manipulates the angle button on the DVD remote control.

In Louise Liliefeldt's piece, *Quarter After*, we used four tracks of audio and video, each beginning at staggered times. Her actions on each of the tracks reflect her specific interests in endurance performance art and body/mind relationships. So, on one track, she is submerging her head in a tank of water, on another she is performing a self-flagellation, on the third she is walking on a bed of nails and on the last track she is staring, directly confronting the viewer. As in the previous performances, the viewer can either experience the performance as separate pieces or intermix each of the video and audio tracks (independently of one another) and discover different connections between the actions.

The entire *Alphagirls* project works in conjunction with the website www.alphagirls.ca. The user of the DVD is encouraged to go to the website to find out more about each artist, their artist statements, bios, clips of the DVD, etc. Once the user has looked at the site (scrolled over a number of links), there is a key that appears on the upper-right corner of the screen. A number becomes visible if you mouse over the key. When users enter this

code into the DVD, they can then access an easter egg or hidden bit of information. This information is available only on Tanya Mars's performance. When the code is entered, an additional 'secret' track of video is available to the user.

Overall, the technical DVD aspects I was dealing with were so new at the time that some of things I had wanted to do could not be achieved.

MH: *The Basement Girl* (12 min, 2000) is a beautifully crafted brief about a young lonesome in her apartment grieving the fresh wound of a relationship suddenly ended. She turns to TV to find a way to begin again. Why is the text in French and why the oversize subtitles?

MO: To answer your question, I feel that I have to go back a few years before *Basement Girl* was made in 2000. After I finished my feature, I was exhausted and seriously wondered if I could ever make another film. In the meantime, I was hired by MAC Cosmetics to make a video, and what started as one project continues today. I've now done over 100 videos for them. This experience pushed me into video, and it was thrilling to have the opportunity to make work someone actually paid me for. One of the projects I did was a feature-length basic-training video for all new MAC employees. I co-wrote the script and turned the somewhat dry information into a little story modelled after an Aaron Spelling–type show, with perfect-looking characters and their perfect lives, almost a nod to Paul Wong's video *Prime Cuts* (1981). This video had to be translated into six languages and I supervised all of them.

With the MAC videos under my belt and various languages buzzing around in my head, I decided to make *Basement Girl* into a 'foreign film.' I had dealt with the Japanese language in *The Displaced View*, and a bit in *Skin Deep*, but here I wanted to use French, as a good Canadian, and give another level of meaning to the film. In the French voice-over, the Basement Girl's ex is actually a guy, not a woman as in the English version. Echoing some of the male references in the English version, it was my little subtle (subversive) statement on bisexuality.

The French language (for those audiences who don't understand French) further transforms the way the video is viewed – from the perspective of a foreign film. When an audience goes to a foreign movie, there are different expectations at play and different readings that can be made. By dealing with TV imagery in a 'foreign' context a shift is made in the audience's relationship to familiar or popular North American culture.

As far as the subtitles, that was a bit of a technical thing. Although we shot most of the film in 16mm, we also used my fave toy camera – a modified Nintendo Gameboy camera, which ended up as a video element. I transferred all the film to video, cut the piece, did the titles and then transferred it all back to film. The mistake I made was not testing the size of the video titles in terms of the eventual film transfer.

MH: The voice-over recites, 'For now it is only the space she inhabits that is real.' She is 'outside the picture' and also 'outside life,' merely an observer. She watches TV not to lose herself, but to learn how to desire again. Clips of TV girl-girl love are recast in luminously recoloured sitcom fragments. Why the extensive reworking of this familiar footage, and how did you collect these moments?

MO: I had planned to use pop-culture feminist icons in the film, such as the Bionic Woman, That Girl and Mary Tyler Moore, so I just kept popping tapes into my VCR and recording every show I could get my hands on. From that material, I selected the scenes or reworked moments to give it lesbian content.

There is no question that for women of my generation, '70s TV shows like the ones I've mentioned impacted the way we saw ourselves. We were no longer stay-at-home moms waiting with cookies and milk; we were now career women living on our own, with problems and relationships. I can't begin to describe how powerful I found Mary Tyler Moore as a role model when I was young. I wanted to pay homage to them and also insert the reality of the Basement Girl into the whole picture.

MH: *I Have No Memory of My Direction* (77 min, 2005) is a Japanese travelogue impelled by your voice-over and first-person shooting. In the opening shot, you say in voice-over, 'When she recalled that moment, their faces would reappear to her, suspended in the oxide-coated Mylar tape like a strange, three-dimensional puzzle, the pieces would continuously rearrange themselves, depending on the clarity of her vision. But they never seemed to tell the entire story, the one she knew was there, hidden in the magnetic recording.' Here you suggest that our video prosthesis has replaced

memory, or become memory. 'Her' seeing relies on the clarity of her vision, but all she is seeing belongs to the videotape. Do you feel you are creating memory with your work?

MO: I am trying to remember by making work. In *I Have No Memory*, I am using a dream landscape as the foundation of memory, which like dreams can be elusive, illogical, emotional, confusing, etc. In reference to the opening scene with the young girls by the shore, this scene stands in for a 'frozen moment' in time. But the voice-over describes this memory/moment as unstable: it's ever-changing, mutating into other bits of time, other stories. The 'real' story of the girls is not visible to the naked eye or the camera. No matter how hard the narrator tries to recall that moment, there will always be something missing.

Since the meaning of 'memory' is the ability to store, retain and subsequently recall information, as an image-maker I am constantly and unconsciously remembering things in a kind of linear narrative or filmic timeline of sorts. Sometimes the whole sequence is readily available, sometimes only a small detail or close-up is trapped on the edge of forgetting.

MH: And how is this related to the film's larger project: to see through your father's eyes?

MO: You are assuming that the narrator in the video is me, and that the character of the narrator's father is really my father. There is some truth in this personalization and some fiction. In this case, the narrator wants to try to see Japan and the rest of the world through her father's eyes. The commonality here is that the narrator's father was a photographer while she is a videographer. In a sequence that appears relatively early in the video, the narrator recalls, 'Her father was always behind the lens, not in front of it.' Visually, we see a montage of photographers and videographers shooting on the streets of Tokyo, mostly in the Harajuku district, where fashion-magazine photographers take pictures of the latest trends. As the narrator/audience observes the crowds, she tries to imagine seeing the world through her father's eyes.

I Have No Memory of My Direction

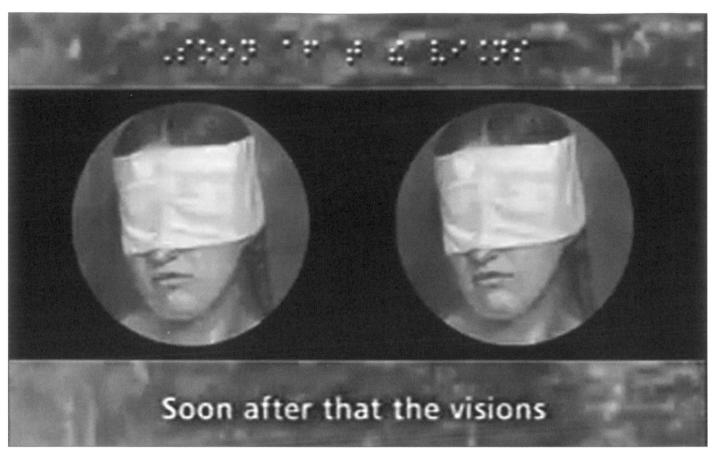

Slightseer

I Have No Memory of My Direction

'She imagines that she has inherited his way of seeing. She imagines that she's behind her father's viewfinder. She sees his eyes, moving like a camera, capturing the world around him. The process of turning information into pictures, memories.' Later, while the narrator is caught up on the Hachiko trail, she supposes that she and her potential new employer, the son of a famous director, share the same desire. 'Each of them wishes to see through their father's eyes.'

For the narrator, the camera or instrument of recording becomes both the common bond between daughter and father and a 'third eye' of possible distortion, making it more difficult to locate a clear image of what or how her father saw things. But the narrator believes that perhaps she has inherited something from her father and that this something is located in how she sees the world. Further, because the tape is set in Japan, the audience assumes the father was either born in Japan or has spent significant time there.

But later in the video, the narrator points out that her father has never actually been to Japan. 'Here, 10,341 kilometres away from her father, in a place he has never been to, she is trying to uncover a part of him she could barely conceive of. It wasn't very practical.' This kind of contradiction or confusion is typical for the dream structure of the entire video. In the end, the narrator's quest to see through her father's eyes as a way to try to retain or hold on to his fading memories is not realized. 'But she would never be able to look through her father's eyes. She would only inherit the dim collection of half-imagined tales – a re-enactment of memories.'

The narrator has been saddled with the burden of being the guardian of her father's memory. Her grandmother gave this task to her, but in adhering to the dream structure, her grandmother is dead and the message is communicated to the narrator by an Italian businessman who she casually meets in the smoking lounge of a Tokyo department store. This idea of being a guardian for someone else's memories is connected to how she imagines her father's way of seeing. She believes that if she can see like her father, then his memories might become more defined. The urgency of this task is pressing due to the fact that the narrator's father is suffering from Alzheimer's – the disappearance of memory.

MH: You call photography a 'blind witness.' Is this being present without seeing also tied to family life?

MO: The quote is: 'She searches for the connecting strands of thought – war, cloning, photography. War, the ultimate destruction of the human race. Cloning, the definitive statement of our fragile egos, the preservation and perpetuation of self. And photography, the blind witness to our arrogance.' These statements refer to the beginning of the sequence that comments on the media construction of war images. War imagery is understandably horrific, but the realities of the unimaginable scenes are made 'unreal' both in our inability to logically and emotionally process such images and by the visual treatment of war by the mass media. It has become commonplace to see video game–type animations, highly manipulated re-enactments, which stand in for the 'real' unpalatable truth. And yet, even when the media shows 'the truth,' footage courtesy of various military sources with blacked-out information on the screen, green night-vision footage, this 'hyper-real' information is again made unbelievable by the distancing effect it has on the viewer.

MH: Why do you call Akihabara the 'birthplace of manipulation'?

MO: The quote is: 'Deeply disappointed, she finds herself transported to Akihabara, Electric Town, the birthplace of manipulation.' Akihabara is a section in Tokyo that is known as Electric Town – a kind of geek paradise. The neighbourhood is littered with electronic items, gadgets, appliances, games and porn. Multi-storey shops tower over street vendors hawking everything from vegetable dicers to spy cameras. This is the area of town where the narrator goes to find a replacement for her broken video camera. The narrator is ideally searching for a camera 'that will record her imaginings. A kind of camera obscura for dreams' – one that might be able to record what she imagines her father seeing. Naturally, she would go to Electric Town, since this is the place where it will be, if such a thing exists.

MH: It's the fall of 2006, and all over the city screen stars are gathered to sell their smiles at the international festival. I'm wondering if you might leave us with a mention of your latest project, which finds you taking yet another unexpected turn.

MO: My current project is a collaboration with Blair MacKinnon, a website producer and digital videomaker. It's an online movie-viewing website, available at www.amovieaday.com. Each day we post a new short 'movie,' between 30 seconds and one minute in length. It started as a long-term project of mine to see if I could produce 365 'movies' over the course of a year. I started in November 2005 and will be finishing in the next few months. I'm down to the last 70 or so. I primarily make the movies on one of my favourite toy cameras at the moment, the Vcam Now, V.1. Intended as a diminutive slice of life in short form, the daily movies provide a brisk commentary on the world around us: at times funny, often thought-provoking, sometimes unsettling. Each day a new free short movie will be posted online at 12:01 EST. Every movie is unique and the collection spans a wide variety of subject matter and digital aesthetics. Specifically designed and conceived for the tiny screen, the movies can be downloaded through iTunes and played on cellphones or iPods. Inspired by an old newspaper concept featuring 'today's thought' or 'a smile a day,' these miniature movies are meant to be consumed daily, in between coffee and a doughnut.

Midi Onodera's Films and Videos

Reality-Illusion   7 min 1979
Contemplation   6 min 1979
Untitled   7 min 1979
Filter Queen   7 min 1980
A Film   6 min 1980
Food Trilogy
   What's for Lunch Charley   4 min 1981
   One Burger, Hold the Pickle   3 min 1981
   Après Diner   3 min 1981
Home Movies   1981 (3-projector installation)
The Bird that Chirped on Bathurst   4 min 1981
One If by Land, Two If by Sea   10 min 1982
Endocrine   15 min 1982
Home Was Never Like This   9 min 1983
Idiot's Delight   5 min 1983
Ville? Quelle Ville?   4 min 1984
The Dead Zone   2:30 min 1985
After Car Crash, Woman Kills Two   1:30 min 1985
Made in Japan   2:30 min 1985
Ten Cents a Dance (Parallax)   30 min 1985
Then/Now   30 min 1988
The Displaced View   52 min 1988
General Idea – Artist's Profile   3:50 min 1989
Heartbreak Hoteru   30 min 1990
David Cronenberg – Artist's Profile   3:50 min 1990
A Performance by Jack Smith   5 min 1992
Skin Deep   85 min 1995
The Basement Girl   12 min 2000
Slightseer   3:20 min 2001
Nobody Knows   3:15 min 2001
Alphagirls   3 × 15 min 2001 (DVD)
I Have No Memory of My Direction   77 min 2005
365 Short Videos   (30 sec–1 min each) 2006

Distributed by Women Make Movies, Canadian Filmmakers Distribution Centre, Vtape, Moving Images and Domino Film and Television International (*Skin Deep*).

Midi Onodera is an award-winning Toronto-based filmmaker who has been directing, producing and writing films for over 25 years. Midi's work has been critically recognized and included in numerous exhibitions and screenings internationally. For the past year, Midi has been working on making a video a day for 365 days. They can be viewed at www.midionodera.com

JOHN PRICE
HOME IS A MOVIE

He looks like someone who is always getting off a horse or exiting a scuffed motor car with the scenery whispering behind him in delight; he has that rugged kind of handsome about him that makes you trust him with things – maybe there's a leak that needs fixing in your life, or maybe those thoughts never had a roof at all and it's time to call and ask him to come over and have a look.

He belongs in a kingdom of geeks, all bent to a narrow geek task. In his case, it isn't golfing shoes or birding or obscure jazz dates that wind him up – no, he loves the machines of cinema. He shows me this little wooden box with a handle – oh man, it's a 35mm camera, not unlike the ones that got it all started at the turn of the last century. He has to crank the film through by hand, and he can't look through the lens to see what the camera sees; instead he has to feel his subject. It's not a point-and-shoot type situation: he has to take a stand and put it up on three legs and start winding. When it's done, he likes to invite friends over and show these large-gauge manufactures in his living room. I'm full of barbecue and conversation, and the projector sounds like a spaceship starting up, and now there are pictures, no larger than this book, projected against John's living-room wall. Kids rush in and out of the light and together we make the soundtrack.

His pictures are gathered between births, after buying ice cream for the kids, before going out into the neighbourhood with his boy and seeing everything for the first time again. He can't spend long months in the edit room anymore, watching the pictures slowly dry out and separate and come back together again, poring over past moments to see what secret codes might be unwrapped so they can speak to each other. Paternity has ushered in a new body of work that refuses an engineered escape, a release from the too many pressures. The all-hands presence required by his children has passed into his shooting, his hand-processing, his selection of stocks and assembly of rolls. Second guesses are behind him; there is no forever and ever or once upon a times, only now. He is filled with eternity and shares it when he can, admitting it into his little crank box of a camera and then pouring it out again. When it's time to show things, they come straight from the camera, or else are blown up in patterns of recognition. And then he splices the rolls together, and if the film gets scratched or ruined on its way through projectors, then it will have to wear the scar or surrender to destruction. There's no time to look back, and he wouldn't have it any other way. He's ready.

MH: Could you talk about how you got over to China to do *Making Pictures* (12 min, 35mm b/w, 2005)?

JP: In April 2005, I was hired by Peter Mettler to assist on a project he was shooting for the documentary filmmaker Jennifer Baichwal called *Manufactured Landscapes*. The subject of the film was Canadian photographer Edward Burtynsky, who was on his way to China to revisit some of the locations he had previously photographed and to make new images of how the landscape had been transformed.

Having seen Ed's work, I had a reasonable idea of what to expect. But the scale and density of these landscapes was more staggering than any photograph could possibly communicate, and our small crew for the most part enjoyed unobstructed access. From the largest construction site in the world (the Three Gorges Dam project) we travelled upriver past cities in the process of being completely rebuilt. We flew to one of the largest coal-distribution centres (an 18 km² coal mountain range), one of the largest aluminum recycling facilities, one of the largest shipbuilding facilities and one of the largest factories. In transit between these colossal sites, we followed Ed to Beijing and Shanghai, where he documented neighbourhoods slated for 'urban renewal' – a government term for the demolition of older districts in order to build higher-density living space. There we found people living in houses without walls – a tightly knit community that cooked, cleaned and carried out their lives in the small alleyways and streets.

Though I was extremely preoccupied with the technical work that had brought me to these places, there were moments of stillness when I was able to observe. I tried to imagine 1.4 billion people existing in the throes of a full-scale industrial revolution. Coal remains the primary source of electricity, the skies are perpetually grey and half the water supply is toxic. Edward was an encyclopedia of ecological facts, and the hard numbers he dished out between long meals sponsored by the local cultural-relations people or factory owners suggested an unsustainable future. Yet there we were, feasting like Caesars in ancient Rome. During the three weeks of intense travel, I cannot recall experiencing hostility from anyone who inhabited the landscapes that Edward was making pictures of. Government officials opposed interviews with holdout groups in Beijing and Shanghai, but wherever we went, people were generally curious and open, especially the children.

With me on the trip was a Super 8 camera that I pulled out when the others were waiting for their moments to happen, for their light to change, for their rain to go. Small windows of downtime came and went quickly, but through them I was able to do my own looking. I saw people working in very strange conditions and living a vastly different experience of time, and I also saw in these same spaces an artist and a film crew at work observing. It is this contrast that the film explores. As Ed liked to put it, it 'kicks open' some complex questions about 'making.'

I created shots on the optical printer from the original Super 8, blowing it up to 35mm, fading in from white into a still frame of Ed or a peasant or a landscape, and then it comes to life for a bit and then usually ends on a freeze frame of a child or a group of children. It was an amazing process that way, no Final Cut Pro or Steenbeck, just the original Super 8 processed as a negative and a bit of guesswork.

Pointing cameras is a tricky territory, and it leads me to think about this China movie. More than anything, for me it's a spectacle. The home movies of my son Charlie (*Party #1–4*, 4 x 2:45, silent, 2004–6) and *ten thousand dreams* (6 min, 35mm silent, 2004) rest closer to me somehow – they make me smile, but not the programmers. So what then is the project of making images? Communication? What makes a balanced movie, a balanced image with 'appropriate' distance? The concept of 'engagement' has been floating in my head a lot – and how much of the sadness I felt while looking over there (in China) was a function of our constant movement. I would like this to end up in the film because I don't see it now. *Making Pictures* reflects the sadness but not the vastness, and I am feeling that the transitions between sites could be useful ... Who knows ...

MH: Props for the show at the Cinematheque! Doesn't it seem like your work is beginning to get around (perhaps more than just beginning, but flowing, insisting, rushing forward)? It is well deserved. Looking forward to seeing movies new and old. I spent the day with Steve Sanguedolce re-recording the voice-over for our *Mexico* movie, the one we 'finished' 15 years ago. Yes, the remaking process is ongoing, but we are making headway, and it's fun besides.

JP: I'm working on six new movies for the show and have been so busy with the physical process of blowing up that I have spent little time thinking about the meaning of the pictures. It may end up a bit of a disaster as I am not planning on sound. Once the images are done, I might, time permitting, experiment a bit. One of the main issues for me at the moment is the desire to show more personal moments/home movies, and those are not really the ones that seem to be in demand on the screening circuit. The things the programmers seem to like lately are the more structural/structured works, the gun movie and the Falls movie especially. Some of the new ones are not at all like them, and the exhibition road may come to an abrupt end. Despite these insecurities, I am chewing through film stock like water and there is work getting made, so this makes me feel like it always does: alive.

The program will focus primarily on hand-developed diary material shot between 2005 and 2007. The starting point for making all of these pictures was an unscripted moment that presented itself while a loaded camera was in my hands. Often there are questions in my head about the nature of experience that inspires the looking: questions about power, violent behaviour, social hierarchy, the arbitrary and often deadly circumstances of one's birth. How do a fishing camp in a remote corner of Newfoundland, a duck-hunting camp in Quebec, Sachsenhausen concentration camp on the outskirts of Berlin, an aluminum-recycling facility in China, a small town in northern Saskatchewan and my seven-day-old baby daughter interrelate? Is it possible to create a coherent screening with such disparate material? At the moment I am less interested in 'finishing' work than in exploring the process of how the dialogue between the photographic texture of the material and the subject of the frame can communicate some-

Making Pictures

thing essential about humanity. The work for this screening will be presented in various states of completion and from a wide array of subject matter. Much of it will be blown up to 35mm for exhibition. The process of blowing up material is the editing; it is a decisive and expedient way to create work that places emphasis on the specificity of the hand-developed material while distilling moments from the raw camera rolls.

What is the plan with your *Mexico* film? A complete reworking? A 35mm blow-up? It must be really good to be able to work with others, especially if it's fun. I wonder if I too will go through a major reworking phase – that's frightening, having older things change into different, more perfect things. Is that it? The sense that you can apply experience to create something better. There are so many things I would change, painfully painful things, but then to get new optical sound and new prints, yikes ...

According to the Internet Movie Database, Lumière's film at Niagara Falls was the first ever shot in Canada. My rolls from the day we went look pretty good. Are these the last handmade 35mm films of the Falls? Soon heading north to do cinematography on a doc about Aboriginal youth at different latitudes of Canada: gas huffing, crystal meth, fast food ... could be really weird.

Three months later, I'm watching from my window as the leaves float in yellow eddies around the tree in the park. I've processed the last of the Falls footage and will start into the Olympic Stadium rolls this afternoon. It's nothing as dramatic as your day, for sure. There's a song that Charlie and I sang at the drop-in that sounded like, 'a smooth road, a bumpy road, a smooth road, a bumpy road ... a hole.' There was delight when I'd open my legs and he'd fall through. For kids, the beasts are adults, and words like *no* and *spinach*. It's hard to imagine how complex our desires become, the healthy ones and the unhealthy ones, though both can be satisfying in the moment.

Later I felt like I had been run over by a truck. I packed all the processing gear and picked up Charlie and fed him dinner and

Lea's cab arrived and I kissed her goodbye and bathed with Charlie and read him stories about curious monkeys and played him slow notes on an acoustic guitar and watched as his eyes became heavy with sleep and fluttered and closed. It's my favourite moment with him, and it makes me cry almost every time.

Months later. Just processed some 35mm Ektachrome from my latest trip to Niagara Falls. It's mostly black and white except for the one roll of colour which shows this big guy in an orange shirt backing up into the frame from one side with a digital still camera poised and ready while hundreds of others snap away around him. It's the first time I've processed colour reversal as a positive, and it looks amazing. The colour shot introduces a series of black-and-white rolls that are mostly just grain studies revealing the Falls through long drifts of focus. It's called *View of the Falls from the Canadian Side* (6:56 min, 2006).

MH: Great to hear things are smooth with Charlie. The whole notion of children is still a bit science-fiction to me, but the more I see them, the more documentary they appear. And yes, I can imagine his technological childhood and digital emotions (he loves me, he loves me not).

gun/play (9 min, 2006) brings together three single-roll 'portraits': the first shows a boy circling with a toy gun, the second a hunting trip with dad, and finally a boy alone on a beach. Can you talk about these moments, and how your haptic, tactile cinema (changing up film stocks and chemistries) grants to each of these scenes an individual impression?

JP: This haptic thing applies more directly to the rolls of my daughter that I am working on. The placenta on the grass, the musty smell as I transported it in my hands out to the backyard rests etched in my memory. Lea gave birth to a girl, her name is Estelle. No middle name yet. Healthy. And afterwards a placenta film – the act of seeing with one's own heart. It is such a beautiful organ. Once Lea was tucked in after the birth, I took what remained and laid it in the grass in the backyard – colour film! Have you ever seen one of these things? It is like the root system of a tree, known as the *arbor vita*, and from all of these roots stems the umbilical cord like a thick old telephone cord filled with blood. The landscapes of her pimple-riddled skin at a week old on some expired 4X black-and-white reversal stock (processed as negative), with its luminescent glow around each grain.

But I am supposed to be answering about movies from the past, which are receding as fast as childhood. The gun movie came so quickly and the individual moments were unlikely partners, shot ten years apart. It was the last roll that inspired the film. We were returning from a short vacation up in the Gaspé and decided to take a final moment on the beach before the two-day drive home. There were three adolescent boys building a castle on a wide sandbar while their father quaffed an ale. As the tide came in, they became more frantic, until the tide levelled their

structure. One of the boys remained, stumbling around in the water. I had shot quite a few rolls of black-and-white during the trip and found only one roll (of colour negative, which I rarely shoot) left in the trunk of the car, the Kodak 7245 that had just been discontinued. I loaded and shot it and actually took it to one of the big labs for processing, feeling it might look interesting without the accumulation of dust and dirt that can result from hand-processing. Technicolor offered to strike a second copy when I mentioned to the timer that it was overprinted. Instead, I took the original negative and made a 16mm positive on black-and-white optical sound-recording film (Kodak 3374). From that I made a 16mm internegative using the same stock, then I made a 35mm print. With each generation, the contrast increased and the background disappeared. Now it looks the way I remembered it. A slightly overweight teenager performs a strange battle-scene re-enactment/dance macabre in a shallow pool of water. He would drop to his knees, gather up a substantial handful of wet sand and hurl it into the air. As the mud returned to earth, he

gun/play

pretended it was a hail of bullets and crumpled as though he had been hit. He kept repeating the gesture, and by the time the film had run out through the camera, I had three solid moments.

The boy with the rifle is my nephew, who was just playing with his gun one summer afternoon, and the hunting sequence was a Thanksgiving weekend at my stepfather's hunting lodge. The guy smoking is an old buddy of my stepfather's who co-owns the camp, Mel Yull. I have been going there since I was 15 and finally brought a camera. Mel and his dog were about 200 yards away across the marsh, so I threw on a 150mm lens (the longest telephoto that Bolex manufactures) and shot hand-held through the reeds and mist. He is an exceptional hunter and can 'call' the ducks in from afar. The birds that get shot down in the film seemed miles away when Mel started blowing through his wooden reed. Over the space of ten minutes, they circled closer and closer until finally they were in range. Then he and my stepfather let them have it. I was surprised that the falling birds were recorded on the film, as the viewfinder in the Bolex was really dark, and by that point I had changed lenses to a 10mm, so they were just tiny specks in the frame. I think that shot really binds the hunting sequence, seeing these animals falling out of the sky.

I'm working on an extension of this movie that mixes hunting iconography with very personal moments of Charlie coming into contact with the passing of these animals (*Camp Series #2*, 8 min, 2007). There are deer and elk heads stuffed on walls and taxidermied ducks. My wife tries to shield him from these visions while my mother celebrates them.

Then there is another film about the fishing trip I took with my dad over Father's Day called *Camp Series #1* (12 min, 2007). There were three father-and-son groups, along with the president of the Atlantic Salmon Federation, at a very remote fishing camp in Newfoundland.

At the dinner table, my father regaled the room with the story of how he was on a fishing trip when I was born. He said he bought my mother a colour television set before taking his leave. To hear my father recounting the episode with a measure of pride was surreal. I put myself in his shoes and scratch my head – no wonder he was so out of it when we were kids. If I had missed the birth of my own child, I think the guilt would have followed me to my grave. It's a question I really must ask him one of these days. The meaning of having a child, of owning that responsibility. Now that I have kids, the anger has been transformed into wonder – but his father held the same prehistoric notions of fatherhood. How to express these feelings without a didactic text, allowing small gestures to provide clues and tell the story? Intuitively, I feel it's all there, but the guy onscreen is my dad and each look is so loaded.

I shot a pile of rolls on the trip with all kinds of emulsions and textures. I have been toying with sequencing on the computer, but I feel so different about the images while making print exposure tests from the negative. Sometimes I am inspired to print a shot because of the texture of the negative and not how it will fit into the 'narrative.' That's the strangeness of the computer for me: it begs me to create story rather than focus on texture. When I process film by hand, there are so many factors that affect the resulting texture. I generally shoot with film stock that I get for free (outdated colour reversal, short ends of lab printing stock, stock that has been deemed unusable by those who have invested heavily to ensure tight control and strive for a seamless-looking reality). I am never absolutely sure how the emulsion will react. Aging affects stock in different ways: increased base fog, decreased contrast and sharpness, oxidation of the colour dyes. Often I am developing the films with chemistry not designed to 'work' with that particular stock. The results vary tremendously. The more one experiments with a process, the more confident one becomes that the result will yield a positive outcome if one is inclined to continue with the experimentation.

The third film in the cycle, *Camp Series #3* (8 min, 2007), was shot at the concentration camp on the outskirts of Berlin. A large group of cops were touring the memorial; it felt really eerie, and I had a couple of rolls of Super 8 with me. It came together in a week, from the rough video transfer to the 35mm print. Its structure seemed very clear as soon as I saw the transfer with its dark and grainy and slowly repetitive gestures. These horrific atrocities were committed so recently. There's a sequence of various walking surfaces, including a boot-testing track where a leather company had prisoners walking in their boots for 12 hours a day to gauge wear and tear. There are hanging poles and medical examining rooms, but most frightening was an execution bunker lined with logs. Some of the camp had been restored, and this idea haunted me for some reason that I am still not able to articulate. I think that's why the movie exists.

MH: You have made several movies about masculinity – it just struck me that the many movies featuring your son Charlie could be included in this category. One of your earliest films was about your father, *The View Never Changes* (6 min, 1996), while another shows dancer Michael Dolan, *nine + 20* (10 min, 16mm b/w, 2001). These films approach their subjects in very different ways. Why these two folks, and how did these movies find their shape?

JP: When I got to Concordia University, I started asking questions that silenced answers, sometimes in my head, sometimes with a camera. Both movies were made during this period.

I went down to visit my father in New York at some point and took my Super 8 camera. I got to his place in the country and no one was home, so I sat waiting. Eventually I loaded the camera and started shooting the house and trees. He showed up a couple hours later with a newly born puppy. I had never seen him act like that, so loving and enthusiastic about every move the animal made. There's a shot during the little dog-dance sequence where you see his hand with a piece of material – I think it's some kind of retrieval exercise toy – and he's trying right off the bat to groom the dog into a champion. That's the issue I had with him forever and still do: his understanding of success involves money and prizes, something I never delivered to his expectations. I would have to be on the podium of some glitzy, commercial, 'recognized' deal for him to appreciate what I have spent a lot of time doing. Either that or a job where I make more money than he does. So there lies the notions of masculinity you mentioned. The new fishing movie is another approach, but I'm not afraid to get closer to him now. There are several moments where he looks around for me as I am shooting, for acknowledgment or approval or something.

After I shot those two rolls of Super 8, I interviewed my mother, who let loose about how he left her high and dry after the wheels fell off their marriage. She said some very hurtful things, and I spent a huge chunk of time trying to find some kind of balance in the text – a story I could live with that pointed to the roots of his emotional imprisonment. The images were cut in a week or so, and the sound took six months.

In *nine + 20*, Mick was just a lovely man going through an extremely challenging time. Trying to figure out how to be generous with his love while being consumed by the physical and temporal demands of being a member of LaLaLa Human Steps in Montreal. He had just joined the company after a series of intense auditions and was still insecure about his ability to perform at that level. We had a really strong connection and mutual respect for each other's creative process, and we were also at a very similar point in our lives, grappling with the concept of being in a committed relationship.

Before I left the city to return to Vancouver, I asked if he would be open to collaborating on an improvised film experiment. With a Super 8 camera and a cassette recorder, we walked up Mount Royal, shooting as we climbed. There was no rehearsal or preconception. When we got up to the observation viewpoint, I placed him in front of me, turned on the camera, and he started to move. I moved with him, and for those three minutes we explored the space. The roll ran out as he came to a stop in much the same position as he had started. He wanted to have another crack at it, but by then a busload of tourists had flooded the area. We ended up in the huge cemetery on top of a decrepit mausoleum with the audio tape rolling. I asked him a series of questions and that became the raw material for the text. Like *The View Never Changes*, the pictures were done in a week, but the audio involved hard labour. Maybe that's why all of the new stuff will be silent. Pictures are so easy for me at the moment; the subtext of a gesture is so transparent now. I am optimistic that this clarity will be shared by those who see it.

MH: *Remembrance Day Parade* (2:45, silent, 2005), *Fire #1 – #3* (3 × 3 min, 16mm silent, 2003), *427 & 401* (3 min, b/w 16mm silent, 2001) and *P.N.E.* (2:45 min, silent, 1996) are all silent, single-roll, hand-processed 'trip' movies, dishing up 21st-century psychedelia. Sure, the close candle watches of the *Fire* series are lovely, the highway trek of *427* is hallucinatory, not to mention the smeared, colour-challenged marchers in *Remembrance Day Parade*. They are all beautiful, but is beautiful enough? They feel like sketches, not movies unto themselves but lovely fragments – is that okay? Or should every movie aspire to be The One?

JP: The parade, the sunset and the *P.N.E.* movies appear as they came out of the chemistry. I exhibit the camera original because I have attempted to make internegatives and the resulting print always looks dead. They are accumulating dust and dirt and some scratching, but, surprisingly, the colour has not faded. The sunset

is one of my favourites because it was such a surprise. It was the last roll I shot before reaching the Cascade Mountains on my way back to Vancouver one year; there was a forest fire somewhere in the area and the light was incredible. I checked my film stash and had only the 3 ASA colour print stock left. I was quite upset because the light meter said there wasn't nearly enough light to record an image. Driving alone, I shot with the Bolex camera one frame at a time, exposing each frame for one second. By the end of the roll it was dark out and I packed the camera away and slept by the Grand Coulee Dam. I thought to myself that even though there would be no silver record of that experience, it was etched in my memory. A year later I finally got around to processing the roll. I had smoked a joint and had some fresh colour chemistry, so I decided I would push and solarize the bejesus out of it. The result had nothing to do with what my eyes had seen that day, but light had reached the film, and I discovered that even this slow colour print stock could be used in low light.

The *Fire* movies were made around the same time I found out I was going to be a father. My girlfriend went out one evening and I just needed to make something. I took a candle into the bathroom and blew a roll of colour print and processed it right away. I had done some rewinding and double exposures and decided to make a small series. For #3, I drew a storyboard, which I never do ... but there were quadruple exposures and I wanted to try and make it as 'narrative' as possible using only a single candle.

I had been fighting to create a shape with *Passages* (24 min, b/w, 2003) for a long while. It is a film journal assembled from nine rolls of black-and-white 16mm film that I shot on an overland journey from Switzerland to Turkey. It is a travelling meditation on the direction of our culture that places images of ruined Roman and Greek settlements beside simple observational moments shot in the cities, towns and villages along the way. *Passages* became the last 16mm film I made with an optical soundtrack and I have never looked back.

The *Fire* movies were a reaction to this, an attempt to find beauty using the most basic means, without editing or sound. They were so rewarding and pure. Though largely unseen, I showed them to friends at home.

Now I spend so little time thinking about the movies and all the time doing them. If the shot looks good, I'll blow it up; if it doesn't contain some moment, then I won't. There is usually a balance between texture and text. Looking through the viewfinder of the optical printer at a negative image is where the editing occurs, and working in 35mm makes decisions easier because it carries more weight (and relative expense). If I do not feel strongly about how an image might function with the others in a series, it gets left behind. It's good for me not to work these pictures to death.

The postman just brought some regular-8 Kodachrome that I shot of my

View of the Falls from the Canadian Side

dad and his dogs out in the country, and I'm excited by how soft the texture of the stuff is, how my dad's creamy bald head glows and how the blue sky behind contrasts his dark-red bow tie. I shot him as he was rushing off to a church committee function and he was rounding up his dogs to stuff them in his car. Maybe someday I'll have time to work with it.

Printing up a home movie tomorrow before the baby comes, a 16mm roll from Charlie's third birthday party which will be the last work for a bit. Lots of film waiting, the Bolex is clean and ready, storks in flight.

MH: Home movies have been a fringe-movie staple, from Mike Snow's 45-minute zoom in *Wavelength* to David Rimmer's movies shot entirely out his windows, from the mourning pictures of Phil Hoffman to the family trysts of Ann Marie Fleming and Richard Fung.

four + 1

Your approach moves in the same direction, gathering footage without a movie in mind, content to open to events as they unfold around you. It was a surprise to come over for lunch on Sunday and have a movie finished the next day, part of a suite of four silent, one-roll movies called *Party* (*Party #1, Party #2* ...). Each is child's play, featuring backyards full of children looking and being looked at. These early-education primers are typically wound through the camera several times to show these familiar faces growing unfamiliar through multiplication – everything is new.

JP: There is so much cruelty these days compelling me to act, to try and express something essential about what is in store for my kid. In Lebanon and Palestine and Darfur, pictures show dads carrying their kids away from home to avoid the killing. There are dead children on the cover of today's *New York Times*. Those were the images that followed me to a commercial I worked on over the weekend to promote the Canadian MTV channel. Frivolous bullshit for $500. Oh yeah, I interviewed for a teaching job at Sheridan College, ho ho ho. I didn't feel like they were looking for someone young and idealistic. One of the final questions was how I felt about being the 'face' of cinematography at the school ... Hmm. The only thing I want out of teaching is to see a couple of students make amazing images that mean something. To be proud of their work ... Fuck.

Two months later. We're in Saskatchewan playing bingo and filming ravens and elders and kids in hoodies sleeping in class. Everyone is very friendly and open. I feel free to shoot, but the director often shuts me down, saying, 'We don't need this,' as a kid skips along a snowy street, or a snowmobile breaks the openness of the landscape. It has been a bit frustrating being under the control of another, and I think it will be reflected in the film. I am trying not to get too invested, but when I see something essential and can't record, it it makes me crazy.

Yesterday we went to a really small town where we arranged to shoot some Métis fiddle players. They were very young kids dressed up in 'traditional' outfits. The 'teacher' was a white man

with either Parkinson's or alcoholism and had them scared stiff. '*Play it with a little gusto!*' They were terrified and terrible because of it. There was a moment where he removed the kid we were trying to focus on and elected another student. The poor kid slunk into the background and covered his face, all caught in a wide shot of the white teacher showing the new kid exactly 'how to do it.' I am in the school right now writing email as the director takes her grandma to the hospital in the next town for an ultrasound. I'm trying to shoot the kids in their unnatural habitat – gotta go quick as the kids are coming out for recess. Two more days here and I will be home.

A month later, just a little story that is weighing on me as Charlie naps. I found out a couple of days ago that one of our 17-year-old subjects up north is lying brain-dead in an Edmonton hospital after being launched from the back of a Ski-Doo during a four-in-the-morning drunken excursion. The guy who was driving died instantly, and she lay in the snow for three hours before someone found her. If she lives, she will lose her legs and hands, but apparently her survival is not likely. It's so sad. We interviewed her in her room in her empty house where she had scribbled poems about friends' suicides on her wall. Winter light fell coldly on her cheek as she told us the story of her broken life. She was living alone in her father's house while he was in Yellowknife on an alcohol-rehabilitation program. Her mother didn't live in town, nor did her sister. She wanted simply to have a job where she could save money to buy her mom a house.

When we flew out of town, she was at the airport waiting for her dad to arrive on the plane that would take us away. He had dropped out of the program. I had the camera rolling when he walked in. She hugged him hard and he stood there stiffly. He granted us a few words on-camera, like the rest of the parents had, but as we got up close I was hit by a wall of stink. He was blasted and had no desire to be present for his girl. She was trying so hard to put him in a good light, it was savage ... and then we got on the plane and took off. The sound recordist broke down. I felt horrible for her too, but now I am a bit confused. We shot an interview with an elder here in Toronto yesterday – the film continues somehow, but I wonder now what the lesson is. I've been skating a bit with my pal Charlie and that makes a lot more sense. We eat and nap and read books and life is so good. And then it's not. The horror is so abstract, because we're not in the room with her anymore.

MH: How many documentaries have stumbled over this problem, of trying to get people to act more like themselves? How to keep the camera rolling long enough so that composed faces give way to something else, something like life happening, in all its sad, ugly, lovely, hopeful and hopeless moments? I wish I could say I was engaged in something like that with my own work, instead of carefully stage-managing all of my pictures (and no doubt, alongside it, my emotions and relationships).

JP: Every situation is so complex and words never find perfection in matters of the heart. I think images do a better job. When I was trying to figure out if I was ready to have children, when Lea was newly pregnant with Charlie, I was still completely unsure about it. One night at my old studio, I was watching some home-movie footage of my nephew's christening. There was a shot of Lea with my other nephew holding a flower out to his chin and there was a smile on his face that gave me the answer. She will be an amazing mother. That night we cried with joy, and the questions disappeared. There is no time to look backward these days – the branch in the road recedes at an alarming rate.

John Price (b.1967) has produced experimental documentaries and diary films since 1986. After graduating with an MFA from Concordia University in 1996, he worked in the commercial film industry as a camera assistant to pay off loans and buy a Bolex. While gaining experience with professional camera and lens systems, his daily contact with motion-picture laboratories led to extensive experimentation with self-processing and optical printing. Guided by presence and intuition, his alchemical approach to a diarist practice has resulted in a body of work that is a textured, closely observed survey of human ritual.

He has received support from the National Film Board, the Canada Council for the Arts, the Ontario Arts Council, the Toronto Arts Council and the Liaison of Independent Filmmakers of Toronto, and has been exhibited at festivals and galleries internationally. He has also produced film projections for opera and dance and teaches cinematography in Toronto, where he lives with his wife and two children. www.filmdiary.org

John Price's Films

Dread   6 min 1992
Outlet   6 min 1993
View/Watch/Look/See   10 min 1995
The View Never Changes   6 min 1996
P.N.E.   2:45 min 1996
Sunset   2:45 min 1997
Wreck   4 min 1997
Nation   5 min 1997
Agate's Party   2:45 min 1998
Remembrance   6 min 1999
West Coast Reduction   4 min 2000
After Eden   30 min 2000
427 & 401   3 min 2001
nine + 20   10 min 2001
Beati Mundo Corde   8 min 2002 (with David Armstrong)
fire #1–#3   3 × 2:45 min 2003
Farewell   2 min 2003
Devry Series #1 & #2   2 min 2003
Passages   24 min 2003
The Vanauley Project   4 min 2004
ten thousand dreams   6 min 2004
Party #1–4   3 × 2:45 2005–06
Remembrance Day Parade   2:45 min 2005
Making Pictures   13 min 2005
The Almanac   52 min 2005
eve   6 min 2006
gun/play   9 min 2006
View of the Falls from the Canadian Side   6:56 min 2006
Intermittent Movement   35mm, 7 min 2006
Untitled   6 min 2007
The Camp Series   25 min 2007
Making Pictures #2   5 min 2007
naissance   10:58 min 2007
the boy who died   7:35 min 2007
Rolls   12 min 2007
four + 1   3 min 2008
sea series #1–2   s × 2:45 2008

Distributed by Canadian Filmmakers Distribution Centre.

When we speak, he appears vaguely uncomfortable in his lanky frame – I suspect because it is not perfect. When will he be perfect? Every word leaves his mouth reluctantly. 'Can I take that back?' Never mind that he is one of the most uncommonly articulate speakers I have ever met, he is most comfortable speaking in the dark, in one of his performances, or in an artist's talk, when everything has been scripted and rehearsed. I know this so well. How much better for me relationships could be if only we both knew our lines. If only we would stick with our roles, and ensure that tomorrow looks as much like today as possible.

He is best known for making performances with an overhead projector, that outmoded school tool used to produce diagrams and charts, scribbled over with hothouse colours. Daniel produces meticulous line drawings and 'animates' them by moving them by hand across painted backdrops. The point is not to fool you – you can see how it's done easily enough, but that only adds to the charm. It is made at home, by hand, and worked on until a whole world appears, with characters that appear in a series of frozen glimpses, narrated by that smooth monotone. There is something nearly unbearable in all this, some overly sensitive surface that shows itself as heartbreak. It is a special kind of sadness he needs to share, not the anguished stab of a loss, but a beauty glimpsed through tears. He constructs a world of characters and stories, but they are always broken, and hurt, and their triumph is not an ability to overcome this hurt, but to speak out of it, to show that something else can grow in this bruised and left-behind place.

MH: You have recently been commissioned by Lorri Millan and Shawna Dempsey at the Winnipeg Art Gallery to produce a short video. Can you talk about what you've done?

DB: *Artist Statement* (5 min, 2006) is a computer animation based on a live performance I developed for the overhead projector in 2004. While reciting an artist statement, I would make a drawing on the projector. The monologue from that performance is now the voice-over for the cartoon, which describes and parodies my personal approach to artmaking.

> I used to get such a rush doing this. Ten years ago, if I were feeling even remotely anxious or depressed, work would bring an instant sense of relief and satisfaction. But now I'm just like all the rest, and working here has become the dull habit of a lonely man ... I don't know why I'm showing everyone this, because I'm actually quite embarrassed by frank expressions of sex and emotions, but I always knew that one day I would personally risk public humiliation by saying certain things and by being gratuitously honest. I hope in my work to do this – to express myself unnecessarily. I'm not posing as an outsider or a rebel. Nor do I ever concern myself with the advancement of my career. My work's not like that. I'm just trying to say those things that people in their daily life find so difficult to express. I think it is possible to reveal the truth for other people in this way. Or at least show them how to get it. [text excerpt from *Artist Statement* by Daniel Barrow]

MH: What do we see in your movie?

DB: This video cartoon shows a young boy making drawings at school. Everyone from the class, including the teacher, crowds around his desk. He's drawing cock. They start clapping and chanting to egg him on. Suddenly he feels pathetic because the crowd is titillated, which is not what he intended. So he starts over. He draws a figure hanging off a branch – the lonely man. The man lets go of the branch and falls into a well. Then we see me at the computer looking at pictures of cartoon fags. Charlie Brown is a guy who spent the first five years of his life in an incubator. I'm then using the mouse to draw an ass getting wiped on the computer. Then a cursor finger-fucks the ass. When the finger comes out, it's covered in shit, and writes, 'I don't want a job' in shit. There's some cock-sucking. The kid writes, 'I want to be touched.' Deeply moved, the entire class bursts into tears, which pleases the boy enormously. The lonely man emerges from the well with a rope hanging off his dick. A kitten hangs on to it for dear life. Saved. The boy rocks. The End.

MH: How do you develop your stories?

DB: I begin with a series of visual ideas that excite me. As an artist, I'm always searching for innovative ways to convey a narrative, but audiences don't always follow the trail because they're distracted by other things: my presence in the room, the technique, as well as the numerous visual gags I make. My methods are very simple but visually dense. I'm still learning to write for a listener and not a reader.

I see my work existing somewhere between animation and comic-book narrative. My interest in minimal movement can be traced back to *Rocket Robin Hood* – a television program from the '60s that branded itself on my mind as a kid. When I was an undergrad I became obsessed with the idea of collecting these childhood pictures; later I understood that my process is simply an attempt to refabricate these formative images. Few of the stories on *Rocket Robin Hood* really interested me. I was inspired instead by the strange, minimal gestures, and the way scenes were constructed. The backgrounds and characters were often recycled from other stories and drawn by animators with radically different drawing styles. Often the characters wouldn't move at all – the story would unfold in a series of stills or gestures comprised of two or three frames. I am not very interested in perfecting complicated movements – I took a classical animation workshop recently and couldn't get into it. My animation acts more like a storybook, using strategic composition and simple movements and repetitions to convey narrative.

MH: Why did you go to art school?

DB: It took me a long time to get there. I typically made the grade in elementary and high school, and while I didn't feel pressure to become a doctor or lawyer, there were unspoken obligations that I created for myself. I was a very obedient child who found it difficult to submit to my desires. This all has to do with growing up gay, actually. At 18, the idea of going to art school seemed like an undemanding, indulgent goal. I studied physics, and then design, with the idea of becoming an architect. Later I switched my major to art history, hoping to become an academic. Finally, with encouragement from a good teacher, I switched to a studio major. I still notice myself edging around the periphery of the things I really want for myself.

MH: Did your work in art school relate to what came after?

DB: Absolutely. I began making overhead projector pieces while I was still an art history major. My Byzantine/Medieval professor was an ex-nun who had taught art history since the 1950s. Over a span of decades she had perfected a series of very structured, pedantic lectures. She would begin every lecture with two images on slide projectors, asking us to compare and contrast. We were not allowed to take notes while she lectured because she wanted everyone to have the same notes. Periodically, throughout her lectures, she would turn off the slide projectors and dramatically walk across the stage to an overhead projector where everything she had just said was condensed to point-form notations. She had beautiful handwriting and a soft, lilting voice and, of course, the supernatural images were very evocative as well. There was something so delightful and cozy about these juxtapositions. I began working with the overhead projector as a way of mimicking her lectures. My first performances parodied Christian lectures about God's relationship to artmaking. I intended them to be archly ironic, but people took me very seriously. I immediately received an offer from a classmate to perform in a church, which I pretended to accept. Gradually these overhead-projector pieces became more narrative and pictorial.

MH: Did you similarly develop your drawing style at art school?

DB: No, drawing was not considered a serious activity. From the time I could hold a crayon, I've been passionate about drawing, but in art school I felt obliged to maintain a poetic distance from process. Besides, my drawing style already seemed mannered and cultivated. So I spent a lot of time working with other people's drawings. For example, I once came into the school late at night and videotaped all the bad first-year students' figure-drawing projects taped up in the hallways. They all featured the same model from different perspectives. I used fans to animate the

paper and recited a monologue about acne. The end result was an art video called *The Sorry Entertainer* (3 min, 1994).

In my thesis year I asked everyone I knew to draw a picture of me picking a rose from a bush, especially those with naive rendering skills. This was in the early '90s and the burgeoning of 'tard art.' I animated these drawings in *Black Heart's Desire* (5 min, 1995). Actually, I still really like that video.

MH: How has your process developed since you left the school nest?

DB: Well, maybe not that much. I've continued to aspire to unique approaches to storytelling, most often using an overhead projector. Specifically, I have created and adapted a series of comic-book narratives to a 'manual' and live form of animation by projecting, layering and manipulating drawings on mylar transparencies. My original drawings are on paper, and these are transferred to

Every Time I See Your Picture I Cry

mylar with a photocopier. I always work in black and white first to work out the sequencing and gestures, because they are about a fifth of the cost of colour photocopies. While I feel I have less energy, my work is more ambitious than it was in art school, but no less tortured. The themes are still the same.

MH: Your performances are filled with personas, masks and characters. How do you go about inventing them?

DB: When I'm starting a new piece, I cast roles in a sense – I think of who the character is and who I would like to be when I perform. Normally the answer is Quentin Crisp or Vincent Price. In *Looking for Love in the Hall of Mirrors* (26 min, 2000), Vincent Price is cast in the role of the protagonist (who doesn't have a name). It's the story of an elderly man who moves to the city for the very first time, leaving his parents behind on a farm. It is told in a series of letters to his parents. He's a failed artist and is busy installing a series of paintings in a gay cruising park amidst the trees. In all of my stories (and many of my favourite films), the protagonist is a failed artist, and the artwork possesses a transformative power.

> Dear Mom and Dad,
>
> I think most artists find it difficult to distance themselves from their subject. But perspective is only difficult to maintain when words or images are inspired by features that have become integrated into the core of one's own identity. Love and sex have not been a part of my immediate experience and so bringing them into clear focus is for myself entirely possible.
>
> Maintaining this kind of poetic distance for so long has meant that I have developed a kind of immunity. I often imagine myself as the harlequin Gilles in the paintings of Antoine Watteau. I stand white with candour amidst the autumn scenes of transformation and lovemaking that surround me. I feel exploited, vacant and indifferent. The sad clown as tragic hero. Beauty often moves people to tears but I'm told my work effects this process in reverse. Quite a feat I think. [text excerpt from *Looking for Love in the Hall of Mirrors* by Daniel Barrow]

MH: In the same performance you say, 'In the end it's really not all that difficult to be a bit different. It's not that different to be a bit different. In the end it's not all that scary to walk off the beaten path.' But your work is filled with lonely, self-loathing monsters, hideous transformations, illness and brutality, insisting that nothing could be more difficult than to be 'a bit different.' This difference is the root and cause of a hypersensitivity, symptom of all the ways you don't fit in, motor for your artmaking. Without a feeling of loss, of disaffection, of not belonging, you wouldn't be an artist, would you?

DB: I think of all of my stories as parables. Each of my protagonists undergoes a profound, though often minor, spiritual transformation. In *Looking for Love*, the hero ultimately realizes the interconnection of all things and is, at least momentarily, freed from the stress of getting laid or finding a boyfriend. The transformations in my stories may be ostensibly monstrous, but my intention is to point to something profound and beautiful. I am not sure what kind of artist I would be if I were not plagued by fear, anxiety and doubt. I suspect the quality would improve.

MH: Vincent Price is one of your favourite actors, and his highlight role remains the decadent, overly sensitive brother in Roger Corman's *House of Usher*. Price recites these lines from the Poe short story that is the basis for this movie: '... any sort of garment other than the softest silk is agony to my flesh, Oh it assails me

constantly, and as I said before, sounds of any degree whatsoever inspire me with terror ... ' He is, like all of the protagonists in your work, an artist. Price appears in this role as a recluse, temperamentally unsuited for a populace that is too loud, too brutal, too vulgar. His overdeveloped and over-refined sensibilities have been honed in solitary: is this what you identify with so strongly?

DB: Yes, you're exactly right. *Against Nature* by J. K. Huysman is a book that influences so many of my character constructions. In the Huysman novel, a fabulous misanthrope decides to lock himself away from the rest of the world, committed to relate only with beautiful objects and never other people. I'm not sure if Huysman read Poe, but it seems pretty likely. Roderick Usher, like Huysman's anti-hero Des Esseintes, is enslaved by his incredibly refined senses and can only hope to heal himself with art. He paints by candlelight, plays the lute very softly and lives on a diet of pallid mash. It's a fantastic dream of mine: not to need other people and to commit myself to perfecting a lifestyle. This is all perfectly and stylishly realized by Vincent Price. Many of my protagonists, particularly Hillbilly from *The Face of Everything*, attempt to cloister themselves in this way.

MH: Could you describe *The Face of Everything* (45 min, 2002)?

DB: *The Face of Everything* is an overhead-projector performance inspired by the life of Liberace's chauffeur and lover, Scott Thorson. The central theme of their relationship was that Liberace convinced Scott to undergo a series of plastic surgeries to make him look more like Liberace. This is detailed in the autobiography Scott wrote about a year after Liberace's death, entitled *Behind the Candelabra: My Life with Liberace*. Scott alleges the plastic surgeries were intended to produce a familial resemblance so that the couple could pass as father and son. I was captivated by the story's popular, tabloid appeal but even more excited about the symbolic potential. Perhaps because I principally draw faces, I think of the face as a template or site of profound transformation.

Catalogue of the Original

166

MH: Why did you name your entertainer Devo instead of Liberace?

DB: *Devo* is the male Italian form of *diva*, but also a band I greatly admire. I was trying to confuse the audience's cultural references. I regret that now. It didn't work. I wanted this character to be an amalgam of Liberace and someone authentically cool, like Devo. I quickly realized that people weren't getting this. In fact, they were missing most of my deliberate references. While *The Face of Everything* is not really an adaptation of Scott Thorson's life story, it is a reimagining of the story. It's set in the 1970s and incorporates many real-life celebrities from the same generation – like Kristy McNichol, Bunny Rogers and Liz Renay. After touring *The Face of Everything* for six months, I decided to create an introductory slide show (and then a trading-card series and single-channel video) called *Catalogue of the Original* to expound upon these peripheral characters and references. It's not necessary while watching *The Face of Everything* to know the history of Little Miss No-Name, for instance, but it adds dimension to the story.

MH: Who (or what) was Little Miss No-Name?

DB: She was a doll introduced by Mattel in 1965, designed by Deet D'Andre, a famous doll artist. She wore a burlap sack and had a plastic, removable tear, her hands extended as if to beg. She was a tragic figure that Mattel hoped little girls would care about. Perhaps they were smart. The television commercial featured her barefoot and shivering in a snowstorm, begging for help. Ultimately she didn't sell well, but I found many online testimonials by grown-up little girls who were incredibly moved and connected to this doll. I'm interested in characters or effigies suspended in tragedy. Little Miss No-Name will never be happy – every time you play with her she'll be disconsolate. There's something at once disturbing and attractive about that.

MH: You present these biographies with hand-drawn portraits on one side of the screen and a handwritten text on the other. You read the text out loud, and I read it onscreen, right along with you. You begin with Dismal Desmond, a melancholic dog. You move on to Liberace's chauffeur/lover, a trio of B celebrities (Margaret Keane; Rip Taylor, the crying comedian; Charles Nelson Reilly, star of *The Gong Show* and Bic Pen commercials), and a couple of self-invented queers: Bunny Roger, who wore a chiffon scarf in World War I trenches, and Quentin Crisp, the Naked Civil Servant. The actors you introduce are curious – all have gained recognition, though for the most part in the lower tiers of entertainment media.

DB: With the exception of Kristy McNichol and Liberace, these are under-recognized figures who mean something to me personally. Quentin Crisp is one of my biggest influences, especially as a writer and a performer of monologues. So much of my work is an homage to him. I've memorized several monologues from his amazing albums and used to recite them in front of the mirror. I might perform one tonight but I will probably ask to have the lights turned off because I've never become accustomed to being watched while I'm performing.

MH: That's a curious attitude for a performer. Crisp has a quality of lying outside the flow of events, in a place he's invented all by himself.

DB: He refers to this as 'becoming a stylist.' I began reading Crisp at an important moment, early in my university education and shortly before he died. I still relate strongly to his philosophy and sense of humour. Crisp can simultaneously inhabit tragic and comic perspectives, pride and shame, more effectively than anyone else I've encountered.

MH: Your performances channel received media wisdoms in an unusual fashion.

DB: This is again because my work is an attempt to recreate some experience I had as a child, and usually that's a media experience, something I vaguely remember from *Chico and the Man* or *Sesame Street*. My response to these images used to have branching consequences. I am now less vulnerable to the power of images, perhaps because I can be very jaded and competitive. It's so incredible to me that YouTube exists, because now these images are all at my fingertips, but in university I was fiercely searching. I videotaped *Sesame Street* three different times a day, every day, for about nine months, to find a specific, short, surreal animation about the letter E.

E
E
See
Me

Catalogue of the Original

Eating a peach
Sitting on my eagle
Chasing a beagle
To the queen on her knees
Under a tree
By the sea
She was looking for her Easter egg
Having a dream about eating ice cream
In the Land of Steam
When a baby seal
Tickled her heel
She let out a squeal
And woke from her dream in time to see
The eagle and me
Flying away with the Easter egg
Over the evening sea
Hee hee hee
E
E

MH: I'm amazed you can remember something so non-narrative. Often it is some element of story that lingers, but this clip features a world in a constant state of flux and transformation.

DB: Twenty-five years after I saw this animation, I made a music video for the Hidden Cameras called *A Miracle* (3 min, 2003). I realized only recently that the story is directly inspired by this *Sesame Street* animation. It's about a young boy who awakens late at night to create shadow puppets on the walls of his bedroom. In doing so, he summons a magical creature who feeds him a spoonful of honey and then swallows the boy whole.

Every Time I See Your Picture I Cry

MH: How do you go about creating a new performance?

DB: Story development occurs as a process of stacking and sifting ideas. I begin with a considerable volume of visual ideas and develop a story by experimentally appending them to each other. My hope is that the best ideas will rise to the foreground and the rest will ultimately form the periphery. Only when all of the visual ideas have been organized do I start writing the script.

The visual narrative rarely lines up directly with the monologue anyway. For instance, when the protagonist in *Looking for Love in the Hall of Mirrors* is painting in the forest, his interior monologue describes his relationship to love and sex. Often the voice-over text is mined from journal excerpts that are customized to fit the narrative. I'm not writing the way a novelist would write. I've never written a proper script either. Instead I allow a story to emerge in the process of constructing a consistent visual and emotional atmosphere.

MH: You use a variety of techniques to grant your still pictures movement, most often by physically moving a coloured transparency figure over a background. But you also lay two line drawings of the same feature overtop each other, with cross-hatched lines running in different directions. When you move the top figure, it appears animated.

DB: I thought I had invented this technique, but later learned that it was a standard effect in late-19th-century Victorian magic lantern shows. And I'm sure there are precedents to that. Everything I am doing now has a magic-lantern parallel. The effect you're talking about is popularly employed in contemporary lenticular postcards. Lenticular images are the ones that seem to move when you change your perspective – like the winking stickers from Cracker Jack boxes or the small billboards in airports that change their message depending on the viewing angle.

MH: Can you tell me about *Every Time I See Your Picture I Cry* (45 min, 2008)?

DB: It's the performance I am currently working on and the most ambitious project I've ever undertaken. The central character is a garbageman, and like all my other protagonists, he's also a failed artist. It's recently occurred to him that he would like to start a new creative project: an independently produced phone book. He's gradually assembling a large catalogue in which each citizen will have a page of the book devoted to the story of their life. He collects personal information by sifting information out of their garbage. What he doesn't realize is that he's being followed by a deranged lunatic who has recently escaped from a mental asylum. The lunatic is killing each citizen the garbageman enters into his phone book, thereby rendering his efforts obsolete.

The garbageman includes an illustration of each citizen in his phone book, but because he's not interested in relearning how to draw, he simply places tracing paper over his subject's window and traces a portrait. Because he works very late at night, most of his subjects are featured asleep or watching television. But in one scene, the garbageman traces two lovers making out on their couch.

Every Time I See Your Picture I Cry

As he leaves the frame, the camera pans and becomes a point-of-view shot, very much in homage to John Carpenter's *Halloween*. We see the serial killer's perspective as he enters the couple's home and slaughters them. Then he writes 'I don't want a job' on the wall with the couple's blood.

> I'm alternately drawn and repelled by the idea that there is poetry in squalor. The theme of complete desperation is compelling in stories, and has been gaining popularity for years, but the idea that life is only a test of our capacity to cope with the depths of human misery is to me outrageous because I feel like I'm capable of so much more. Periodically, people like Helen Keller come up with interesting comments like, 'Our greatest challenges in life will one day be known to us as our greatest teachers.' But in truth no critically ill or wheelchair-bound person has ever learned so much from the experience that they encouraged others to seek it out first hand. [text excerpt from *Every Time I See Your Picture I Cry*]

MH: You've just shown me a clip from *Song of Bernadette* (1943) in which an older nun complains bitterly to young Bernadette that she was not the one chosen to receive visions from the Virgin Mary. She has worked hard, worn her fingers out on prayer beads, but instead the Virgin has appeared only to Bernadette. Why this clip?

DB: It's one of my favourite monologues and very similar to the Vincent Price monologue from *House of Usher*. Like Roderick

Usher and Huysman's Des Esseintes, Sister Vauzous, played by Gladys Cooper, renounces social comforts because she is in pursuit of an aesthetic ideal. Roderick Usher isolates himself in order to cope with his sensitivities. Sister Vauzous similarly isolates and tortures herself in an effort to become sensitive to the divine:

> In all our sacred history the chosen ones have always been those who have suffered. Why then should God choose you? Why not me? I know what it is to suffer. Look at my eyes. They burn like the very fires of hell. Why? Because they need sleep, they need rest, which I will not give them. My throat is parched from constant prayer. My hands are gnarled from serving God in humiliation. My body is pained from stone floors. Yes, I have suffered, because I know it is the only true road to heaven. And if I, who have tortured myself, cannot glimpse the Blessed Virgin, how can you, who have never felt pain, dare to say that you have seen her?

Gladys Cooper is one of my favourite actresses. I think in early cinema, actors typecast themselves because it paid well. While some actors made their careers playing swishy, gay waiters, Gladys Cooper, at least later in her career, became well-known for effortlessly depicting stone-cold, thin-lipped, aristocratic bitches. Her characters in *Bernadette*, *Separate Tables* and *Now, Voyager* (all favourite movies) are virtually indistinguishable. I often want my characters to be angrier than I can realistically depict them. I soften their edges because I don't have the confidence or dramatic talent to pull it off, but if I could, I would hire Gladys Cooper to play the part of my garbageman.

MH: Daniel, do I even need to point out that you are identifying with the 'wrong' character? Of course it is the lovely Bernadette that you are supposed to become as the viewer. She is virtuous and holy – even the Pope says so. The character you feel closest to, on the other hand, is ugly and mean-spirited, and gives the innocent heroine a difficult time. Can you talk about your identification with 'bad/wrong' characters and how your own narrative work is founded on strategies that might lead viewers to share your view?

DB: One of the themes that unites all of my storytelling is spiritual redemption. *Song of Bernadette* is a biography of St. Bernadette who, as a young girl, sees the Virgin Mary in a garbage dump. The Virgin tells her to dig in a certain spot, and a fountain bursts from the hole. The Vatican finally concludes that the waters have magical, healing properties, but at the time Bernadette was ridiculed. While Bernadette has no interest in becoming a nun, once the Vatican endorses her claims she is forced to join the convent, where she is reunited with the jealous, bitch nun who taught her in elementary school.

Of course I identify with Bernadette throughout most of the movie. But when Gladys Cooper, playing the bitch nun, delivers her monologue, I think we are meant to identify with her. All of my characters traverse the archetype of bitch skeptic and ultimate sinner, and then wake up on the other end to realize they are redeemable.

I've never been able to embrace any particular religion – probably because I am terrified by conceptions of hell and they all include at least one. For a person who has never even been to church, outside of the occasional wedding or funeral, I think about hell far too much. As an explanation, it seems entirely conceivable and even likely. The tragedy of this city came with everyone's consent; my individual shortcomings and failures are no accident either. We're all secretly in love with evil, and many of us try to sustain pain or dwell inside suffering. We're all bound for some dark, tight place, and we probably all deserve to die. [text excerpt from *Every Time I See Your Picture I Cry*]

MH: Talk to me about *Winnipeg Babysitter* (180–190 min, 2005).

DB: *Winnipeg Babysitter* is an ongoing archival project that began in 2003. Over the last three years I have been researching, compiling and archiving a history of independently produced television in Winnipeg, Manitoba. The result is a hybrid between an overhead performance and a feature-length documentary. There are two projections in *Winnipeg Babysitter*. The main theatre projection features unique vignettes from a brief synapse in broadcasting history when Winnipeg cable companies were mandated to provide public access as a condition of their broadcasting licence. I use an overhead projection to superimpose text commentary on the video image. The overhead texts act as footnotes to the main projection. I used an overhead projector instead of making a video documentary because I wanted to showcase a kind of specific '80s formalism – I didn't want there to be any confusion between my intervention and the original image. The scrolling commentary describes the stories behind the featured public access programs. The experience is a bit like watching that VH1 show, *Pop-up Video*.

This is another project of collecting formative images. I watched all these shows as a kid and desperately wanted to see them again. I also felt certain there was an audience for this material beyond Winnipeg. But finding the work wasn't easy. The local public access archives were destroyed when larger cable companies gradually bought the smaller ones. Consequently, the programs could only be found in the VHS collections of the original producers. In cases when these producers did not save their own work, I had to rely on television collectors, fans and enthusiasts. In this regard, I consider *Winnipeg Babysitter* an archival project that restores a previously lost history.

The work is located in an under-recognized zone outside the mainstream of art and video circulation. While some of the artists from the program have since established tremendous critical success (notably Guy Maddin, Kyle McCulloch and the members of the Royal Art Lodge), it's important to me that the audience understand that every producer included in this program was driven entirely by creativity and enthusiasm, without any commercial participation in either the art world or the television industry. The artists of *Winnipeg Babysitter* are unified by the idea of presenting work voluntarily in a public realm.

I am still looking for certain programs, and in this sense, *Winnipeg Babysitter* is an ongoing project. Most of the original producers kept copies of their work in VHS, but only the episodes that aired since the advent of the consumer-grade video recorder. This means I have been unable to locate any footage before 1981. I would still like to present some television work that appeared in the 1970s. Glen Meadmore, for instance, was a Winnipeg performance artist and is now a big part of the Vaginal Creme Davis crowd in Los Angeles. I've never seen it, but he is infamous for creating a television program called *The Goofers* (later *The Glen Meadmore Show*). The story goes that Glen sat in front of a television camera staring back blankly or silently picking at his acne for 30 minutes each week. My theory is that he introduced to the Winnipeg public the idea that public access television could be weird enough to be art.

MH: How did you go about finding the artists for *Winnipeg Babysitter*?

DB: I located most people by simply looking them up in the phone book. However, in some cases I could only remember the producer's first names, like Louise and Mary from *The Cosmopolitan Time*. Louise Wynberg and Marion Clemens were two senior citizens who produced the longest-running Winnipeg cable show. It was one of the first shows to be picked up and one of the last to be dropped from the schedule. *The Cosmopolitan Time* started off as an interview program and gradually became an all-request music program. Marion played the drums while Louise played piano and organ simultaneously. She had an encyclopedic knowledge of music, so when people would phone in and request songs, Louise would be able to either play it or fake it. Mostly callers would request good-time oldies like 'Somewhere My Love' or 'Spanish Eyes,' but most people of my generation remember the requests for ABBA, Deep Purple or Led Zeppelin. They stopped taking live requests when an obscene caller ruined everyone's fun. Undaunted, they began to take requests by mail. By then, they knew what everyone wanted to hear.

The Cosmopolitans are Winnipeg icons because everyone grew up watching them. They were ubiquitous on that station. They had an enormous fan base amongst senior citizens, but also had a cult following amongst people who thought they were camp or funny. They wore matching gingham outfits and blond pageboy wigs, and every so often they would invite the students of their music school (children) to join the band.

MH: Were they surprised to hear from you?

DB: Louise has died, but Marion seemed relieved when I contacted her, which is a common response. Producing a DIY television for a couple of decades becomes a part of one's identity, especially for Louise and Marion, who loved performing so much. Marion was a little cautious initially, but she was still very excited to watch the tapes with me. We've since become good friends. She let me out her at the age of 81, which was such a monumental and daunting honour. I think most of their neighbours assumed Marion and Louise were sisters, especially during the 1950s and 1960s. This was the first time Winnipeg came to know them as lesbian partners.

MH: Was it difficult for Marion to cross that line with you?

DB: I was very nervous about asking, but she immediately said yes. Because she and Louise were pretty closeted their entire life, I don't think people extended the appropriate sympathy to Marion when Louise died. She knew of only one other lesbian couple in town and resolved after Louise's death to find others. In her late '70s she learned to socialize as a gay woman. I met her four years later, so by then I think she was a little more comfortable.

MH: You present this material in a live screening format, with text interventions written by yourself.

DB: It was important to avoid a program of lampoons. It's incredibly popular now to profile lemons and have a good laugh. Obviously, in some cases I'm showcasing a particular brand of kitsch or camp, but I also want people to understand that in every case

there is a touching backstory. I treat the artists in *Winnipeg Babysitter* with the same integrity a curator would in a gallery. So much of this material was ahead of its time.

I decided to use an overhead projector to moderate an audience's experience – to render a campy memory inspiring and emotional. The whole program has the stain of tragedy, because large conglomerates have gone to such nefarious extremes to end public access television. I really want the viewer to inhabit the twin perspectives of comedy and tragedy at the same time.

MH: Can you tell me about your forthcoming *I've Never Felt Sexually Attracted to Anyone at All?*

DB: It's an animation that will take shape either as a video, or more likely another overhead performance. It narrates the story of a young, aspiring fashion model who is slowly dying from a severe allergy to his beloved cat.

So far, I know that the protagonist will be introduced as he is pictured reading a fashion magazine in a veterinarian's office, waiting for his cat to be neutered. The article asserts that hairy and 'funny-looking' men are the most desired models on the catwalks of Europe. To a certain extent, this article acts as a foreword to the performance. Though this guy is almost 17, he is without body hair. *I Have Never Felt Sexually Attracted to Anyone at All* describes his various attempts to embody the latest paragon of male beauty and his cat's recovery from castration. Sometimes their efforts will resemble artistic practices; ultimately, however, their private rituals explore the simultaneous experience of deep shame and pride, and a quest for a kind of sublime identity.

The protagonist is, like all of the others, an artist of sorts. So far he makes drawings of bearded or hairy men on rolls of paper towels. I have been developing the outline of this story by replicating and documenting the processes of this imagined, narcissistic protagonist. For example, I have been making drawings on toilet-paper rolls, boiling mirrors, etc. This is how I will begin to hem together the story of a young man who is both deathly allergic and yet romantically beholden to his pet cat.

The piece expands upon the dualistic themes from my previous work: beauty versus ugliness, shame versus pride, indulgence versus purity, and the balancing of one's talents with advancing physical shortcomings. All of my work is designed to pair popular imagery from the cultural and technological past with emotional, usually melancholic content; in doing so, I simulate a return to a nostalgic media experience.

MH: Your presentations are models of efficient, perfectly rendered, articulate and touching experiences. Perfect. Has your work always been – will it always be – just exactly perfect?

DB: I reluctantly hope so. Being a perfectionist has brought a pronounced level of anxiety to my practice, though I know it is more difficult to progress if one is obsessively trying to avoid mistakes. In this regard, I hope one day to experience a breakthrough and become more satisfied with my work. Having said that, I hope to maintain a certain level of 'completeness.' I like that you describe my work as 'efficient,' which offers a more accurate description. My best work maintains a rigorous, pedantic structure that's not likely to change.

Daniel Barrow's Media Work

Untitled   1996 (4-monitor installation)
Showcase   4 min 1992
Circle Square   15 min 1993 (performance)
Moonwalk   4 min 1993
The Sorry Entertainer   3 min 1994
Black Heart's Desire   5 min 1995
Party Killer   4 min 1995
Backwash   4 min 1995
The Individual   4 min 1996
Untitled   5 min 1997 (with Sheridan Shindruk)
The Castle and the Cell   1998 (3-monitor installation)
The Wallflower   14 min 1998 (performance)
Looking for Love in the Hall of Mirrors
    26 min 2000 (performance)
The Face of Everything   45 min 2002 (performance)
A Miracle   3 min 2003
The Face of Everything   26 min 2003
Catalogue of the Original   9 min 2004
Artist Statement   3 min 2004 (performance)
Snowglobe   2004 (installation)
Artist Statement   5 min 2006
Winnipeg Babysitter   180–190 min 2005–present
Every Time I See Your Picture I Cry   60 min 2005 (performance)

Distributed by Jessica Bradley Art and Projects and Vtape.

Daniel Barrow is a Winnipeg-based media artist working in performance, video and installation. He has exhibited widely in Canada and abroad. Barrow is the 2007 winner of the Canada Council's Victor Martyn Lynch-Staunton Award and the 2008 Images Festival's Images Prize. www.danielbarrow.com

WAYNE YUNG

MY HEART THE TRAVEL AGENT

He is standing in a meet-and-greet at the Oberhausen Short Film Festival as the scrum moves out of the hall, with a lot of shiny metal hanging off his face and a serious haircut and an upright slouch that looks like the whole city of Köln has managed to tuck itself up into his body. We talk for just a moment before I race back into the theatre, desperate for the movie to open, for someone else's life to start so that mine might be put off for some more suitable hour. Wayne looks so hip and up into it all that he makes me want to run back into my hotel room and read books. Not that books aren't life as well – some of my best dreams turn around the reading of books, sleep narratives, fractured and delicious. But Wayne has no need of these diversions. At least, he doesn't create a Berlin Wall out of them: he is right there on the front line of his life. Who else would have kicked off a 'career' in the fringe with a movie called *Peter Fucking Wayne Fucking Peter*. Co-starring his boyfriend, of course. Co-starring himself, of course. What better way to muse about identity politics and the fabled passivity of gay Asian males and the sticky negotiations of relations where one is HIV positive and the other isn't than in the midst of a slamming butt-fuck?

Wayne's work might be read as an oblique autobiography – certainly he has been unafraid to appear in tape after tape – and so we have watched him age, not that he's old by any means, but he is not so entirely young anymore. There are a lot of years and lovers between *Peter Fucking ...* and *My German Boyfriend*, for instance, and his aesthete sensibilities have been sharpened in the decade-plus to a fine point. He is not afraid of beauty, to arrange and layer and wait for the light until yes, now, exactly now. And because pictures of guys like Wayne aren't exactly crowding out the billboards – I mean good-looking Asian gay male hipsters, or even not so hipster – Wayne has an issue. His short tapes (and what's wrong with short?) fly in the face of this exclusion, pointing out some of the cracks in the corporate megapixel that is trying to recast us all as part of a global village. Watching him brave his way through these videotaped moments is a bracing reminder that there is another heart beating in the next room, and it's not your heart, and not your room either. It touches me, it moves me, and then I want to read him telling me all about it.

MH: Did you always know with the fierce unbending will of a child that you would make pictures? Did you have an early significant picture encounter (or did you feel, as you were moving past childhood, that it was difficult to keep parts of yourself from becoming a picture)?

WY: I grew up in Edmonton; after my parents divorced, my father and I lived together in my grandfather's basement. Each room had just a small window, high up on the wall, which let in a narrow beam of sunlight, like a spotlight in the dark. I remember once standing up on a chair, trying to peer through the window, and seeing only weeds growing in front of the glass, and the fluffy white clouds high up in the sky. I started crying with a vague frustration that I was missing out on something, that something wonderful was going on, somewhere out there, without me. It wasn't like the door was locked; I was free to run out to the local playground, or to the corner store. But I had this vague feeling that there were many things I couldn't do, things I couldn't even put a name to, as long as I was ten.

Ironically, I connected this to the feeling I had when I played my father's ABBA records. So maybe it was a just a premonition of my future gay life! Anyways, I think it was this particular feeling that drove me to leave Edmonton, and then Canada. It's this feeling that often motivates me to try new things – the feeling that, otherwise, I'd be 'missing out.' Living the life of an artist, and of a videomaker, has let me try a lot of things I might not otherwise.

I can't say I always knew I'd make images. I started reading for pleasure at a very young age, finishing at least one novel per week; so when I turned 14 or 15 I decided I wanted to become a writer myself. Later, in high school and college, I took some classes in creative writing, as well as acting. Finally I went to art school and became a visual artist and performance artist. It wasn't until I was 23 that I discovered videomaking, which allowed me to pull all these creative impulses together. Video allowed me to tell stories, which is what I wanted to do in the first place.

I can't say I have this innate, burning desire to make images. Much depends on the pleasure I derive from the process, from collaborating with my peers and meeting members of my audience. After moving to Germany, I temporarily lost the urge to make videos because this pleasure was missing. I spent the first few years trying to find it again. I've come to realize that video projects are my way of playing with my friends, who also happen to be artists and videomakers. We discuss ideas over late-night noodles, we get together to do spontaneous projects, we have a good time. I miss that. Without this external input, my internal engine simply loses interest in making art; I don't make it just for myself.

I think an artist is just kidding himself if he says he doesn't care if the audience rejects his work. Actually, even 'rejection' is a response; the real problem is when there is no response at all, when no one cares to look at your work, and it never gets noticed by anyone. Most artists would give up if they were really just 'making it for themselves.' For me, the audience is the other half of the equation; I see artmaking as a dialogue, not a monologue.

MH: In an essay called 'Centre the Margins,' Richard Fung talks about the absence of gay Asians on movie screens. He goes on to write: 'In my own video work in the area, I have seen the most important task as the representation of gay and lesbian Asians as subjects, both on the screen and especially as the viewer. I believe that it is imperative to start with a clear idea about audience. This in turn shapes the content of the piece.' Do you feel the same? Do you begin your work with a clear idea of the audience, and the political arena your work is entering into? Do you feel the responsibility implied in Richard's remarks about his own practice, and does it similarly shape the form and content of your work?

WY: Richard Fung was the first one to use video to describe the issues of gay Asian men, and he played a major role in inspiring me and other gay Asian directors; there are probably about 30 film and videomakers in the world who have shown specifically gay Asian characters onscreen. This is from the thousands of other directors who show gay characters of other races, the huge majority being white characters. Most gay Asian directors know each other personally, since we meet at film festivals, which often put all the gay Asian films into one special program. This 'ghetto programming' has both good and bad sides: on the one hand, it's an easy way to get an overview of the gay Asian scene in one show, but on the other hand, it means other programs (the 'sex' program, the 'family' program, the 'religion' program, etc.) can remain all white.

Richard was a big influence on me as I was starting out, especially his essay 'Looking for My Penis: The Eroticized Asian in Gay Video Porn.' I do feel a certain responsibility to present gay Asian men onscreen and am often critical of others for using all-white casts, especially when it's not essential to the concept.

I recently read a draft script about an old man confronted by four young women on the street, written by a director here in Germany. When I spoke to her, I suggested it might be interesting if all the characters were Turks, who form a large minority in Germany; there were no clues in the script that would have prevented this. She was very surprised by my suggestion; it hadn't even occurred to her. But I was surprised by her surprise; she herself is a Persian who grew up in Germany. In the end, she never did produce that script, but instead moved on to another one, which also features only white German characters. And so it continues – German movies fail to reflect the reality of the street; the population here is about ten percent foreign, but that's certainly not visible onscreen.

I don't believe a non-white director should be 'required' to cast non-white actors, but if we all continue to avoid using non-white actors, then we simply perpetuate the larger system that makes us invisible.

Minority directors are in a peculiarly privileged position, precisely because we're minorities living in the context of a majority. I know what it's like to be Chinese-Canadian and queer; but I also have a very good idea about what it's like to be white and heterosexual, because I've been consuming white heterosexual media for my entire life. I'm quite confident that I could write believable white heterosexual characters, based on this lifelong exposure and my daily interaction with white heterosexuals. But I'm not at all confident that a white heterosexual could write a believable non-white character, or a gay character, especially if they've had no intimate exposure to such people, or to the media made by them. For me, the question of race and representation can be asked in three directions: who is making the image? Who is represented in the image? Who is consuming the image?

A friend of mine, who's also Chinese-Canadian, once told me about something that happened when he was working for a queer film festival. The programming committee was debating a gay Asian video; my friend thought it was great, but the other committee members didn't appreciate it at all. The others were not Asian and simply didn't get the humour. So my friend had to push for it, and finally got it into the festival. It was put into a program that attracted a large gay Asian audience, and it turned out to be a big hit. If my friend had never been on that committee, the tape would have been rejected, and this audience would have been left with yet another tape about gay white men.

My third video, *Lotus Sisters*, was an experiment in addressing a particular audience: gay Asian men in North America. I let the onscreen characters use the slang and inside references that only we would understand, and consciously chose not to 'subtitle' it for the benefit of 'outsiders.' In the end, I think it was only semi-successful; the text was difficult for many gay whites to understand, and opaque for heterosexual audiences. Since then, I've tried to find a balance: there should be something satisfying for a mainstream audience, but a bonus layer of meaning for non-Asian queers and a super-bonus layer for gay Asians.

However, gay Asian issues have become less and less central to me, especially since I moved to Germany. A lot of that has to do with the audience here. For white Germans, gay Asian subjects may be interesting on an exotic level, but it has little personal relevance or application, since hardly anyone actually knows an Asian in real life. And for the few gay Asians who do live here, my voice is also quite alien; most of them come directly from Asia, and when they hear my native English accent, they put me in a different category, that of a privileged 'Westerner.'

But even if I was still living in Vancouver, surrounded by my gay Asian-Canadian community, I'd probably be drifting away from this topic anyway. I feel like I've said everything I wanted to say on the subject of being gay and Asian. But I'm still trying to settle on my next topic.

1000 Cumshots

Chinese have been in Canada for well over 100 years, and now form about a third of Vancouver's population. The city once had a reputation for being very 'British,' but is now well-known for being very 'Asian.' In truth, Chinese-Canadians are assimilating very quickly into mainstream Canadian culture; my generation generally speaks little Chinese, and I think the next generation will speak only English. It's a natural consequence of a school system where everything is taught in English, and we study Shakespeare instead of Confucius. Chinese cultures have heavily influenced the cuisine of Vancouver, but less so the culture.

Nowadays, my audience seems to be gay white Germans, as well as the 'general' German mainstream. This has also necessitated a shift toward working in the German language, as in my latest work. However, I still cringe at the idea of portraying only white people, and make an effort to include non-white faces onscreen. Perhaps not always Asian faces (they can be very hard to find in Germany), but certainly people of colour.

Davie Street Blues

I see Wong Kar-Wai's *Happy Together* as an inspirational example. Although the two main characters are gay Hong Kongers, I wouldn't necessarily classify this as a 'gay Asian' movie. Being Asian is not the issue, and being gay is not the issue either. In this film, racial and sexual identities are not a major subject of conflict or analysis. And yet, nonetheless, it is very pointedly not just another story about straight white people. *Happy Together* is not limited to some Asian or queer ghetto; it manages to speak universally, transcending its specificity.

I do think very much about my target audience. For me, artmaking is a dialogue between artist and audience. I see it as a kind of contract: they give me a few minutes of their time and I give them some entertainment, usually in the form of sex and comedy. If they don't come away entertained, then they probably won't come to my next screening; they might even walk out before it's over, or simply tune out. But underneath the entertainment I still try to slip in some of my more political statements.

MH: *Peter Fucking Wayne Fucking Peter* (4:31 min, 1994) is a home-movie essay, and a boldly personal sexual encounter. Did you worry about making something so intimate and revealing? Its blurry, handheld haziness seems a guarantor of its authenticity. It insists: this is really happening, and we're really feeling this. Sex appears as the final assurance, the last stand of truth.

Your movie is, amongst other things, a love letter to Peter, an HIV-positive white man. You are HIV negative, and you say at one point, while he is fucking you, that this condom isn't enough to contain your fear. What a powerful moment this is to share with us. What led you to speak about this, and how did you negotiate this 'scene' where, in the end, as artist and editor, you would 'top' him – in other words, have control, the final say. I'm wondering what this moment feels like now, with a distance of ten years and a world of difference in treatment options. Not to mention the many who have died.

The issue of interracial desire is already here, at the beginning of your work, and continues to bring a strong questioning presence to much of what follows. In later work you describe the racism that keeps Chinese men from each other, but here you are on much more tender and immediate terms. I realize this is an impossibly large question, but can you elaborate on how your thoughts have changed over the years about this? Is that part of why you make movies?

WY: I rarely look at my early videos anymore; when I introduce people to my work, I generally begin with *Search Engine* (1999). But recently I was invited to do a lecture for a Queer Studies seminar here in Cologne, so I decided to focus on the early works, because I find them to be much more 'queer' than my later work. After several years of ignoring *Peter Fucking Wayne Fucking Peter*, it was a bit of a shock to see it again. It's almost like the tape was made by someone else: someone much more naive and idealistic, with a lot more daring and recklessness. Twelve years later, my videomaking has become polished and considered, and I'm a lot more careful about what I say.

It was my first video, at the age of 23. I had just attended a series of weekend workshops at Video In Studios in Vancouver, taught by Lorna Boschman and Paul Lang. My grip on the technology was quite tenuous; in this video, every transition is a fade to/from black, because I forgot how to do a dissolve between two shots (this was back in the days of tape-to-tape linear editing). The sound quality is quite poor, because I recorded the voice-over by speaking directly into the camera microphone while sitting in a closet late at night when everyone else was asleep (we were spending the weekend at a beach house, and I'd borrowed the Hi8 camera from our host). The music was recorded after everything else was edited; luckily Peter knew this musician, Glen Watts, who was able to pace his accordion-playing to match my voice-over.

When I look at this video, the thing that really shocks me is that Peter actually agreed to do this! After all, he was 18 years older than me, and not nearly so naive as I was. We had just started dating four or five weeks before shooting this scene. There wasn't any script yet – I wrote that after the fact. I guess I wanted to collect some footage, and let the editing ideas come later.

It was only after I showed the finished video to Peter that I actually asked his permission to show it in public. I was quite prepared to keep it private if he felt uncomfortable with it. But he said it was okay, as long as it never showed in his home city, where his friends might see it! So I never did show it in Edmonton, and Peter has never had to sit in an audience watching this tape.

A few months later I made *One Night in Heaven*; Peter was in that one too, as well as Paul Lang. Again, I'm a bit startled by the freeness and spontaneity of my working style back then. I had originally planned to set the story in Stanley Park, but it snowed the day before the shoot, so I quickly rewrote the story to work indoors. The location was in the storage lockers beneath Video In Studios.

I guess I dated Peter for about a year and a half. It was a long-distance thing: he was living in Edmonton, and I was in Vancouver. He was an artist himself, so we did a lot of projects together, not only video. It was only my second serious relationship; Peter had certainly had more lovers than me, having had a very active gay life in the 1970s and '80s. But in a way, he was almost as 'young and eager' as I was: since testing HIV-positive, he'd been having very little sex, let alone romance, and wasn't sure he'd ever find love again. That happened to a lot of HIV-positive men back then: they were just happy to survive, not daring to ask much more from life. There was a lot more stigma back then, and few HIV-negative men would knowingly date an HIV-positive guy.

I was also quite lonely when I met Peter. I'd been living in Vancouver for six months already, and it was my final move out of the family nest. I still hadn't found any sex, let alone love, in my new city; I was nervous and unsure of myself. Like many gay Asians of my generation, I also had very low self-esteem, and doubted that I'd ever have much of a love life. At the age of 23, you can be very pessimistic about your future! So when I fell into this romance with Peter, it was like an unexpected gift, and I went wild with passion.

In this relationship with Peter, I never felt that I was 'less' than him. Certainly he had more 'power' in certain areas: he was white, and he was an older and established artist. But I had the advantage of being HIV-negative, which was much more significant back then, and I was young in a gay culture that glorifies youth. We were both aware of these power dynamics and discussed them openly; that was an important part of being together. Since it was a long-distance relationship, a lot of time was spent on the phone.

After Peter (who, by the way, is still healthy and active), I had a couple of other serious relationships with HIV-positive men.

This was before the 'cocktail' medications came out, so there was still a lot of fear, and my other positive boyfriends did not deal with it so well (one became addicted to Catholicism, the other to cocaine). Ironically, since the emergence of the new meds, I haven't had any serious romances with positive men. It's not that I particularly avoid positive guys, but I think maybe they've begun to avoid negative guys. Now that they have their own strong social network (and even 'pride'), they don't really need to look outside the poz scene to find love and sex. It's probably just easier if both partners happen to be HIV positive.

None of my lovers has actually died yet (at least, I've never been around to see the obituary!). I've lost a few distant acquaintances to AIDS, but no one very close, so I've never had to go through that whole process of hospital visits, homecare shifts, funerals, etc. So I guess I've been very lucky. The subject of death and mortality is slowly creeping up on me, but only because I'm seeing myself getting older, and my friends and relatives are getting older too.

MH: In *Lotus Sisters* (4:59 min, 1996), one man says, 'Having sex as an Asian is important. We've been desexualized and now I have to show the world. I'm having sex for everyone.' This sounds like a manifesto for much of your video work. Do you feel that you are a sex activist? Are your pictures 'correctives' that work to counter mainstream impressions, perhaps even impressions that are not so mainstream? Where does the stereotype of the asexual Asian come from and why has it been perpetuated?

One of the two men in *Lotus Sisters* says, 'We're all closet sticky.' What does that mean? We see a couple of boys hanging out at a diner, lounging on the floor at home, cracking up and making out. Their moments are interrupted or juxtaposed with stolen media moments. Where are these other pictures from and why do you present them so insistently?

WY: *Lotus Sisters* was my third video and the first that dealt with the idea of a gay Asian community. One of the reasons I moved to Vancouver was because I wanted to get into this amazing Asian-Canadian cultural scene, which I had first experienced in November 1993, when I came over to do a performance piece at the Racy Sexy show. I moved to Vancouver in January 1994, and, for the first time in my entire life, I started making friends with other Asian-Canadians. That was a personal revolution for me; I had grown up in Edmonton avoiding other Asians, because I was essentially ashamed of being Asian.

Song Pae Cho became one of my closest friends, and he introduced me to Winston Xin; both agreed to appear in *Lotus Sisters*. Song was moving to Korea, so I wanted to use this opportunity to get them together on tape. They themselves were just friends, not lovers, but they had no problem 'pretending' for the camera.

Through them, I had my first 'practical' experience of what it meant to have gay Asian 'sisters.' These two were very much role models for me, of what kind of person I wanted to become: political, self-confident, funny, ironic, alternative, sexy. I'd never met such interesting gay Asians before; I never even knew that gay Asians could be interesting! And when we sat together in the noodle house late at night making sassy remarks about boys and politics, something new started emerging in the space between us: a hybrid subculture. It combined being gay with being Asian-Canadian; we had a particular slang (such as 'rice queen' and 'sticky rice') and a particular attitude (a defiance that was both political and self-consciously ironic). I know we weren't the first ones in Canada, but these two were the first for me.

In 1995, I did my first curatorial project, a program of videos by gay Asian men, for Vancouver's Out On Screen festival. One of the main themes at the time was our relationship with gay white men (other races were never addressed in these videos). The basic pattern was: my 'rice queen' done me wrong, but then I went 'sticky,' and now I'm happy and liberated (*rice queens* are white men who go for Asian men; *sticky rice* refers to Asian men who go for each other). Or, to quote Marlon Riggs (as we often

Chopstick Bloody Chopstick

did back then): 'Black men loving Black men is the revolutionary act of our times.'

Although I found this idea very seductive in its simplicity, I also knew it was too simplistic; all my sex and love had been with white men, and I couldn't say it was all automatically invalidated by this history of racism and (post)colonial (self)oppression. And, although Song and Winston portray 'stickiness' in my video, neither of them were themselves particularly sticky. So when Song says, 'We're all closet sticky,' he's also being ironic; stickiness may be a political 'ideal,' but it doesn't necessarily match the messy realities of our real love lives.

When Winston says, 'I'm fucking for everyone,' he's confronting the desexualization of Asian men in North American media. It was something we were all keenly aware of, and it had had a powerful effect on me: in my entire life, I'd never had any role models who showed that Asian men were sexy and

desirable. On Canadian TV we were laundrymen and kung fu stars, but no one ever fell in love with an Asian man. This has emerged as a major motivation for my work: to show Asian men as sexy, Asian men who are there for their own pleasure, and not (only) for the pleasure of white men (as seen in the specialized gay pornos designed for rice queens). It's about taking control of the media, and of our own representation; when the media is controlled by white men, it naturally reflects only their agenda.

In *Lotus Sisters*, I appropriated clips from *The Joy Luck Club* (featuring Chinese-American women) and *Farewell My Concubine* (featuring homosexuals in Mainland China). It was my way of 'cobbling together' a gay Asian-Canadian media culture; since we were essentially non-existent in Canadian mainstream culture, I identified with the nearest approximate images. I am not a homosexual opera singer in China, nor a Chinese woman in San Francisco, but there are certainly aspects of both that I can relate to.

But in the end, these things are very campy too: this melodramatic (and gorgeously costumed) opera tragedy appeals to the drag queen in anyone, and almost every Asian-Canadian recognizes their own neurotic immigrant mother in *The Joy Luck Club*.

Looking back, I realize that what I had with Song and Winston was very particular to that time and place. It's not like every gay Asian in Vancouver shared this campy/political point of view; in fact, very few did. Here in Germany, I've mostly met gay Asians from Asia, and they generally don't share this taste for politics and irony. When I visit Canada nowadays and see the younger generation of Asian-Canadians, they seem much more self-confident than I was at their age, both sexually and socially.

I still see Vancouver as my 'homeland,' and the only place in the world where I don't feel like a minority.

MH: *Search Engine* (4:08 min, 1999) begins with a bevy of scrolling personal ads, and when these are exhausted, another set of titles appear saying, 'When I grew up there were no Asian men on television. There were no Asian movie stars. No one ever fell in love with an Asian.' Then a series of titles announce: 'I want to be a sex object.' Is desire constructed through the image? Do you feel that our bodies are made of pictures – and that by changing pictures our bodies and their possibilities will also change? Are movies necessarily, inescapably, political? Why don't you make feature films, where your 'messages' would reach out to a broader audience?

WY: Before internet chat rooms and phone chat lines, there were personal ads in the classified sections of gay newspapers and magazines. I used to read and collect any ads that mentioned gay Asians, either as subject or object. In the entire newspaper, this was often the only evidence that gay Asians existed at all; the rest of the paper (especially the ads for parties and porn shops) depicted the gay scene as entirely white.

Of course, it wasn't just the gay scene – mainstream TV and Hollywood movies were the same. All the important roles were filled by whites, both in front of and behind the camera. If an Asian man appeared onscreen, he might be a kung fu master or a cook – in any case, not romantic, and certainly not sexual. I do feel this had a major effect on the formation of my own sexual self-image; there were no media images that affirmed that I, as an Asian man, could be sexy.

And this didn't affect just me, it also affected my non-Asian schoolmates; they made it perfectly clear that they believed Asian men were not to be taken seriously in the field of dating, romance and sex. When I was a teen, everyone watched the film *Sixteen Candles* (1984, written and directed by John Hughes), which included the infamous character Long Duk Dong, an Asian exchange student who was the butt of many jokes. Suddenly my teenage peers were calling all Asian men 'the Donger.' They thought it was hilarious, and I just wanted to crawl into a hole and hide.

For me, making images is necessarily a political act; it's about taking control of the means of image production, a control that has largely been exercised by white men. A movie like *Sixteen Candles* may be marketed as a 'universal' story for teenagers, but it's not universal: it does not speak to non-whites. The story itself was not about whiteness per se, it was about the teenage insecurities we all go through, regardless of race; but nonetheless, all the main roles were filled by white actors (as usual), and the one Asian actor was presented as a laughingstock.

A fellow video artist once told me about a filmmaking handbook in which Hollywood producers advise against casting a non-white actor unless it's essential to the role. A 'normal' story (one where race and ethnicity are not an explicit issue) should simply use white actors only. When expressed so directly, this advice sounds shockingly old-fashioned and racist, but, actually, I think it's still pretty standard practice in mainstream film and TV. Non-white casting is still considered a cutting-edge 'statement.'

I once thought I might make narrative feature films, but I'm not so sure now. Part of it has to do with my working habits; I've discovered that I don't really enjoy the process of commercial filmmaking (script development, coverage shooting, continuity editing, etc.). And I'm not interested in telling 'fictions' just for the purpose of 'entertainment.' There's already lots of other directors who are hungry to do that work, and I'm happy to sit back and watch them do it.

But more importantly, I don't see the burning need. For whom would I be making the feature film? Straight white audiences? Why would I want to serve them? I don't believe I'm going to change their minds about anything; movies like *Brokeback Mountain* sold well to gay-friendly audiences, but hardly made a dent among the homophobes. I once thought I might like to make a feature film for the gay film festivals, but now I understand that the gay audience is just as bourgeois as the mainstream audience,

and is mostly just interested in pure entertainment. Nowadays there's a steady supply of gay dramas and romantic comedies to serve this demand. Well, there are still very few feature films with gay Asian men … but honestly, most gay Asian men are the same as most gay white men: they're not interested in politics at all, they also just want light entertainment, which I'm not really interested in producing.

I think the only people who might possibly 'need' my kind of work are gay Asian youth, or gay Asian men who are still struggling with their self-esteem and self-confidence. But I can generally reach them by making these small video projects that are screened at gay film festivals in shorts programs. For me, that's enough; I don't really need to distribute my work in every suburban cinema in North America.

I enjoy today's fragmented media market; we're no longer forced to consume the same bland fare of the traditional three major American TV networks. We can turn to various webcasters, specialty DVDs and alternative film festivals, each with a relatively narrow target market. As an artist, I can choose to speak directly and intimately to a gay audience without having to get the permission of some heterosexual Hollywood producer, TV network executive or the manager of your local Cineplex. I can freely use words like *rice queen* and *darkroom* and expect my audience to understand because they're gay; if it was a mainstream audience, I'd have to add subtitles, or drop these words completely.

MH: In *The Queen's Cantonese* (32:41 min, 1998), you adopt the serial form of a Cantonese language lesson to dish the fragmented story of a Chinese/European boy-boy couple vacationing in Vancouver. This overheated melodrama, winningly played in stripped-down sets and ravishing lighting, leads one to wonder whether being with a white guy is really okay. In the end, they both fall for the same man, everyone winds up at the baths, with serial bed exchanges and agonized recognitions. At last, the two Asian boys stroll off together. Did you begin with this story and then decide on the language lesson as a framing device? What led you to adopt this form? At one point the female narrator recites, 'To speak Cantonese you have to be able to think in Cantonese.' Do you believe, à la Lacan, that the unconscious is structured like a language? This work is very accessible, the clearly delineated characters 'say what they mean,' there is a transparency of word and picture often missing in fringe media. Is that a conscious choice on your part because of an audience you don't want to lose?

WY: I wrote *The Queen's Cantonese* in collaboration with Winston Xin, who also appeared in *Lotus Sisters*. The concept emerged from the banter and jokes we shared over midnight snacks at the noodle house, when we talked about guys, sex and life in general. Although we both came from Cantonese-speaking families, we ourselves spoke the language poorly, having been completely assimilated into the English-speaking majority. So when we sometimes dropped short Cantonese expressions into our conversation, phrases we remembered from our childhoods, these words became ironically recontextualized by the gay subjects of our adult conversations.

The Queen's Cantonese became a way for us to reconnect to our lost childhood language and adapt it to our contemporary needs as adult gay men. The project was also a way to place gay Asians at centre stage, in a Vancouver gay scene where we were still largely marginalized. So I 'redesigned' various gay milieu to reflect a campy Cantonese influence (e.g., a gay bar with mah jong players, a cruising park within a bamboo grove, a gay bathhouse with dim sum carts). This portrayal of Vancouver as a 'Pearl of the Orient' was also inspired by a quote from Christopher Isherwood, where he says that his literary portrayal of Berlin was not strictly true-to-life, but rather reflected the 'heightened' Berlin of his fantasies, skipping over the drab and tedious details of his everyday life in Berlin.

The 'language lesson' format served several purposes. On the one hand it was economic and practical: language lesson videos have notoriously cheap production values and unrealistic acting, allowing me to disguise my lack of resources and directorial experience (it was my first time directing scripted dialogues). On the other hand, it was a format that was both didactic and dramatic, allowing me to communicate a lot of information efficiently and humorously. Many viewers immediately recognize the format, having been exposed to language cassettes before; *The Queen's Cantonese* acts as an antidote to the boring dialogues of such programs. Even more, it's a critique of the heterosexism ('I would like to buy a gift for my wife'), classism ('Where is the nearest four-star hotel?') and prudery (no words for flirting) that are the implicit agenda of these videos.

At various points in my life I've spoken Cantonese, English, French and German, and my thought process is a nearly constant flow of words. Although I believe that any idea can be expressed in any language (with varying degrees of efficiency, depending on the subject matter), I find that each language evokes a particular mood, and this shows up in my work. For me, Cantonese connotes a certain casual familiarity (as in *The Queen's Cantonese*), as well as an emotional moodiness (as in *Davie Street Blues*), but doesn't have the overintellectualized precision of German (as in *Miss Popularity*). Of course, this also reflects my own life experience, having used Cantonese as a childhood language, and German as a language of postgraduate studies.

However, as a visual artist, I also believe there is another thought process that is entirely wordless. I edit videos according to a visual logic that can't really be translated into words; words aren't really efficient (or sufficient) in explaining why one image works and another doesn't. There is a famous anecdote about the dancer Isadora Duncan, who was asked by a newspaper reporter to summarize her latest dance in just a few words. She replied, 'If I could express it in words, I wouldn't have to dance it.'

The Queen's Cantonese has emerged as one of my most popular pieces. It was a kind of 'service' I undertook for the gay Asian community, providing them with an artwork that tries to speak to their specific realities and concerns, in an entertaining format they can easily enjoy. It's a video many have gladly purchased for private use, more so than any other video I've made. It's a kind of 'love letter' addressed to an entire community. But gay Asians are a fickle audience (like any other), with no particular loyalty to me and my artistic production. Whenever I make something 'arty' (such as *Angel*), they largely avoid the show and are replaced by an 'arty' crowd. I don't have a problem with that, since I don't expect (or desire) uncritical loyalty from any audience. I don't have an allegiance to a particular audience either; sometimes I want to serve one crowd, sometimes another.

MH: *Davie Street Blues* (12:37 min, 1999) is a mini-narrative love lament, its grainy tableaux featuring a hyperactive white clown and an unmoving Asian stoic played by yourself. Why the long static shots and narrative burlesques? And how did you shoot this? It looks fabulous.

WY: *Davie Street Blues* was my homage to the films of Hong Kong director Wong Kar-Wai; some of the scenes were direct 'quotations' from his work, particularly *Chungking Express* (1994) and *Fallen Angels* (1995). This is also why I chose to do the voice-over in Cantonese (which I can speak only haltingly) and shoot it in 16:9 aspect ratio; I wanted to evoke the feeling of watching a subtitled, art-house movie.

The decision to use long static shots was partly practical, partly artistic. On the practical side, I designed this as a no-budget project to be shot in less than 24 hours, with just two crew members: Clark Nikolai on camera and Nickolaos Stagias doing everything else. We shot guerrilla-style, using available light, with no shooting permissions for any of the public locations, so

this forced a lot of practical limitations on what the cameraman could do. For example, in the café scene, we performed in a real café during normal business hours: I went in, bought a drink and sat down in front of the window; a minute later, Stuart Folland (my co-star) joined me, performing in character. Meanwhile, Clark was out on the sidewalk with the video camera, shooting through the window, and Nico was holding an umbrella over his head. We did the shot in one take, and the café staff didn't even notice what was happening.

On the artistic side, I wanted to strip the picture down to the basics, using none of the compositing, graphics work or special effects of my previous (and later) videos. It was all just straight cuts, like in a classic art-house movie, with the visual interest being driven by the actors' performances. We shot it on MiniDV, sometimes using a very slow shutter speed to compensate for low light levels (also a technique used by Wong Kar-Wai). Using such a small camcorder was also conducive to this fast, highly mobile, guerrilla style of shooting.

The stillness of the main camerawork reflected a certain emotional state I was experiencing. My romance with a visiting film student had recently ended in heartbreak, and it was taking me a long time to accept that it was over, even after he'd already moved back to Zurich. I was at an emotional standstill, waiting for the day when I'd finally stop thinking about him; so this video project represented a kind of post-breakup therapy for me.

MH: *My German Boyfriend* (18 min, 2004) looks so beautiful; every landscape and building and face is glowing and perfect and arranged. The movie begins with high expectations about your three German dates-to-be, each disappoints in his own way, and then you meet a man who eventually marries you. Desire is so messy and misbehaved – how does it relate to the perfect aesthetic world you have composed? How do issues of control (which make this perfect world possible), expectation and desire work

together, or do they? 'He wasn't part of the script,' you say when you fall in love with one of the actors, and he can't tell whether he's acting or not. By making the movie, you put your own 'real' love at risk. Can you talk about the line between art and personal life, between public and private. Why do you take such risks?

WY: I shot *My German Boyfriend* in Berlin during the summer of 2002, but didn't edit and release it until 2004. It was funded by the Canada Council for the Arts; in my original proposal, I stated that the first part of the video would be scripted and that the second part would be a video diary documenting the process of making the first part. So I couldn't really plan what the second part would look like until the first part was already shot. And I couldn't write the script for the first part until I'd actually arrived in Berlin to do the necessary research concerning German/Asian stereotypes. Much of the project developed spontaneously on location.

In the first four minutes, you see at least 20 locations; it took weeks of exploring Berlin, searching for locations that best 'represented' the city. My general shooting plan was to book my cameraman (Kai Scharmer) plus one actor for the day; we would put on our costumes, go visit various pre-selected destinations and simply shoot scenes whenever and wherever I felt inspired. So even though the shots may look meticulously planned, most were the result of serendipitous discoveries. Whenever I saw a beautiful place, I quickly sketched out an action and a camera position, and we'd try it out in various ways until it finally worked.

We always shot more than I needed, and we did a lot of scenes that didn't make it into the final edit. That's one of the pleasures of working with such a small team and using MiniDV: we can play around and use up lots of videotape, without needing to spend a lot of money. Again, we shot without any shooting permissions for the public spaces, and to the casual passerby, it really looked like we were just friends on a fun, spontaneous outing. When

My German Boyfriend

doing scenes in public, I don't like having assistants standing around behind the camera because it attracts too much unwanted attention.

I dislike drawing storyboards, and usually work without them. A few days before the shoot, I usually do a camera rehearsal with my cameraman, so that we can work out the basic style. After that, I don't control him much, since I'm too busy directing the action, as well as performing myself. I have to trust that he's doing a good job, especially when I've supplied only a vague script outline. During a video project, my closest relationship is always with my cameraman.

My German Boyfriend, like most of my work, involved a lot of personal emotional risk: I record myself in romantically intimate situations and reveal autobiographical confessions in the narration. This is partly a political action, inspired by Richard Fung's call to diversify the visual representation of gay Asian men; since it's often impractical or impossible to get other Asian men to do these gay scenes, I usually end up using myself as the 'model' gay Asian. It's also an artistic decision based on my own understanding of the best way to be a artist – I have the most respect and admiration for those artists who take the biggest emotional risks. Perhaps it's also because, deep down inside, I'm actually a control freak, and I'm learning that art (and life) are much more interesting when you give up control and let random accidents happen. I get a kick out of proving to myself that I'm not limited to my own personal 'boundaries' and that I can overcome my own fears.

This is a peculiarly Canadian style of video art, closely related to American work, which I rarely see here in Europe. European video artists seldom put themselves in emotionally vulnerable positions; they tend to prefer being cool and in control. Here in Germany, my videos seem jarringly out of place; few German artists would reveal such private details onscreen. In contrast, many Canadian video artists seem almost addicted to self-confession, and it can be like a competition to see who can take the biggest emotional risk. My own early models included Paul Wong, Paul Lang, Ken Anderlini, Kiss and Tell, Laurel Swenson and Maureen Bradley: all queer Vancouverites who weren't shy about their own vulnerabilities.

Mixing my personal and artistic lives has become second nature to me, and everyone who's close to me knows they might get pulled into one of my projects. I'm actually surprised at how rarely this causes conflicts, but I guess people who place a high priority on anonymity are not the type who would hang around with me. I am drawn to people who show a lot of emotional courage, and to boyfriends who trust me enough to allow me the freedom to be the artist I want to be.

In *My German Boyfriend*, there are scenes of me kissing the actor Frank, who I ended up falling for. Much of this footage is actually from camera test rehearsals, where the goal was simply to develop the necessary romantic chemistry for the video performance. Somehow the line between 'pretending to be lovers' and actually wanting to be lovers got very blurry; it's like that psychology trick of putting on a fake smile to cheer up your actual mood. In the end, I'm quite ready to 'exploit' this phenomenon to produce good footage. The actor Donald Sutherland once said that he had to develop a 'romantic' relationship with his director, even if it's between two heterosexual men, in order to produce good footage. I see this in my own work too: the best 'performance' is usually the one that isn't actually being 'acted.'

MH: In your *Field Guide to Western Wildflowers* (5:37 min, 2000), the camera turns around you and a succession of men locked in

a kiss. Behind you is a turning sky filled with flowers identified by their common name, Latin name and an associated quality (Honesty, Anticipation, Reconciliation). Where are these names from and how did you come up with the idea for this tape? How did you structure the running voice-over? And what does this picture-perfect world have to do with desire?

WY: I got the idea for *Field Guide to Western Wildflowers* one morning over breakfast, as I was joking around with my friend (and fellow video artist) Clark Nikolai. The idea of using flowers in the background was actually just a random placeholder; I didn't know what I wanted in the background yet, so I just said, 'Flower,' expecting I would get a better idea later. Of course, I never did. Collecting flower images became a long and tedious obsession, as I painstakingly scanned and cut out each one.

Field Guide to Western Wildflowers refers back to the old flower language of the Victorian era, when every flower had a traditional meaning, and it was common to send carefully prepared bouquets in order to communicate a coded message (e.g., red rose means love, white lily means purity). However, in my video, I only sometimes kept the traditional meanings; other times I invented entirely new meanings (e.g., periwinkle means codependence), with an eye toward their relevance in describing contemporary gay romance.

My original goal was to kiss 99 guys for this video. I prepared a small invitation card describing the project, with mock-up photos of me kissing Clark. Then I gave copies to three of my friends, who had four weeks to go find 99 volunteers for the shoot. In the end they managed to get 64, which turned out to be plenty. The most successful recruiter (or should I say 'pimp') was Clark, who invited all his bear friends; I often get comments that there seem to be a lot of beards in my video. Clark invited

Field Guide to Western Flowers

around having an Asian partner; if a white guy 'unexpectedly' takes an Asian lover, his white friends might say, 'But you're good-looking – why go for an Asian?' This video is a statement of 'pride,' showing men who aren't ashamed of kissing an Asian, and who aren't afraid to talk about it either. On a personal level, it was also a kind of farewell to Vancouver. I was planning to move away after finishing this video, and this was the last chance to kiss every boy I'd ever had a crush on!

MH: In *Miss Popularity* (6:20 min, 2006), you delve into the murk of multiple relationships, taking an approach that is both lyric and documentary. You use a raft of black-and-white found footage from the 1950s, common currency in fringe media, but unusual for your work: why lean on these borrowed tunes? You close with a forest kissing idyll showing you and a German man. After the distance provoked by the found imagery, was this scene a way to bring the movie 'back home,' to give it roots in the present?

whoever he met at the bar; later he told me some pretty interesting stories about guys who declined to participate because they would never kiss an Asian man. It's unfortunate I had no access to them – it would have made an interesting interview.

The shooting day was eight hours long, divided into ten-minute slots; every kisser knew his pre-assigned time, so that he wouldn't have to wait too long. Traffic was controlled by my receptionist, who sent me each kisser, one at a time.

First, I sat with the kisser and showed him a 'menu' of 11 types of kisses, asking him to draw the line. Some wanted only a cocktail kiss in the air, others wanted dry kisses on the lips, while a few wanted the whole menu (one even bit me in his passion, which was inconsiderate, since I still had hours of kissing to do). After shooting a two-minute kiss on a rotating platform (one guy nearly fell off), the kisser went to the next room to do a brief interview with my friend Winston Xin. The theme was: "Tell me about your first Asian kiss.' Since this topic was known to everyone in advance, some took the opportunity to deliver a prepared anecdote (two guys even wrote poems). Others admitted that their very first Asian kiss had happened just now, and spoke about that. Clips from these interviews form the audio track of the video (beneath their voices is an old Japanese cabaret song from the 1920s, about a woman who sells melons on the street). The interview stories ranged from sweet and innocent, to exotic and fetishized, to complete surprise that an Asian kiss could be just as hot (and just as normal) as any other.

Politically, I was motivated by the idea that no one ever kisses the Asian man onscreen, especially not in the gay media of North America. I wanted to show that gay Asian men are not romantically invisible, and that a wide range of other gay men can appreciate (and have already sampled) the romantic potential of the Asian man. In North America, there's still a certain shame

WY: I'm frequently inspired by watching the work of other artists, and interested in sampling new visual styles, even if only for one project. The found-footage style of *Miss Popularity* was inspired by the work of Steve Reinke, who I met during his residency at Video In Studios in 1996, when he made the video *Everybody Loves Nothing*. It was Steve who first told me about the Prelinger Archives; ten years later, I discovered that these archival films were now available as downloadable movies, which gave me my first opportunity to play with them myself.

Miss Popularity deals with the theme of polyamory, with which I started experimenting in early 2005. Of course my boyfriend(s) knew about it, as did some of my closer friends, but it was hard to discuss openly, due to the social disapproval surrounding the idea of multiple relationships. The power of social disapproval formed the background of many educational films of the 1950s, which tried to teach teenagers the 'correct' way to behave as respectable young men and women. This black-and-white world provided the perfect springboard to begin my video. After starting with pure found footage, my own voice is gradually inserted: first through graphic titles, then through voice-over and finally through camerawork; in the end, there's no archival material left – only footage of me and my (second) boyfriend Frank. The video progresses from archival to contemporary, from heteronormative to queer, and from societal to personal.

Miss Popularity represented a milestone for me, being the first finished project that was entirely motivated by my life in Germany. (I'd already completed a few other tapes here, but they were all projects that were initiated in Canada.) I made it in the spring of 2006, after becoming depressed about not making anything in my first three semesters as a postgraduate student at the Academy of Media Arts in Cologne. I was now facing my fourth and final semester, so I decided to whip out a short video during the semester break, just to prove to myself that I was still capable. In the need for speed, I fell back on the tried-and-true artistic strategies I'd learned in Canada (i.e., no-budget experimental video, using personal/confessional voice-over). In the end, *Miss Popularity* has done quite well on the festival circuit, especially in Germany, where this peculiarly Canadian (or generally North American) strategy still stands out as something unusual. But I'm still trying to find my way here, as a Chinese-Canadian video artist who has now chosen to live in Germany. I'm still trying to find my genre, my subject, my audience and my voice in general. But in the end that's why I had to leave Canada, although I still love the place: I needed this new challenge, as an artist and as a human being.

Wayne Yung's Videos

Peter Fucking Wayne Fucking Peter   4:31 min 1994
One Night in Heaven   5:56 min 1995
Lotus Sisters   4:59 min 1996
Surfer Dick   3:20 min 1997
The Queen's Cantonese   32:41 min 1998
Angel   4:47 min 1999
Davie Street Blues   12:37 min 1999
Search Engine   4:08 min 1999
Field Guide to Western Wildflowers   5:37 min 2000
Chopstick Bloody Chopstick   14:19 min 2001 (with Shawn Durr)
An Atlas of the Moon   4:38 min 2001
The Photographer's Diary   26:16 min 2001
My Heart the Travel Agent   1:30 min 2002
1000 Cumshots   1 min 2003
Postcard to an Unknown Soldier   4:27 min 2004
Shan Xia Di: Under the Mountain   39:51 min 2004
My German Boyfriend   18:29 min 2004
Miss Popularity   6:20 min 2006
Asian Boyfriend   1 min 2006

Distributed by Video Out Distribution.

Wayne Yung is a writer, performer and video artist who has explored issues of race and identity from a queer Chinese-Canadian perspective. Born 1971 in Edmonton, he later moved to Vancouver and is now based in Germany. www.wayneyung.com

JAYCE SALLOUM
FROM LEBANON TO KELOWNA

For a committed politico, he sure talks a lot about beauty. His camera glides over surfaces, it caresses the light from a bus window, the way a hand falls halfway out of the shade, offering only the promise of another secret. And it's a good thing, because this beauty permits him access to what he's most interested in, and it allows him to endure, if only for a moment, that which cannot be endured: to hear the stories of survivors.

Beauty is complexity, he says, and I can only nod, trying to catch the long sentences as they float past. Most of all, I am grateful he is doing this work; the situation of the Palestinians, for instance, is far too important to be left to journalists, who for the most part have given up even the attempt to provide a picture of these stateless exiles. In the wake of so many pictures dedicated to erasing, of making invisible, he reverses the field. What does it mean that we are able to turn to Jayce's tapes from ten and 20 years ago and learn more about the present situation in Lebanon than any up-to-the-minute broadcast? He lays bare the mechanisms of seeing, the histories we carry with us when we try to enter the city of Beirut, or the Okanagan Valley. His seeing issues these truths like a wound that will not heal, a speaking wound that refuses to close (DeLillo: 'The past brings out our patriotism ... we want to feel an allegiance'). In his considered reflections on reflection, his careful walk through the minefields of metal and language and casual misunderstandings and power, he holds up in front of him a beauty to make the next step. When the suffering is too much, when too many innocents have been slaughtered, he uses this beauty as a shield in order to get close – he needs to get close so that it is possible to look and to see, to bear witness, to tell the story.

MH: Your beautiful and harrowing tape *untitled 3b: (as if) beauty never ends..* (11:22 min, 2000/2002[1]) is anchored by the voice of Abdel Majid Fadl Ali Hassan (in Burj el-Barajneh), a Palestinian elder who has been living in refugee camps in Lebanon since 1948. Here is an excerpt:

> So we walked, and I kept looking around in wonder and amazement, I couldn't believe I was back on my land. God is truly great. When we got to Kweikat I bent down and kissed the soil. We headed to the cemetery and I noticed the untended grass and weeds. I also saw the barbed wire fences that the Israelis had erected to stop the Feyda'een from returning. We reached the areas where our homes used to stand, they had all been demolished with nothing left but the foundations of the houses, standing bare of the stones which had been stolen. Pine trees had been planted among the ruins. We continued walking through these former houses and yards. While looking around I felt as though I could hear something, I imagined that my house

was speaking to me. 'Are you aware that it was my arms that received you the day you were born?'

We never see the speaker. Instead you show us fish moving in slow motion, shadows passing over flowers superimposed with the remains of an Israeli-sanctioned massacre: corpses lie on the streets of the Palestinian refugee camp of Shatila[2] and the contiguous Sabra neighbourhood. The exile who has come home, and the landless who will never go home again. Why do you offer us this juxtaposition? Can you talk about these massacres, which are both widely known and absolutely repressed? Where did this footage come from, and has it been widely distributed?

JS: The *untitled* tapes are part of an ongoing videotape without end. I originally intended for the *untitled* videotape to start at time code 0:00:00 with continual additions of edited material until I died. I had hoped people would screen or order it by sections they would designate, e.g., 0:10:30 to 0:40:02. Later, I realized this would make distribution practically impossible. So I divided and produced the tape in parts, most of which are available individually as single-channel works or shown together in an installation context. *untitled* extends and continues my series of projects addressing social and political realities and representations. It isn't modelled on the viewing of art (e.g., painting), but on an approach to research or reading, an active living archive. The parts play off each other, creating a literal and imagistic experience of the physical/visceral and of the underlying subjectivity experienced through the body, as crisis, place/nation and metaphor, or in transition and shift, and in the recounting or enunciatory nature of the interstitial site.

To get back to your original questions, in September 2000 I videotaped 40 hours of conversations with Palestinian refugees in Lebanon at six different camps spread from north to south. It usually takes me several years to make a tape, to continue research and to consider the issues and implications, so the material was still sitting on my shelves when, on April 3, 2002, the Israeli army started its attack on the West Bank Palestinian town of Jenin and its refugee camp. Slaughters were carried out and covered up as usual, and any attempt for a timely investigation by the International Red Cross and the UN were refused by the Israeli government until they could literally bury the damage. I was moved to get some part of this material out because it represented one of a series of massacres that Palestinians have been subjected to and that then Israeli prime minister Ariel Sharon was either directly responsible for or implicated in since the Naqba (catastrophe) of 1948 and the Qibya massacre in 1953. The footage of the Jenin incident that was released was ultimately so reminiscent of the footage of the Sabra and Shatila massacre (1982) that it made sense to collapse the space of time and to make an homage and commentary on this series of ongoing atrocities against Palestin-

---

1 Date shot/date edit completed.
2 Shatila camp is situated in southern Beirut and was established by the International Committee of the Red Cross in 1949 to accommodate the hundreds of refugees who poured into the area from the Galilee in northern Palestine during and after 1948. There are currently 8,212 to 12,235 registered refugees living in the camp.

ian people. In the installation you see what we call '48 *Palestinians* (Palestinians who were forced to flee their homes in 1948 speaking their stories of dispossession). You see Abdel Majid telling the story of visiting the site of his village 30 years after it was destroyed. And you see an elder woman, Nameh Suleiman, talking about being displaced once, twice, three, four times, from her home in Palestine, from South Lebanon, from the mountains and from camps destroyed in the Lebanon war. You see and hear them talking on a video monitor while the visuals of *part 3b* are projected as ambient imagery along the walls behind. In the single-channel piece, Abdel Majid is never seen talking.

People have been documenting other cultures long before the invention of film and photography. Napoleon took a fleet of engravers (as well as engineers, historians, archaeologists, architects, mathematicians and chemists) with him on his flagship, *L'Orient*, when he invaded Egypt in 1798. This could be seen as the start of the ethnographic tradition. The depiction of other cultures as a part of a continuum. Leaders would bring painters, engravers and printmakers on their invasions to document their exploits for purposes of heroism and imperialism under the guise of scientific knowledge. Now they bring a coterie of embedded journalists.

As we've come to know the Palestinian condition, it's been represented very one-dimensionally, as a corpse, a culture that's destined to die or that is already dead. If you're Palestinian, you're subject to many layers of annihilation: there's cultural genocide and practical genocide. The aim is disappearance. The images we've come to recognize as Palestinian are stereotypical and thin. There's little recognition that it's a rich life; even if you're living in a camp, you would still have a garden and other experiences of nature and aesthetics. Beauty continues even if you're under curfew, elements of pleasure remain – otherwise you wouldn't fight to go on living.

The tape (*part 3b*) explores two dominant motifs or guiding metaphors: flowers blooming in slow motion, and the process of *imaging* the corpses from Sabra and Shatila. That 1982 massacre of Palestinians was undertaken by the Phalange militia, a right-wing Maronite Christian-based militia in Lebanon (allied with Israel). Shatila camp and Sabra neighbourhood were surrounded by the Israeli army, and Israeli Defense Minister Ariel Sharon gave the green light for the Phalange to go inside to do their dirty work.

The massacre footage was given to me ten years later, when I was working in Lebanon in 1992; I was there for a year, and people would offer me things I might be able to do something with. It was given to me by a stringer who shot it while working for Agence France-Presse. I did research at the Communist TV station (New TV) in West Beirut that was there at the time, and found that journalists travelled in packs, like heat-seeking missiles, to find the corpses. I found multiple versions of these shots of clumps of hair lying on the ground, hats, canes or bodies, hundreds of them nearly identical save for a slight difference in parallax, shot standing a few degrees apart, hovering, framed so they don't show the other journalists who are there.

Even though the tape is a eulogy of sorts, a *figure* of recognition that the flowers indicate, I wanted to evacuate these forms of representation: the corpse and the flower. I wanted to make one disappear into the other, emptying out the usual representational tropes via juxtaposition and other devices, thereby complicating them. The picture becomes more complex with the exoteric and inherent layering. Complexity is the basis for beauty – beauty is never really simple. If it's meaningful, it is complex.

MH: Is the footage well known?

JS: No, not in this state. The news media would have used only seconds of material. However, fictional or not, one has an image recall of the massacre; by name it was pretty well-known, but once you've seen massacre footage, such as in Lebanon, or Iraq, where one bomb explosion in a market is difficult to distinguish from another, they start to transpose themselves onto each other in the viewer's mind. The massacre was large: between 2,000 and 3,500 people died or were disappeared, and many bodies were never found. The juxtapositions throughout the tape represent aspects and intersections of the story but are not ostensibly related. The Times Square LED ticker tape, for instance, makes connections with geopolitical global relations underlying the events, notably the globalized war against social struggles, the dominant news media and the machine of capitalism – the military-industrial complex we are all subject to. This LED display describes peace talks in an East Timorese context, which evokes the so-called *Middle East peace process*, which was never really about peace but a cyclical form of Palestinian capitulation.

The slow-motion blooming flowers, mostly orchids, are shot in my home studio – domesticity is woven into the making of this tape. Abdel Majid was taped in his living room with children milling about, people working in the kitchen and guys seated around the edge of the room. He's probably told this story hundreds of times, and the guys listening have surely heard it almost as many times; nevertheless, everybody is in tears by the end of the telling, whether they're hearing it for the first time or a myriad of times. It's part of an oral-history tradition that's survived multiple dispossessions, and it's part of a domestic setting within the camp, which is like a transposed village. This doesn't occur so much now, but when people fled Palestine in 1948, inhabitants from the same villages gravitated toward particular camps. Within the tape, I want to show how larger geopolitical and social aspects of survival, conflict and beauty are reframed in our daily lives.

MH: We never see Abdel Majid, though his voice floats over the dead bodies lying on the streets, as if he were a ghost speaking.

JS: It was a deferment; he appears in the installation, not the single-channel version. I've accepted not having his image, though I always want to have a recognition of the subject in the tape – not having it visually doesn't lessen his presence. Without

I imagined that my house was speaking to me..

untitled part 3b: (as if) beauty never ends..

a visual referent, you're not able to slot him into a certain type of person: Arab, Muslim. I don't think people try to imagine what he looks like while watching; the other imagery fills the visual need, though afterwards they may wonder. But it does create a space where the story can be paid more attention to by the viewer: it's more visceral having these images and this text messing with them intellectually and somatically. I like working with a combination of visceral, formal and literal elements.

MH: The tape is punctuated with blank spaces, underlining the fact that something is missing, that everything cannot be shown here. There are partial gestures – hats without heads, shoes without feet. The hole in the wall offers another viewpoint, another aperture to see the city. This shot suggests to me that no matter how painful, there's no use pretending the wall is still intact. Instead you move toward the wound, the hole, and look through.

JS: The wall is on the edge of Shatila. It's shot ten years after the massacre. What we're looking through is a sniper's hole; it could have been a shell hole originally. We're looking out at the camp, which is part of the city, a specific zone. Camps are quasi-autonomous, neglected and denied spaces. To the Lebanese they are a type of no man's land because they have their own internal governings and structures, depending on which Palestinian party is in control. The demographics of the camps in Lebanon have diffused a little since the war; other people are also living there now, like Lebanese displaced from the south and Syrian labourers who can't afford to be anywhere else.

The wound – a lot of this work is about how to visualize absence and loss. Imagistically, ruins are so easily fetishized. However, they can also be used more potently, representing a past that had been, and what's going to replace them. In *part 3b*, I use them metaphorically and literally in talking about dispossession, absence, denial and neglect of the Palestinian population seen through this void in the structure.

I use black frames a lot in the videotapes for a variety of reasons, initially to break the relentless naturalism of film. When you're watching a narrative film, it all seems to flow and there's no reflective point, so the black breaks up that rhythm and creates another rhythm that is more related to the conceptual trajectories of the piece. There's a structural element as well – it's like in early structuralist film with black-and-white leader, but with content. At its most basic level, the use of black is structural, though it becomes indicative of absence. When speaking about the Palestinian people, their absence is very particular to political situations: either they're left out of the equation, or they're only incorporated when there's an acceptable subject. Like in the negotiations that the West directs between Israel and the Palestinians, where the West (and Israel as part of the West) decides who is present and who is absent at the table, who is acceptable and who is not acceptable. It's not a matter of the Palestinians choosing who they want; even going through the democratic process of having an election is still not sufficient, so they have to rearrange their government again to make it somewhat passable to their own people and to try to placate the powers that control whether they live or die. Absence is very real, it's not just nothingness – absence becomes a political fact that determines survival. When the camera pans to the wall in Shatila, it carries references to history, absence and perception. Perception ties all the works together – it's with perception that we produce articulations that formulate and support policies. That's why confronting the perceptual process is so crucial: it can challenge, feed and lead people along, creating a more informed or intricate discourse by way of perception.

MH: Your movie is very beautiful and lyric – were you concerned that people would wonder why isn't it more transparent? Why not a more conventional documentary approach that would deliver a clearer message?

JS: My work situates itself partially in reaction to the conventional ethnographic form we've come to know as documentary – and the information technologies that followed. I work to raise questions, to insert propositions and to counteract the fulfillment of knowledge. People are only ever seeing an excerpt; the work is inadequate on many levels, as far as fulfilling their needs. I want them to acknowledge that the tape is partial, representative of a much larger body of information and experiences. In the stream of their life, it acts as an interruption in a canon of thought, suspending presumed understandings. In these situations or conditions or examples or themes, I don't think a total *understanding* is possible, or even what we're aiming for. With the subjects/people in all my tapes, we can only imagine what this life was/is like – in fact, we can't imagine it. We can only have a very partial glimpse or fragments of understanding at best. It's more about other things, like materializing an approach to the material, developing a sense of the situation on the ground, addressing specific representational issues, articulating the various positions and relationships, and finding an empathy for the subjects. The work is designed for what I've called 'productive frustration.'

MH: You open *This is not Beirut/There was and there was not* (49min, 1994) with a series of possible approaches to 'Beirut,' via home movies, for instance, newsreels, TV clips and a large array of postcards that contrast the ancient ruins of the old city with hypermodern hotels and plazas. In a scrolling text, you offer a collection of epithets: 'The Paris of the Middle East, the Switzerland of the Middle East.' To enter the city, and to enter the picture of the city – in these always-shifting views, you suggest that one entry is not possible without the other.

JS: It's not possible to have a singular entry, because every entry you make is prefaced by a plethora of others that have come before you. One of the reasons I chose to work on Beirut and Lebanon is that historically it's a place that has been occupied by various military forces over centuries, sometimes several at one time, like in the 1980s, when there were French, American and Italian troops, United Nations forces, Israeli and Syrian armies, Palestinian fighters and 16 confessional divisions of Lebanon, most of them with their own militias. There have always been powers at work, from large national and multinational units to tiny gangs, and assorted resistance groups. You can't enter Beirut without an accompanying history. Even if you don't think you're carrying this with you, as soon as you arrive, your history, or whatever you represent to them, is acknowledged by others. Whether you choose to represent that is not really up to you in initial encounters.

MH: There are other cities in the world that similarly offer histories of occupation, so why Beirut?

JS: In 1983 I purchased my first VCR to record TV footage that I photographed and used as large stills in photo based installations. This work focused on constructions of the male psyche, how media influences our understanding of ourselves and our world, and how it influences our perception. This subsequently became the video footage for my first videotapes (1984–87). I continued to use TV footage critically in the tapes that followed. *Introduction to the End of an Argument* (41 min, 1990) deals with how the 'Middle East' as an object for study, engagement, discourse or exploitation was and is constructed in the West. The tape is still in circulation, because the same representations continue to be recycled and reproduced. With that tape, the previous, *Once You've Shot the Gun You Can't Stop the Bullet*, and the later *This is not Beirut*, a lot of the questions were about issues of the psyche and the construction of representation and how those representations were used in the actions of our governments. Where have our tax dollars gone, who are we supporting, who does that affect, where are we displacing people, who is it funding? Those

questions were aligned on a practical and a conceptual level: how does representation construct meaning and how does that produce or inform identity and larger political processes?

This led me to thinking about other sites where this process was enacted: geographies, histories, countries and cities ... and to Beirut. Beirut is the epitome of the historic city. The other reason I wanted to go was because my grandparents were from Lebanon, from the same little village in the Bekaa Valley. I was curious to see what relationship the conceptualization and actuality of this place had to me and my own alienation. I developed several projects to carry out in Lebanon in 1992, just as the civil war was ending. Beirut was relatively peaceful then. South Lebanon remained occupied and was in people's minds only when there were major events, like when the Israelis would break out of their 'insecurity zone' and bomb a power plant near Beirut or recommence shelling Lebanese villages and highways with their cannons and jets. There was a resistance movement, Hizballah,[3] which had taken control that ultimately drove the Israelis out (in May 2000).

Postcards introduce interesting past lives. You had these pre-civil-war postcards, made before 1975, filled with bright, dye-transfer colours, typically idealistic promotions. They were hard to find, sometimes appearing in shops that were reopening, in dusty corners. The Tourism Ministry, hoping to regenerate business, went back to photograph the same locations. In one shot in *This is not Beirut* at the Place des Martyrs (where the Ottoman Turks hung Lebanese nationalist resisters in 1916), I hold out one of these pre-war postcards in front of the lens, then move it away to show the site in its present-day state. It's since been flattened to make room for what I'd call a mythically inspired neo-orientalist souk-like mall environment, whose shops are so expensive that the people who used to frequent this most public of all plazas or who lived in the neighbourhood can't afford to shop there now, but for the visitor it looks spectacularly exotic, and the setting itself has more recently been appropriated by Hizballah supporters trying to force the government to fall. It is likewise on the Green Line between East and West Beirut, where opposing militias fought and set up sniper posts. There are Greek ruins and Phoenician ruins buried there along with contemporary ruins – mid-20th century, it used to be a very modern square. I have a postcard of the square with a marquee advertising a Jean-Luc Godard film with Brigitte Bardot (*Contempt*, 1961).

The Lebanese were always proud of their cosmopolitanism; they would adopt what they saw as the best part of the cultures that occupied them. It's an interesting sort of pride built on knowledge passed on through interactions with their occupiers and places they've been influenced by. It's similar to the way that Islamic, Arab and Middle Eastern culture and science spread through Europe from the 11th to 14th centuries. It was commonly referred to as the Dark Ages because knowledge came from elsewhere; it wasn't until the 15th century that Europeans took that

---

3 Other spellings include: Hizb'allah, Hizbullah, Hezbullah, Hezbollah.

knowledge and developed it for themselves, and that was named the Renaissance (rebirth).

I would take these pre-war postcards down to the square to show the kids who were hawking their wares, coffee and snacks and things, and we'd talk about these finds, and by the end of my trip the kids had started collecting postcards themselves and developed their own little cottage industry, trading them like baseball cards and selling them to recently arriving tourists and returnees. In the videotape, the postcards are a comment on the multitude of possible entries and layers of reality, juxtaposing the ideal and the actual, the aggregate mythologizing that goes into the construction of a representation of a country (internally and externally). It points to the way certain things are buried in order to reveal others that are more attractive. When they demolished this area, the Bourg, they carted away the ruins, leaving select histories visible while burying others. It all depends on what the power of the moment decides.

In a colleague's archive in New York, I found old black-and-white film footage made by a tourist from Florida and his wife and a friend who came through the Mediterranean by steamship in 1932. These home movies see them arriving in the port, and views of Beirut that no longer exist. It was important to show this paradigmatic touristic approach, seeing what they can capture in a few hours before leaving again. They ham it up with the Natives, get them to pose; he shoots his wife and his wife shoots him with the friend. It's the beginning of the modernized form of the Disneyfication of cultures that are set up as a tourist industry, for consumption. It shows us how cultures are consumed on a fundamental, primary level, visiting and capturing images that can be shown to friends and family. What they recognize as worthy subjects are their own expectations – they look for what they expect and take pictures of it. They have in mind that Natives look like this, the temple looks like that, they want to have pictures of themselves in front of the mosque, and labourers carrying stuff. It's not unlike when Europeans went to Africa and made photographs with a pygmy standing under each arm as a juxtaposition of scale and hierarchy. They are captured. Whoever has the camera has the power. These images demonstrate colonial power relations.

Later in the tape, I look at the reappropriation of 'Western culture'[4] in Lebanon. You see clips from Lebanese TV showing Charlie Brown and Lucy, who asks him where he's going and tells him to be careful. It's followed by a music video where people can phone in tributes, such as to a girlfriend or boyfriend who is having a birthday. As the videos are played, people's names

appear in a large coloured font on the screen. It's a Western music video but it's been mixed back and redesigned into a local interaction unique to that moment in Beirut – pop culture becoming part of the cultural fabric. In other short TV clips, characters express alienation as they come upon foreign cultures, in the dialogues of Captain Kirk and Spock from *Star Trek*, or the Teenage Mutant Ninja Turtles' introspective quips. In these partially humorous bits and throughout the tape, I'm positioning myself as a part-time orientalist,[5] visitor, sometime tour guide, artist, native and/or other.

The entry into the city is replayed in another sequence where a chronology of headlines appears as a series of scrolling texts, each of which characterizes Beirut/Lebanon in six words or less. In the pre-war period, the list includes 'Paris of the Orient,' 'City of Bliss,' 'Crossroads of Civilization,' etc. During the civil war, titles announce, 'City of Regrets,' 'Bastard French,' 'A Byword of Barbarity' and 'Lebanam,' comparing it to Vietnam. In the

This is not Beirut/There was and there was not

post-war period they shift to 'Une Ville Qui Refuse de Mourir,' 'Mille fois morte, mille fois revecue,' etc. This sequence allows us to look at these singular descriptions that have been applied from Vietnam to Lebanon, from Lebanon to Yugoslavia, from the former Yugoslavia to Iraq and Afghanistan, whenever so-called Balkanization or conflict occurs. Our systems of understanding are so limited, we transplant metaphors from one zone of conflict, superimposing them onto another.

MH: Is that because media shorthand demands that complicated situations are reduced to headlines or is it part of a status quo politics in which mainstream press colludes with the reigning

---

4 I don't mean to suggest that 'Western' and 'Eastern' cultures are ever exclusive of each other; on the contrary, this nomenclature is basically a fictional categorization used only for broad sweeps and generalizations – in fact, hybridization is extensive and was always a historical feature since contact, influences running in all directions.

5 'Orientalist' as elucidated by Edward Said in his book *Orientalism*, 1978. Orientalism is the discursive body of studies of the Middle East/West Asia in all disciplines, usually tied to imaginative, imposed or imperialist designs.

empire (by continuing to report whatever national leaders say as 'news,' for instance)?

JS: It's both. They feed off each other. Whatever the media dishes out is due to our acceptance of what is being produced; it regurgitates itself, and we short-change ourselves. The foundation is our education system – that's where passivity and conformity are ingrained, that's where we learn to accept what we're told uncritically. We are trained to accept that we're not going to be able to know about a lot of things, that we'll have to rely on experts. We're taught to specialize, not to develop fluid patterns of recognition or to accept encounters that aren't instantly understandable. We are not taught what to do with experiences that require contemplation, investigation and reflection, that are not prepackaged.

MH: You're suggesting that we concede large areas of our lives to experts: the plumber fixes the bathroom, the news anchor fixes our view of the Middle East.

JS: Or to patterns that have been provided for us, or that we've accepted and have become normalized within our way of living. They are so systematized and naturalized, we don't recognize them as ideologies anymore. Part of our ideological apparatus says we're not equipped to analyze complex political situations – we're looking for someone else to do that work and then we'll adopt it as our own. We're a very controlled and well-behaved society. We're afraid to ask questions that might disturb people – that's what happens in a repressive state.

MH: There's a wonderful moment when co-conspirator and fellow artist Walid Ra'ad is speaking to you in a parked car about the traditional problems of ethnography. The camera pans away as he's speaking, taking in the neighbourhood before returning to him. This shot suggests: foreground or background, where should the focus be?

JS: How do you map a people or a territory? A distinction between background and foreground is antithetical; they are inextricably fused. One of the threads in this tape is the inadequacy of representation. There are scenes of note-taking, scribbling, sketching, demarcating and accounting: there are multiple references to the way diverse forms of representation have historical precedents for imperialistic purposes. How do you map in a way that is not about possession or ownership or occupation, how do you map to create contiguous, overlapping and integrated zones of contact, and map in an intelligent way that can critique and complicate the process while you're doing it? Ethnographies are another form of mapping, the camera is used scopophilically, an exacting and extracting way to interface with culture and society. The discussion continues with Walid when the camera pans away. He's not central to the frame anymore. This theoretically introduces the rationale behind a supposedly benign pan. We're talking about producing local knowledges and whether anyone is well-placed to make those representations. Is it the anthropologist's 'native informant,' an outsider or some combination? Cinematically, the pan is used to capture landscape, to locate and position; in addition it's used militaristically to map out territories that will be invaded and destroyed. My camera movement recognizes the problematization of the pan and at the same time shows the neighbourhood and tries to make evident our positions there.

Walid plays the role of my alter ego. We have conversations throughout. I'm not setting up a polemic between the two of us; he's re/presenting matters I'm questioning and vice versa. I invited him to come to Lebanon with me to work as my assistant for the year; because we were working so closely, halfway through I asked him to co-direct *Talaeen a Junuub/Up to the South* (60 min, 1993), which was the start of his work in video.

MH: Here's another quote from someone you speak to: 'I've noticed in your field that there is something called representation. In Arabic there isn't such a word.' What does this mean?

JS: It's a combination of things. I often went off on my own, rambling about taping, and photographing. Walid left me for the last few months and lent me a car of his family's. By then I had learned to manoeuvre on Beirut roads where everybody drove in every direction no matter what lane you were in. There were no observed stop signs or working traffic lights, it was all hand gestures and car horns. You had to drive fast and aggressive, an interesting chaos indicative of the situation within the country.

The shot you're referring to was next to the Place des Martyrs, in a building on the Green Line that was occupied by the Syrian army. Locals believed these bombed-out buildings were strewn with land mines, but I would go into them as long as there were footsteps in the dust in front of me. I'm walking up the stairs of a building that's partly in ruins, joined by a couple of Syrian soldiers I met outside – they're pretty casual, though still in uniforms with AK-47s (submachine guns). There weren't many people who would walk around this area, let alone with the Syrian soldiers. Some would see them as allies, while others regarded them as occupiers, depending on what constituency you identified with. As a foreigner, my position was much more difficult to pin down. In this case, I assumed the role of a tourist with cameras, Lebanese heritage and of Syrian origin,[6] so they were happy to show me around and relieve their boredom. So we're walking up these fractured stone stairs together, in this dark, reverberating chamber, light piercing through bullet holes and where windows once stood; the image is shaky and askew, shot from waist level. There's a metaphorical dimension as we climb toward the top, trying to reach an unknown summit of understanding, a climax in this rambling conversation I'm having in my broken Arabic. I'm talking and taping and climbing the

---

6 Just before my grandparents and uncles immigrated from the Bekaa Valley, it was still part of Syria. The state of Lebanon was 'created' by the French Mandate in 1920 and granted nominal independence some 25 years later.

stairs at the same time. There are key words that come up in the conversation; we exchange names, they tell me where they're from, one is from near Jordan. Oh yeah, do you know so-and-so, I ask. I tell them my name and he tells me that he's named Jihad; I pause wonderingly and mumble, 'Oh, Jihad!' There are funny little slips of moments inside the circular stairwell, climbing, there's understandings and misunderstandings, connections and disconnects all the way through that have meaning and add to the layering.

To highlight the difficulties of articulating the project of representation, I superimposed the audio from a conversation Walid and I had with a few guests in someone's living room where we talked about what we were trying to do in Lebanon with our projects. I say it's questioning and producing representations; a professor and journalist friend of Walid's asks, 'A representation of what?' to which I respond, 'A representation of representations.' They laugh uproariously. Walid exclaims in Arabic, 'No, no, he's right, that's what we are doing!' Then the friend says that in Arabic there is no expression for the way we're using the word *representation*. He goes on to say he's going to invent this word. That's when we arrive at the building's summit, this Babelian tower. You expect a sign that you're arrived somewhere significant. There's the bright blue sky and the brilliant rays of the sun pointing through the rubble of shattered walls on the top of this fragmented spiral tower, but that's about it. Representation, alienation, connecting, disconnecting and assumptions carried with us – this tape tries to produce something analogous to what we were trying to do and the complexity of our positions.

MH: You went to Beirut with a project to lend cameras to people you would meet along the way. You discuss this in a long chat with Walid while driving around Beirut, trying to decide whether this project is still worthwhile.

JS: At various times in this tape, we're talking about the projects, the proposal, the tapes – there were two single-channel tapes made there that I see as complementary: *Up to the South* and *This is not Beirut*. What I did with one tape I couldn't have done with the other. *Up to the South* speaks more straightforwardly about specific geopolitical questions and has subjects directly addressing the viewer at the other end of the camera. *This is not Beirut* is more self-reflective and self-reflexive in style – although both tapes are equally conceptually based.

The premise I received funding for to go to Beirut was to take five Hi8 video cameras, an editing suite and tripods, etc., to develop projects with whoever wanted to make tapes, at this point in their lives after the 'civil war.' From these tapes I would put together a program that could be brought back and shown and distributed. Discussions as featured in *This is not Beirut* questioned the point of doing this – once again we would be creating images of Lebanon for consumption in the West. Would this simplify the situation for viewers, and why would we want to do that, especially because we're critiquing what this involves

anyway. Do Lebanese know more about this situation than we do, just because they're here (in Lebanon)? Who has the position of knowledge that you want to privilege, and why do you want to privilege that knowledge over another? We knew that whatever was released would be taken as fact, as *the* reality.

MH: Especially if the work is produced by folks living there.

JS: Yes, it would be more 'authentic.' A discourse of *authenticity* is recurring these days – the more Lebanese you are, the more purity points you receive. Programmers are returning to simplistic notions of identity as a criterion of quality: was s/he born there or just passing through? Instead of asking what the levels of engagement are within the work.

The project could never be exactly defined. I wanted there to be ambiguities; people were wondering what exactly it was, and Walid was challenging me, and together we were challenging the project, whether it should still go on. In totality, this 'Lebanon' project was very multifaceted: the production of 16 videotapes produced by individuals through the workshops in my studio, the two single-channel videotapes, my large photography and text project (*sites + demarcations*) and collecting objects and footage and using them in a preliminary layout for the intensely dense and complex installation *Kan ya ma Kan* (1988–1998), with five videotape loops and half a ton of material/documents/reproductions/files. We held video workshops regularly; on weekends people would come and drink Scotch and we'd show tapes of video artists. People became friends and hung out. It's a very hanging-out type of culture. Wherever we're trying to work, there are layers of politics we can choose to embrace or not, it doesn't matter what area we're working in. I think that's what determines a work's level of engagement: how it chooses to interact with the possible access points, the multiple layers that people can enter into the work, and what it does with those layers of expression, information and articulation.

Numerous shots in the two tapes were made through car windows as we travel in a vehicle that represents both a physical and metaphorical separation from the landscape and sociopolitical sites we pass through. Walid's distance is slightly more ambiguous because he grew up in Lebanon, but a lot of his recent life and formulation of his process occurred in the United States. This type of gaze, this view(ing) – out the car window – recognizes and marks distance, shot through the reflecting, dusty glass, visually impaired. So much of the tape is shot through layers, reflecting upon the mediation involved, the strata of perceptual filters between understanding and encountering of any sort.

MH: The camera often provides a passing glance or partial look. You set the camera down on a table in a bar, and while people are speaking we see only a pair of hands, or a sleeve. You refuse the whole picture, always insisting on the fragment.

JS: Is there such a thing as a 'whole picture'? I don't think so. Every frame, every image, is a fragment of some larger whole and every whole, a fraction of something else. Each fragment, each frame, acts synecdochically, as signifier and reference, literally and metaphorically.

MH: *Up to the South* begins provocatively with a woman saying, 'If I simply wanted to refuse, I would not be doing this interview. But if I don't do this interview I cannot express this refusal. You put me in an uncomfortable position because even this refusal you will use to your own advantage.' Damned if you do or don't: is this the position of the post-colonial subject, the one who does not sit behind the camera but in front of it? Why did she feel there was no way for her to say what needed to be said?

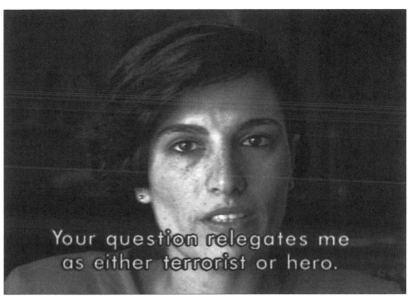

Talaeen a Junuub/Up to the South

JS: The paradox is that if you resist speaking or refuse to speak in fear of being co-opted, there is no way of anyone hearing or recognizing your refusal. Your resistance may go unnoticed. The point is that anything you say can, and perhaps will, be used against you by the media, academia and other information/knowledge industries outside of your control. We wrote this opening sequence as well as the ending sequence with Zahra Bedran, the women performing these parts. The ending sequence refuses to accept Lebanon as a laboratory for others to exploit.

MH: A Lebanese resistance fighter, imprisoned for four years, tells us that the compound where he was incarcerated (El Khiam detention centre) used to belong to the French, then passed into the hands of the Lebanese army, the Palestinian resistance, the Lebanese National Resistance Movement, and then the Israelis.[7] He says, 'It's strange how this centre's history reflects the history of my country. This country upon whose sovereignty so many have infringed.'

JS: The significance of the centre in this clip is how it represents the flow of histories. You don't really need to have a visual depiction of the centre – its physicality is important, yet conceptually it's secondary. Subsequent to the making of *Up to the South*, the centre was liberated along with South Lebanon in 2000. It was then controlled by yet another party on this stage, Hizballah.

MH: A woman from Kfar Roumane describes an Israeli shelling she was certain she wouldn't survive, then she emerges from the bomb shelter to find everything in her town burned and destroyed. You cut away from her and show us another lingering pan of the valley as she recounts, 'If you could transport the land, and the soil, people would have packed it up and left a long time ago.'

JS: This is a common sentiment. The attachment to a land that all of your known ancestors have called home. Where generations have literally built their lives. There is a word you hear expressed in the south, and in Palestine, *Sumud*,[8] which translates roughly to *staying put*, steadfastness as a form of resistance, staying and working your land come hell or high water, 'cause if you leave it, it will surely be occupied and stolen by the Israelis.

MH: In the second half of the tape you enter the occupied south and show us the town of Khiam and some of the impossibly brave who have survived its brutal detention centre. They speak of their systemic torture by the Israelis (and the SLA – South Lebanese Army – a proxy militia set up and controlled by the Israeli forces to give a Lebanese facade to the occupation of South Lebanon), all of the detainees being held without trial or representation, men and women from the ages of 12 to 70, all tortured. It is a shocking and saddening medley of testimonies. You maintain the quick pace of the tape even here, though; each is granted their moment – they come alive as individual subjects, but you don't linger; their stances are cross-pollinated, gathered and collected together. By way of contrast, in the very next scene, you offer a luxury of time to a French-speaking citizen philosopher who says, 'But to defend myself, I have to become someone else, and thus I risk losing myself anyway.' Could you talk about this juxtaposition, the way you found the detainees and how you approached taping them, and what he means when he says, 'And this is the profound mentality of those who resist; they resist within their image, from their identity.'

7 El Khiam detention centre was originally built in the 1930s by the French as a barracks and horse stable. After the French withdrawal, it became a base for the Lebanese army. When Israel invaded Lebanon in 1978, they occupied the south and converted the base into an Israeli/SLA detention and interrogation centre, officially opened in 1985. It continued until May 24, 2000, with the liberation of South Lebanon and the retreat of the Israeli forces. Hizballah then turned the place into an ad hoc museum and commemorative centre open to the public. The Israeli Air Force destroyed the centre during its invasion of July 2006.
8 Alternate spellings of the transliterated Arabic word include: *samoud, sumûd, summud, samud*.

JS: Roger Assaf, the French speaker you mentioned, is able to articulate and theorize many of the experiences we present in the tape. This is placed close to and surrounding the accounts from the resistance fighters and ex-detainees. We wanted to have multiple levels and conceptions of resistance represented and spoken, just as we wanted to have disparate ways of theorizing and articulating experience presented and juxtaposed. As many of the subjects are multilingual, they were free to choose whichever language they preferred for each taping or section of speech. Each subject has her own enunciatory manner or methodology. There is no one way of describing a condition; the various positions people are coming from, and the ways in which they speak or perform are additive, producing a richer, fuller encounter with their experiences. Each voice we present is important and recognized and adds to the complexity and layers of issues being dealt with.

We met ex-detainees through contacts we were working closely with and through detainee organizations and their supporters. Most were more than agreeable to tell their stories on tape, to start building a recorded oral history around these events. At that time there was practically nothing being shown outside of Lebanon about Khiam and the detainees – this was one small project they could participate in.

As for the last part of your question, Assaf attests that, at that moment and the contiguous history before that moment, those who resisted did not become other than who they were to resist. They resisted from within themselves and their own philosophical and other beliefs. He's saying the danger in resisting *or* invading is that you may lose yourself and become someone or something else in the process.

MH: You continue these deliberations on the representation of resistance with a long interview deconstruction, in a tape made years later. Can you talk about how that happened?

JS: *untitled part 1: everything and nothing* (40:40 min, 1999/2002) is a videotape of a conversation I had with Soha Bechara, ex-Lebanese National Resistance Front fighter, in her Paris dorm room. It was recorded during the last year of the Israeli occupation, one year after her release from captivity in the El Khiam torture and interrogation centre (South Lebanon), where she had been detained for ten years – six in isolation. She was captured in 1988 for trying to assassinate the general of the SLA, Antoine Lahad. Revising notions of resistance, survival and will, the overexposed image of her, as the *survivor*, speaks quietly and directly to the camera – not speaking of the torture, but of separation and loss, of what is left behind and what remains.

When I was in Lebanon in 1992, Soha was still in detention, and I would see posters of her around the country. When we went to visit people in the occupied south, people would have her picture next to their sons and daughters who were martyred in the war. She was one of five or six women who were legendary, part of the mythology of the resistance. Their images and storylines were used by the resistance movements for propaganda and patriotic purposes, but unlike the others who had died, Soha was recognized as a living martyr.

MH: Did she have any idea this was going on?

JS: I'm sure she knew her image or persona was part of a gesture of recognition that included other women. The secular resistance LNRM (Lebanese National Resistance Movement) and the PPS (Partie Populaire Syrien) made several dynamic and fervent films featuring women martyrs. Some were confessional[9] films and others pseudo-documentaries of incursions and commemorations of operations[10] carried out. A few had more narrative elements bracketing them, including a sequence of *Brides of the South*,[11] with women dressed in wedding gowns, standing on beautiful hilltops in South Lebanon, facing the countryside proclaiming their allegiance.

When we made *Up to the South*, we went to the occupied area and worked with people who knew Soha. The tape shows the El Khiam detention centre and talks about the conditions there. It was one of the few videotapes, and the only art video at the time, that talked about the occupation of South Lebanon. It was a non-story in the West. Why? There was no value in America reporting that Israel had an occupying army operating torture and interrogation centres, that villagers could only stay on their land if a member of their family collaborated with them, otherwise they were expelled or detained. The stories we usually hear are the ones the media and ruling powers want us to hear; hopefully there are other forums of information. People have a limited capacity for reflection – if you think of all the atrocities happening now, it can render you incapable of doing anything.

In 1995, Mireille Kassar, a Lebanese artist living in Paris, organized a clandestine screening of *Up to the South* at the luxurious theatre of the Institut du Monde Arabe in Paris. They wouldn't sanction an official screening, so we used word of mouth to spread the news of the event. There was a huge turnout and a long discussion followed the film. Even though I don't see the tape as a documentary, there is a level of information that people grasped intently. After the screening, Mireille and I became friends and, unbeknownst to me, she later formed a committee that worked for the release of Soha and the other detainees in El Khiam.

Four years later I'm in Brussels for a show, having just shot *untitled part 2: beauty and the east* (50:15 min, 2003), in the former Yugoslavia after the NATO bombings. Mireille called to say Soha was living in Paris because shortly after her release the French government offered her a bursary to study at the Sorbonne.

---

9 Videotaping sessions of fighters talking directly to the camera explaining their actions to their families, their parties and others before they carried out their 'sacrificial' acts of resistance.

10 Military actions of the resistance fighters, attacks, bombings, assassinations, etc.

11 This is not an actual film title but a description of the women resisters that was used in many films, posters and media discourse.

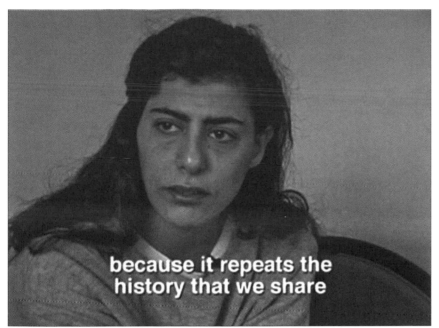

because it repeats the
history that we share

untitled part 1: everything and nothing

There was a gallery exhibition of artworks that had been smuggled out of the detention centre, like necklaces made with olive pits, embroideries with threads they would pull out of their shirts and weave, and charcoal drawings and writings on toilet paper given to the Red Cross and smuggled out. Mireille suggested I come to Paris and screen *Up to the South* at the gallery where Soha and Rabab Awada, an ex-detainee in the tape, could speak after the screening. I went, and Rabab and Soha talked about the continuing occupation of Lebanon and the detention centre, which was still operating full force. It was a good screening and impassioned discussion. Soha and I then took off to talk over a Lebanese dinner.

We had a nice long chat in my bad French and her little bit of English, and I was pondering during dinner: should I ask her or shouldn't I? Should I tape her or not? I asked her, look, now you're being filmed to death, you're telling your story over and over again to the news media, I really understand that you may not want to be taped anymore, and I don't want to be part of the feeding frenzy. We discussed this a bit, she didn't think anything of it and said come on over tomorrow, I'll make you breakfast (a Lebanese dish, *kishk*), and we'll do the taping before. In the tape she states that part of her mission is the talking about it (the detention and occupation) so others can know – this as a form of resistance.

She lived in the suburbs in a small dormitory just a little larger than her old cell. I brought her roses, but you don't see me give them to her because it's not the kind of encounter where you walk in with cameras blazing. She puts the roses on the desk near the door on a three-foot-high pile of dead flowers. I asked her if she would put them in water. She said, 'No, I don't put flowers in water,' and then tells me the story of why. During the taping I get her to tell me the story again. We go further into her room (there is only one room), and I set up the camera and start taping to see what'll happen. I didn't have any concept of how I would

use the material. I knew I didn't want to ask her the same questions she had been asked a thousand times: what were the interrogations like? How did they torture you? Where did they torture you? For how long did they torture you? These are the desires of the press, the most spectacular details. They don't ask questions about what it meant for her to resist. Press stories are short, highlighting the most explicit situational pornography. The press is the pornography of politics, in the same way that storm recordings on the weather channel are called storm porn by people who make them. They're dealing with quick sensational bites that keep the audience from changing the channel. That's a pretty cynical view, and there are exceptions – leave it to say I wasn't interested in asking what she'd been asked previously.

During the taping I didn't understand what she was saying: she was answering me in Arabic and I was asking questions in French. My Arabic has about a 30-word vocabulary at best: left, right, straight, go, stop, how much is it, what does it cost, etc. Whenever I tape somebody I ask them to speak in the language they're most comfortable with. Sometimes people choose their original language, sometimes for tactical reasons they'll choose another language because that's what they want to 'perform' in. These are all performative collaborations: the more they speak, the more professional they become at it, in terms of the role they have. As soon as I turned on the camera, I could tell that Soha had this image of a resistance fighter that she was speaking from; she had a role to play that she handled very well, and that she was used to doing. I wanted to ask questions that would recognize both her story and her representation, and in addition would make this representation malleable. I wanted to create this permeable representation that she would enter and leave, that viewers could enter and come back out of, an elastic image that would provide moments for her to open and close, so that we're encountering more than just a role she takes on. So I asked questions about how she lived in the detention centre and now in Paris, and before in Beirut, and about the triangulation, what the distance means between the three sites.

Whenever I'm taping conversations, I'll try to set it up so viewers can be brought into the encounter, so they're intimately engaged. I place the camera right here, between us – as a subject you have to look through the camera lens to see me. Occasionally, people try to look around it, then after a while they settle down and talk through the lens to the potential viewer.

MH: Isn't this the promise of every picture, that it can be seen later, cherished and recorded? You tell her that the interview will be translated, that you don't understand now, but you'll understand later. Does this deferral also relate to the resistance itself?

JS: Is every picture worth saving and viewing? There are no promises with videotaping. Who knows if you can ever make anything valuable out of what you shoot, gather or collect. I never know how or if something will be used till much further in time, and even if the clip will make it this far, after time passes in life, after repeated viewings during logging and editing.

Perhaps the goals of the resistance are ones of deferral, but real. You wouldn't take up arms or resist if you didn't feel the outcome would effect positive change. All in all, resistance isn't that complicated: you have an occupier and an occupied people, and a resistance that grows out of this. Of course there are factions that develop – the LNRM was made out of all sorts of secular groups. With the later invasion of Israel in the early 1980s, the Islamic militias started to get stronger. Because the Israelis occupied primarily Shiite villages in the south, Hizballah grew with the support of Iran and Syria. Hizballah decimated the other resistance movements by 1985, and eventually any resistance, by even the smallest pod or cell, came under the umbrella of Hizballah, which was a powerful position for them to be in.

I was familiar with this history. My point wasn't to talk about how the resistance was formed, but ideas of resistance, and what it means for us: how can we be resistant, what different forms can resistance take? After her release, Soha continued to see herself as part of the resistance: she was going into international law at the Sorbonne and talking about the conditions of the detention centre and in Lebanon. I see the tape as part of a resistance, a very mild form – it's just a videotape, not a Molotov cocktail. Though I'd want my work to have fiery effects. My work resists status quo conventions and understandings by embracing multiple ways of approaching and engaging systems of 'knowledge.'

Even though I shot this in 1999, I knew it might be a few years before I got it out; my work takes time to produce, sometimes it feels like forever. So when I said I'll understand later, it meant I'll have the distance to have a broader appreciation of what she's saying. As opposed to the news industry, which has a demonstrated antipathy toward time. Instead of valuing only immediacy – i.e., after five minutes it's worthless – the distance that time provides would make the experience clearer for me and provide a better position to approach the material. Time provided a necessary distance.

MH: It's reminiscent of a comment by Godard, who recommends that television be seen only ten years after broadcast – then it becomes clear what is happening. In one of the many touching exchanges in the tape, you ask her what she would title this encounter.

JS: Soha says she doesn't like titles. She says, 'Normally you are the one who decides ... if it was up to me, I would name your film "untitled."' I've used this for the video project's overall title and as a way to thwart the packaging or commodification of the videotape as an object. With each part I don't normally use beginning or end credits, as the videotape parts are actually pieces of one long continuous tape. This part is subtitled 'everything and nothing,' taken initially from earlier in the tape where she says, in reference to leaving Khiam, 'In my opinion I left everything and I left nothing at the same time.' Meaning, they had nothing in the camps, no material possessions, nothing resembling a 'normal' life – she left that, but she left all of the other detainees that she had become so close to, that had become the world for her, so when she was released, she was leaving everything as well.

MH: She says she's closer now to her fellow detainees left at Khiam than she was when she was detained there. 'If one loves, distance is not a factor. It is the decision itself which is determinant. You decide for yourself whether you want to assert distance or abolish it, be close or far, or become dedicated or not.'

JS: It's a question of discipline and will to determine how close you're willing to get. You hear about a massacre and decide whether you're going to let that impact you. Today there is war going on in Palestine, Iraq, Afghanistan, Sudan and other places of lower-intensity conflict or that we hear of less frequently – we have to decide how to go on living, how involved do we get or can we get.

In these types of interrogation and torture centres like Khiam, you choose if you're going to try to survive, and Soha decided she was going to use every minute to become stronger and more reflective and to develop whatever she could within herself. She was going to make the utmost of her time there, no matter how arduous, whether she lived or not. She was very disciplined: she exercised every day, literally climbing the walls in her isolation cell, which were so close together she could put her feet onto opposing walls and climb up and down for exercise. When she was in a cell with other women, they would share their stories, recite poems, sing songs, create narratives out of any remembrance. I think she refined her sense of purpose and was able to develop a form of acute reciprocal articulation that took a lot of practice and determination, and the necessity of love became all the more apparent.

MH: 'We represent the resistance, the detention, the occupation and a generation that lived the civil war ... ' She talks about being bound hand and foot in an isolation cell measuring 90 cm by 90 cm by 90 cm. There is no blanket or mattress, but, impossibly, a rose. She feels the rose doesn't need to be put into water to be 'recuperated.' She steals a slice of cardboard to frame the rose and offer it as a present to a Palestinian girl, but the guards catch sight of it and burn it. 'We were not allowed to make or keep any objects that expressed ourselves, our states of being or ideology in any form.' Can you tell the story of the rose?

JS: Ah, the rose. Well, you've summarized it quite well already. The rose was slipped through an air space in the door by a Palestinian detainee, Kifah. Soha contemplates the rose and thinks, why should it be put in water, it is beautiful in itself. Trying to revive its original meanings is futile, they were lost when it was cut; one could embellish the cut rose in many ways, but that would be altering its natural state. In spite of it all, the 'rose remained a rose, it kept its beauty, and radiance, even after it was burned.' That's when she decided that when someone brings her flowers she won't put them in water.

MH: I'd like to switch gears for a moment and return to an earlier moment in your body of work that also turns around an interview with a woman, *Episode 1: So. Cal.* (33 min, 1988). Here the speaker is Aida Mancillas, a Chicana woman who falls in love for the first time with a rich teenager. Her non-stop voice-over describes a fairy-tale story with a cruel twist of class and race. 'I was fascinated by him but I didn't like him at all.' Her dreamy tale of youth and beauty is punctured by unexpected observations, like the fact that every time she sees him she becomes physically ill. Because you let the interview run for so long, the viewer can feel the way the flow of her speaking works to cover over these breaks.

JS: I made that tape in San Diego when I was going to grad school, and this was *Episode 1* – predating the start of the *untitled* series by 11 years. I thought I would continue to make episode two, three, four … but that same year (1988) I went to the Middle East for the first time and started working on other projects there. As I mentioned, all the tapes before this deployed re-edited television footage; this was the tape where I made a bridge between someone's recounting of their experience, their articulation of their history and subjectivity, and prepackaged forms of histories and subjectivities as consumable objects – television objects meant to produce our psychic condition as humans and consumers. This was the first time I broached that division: I let Aida speak until she was finished, and that became the length of the tape. You never see her, the same way Abdel Majid is never seen in *(as if) beauty never ends..*

Her voice is paired with Southern California regional landscapes, from the car, from sites travelled to, and from television sets in motel rooms, to get a sensation of the land and cultures where the story is located, to situate her speaking. Even though the body is not visible, it's felt, and the drive produces an out-of-body experience. When you come from an immigrant culture, you learn how to render your body and subjectivity invisible. A form of internal ethnocide takes place (and external when forced by the dominant culture). Linguicide occurs when there is no public space to embrace your language. The repression she describes as a Chicana, a Mexican-American woman, is a fundamental story for Southern California. At the time of the taping, there was a resurgence in cultural recognition of the Hispanic communities. There was the formation of the Border Art Workshop (Taller de Arte Fronterizo), for example, one of a few collectives and art projects developed to do cross-border work between Tijuana (Mexico) and San Diego. You can take a streetcar from San Diego and get off and walk ten minutes and then you're in Tijuana. They're each distinctive cities, but there's a lot of criss-crossing, which has become even more formidable now because of the increased official and vigilante American border patrols.

When she tells these stories, she relates her body's reaction to social circumstances that are tied into racial/ethnic/class divisions which she internalizes. Her illness becomes another form of representation of the experience she's encountering.

MH: In the tape's second chapter, she describes the reaction shot, a summer affair with a working-class guy, a scooter-riding mechanic in Spain. She describes it as the happiest time of her life, and he becomes the image of the person she should be with.

JS: It's only the person she feels she should be with at that moment. It probably helps that she's in Spain and that someone speaks her language, that the context she's surrounded by is so contradistinctive, new and yet somehow familiar.

MH: The third act takes a different turn: the serial love story veers off into someone else's life. She talks about her friend Carol, whose father is a napalm dealer and a 'monster.' The two friends drift apart, Aida gets married, and news of Carol's shotgun suicide is initially kept from her. When she finds out, she is devastated and lapses into depression.

JS: I didn't predetermine any of this sequencing, it was based on the encounter. This was Aida unpacking her stories. It was important to introduce the arms manufacturer, because it brings more levels of understanding to the landscape of southern California. It allows us to talk about the military-industrial culture within the very grounded, local story of her life. It's the same thing I'm trying to do with the shots of the media, the landscape, the passing buildings, the palm trees: to offer more reflection on a site that isn't far from Nevada and other places of military-industrial manufacturing and bomb testing. I made a second audio tape with Moyra Davey, a friend of mine, which was to have been the basis for *Episode 2* – another portrait of sorts, of an unrelated life – but that was never finished, as I soon left for the Middle East where I shot footage for what was to become *Once You've Shot the Gun* and *Introduction to the End of an Argument*. These two tapes, *Episode 1* and *Once You've Shot the Gun*, could be seen as bridging pieces between the earlier found footage/media deconstructions and the work where I'm focusing on specific subjects in, and locations of, conflict, post-conflict or interstitial zones.

MH: Over the FBI copyright warning you scrawled, 'Copy this tape.' Why?

JS: I was going to do this with all my tapes, refuse proprietorship and make them available for mass distribution and duplication. The idea of copyright was always problematic; I disagree wholeheartedly with the commodification of video, making it into an object. Though my tapes are packaged and sold and rented, I don't like fetishizing them as objects. That's one reason why *untitled* is an open-ended project; it's more reflective of a life and the lives of people I encounter, where experiences flow and grow into other experiences – it's more lifelike.

MH: How would you feel if chunks of your tapes showed up in someone else's work?

JS: It depends on how it was done and with what footage. If it was of people speaking who had worked with me, and was done without acknowledging where it came from, without contextualizing it as part of another story, that would be troubling. When I'm taping people, I feel there's a responsibility to their subjectivity and stories, and this must be viewable, it must be evident. As I'm taping, they understand I'm going to let their story be heard; I feel a responsibility to do that within the context in which they are speaking.

MH: *Once You've Shot the Gun* (8 min, 1988) is framed by two extraordinary audio texts. At one point, a man says in voice-over that he visits a family where the man begs him not to rape his wife and to kill him instead.

JS: This is an ex-Israeli soldier telling the story of breaking down the door in an assault on a Palestinian family's house. The man he assails is afraid his wife will be raped, and to avoid this he offers himself to be killed. I videotaped the soldier when I was travelling in Palestine/Israel in 1988 (the same trip where I continued to Lebanon for the first time). I shot 30 to 40 hours of footage from several refugee camps, villages, cities and points in between and tagged along with an NBC news crew from Houston, Texas, which was there on a week-long 'eyewitness' tour. We visited representatives of different movements, including Peace Now, which the ex-soldier was part of. After the news crew left, I remained in Palestine and stayed in Jabalia refugee camp on my own for two weeks with a family I'd met through a friend. Later in the videotape, my girlfriend at the time tells the story of a dream where the lower part of her face disappears.

MH: She can't speak and doesn't understand why. She decides to undergo an operation where the doctors peel away all the flesh from her face and realize she has no jaw.

JS: Much of this tape is about living with anxiety, alienation and denial, or the inability and construction of it and the allowances made. I combined footage I shot with fleeting images from TV in order to look at alienation when encountering other cultures and individual people. It was shot in travels through 16 cities or towns like Jerusalem, Beirut, Byblos, Jouni, Kelowna, Las Vegas, Limassol, L.A., San Diego, Phoenix, N.Y.C., Portland, San Felipe, Tijuana and Vancouver – though you may not be able to recognize them. The tape offers fragments of those passages – a woman's hand brought to her chest, dark glasses settled onto a table – gestures that produce a physical closeness, and then a

visceral pulling away and separation. The skin is peeled away to only to reveal absence. Throughout the tape there are references to personal and political aphasia; it's impossible to speak about these moments in a language we understand, so we develop another language in order to have speech. This process involves anxiety, distance and separation, moments of empathy and connection, love and pain – it's a real mélange. A relationship was a familiar way of looking at alienation – you can get so very close to someone, but how deeply do you actually know them?

MH: This tape is stunning and necessary, a beautiful lyric that restages a relationship across a fragmented landscape. It's all so very beautiful – can you talk about beauty? Is beauty a political subject, or is it possible only when talk of politics is retired? Can we afford beauty, does it clarify or blind?

JS: You have to have beauty. Trying to describe it is almost futile, and problematizing it is necessary. I want to make pleasurable and engaging and sensual tapes, I want to draw people in. Although the work may be painful, there are moments of visual pleasure, but you can only get so tactile with videotapes; it is very difficult to work with them beneath the skin – the surface of video is always the starting point, but this impermeable layer must be scratched away to get beyond it. Beauty is a form of nourishment. If there were a Canada's Food Guide that listed the five essential ingredients to live, it would have to be included. I'm not talking about conventional attitudes of beauty, but a richness and complexity of life, incomprehensible to a large degree, but very rewarding. Moments of the sublime or the awesome when you're encountering nature or moments of sensual pleasure or visual pleasure. Why do I weep when looking a painting of Monet's piles of wheat in a French winter field? What's with that light, what does it draw out in you? It's the layers upon layers upon times of reflection and connection, the meditative, the inexpressible: these things connect to your life and deeper to past lives, next lives, other lives. That's what beauty is for me.

There is a caveat, however, as in *untitled part 3b: (as if) beauty never ends..*, the notion of beauty is negated with the *(as if)* segment of the title, as if meaning *of course not*. Beauty is subject to ending like any aspect of life, as it requires a subject to engage with.

MH: In *untitled part 2: beauty and the east*, a medley of voices opine about Eastern European identity, borders and nationalism in the former Yugoslavia after the NATO bombing. One talking head follows another. There is a distinctly erotic subtext in this work: there are so many beautiful women speaking, and they speak so well, with such precision and clarity. 'It is very interesting not to believe, not to share illusions anymore.' 'I can't identify myself with a national state.' 'Some people are only an image, others can think and talk.' On the one hand, this tape is all talk, and on the other, the return of the repressed. This tape is ripe with longing, with a need to have a body, to become a body, to embody these ideals and this history perhaps. Can history also be the story of a romance?

JS: In fact, all of the quotes above, if I'm not mistaken, are made by men, whom you could also say are beautiful. The body politic – is this the body you are conflating with the sensual body? Beauty, as I have described it, is such an oblique, subjective, abstract thing – perhaps it suggests possibilities, or hope, a yearning for another state. The nation-state is a romantic notion, all too impractical and forced upon us and others. Its dissolution and reconstitution can likewise be seen that way. The narrative of history and the narrative of love, both are constructed fictions to live for or with – it seems both are necessary for hope.

MH: *untitled part 4: terra ~~in~~cognita* (37:30 min, 2005) is a commissioned work. Can you describe how it came about?

JS: I'd always wanted to make something in Kelowna, where I was born and raised. Then the opportunity came up. The Alternator Gallery won a public art competition offered by the City of Kelowna looking to celebrate its centennial year of incorporation in 2005. The gallery's proposal was to invite five emerging artists to make five-minute videotapes, and two senior artists to make 15-minute pieces about an aspect of the area. Proposals for the five-minute pieces would be juried, and for the senior pieces they invited Dana Claxton and myself. These would be put together on a DVD compilation and released as a commemorative disc. For me, the foremost thing to feature in the compilation was First Nations' voices from the area: I wasn't sure in what way to approach that. I called up Dana, who is a Lakota (Sioux) artist from the Prairies, and asked if she would be interested in collaborating, but she declined and said, 'You go ahead and do it, you're from there.' Initially, I proposed a project to the city that would combine First Nations' histories and immigrant stories from Kelowna and the (Okanagan) Valley. Like all my projects, once I started taping, it took on a life of its own.

My grandparents emigrated to the Prairies from Lebanon in the early 1920s, and my parents grew up in south Saskatchewan before they left their farms and went to Quesnel and then the Okanagan to raise a family. In this project, I hoped to be able to tease out and confront some of the geopolitical implications of colonization, settlement and immigration. There were different periods of encroachment, with people arriving from the late 18th through the 19th century for a variety of reasons and with different expectations; how do First Nations of the area (the Syilx) people view the period before contact, at the point of contact and afterwards?

For a few years I had been running art and video drop-in workshops with a collective I

started, desmedia, in the Downtown Eastside of Vancouver, where I met Warren Wyss, brother of Cease Wyss, a Squamish filmmaker/media artist. Warren relocated to the Okanagan, working with peoples' sweats, on recovery, part of a healing circle. I headed to Kelowna in February of 2005 for ten days of shooting and hired him to do second camera. He lined up several people he knew for us to visit. I also went through official channels, calling the band offices, and met a few people that way. After the taping of the conversations started, I realized it didn't make sense to combine the Native and non-Native stories; there was too much compelling material and the need was so great to present the Syilx (Okanagan) position however best I could. Their stories aren't known at all; it was imperative to have them as a principal part of the compilation and embraced as part of Kelowna's history, albeit a neglected part in most of Kelowna's eyes.

Whenever I start a videotape or get invited to produce a new project, I try to figure out what the most critical issues are to be involved with in a local context. If I'm going to devote my time to a specific situation, I want it to have resonance, like in South Lebanon. What are the crucial contentions? Who are the figures to represent the essential areas/fields of representation I want to feature? After being there for a while, you figure that out, you shoot and gather and listen and learn. I make annual trips to Kelowna, and nearly all of my family is still there, so I had a sense of things. When I grew up, it was basically an apartheid state – it still is, like a lot of Canada. The only Indians you meet are usually the disenfranchised urban Natives on the street. You don't really have a lot of encounters with Native culture unless it's ceremonial, for consuming at a festival, or an opening dance at a conference. I grew up on one side of the lake; when it was colonized, the settlers pushed the Indians onto the worst land and took the most fertile areas. The actual town site of Kelowna was part of an area that had been left as a bears' habitat; it was sacred

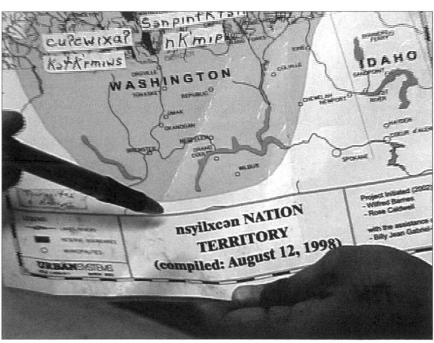

untitled part 4: terra ~~in~~cognita

land and the Natives respected the bears and left this space for them, rarely encroaching upon it.

The day before the premiere screening, City Council viewed the video works and deemed the project inappropriate for their sponsorship. They based their rejection on my videotape and tried to censor the entire project's screening. That was four in the afternoon, with the screening scheduled for the next day. I called the Alternator Gallery and said, 'I'm coming to Kelowna anyway, my flight is already booked, you need to get another space, let's do it in your hallway or rent another place, because people are going to be coming from up and down the valley to see this work.' They called me an hour later and said, 'The board's okay with that, we're going to arrange an alternate screening site.' The next day, the day of the screening, we were actually able to take over the city's main theatre for the event – the original venue – after finding out the City had cancelled their booking.

Previously I had arranged for Roxanne Lindley and her extended family to come across the lake and make an official Syilx welcome – a welcoming to our land. (Roxanne is the Westbank Band's cultural advisor and is featured in the tape.) This is never usually done at our official cultural events, but we should be doing it as a matter of protocol; there should always be an acknowledgment of territory, of whose usually unceded land we are on. Those who have native rights to that land should be invited and asked if they want to give a welcoming to the visitors who are coming. For Roxanne and Chad and her extended family, it's a political statement, which is also very hospitable; it's engaging on a level that people appreciate. Their welcoming song also opens the tape, in which Roxanne says we're all beautiful because we're all from this land.

So we do the screening and hundreds have come, including chiefs and representatives from four Native band councils from down to Penticton and up the valley to Vernon – news coverage about the attempted censorship increased the interest. In effect, what the City was saying to the First Nations people – the Syilx – was that they could participate in city events, dance, sing and make and sell crafts, but we don't want to hear about your histories, or know your stories, as part of our official history.

Roxanne and her family and friends did their welcoming song, and all seven works were screened. There was a discussion afterwards about the tapes and about the meaning of the events surrounding the reception of my piece. There was an awesome energy in the theatre. Near the end of the discussion, Chad Paul, who is in my piece, got up and said, 'Jayce, if they don't want to have you on this side of the lake, well, you're welcome to our side of the lake anytime.' Following the screening, there were six weeks of press battles back and forth while the Alternator negotiated with the City's public art committee. In the end a compromise was reached and the Alternator was not paid the rest of the monies owed to them by the City and the City washed its hands of the DVD project, letting the Alternator have ownership of the compilation rights. The power of unambiguous voice to connect, the subtlety of their speech, and a direct engagement with the

'subjects' proved too compelling to ignore by all who saw the tape or participated in the surrounding discourse. Throughout this process, and afterwards, the tape was definitively accepted by Elizabeth Lindley Charters, Roxanne, Chad and the others in the tape as their own film, something that spoke to and from their lives. I couldn't have been paid a higher compliment.

MH: Unlike with your Beirut tapes, I really have to look for you in this work. Of course you are behind the camera, and occasionally you say *yes* when a subject is speaking, but for the most part, you deploy the conventions of documentary as a shield, to block my access to you. In *This is not Beirut*, Walid asks, 'What is your point of identification?' which I took to mean: why are you here exactly, and how do you show this reason in the way you present the subject? Why was it necessary to show yourself in Beirut but not in Kelowna?

JS: Why do you have to look for me, my corporeality? I reject and refuse this conviction, that first there has to always be an obvious presence of the artist or filmmaker easily and readily available for the viewer to engage with, like the artist always has to have a neurosis to work out in some hysteric or masturbatory way to exorcise their demons or more banally to navel-gaze like much contemporary artwork – that which I refer to as 'vacuous conceptualism.' Second, I am present in every moment of this tape; whether you recognize it or not is not an issue for me. In every video frame (one-thirtieth of a second) you can find my presence, in every field (one-sixtieth of a second), in the framing of every response, the asking of every question, and every aspect of this production.

People have often asked me about my earlier work, the television montages, for example: 'Where are you in this work?' Every edit reflects upon the maker, every moment of blankness and space and rhythm that you're sewing and suturing the piece together with is autobiographical. My presence is physically manifest while making the work. You can read the tape all the way through as the maker's mark even though the *story* is about other things. I reject that unless you're seen or heard, or your hand is more evident, that the work is any less personal. In this tape I didn't want to be a visible subject, or to bracket discussions with audible questions. The only time I offer commentary is when we're out in the field and I say to Elizabeth, 'So they were trying to separate them, right, from the culture?' and she says, 'Yes ...' and elaborates on how the settler governments did that. With Chief Dan Wilson in Vernon, I say, they were 'dispossessed twice,' and he replies, 'Yes, dispossessed twice from their homelands.' He's talking about how, under the Indian Act, reservation land was given to a few families while other families were left 'out in the cold,' so that many wound up in the urban centres with nothing but their names. The video image appears like a viral landscape, skin that's peeling back, revealing more and more layers. My presence is concretely there, it is felt, barely audible and not ostensibly seen – visualizing my image so superficially is not an imperative in my work to date.

Working on the project was personally significant. I was able to reconnect with a landscape I knew well, the valley where I was nurtured as a child, the fields, trails and the lake. Kelowna was quite small back then – nature was very accessible. Roxanne and the others sensed they could work with me; our shared appreciation of and respect for the land helped provide the level of trust and intimacy that's necessary for this kind of work.

MH: Aren't your subjects more transparently staged here? In the Soha interview, you interrogate the mechanism of the interview, while at the same time conducting an interview – both are at play. Here the interrogation is absent, which brings the work closer to traditional documentary work.

JS: If you look further through the image, you might think of this in another way. Traditional documentary makers would probably find all kinds of fault with this piece: the use of black frames, the non-synchronous sound, the diverse mix of editing and shooting styles, the rapid cuts, the degraded low-budget pixilation effects, the camera positions and handling, distancing/mapping shots from the car window, no seamless narrative nor a voice-over – telling people what to think – the denying of a linear naturalizing structure and negating the formal fetishization of the *real*. I could go on. Suffice it to say, in each tape that I make, I choose what I feel are the most appropriate visual, audio and conceptual tools for the specific ambitions and objectives of that work. I challenge myself not to repeat the methodologies I've used before in the same way or to become formulaic in my practices – this would be the death of me. I ultimately disagree: there is an 'interrogation' taking place here, maybe not enough on the level of 'image' for you, but dialectically into the discourses of history, colonialism, Aboriginal voices, and our settler nation's continued denial and effacing of those histories and articulations.

MH: Yes, but the subjects are often centred, and they appear whole. This is all there is; the questions around what we can know – of the fragment, of what is being left out – are not so much in play here.

JS: I didn't want to disturb these stories so much – the subjects spoke from where they lived. I wasn't interested in messing with their voice – we've messed enough with their territory already. Even so, the shots or clips in the tape do speak to me as fragments. They are only parts of a much larger discourse, they represent my engagement with only *a beginning to hear*, a set of voices to start listening to and to make tapes out of – for me as a maker to start from, and for audiences to begin a process or period of reflection at the moment of viewing through this. Yes, there are seemingly whole thoughts here, complete sentences, and some centred imagery, but each of these functions like signifiers, synecdochical and metonymical pointers to all that is left unsaid, the multitude of other pieces, nuances and multiplicity of what could be said, to the cultures that have been oppressed,

the discussion of hybridity and the non-monolithic, collaborations and corruption, the ethnocide, linguicide, attempted genocide, and to the historicide that colonialism enacted and neo-colonialism shares the history of.

MH: Haven't we seen too many Native stories told by others? Many of your landscape shots are so beautiful, but aren't these non-Native views part of the problem? Isn't the crux of the Native/non-Native conflict about land – not only who owns the land, but how is it seen, who makes it visible and to what end? Is part of the point of your tape to bring us to a place where we can see the land differently? How do views of the land shift according to your three-part pre-contact, contact, post-contact template?

JS: These three historical periods work as referents in *terra incognita*, though they are not detached and separate from each other, all having resonances and significant effects in subsequent periods. To arrive at the contemporary condition of Kelowna, which epitomizes the condition of a lot of North American communities – large towns, not quite cities despite mall-invested arteries, rural life omnipresent within its boundaries – I utilized a range of treatments of the land imagery as well as blurring, overlapping, reinventing anew these treatments from time to time, and confounding the reliance on any one reading or interpretation of the land, whether city, residential, industrial, commercial, development or rural lands. For example, to map out a sense of the colonized land from contact into the initial settlement period, I used fast-motion car shots of the current residential neighbourhoods and strip malls along the highway – with the occasional dry Okanagan mountainside in the background peeking through – accompanied by accounts of this historical period and the initial loss and privatization of land, tying this into the present developmental circumstances.

I've been accused of or criticized for producing work with people who are identified by others as not part of my identity profile, or for introducing or bringing into the discourse, into the fold, issues and points of history that others would rather continue to hide under the rug. This has been a continuum in my work and will continue to be. We all have to account for our histories. There are many powerful Aboriginal filmmakers and video artists in Canada, such as Alanis Obomsawin, Zacharias Kunuk, Annie Fraziér Henry, Dana Claxton, Loretta Todd, Barb Cranmer, Cease Wyss, to name just a few. I'm not sure how many of them you've interviewed. There are powerful storytellers out there. For me it not a question of speaking for others (appropriation) versus carving out a space for suppressed voices (emancipation) – it is much more complex than that. I speak in affinity with. My videotapes are collaborations, there is an exchange, a sharing and a trust developed and evidenced. The conversations themselves reveal this, it's how this tape is made, performed, shaped and realized, and it's what we as subjects are saying that is important, not the fact that I am from that locale or not, or whether I am black, white, red, yellow, brown or an undefined shade of grey.

Exclusivity, defined however you want, is occasionally needed for periods of time, regrouping, regathering, solidifying, but this praxis will ultimately prove limiting. I am opposed to facile distinctions and categorizations of identity. We who have privilege in the art world, academia, literature or in popular entertainment and the press – who have an acknowledged voice, and are heard from time to time – need to reflect deeply on what we are using our speech for, what social paradigms we are reinforcing, supporting, challenging or subverting, what confrontations and changes we are proposing to, or producing in, the political and ontological systems that be. How we can we work in isolation, independently and together to enact constructive sustainable change? Affinity-based production, collaboration, a building of allegiances, solidarity and a shared purpose – cross-cultural work provides a site for these uneasy conjunctions, negotiations and unpredictable journeys to take place.

Jayce Salloum's Videos

'..In the Absence of Heroes..' Warfare/A Case for Context –
   Introduction   60 min 1984
'..In the Absence of Heroes..' Warfare/A Case for Context
   43 min 1984
'..The Ascent of Man..' Part 1: Silent Running   4 min 1985
'..The Ascent of Man..' Part 1: Silent Running – Appendix   4 min 1985
'..The Ascent of Man..' Part 2: Conditions of Mercy   6 min 1986
'..The Ascent of Man..' Part 3: Acts of Consumption   8 min 1987
Episode 1: So. Cal.   33 min 1988
Once You've Shot the Gun You Can't Stop the Bullet   8 min 1988
Introduction to the End of an Argument/Speaking for oneself.../
   Speaking for others...   41 min 1988 (1990) (co-director Elia
   Suleiman)
Talaeen a Junuub/Up to the South   60 min 1992 (1993)
   (co-director Walid Ra'ad)
This is not Beirut/There was and there was not
   49 min 1991–92 (1994)
untitled part 1: everything and nothing   40:40 min 1999 (2002)
untitled part 2: beauty and the east   50:15 min 1999 (2003)
untitled part 3b: (as if) beauty never ends..   11:22 min 2000 (2002)
untitled part 4: terra incognita   37:30 min 2005
untitled part 5: terra cognita (working title)   2007
untitled part 6: footnotes to a book of setbacks (working title)
   ca. 75:00 min 2008
untitled appendix i: lands   20 min 1999
untitled appendix ii: clouds   15:35 min 1999–2001
untitled appendix iii: other   6 min 1999–2003

Distributed by NMI/Monte Video, Video Out, Heure Exquise!, Argos, LUX, Video Data Bank.

Jayce Salloum has worked in installation, photography, video, performance and text since 1975, as well as curating exhibitions, conducting workshops, organizing collectives and coordinating cultural projects. Salloum has exhibited pervasively at the widest range of local and international venues possible, from the smallest unnamed storefronts and community centres in his neighbourhood to institutions such as the Museum of Modern Art, New York; National Gallery of Canada; Centre Pompidou, Paris; the Rotterdam International Film Festival and the Biennale of Sydney. His texts have appeared in many publications such as *Third Text*, *Documents*, *Framework*, *Fuse*, *Felix*, *Mix*, *Public*, *Pubic Culture*, *Rouge.com.au* and *Semiotext(e)*.

JEFF ERBACH

SOFT LIKE ME

want him to play for my team. I want to offer him his own car, his own studio and assistants, and all the fancy lighting gear he needs to make those large-gauge, beautiful pictures he produces. Instead, Jeff Erbach continues to work in a wilderness all his own, not quite an experimentalist, not quite a storytelling machine. Perhaps it is enough that he has produced some of the most visceral, striking pictures on the fringe. They show young boy slaves in metal harnesses, white-smocked girls with missing eyes, underground lairs devoted to meat. It is hardly necessary to add that these imaginative flights are grounded in documentary, like all necessary fiction; it is a world he has lived, and then sculpted again out of light, with actors and crews and truckloads of gear. Jeff has an expensive imagination. But in order to show the trials of childhood, or the prison house of adolescence, he has summoned an army of ghouls, reincarnated cadavers and displaced genitalia. He is not afraid to open the wound and share, to stand up inside the infinite space of the frame and make the first mark that will allow us to go back, to speak the myth (not the story) and tell us why.

Over and over again he presents us with situations that are so far from our understanding that at last we have to say that it is also the mirror. Yes, that's me. And me again. He refuses to look away, his well-lit cinema is a long stare into the grotesque, the misanthrope, the malformed. He shows us, he insists, that we are also these nightmares. He embraces them with tenderness. He searches not for the moment when we are witty and the good humour is dripping from our lips and the lighting softens our creases – no, he is only interested when we are covered in our mistakes, hardly able to speak at all. While my zombie is busy being born again, while parts of my body have issued declarations of independence. The winters are long where he comes from, long enough to nurture this cruel kindness. Won't you have a look?

MH: Many independent moviemakers, on and off the fringe, like to go take their cameras for a stroll. Oh, look! And then they do. Some bright or not-so-bright idea might occur to them, and off they go, venturing forth in some post-home-movie mode, to seize the day, or admit some moment of it into their viewfinder sights. Moviemaking can be spontaneous, or occur as a matter of gathering material; shooting can happen with no particular end in sight, the way someone else might sit down and sketch a flowerpot, over and over. You seem entirely resistant to this mode of production (I wrote 'protection'!) – holding a camera means a crew needs to be at hand, grips and lighting people and actors. Why is that?

JE: I'm actually not at all resistant to other modes of production. I simply cannot create any other way. I wish it weren't true, which might surprise people.

I like the personal, intimate feeling of handmade films. I like the accessibility and immediacy of video, but I can't make either kind of work. I've tried. Invariably, I'll take out a video camera with

every intention of gathering some images, only to find days later that I haven't shot anything, still waiting for those three actors to show up with a van full of lights. I rarely even take still pictures. Alas, I'm too far tied to using the traditional craft of filmmaking, exploring how the acting, pacing and photography can work in balance to bring visceral, mind-numbing, pseudo-stories of timeless other worlds to the screen. I have the utmost respect for visual artists who work with film, but will forever watch those works knowing deep down that it's not me. They are like sculptors and I'm a construction foreman yearning to be an architect.

I've become incredibly self-conscious about my films and feel isolated in my approach. Artists who explore film as a plastic art, filmmakers who process their work in a bathtub, draw on it, run around gathering images themselves, sometimes have little capacity to see the artistic nature of what I do with lighting, staging, acting, pacing, etc. Conversely, film-industry types recognize typical characteristics of narrative filmmaking in my works, but are then baffled when the movie proves resistant to the icy demands of 'storytelling.' Where is the hero, character empathy, resolution? I'm not a storyteller, and don't understand why it's expected of my work. How else to measure one of my films, though, because it's not experimental, so it must be a failed attempt at storytelling. That one sentence might sum up what I will one day call my 'career.'

So, neither a film artist nor a film director. I'm in cinematic purgatory, entirely self-imposed, which makes it much worse. On more positive days I think my work might be unique, but the cold, blank stare of my resumé, lacking any screening at a major festival or even a single Canada Council grant, always lights my matchstick confidence. It shouldn't matter but it does. Every artist knows it does, and many filmmakers thrive on it. If I could change two things, one would be to find a love of working without lavish cinematography or the beauty of truthful moments in acting, and the other would be to develop a head for the self-adoration common amongst white male film directors.

I'm now feeling like this wasn't the answer you thought you might get and that I've split off into how my work is received versus why I make it this way. If I'm being truthful, I suppose it's because I have no idea why I do it this way. I often wish I didn't, but continue to do so anyhow. Such is love.

MH: Of course it's true, your movies have the production gloss of story movies, with big-screen smarts and actors and cameras that move in a reassuring and controlled fashion. And there's a story all right, but it's not right up in the centre of the frame where I can take a bite out of it. Instead, something else asserts itself, time and again, like a virus that has attached itself to the host. This leads, all too quickly, to a problem of naming. What the hell is it? Your absence from major fests clearly narrates this confusion of categories. And yet you refuse to budge, and keep turning away from the storytelling confines of genre that permit viewers and programmers alike an entrance door with easy handles. Does it have to be so difficult? In other forms (like the novel, for instance, or in painting), stories may be conjured in impressionistic smears, or dispensed with altogether, but movies in wide release require a marshalling of resources that render them conservative by nature. While working with actors, is the thrill in being able to throw your voice, to find it in the face of another, or the way someone sits on a couch, stares out a window?

It would appear you've been seduced (come here, be part of this) by movies you've largely rejected. I know you're not a story-teller, but wonder if you might venture one anyways, something about an early encounter (or two or three) with pictures that proved formative.

JE: I'm extremely curious about everything, a curse that prevents me from ever spending enough time in any one place. So I make films with as many elements of control as I can. I'm fascinated with cameras, lenses, photography and image making, so I try to make films that are lavish and full of detail. I love history and geography, and so my films reference both. I am a closet psychologist, so working closely with actors to illuminate the deep emotional subtext of a script is incredibly rewarding for me. I love the artistry and theatricality of makeup, costumes and set design. My filmmaking style might be a product of my voracious appetite for learning. When these disparate elements come together, I can convey a world entirely created in my imagination, allegories for contemporary living. Oh, yes, I'm obsessed with myths and fables.

I grew up in a sheltered suburb of Winnipeg, known throughout the city as a bizarre backwater. My cultural experiences were limited to the endless parade of forts and museums we'd frequent on our intrepid family vacations. To the very date that I decided what I would do with my life, I had not set foot in an art gallery and I considered *Jaws* to be a work of high art.

With four months left until graduation, there was a palpable sense of panic among those who hadn't yet decided what they would do after high school. I toyed with the notion of being a paranormal investigator, but encounters of the bizarre had become too usual. I sat in my social studies class and wrote out the two things that most interested me. They were science and, almost inexplicably, art. I couldn't imagine going to university to study science, a ridiculous decision since I was very fond of research and essay writing. Now left with an 'Art' headline, I wrote out all of the artistic disciplines I could think of: dance, singing and music, poetry and writing, theatre, film, painting (not visual art, just painting, a sign of my incredible naïveté). Very quickly, in a two-minute span, I had eliminated all of the disciplines where I was utterly feeble and was left with theatre and film. To the casual observer, this would have seemed like complete rubbish. Here was someone who should have gone to university and pursued religious studies or become an English professor, but instead was considering a career in the theatre without ever having seen a live play. It was too much. Through fate and sheer lunacy I decided that I would try to make films.

I discovered the films of Ingmar Bergman and spent the summer at my job in the scrapyard sitting in hollowed-out cars with my head full of cinema. On the brink of being a camera jockey, I suddenly veered headlong into making my own films. And then at last I made a feature film, only to dive into work-related depression, realizing that I simply don't 'fit' the film system. I know that I wasn't 'born' to make films like some always crow on about. I think if I get very lucky I could become someone like Michael Haneke or Aleksandr Sokurov and make films that resemble stories. If I'm unlucky, something else will grab my attention, and I will have made my last film.

MH: I've seen your work a few times under the umbrella (the shadow?) of 'movies from Winnipeg,' a city you happen to live in. Most work, most of the time, is not shown this way. My small mutterings, for instance, have never been gathered up in a made-in-Toronto fest. Does the regional identity tag still feel sweet, or are you tired of the company? Do you feel there is a shared sensibility, if not amongst every last trademarked and tattooed director, then at least amongst some of your neighbours, some of the time? Those big skies, unrelenting winters and too much late-night television – you tell me, does it add up to: *we belong here, we see it like this?*

JE: You're going to make me reminisce. There was a time when I was proud to be part of something here in Winnipeg. There was a group of people – editors, designers, grips, cinematographers and directors – and we all helped each other make films. It was real magic, even if not every film was a complete success.

Now there's an odd feeling to being lumped in with all sorts of other films. While people outside Winnipeg are too quick to attribute small things to being definitive of a Winnipeg film, people inside Winnipeg are very careful not to be seen as being too derivative (there are some exceptions, but no more gossip).

People always think that Winnipeg films are all very dark, bizarre, surreal or absurd. Some are, but I could list you dozens of local filmmakers whose works challenge all those preconceptions. For unknown reasons, no one charts those filmmakers. I could be facetious, and certainly more entertaining, if I droned on about the weather, the isolation, the depravity and self-consciousness of Winnipeg makers, but it's all too much rubbish. There is cold and isolation in Regina and Edmonton. Depravity is wide-spread, and Toronto is the most self-conscious city in Canada.

In reality, there are two reasons why Winnipeg filmmakers make so much interesting work. One is funding. Aside from the übercompetitive federal arts grants, we also benefit from one of the best provincial arts councils in the country, where funding is stable and considerate. Add a healthy civic arts council, small funds from the local media arts centres and a ridiculously low cost of living, and there's enough money to have a go. Secondly, when no one is interested in developing local directors, you quickly realize there's no hope whatsoever in being a professional filmmaker. Success, whether in movies, music or visual art, is measured by innovation and artistry. The message of Winnipeg is: be true to your heart. Make work for decades and die lonely and impoverished, but know that some of the work was good and there were hot summers along the way.

I feel like I'm ruining Christmas, but it's not the water or the weather, it's cold cash and a sense that short films are not 'calling cards' but an art form worthy of exploration. Even Winnipeg filmmakers disagree with me on this issue, but I've heard no other reasonable explanation. Don't be taken in. Some Winnipeg filmmakers have a fascination with promoting themselves in the context of a burgeoning renaissance of filmmaking from a small, backwater prairie city called Winnipeg. Of course they disagree with me, so talk of weather and skies and magic persist.

Gavin Frogboy

MH: *Gavin Frogboy* (10:20 min, 1994) considers an isolated, frog-identified mute boy. The product of a broken home (Ma locked him in the basement, then left him for over-the-hill party boy Dad), he looks to nature for possible behaviour models. He is mostly shot in tight interiors, listening to others speak or have sex through the walls of his confinement (or is it their confinement?). Language is a scalpel that has not cut him yet, and in its absence he is left outside the tribe, seeking escape. The opening chase scene with an overgrown fly suggests he is not alone. Is this another allegory for adolescence? Why the B-movie bug costumes?

JE: Gavin Frogboy is my mole. When you have a mole, depending on where it is, it can be charismatic. You might even have a Cindy Crawford mole, which is darn sexy. But it's a mole, so it will invariably revert to what moles do: grow larger, discoloured, hairy, ugly, and they may kill you. I look back at this film, something I created out of sheer boredom when I was considering being a camera person in the film industry, and love it despite its flaws. It is, after all, mine.

While Gavin was locked in the bathroom escaping to other worlds with his large frog costume, I was doing likewise with a 16mm Arri BL. Gavin ran to the swamps and I ran to the local film co-operative – equally mushy and dangerous. I wore the rags of a filmmaker for the first time outside of school, listening closely, trying to make sense of things. It is easily the most autobiographical film I've made, which I hope stands on record since I'm asked that question of every single film I make.

I only made two films in this particular style before I couldn't control it anymore and it mutated all on its own. They were my student film (*Mr. Twenty Five Cents*) and this one. The dominant idea involved taking on alternate personalities and escaping to fabricated new worlds. Maybe Gavin has a broken mind, maybe he was never fully a person, but either way he is also partly a frog. Other boys were partly giant bugs, or lizards, but always things that boys had natural affinities with. Little boys have tiny worlds, so their escapes are limited to what they know best.

The parents are oblivious, a short nod to broken homes. Cavi-

ties of the house might as well be miles apart; the bathroom is the refuge of the frog, while all other rooms belong to Dad. Sex is heard but never seen or understood by poor Gavin, who might be more inclined to spread seed over a pile of eggs. Could a lack of sexual comprehension infect your sense of place in the world? Possibly, since sex is the most revered and celebrated form of communication between two people.

All in all, the film is quaint. It shows characteristics of where I was headed and might be the most 'commercial' of my projects. Writing about it is like talking about my garden, you know? It's there, I slaved over it, it's pretty ...

MH: *Under Chad Valley* (8:30 min, 1998) shows a pair of butchers hard at work in a subterranean doomscape. One makes a wordless sexual advance; the other, distracted by the prospect of having a body again, chops off the end of his finger. He retreats into an icy chamber, watched by two hungry girls dressed, like the butchers, in shapeless white smocks. At last, the active butcher pulls a stream of yolk out of the other's mouth. Why the sudden ending? It felt like we were just getting warmed up. Where and what is Chad Valley? The movie is structured as a spiralling series of crescendos, in cycles of tension and release. Can you talk about how you shaped the film? This is my fave movie of yours because of its wordless refusal of plot, its drop-dead gorgeous cinematography, its always twilight mood. Even its that's-all-folks celebration of the fragment makes me feel relaxed all over. At last, large-gauge filmmaking can be used to show a situation, granting equal attention to foreground and background, looking from both sides of the picture.

JE: Maybe I named it prophetically, because this piece remains relatively unseen, buried in a plastic bin in my basement – *Under Jeff's House*. Not really a horror film, not experimental, but not sufficiently queer-themed either. Unclassifiable work is simply not a good place to be.

Why so short? The most painful question of all. Unfortunately, I had to build sets, pay actors and painters and props and camera people and do a soundscape and make final prints. It costs a fortune to make films like this. Video artists get the same amount of arts council money as I do for sitting in front of a computer. Maybe that's why large-scale filmmaking practices aren't regularly applied in this fashion.

As for the process of discovery, I sometimes find little things as I go along, but for the most part it's all laid out in advance. Once the two or three days of shooting have passed, I can't redo anything. This style has great limitations.

I wanted the metal casement for the butchers to be underground, hidden from view, a love that is unseen and unheard. What's lower than a valley? And there should be meat: chops and loin and fingers and dicks. Slaving away at the chopping block is aggressive, ridiculous and cliché, but it's an idea I can repurpose, like the man with a penis-arm. The freezer could be a gloriously theatrical space, the hanging carcasses gashed with huge vaginal openings – a tank full of every conceivable notion of penetration, flamboyance and bodily fluid.

I figured two little kids could tootle around the tank, clearing up the scraps, small pieces of meat collecting even smaller pieces of meat. They watch the proceedings closely, but their eyes are blotted out, thus protecting their identities. Children shouldn't be subjected to the lust games of fatally attracted butchers.

This is where my issues with conventional storytelling are clearly on display. Not just here, but in all of my films, there's a sense of catching only glimpses. I'm a huge fan of vignettes stitched together to convey a pseudo-story. You get a feeling for it, but it's not straightforward. It's not experimental, but not narrative either. Even Nicholas follows this device to a point. The pacing is immersive and you fall into it like a warm bath. *Under Chad Valley* might be the most successful of all my films in this regard.

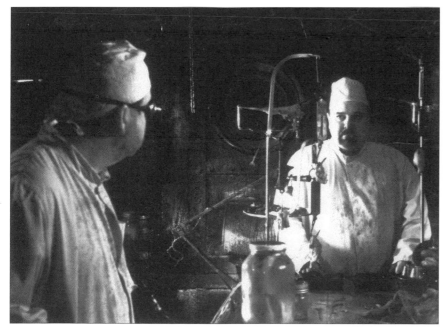

Under Chad Valley

MH: *Monday with the Martins* (4 min, 2000) is a marital study of sexual conspirators. While the Missus is busy downstairs watching porn, Mr. Martin tries to repair a cock that happens to extend from his right arm. These eruptions are punctuated by glistening, soft-focused tracking shots over mysterious moments of domestic architecture, as if the house were alive and paying attention. Of course, I can hardly remember this movie. I saw it with you last summer, and I am groping through my extremely soft ability to recall. What led you to the Martins? Movie sex mostly consists of barely lit shots of perfect bodies in missionary position, with requisite pans to windows, candles and sheets. These couplings are shown without a hint of the awkwardness, shame or rage of real sex. Your movie takes some of this task on: how do we show what we want? I took this as a mini-essay about sexual representation, so why the dramatic setting? Why even the rescanned moments of porn hyper-reality, the exaggerated moanings of sex/death, the strictly observed boundaries between top and bottom, the acrobatic exploits of folks who can produce the fantasy of being purely, absolutely a body? And to risk asking the most obvious and boneheaded question of them all: why does this man have a hand for a penis?

JE: This is a strange little movie for me. First of all, aesthetically it doesn't really relate to anything else I've done. Second, it was by far the least expensive, shortest shoot I've ever had, yet in my personal order of appreciation it ranks as the youngest daughter.

I was an artist in residence at the time, and the organization wanted the artist to create work during the residency. The funds available for the work were scant. So I whipped up a two-day shoot with two actors I know (actually, Mr. Martin is long-time collaborator and picture editor George Godwin) and shot it on one roll of 16mm film. I had seen some great Sokurov films, like *Mother and Son*, and wanted to try adding lighting gels directly on the front of the lens, smearing it out with K-Y Jelly (not Vaseline, which tends to darken the image).

A man with a hand for a penis. It's not very original, but I don't pretend that it is. Instead, I wanted to take the idea a step further; what would it be like for a husband and wife if the husband had this more useful, functional appendage? It seems to have a mind of its own, unzipping his pants and trying to escape. He needs to suppress the sex, to hold it in, but it manifests in other ways. The wrapper is an s&m-looking bondage piece – and the sex starts to bubble. The wife, on the other hand, is either sexually frustrated or persistently horny. And what's the difference there? The barometer is busted; pleasure and pain comingle when your man is able to stimulate your clitoris and penetrate you at the same time with the same tool.

Porn is one of those things I find boring, unless taken in small doses. I suppose that's why the internet is so popular, because you only get those 20-second clips, which is really all you can take. The average viewing time for pay-per-view adult films in hotels is about eight minutes. There's something in that. Even discussions around porn, its dissemination and production, are utterly boring. There's something deadening about porn, something that turns off the tender, soft part of people. It's the hard, hairless bodies retooled for singular purpose, the repetition. When two people kiss, it's more electric than any love scene in any Hollywood film. They smashed through the muck. Sex, like films, is meant to be experienced. When it came time to gather the porn for Mrs. Martin to watch, I knew that, no matter what I found, it wouldn't be titillating enough. So I tried to repurpose it. I looked for images that captured the reptilian part of sex, the jungle-gym part, all arms and legs and new positions. I made porn into porn, exposing it for what it really is.

But why does he have this extra arm? I can't take full credit for the idea, so can't fully explain it either. It's like saying 'Bloody Mary' 13 times while looking in the mirror, it's a story that runs through the culture. Men have this floppy tool they use for peeing and copulating and pleasure, but it's also the centre of fixation and power. You'd think it would be a more developed organ, something more impressive! I like the dichotomy, and exposing it for what it is, a ridiculous-looking extension that embodies so many base feelings. So I've added this extra function to the penis, both reducing its role and elevating it at the same time. In the process I'm asking men and women to, well, think about dink.

MH: *The Nature of Nicholas* (90 min, 2002) exists in a strangely suspended state between childhood and adulthood. Two not-quite-teen best friends strike a variety of poses: slouching against school lockers, conversing at a party, standing with a baseball bat perched over one shoulder. Can you talk about creating pictures from other pictures? (Are we condemned to them? Is there no way out?) What drove you to start this movie?

The Nature of Nicholas

JE: Acting, like filmmaking in its infancy, is measured in scales of naturalism. Actors are supposed to capture emotion and deliver truthful performances. Awards are given to those who can mimic something they're not, who can make a show of their performing, whether it's the queen of England or someone with a disability. The acting in this film is subtle, mainly because these kids are turning over complicated issues for which they have few answers. I wanted the actors to be themselves but also to reflect the film's feel and content. It's a very different way of working, and one I'm still trying to perfect. The persistent poses, frozen, but only for a second, reflect boys on the cusp of manhood, mimicking the images they aspire to, or holding on to the childhood images they hope not to lose.

MH: There is a curious space around the dialogue – a silent beat follows nearly every sentence, lending the proceedings a deadpan suspense. Why the absence of sound overlaps, the careful diction, the wide-open spaces between the words? Is this prairie landscape turned into a grammatical device?

JE: All that silence makes for short valleys in the dialogue, a persistent rising and falling where lines spring up like shoots of wheat. It feels truthful but also strange, and so the acting manifests in the same way as the photography or the sets. More to the point, it is truthful, but through a prism that might help to illuminate new truths. That's the essence of what I do.

MH: With her hair flip and perfect outfits, Nicholas's mother always looks 'on display,' or just 'on,' though her performances are mostly at-home appearances. She seems another manufactured product of the 1950s, holding faith with a utopian science, dishing ice cream and Jell-O and homilies with a studied cheer to her only son. Her life is a style, and this modernity covers her inability to grieve her dead husband. He has been left behind, it seems, in modernity's inexorably cheery march forward. Can you speak about her role as modernist cipher?

JE: The mother essentially wears the same dress for the entire film, but in different colours. These outward appearances hide her inner turmoil. In this way, she acts as a counterpoint to Nicholas's struggles. She hopes to move forward by pursuing a new boyfriend, getting a new house and maintaining a uniform, but delicate, presentation.

MH: After the two boys kiss, one of them turns into a zombie. I'm no Syd Field expert, but this looks like the 'climax' of the first act. Why the zombie subplot? And I'm wondering if you could fill me in about the three-act structure of dramatic movies. Is there no way around that?

Soft Like Me

JE: Essentially it's the same model that's been used in films for decades and so doesn't interest me. You start by setting up the main goal of your hero. This is usually done in the first few minutes. Despite viewer sophistication, we're still watching the same kinds of films that were made at the dawn of narrative filmmaking for people who had never seen moving pictures.

I appreciate that this film seems to head in one direction, only to make a sudden, unexpected turn. I call it a 'cathartic cinematic event.' I'm often accused of a fairly heinous crime of creation: making work for no reason other than attention-seeking, being a 'bad boy,' trying to push people's buttons. There is, in my mind at least, a massive double standard going on. I could name several filmmakers who do precisely that. They take an issue and come up with some controversial way of presenting it. I'm accused of doing what I've never done, while others get all the attention they seek. It's strange to me. I should be more specific, but I can't even talk about it anymore, it's so completely boring.

I've mixed, imploded and repurposed the iconic symbology of common genres. The coming-of-age film, where tweens stumble charismatically into teendom, is an offensive mythology grounded not in truth but in pedestrian escapism. I don't remember winning over cute girls with my humour and integrity, or performing a superficial makeover that suddenly impressed former bullies. No, we all know the truth, which is that travelling through puberty is a period of cold self-discovery. Though this film has the paw prints of fantastical surrealism, it's actually grounded in real experience. Shame, guilt, disconnection, unrelenting parental pressure – now, that sounds like puberty to me!

The decaying body, which I've alternately called the 'zombie,' the 'ghoul' and the 'monster,' is all of these things and more. Unlike other 'zombie' films, where, at best, the zombies are symbols, my little green bodies are metaphors. A metaphor is more complicated, an open-source project where everyone can contribute to its meaning.

Decay, for most, is a terrible thing. Artist Damien Hirst believes it's far more frightening to people than death itself. I think there's beauty there too. As does he. It's a rejuvenating, life-giving process, where nature presses itself against living tissue. When I die I want my loved ones to put me in a car and drive me out to the prairies, where they'd dig a hole, drop me in and cover me up. Back to the place from which I came. Of course it's completely illegal, so I guess it won't happen that way – wink wink.

Decay could be seen as a process of natural change, even progression. Now I've illuminated where I'm headed, I'm sure you can see it. The march through puberty, bubbling sexuality, tender but guilty feelings for your friend, all wrapped up in metaphor. There's more, though. There's also a duality, a physical separation where one body blossoms while another descends into the muck.

My wife just asked me what I'm doing, so I told her. She said, simply, that boys love zombies. Her idea is that the representation of reality conforms to your limited idea of it – in the boys' case: baseball, comics, girls and zombies. These few paragraphs might be more than I've ever said about the film. The more I say, the more I ruin it. When the mystery of a piece is gone, there's little left, a fact that leaves me extremely coy about explaining away everything. For example, I haven't even talked about the subtle Christian elements: the baptism, journey to knowledge, death and resurrection under the guide of a father figure. That's as far as I should go! The only artists I trust less than those who don't understand their own work are those who understand every little bit of it. What a horrible, plodding way to create.

I wanted to make an unapologetic prairie film where a boy comes to terms with his own identity. That idea, over time, started presenting itself to me with another boy who was decaying. I thought maybe Nicholas found this other boy, but soon realized that they knew each other. It all went from there, little threads that made the giant ball of string. This might explain why I have such a difficult time getting more films made, because it's all exploratory for me, even while we're shooting.

MH: *Soft Like Me* (25 min, 1996) is set on a boy farm where preadolescents are harnessed and put to work in the fields. At night they are hung up like farm implements, kept in check by a lordly fop and a devouring maternal presence. The beast is doubled by a young girl who offers escape, but like all innocence here she is brutally slaughtered. You offer a harrowing vision of growing up on the prairies, all the more unsettling for occurring in the high-key afternoons of summer. Is there no way to create desire without top and bottom? Why these childhood reflections, and what does the title refer to? (If I were a father, and mercifully that will never happen, this is what I would name my first son.)

I remember the first time I ever watched this movie, with all of its young boys lined up in their harnesses for inspection, an image that still disturbs. It makes me grateful I've never had sexual feelings for a child, though this is an undercurrent that runs through much of your work. Surely by now there have been charges levelled at you: pornographer, pederast, exploiter! I can imagine stills from your movie showing up on some bent-up websites. Do you worry about that, or is that another way of saying, 'Censor me'?

JE: Desire and innocence are not mutually exclusive ideas. Children, prepubescent young adults, whatever they're called, are expected to be without desire so they can remain innocent. In a culture where even casual body-touching games are taboo, the notion that a 12-year-old wants to put his dick in someone seems outright criminal. I fear we're headed down this path, where any and all discussion around childhood sexuality and development is derided as pornography. When I was 12 years old I wanted to nail half of my class (don't tell the Ellis twins). Why can't that be expressed? It's a very real and crucial period in people's lives. I could go on about the influence of ultra-conservative ideology on morality and sex in Western culture, but the point is so obvious. If it wasn't, watching *Soft Like Me* should clarify things nicely!

The title is mainly a visceral moniker. It could be the words of the boys in the camp, or the warden himself, or the words of the viewers who get a sinking feeling from the film. It was the beginning of something for me, trying to find a way to synergize pacing and acting and content.

As for my work overall, I know full well there is a certain market for my work that exists outside the beltway of sophisticated taste. It doesn't matter to me. My work irregularly appeals to queer audiences, horror fans, cinephiles and super-weirdos. I don't believe I've ever fetishized any of the imagery in my work, and those seduced by the images are sometimes oblivious to the messages. Every year there's another narrative moment at the Cannes Film Festival where the actors have graphic, unsimulated sex. This is far more egregious than anything I've ever done. I'm talking about painful, beautiful periods of young people's lives, not filming two people fucking for a boring porno trend.

I've actually written a new larger film that is about parenthood. I hope to make another short film soon about puberty in teenage girls, and I'm writing another film about imagination and interconnected dimensions. Slowly, my central protagonists are getting older and my work is branching into new areas. Why so much work about kids? *Under Chad Valley* was about two butchers and *Monday with the Martins* is about a husband and wife. In actuality, only about half of my work has centred on children or teenagers. Maybe that's a lot, I dunno. I do know that I simply gravitate to the subject. Making films about two adults hashing out their relationship in an apartment bores me to tears.

Jeff Erbach's Films

Mr. Twenty Five Cents   8 min 1993
Gavin Frogboy   10:20 min 1994
Soft Like Me   25 min 1996
Under Chad Valley   8:30 min 1998
Monday with the Martins   4 min 2000
The Nature of Nicholas   90 min 2002

The Nature of Nicholas distributed by Domino Film and Television International Limited, short films by Tiny Sumo Entertainment.

Jeff Erbach is an independent filmmaker from Winnipeg. He has made several short films and the feature film *The Nature of Nicholas*. His films have won awards, played all over the world and earned him a retrospective at the Canadian Film Institute in Ottawa. He has several projects in development while he continues his work as the faculty director for the Academy of Acting in Winnipeg.

SU RYNARD

AFTER SCIENCE

Her work is sharp and pointed and rich, every high key surface lit and lavished and exposed. The shadows have been cast away by these careful, set-decorated ministrations, or perhaps they appear as white shadows on a white ground, hardly visible. It was clear even from her very earliest efforts that she had visual chops. There were lingering pans over emptied party tables, the left-behind glasses and half-eaten cakes more eloquent than a thousand miles of after-dinner chatter. There were shots of emptied apartments and walls that were chilling in their appearance. Somehow she had the gift to make objects speak, to take the backdrops and props of our lives and grant them a place onstage.

And there were strange rumours – that she was the child of Joyce Wieland and Michael Snow, for instance; that she had been created in order to make art, product of the primal couple of Canadian media art. Crazy shit like that, not a word of truth in it. Even so.

Like Midi Onodera, Su is another tech geek, and held down a job at Charles Street Video for many years. Charles Street (which has not made its home on Charles Street for many years now) is part of a chain of artist-run production centres that grant access to gear and cameras and lovely edit suites, and help relieve the feeling that you are the only one interested in these strange formulations. Video's restlessly changing technologies have made it particularly difficult for those, like Su, who were expected to help others make their small-screen dreams come true. That she has kept herself on the frontiers of understanding for so many years now is testament to her perseverance and tenacity. How much easier it would have been to turn those skills into an industry placement, settle in with a broadcaster and a mortgage. Instead she has chosen the road not taken, and produced, over the past couple of decades, a body of work that offers models of behaviour and understandings, that allows us to see ourselves, refracted in the beauty of a world where background and foreground have achieved a rare equilibrium.

MH: You are known for your densely poetic short work. Why did you take on the feature-film project Kardia (85 min, 2005)? Why did you want to make this film in particular – are its themes and events close to your own experience?

SR: For many years I have worked across several disciplines and across a range of approaches: dramatic, experimental, documentary and installation. The idea dictates the form, and Kardia is no exception. I wanted to tell a complex story and I needed to use long-form dramatic narrative to do that.

You described the short films and videos as densely poetic, and I believe this is also an accurate description for Kardia, as the film is visual, lyrical and ephemeral. It is more of a meditation than a traditional narrative. The word kardia derives from the ancient Greek meaning heart. Thematically, the film explores the heart – physically, culturally and emotionally. The events of the film are both told and imagined by Hope, a pathologist, whose story unfolds within one moment in time – the brief instant when her heart stops. Her journey becomes both the telling of a childhood tale and an examination of the heart as soul and psyche.

Why this film in particular? Kardia is fiction, but I gave the characters many things from my personal life. For example, my father was in the air force and we (a family of eight) lived in a tiny house on the Downsview air base. Like the character of young Hope, I grew up surrounded by airplanes and Popular Science magazines. At the emotional core of the script is a father-and-daughter story. My father died of heart failure, and to some degree bereavement fuelled the writing process. My first video artwork, Absence (1986), is created from that same place, so I guess this is part of who I am.

MH: Kardia is partly set in the 1950s, when the hopes of a utopian science remained intact. The atom had been split, the moon was within reach and time-saving domestic appliances promised liberation from mundane concerns about survival, freeing 'us' (those privileged to enjoy the benefits) for better things. What is it about this time that compelled you to recreate it so faithfully? How did you research the minutia that would need to be collected (the stray objects on a table, the pattern of a rug, the look of a sofa)?

SR: In Kardia, a fictionalized version of an experimental surgical procedure called 'cross-circulation' is depicted. This is why 'the past' in the film is set in 1955, when these operations occurred. At this time, Dr. Walter Lillehei at the University of Minnesota Hospital performed 49 open-heart surgeries on infants and children with congenital heart defects, using an experimental procedure called 'cross-circulation.' Cross-circulation was a procedure where a young heart patient (often an infant) was connected, via a series of tubes and a pump, to a healthy adult. The patient relies on the healthy person's heart and lungs to keep them alive during the operation. These operations were performed before the invention of the heart-lung machine, when opening the heart would mean certain death for the patient. The famous blue-baby operations, as well as the first heart transplants, were big media events and very much in keeping with the 1950s utopian science mentality you describe. Importantly, in contrast to this era of idealism, a portion of the film is set 50 years later, in the present, around 2005. Here, the protagonist Hope is a scientist in crisis. She questions the scientific thinking that is synonymous with her worldview and asks, which is true, an empirical truth or an emotional one?

But back to the 1950s. You are correct in suggesting the 1950s elements in the film are faithfully recreated. I'm very detail-oriented in all my work, and for the most part, these details are written right into the script. For me, the details are the syntax of visual language. For the film to be fully understood, it must be simultaneously read on different levels – the visual story as well as the narrative. Visual meaning is created through a combination of colours, objects, textures, tones and shapes. An example

Kardia

in *Kardia* is an exterior scene where the baby, in a state of distress, is lying in her carriage looking up at the branches of trees. Here, a detailed image of tree branches against the sky transposes into the branches of capillaries in the human heart. The sequence bridges past and present, folding the exterior world – the landscape where the characters exist – into the internal world of a biological landscape.

When visualizing the script, it was important that the props, set and overall look of the film not be generic or picture-perfect. The characters are less than perfect. The dad is losing his eyesight, and Hope has a defective heart. The father's deteriorating sight also impacts the image language in the film. His world is textured with varying depths of field, with magnified and soft-focus images. These textures also serve Hope's story, as they evoke the act of remembering. This kind of cognition is never clear or concise.

To research the details necessary to recreate the past, I created a collage book of images with old family photos, magazine tears, images shot with old Kodachrome film stock – anything that spoke to me in terms of the kind of detail I wanted to see in the film. But because of the scale of the project, I certainly didn't execute this on my own. I owe a great deal to my art department, led by Aidan Leroux, and to the director of photography, Kim Derko, an artist in her own right. Ultimately, the act of the recreation was a collaborative one.

MH: *Kardia* occurs largely inside institutions, often in a medical lab or hospital, and the arrival of a social worker/surrogate mother turns the home into an institution as well. The main character makes it only a few steps from her workplace before she collapses with a heart attack. She is claimed and marked by the institution, finding it impossible to leave the prison house of language and work behind. Can you comment?

SR: Your question gave me a flashback. In 1988, I made a video art tape entitled *1932* (8 min, 1988). In this work, a woman moves through a series of institutional spaces – home, school and church – ritualistically acting out a succession of unremarkable tasks and chores. In hindsight, I can see that this work is a little oblique in its intended meaning, but I was trying to create a portrait not defined by the innate nature of an individual, but by the institutions and rituals that surround us. So yes, in a way, placing individuals in institutional settings of one form or another is something that reoccurs in my work.

In *Kardia*, Hope works in a confinement of her own creation. At the beginning of the film she collapses. Her collapse is visually associated with the image of a feather falling. She states, 'At the time of death, the heart would be placed on a scale and weighed against truth. Permission to proceed into the afterlife was granted only if the heart weighed less than a feather.' She is referring to the Egyptian Book of the Dead, and the belief that in order for a soul to pass into the afterlife, it had to be pure in spirit, as light as a feather. At the end of the film, Hope discovers the truth of her past and reconciles this with her science and her self. This allows her to pass into the afterlife. The beginning and the end of the film describe the same moment, the moment of death.

MH: Can you speak about the role of technology in your movie? When the baby is found, the new 'father' makes a photograph, which appears in the newspaper – newspapers and microfiche play a role – and the central scene is a new heart procedure requiring the very latest medical technology. The lead often speaks into a tape recorder, which is her primary company, her mute listening companion. Between the two time frames of the movie, how does the idea of technology change, or does it?

SR: Memory, technology and biology are inextricably linked in the film. The quest of the protagonist is to piece together fragments of her childhood in order to understand the bond she shares with the man she believes to be her father. With a photograph as her only artifact, she sets out to unravel the mystery that surrounds her early life. We generally accept that photographs record past 'truths' and are in fact authentications of the 'real,' but are they? In *Kardia*, the origin of the photograph is in question. The dad takes a photograph of himself with the baby. Or does he? Perhaps the newspaper reporter took the photo? Are they not the same image? Memory is never a crystal-clear version of the past. Memory is reinterpreted through experience, history, desire, technology and DNA. Hope's story becomes a combination of reinvention and erasure.

In the film there is an overhead shot of an adult male and a baby in a 1950s operating room. Their bodies are linked by a series of plastic tubes and a mechanical pump. Blood travels through the tubes and creates an extracorporeal circulatory system through which the adult keeps the child alive during the operation. This system is a kind of Frankensteinian biological/technological umbilical system that, in the film, creates the mysterious and complex relationship between these two characters. They are not blood relatives, but they in fact do become related through blood. This image is also a central metaphor in the film's exploration of the heart and its relationship to the questions of body and mind.

Hope struggles to resolve the mystery of her past, and the technologies you describe are the means by which she both processes and accesses her memory. But the technologies in the film fluctuate as Hope states, 'Our history is encoded in our cells. Our memories are stored in our tissues ... But my blood was mixed with the blood of another ... ' So where does the truth she seeks really lie?

MH: Video's pioneering moments featured low-fi, black-and-white, no-edit, 'real time' shots, a rough-and-ready, do-it-yourself, turn-the-machine-on-and-go aesthetic. And then you come along a generation after video's beginnings with your immaculately lit, carefully staged manufactures, and a painterly sensibility. I'm guessing you didn't turn to film at this moment because it was a boys' club, whether in the labs, the co-ops or the schools. And more than that, film was genrefied – filmmakers made docs, features or solo avant outings. Your work seems something in between. I'm guessing your productions are more like fiction creations, with a crew and storyboards and dolly tracks and intricate lighting. But they steadily refuse narrative, collecting carefully chosen fragments and juxtaposing them, leaving the connecting threads empty. They are vehicles for producing pictures, successions of tableaux, though our usual viewing expectations of time-based media insists (no matter how successful your strategies) that there must be a story behind all this. Can

you talk about your relation to storytelling and the composition of pictures, especially in your early work?

SR: I studied at the Ontario College of Art in the department of Photo/Electric Arts from 1983 to 1985. At that time, the department was cloaked in a McLuhanesque philosophy that also embraced the ideal of the renaissance artist – an individual who was well-versed in art, science and technology. Instructors encouraged the creative use of technology: soldering irons, circuit diagrams, microchips and voltmeters were our tools. I studied both video and film, but quickly gravitated toward video. I was fortunate to be surrounded by a very talented peer group: Steev Morgan, Dennis Day, Robin Len, Jan Levis, Carl Hamfelt, Laura Kikauka, to name a few.

I was initially attracted to video because of the malleability of the image itself, especially in post-production. The technology at that time was very rudimentary but open-ended. To achieve the results I was after with film would require chemical interventions, but video was electronic. The electronic image allowed the development of a kind of signature aesthetic in much the same way a painter might develop a style.

When I left OCAD, I joined Trinity Square Video, where I was on staff for two years, then Charles Street Video, where I worked for almost seven years. I became one of those equipment geeks you describe, and all of my early works were produced through these facilities. In terms of my production process, the colour palette, texture and feel of the work were all considered very early on. I found locations or created environments and gathered props largely sourced from my personal lexicon of people, places and things. I made shot lists and image charts, as well as diagrams for camera placement – gathering all the ingredients necessary to create the visual world. I sometimes did the camerawork and edited myself. Editing was central to the creative process, as it was always the final stage of writing.

In making these early works, I was not interested in naturalism or in documenting or representing real life. Video was seemingly free from the conventional devices of traditional narrative. Exhibition was in the context of the visual arts – art galleries or dedicated video festivals. In galleries, viewers received the work much as they would a painting or a conceptually based work of art. I never thought to tell a story. The process of making a video was intuitive, delving into an internal world of subjective experience, rather than the objective world of telling. I focused on creating a sensory experience and rendering this through an emotional tone and space. The resulting short works belong to an art of the unsayable; each is more like a poem than a story. They aim to create impressions rather than statements, adhering to an internal logic and structure. Each video is a solo act, struggling to define its own unique image language. All of the work is imperfect.

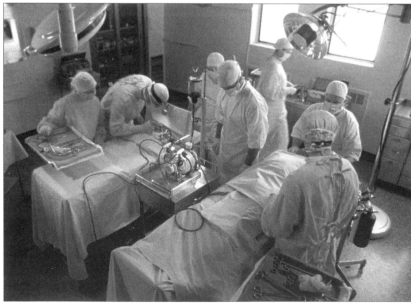

Kardia

MH: *Within Dialogue (Silence)* (5:40 min, 1987), *Absence* (5:30 min, 1986) and *1932* (9 min, 1988) are three early works that bear a nearly familial resemblance. They are extraordinarily restrained, content to show moments that occurred before or after some event has taken place, delivering us a trace, a mark, but refusing to grant this mark a history. In *Absence*, a pair of digitally altered lips separates from the face it used to belong to, in order to mouth the title. There are long tracking shots across a birthday-party table, but the guests have already gone home. When the woman returns, she is in some nowhere place, an empty room, a world in which she is the only inhabitant. The end is ambiguous – she turns from a wall, toward what? Do you feel this movie is deliberately incomplete, that suspending its narrative allows viewers a place of entry?

SR: *Absence* is a work that describes or defines absence as a state of loss. The video does not adhere to a narrative structure, but to the experience of memory and the unconscious. The images arrive as fragments, not grounded in a story-based meaning. The soft, grainy textures, intense colour palette and use of slow motion and dissolves, along with the juxtaposition of unexpected sounds, combine to evoke an overall impression of absence.

Sound plays an important role in *Absence*, as it does in all three of the works you describe. The sound is never naturalistic, nor did I make use of the sync sound recorded with the image. An original soundscape was created in post-production. In *Absence* we hear a collage of voices, laughter and murmurs – the sounds of an intimate gathering, but the image sequence shows the emptiness of the party's aftermath. This dislocation in time immediately sets the image in the space of memory, or unconscious desire, creating a feeling for what might have been.

The 1980s were also a time when film theory and semiotics were a part of the discourse of image-making. I briefly flirted with these notions, and this influence can be seen in *Absence* more than in any other work. For example, there is a sequence in which the woman both finds and loses herself in the mirror. In this context, the duality of her presence and absence represents female subjectivity and the construction of the self.

Absence was also my first work that screened internationally, and with the support of the arts councils, I had the opportunity to travel with the work, both in Canada and abroad. This opened up a new world for me. I took in video by artists I had previously never heard of: Susan Britton, François Girard, John Gurrin, Chantal Akerman, Dalibor Martinis and Sanja Ivekovic. All of this, in some way, made a lasting impression.

MH: *Within Dialogue (Silence)* feels the most storied of the three movies mentioned. A couple sit at a table, but again you make a curious and beautiful decision and don't focus on them at all, but on the objects that surround them. These objects (the cutlery, the dishes), which are usually the 'ground,' overtake the importance of the 'figure.' The middle of the movie is filled with shots of an emptied apartment, a sign that their incompatibility, their

inability to speak to one another, has led to breakup and departure. Somehow they need a story in order to get along; without stories, they are just more brightly coloured objects moving in space. The woman walks along the side of a busy highway and takes off her jacket, earrings and shoes. The end of the movie returns us to the restaurant where their first words are spoken, a brief exchange of banalities that shows them at cross purposes. 'I want more coffee.' 'I want to travel.' They are speaking, but not about the same thing, at the same time. Language has been reduced to the level of noise, or signs that have stopped working. Can you comment?

SR: *Within Dialogue (Silence)* portrays the empty, material lifestyles promoted in the late 1980s. Like *Absence*, *Within Dialogue (Silence)* shares more with poetry than with storied narrative. It is an expression of the intangible, a distilling of moments vaguely apprehended. Here, seemingly disparate images combine to create a layering of meanings that resonate and form connections.

The visual 'vocabulary' used in *Within Dialogue (Silence)* departs from *Absence*, in that the textured space of memory is replaced by the sharpened edges and piercing sounds of a dislocated reality. Defined by crisp editing and bold colours, the sequences with the man and the woman bracket the body of the tape. In the opening montage, they do not speak, but move objects on the table, like a game of chess. At the end, they speak but do not communicate. The emptiness (silence) of the words, like the lifestyle portrait itself, is vacant. In the more subdued body of the tape, the young woman moves through a world of silent interiors and urban detachment. Standing at the edge of the freeway, she sheds her possessions in what could be interpreted as an attempted escape, a suicide or a leave-taking. It is dispassionate, almost mechanical, yet at the same time desperate.

The soundtrack consists of an oppressive tonal quiet that is punctuated by sparse intrusive sounds. The high-pitched whine in the apartment kitchen, the ominous rumblings of the highway, the brief disjointed conversation – all are intended to accentuate the woman's alienation and the viewer's unease.

It may seem odd to gravitate toward the intangible, without feeling the need to have the work explain or complete itself. But how do we experience art? Meaning is created between the viewer and the work. One completes the other.

The premiere screening of *Within Dialogue (Silence)* happened in July 1987, along with new tapes by three like-minded video artists: Rhonda Abrams, Dennis Day and Tess Payne. We dubbed ourselves 'the four redheads' (we all had red hair) and staged a screening in a warehouse space at 60 Bathurst (a building now replaced by condominiums). We came together via the practical and somewhat accidental fact that the work was being produced at the city's two video co-ops (Charles Street Video and Trinity Square Video) at roughly the same time. These works were not thematically linked, but were unified in that they abandoned what you described as the rough-and-ready, do-it-yourself aesthetic, which in Toronto at that time was associated with political importance. Instead, the work espoused both a unique voice and a stylistically diverse, aesthetically rendered personal vision. The screening was attended by throngs of people, as many as could be packed into the space, and the success of the evening was testament to the excitement generated by such independent ventures at that time.

MH: *1932* follows a few daily moments of a woman at home, picking up a bottle of milk, setting a table, dressing. These scenes are intercut with pans across emptied school desks, or a hand sealing a letter with wax. There are hidden symbols, mysteries without keys, clues without revelation. She goes to a confessional where she recites a short Hungarian prayer. Clearly, something has happened, she is experiencing the aftershock of something, but instead of using your movie as a stage for her subjectivity, to proclaim 'This is what she is,' you deliver us to the mystery of another person's life, which will not simply be laid bare by a camera, opened like a cadaver so that we can examine the contents. In other words, it refuses the founding tenets of biography itself. Why?

1932

SR: Characterization, or the story of an individual, didn't really enter my mind when I was making *1932*. The piece consists of a series of tableaux and is structured like chapters in a book. I tried to draw attention to the institutional spaces that surround the woman (domestic, school, church), that define her in terms of her role in society. Other scenes suggest memories of significant events (a death, a letter, a confession). These moments shape more intangible kinds of spaces that both inscribe and confine the individual. We may not learn much about the woman's 'story,' but we do experience, through tone and rhythm, something of her isolation and grief.

While making this video, I saw a reproduction of a series of black-and-white photos titled *Rites of Passage*, by Hollis Frampton

and Marion Faller. The series consisted of 20 photographs of identical wedding-style cakes. What made each photo different from the next was the single, plastic, iconic decoration on top of the cake. I was moved by the way these formally linked, serial photographs suggested a narrative – from stork to funeral urn, birth to death – the passage of life demarked simply by a series of celebrations. I also saw the Chantal Akerman film *Jeanne Dielman* for the first time and was very affected by its quietness, the rhythms of the unhurried editing, the careful compositions and beautifully constructed shots. I was inspired by how, in both of these very different works, structure and visual language is utterly integral to meaning.

I'd like to return for a moment to the question of narrative that you raised in connection to all three of these videos. In the midst of considering these questions, I received an email from someone who had just seen *Kardia*. She loved the fact that the film is about something so interior (the heart – literally and figuratively). She mused that because the narrative hinges on moments of stillness, interiority and the small epiphanies that occur when a character realizes a truth (as opposed to external worldly conflicts), the film is a kind of 'anti-film.' Her comments made me see that the relation between these early videos and *Kardia* is quite strong – each is shaped by an internal edict that ultimately disobeys narrative.

MH: *Signal* (3 min, 1993) intercuts a sailor making semaphore flag messages with a woman undergoing an eye exam. It is filled with carefully created close-ups, with an exactingly executed high-tech polish. It shows us two worlds where every eyelash is in place and every instrument is wielded with precision. These are environments that demonstrate the beauty of control, and the control of beauty. Though the splendour that is everywhere in evidence is invariably reined in, 'uniformed,' harnessed, tied down. It is also a luxury that resists narrativity. Who is the woman in the eye exam? Why the sailor? What are the messages being delivered, or even the relationship between these two gestures? I think the signal on display is the way in which beauty is corralled.

SR: *Signal* is an allegory of sight and perception. The work explores the idea of seeing and was inspired by annual visits to my ophthalmologist. During these eye examinations, my doctor carefully performs a series of tests and measurements to check the health of the eye. I began to think about how modern medicine increasingly relies on new imaging technologies that allow one to see the body not just from the outside, but from the inside. I wondered how these technologies, unavailable in previous centuries, have allowed us to visualize and represent what was previously not possible to see.

Signal juxtaposes two scenarios – a woman undergoing an eye examination and a sailor signalling in semaphore code. Semaphore is a kind of language, a system for sending messages

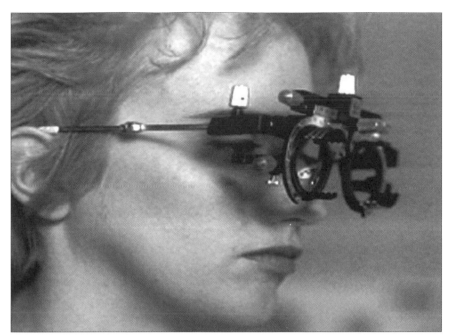

Signal

and Watson, for instance, who uncovered human DNA. Can you talk about how you found the form for this movie, which packs more information in its 12 minutes than many do in feature-length mode? Eugene is a short form for eugenics, the 'science of human improvement.' This widely held truth was responsible for state-mandated sterilizations around the world and used to underpin racist laws and practices. Why are all eight Eugenes white, and why is there so little discussion about race? Why do the men appear with shaved heads, turning in space, while a woman in a lab coat (are all your heroines wearing the same coat, working in the same lab?) tells us the story?

SR: *Eight Men Called Eugene* is a faux documentary. It playfully interweaves fact and fiction while unravelling the work of eight genetic scientists. In the art and indie film/video world, the 1990s was the decade where the once highly contested and formally disputed territorial distinctions between film and video collapsed. *Eight Men Called Eugene* freely mixes the two mediums. The look was inspired by the 16mm educational science films we watched in grade school. These films used techniques such as time lapse, archival footage, graphic information and, of course, a knowledgeable presenter. *Eight Men Called Eugene* humorously reinvents this form.

When I was writing the script, the human genome project was well underway, but public awareness of the project was just beginning. Many of the social issues that came to the fore 60 years earlier with eugenics were being revisited. In the early part of the last century, eugenic ideals were very prevalent in Canada and associated with health and social good. Their practical application could be seen everywhere – from identifying criminals to reducing health-care costs. These ideas were accepted and promoted by governments in the same way we embrace low-fat diets today. Much to my chagrin, early feminists were often strong proponents of eugenics, and the 'Fitter Family' presented in Eugene is not a hoax.

To answer your query regarding questions of race, rather than focusing the piece around this issue, I was interested in the dangerously insidious and widespread social eugenics that we, in our history as Canadians, embraced.

Hadley Obodiac plays the role of Dr. Wanda B. Langton. With an ironic text and deadpan delivery, she takes viewers on a rapid journey from the quiet origins of early genetics to its implications in the present technological era. The structure of the piece is much like chapters in a book, with each Eugene spearheading a new decade of ideas. I cast young men with shaved heads to play the eight Eugenes. They are shot on a rotating pedestal, in a black, non-descript space. This is a reference to how one might look at a scientific specimen – observing it in a neutral environment

using flags. Each gesture communicates a letter of the alphabet. The woman who undergoes the eye examination reads the letters on a Snellen chart. The ophthalmologist looks inside the woman's eye, and the viewer visually enters the body. The image inverts (as per the mechanics of our eye), and we experience a sequence of images that playfully represents seeing and the processing of language. One of the images is a moving X-ray image of a cat – a modern medical visualization. The military figure is juxtaposed with a medical scenario to suggest the idea of the body being the 'final frontier.' Is colonization now advancing inside the body? The graphic text superimposed over the sailor suggests this, as the letters spell the words body and battleground.

Signal was shot with short ends of 35mm film, on the oldest, cheapest, non-sync camera we could find. The crisp black-and-white image of the sailor was inspired by text fonts, and shooting emphasized the graphic nature of his flag signals. The colour palette of the doctor's office uses soft blues, greens and brittle whites, which are often found in medical scenarios. I combined this with a hint of red to evoke the interior of the body. The exacting visual language you describe builds a lateral narrative rather than a linear one.

Signal was a pivotal work for me. This newly formed interest in using science (in this case, medical science) as a departure point for artistic inquiry informs many of the video, films and installation works that follow. Importantly, the simpatico sensibilities of the creative team of Robin Len (graphic design), Kim Derko (cinematography) and Phil Strong (sound design) were key in executing this piece, and several others in the future.

MH: *Eight Men Called Eugene* (12 min, 1996) features a dazzling display of animated pyrotechnics laid over the eight men of the title, who appear in brief, neo-biographical vignettes. They appear as 'types' of a radiant science, pioneers and explorers – like Crick from all perspectives. The Eugenes are stand-ins for real scientists (or scientific concepts) and their modern-day, skinhead look helps to draw an uncomfortable parallel between a eugenic past and the genetic future.

You ask about the women in the white lab coats. It is true, people dressed in white lab coats often inhabit my videos and films. Before *Kardia* (when the pattern became undeniable) I never really thought about why, it just happened. But, if I have to analyze it, I would say that the person in the white lab coat is a stand-in for the artist, or the creative process itself. This person is always examining, exploring or discovering some situation and relating these ideas in new ways. Science and art are both processes of discovery. There are also significant events in my life that shaped this perspective. As a young child, I wore a Frankenstein-like, leather-and-metal leg brace that stretched from my hips to my toes. At night, with my body quiet and my mind active, I imagined the whispered mysteries I heard in doctors' waiting rooms – 'blue babies' and 'iron lungs' – stories from bygone days that I imagined quite literally. These experiences created empathy for human frailty, and a fascination with the relationships between philosophy, biology and medical science.

MH: *Strands* (22 min, 1997) is a drama that draws together many concerns familiar in your work: an institutional lab setting, a clean, high-tech look and a female scientist as the lead character. Helen is a DNA specialist who manufactures a fellow blond geneticist, but she becomes increasingly disconcerted as her Frankenstein's monster proves to a be a bit smarter, a bit funnier and better liked than herself. And somehow they have come to share the same memory – in short, she has created a better version of herself. Into this controlled environment, where everything is in its place, this eruption (be careful what you wish for) is solved by a bathtub drowning of the unwanted double. Can you talk about what led you to make *Strands*, and the circumstances of production?

SR: While works such as *Bug Girl*, *Eugene* and *Kardia* use science as a departure point for artistic inquiry, *Strands* fits comfortably within the science-fiction genre. In 1996–97, I attended a directors' residency at the Canadian Film Centre. I wanted to further the concepts explored in the earlier work, and worked with writer Tricia Fish, and later Shelley Eriksen, on the script for *Strands*.

Strands is a darkly humorous tale about friendship, jealousy and possession. It is the story of Helen Critteck, a lonely scientist who decides to create a best friend. *Strands* was inspired by Mary Shelley's 1818 novel *Frankenstein*. Shelley's novel is very much a social commentary on science and nature and the process of socialization, and I was attracted to these themes. We updated the

story by making the doctor female and setting it in the world of genetic science. When we were shooting, the news of Dolly the sheep (the first mammal ever cloned) broke, and all of the sudden our script did not seem so far-fetched.

Rather than using a mechanical model (electricity, wires, bolts) for the creation of the monster/clone, I chose a more contemporary analogy and worked with a biological model using fluids (as in test-tube babies and petri dishes). Halley, the creation, is born, and later dies, in water. We also brought watery images into many scenes in the film – test tubes and beakers in the lab hold colourful fluids, and a watery image is reflected in the windows of the lab. This visual theme of water as life contrasts with the other physical spaces in the film; Helen's apartment and lab feature icy colours, and the black, shiny, near-modernist surfaces that embody her austere personality. I also worked carefully on how to express the relationship between Helen and Halley within the structure of the shots themselves. How is Helen's world is defined with and without Halley? With the DP, we developed the idea of a balanced or unbalanced framing of the two characters, depending on the status of their relationship. When things are going well, the two characters occupy the space in tandem. When the situation becomes unbalanced, there are scenes where the camera 'corrects' the space, panning over and giving the entire space of the lab to Halley. Inversely, near the end of the film, the camera movement gives the space back to Helen.

MH: When I went to film school, I was surrounded by men, and even those who had nothing to say (most of us) had no difficulties saying it over and over again. 'I am angry. I am so alone. I am confused.' The small media-arts scene I was involved in seemed slightly better; women headed up some of these admittedly small concerns, but even so, the artists, festival organizers, arts council administrators and curators were mostly of the male persuasion. I'm wondering what kinds of challenges you've faced (a too

Strands

Absence

the NFB. This was not necessarily a goal of mine, but this door was open when others were closed. Being flexible in this way has helped me do the thing I need to do the most, which is keep going.

The recent fact that anyone can buy technology at the corner camera store and operate it themselves certainly has opened up the doors to many, including women. My experience in the independent media-art scene is much better than in the industry, as there are more women, a more progressive atmosphere and fewer gatekeepers.

On another note, I believe there are often differences in how women experience the world, and this can be reflected in the style, the way of seeing, storytelling, subject matter and creative process in general. Because women's work is underrepresented in every way, there is less dialogue around the work, less affirmation and understanding of certain aesthetics or voice. A recent review of *Kardia* stated, 'To say that this is a very feminine film is not merely to state that the film was written and directed by Su Rynard but to say that it is feminine is in the best Jungian sense of Anima, that feminine principle, that is an integral part of women and men.' This review was written by Peter Malone; he saw the film in Iran and wrote the review for a British-based international organization. His review was very positive, but my experience distributing *Kardia* has been uneven. Yes, the film garnered two prestigious international awards, but it has also been overlooked by many. I believe this is due in part to the innate female perspective and treatment of the subject matter that this reviewer noted.

You ask about my work with Kim Derko. Kim is an exception, as I find that most of my colleagues in the field are men. Generally speaking, the men I work with are very supportive, they are my confidantes and companions. As a DP, Kim Derko must both head a camera team and direct the lighting team. These teams are invariably made of men, but to Kim they are 'family,' and the bonds are incredibly strong. Sometimes when I'm on a project, working alongside my male colleagues in utter harmony, it may seem like a contradiction to the statistics and examples I laid out earlier, but I don't think so. This is an example of how it could and should be. In these moments, my tiny corner of the planet is working well. It doesn't mean that systemic problems don't exist, but it does prove that they don't need to.

large question, I realize) as a women artist (could you be specific? an instance?). Are there glass ceilings in place in fringe media world along with the corporate world (for instance, women directors for Canadian television is not so common)? You often work with women (Kim Derko as your DP, for instance) and often feature women performers – do you feel your movies are a picture of a feminist community, or has the F word become unspeakable? Do you feel that your work will make it easier for other women to come along after and realize moving pictures of their own?

SR: Mike, your question has caused me some anxiety and I've been avoiding answering it. Media arts, film and video are extremely competitive fields. Production resources and dollars are scarce and space for exhibition and distribution space is limited. There are many challenges for everyone. But yes, the field is particularly tough for women.

Each project is a process. Each work points the way to the next. You need the opportunity to practice your craft, to excel and gain experience, and simply get better at what you do. In a field where there is less opportunity for women, women simply get left behind. This is not new information; it's tedious to say it, and heartbreaking that it still needs to be stated. In Canada, women make up 51 percent of the population. In film programs in universities and colleges, 51.6 percent of students are women. In the film and television industry, women account for 10 percent of directors and 88 percent of clerical workers. In my experience as a director who works freelance in the film and television industry, it's beyond 'glass ceiling' – it's more like a titanium vault.

My work is a combination of low- and high-budget, film and video, gallery installation and theatrical film. There have been times when switching gears (or genre or medium) is a necessary tactic. For example, in 2000 I directed a feature documentary for

Su Rynard's Films

Untitled – A Tape About Memory   4 min 1985
Absence   5:30 min 1986
Within Dialogue (Silence)   5:40 min 1987
The Greatest Thing   1-min loop 1987
   (co-directed with Dennis Day and Christine Martin)
1932   9 min 1988
What Wants to Be Spoken, What Remains to Be Said   25 min 1992
Sexual Healing   24:17 min 1995
Signal   3 min 1993
Big Deal So What   25 min 1995
Eight Men Called Eugene   12 min 1996
Strands   22 min 1997
The Day Jesus Melted   3:15 min 1999
Dream Machine   76 min 2000
Bug Girl   5:47 min 2003
Bear   9:15 min loop 2004
Kardia   85 min 2005

Distributed by the Canadian Filmmakers Distribution Centre and Vtape.

Su Rynard's films and videos have been exhibited in festivals and art institutions around the globe. Her debut dramatic feature film, *Kardia*, was awarded the prestigious Alfred P. Sloan Feature Film Prize. www.kardiathefilm.com

MONIQUE MOUMBLOW
DOUBLING

No doubt we have stood in the same room, looking in the same direction, admiring the view, but I don't think we've ever met. After a couple of decades in the fringe, this isn't entirely unlikely. Certainly I have been present often enough when her work is being served up, most usually as a dish amongst others, in the midst of a festival program in the Impakt Festival in Utrecht, or closer to home, in the cat-inhabited bike-repair/theatre palace of Cinecycle. The question of her presence and appearance haunts all of her work, and because she is a reliable performer, whether onscreen or not, I feel as if I know her, though her practice is far from autobiography. She is part of an art-school generation that had the chance to study their mothers and fathers, and working through the inevitable anxiety of influence could arrive at some collection of personal tics (or style) that would contain and release a personal practice.

Here is a long riff by early video-art maestro Vito Acconci, as he laid it out in a talk for a Toronto audience in 2005.

These new video pieces were focuses on making the self, this was the 1960s remember, and there was a lot of talk about the self. How do I prove I to others? How do I find my body, by finding myself? How do I find the space I'm in, how to occupy a self? How do I find every inch of my body? The body as space as instrument, how does my body survey space around it? There was a stress in this work on the body, how the body adapts, takes shape or resists or reacts according to these stresses. *Trademarks* was a performance in which I 'found myself' – I would bite each part of myself, apply printer's ink and make prints of these marks.

Video offered simultaneous feedback, you can see what you're doing while you're doing it. Video as mirror, to see what you can't see. Movies were landscape but video was close-up. When he was asked why he never used close-ups Charlie Chaplin answered that there was nothing funny about a face 15 feet high. But TV delivered new faces, made looking at new faces possible. Jack Nicholson and Robert DeNiro wouldn't have been possible without television. The monitor is the size of a person's face, it offers a face-to-face encounter between artist and viewer. Then there's this question: where am I in relation to the viewer? Am I below the viewer, beside them, opposite the viewer? I take a position vis à vis the viewer in each videotape. In front of the camera.'

Monique has mastered the art of appearing and disappearing. What do they call it in a magic trick when you return the missing item, the bird that has flown back into the sleeve, the subject chopped into bits, the escape artist missing from the tank? The prestige. Monique is master of the prestige. She shows us the missing signature, and then she brings it all back again. This return, this journey of recovery, allows the viewers to settle back into our own bodies, to inhabit ourselves as if we were another. *Je est un autre.*

MH: Video art is such a rarely seen momentum, marginalized even in the art world, where it might have felt at home. It has never secured a perch on television, and theatrical screenings are rare. What drew you to this rarefied field?

MM: I'm a reluctant video artist. Every time I finish a tape, I say this is the last one and I'm just going to focus on writing from now on. But a few months later I'll find myself in the middle of another project. So I guess something keeps drawing me in.

I started out doing performance art, but I never really resolved this idea of an 'audience.' Something about the relationship between a performer and a live audience didn't sit well with me. In certain performances, where there is too much attention given to the exchange between the performer and the audience, things become too restrictive, or too much about that interaction, for me anyways. So seeing early, performance-based video art (in particular works by Vito Acconci and Colin Campbell) was probably what first drew me to the medium.

I think that was my initial impetus for making videos, but my more recent work has really veered away from my earlier, performative tapes and become something quite different.

MH: *Winter Fruits* (2:30 min., 1992) is your first public work, a beautifully lyric short, downright filmic in its concern for texture, rhythm, colour and composition. These days, when video art is produced by the kilo, the detailing and craft of this piece is especially striking. It appears deceptively simple, mixing butterfly pictures with a shopping trip. When Canadian fruit is sent to Chile, the enclosed apple is regarded as the most exotic of all fruits; when Chilean fruit is opened in North America, a black widow spider crawls out unexpectedly. This exchange between different parts of the world suggests that meaning is context-bound, and also hints at the relation between viewer and viewed (who is watching? from what place?). Can you talk about how this work came about, why the butterflies, and why the two pictures of the globe that appear at the beginning and the end, as a kind of framing device?

MM: It's funny that you talk about the tape as being filmic. The one thing I remember about making the piece is that I really wanted to use a dissolve. But it was made in a primitive edit suite that had only two decks: a player and a recorder. There was a live feed from a studio camera in another room, so on the fly, I reshot the image of the butterfly off a television. The footage was probably dubbed a couple of times to get the timing right, so it all ended up being pretty degraded.

The image at the beginning of the tape was the earth, but the one at the end is actually the moon. I liked that they could be read either way. It is, as you note, a piece very much about context. My partner, Yudi Sewraj, is from Guyana and he told me that each year his aunt used to send the family a box of apples for Christmas. As a child, he thought they were the most delicious and exotic fruit he'd ever tasted. To me, apples seemed boring and ordinary. The tape began from that simple story and the juxtaposition of the urban myth of finding a black widow spider in a bunch of grapes.

The butterfly was originally an image I used in a performance with Anne Russell. Anne uses a pair of butterfly wings to transport herself across the surface of the moon. I think this is a pretty common image – a moth against the moon. My interest in butterflies at the time had to do with their use as a symbol of something exotic/feminine, but in a pretty clichéd and often humorous way. I was also interested in Nabokov's use of the scientific word *nymphae*, and its connection to the term *nymphet* ... but I'm getting a little off-topic here. Anyways, the initial inspiration for the images in this video was a plastic butterfly I saw on the side of a house. I don't know if it's still the case, but in Nova Scotia people used to attach giant, colourful butterflies to their houses. On grey days, in the middle of winter, it was funny to see all these tropical-looking butterflies. So when I came across this very bizarre National Geographic footage of a bird eating a butterfly off a tiny conveyor belt (I could almost picture it as a juicy little mango in some supermarket), it brought the two stories together.

MH: *Winter Fruits* narrates something about the myth of stereo, the mystery of speaking or hearing two things at the same time, or the ability to maintain contradictory thoughts. The title is already a tip-off, along with the exotic apples. Can you comment on these dualities, and how the montage works to complicate either/or binarisms (it suggests we don't have to make a choice between this and that, but instead can allow both thoughts to exist at the same time, in stereo).

MM: Two contradictory thoughts ... I think these kinds of odd juxtapositions are always circling around in my mind. Not like a stream of consciousness or anything like that. I could never write that way, I'm way too uptight. It's more like having two incongruous things exist side by side in a very controlled manner. Things that are very peculiar to me, like Cheerios and urine, or sugar and glass.

I'm fascinated with the idea of doubling; it's something that's always been a part of my work – two voices or two conflicting narratives. But beyond any philosophical implications, I guess these dualities are also a strategy. A place to work from. What does a butterfly have to do with fruit? What does fruit have to do with the moon? You start from there and work backward to find threads that connect them.

I don't know if I can comment specifically on the montage of *Winter Fruits*. It's been so long since I made the tape. But for me the montage always has to undermine the text (or dialogue or voice-over). Otherwise what's the point? I never see the montage as illustrative of the text. It's much more fun when it's doing its own thing. I think all the elements in *Winter*

Fruits are simple, but the different directions you can go with them are complex because they are all allowed to exist, as you say, in the same space.

MH: Lao Tzu wrote, 'The name of a man is a numbing blow from which he never recovers.' Your *Liabilities – the first ten minutes* (10 min, 1993) suggests that naming is a liability, and is an essentially transforming agent, a screen through which one views and collects experience. There are two characters – Anne and Monique, who are alike except for their names, but this single difference sets them off on very different paths. Can you comment?

MM: I had never heard the quote by Lao Tzu before. It really struck me. Naming has always been an obsession with me, maybe because I have mixed feelings about my own name. I never really felt like it belonged to me. But on the other hand, I have no desire to change it. I don't necessarily dislike it; I just don't feel like it refers to me. I have twin daughters who are 19 months old. When we were trying to choose names for them, I was a wreck. I was so overwhelmed by the responsibility of it. Especially because of all the work I had done with Anne on the *Liabilities* tapes. Every name that Yudi and I looked at seemed like it had the potential to destroy their lives. This one was too difficult to pronounce, that one would be too easy to make fun of, etc. We were in hospital for a week and we still couldn't settle on a name. The nurses had to refer to the girls as 'Baby A' and 'Baby B.' Then one day I realized that if we didn't make a decision soon, the names A and B were going to stick. So we did, and I think we did okay, but sometimes I wake up in the middle of the night thinking that maybe we should have named them something else.

I really do think that naming is a liability. The work with Anne began with a very simple premise – how each of our lives would be different with another name. Nothing more complicated than that. It started out as a series of somewhat improvised video letters between us, and later became a tape.

Liabilities – the first ten minutes

MH: Butterflies return in *Liabilities: the first ten minutes* as an iconic motif and holdover from *Winter Fruit*. You appear both as yourself, Monique, and as Anne. When you are dressed like Anne, you appear in a photograph with butterfly wings. When you sift through a box of things Anne sent you, you pull out a pamphlet about butterfly and insect worlds, and another book called *Butterfly*, which Anne wrote under the pseudonym Kathryn Harvey. What is it with all these butterflies?

MM: Hmm, the butterflies ... I can't comment on Anne's interest in butterflies. I think it's pretty unsophisticated. Well, maybe unsophisticated is an unfair way of putting it. Let's just say it's an unconscious obsession. She has an enormous collection of butterfly paraphernalia. It's huge, nutty. If something has a butterfly on it, Anne buys it. There are candlesticks, bags, wind-up toys, linens, books, cigarette lighters, toilet paper ... A number of years ago we put together an installation in Halifax of a part of her collection. On one evening, Anne gave a reading from *Butterfly*, a romance novel she claims to have written. In the book, Butterfly is the name of a brothel where women go and have sex with male prostitutes. It's very campy. It would probably make a great film.

My own interest in butterflies really started with *Lolita* and the history of Nabokov as a butterfly collector. This strange blurring of his art and life. I was interested in the connection between three words and their origins: *nymph, nymphalid, nympha* – referring to a young girl, a butterfly and the labia minora. I think that every time a butterfly appears in this work, there is a quiet reference to something a little dark, but with a sense of humour. If that makes any sense. The exact meaning of the butterflies isn't specific. It mutates with each tape. They operate more as a marker.

MH: Your doppelgänger Anne writes in three genres: travel, scientific discoveries and romance novels. These three suggest discursive fields (or is it the body – the legs, the heart, the brain?). Why these three?

MM: Again, I can't really answer for Anne about these three genres. I doubt she would consider them discursive fields. It's all blurred. If you look at Anne's writing it would be difficult to tell what was a romantic story and what was a paper on her scientific research. She gave a talk at the Nova Scotia School of Art and Design; there is a section about this in the video. She showed about half an hour of slides of the 'Blaine' family. (I don't believe this family is in any way related to Anne.) The presentation wasn't funny or interesting enough to be theatre, and even for an art audience it lacked enough content to be a 'good' performance.

MH: Anne is described as a recluse (shut-in Monique, perhaps), receiving most of her information from TV travelogues and coffee-table magazines about exotic places. Even these information-dispensers are displaced, at a distance.

MM: Yes, Anne is a recluse. She's a kind of modern-day Jules Verne. (He never left France in his entire life.) But unlike Verne, Anne has quick and easy access to any information about anywhere in the world. It makes her a good liar.

I think there are layers of distance going on here, both in Anne's existence as a recluse and my barely concealed hostility to her. Anne communicates to me through letters and video, but never in person. I have never written back to Anne. However, in the tape I do talk to the audience about her. I think this distance speaks a lot about naming and our fragmented self/selves.

MH: *Liabilities* ends very abruptly; it seems as if there's going to be more to it. This cut (the end) produces and maintains the mystery of the doppelgänger, the double, as if, despite the calm recitations on offer, you must not, dare not, say any more.

Joan and Stephen

MM: Yes, there is more. And yes, I probably shouldn't say more. Most of it is off-camera. It's an ongoing project. I really don't know if I'll make more tapes with Anne, but there are appearances. She usually goes out every year on her birthday. I still get letters from her and, of course, the occasional postcard.

MH: *Joan and Stephen* (12 min, 1996) features a framing narrative, conventionally shot, which offers a glimpse of a parental couple eating and groping at the stovetop while their daughter looks on through an overhead grate. The bulk of the movie is taken up with shots of you in bed talking about your imaginary boy: 'If I'd been a boy, my parents would have named me Stephen. I can't really picture being male, so I decided to invent you.' What is the relation between these two sets of images?

MM: For fun, let's just say nothing, that there is no direct relationship between these two images. But after saying that, of course once you put two things together, there is always a relationship between them.

Sometimes I think the real relationship between these two sections is more about film and video than about the content. These sections play off each other and our expectations of what film or video is. For example, the first section is in black and white and it's shot on film, so we assume it's a flashback scene, and the second part is on video and hand-held, so it must be intimate or confessional. And the tape does fit neatly into both of these assumptions, but when you begin to look at it more closely, maybe it doesn't.

The video has every combination of watching or being watched. The distanced third-person perspective, elements of surveillance, as well as this '70s art-video aesthetic where the performer is watching you, the audience. It's a game on many different levels. The two sections are really playing out the same game, but from different perspectives.

Just for the record, though, there is definitely no narrative tie-in between these two parts. It's funny how often people have tried to create a continuous narrative with the piece.

MH: You bring the camera into bed with you where it's close by, almost touching. Your fictional double addressed through the camera is masculine, but this double might also be seen as camera or viewer. Your words conjure 'the male gaze.' You invite us into your bed to talk it over, to talk to us, to grant us various attributes and tastes (toast and coffee in the morning). Eventually you speculate that 'he' (also 'us,' the viewers) is mostly blind, and that the initial frisson of pleasure arrives with the avoidance of being watched. But the deeper pleasure, you note, is that you are free to look without being seen, which of course is exactly the state of the audience. We can look at you without being seen. In this sense you, the performer, are blind; you can fill the room with your words, but you can't enter the room to see who is watching.

MM: My blindness is the irony of the whole thing. All I really want is a 'blind' male gaze, and by that I mean an uncritical gaze – a gaze that isn't cruel or doesn't scrutinize. Throughout the tape I go about trying to construct that, first by making Stephen blind and then by taking away his body. In the end I'm left with an outline on a mattress and an audience I can't see.

It's true, the audience does have the pleasure of seeing without being seen, but I think there is a rupture there. The tape makes the audience uneasy and I don't think it's simply because of this idea of a 'returned gaze.' There is something else going on, but I have difficulty putting into words exactly what that is.

MH: Later you trace the outline of the missing body 'like the silhouette of a murder victim.' This tape expresses a longing for embodiment, in its references to early video art with its one-camera/one-person bodily evocation; it rereads this history as a longing for a lost body. (Or suggests that fiction is necessary to

move outside the solipsistic modernity of the monad, the one.) Can video help return us to our bodies?

MM: Stephen's body is an absent one. I used to think his outline on the mattress was about longing for a real body, someone to fill that outline. But I realize now that the only way for any intimacy to exist within this tape, at least on my terms, is for that body to remain missing. And in a funny way, Stephen's body is really the body of the audience. So when I speak to Stephen, I am speaking to you. I am tracing your outline on the sheet. I am taking away your body so there can be something shared between us.

Can video help us return to our bodies? Perhaps. Sometimes, though, I'm not sure I want to return to my body. It seems too frail, too messy, too complicated.

MH: Do you believe it's necessary to make pictures of catastrophe – for instance, the images that accompanied news of the tsunami disaster? How do artists' pictures relate to this global media? They are so small, are they worthwhile at all? Do you worry that your pictures are only shown in venues where the converted are already seated? Do you feel, as a First Worlder of pictures, that your pictures carry a political responsibility?

MM: No, I don't think it's necessary to make images of catastrophe, but I don't know how to imagine a world without them. We live in such a culture of images.

Outside of financial reasons, I've never worried that my videos are seen by only a few people. I'd love to have a bigger audience if it meant I'd make a little money, but usually I'm pretty happy if two or three people turn up at a screening. I suppose I do aim for a kind of integrity to what I do. Maybe 'integrity' is too pretentious. I just don't want to make 'bad' work, whatever that means. Is what I do worthwhile? I don't know. I think I used to have a clearer sense of what was worthwhile and what wasn't. As I get older, things just seem more complicated.

Within my own work, my pictures carry a political/personal responsibility, but I recognize that I have very little control over where these images will end up, or how they will be used. They're on video. I have tapes at libraries and distribution centres. Anyone can make a copy and do what they want to with the material.

I suppose I'm pretty hypocritical here. I'm totally comfortable using pirated footage in my own work, but I'm not too happy about the possibility of someone else using my images.

MH: *Three Waltzes* (7 min, 1998) hosts a literary structure. You present three visual tableaux sequentially, followed by a section entitled 'Notes' that reflects on, or seems to reflect on, the 'purely visual' experience of the 'three waltzes.' Did this structure arrive out of the material or vice versa?

MM: I think it was actually both. I had a very concrete idea of the structure before I began working. But the video became even more tightly structured when I began editing. The piece was

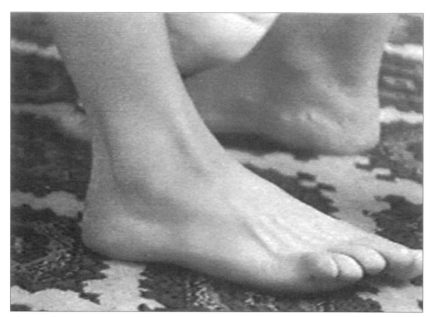
Three Waltzes

originally titled *Five Waltzes* and there were going to be five short sections. I had wanted to construct the whole piece without using any language. At that point, I felt I relied too much on my writing. So I edited five self-contained sections, which were made up of very simple actions and music. When I watched the finished edit, though, it felt somehow incomplete. I wanted to include some kind of text, but I didn't want it to interfere with the immediate experience of watching the three sections. I was reminded of the idea of notes, like an afterward, but I also thought about 'notes' in reference to music. I think placing the text at the end of the tape goes back to something we talked about earlier. A desire to have the images and the text working against each other. In this case, that's achieved by displacing the words.

MH: The first dance shows a woman pulled up off a chair by another over and over before they swap roles. Both wear elaborate leg bandages. Why do they never look at each other? (Because they are 'only bodies'?) Are social interactions always so coded that role-playing is the best we can do? (Is there no self to which we return, only the frames of presentation we have inherited?)

MM: I don't think I ever gave directions when we were filming this section. That we never looked at each other is just what happened. I'm not sure why. Perhaps it was because we were very focused on what we were doing. In the end, though, the lack of eye contact is really important and foregrounds the fact that they are just bodies, like you say. They are injured bodies or, more specifically, bodies faking injury. The fake injury is a visible sign of something hidden.

MH: The first note relates a longing for illness (and its easing of responsibility and blame – 'How can I be guilty? I'm sick!'). It specifically mentions wanting arthritis so you can get off a chair like your grandmother did. Is this gesture the punctum (is there

a moment in someone's life that looks back at you, claims you, demands you?)? Is that the connection between 'you' and 'your grandmother' – the way you get out of the chair – a relation that can be practiced and rehearsed with others?

MM: *Punctum.* Oh yes, definitely. I sat on this section for ages and wasn't sure I wanted to include it in the tape because it was so particular to me. I didn't know what kind of meaning, if any, an audience might take from it.

A longing for illness was somehow frightening to admit to. It seems perverse to wish for pain and suffering. I felt that on some level I was making fun of my grandmother's severe rheumatoid arthritis, which in my childhood was all wrapped up in this horrible, heavy, Catholic guilt, all centred on the idea of bearing pain stoically. Maybe *making fun* isn't quite the right phrase, it was more like having fun with something that was so serious. I still feel slightly guilty about it. I know that probably sounds extreme, but showing this tape to my mother was more uncomfortable than showing her a tape that was sexually explicit.

The longing for illness wasn't about avoiding responsibility and blame, it was more like a child faking a flu to get a little attention. Any attention. It's funny, but as I'm writing about the piece I'm reminded of how much all the sections are about feeling invisible.

Here are two people pretending to be crippled, helping each other get out of a chair. Neither one really needs help. But if they didn't need help, there would be no point to their relationship. The connection between me and my grandmother is that gesture of rocking.

MH: In the second 'waltz,' two people stand in a room. She drops dishes on the floor while he stands with his back turned to her, trying to remain oblivious. Her face is blurry – I think you've done something to the image to manage this blurriness. Can you say why? She's the actor and he's the reaction shot. It looks like an allegory of traditional gender roles: she's all feeling (all body), while he's in his head, waiting to do something else, anything else. Of course they have problems, but he can deal with them only by turning his back. He can't hear what he hears. He can't see what he sees. Is that a reasonable reading of the scene?

MM: I think the fact that her face is blurry shows her in-betweenness. She's not a ghost, but she isn't completely there either. When I first blurred the face, I worried that the effect was so subtle that people might think it was a glitch. I really don't think I consciously knew what I was doing when I added the blur, but it felt somehow wrong to have the face visible.

He can't hear and she can't speak. It's a game that asks who takes responsibility. Describing this scene in terms of traditional gender roles is interesting. It's the typical image of an angry woman and a man ignoring her. But there's something different this time. It's flat. The act of throwing dishes should be violent or aggressive, but it seems born out of boredom rather than any domestic tension. There's a humour in the lack of emotion, which I think is what makes their relationship very similar to the other sections. They're playing out prescribed roles.

Whenever I watch this section, I'm reminded of going to an opening at YYZ in Toronto – I think it was for Tom Sherman, around 1987. While we're watching his tapes, an elderly couple comes into the gallery. They're having an argument. Or she is. She's yelling at him and he is completely silent. He's actually pretending he doesn't know her and of course it's obvious that he does. It was very embarrassing. The weird thing about the whole incident was that it felt so staged I'm still not sure if it was a performance. It felt like it was part of the work. It was quite surreal.

Kevin

MH: The second note is entitled 'Poltergeist.' It reads, 'When I go to a party no one remembers I'm there.' The woman (the one who is all feeling, all body) doesn't exist, so he can't hear her. Her experience is not her experience, because she needs him to affirm it or, at the very least, not to erase her moment as it occurs.

MM: I think it goes something like this: *I don't say anything. But on the other hand, you didn't ask. If you asked, you'd give me the space to answer, or to speak.* I don't think this is entirely about gender for me, but it's definitely about relationships. How we erase or don't erase each other.

MH: The third 'waltz' shows a pair of couples posed in front of the camera, then walking the streets. They pass one another 'accidentally,' and this moment is replayed three times. You and Yudi are one of the couples – is this important to know? Why this

accidental meeting (in our meetings with one another, is it never our bodies – only looking and language – that intersect)?

MM: Is the fact that it's Yudi and I important? I think it is if you know. It inevitably changes how you read the scene. But if you don't know, then it's not important.

This section is about doubling in a very particular way. Yudi is Indian and I am white. It's a marked unit. Whenever we were out together and spotted a couple with the same makeup – i.e., Indian man, white woman – we'd point it out and joke about it, in a very dark way. We'd say, 'That relationship's not going to last,' or 'You look happy now, but wait a few years.' I'm not sure what the joking was about. Maybe it was like a nervous laugh or a way to speak about our own tenuousness as a couple.

This accidental meeting occurs through looking. The gaze is repeated three times in closer and closer detail. The cross-flirting with the eyes was like swapping, or the suggestion of it. The idea that perhaps their relationship is no different from ours. It's interchangeable. Seeing your double is supposed to summon the uncanny, but somehow it doesn't here. The music that accompanies this section is constructed from samples of an orchestra tuning up. It begins quietly and builds, but the climax never really occurs; the image just eventually becomes silent.

MH: *Kevin* (8:30 min, 2002) opens with your parents singing a fragment of an old miner's song, 'Sixteen Tons' ('I sold my soul to the company store'). The song is about a man who makes so little for his back-breaking work that he is condemned to work forever. Why this song?

MM: I worked with my parents on this project for quite a long time. I think we shot off and on for about a year and a half. At first they were having a lot of fun, joking about being the stars of a big movie, etc. But eventually they got sick of the whole thing and would start to groan every time I pulled out the camera. I was at a loss for what to do to make it fun for them, so one day in the kitchen I asked them to sing a song. I have no idea why my father started to sing this particular song, and you can tell that neither one of them knows the exact words.

Anyway, the song was only meant to be an exercise, and I never intended to use it in the final video. But when I began editing a year later, I decided to include it as a framing device. The video opens with the parents' song and then ends with Kevin's song.

The opening song speaks about a number of things. I guess every child imagines that their adult life will be different from their parents. They're going to have lots of money, no responsibility or hardships. There is really very little about my parents in the video. I tried hard to edit out any details about them or their lives, but the song offers a little hint.

MH: Throughout *Kevin*, your parents tell stories of the incorrigible Kevin, the bad son, while we watch home-movie moments of you as a child. When I was growing up and felt my parents were misbehaving, I imagined that my real parents, the origins of sweetness itself, were locked and bound in the upstairs closet, while their evil doubles were free to torment me. You pull a reversal on this familiar childhood terror, reattaching your childhood moments to Kevin. Your mother tells us they had two daughters, so these stories of a bad-seed boy couldn't belong to them, only to your reconstructed fiction. Once again there is a pull of naming and identity, and a longing to be someone else at the same time. Two be or knot to be.

MM: From the beginning, I really wanted this project to be a collaboration. My parents and I would create another child. Conceptually it was like going back and having a voice in how you were going to be raised. In your own becoming.

I did have an imaginary brother named Kevin as a child. This seemed like a good starting point for the project. But when I started taping, it became clear that nobody remembered much about him. There was a general amnesia about Kevin. I was interested in the moment Kevin disappeared, or when I stopped talking about him. My parents couldn't remember. It pissed me off. I thought they should have been paying attention, but of course that's my own self-centred perspective.

So instead we started working with pure fiction, making up stories about a little boy named Kevin. It eventually became clear that wasn't working either. The stories lacked any kind of spark. So finally I said, 'Let's talk about something I did as a child and use the name Kevin.' It was funny. As soon as we changed my name to Kevin, it was quite liberating for both my parents, and especially for my mother. All of a sudden she started telling all of these terrible stories. I guess she couldn't have attributed them to me, but once it was somebody named Kevin, it was okay to talk about anything.

I think it was one of those projects where you encounter so many dead ends, but somehow you eventually find the direction where you should have been headed in the first place.

While filming, I heard two separate stories in the news about children who had somehow managed to get in the family car and drive away. The one that stuck in my mind was a five-year-old boy who had woken up in the middle of the night and got the keys to a car parked in the driveway. He managed to get behind the wheel and drive several blocks before the police apprehended him. They thought it was a drunk driver because of the way he was swerving back and forth across the road. They were shocked to discover that it was a little boy. When they asked him what he was doing, he told them that he was going to the store to get some Froot Loops.

That Kevin's escape from his family would be accomplished by just getting in the car and driving away seemed so perfect and simple. I wish it were that easy. The ending of the piece was really important for me. I wanted it to be a complete break from everything that happened before. The entire song plays, and people have complained about it being too long. But it's about moving into another space, one that is more evocative than narrative. It signals a shift rather than a conclusion.

MH: I'm wondering why you worked so hard to erase any moment of your parents' intimate lives; you are family, after all, and this home movie is set inside their home. Did you feel you would be betraying them by showing who they 'really were,' or perhaps there is some larger secret that must be kept, the secret that arrives with every camera and every picture?

MM: I don't think I worried about betraying my family by revealing too much. But because they are family, I was conscious about not depicting them in a way that they might be uncomfortable with. In the end, though, the decision not to allow them to speak about themselves was a way to define who they were through Kevin. It also put the emphasis on how they addressed the camera (me), which is really the subtext of the piece. *Secret* is a good word. A picture that doesn't hide more than it reveals is not that interesting.

MH: Yes, I couldn't agree more. The way an image keeps its secret is much of what creates a 'real' image, as opposed to the virtual ones that continue to surround and bewilder.

Having Coffee with No One (4:30 min, 2002) opens with an empty chair and a siren, a promise but also a broken date (and a portent of catastrophe, a distant unglimpsed difficulty). Is every movie like a date? Could it ever be that private, that small? Is it perverse to imagine that this movie (or any movie, really) could be just for one person? The movie goes on to show scores of

Kevin

waiting tables, with the same empty chair waiting, always waiting. Where are all these tables? You show us an image of the good life, a travelogue of cafés, but something is palpably missing, displaced.

MM: I don't think it's perverse to imagine that any movie could be just for one person. I think I always write with one person in mind. This video is a very intimate letter to one particular person. Other people can listen in if they like. Or pretend that I'm speaking to them, or that they are the one writing the letter. I think we always identify with multiple positions in a film.

I was doing a residency at the Paris Studio, working on another video, when I shot this tape. It was a little side project, something to get me out of the studio. In the end, though, *Having Coffee with No One* was the only tape I finished. I abandoned the other, longer piece.

There is something solitary about cafés in Paris. There is a social scene around the bar and the neighbourhood aspect of cafés, but somehow it's different than home, and solitary is the only way that I can think to describe it. Or maybe that was just my perspective as an outsider.

I have a very old, clunky video camera, one of the first digital video cameras ever made. It looks like a still camera. So it was very easy to set it down on a table and record. People just thought I was a tourist taking a break from sightseeing. After walking for an entire morning, the cafés were a moment to sit and be alone. But I was never really alone. Is anyone ever alone? We're always thinking of someone. There is always that presence or ghost beside us. I emphasized 'No One' in the title, because the 'No One' is obviously someone.

MH: In its one-note insistence, art as permanent refrain, this is a movie that might once have been dubbed structural, owing to its predetermined shaping strategy. This strategy signals a departure from your other work (doesn't it?).

MM: Yes, this tape is a departure from my other work. I like thinking about it as being structural, and I would love to make more like it. I've shown it to a few people, and halfway through they asked if this was really my film. I guess it seemed so different from anything I'd done before.

I enjoyed the fact that the piece had a very tightly defined framework. Once the framework is in place, you go about fitting all the pieces into it. You've got your boundaries, and once you've reached them, the piece is done. It's finished. The tape is what it is, nothing more, nothing less. There's no agonizing over it. There's a kind of freedom to working that way.

MH: Is the self only completed, or realized, in the presence of someone else?

MM: I think so. But it can also be completed in the 'imagined' presence of someone else. But maybe I don't need to qualify that, maybe that goes without saying. If I could sum it up, though, I think that is what all my work has often been about – completing oneself through an imagined presence.

MH: A series of intertitles changes the café mood: 'I have this image in my mind. Your hand is resting on my chest and my face is buried in your neck. I'm not sure if this qualifies as a sexual fantasy but it's the only thing that comes to mind and we don't get any further than that. I don't want to see us together like this anymore. It's too disturbing.' What does the title 'I don't want to see us together like this anymore' mean? And why the text insert?

Having Coffee with No One

MM: The text is actually very literal. I don't want to see us together 'like this' – i.e., together as we are in this tape. Me here, you in my head. I don't want to be stuck in this impasse. It's too disturbing.

Why the text insert? I guess I didn't know how to communicate this thought without text. I wish I did. I wish the initial pictures said it all and the final video was just a series of empty chairs. I've always preferred silent films, or films that were close to silent.

MH: The text arrives as an afterthought, a reflection on the image. Why this mode of address (which once again restrains or represses any notion of the body)? If we saw a body, or part of one (like a hand, for instance), would that ruin everything? Are pictures produced only to make up for what isn't there? (Derrida writes, 'When something is missing, language speaks.') By extension, personal deficiencies become the crucible of artmaking – do you feel this? If you were unhappy, would you make more work? If you were perfectly content, would there be any need for pictures?

MM: If we saw a body, even a fragment, it would ruin it. The missing body is so important in this tape. I've only ever loved missing bodies, really. Isn't that how it works? Isn't love constructed through absence and longing?

If pictures are made to make up for what isn't there, then I suppose there is a kind of perversion to this work, because I'm photographing an actual absence. Freezing it in that state and forcing it to remain absent.

I hate thinking about whether I would make art if I were happy. It's so hypothetical and I can't really imagine ever being perfectly happy. Personal deficiencies are usually my initial impetus, but after that it gets complicated. I make work for lots of reasons. Lately, I feel like I'm still making videos out of habit. It's what I do. That sounds terrible. That making art is just habit, rather than anything more important. But maybe it's okay. If it were too weighty, I'd feel paralyzed. So I keep putting out these little things and hopefully there is some relevance to them.

Monique Moumblow was born in Hamilton, Ontario and received a BFA from the Nova Scotia College of Art and Design in 1992. Initially, she was primarily interested in performance and worked collaboratively with Anne Russell. In 1993, Moumblow moved to Montreal where she began to focus on single-channel video. Her tapes have screened at festivals and galleries in North America and Europe and are included in the collections of the National Gallery of Canada and the Netherlands Media Art Institute. www.moniquemoumblow.com

Monique Moumblow's Videos

Winter Fruits   2:30 min 1992
Liabilities – the first ten minutes   10 min 1993
Joan and Stephen   12 min 1996
Plug   4 min 1997
Three Waltzes   7 min 1998
Accordion   2:30 min 2000
Sleeping Car   5:38 min 2000
Having Coffee with No One   4:30 min 2002
Kevin   8:30 min 2002
January 15th   3:50 min 2004
Oh My Darling   4 min 2006

Distributed by Vtape, Vidéographe and Video Out.

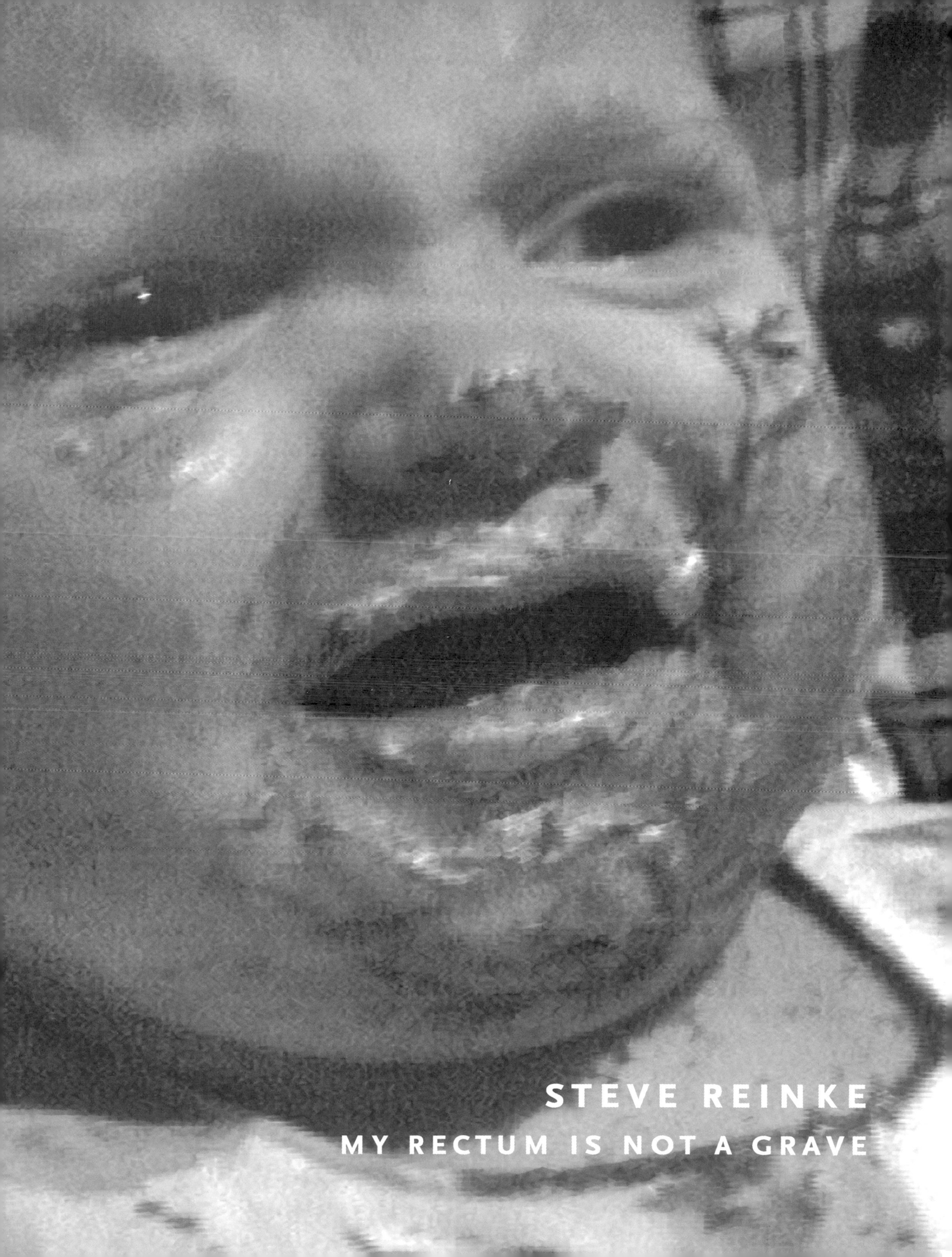

STEVE REINKE

MY RECTUM IS NOT A GRAVE

It's his voice you notice first of all. You can't help noticing. Beuys had his uniform, Warhol had his silkscreen, Steve Reinke has his voice. It is a kind of signature, a costume for the masquerade of personality, but more importantly: a guarantor of pleasure. Listening to this voice, I imagine again the thousands of moviegoers who once swooned at the sight of Garbo's face, that mask of light that trapped everyone who passed into the Medusa stare of cinema. Like Garbo, Steve's voice manages a universal appeal and an individual promise, a promise no less real for remaining always a secret.

Reinke's voice offers us an oblivion, a delirium, that is peculiarly Canadian. If Americans are television and movies, Canadians are radio. Reinke's is a voice without range, always set at medium, its entire expressive register limited to a few mild bursts of acceleration. There is nothing flashy here, nothing of the diva in this voice, nor would you ever want to hear him recite Shakespeare. If Reinke's voice is perfect, it is a perfection that brooks no variation. He offers you a five-star dinner, and it will be just the same night after night. Like the uniform of Beuys. The silkscreens of Warhol. Reinke's voice is the monotone of the inner dialogue, the siren call of conscience, all dolled up in a fantasia of seduction, intractable, compulsive and omnipresent. Like every voice of conscience, it never stops. Or never for long.

He burst upon the art scene with his first movie, *The Hundred Videos*, which set a new standard for Canadian media art. Filled with stolen pictures and the superior intelligence of his speaking, they were word-smart, funny, critical and seemed to be in a constant state of display. Moments of the work could be found at every festival and gallery collective and new-works show, and soon, even though he was only 'beginning,' there were calls for retrospectives near and far. Richly deserved. He has endowed the field with a rare insight, and remains the most important Canadian media artist of the 1990s, though his work since *The Hundred Videos* has raised the stakes of his own considerable practice.

MH: From 1992 to 1997 you worked on *The Hundred Videos*, a low-fi epic that calmed your superego interdiction to 'complete 100 videos before the year 2000 and my 36th birthday. These will constitute my work as a young artist.' You immediately cleared the table for new work, beginning with *Andy* (9 min, 1996). What's the relationship between the two?

SR: I finished *The Hundred Videos* in 1996. I'd been working on them since 1990 and had originally thought it would take me until 2000 to finish them. Ten a year for ten years, and then I'd have a body of work as a young artist and be ready to move on to more mature work. The series allowed for a proliferation of images, proposals and desires without getting bogged down in a single idea. I wanted to be fast and cheap and follow whatever caught my attention. As an artist I've always proceeded by telling myself two lies: that the images already exist independently of my authorship (I'll say more about that later) and that I'll make

something really good in the future, and the work I'm doing presently – whatever it might be – is a preparation for the real work, which is endlessly postponed. *The Hundred Videos* were great for me in this respect: a series of short works that present themselves as sketches, proposals or little wishes.

But I had a couple of interests that couldn't be accommodated within the series, mostly because it seemed to me that each of the components should be very short. The average length is under three minutes, while the longest (a re-edit of a documentary I shot in 1984) runs about ten minutes. While many of *The Hundred Videos* were concerned with ideas of documentary representation, the short running times didn't really allow me to engage directly with documentary production.

The other avenue *The Hundred Videos* didn't allow me to explore in-depth was work based on following predetermined instructions, like the compositional methods of John Cage, the early process pieces of Steve Reich or structuralist film. Doing this work is like a hobby for me. I like to establish a set of procedures (a heuristic) and begin the process of carrying it out, usually as a transformation or remapping of a particular film or piece of writing. Often I don't finish the projects, and usually don't release the ones I do manage to finish. Here's one I worked on a few years ago and have a yen to complete: I began reading Joyce's *Finnegans Wake* into my computer. A voice-recognition program transcribes the text. Because most of the book is not really in English – it's made of neologisms from a wide variety of languages – the computer transcription bears little resemblance to the novel. Though in its own way it is a more rational, readable text, as it is now limited to a basic English vocabulary. I managed to read the first third into the computer. It was lots of fun to read out loud and it's doubtful I would read the thing on my own; reading *Finnegans Wake* is not necessarily its own reward – one benefits from having an ulterior motive. It is perhaps the ultimate modernist writerly text: to read it is to recompose it, to write it over again. This project literalizes Barthes' distinction between the readerly and writerly. At first I got the computer to read back my transcription, but the monotony of the voice became quickly tedious, and besides, Mac voices are overused. So instead I read and recorded the transcription. It sounds very good, like an endlessly obscure bedtime story. So far it takes close to three hours (I recite it fairly quickly), but if I finish it, I expect it will be upwards of ten. With a lot of compression it should fit on two MP3 CDs or an iPod and be at least as good as any John Grisham book on tape. I would also publish my transcription, giving it the title my voice-recognition program gave it: *Finnegan's Wake*.

Of course it wasn't only length that hampered my engagement with documentary production, but also a general inability, or even refusal, to engage with people as documentary subjects. Although I'm continually tempted by the observational documentary, I seem to be unable to actually make one, at least with people, though I think I would have no problem with plants or animals. *Andy* is a compromise – a documentary, I suppose – but conceptually simple and completely preplanned. Andy had heard my work contained pornographic images and wanted to be videotaped masturbating. (He had already starred in a few amateur porn productions.) My previous sexually explicit images had all been appropriated. I'd never shot sex, but was certainly willing, even eager. At the same time, I thought that shooting a solo scene might be fun, but not interesting enough to be a tape. Both Andy and I were interested in making a public tape, not just a private sex thing. The two things Andy was most proud of, and most fond of showing off, were his large penis and his well-decorated apartment. I thought it would be good if the video showed him masturbating in his living room while he discussed his decorating choices (in voice-over) as if he were giving an in-depth tour of his apartment. These two modes of self-presentation, home decorating and sexual exhibition, parody one another, and perfectly encapsulate a particular

Echo Valley

contemporary, urban gay male way of being. I think of *Andy* as an ethnographic portrait: Andy is not only an individual but a type, an exemplar. The tape makes fun of Andy's exhibitionism and decorating proclivities equally, but he got it right away and thought it was very funny. It takes a real fag to be Martha Stewart and Al Parker at the same time.

MH: *Everybody Loves Nothing (Empathic Exercises)* (11 min, 1996) continues your recycling of pictures, familiar from *The Hundred Videos*, but now drawing from the Prelinger Archives. Mostly your work has rerun TV moments (Oprah Winfrey) or clips from widely available docs (*Lonely Boy*) – why this search through musty archives?

SR: I'm more of a browser than a researcher. In terms of any particular discipline, I am a dilettante rather than an expert. I have some research skills, and have used them for employment occasionally, but generally prefer a less structured relationship with the archive. The trouble with archives is that they are well-organized and strive for comprehensiveness: you will find whatever it is you are looking for. But I'm more interested in finding things I had no idea I wanted (a category that includes things I had no idea existed, as well as things I did not consciously think of).

I used to think that the destruction of an archive, museum or library was a horrible thing. As a child reading about the Seven Wonders of the World, I was traumatized by the burning of the library of Alexandria. Now I'm not sure I care. All those grand collections seem overwhelmingly oppressive. We should just get rid of them and start over.

Rick Prelinger (of the Prelinger Archive of Ephemeral Films) has nothing against browsing. I arrived looking for films documenting brain surgeries prior to my birth. He has a number of them, and they were exactly as I'd imagined from their descriptions, only better. But they were never used in the end. For reasons of expediency (I forget why), I culled all the material I

used from a few hundred 3/4-inch video transfers he had in the main office. I'm not sure if I had the central idea for *Everybody Loves Nothing* at that point. I think I just dubbed whatever clips caught my eye. A lot of the material was from the Levy family's 16mm home movies. They took annual vacations to faraway places, which they documented far more proficiently than most amateur vacation films. They're famous bakers in New York; I think their motto was/is something like 'You don't have to be Jewish to like it.'

Everybody Loves Nothing (Empathic Exercises) is the video of mine I like the least. I've been tempted to pull it from distribution, but it's been one of the most successful, being purchased for broadcast (which rarely happens with my work, partly because of its sexually explicit imagery and/or issues of copyright) and winning the Telefilm Canada Award at the Images Festival. I think I dislike it because I stoop to cheap, seductive tricks so often, most particularly slowing down footage until a clip ends with a freeze-frame as the subject looks directly at the camera.

MH: *Echo Valley* (8 min, 1998) features an episodic portrait series. I appear in one sucking a candy cane. I remember the shooting was brief and casual; you assured me at the time that you would make up in words what might be missing with pictures. Can pictures be recaptioned to mean anything at all? Do you wonder, like Walter Ong, that if a picture is worth a thousand words, why does it have to be a saying?

SR: Interesting you don't ask whether pictures can be captioned indiscriminately, only recaptioned. Your question supposes that images arrive precaptioned, which I think is true: every image derives meaning only if it is already caught in the webs of discourse. Pictures mean nothing without words. In fact, they are not even pictures.

What I added to the images of *Echo Valley* are small written monologues, a parallel stream of information that can be

Echo Valley

attributed to the person pictured, or to the artist as implied narrator. I hope it's also unclear which text belongs to each character.

MH: From Marcel Duchamps' *Anemic Cinema* to Richard Serra's *Television Delivers People* (and many more besides), there is a future-past of motion pictures comprised exclusively of text. Could you talk about how *Incidents of Travel* (10 min, 1998) fits into these heritage moments?

SR: Moving pictures without pictures always seem sophisticated to me. Both works by Duchamp and Serra might be named conceptual, a term I hate more and more. *Incidents of Travel* might be called *Anemic Video*. It is a sluggish piece, low blood flow. The soundtrack is the most annoying pop song, 'Popcorn' by Hot Butter, a Moog synthesizer piece from my childhood slowed down many times, but with the original pitch maintained. The text, which fades up from white, is from a two-volume travelogue of a Victorian adventurer, John L. Stephens' *Incidents of Travel in Yucatan*. (Robert Smithson has also worked from the books.) As was the style of the time, the table of contents contained descriptions of the contents of each chapter. I included only the descriptions that do not contain proper nouns (names of specific people or places) or strong actions/events. What we are left with is a string of short descriptions of nothing in particular, evocative of an episodic narrative but not in themselves constituting a narrative. It is my hope that the video leads viewers to imagine a context for the descriptions: it is meant to be evocative, opening a space for antique imaginings, lost wonderments reglimpsed.

MH: *How Photographs Are Stored in the Brain* (8 min, 1998) seems like a departure for you. There is a no voice-over and the tone feels nostalgic, even romantic.

SR: Nostalgia is a strange thing. It comes up all the time when people talk about art. History has disappeared and left us with only nostalgia. We remain ignorant, but filled with intense, if vague, emotion. We want to return to a home we never experienced but can almost remember. A few years after making *How Photographs Are Stored in the Brain*, I curated an exhibition for the Argos in Brussels called *Attack (Retreat)*. The premise was that popular culture's most powerful force for interpellating us is nostalgia. One would have to be heartless – inhuman even – to escape its heart-tugging force. It cannot be attacked directly, for every attack is regarded as hollow cynicism. But where attack is not possible, one might be able to engineer a strategic retreat.

I said earlier that an archive is a horrible thing. But a collection, especially if it fits into a box that is easy to carry away, is a fine thing. A friend of mine found a box outside a recently sold house in Toronto containing 20 old 78s, a photo album and personal correspondence. The photos and music were used for *How Photographs Are Stored in the Brain*, while the correspondence and a few of the photos were used in my only interactive CD-ROM, *Mr. Green*.

MH: I have seen *Fireball* (5 min, 1999) many times now, and while it hovers always at the border of coherence, it never arrives, it never makes any sense to me at all. Steve, help me out with this one – what does the title refer to? What are these strange goings-on? Who are these artists and why should we care?

SR: As in *Echo Valley*, I wanted to have monologues that seemed perfectly and profoundly attributable to their speaker and then spoken again by someone else with the same effect. A floating monologic perspective that could be multiply-voiced, pertaining to anyone. In one of *The Hundred Videos*, 'Jason,' I interviewed a heavily tattooed guy. I wanted to make a documentary portrait, but what he said didn't satisfy me. I wanted the tattoos to say things that were as interesting as he looked. (I wanted him to voice my projected desire back to me. I wanted him to live up to his image. After all, isn't a tattoo an advertisement or exteriorization of something?) So I wrote what I wanted him to say, and he said it. Suddenly it was clear to me why it would be interesting to work with people in front of the camera, or even to make small dramas. But so far I've stuck to the monologue. One of my main concerns at the time was to find ways to make the monologue, to use Bakhtin's terms, dialogic rather than monologic.

Fireball came out of a project I made for a group show of public, interventionist work sponsored by Mercer Union in Toronto. I printed about a dozen monologues on little cards, took to the street and asked people to recite them for me. The results were not so good – everyone was flat and stumbling, and in the end there was nothing usable. But I took the monologues with me to Berlin where I was staying for a few weeks to participate in the Frank Wagner exhibition *Fleeting Portraits*. I gave a talk at the Hochschule, where I recruited people (mostly students) to participate in the video. I spent an hour or so taping them in their homes, and then either wrote something for them or gave them one of the existing monologues to recite. The monologues I wrote appeared to be about each person specifically, but could also be endlessly transferable – that is, anyone could recite them and they would seem just as particular.

I'm very fond of *Fireball*, though I may not have many reasons to be. It was crudely edited on Premiere in a few hours (a program I have never used before or since) with star wipes between each scene. I know it can seem like a lame travelogue – or worse, an obliquely political tape about life in post-wall Berlin – but for me it is about throwing my voice, a particularly mediated self-portrait presented as a documentary of others.

MH: *Spiritual Animal Kingdom* (26 min, 1998) raised the bar for your work, showing a new commitment to old-fashioned cinema values (framing, montage, complex sound work), along with a shiny pop gloss. Its train of episodic fragments has become a model for some of your subsequent release.

SR: However much I like my work since *The Hundred Videos*, they seemed to me an idiosyncratic collection of shorts. I wanted something more substantial, made with a presence and authority that would be able to seduce an audience into sustained, thoughtful engagement. *The Hundred Videos* was, in this respect, an ideal structure for me: individual components could be slight, while the overall project was grand. *Spiritual Animal Kingdom* is something like that: a container for an arrangement of individual, modular components. Not to say that the components don't belong – it is important that they work together to form a whole that is coherent (thematically and otherwise) – but some modules could be removed, others added, their order shifted. The structure isn't closed like works based on pattern or epic myth.

It was made for the Montreal Biennale. In large group shows, people spend very little time with individual works. My tapes usually screen in theatrical settings, which ensure that audience members will most likely see the entire piece from beginning to end, from a single, comfortable seat with minimal distractions. In galleries and museums, people walk in and out quickly. Small wonder that gallery video tends to be simple and bombastic: a single overwhelming image (or bunch of images run against a single piece of music). They are all presence and affect, with no discursive development possible: no arguments, stories or even descriptions, just a single performative gesture, a painting or photograph that changes over time. *Spiritual Animal Kingdom* is a work one can enter at any moment. I tried to seduce the audience into staying until they've seen the whole thing by making the modules short, snappy, colourful, humorous and full of familiar hits from the '70s.

MH: *Spiritual Animal Kingdom* begins with a wavy abstract light and your voice: 'I went to the doctor and said, "Doctor, I'm not depressed now or anything, but I feel that at any moment I might fall into a deep depression. I guess I'm feeling kind of vulnerable, and I have a lot of things I want to get done so I don't want to become catatonic – or even lethargic – and be unable to finish them, so I thought I could start hedging my bets by starting on the Prozac now."'

This voice is yours but not yours; it isn't the voice you answer the phone with, for instance. Could you elaborate on the difference between 'acting' and 'performance'? A friend recently said of the late Colin Campbell, who appeared in nearly every one of the 50 videotapes he produced, that his chops weren't good enough to be called 'acting'; never mind the wigs and makeup and increasingly complicated narrative scenarios, he was definitely 'performing.' And you?

SR: Maybe it's something like this: actors try to be other people, while performers remain themselves, or aspects of themselves. They're not trying for transformation or mimicry, but merely to exemplify some aspect of something that gets refracted through them. (Kind of like self-portraiture.) Never trust an actor. But a performer? Just sit back and enjoy the show.

MH: There is an interest throughout this tape in abstract forms. Some segments remind me of the work of the Whitney Brothers, or the computer abstractions of Larry Cuba. Some of these folks claimed for their work a 'universalist' consciousness that could be expressed, at last, by pictures liberated from the burden of representation, from having to show something. Others felt these abstractions, painstakingly produced using complicated machine manoeuvres, signalled a triumph of science, or some melding of science and art. Where do your abstractions fit?

SR: I had a student at CalArts who was doing very similar animations. She would write her own algorithms. It was a long,

How Photographs Are Stored in the Brain

complex process that involved a lot of specialized knowledge and labour. I used an inexpensive consumer program called Bryce that was intended to generate cheesy science-fiction landscapes. I let it run more or less randomly and chose the animations that pleased me. The student had just moved from Germany to California, and this shift, from a quasi-scientific, intensive craftsmanship to a disinterested choosing of pre-existing elements, seemed to her to encapsulate the two cultures.

At this time I wasn't really thinking about animation at all. Work I made later engages directly with the history of abstract animation, but at this time my concerns were almost exclusively in the realm of the literary, discursive, rhetorical. The animations in *Spiritual Animal Kingdom* were meant to be wallpaper for the monologues, things to catch the eye. Perhaps they might pacify the viewer, offering a kind of pleasing submission while their ears opened up. They were meant to prioritize the voice and enhance the tone of particular monologues: a few pulse violently with garish colours, others have a more peaceful palette and flow rather than pulse, etc. They also have a structural function: all the monologues that begin 'I went to the doctor' have their signature wallpaper/animation, as do the 'When my father died' monologues.

I thought of the work as having a warp (of individual moments and impulses) and a weft (of themes, methods and loose narratives). Here are some of them: the death of the father; subsequent visits to the doctor; chronology of the narrator's self-consciousness from kindergarten; popular culture torqued into a kind of comic pathos; loss and nostalgia linked to a muted libido; sudden eruptions of aggression that immediately subside or are sublimated; etc.

MH: *Spiritual Animal Kingdom* is haunted by the death of your father, which you announce several times in the movie ('When my father died, we discovered he was a masochist ... ' and later: 'When my father died, we got rid of all his hats. Now I wish I had kept one. Whenever I see a man wearing a hat I think it must have once belonged to my father. He had quite a number of them, a dozen or so. Mostly baseball caps.') The doctor jokes in which you request medications; the brilliant, racing voice-over deliveries; the disgust and fascination with the body (which continues into the abstract sections, as if the thought of the body were too much, because every body would return you to his) – all appear to derive from this fact. Like the announced death of your mother in *Sad Disco Fantasia*, it is a conceit, a fiction. In a Canadian media art context in which personal, confessional videos are not uncommon, why riff on these red herrings, why this elaborate construction and why the need to strike a pose that appears so very personal?

SR: Well, my father did die before I made *Spiritual Animal Kingdom*, so the joke's on ... well, somebody. I use the confessional as a fictional mode. I use whatever experiences (interests, desires, methods, materials) I have access to, but I am not making autobiography (or self-portraiture). I don't find myself that interesting, and if I did, I would keep it to myself. In fact, that is my new

teaching motto: 'Keep your self to yourself!' Which is perhaps slightly more helpful than the previous one: 'Artists have no intentions.'

Unlike the narrator of *Sad Disco Fantasia*, my mother is still alive – I just talked with her a few days ago. I am interested in the ideas of the death of the father and the death of the mother as they play out against other ideas, images, sensations, possibilities. I am not interested in making personal stories that recount instances of particular events. Claims toward authenticity disgust me. I want to cut through a social/cultural fabric that seems entirely constructed (warp and weft) from various hypocrisies.

MH: *Afternoon (March 21, 1999)* (24 min, 1999) is set entirely inside your apartment, a duet of camera and maker, playfully turning the space through your lens. At one point you open your shirt to reveal your chest and say, 'Oh, I've got more in common with Vito Acconci than I thought.' Vito seems father to your musings, and I wonder if you could speak of the importance of ancestors, tradition and the individual talent.

SR: Although Vito Acconci is central to my work, I'm not sure how much this particular video was influenced by him. With the in-camera editing, seemingly straightforward record of someone making their way through the world (even if the world in this case is reduced to a tiny studio apartment) and comic persona, it owes more to George Kuchar. Still, the reference to Acconci works in a couple of ways. In the video I toy with the audience about showing myself. My body (or someone's body) is central to the work – the camera is clearly an extension of the narrator/artist/protagonist's body – and I show fragments of myself, but never my face. For the Acconci joke, I am lying on the couch and unbutton my shirt to expose a hairy chest and claim that my similarity with Acconci may be as much physical as anything else. It insists that *Afternoon* be read within the historical context of video art. It divides the audience (as humour often – and citations always – do) between those who have a first-hand knowledge of Acconci's work (who laugh) and those who don't. It premiered before an audience of filmgoers who didn't have the capacity to understand it (although it is really very simple and not inherently challenging). Many took it as some kind of provocation, as often happens when audiences are faced with experiences outside the realm of their possible expectations. For an art or video crowd, it is easy to make sense of; they might think it is boring, but won't find it unusual or that I must be 'pulling their leg.'

It seems strange, in a way, that the work takes as its fathers Acconci and Kuchar. Surely it must be one of my most self-consciously video-art videos. Ideally, I'd like to assert a much wider set of influences and claim for video the ability to combine stuff from almost anywhere. Video art and experimental film once had completely separate histories, but now that film is dead (and mourned) and video is dead (its death has not been noticed) and we've gone digital, these separate histories seem quaint and irrelevant. New histories are being written, and a new canon is forming. *Wavelength* will be placed beside *The Red Tapes* and no one will think twice. Last year the Whitechapel Gallery in London showed my *Sad Disco Fantasia* with Stan Brakhage's *Dog Star Man*. In years past, such a pairing would have appeared merely idiosyncratic and silly.

When I was much younger and a prose poet, I wondered why my writing was so much like the work of Michael Ondaatje, Christopher Dewdney, Margaret Atwood and Marie-Claire Blais in terms of sensibility and style. I did not believe in national identity (at least not as a defining creative force) and would have preferred to be able to choose who my influences were. Why not write like Beckett, Joyce, Berryman, Genet, Faulkner, Emily Dickinson or Cormac McCarthy? As Gertrude Stein said, there is very little one gets to choose in life, and one may choose from whom one steals, but not by whom one will be influenced.

MH: *Sad Disco Fantasia* (24 min, 2001) opens with the death of your mother, like the famous novel of Camus that begins, 'Mother died today.' But unlike this affectless cri de coeur of existentialism, your work features animal musings, brightly relooped pop moments from the '70s and drenching animations, haunted always by death. Is Charlie Brown correct when he says, 'Good grief'? Is this another of the oxymorons the work explores?

SR: Yes, I believe in the death drive, and will say no more on the subject. (Except that we're all going to die. And not everyone loves us.)

MH: *Anal Masturbation and Object Loss* (6 min, 2002) features a single shot (with edits) that shows a close-up of your hands gluing together pages of a book. In its performative, one-take, non-stop chatter approach, it recalls early video art, as well as your vocation as a teacher. Can you comment? And why do you keep gluing pages from the female masturbation chapter together, repressing once more a feminine erotics?

SR: The video has three components: the voice-over monologue, the action of gluing the book together and the view of the book itself. While the narrator claims to be gluing together all the chapters except the eponymous one, we mostly see him gluing together a chapter on female masturbation. Although the shot is too tight to read any entire page, we get a good view of chunks of the text. That particular chapter had the raciest case studies and used a lot of coarse and provocative language. I wanted viewers to be compelled to read the book's text as well as listen to the voice-over. Of course, they can't read very much until the gluing happens again. The action is itself provocative: the glue is applied with a penis-like stick, the pages pressed together with a repetitive, gentle rubbing motion, then the book is slammed shut,

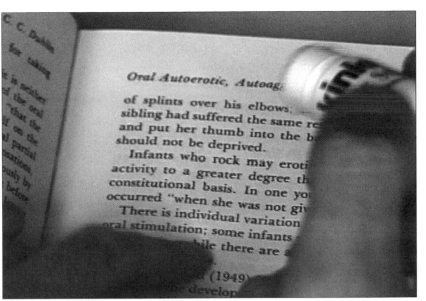

Anal Masturbation and Object Loss

pressed down and reopened. Female sexuality is foregrounded. If the gluing symbolically represents the repression of sexual thoughts and desires (and why not?) it must be remembered that the gesture has a double movement: it first reveals that which it obliterates. As the narrator says, nothing is missing, all the words are still on the page, you just can't access them.

MH: In *The Chocolate Factory* (28 min, 2002) you present a series of drawings showing the victims of Jeffrey Dahmer, along with snippets of Black Sabbath's 'Fairies Wear Boots' and a slowed voice-over. The cruelly repetitive, serial nature of the work is so dull that I have to ask: don't you want to be loved? Don't you long for that moment, after the screening, when strangers will rush to embrace you? How could you make a work so difficult as this?

SR: Do I want to be loved? I am loved well and sufficiently. I don't need any more. There is too much love in the world. I prefer screenings to occur in my absence. I do often enjoy a good question-and-answer session, but questions from an audience member gushing with love are as useless as questions from someone in an antagonistic rage.

Of course, *The Chocolate Factory* is not meant to bore people, although that is undoubtedly often its effect. I don't think it's a difficult work so much as an unpleasant one. Perhaps there's not much to give an audience immediate pleasure. But it is rich and pleasurable beneath its boring structuralist crust! And in the same comic/ironic mode as my other work. The range of images and sounds is small, and their use monotonous. Yet the voice-over can be quite dense and it changes rhetorical mode frequently. The video is sometimes dense and overwhelming – at some points there is too much to take in.

It is partly a sign of the times that unpleasant work (the code word is difficult) seems useless and unbearable. Back in the '80s, difficult work received at least grudging respect. Now it is met with anger: 'How dare you bore us! We must be amused.'

MH: *J.-P. (Remix of* Tuesday and I *by Jean-Paul Kelly)* (7 min, 2002) is a first-person confessional that, unlike most diaries, exists in multiple versions. Can you talk about how you came to this footage, and why you treated it the way you did?

SR: J.-P. was a student of mine. I liked his drawings and asked him to illustrate my video *The Blind Necrophile*, which was based on an early psychoanalytic case history. The video turned out fine, but was unremarkable, so I didn't bother putting it in distribution. (I make too many videos and so have tried to release only the best, or most interesting.) He also illustrated *The Chocolate Factory*. J.-P. made *Tuesday and I* late one night, depressed after a weekend of partying and ecstasy, in a single, 18-minute confession to the camera. His despair is compelling, but 18 minutes is too long – it isn't the '70s anymore. So J.-P. has offered up his confession to anyone who will remix it and make it shorter. I like J.-P. very much, but find the endless self-pity of his confession tedious and annoying, so I must confess my first impulse was to deflate his self-aggrandizement. The material asks for either sympathetic engagement or rejection of empathy. Initially I had dramatic music well up and cover his words at certain points. This worked well but seemed reductively cruel. Instead, I decided to keep his performance intact, but sped up certain sections, initially only those in which he isn't talking. As the video progresses, I also fast-forward through some of his words, and this fast-forwarding gets faster and faster. I was interested in using speed to squeeze sounds out of his body. These sounds produce a parallel monologue.

MH: You told me once that every memory is accompanied by equal amounts of shame; past breakfasts and humiliating sexual encounters are all part of the same sorry past. Why is that?

SR: I am being misquoted/misremembered horribly, although you are almost right. It is not memories and shame (I remember

J.-P.

nothing and feel shame very rarely) but events and embarrassment. Everything embarrasses me. There is something appalling about existence itself, or if not existence, consciousness. I don't worry about it too much. It is a trait I share with many previously shy people – there is a shy/embarrassment switch: either it is all on or all off. Nothing is quite like a humiliating sexual encounter, but I can more honestly say the recollection of eating lunch today is just as embarrassing (and somehow as private) as my last sexual encounter (which might be considered sleazy, but was not humiliating).

My use of the confessional mode in the work may be connected to this – how could it not be? – but I don't think my ex-shyness is the determining factor. Sure, I tease the audience with confession/autobiography that gets invariably displaced. Autobiography joins voice and body together through narrative. Confession interpellates us as social subjects. These basic ways of understanding ourselves seem inescapable but limiting. I want to move through them to something else.

MH: *The Mendi* (11 min, 2006) is a found-footage short that returns to material first used in a couple of *The Hundred Videos*. Do you have an archive of material that you draw from to produce new work? Did you feel that the original material, a CBC ethnographic documentary about a Papua New Guinean tribe called the Mendi, wasn't exhausted by your first approach? Could you imagine continuing to rework this same footage, again and again, in all of the work you would make in the future? Will it never end?

SR: I do still use material gathered many years ago. I don't have that much of it. I actually don't like having to deal with mounds of things. In the early '90s I worked at the University of Toronto, in the Education building, as an audio/visual technician's assistant. Like many libraries, they were getting rid of their 16mm collection. I took a few dozen films, rented a flatbed for a few days and spliced together a few reels of material. Whatever caught my attention. I had no idea what I would use this stuff for. I just knew I didn't want any excess: anything I took was something with a high probability of being put to use. I took these reels and had them transferred to Betacam. *The Mendi* was the one film I kept relatively intact. Every scene was compelling, and I loved the strange commentary, which was definitely feminist, but still alarmingly condescending to the Mendi. Right now, I can just remember one line, 'The Mendi have minds like computers.' I'll continue to draw from all of it, as long as it compels me. I would like to become someone else, or at least develop a larger sense of things, but as it seems I am doomed to remain exactly myself, I assume this material will compel me always. Of course, any particular piece of material could never be exhausted. The question is whether one's interest in working with the material could be exhausted, and I don't think it will happen. I haven't, for instance,

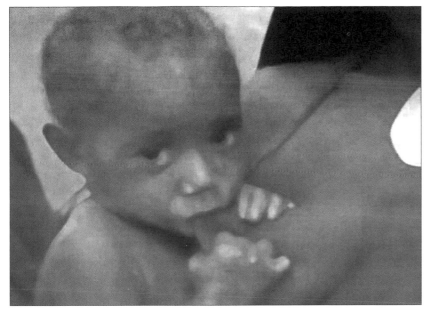

The Mendi

The quote refers to a prism and a darkened chamber. The music during the segment is from Pink Floyd. The title of the *Dark Side of the Moon* album refers to a place of darkness (if not a chamber), and the cover of the album depicts light being pinched through a prism. So when the image resolves into the highly recognizable album cover (for though all the visual material in the section is derived from the cover, it is not recognizable as such until the end), it refers to two separate things: where the music is coming from and what the quote is referring to. Usually audiences laugh when the image resolves, though there was no laughter when you showed it in Rotterdam.

MH: *Ask the Insects* is an episodic work, reminiscent in its shaping strategies to *Spiritual Animal Kingdom*, *Sad Disco Fantasia* and *Anthology of American Folk Song*.

dealt with the voice-over on the original film. Some people, by the way, get perturbed when they see material reused, as if I'm cheating them. I'm happy working with a small bank of images. I never yearn to have massive amounts of material. I would like more footage of brain surgery from the '50s, though.

MH: *Ask the Insects* (8 min, 2005) opens with an intertitle warning viewers about the tricks of light to come, the illusions cast in a theatrical space. It reads: 'Friends, avoid the darkened chamber where your light is being pinched.' Could you talk about the origin of that text, and why it is followed by the album cover for Pink Floyd's *Dark Side of the Moon*?

SR: The quote is from Goethe. He's writing against Newton's theory of colour and light, in particular the prism experiments. For Goethe, the artificial situation of passing a beam of light through a prism in a darkened room could not produce valid results, as it was so far removed from everyday perception/experience. Today, in the age of empiricism, we have no doubt Newton was correct and that Goethe's scientific theories are quackery. Yet there is also something modern about Goethe's stance, which seems akin to phenomenology in its preference for the experience of things as they appear complexly in the world, rather than the abstractions of scientific experiments in which limited conditions are imposed. But, of course, I don't expect many people will recognize the Goethe quote, which is unattributed. In the video, the quote seems to be speaking about the condition of being a spectator in a movie theatre. Still, the two light-pinching apparatuses – prism and cinema – don't seem so different. At any rate, it is always wise to begin with a warning, if only for issues of liability. This is the first work that I've thought of as, if not actually being animation, then being about animation, in particular the relation between the animated/digital image and its possible referents in the immanent world.

SR: When I made *Spiritual Animal Kingdom*, I was thinking of the structure of a variety show on TV. There were recurring comedy bits, musical numbers and bumpers. Everything related to everything else in one of three or four ways. Then I had a section – a giant book a neurologist produced about his wife after she died called something like *The Brain of a Pianist*, slices of her brain carefully photographed. And this material didn't relate directly to anything else in the work, but I put it in anyway and discovered it was fine: it belonged despite me not being able to pinpoint exactly why it belonged. Then I didn't worry about it anymore. I realized I wasn't building an airtight machine, or even a machine with a particular reason to exist, a particular function.

Sad Disco Fantasia is even looser: it is about living in Los Angeles as a kind of flâneur, the death of the mother and the impossibility of home, but many of the sections have nothing to do with any of these. And although *Anthology of American Folk Song* is even looser, I think that on a deeper level it is completely tight and coherent.

All of those videos are about the same length, about 26 minutes. *Ask the Insects* is much shorter, with fewer sections. It seems to me a series of introductions to the graveyard walk. Okay, not really a series of introductions at all. Still, the video seems to have two parts of about equal length: the walk, and everything leading up to it, which is animation (though the narrator, of course, claims otherwise).

MH: In the second episode of *Ask the Insects*, your voice-over states, 'The reader has proved inadequate: simple-minded, easily distracted, and mean and petty.' From the death of the author you move to an inadequate reader, implying of course that the readers of this movie will be inadequate. Do you feel that the work you have made up until now has prepared viewers for what's to come, raising the skills of viewership so that you can make increasingly difficult or complex work? Movies like this are difficult to draw together, it is so wilfully fragmented, jumping from one place to another. What do your musings about burning books, a walk to the yards of grave and school, an abstracted display of processing, the forms of rain and insect life, have to do with one another? What is the relation that joins these into a unity, a whole?

SR: Yes, I still think the idea of an oeuvre is important. Even if the author is dead, other concepts have taken its place, like the signature effect, or a contract between the text and its implied reader(s). Individual works within an oeuvre teach us how to read other works. If we only had one Emily Dickinson poem, it would mean nothing. The poetry of Emily Dickinson only makes sense as part of a larger body of work. Genre can do this as well, of course, but one always wants to exceed genre.

And why not insult the audience? I had already warned them, after all. It is more than their light being pinched.

I hope I'm getting better at whatever I'm doing, but I hope this doesn't necessarily mean becoming more and more complex, like Joyce's path from *The Dubliners* to *Ulysses* to *Finnegans Wake*. That's kind of a modernist, teleological concept. But despite this, my work has become more complex, and I do hope viewers are drawn along. If you know my previous work, for instance, *Anthology of American Folk Song* will probably not seem incomprehensibly strange. The other route, the poet's route, rather than increasing complexity, increases simplicity and succinctness, stripping everything down to the essentials. The two paths are not incommensurable: individual components are often getting simpler and simpler, while the way they function in relation to the others is increasingly complex.

MH: Could you talk about the closing sequence of *Ask the Insects* – did you take this camera walk knowing it would be your conclusion?

SR: The last section is derived from footage I took a few summers ago. I walked the same path I used to walk to school, from kindergarten to Grade 8. The school is at the top of a hill, on the right-hand side. A graveyard is on the left-hand side. When I get to the top of the hill, my father's grave is right there, along with other Reinke stones, so it does kind of look like all the graves bear (bare?) my name.

I did not know what could be done with this footage. Certainly much of the other stuff in the video leads up to it, in various, often obscure ways. The shot of the buck in snow is from *Bambi*. It is Bambi's father telling him wordlessly that his mother is dead. The monologue about abstracting an unidentified representational image through processing gives another possibility for the processing of the walk footage: it could so easily be repressed

through the application of a single filter. The third-last section refers to walking/journeying: 'Every day a bit further, until the horizon is breached.' The second-last section (before the walk) ends with a nonsequitur resolved in the last section, '... like a graveyard where every stone bears your name.' Other sections warn or insult the viewer, speak about the weight of paternal/ancestral knowledge (book burning). Still, all these connections do not add up to a complete exploration of a single theme! The fact that many sections feature precipitation might be of no less relevance.

MH: *The Fallen* (4 min, 2007) is adapted from a four-panel archival ink-jet print you produced called *The American Military Casualties of the Second Gulf War for Whom Photographs Were Available as of October 6, 2006, Arranged by Attractiveness*. How did you make the transition from still to moving image? What about the music?

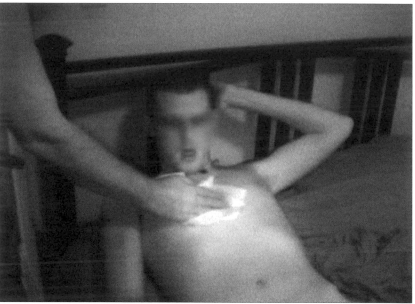

Anthology of American Folk Song

SR: Initially, I didn't think the work could exist as a video. How to rank over 2,600 faces over time? How to do it without jeopardizing the neutral tone of the prints? But they are quite different pieces: the video is more aggressive. You can't go back over any of the faces, which are processed in batches before the camera zooms to the next batch. The video returns four times to the original prints, making it clear that it is an adaptation, an animation of a still image. The pictures were downloaded from the website of the *Washington Post*, and are arranged exactly in order of attractiveness according to me. It exists as a four-panel, ink-jet print, and this is an animated adaptation of that photo work. The music is a recent blues song, 'Goin' Down South' by R. L. Burnside, who, like all bluesmen, recently died. The song has only three lines that are repeated – the title, 'I'm goin' with you, babe' and 'I love being dead.'

MH: The more I see *Anthology of American Folk Song* (26 min, 2004) the more it coheres. It opens with your niece, on the occasion of her first birthday. An opening of innocence then, which quickly turns to something else as she smears chocolate cake over her face and looks distressed. It is her face you focus on, her face is the beginning, but it is met by her ass, 'the end' of the body, and you bring these together via the look of his relatives whose slowed-down speech turns their love into a sinister, looming presence. You continue the themes of beginning and end in the very next scene where you have Vito Acconci announce, 'Let's say the revolution has failed. Okay, the revolution has failed.' Are you also referring to the exhaustion of a certain trajectory or strategy in video? This clip is excised from *The Red Tapes* (1976), after all, Vito's final single-channel tape. You also replay scenes from Joseph Cornell. Do you feel these are father figures or antecedents? (Cornell's body of work consists largely of 'found' and reworked materials; Acconci's work uses video to embody literature, to stage the voice.)

SR: The video is full of excerpts from others. I love the Acconci quote – he appears in close-up, blindfolded, perhaps about to be executed. The title of the video and half its music come from Harry Smith's *Anthology of American Folk Music*. I wanted to map out the mythology of contemporary America (misplaced paranoia, angels, new age, etc.), using Smith's anthology as a model. If all we knew about America was the Smith collection, the country would appear as darkly perverse and psychotic, a view that is both partial and accurate. I wanted to undertake a similar kind of mapping.

MH: Can you talk about your use of the Polaroids in the tape? In one scene you sing a Jennifer Lopez song in a whispery falsetto, while picking up a bevy of hard-ons and showing them to the camera, and then turning them face down, as if enumerating your collection. Why the Lopez song? And why do you reintroduce these pictures with gold leaf applied over their faces?

SR: There are several sections that include pornographic Polaroids. They had been originally sent to a straight swingers' magazine in the Midwest. I bought them on eBay for $80. In many of them, the guys try to establish anonymity by scratching out or covering up their eyes. Polaroids are kind of meaty: they have layers of plastic and chemicals, so the scratching-out can look like a wound. Matter is gouged away. I applied gold leaf to somehow undo this action, to reclaim it, to gild the profane. The song is 'Jenny from the Block.' It mentions Oprah, and I like to mention Oprah in as many videos as possible. The chorus tells us that the singer (Jennifer Lopez) is simultaneously grand and simple, that despite her fabulous wealth, she is still a poor girl at heart: 'Don't be fooled by the rocks that I got, I'm still Jenny from the block.' So now we have two ways to like her. She asks us to love the surface appearance, but to remember that there is something authentic beneath it. She gets to keep her dick and her eyes, while we have to choose.

MH: You play a reworked snippet of Laurie Anderson's 'O Superman' ('Here come the planes, they're American planes ... '), and show an Iraqi building target being destroyed. Cornell's ghostly figures return (it is their destiny somehow to keep recurring) with the quote 'crushed by accident/resurrected by design (Versatile Machine).' Is this quote yours? The broken body of science returns in several forms, most notably the adolescent boy whose body is too female and is given steroids in order to grow hair (do you see this boy as the allegorical figure of America itself?). Later the tape asks, do you remember the astronauts (and the way they carried the hope of a utopian science)? The science that has been used to build the machines of war has been turned on its own citizenry, and the result is an embodied catastrophe. Lying beneath *Anthology*'s fractured and sometimes very abrasive surface is a pointed political critique, taking aim at the American empire. Wouldn't you say?

SR: 'Crushed by accident/resurrected by design (Versatile Machine)' is something I came up with, so it isn't a quote, and I don't know what it means. It has something to do with the recent incarnation of the American military-industrial complex, which wages war 'surgically,' claiming that any damage is accidental, 'collateral.' And then, after all these unfortunate accidents, the same complex rebuilds. So it is a very versatile machine, building and destroying more or less simultaneously, and with sustained profit. But that is just the same old military-industrial complex at a somewhat accelerated pace. The difference is in a people who find it a good idea – necessary, even – to follow bombs with cute air-dropped care packages to demonstrate that they are really nice because they care.

But I can't claim that *Anthology* is pointed political critique – what I'm doing is murkier than that. The hope is that larger trajectories emerge out of the murk that I've been calling 'mythological landscape,' which is really, of course, a psychotic, paranoid, teleologically apocalypse-driven ideology. For the record, though, I love America. Once you get used to the obsequiousness and all. Plus, the food's not bad.

Regarding the Pain of Susan Sontag (Notes on Camp)

Steve Reinke's Videos

The Hundred Videos   289 min 1989–1996
Andy   9 min 1996
Everybody Loves Nothing (Empathic Exercises)   12 min 1996
Echo Valley   8 min 1998
Incidents of Travel   10 min 1998
How Photographs Are Stored in the Brain   8 min 1998
Spiritual Animal Kingdom   26 min 1998
Fireball   5 min 1999
Afternoon (March 21, 1999)   24 min 1999
Sad Disco Fantasia   24 min 2001
Amsterdam Camera Vacation   11 min 2001
J.-P. (Remix of *Tuesday and I* by Jean-Paul Kelly)   7 min 2002
Anal Masturbation and Object Loss   6 min 2002
The Chocolate Factory   28 min 2002
Anthology of American Folk Song   26 min 2004
Ghosts of Gay Porn   4 min 2005
Ask the Insects   8 min 2005
The Mendi   11 min 2006
Regarding the Pain of Susan Sontag (Notes on Camp)
   4 min 2006
My Rectum Is Not a Grave (To a Film Industry in Crisis)   7 min 2007
The Fallen   4 min 2007
Hobbit Love is the Greatest Love   14 min 2007
Election Defeat   3:30 min 2007
Final Thoughts, Series One   83 min 2007

Distributed by Argos, LUX, Video Data Bank and Vtape.

Steve Reinke is an artist and writer best known for his work in video. He lives in Toronto and Chicago, where he is associate professor of Art Theory and Practice at Northwestern. Recent books: *Everybody Loves Nothing: Video 1996–2004* (Coach House) and the anthology *The Sharpest Point: Animation at the End of Cinema* (edited with Chris Gehman).
www.myrectumisnotagrave.com

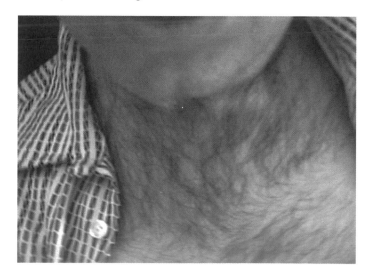

ALEESA COHENE

TWICE-TOLD TALES

She would like to swap the mask of ambivalence for the mask of certainty. After a screening, she pulls me to one side and tells me that our friend Mark is dead – Mark, the relentless optimist and animal activist, the vegan anarchist, the tall handsome editor of my last four features who worked tirelessly and never had a bad word to say about anyone. He looked after others a little too well, and used his kindness to cover up his own difficulties. We will miss him so very much, but after Aleesa tells me, I don't know what to say, and for a moment she does all the feeling for the two of us.

Aleesa's work is related to 'received wisdoms'; it is largely made of footage made by others, and from this archive she extracts, with an uncanny precision, particular moments. While the role of the found-footage artist is hardly a new one (even TV promos feature clip montages culled from the vaults), this is so very different. Aleesa gathers so that she can change the speed of her materials – she lets them settle inside her until they become her pictures. These images wouldn't 'belong' to her any more than if she had gone out and shot them herself. Somehow, her role as an artist involves the recasting of these pictures into moments of her own life. These small instants, grown back inside the body, then become a new alphabet that she uses to write new stories that belong entirely to her. And then to all of us.

Over and over again, she returns to the middle-class home where actions that never happened for the first time recur again and again. This sutured medley, broken and reassembled to show where the cracks are, make evident something of the strain of having to live inside these houses. She shows us the pictures we live inside. She arms herself with her feeling, and then she moves out into the world where everything is a bit too much and overly sensitive, and from these difficulties a politic arrives. The stakes are high, the pictures already overcoded, the machines are waiting. She is ready. After everything that's happened, there are stories waiting to be told.

MH: Has every experience already been photographed? Is that why you use found footage?

AC: Every experience and emotion cannot possibly be photographed – that's why I use found footage. The realms of experience and emotion are infinite, yet so many of us choose familiarity and stability over risk and the unknown. I'm fascinated by how much silence and suffocation there is in each human interaction.

We watch movies to feel something more than we allow ourselves to feel in our everyday lives. Recorded images and sounds double as mirrored echoes where we don't have to look or listen to ourselves, we only have to be quiet and watch the screen. I think this is an everlasting power of cinema. It permits us to be who we want to be, free from responsibility and action. It releases us from guilt and shame. The more I pick through old movies, the more I find a history of this psychological etiquette.

My work aspires to understand why we live in a poverty of emotion and how it can change.

MH: So you feel that becoming like the pictures that surround us could make us more human? What a lovely idea. But don't movies also render us helpless and infantile? It's not my fault, it's not my problem – moviegoing equals actions without consequences, and what could be more dangerous than that? Many sociologists, certainly censor boards and the governments they represent, are quick to point to the negative impact of moviegoing. Do you feel its outpouring of feelings outweighs these disadvantages?

AC: It's both these forces that attract me to using found footage. The tears that stream down my face when I watch *A Birth Story*, coupled with the difficulties I have with so many aspects of parenting, is a familiar disjunct of our technological times. Without the tears, despondency reigns, and if anyone is going to change something they believe is wrong, they have to know how they feel about it first. We live in a society that mistakes cohesiveness for political action and sameness for power. Most movies (at their ideological core) perpetuate this. But I think the emotion we take away from movies overrides their plots. Perhaps that's why stories don't change and people do.

MH: Some would argue that you are doing nothing creatively, you're not adding anything new, only parasitically taking what others have done and reshuffling it before signing the results. How would you respond to these criticisms?

AC: I would argue that everything is made by reshuffling. New buildings are based on parts of existing buildings. Medicine is based on new combinations of chemicals. Nothing is without multiple origins. Origins can be hidden or exposed, and I'm not interested in hiding what I edit. My creative tool is editing, and without footage my art is not visible.

MH: Can you describe your process of collecting pictures? Do you have a source archive from which your pictures are drawn, or are you continually on the hunt, looking out for another, better shot?

AC: I have an archive of shots I've been collecting for the past five years. I'm also always on the hunt. I try to stay ahead of a desperate hunt, though, which always involves a shot that is too specific. I've decided that these shots don't exist – I only want them to. Instead, I have a system of collecting things in groups: people walking down hallways, climbing stairs, driving cars, sleeping, on the phone, taking a bath, running away, opening and closing doors and windows. Once I've grouped clips into thematic categories, I make subgroups of emotional categories. I find sound harder to divide this specifically, so I organize it differently, such as: ambience and texture, sound effects, ethical assertions, emotional expressions, excuses, admittances, beliefs and anyone discussing truth. With each idea I focus on, there are always other

Ready to Cope

fear of chaos. Chaos breeds strictness and strictness privileges sameness. The same cycle exists in the hundreds of horror movies I went through: something disrupts or invades a clean house, a good relationship, a sweet family, a good intention. A desire for goodness is destined for disturbance. This then became my focus. How do we define goodness? How do we protect ourselves from impending doom? These difficult questions took a long time to build a narrative around, especially since many of their qualities are repressed and nuanced.

MH: Is it necessary to arrive at new forms and new relationships in your own life before being able to apply them in your movies?

AC: Yes. For the past seven years my work has been based on the questions *What do I believe? And what am I afraid of that makes me believe that?* The answers to both questions always have something to do with the ideas I trust and the relationships I have.

Lately I've experienced a rawness that is very new to me. I easily lose a sense of myself. I'm overwhelmed by anxiety and hesitation. I guess I feel like I'm fighting a lot of skepticism. I trust fewer people than I used to. I remember feeling something important going on inside me and sharing it with several people, looking for different perspectives and reactions. Now I barely want to talk about important personal things, as though they will change if they get out, as though I'll lose something. The examples I can think of are small and wouldn't make much sense to anyone else.

The person who is closest to me right now is Tema, and she hates the word *integrity*. She understands it as a grandiose idea about Truth and Properness, something no one can live up to even though everyone tries. It's an archetypal vision of 'rightness.' A choice you make one day may seem full of integrity while another choice might negate that integrity. This contradiction is how we are human. The idea of integrity is a static unflinching notion, but to be human is not. She says that the only beings that have integrity are animals. Her distaste exposes the conflict in ways that aren't possible on my own. We argue about it all the time; I feel the conflict is primarily within oneself, a grappling with an inner knowledge of right and wrong. She tries to determine what is most compassionate outside of her personal desires. She spends a lot of time with animals.

When I was first being politicized in my early 20s, feminism and anti-oppression politics taught me to be an ally, to speak from my experience and to hear other people's opinions as their experience and to understand my privilege. It was my responsibility to identify my own prejudices and actions that perpetuate oppression. Dialogue and discussion are necessary to learn how to listen non-defensively and communicate respectfully if an anti-oppression practice is going to be successful. I realize now how deeply skeptical I am and how far apart experiences are from how they get told – how 'owning' an experience invites

categories I create for the footage I find. Generally, though, I'm looking for moments before and after an event. Whether it's anxiousness, anticipation, denial or relief, the emotions that frame actions are points of relation – they might be mine or yours.

MH: Are there some shots that are so powerful, so moving, that you want to make a movie simply so this moment can be felt in the way you feel it?

AC: Yes. These are also the shots I can't put into a category other than 'favourites.' They are moments that are layered with complex and multiple emotions. I often use them to structure a video. The first shot in *Ready to Cope* of the boy picking leaves off the bush is an example. He seems so sad and at the same time paralyzed by his sadness. In the original movie, he had just killed his brother when they were out hunting. His shock and grief are buried by guilt, which is what I believe national security is based on. That's why I chose it to open *Ready to Cope*.

MH: You spent a good while cutting *Ready to Cope* (7 min, 2006) – why so long? Were you looking for a new relation to your pictures, trying to get them to 'make sense' in a different way?

AC: Beginning in August 2005, I scheduled one day each week to edit *Ready to Cope* and *Supposed To*. However, I've found it impossible in my work life as an editor to predict the length of a project. The work I was doing for money often bled into time for my own videos. Juggling this aside, I also encountered many other challenges with these pieces. My first intention was to concentrate on our cultural obsession with uniformity and homogeneity. Once I felt I had collected enough images and sounds and began a paper edit, I discovered that the underlying fear of these themes was far more interesting and pervasive, especially with recent political debate regarding safety and security in Canada. It's clear to me that my own desire for order is very much grounded in a comparisonism and often competition, and how often self-reflection deepens oblivion. In moments I think I'm being straightforward, people seem confused. I've always thought of myself as overly sensitive but often get told I'm not sensitive enough. In the darkest part of this reality, tragedies are compared and compassion is measured accordingly. It feels as though theory and practice are colliding with one another, cancelling each other out. An insidious system of erasure resides at the base of the ideas I trust most. I see it in the world, in myself and in others.

I remember a few days after the second levy broke in New Orleans, I was at a bar with friends. People were discussing connections they had to people affected by the tragedy. One person talked about a woman she knows who was getting ready to leave New Orleans to go to school in San Francisco. She made it to San Francisco having lost all her possessions. She had only the clothes she was wearing and the items in the bag she was carrying. The person telling the story explained that she came from a fucked-up home: 'Her mother collects Barbie dolls,' she said. I got angry with her and asked why that meant her home was necessarily fucked up. The conversation died prematurely (as most conflicts do), but I still think about it. What bothers me most is that a sad situation cannot simply be sad, it needs to be punctuated by morality in the form of what I believe was understood in this case as feminism. Whether or not this woman's mother's Barbie collection was a source of abuse, neurosis, a hobby or art, it cannot define wrongness by itself. Nothing can. Like an anti-oppression framework, feminism is deeply committed to ideas about not generalizing feelings, thoughts or behaviours, and is therefore devoted to reconstructing and redefining power. Yet I'm not sure most feminists or anti-oppression activists are personally committed to the same things. We want to tell a good story, to make people laugh, to be loved. We want things to set us apart and make us feel special. The woman telling the story wanted to hold an audience. For many reasons there's shame in these desires, causing us to hide and to value opinions over feelings. I know I've said many things just like the woman who told this story. Perhaps the reason it stayed with me is because it reminded me of ways I don't like myself.

MH: *Ready to Cope* begins with a voice-over that asks, 'In the history of Canada, has there been a crisis this deep, this merciless?' Where did you find this quotation and what drew you to it?

AC: I found this piece of audio in a documentary about farmers' rights in Canada from the early '80s. It was one of the first things I knew I needed to use. The woman speaking is passionate and honest. I was especially drawn to the idea of a 'merciless' crisis providing a shell for the cyclic relationship between self-protection, denial and national security issues. I'm interested in how drawn we are to wanting and needing mercy when we often can't give ourselves a break.

I also knew that I wanted to establish the ideas in *Ready to Cope* within a frame. When something is named a crisis, there is often more tolerance for emotion, hysteria, speed (or immediacy) and even a kind of abstractness that is not acceptable in a 'professional' environment. *Ready to Cope* contains all of these elements, so announcing a crisis set an appropriate stage.

MH: Your movie is framed by people taking the next step, in high heels and sneakers, inside and out. The effort of going on, of getting up over a paralyzing sense of malaise and anxiety, is everywhere palpable. Much of this dread is centred in homes where doors are ominously approached and hallways are the circulation system of unseen fears. Why have you placed the middle (class) home at the epicentre of these fears?

AC: 'The middle home' is an interesting way to look at it. For me, the home is where most of our unconscious fears are rooted and where we act through and against them. In a lot of my work it functions as a figurative source for the themes I address. As a child, it was in my own home where I first learnt to manipulate, to dwell in insecurities, and mostly to feel the depths of hopelessness and despair. I grew up feeling affected by everything: stuffed animals that had a bad look in their eyes, wallpaper patterns that moved at night, babysitters I hated the smell of and fantasies of running away so I could be a different person. I would put on a dress that I hated, pack a bag and walk out the front door. I remember thinking that if I wore an ugly dress people would treat me differently and I could begin a new life. Nothing felt right, though nothing was ever all that wrong.

But 'the middle home' is a place that is similarly represented by most movies. Unlike my own obscure memories of growing up, the collective home functions as a receptor for collective fears that we can attach to our personal experiences. A creepy shadow in the hallway reminds me of the shifting cloud patterns on the wallpaper in my childhood room. Only now I have an enemy. This same shadow reminds you of an early fear of yours, and in an instant we have a shared enemy.

When I was developing ideas about safety and security for *Ready to Cope*, I knew I had to disassemble why movies can scare us so profoundly. The connections to our early understandings of fear have no explanations for many of us, and illuminate why similar narratives can scare us infinitely. Movies provide us with pictures that we've been waiting to put content into and explanations we crave. Conscious or not, the fear we feel when watching movies must be a continuation of where it all began, but often stripped of its original uniqueness and sometimes capable of providing false and easy answers.

In *Ready to Cope*, I wanted to bring the obscurity of early experiences of fear back into a collective dread and anxiety. What if the creepy shadow is my own? What if I forgot to lock the door and the wind blew it open? I focused on the home in order to ask questions like these and to bring focus to our only true collective enemy: ourselves.

MH: The home shrinks and bursts open until a body falls from the sky, lies on the grass, runs into woods. When images of home return, they are seized with a new pressure and violence; they build until they break in a shattering storm of broken windows and dishes. You close the movie with a trio of shots: a woman puts it all away in her cupboards, a girl bends down, a sneaker leaves the room. It is a powerful ending, especially because the movie stops here. Why these three shots, why are you filled with so much hope?

AC: At the end of *Ready to Cope*, a woman is searching through all her cupboards. Looking for something but unable to find it. In the next shot a girl creeps down and peers under a stall, knowing that something or someone is there. And yes, a man's sneakers leave (or enter) a room, and the movie ends. I never thought of this ending as hopeful, but I suppose it is. I edited the video to reflect the idea that the fear we feel is a fear of ourselves. So I structured the last 30 seconds (three shots) of the video as a reprise of my thesis. The reprise begins with a frantic search (shot #1), a feeling of having lost or misplaced something can feel like you've lost a part of yourself. Then, from within (shot #2), you gather some courage and look one last time. Maybe it's the last place it could possibly be, maybe you hear a strange noise and know it's there. In the final shot, action is required, you must choose to enter or exit. I know that my translation of these images might not be communicated to the audience the same way I've explained it here. But like all my work, I hope it's experienced in flux, as we experience things emotionally. Maybe this is why you feel like I'm hopeful. I think hope is possible only when you know things will change and that you can participate in the change.

MH: The pictures your movies are drawn from are from other people's movies, from a 'public record,' so I'm wondering what your relation to your audience is. Once upon a time you were 'equal,' both spectators in a theatre, or video store patrons. But now you have taken portions of this shared understanding, this visible inheritance, and turned them to your own ends. Are you attempting to activate a new kind of spectatorship? Who are your movies for? Only the usual suspects – those who attend art-video fests, for instance?

AC: I'm of two minds. On one hand, my relationship to my audience is strange. There is so little dialogue about video art (about so many things) and my work speaks to this. So I'm often confused by my audience. Who they are, who I want them to be, what they think, what I hope they think. This confused silence of mine and theirs feeds new ideas for new projects, so it's sometimes hard to imagine anything different, any 'new kind of spectatorship.'

On the other hand, I have a lot of fantasies about who my movies are for and where they could show. I feel like they are trailers for our problems. I think about what it would take to offer art as a public service. I imagine an advertisement:

Feeling anxious?
So are we.
Watch this movie ...
If you feel worse, that's good.
If you feel better, that's good.

My divided perspective is probably why I make work in isolation, but most days I work as an editor with various community groups and other artists to produce videos they want to make. I haven't found a balance, and I'm not sure if there is one.

MH: *Supposed To* (7 min, 2006) has a feeling of barely controlled rage that is smoothed over by its sweet pop electronica and your assured montage. But I'm wondering if you could talk about the origin of this visceral anger – the movie feels like it wants to reach out of the monitor and choke me. Like your other work, this movie is made up of pictures made by others – why is it important to refract your feelings through others? Are you using found footage the way others would deploy actors and scripts?

AC: When I first started thinking about and using found footage, I was also reading a lot about psychoanalytic theories of projection. The idea that we attribute to others our undesirable thoughts and emotions became key for many personal and political questions. Found footage is the cultural source of an ingrained defence mechanism.

Undesirable characteristics are not only being displaced onto other people but also onto animals, inanimate objects and social constructs. We create scapegoats in order to feel better. When I feel frustrated about something in my life, I'll often hate the way a piece of furniture looks. I'll move it around the room hoping to like it better at a different angle, in a different spot. Editing of all sorts has become the manifestation of many of my feelings, anger included. Anytime I dig for the root cause of a feeling, possibilities and combinations multiply. Nothing feels like it exists without its past and future relationships. The origins of my anger exist equally in my past and in movies I haven't seen yet.

Supposed To

MH: Because you work with status quo pictures, are you concerned that the many people who are never represented in movies (the working poor, immigrants, the elderly ...) are similarly missing from your work? Does your work mimic the exclusions of mainstream media?

AC: The images I choose are steeped in representational stereotypes. And the presentation of the work (as you've indicated) is exclusive and limited (video festivals and galleries). These realities weigh on me and at the same time push me to keep working.

I'm always interested in what type of person is cast to play different emotions. There are so many hidden rules. When a horror movie deals with an 'unknown phenomenon,' the main character is usually a white woman with straight brown hair. If her hair is curly, then perhaps she's called the evil to her, and if she isn't white, well, then she is the phenomenon itself. The racist, classist, sexist realities of these movies have been analyzed by many people and it's my hope to continue the discussion using the pictures themselves.

Abscess

MH: A young girl looks into a mirror, but when we see the answering shot, it is a man's face that looks back at her. Throughout this movie you disperse subjectivity between genders and across different age groups. You ask us to unify these experiences, these bodies. I understood the climactic scene where a man crashes through a window as emblematic of this broken subjectivity. As a viewer, my identification is asked to shuttle between the two poles of broken and whole.

Supposed To is carefully structured, filled with rhyming gestures (a hand wipes the windshield of a car, other hands grip a steering wheel, a third shot shows yet another car on the road, though the montage makes it feel as if it's all the same car). Can you talk about the overall structure of *Supposed To*, with its prelude of first steps, its attempted escape, the window crash, the telephone call and the return home?

AC: Like all my videos, *Supposed To* is structured through intuition. I'll write scripts prior to editing, or make elaborate paper edits to structure the argument I want to make, but it always changes during editing. Each shot has its own rhythm and each edit its own metre, so no matter what I want to say conceptually, I'm led primarily by mood. The montage produces a sequence of emotions; the struggle is for the emotions to say what I mean.

Supposed To begins with a scene of a boy helping an old man take off his boots. The old man pushes the boy's bum with his foot to help him get the boot off. The scene is simultaneously sweet and creepy and acts as a prelude for an investigation about obligation and guilt. Following this is a series of feet taking steps through a field, up stairs, in hallways, outside a door. It is a collective arrival by people who, at least in my mind, have come to hear: 'There's a whole machine that works because everyone does what they are supposed to. I found out I was supposed to be something I didn't like.' From here the movie begins unravelling the complexity of work: a suitcase falls, a woman scrambles through her wallet and sees that her ID is gone, another woman falls into a pool, a man in a uniform collapses and shots of losing oneself are interwoven with people at work. A man sits at a table eating bananas in milk as another voice talks about working nine to five and how that 'snuffs out eccentricities' and results in passive aggression. A woman vacuums. A girl looks into a mirror and sees someone else. This continues from person to person, each facing herself in order to see another. People are shocked, confused and frustrated.

This catalyzes a change and escape. A woman puts on her housecoat and another woman looks out the window. A young woman frantically gets into a van, people are packing, and a series of cars driving occurs. A boy sitting in a vehicle turns his head and says, 'Know what I did?' A shot of scattered clothes and broken glass follows. A woman is on the phone, she covers the receiver and says, 'He broke a window.' The escape has prompted a confession about something that hasn't happened, or at least doesn't seem wrong. The confession itself has caused a crime. A series of people fall through windows, and glass is scattered on various floors. A boy is running away. A man lies face down on the shore.

The final scene begins with the phone ringing. A woman picks it up and hears a man's voice saying, 'Time has come to put aside childish things ... ' Three more women are listening on the phone and one says, 'Okay,' in response. The man continues, 'Face up to who you are ... ' Three more woman listen. The man says, '... suspicions of destiny ... ', ' ... surely you must be feeling it ... ' A woman answers, 'Yes, I am.' The voice continues, 'We all have them ... ' and a boy on the phone answers, 'Oh, okay.' The man concludes, ' ... a deep, wordless knowledge.' A woman looking in shock hangs up the phone followed by a series of hang-ups and a boy saying, 'Did I do anything wrong?' Shots of a few people located outside houses appear and a woman says, 'I thought it was all over.' A woman enters a room and takes off her stockings, another woman drops her keys and the final woman drops her coat, returns to a bed, sits down, hesitates to pick up the phone and instead sits in silence and bows her head.

I hope the end explains itself. For me, the scene is very dramatic and enters a new territory – something I will develop more in new projects.

MH: *All Right* (7 min, 2003) is a very unusual hybrid film: part found-footage collage, part immigration polemic. Can you talk about how you became involved with issues of displacement, borders and Canadian immigration? Why did you mix these concerns with found footage, and how does the 'other' footage function in the movie?

AC: The ideas in *All Right* are based on experiences I had doing various types of activist work around new immigration policies and detainee issues after 9/11. I learned about a Toronto Immigrant Holding Centre that is a converted motel near the airport where refugees and immigrants were being held for long periods of time in poor conditions, behind razor wire, without information about why they were there. This detention centre was called the Celebrity Inn and is now called the Heritage Inn. It is a large place where people (mostly women and children) are brought directly from the airport. Reena, my ex-girlfriend, worked with a group that made visits to the centre, played cards with some of the people and worked to get them the aid and information they needed. *All Right* grew out of the reality that refugees and immigrants can be arrested or detained without criminal charges and held indefinitely once they arrive in Canada until they are granted citizenship.

Once I started researching immigration issues in government-sponsored footage, I realized that we have been talking about the same issues in Canada for years. Many of the documentaries I searched through were made in the early '80s and still felt relevant in 2004. I believe that there is an unstated kind of racism in Canada.

When I was in high school, there were a lot of Asian immigrants from Hong Kong in my classes. They had been sent to Vancouver without their parents; many had cars and houses, that's where the parties were. My mother said the reason mothers didn't accompany their children is because they were afraid that their husbands would be unfaithful. She had no Asian friends, so there was no way for her to know anything about the lives of these people, but this story made her feel more comfortable with them being 'everywhere.' Many referred to the new immigrants as the 'Asian invasion.' People said it freely without any shame, without any reference to their own immigrant history. When I was growing up, racism was never called racism, it was simply entitlement and maybe very complex fear. When I started thinking about the characteristics of this shameless racism, many images came to mind. I began looking for movie moments where people are confused, unable to see anything around them. There's a shot in *All Right* showing a guy from his thighs down;

he's on a gravel road and kicks a rock. It's so defeatist, it feels like a powerless, childish gesture. There's a woman wearing a dress searching through a grassy field. The drama of her action foreshadows the fact that she's not going to find whatever she's looking for. A woman turns a corner and runs down a hallway; without seeing who is chasing her or what she's running from, she can only be running from herself.

The movie opens with a boy bending down to kiss something, and a creepy woman's voice says, 'Feel it, it makes you strong.' Her voice provides an emotional anthem for the piece, an emotional calling for the nationalism that the movie takes up later. A woman turns to a man in a car and asks him if he feels it, and he responds, 'I feel things as they come, come on.' This concludes the anthem. He opens a door, and another man walks through a door into a bedroom, suspicious of something being under the covers. He tears off the covers and nothing is there. What stops people from feeling things as they come are suspicions. Then the song begins and the title comes up. We work to make things seem all right, but they never are because we're not present to how we really feel. These fears are also felt on a nationwide level.

I took footage from a Canadian documentary called *Who Gets In?* and officer training movies from Immigration Canada. In one sequence we watch an interaction between an immigration officer and a woman who is applying to immigrate, through the lens of emotional manipulation. They have this exchange.

> 'Because you want to upgrade? Because you want to study computers? Well, I'll tell you honestly, very honestly, I don't believe you.'
>
> 'Sir, but ... '
>
> 'That's what I think. The new employment that you want to find in Canada I don't know what you're going to find in Canada. I'm meaning that I'm not sure that you know what you're going to find in Canada. Because you know nothing about Canada. I would not invest anything if I were you. You will not be going to Canada.'

What he uses to make a decision about her application is based on a judgment on what she knows or doesn't know about a country she's never been to. It's manipulative criteria. They're not having a conversation – he's telling her what he believes, and what she thinks. Based on his judgment of her, he's decided that she's not eligible. When a real dialogue doesn't take place, interaction is reduced to superficial impressions and racisms. Scenes like this helped explain to me why no one knows and even fewer care that a motel has been turned into a covert detention centre.

MH: There is a striking shot where a blond woman comforts a large naked man. Can you talk about the origin of this scene and why you included it in your movie?

AC: This shot comes from one of my favourite movies, called *Brainwash*. It's about a woman (the blond) who takes over a company using psychological tactics that break people down to their rawest emotional selves. The naked fat man is Buddy; she asks him to strip in front of a group of men and then talks him through his childhood sexual abuse as the explanation for his weight. I keep thinking I'll use the whole scene, but I tend to grab tiny bits from it for various projects. She manipulates the employees of the company under the guise of compassion and moral integrity. The shot that I use in *All Right* occurs at the end of the scene. Buddy exposes himself, physically and emotionally, as she encourages him to cry. He does and she hugs him. What stands out for me is the complication behind compassion and care. At the time, this scene felt a lot like what gets called 'standard procedure' by the Immigration Canada, when it is really the excuse for arbitrary treatments.

MH: Your new movies have just premiered at the Impakt Festival in the Netherlands. How was it?

AC: *Supposed To* was a part of a program called *Survival of the Fittest*, which carried this description: 'The rat race of modern life makes ever greater demands on its participants. For the moment, there is no room for compassion with the less talented. What does stress do to people, how far can you go in your ambitions, and what will the future of our industrial society look like?'

The Central Museum's auditorium is a black glass box that makes day feel like night. When you're inside the building you can see the outside darkened through the tinted glass, but when you're outside you can't see in. *Supposed To* screened second in the program. Following the first voice of an old man saying, 'Help me out with these boots, would ya?' there was a loud noise. I thought something screwed up with a speaker, but when I looked over I saw a guy on the outside of the building with a hose spraying the side windows. The projectionist went over and banged his fist on the glass. The man didn't hear the banging and continued washing the window until the projectionist went outside to tell him to stop. The entire interaction was visible from inside the theatre and functioned as a replacement scene for the first three minutes of the video.

When the screening was over, I took a train back to Amsterdam and thought about what had happened. In many ways, it was a perfect live scene for the movie. I've often wondered how I might want to integrate live components into my work. Maybe this is a beginning. Two men were trying to do their jobs and one conflicted with the other. Both men were angry and the audience was watching. I was embarrassed. I was embarrassed for the window washer who was not only told to stop doing his job but was being watched by everyone inside without knowing. I was embarrassed for the projectionist who tried to tell the window washer to stop and in doing so became just as much a spectacle as the disruptive window washing. And I was really embarrassed for myself, as though I had planned the whole thing.

Aleesa Cohene's Videos

Absolutely   8:24 min 2001
Abscess   10:18 min 2001
Alter   20-min loop 2003 (installation)
All Right   7 min 2003
Supposed To   7 min 2006
Ready to Cope   7 min 2006

Distributed by Vtape.

Toronto-based artist Aleesa Cohene produces videos and video installations that seek to occupy the oppositional zone between ideas and emotion, cultural belief and personal integrity. Her work has shown in film and video festivals across Canada as well as in Brazil, Germany, Holland, Russia, Scandinavia, Turkey and the United States, and has won prizes at Utrecht's Impakt Festival and Toronto's Images Festival. www.aleesacohene.com

HO TAM

SEASON OF THE BOYS

If Ho Tam isn't the hardest-working man in show biz, it isn't for lack of trying. When I meet him, which is not so often, he seems always in motion, even when he's sitting in the opposite chair. Already there are new commitments and promises for work that has to be made, and students who are absorbing the precious resource of time and an inner life that is steadily flowing away from him. Who has enough clock for private moments or a day outside of the work flow? Since stepping away from his social-worker persona, Ho has proved himself a tireless producer of paintings and videos. In both media he is a diligent collector of faces, accumulating them the way others build stamp or base-ball-card collections. In *Matinee Idol*, for instance, he gathers moments from the great Hong Kong screen star Ng Cho Fan's 250 films and shows him in a catalogue of emotions. Here he is crying. Here he is laughing. Here he is greeting his long-lost daughter. Ho offers us behavioural studies, as if he were new to this planet; as if, by watching this work, we might also become new, with eyes fresh enough to see the world around us, instead of being content to name everything instead.

The frame of his work is carefully considered. The first step is the most important – it indicates a direction, an intent. After he takes the first step, the rest of the way is relatively clear for him. He simply moves forward, completing the initial gesture until the frame is full, the catalogue is complete, the set has been mapped out. He offers us collections of Chinese barbershops on the Lower East Side. He shows 99 Chinese businessmen, one after another, looking back at a still camera. How are the humans today? Perhaps by accumulating their behaviour, it will be possible to understand their motivations and common interests. Little wonder these catalogues have morphed in his later work into an abiding interest in the portrait movie, whether it's the string-playing cop in Hong Kong or AIDS activist James Wentzy. In the face of globalized pictures, and the globalized subjects and cities they are busy creating, Ho's models for living – his small portraits and possible lives – are more necessary now than ever.

MH: Most art begins with the act of copying: I want to make something that looks like that, or I want to become someone who lives like that. How did you become involved with fringe media? Did you have a significant mimetic moment that led you into the field, and once you got here why would you go on, knowing that this work is so terribly marginal? Aren't you concerned about obscurity, singing songs no one will ever hear?

HT: I am now sitting in a café called Mirage run by a guy from Peru. I visited here [Victoria] during my job interview and apartment search and found it quite soothing. For the last two months I have been working at a frantic pace on my university job and the upcoming show at Paul Petro Gallery and the Reel Asian Festival screening, plus a number of other things. Life is a bit crazy and I really have to get away from home/workstations to gain some form of privacy in order to correspond with you.

I guess I have no one to blame getting into a situation like this. Sometimes I feel like I am at a dead end. I was talking to a friend in Seattle and we agreed that its a hard life being an artist and would never encourage anyone to pursue it unless they feel there are no other choices.

Well, this goes back to your question about where I started. I actually studied to become a social worker. I was doing placement in a community psychiatric program that had an art therapy component. While watching individuals making art, I realized it was what I really wanted to do. That began my downfall.

I began by exploring commercial art and did quite well, but it was not satisfying because I was mostly a tool. I worked and worked and by the end of the day there was no energy to do anything creative for myself. So I went back to work in the community health field as a life-skills counsellor, employment counsellor and then as a case manager. Each of these jobs assisted individuals to live and work outside of institutions. In all those jobs I talked constantly, seven hours a day, making treatment plans and suggestions. During this period I found time to explore art again and began exhibiting in some Toronto group shows.

There were two very supportive persons in my life: Kirby Hsu, my deceased partner, and Carla Garnet, of the Garnet Press Gallery. They were very influential in shaping me to become the person I am today. Without them I would probably have continued to be a Sunday painter.

My work is drawn from my day-to-day experience, and tries to represent the under-represented.

When you speak about fringe media, I guess you mean video/film art. I was interested in all forms of artmaking. But due to my limited training (self-taught with some night schooling), I was mostly confined to disciplines like painting and drawing. I have always been interested in bookmaking and print work. In 1993 I made an artist's chapbook called *The Yellow Pages*, playing with issues around racial stereotypes. It examines questions like: what is a real Asian, or a real Asian experience? Nobody is safe from scrutiny, and I became confused about what I should or shouldn't do. I had made chapbooks when I was a teenager, and produced many flyers in my commercial work, so the print medium was natural for me. The book was Xeroxed and hand-bound by pins and fasteners. It is an alphabetically arranged book (A–Z) with headings corresponding to various qualities typically attributed to Asians. For instance, a picture showing a woman carrying a serving tray with a steaming plate of meat had the subtitle 'Dog meat.' A picture showing a pair of skeletons, one smaller than the other (father and son?), had the subtitle 'Number one son.'

Did I want to copy? I think I have always been copying. My background in advertising and graphics encourages borrowing and stealing images from everywhere. One of the great technical innovations in the '80s and '90s was the popularization of the photocopier. My experience in advertising taught me lots about that. *The Yellow Pages* is a book made from the idea of photocopying. But you have to understand, in those days images were not as accessible as they are today. The act of copying could be painstaking. You had to be very dedicated because it took time and money.

Then I chanced upon a call for submissions from Public Access, an exhibition collective, which had arranged to put video projections into the central train station, and I thought the book could translate well into this new context. *The Yellow Pages* (7:40 min, 1994) installation at Union Station was a ten-foot projection in the lobby, but the station is so huge even this large projection was lost in space. The video used an approach similar to that of the chapbook; both were based on a collage of found images that required lots of research and image collecting via tape and TV viewing.

The Yellow Pages is a tape made in the climate of political correctness and historic facts/fictions. It doesn't present a single point of view, it leaves that to the viewer, but because everything cancels each other out, viewer negotiation is difficult. This was my response to the policing of thoughts and actions. At the time I was just working with what I knew. I had been to film and video screenings but I was not so aware of video art. When I look at it now, the piece is similar to Martha Rosler's *Semiotics of the Kitchen*, in structure anyway.

I am totally aware of my obscure existence. Once upon a time, I read an artist's interview (I think I still have the clipping) that once you practice for five or ten years, you will not have the skills to do anything else. You have to continue being an artist because you're not trustworthy or employable. But then again, I could not think of another job I would rather do.

But I do see myself trying to connect with reality in my own little ways. It may be a very lame attempt. My work does not totally renounce or reject the world, in my opinion. But perhaps it is situated in a neither/nor position that is not understood by mainstream viewers or artists. Do I care? Yes and no. I'm allowed to make only the things I want to. If I were a commercial artist, I would probably make things that had more mass appeal.

The Yellow Pages

It is two days later and I am back in the same café. I am still working frantically on (or just feeling frantic about) the upcoming shows. This is probably the last weekend before going back to work and my trip to Toronto.

I did not make another video for many years after *The Yellow Pages*. I think it had to do with equipment accessibility and my phobia about technology. I was accustomed to paintbrushes and pencils, not cameras, which I picked up almost for the first time when making this work. In 1996 I went to New York City for the Whitney Museum Independent Study Program. I had no space to work because of the studio and apartment situation in the city. I also began to question product-making and the art market. These factors turned me toward video-making again. I made about ten tapes in the four years I lived in New York City.

I'm still trying to reconcile all the different kinds of work I make, discovering how human experience can be shown in each of the mediums I work with. When comparing different mediums, I find video/film liberating for me. Narratives communicate to the viewer in a more straightforward way than painting or drawing. Visual art concerns have become rather alienating. I do not feel that I have to follow a trajectory in video. I could start a new project that has nothing to do with the last. And the work can travel. If I could speak and write English better, I would rather be a writer, but then most writers want to be filmmakers. So I guess it is not so bad, after all.

MH: *Season of the Boys* (3:30 min, 1997) shows a group of shirtless teen Asian basketball players. In voice-over you recite a story about the season of the boys, their beauty reflected everywhere. You say, 'History will repeat itself to no end. Together we shall fight and rebel, following the path that each of us has chosen. But secretly we believe the myth of that special season will return; someday the boys will come into our lives once more and we shall not be alone. Or rather, we ourselves shall become the boys we so often dreamed of, the boys of a season gone by right before our very eyes.' It is a beautiful and moving text. Can you talk about how the idea for this movie came to you?

HT: Most of the tapes I made in the past were not premeditated. I often gathered material, and ideas came later. *Season of the Boys* was made the year after I lost my partner to AIDS. I was in New York City, alone, isolated, and wandered by chance into a basketball tournament. Watching the guys was both exciting and depressing. I was contemplating life and death, beauty and youth, the fragility of existence. I was only 35 then! These questions expanded to gay culture; I was thinking about its shallowness, for instance.

Yes, I wrote the text myself and I am a little embarrassed about it. I sound much older than my age – at least, people who have watched the tape tell me that. Before losing my partner I had a happy-go-lucky attitude toward life. It was particularly hard for me, even though it was not a straightforward path either. It took me a long time to find my art, for instance, and coming out was difficult. But I usually got what I wanted and I was quite spoiled. After losing my partner I started to look at my surroundings differently. I think internally I was either very depressed by the grieving or I had aged ten years. I took on a more critical and contemplative stance. Gay culture is often so youth-and-beauty oriented. There is a hierarchy built into this culture, and certain attributes are considered desirable. I think 'liberation' and globalization have only made it worse. For a long time, perhaps this phenomenon existed only in North America, but now it seems to have spread all over. Since the 'desirer' and the 'desiree' are basically the same person in this situation, we are just victimizing ourselves.

MH: In *Dear Sis* (4:30 min, 1998), you film a young girl on the subway who seems entirely unaware of the camera. How did you film her? A voice-over text narrates a letter from a woman to her sister, hoping to make peace. Why this letter with its sentiments of loss, absence and betrayal?

HT: *Dear Sis* is about human relationships: how one reaches out and another shuts down. I thought of my relationship with my sister while watching the girl on the train. The image was taken with a camcorder on my lap without the family realizing the tape was rolling. Of course, the text is also about race and equity issues, because being born into a certain racial and social class shapes experience. So while the text is personal, it acquires a political stance as it goes on.

I am a middle-aged Canadian-Asian man looking at a young African-American girl. That is a very interesting position. Perhaps I have an idealistic stand that all of us should be equal. Living in N.Y.C. really opened my eyes to the segregations of race and class and the huge inequities that persist. Parts of the city were no different than the Third World. And then there are always

Dear Sis

misconceptions and misunderstandings among the 'Others.' *Dear Sis* tries to offer a glimpse into this scenario.

Season of the Boys and *Dear Sis* were two of my early attempts at working with text. I abandoned these ideas shortly afterwards, perhaps because I became too self-conscious about my writing.

MH: *Hair Cuts* (8 min, 1999) features a catalogue of 110 Chinese barbershops and beauty parlours in New York's Lower East Side. The sheer number is impressive, but you never venture inside, we never see humans or human activities. Instead you present a series of signs and facades. Why?

HT: I was walking through New York City one day and noticed there were many barbershops. I had a camcorder with me and began filming one after another. There are a few shots of the interiors and the 'actions' within, but I never went inside. When I was living in New York, I was very broke and cut my own hair. I was amazed at how popular those places must have been, judging by their numbers. I was also interested in the video itself as a cultural study that related to signs and facades. As I was a noncustomer, this short study of hair culture featured fascination, attraction and repulsion. Interestingly, if you look carefully at the shop posters, most feature Caucasian models. Perhaps it speaks to how we want to look and what constitutes ideal beauty.

MH: Could you tell me about *Pocahontas: TransWorld Remix* (4:20 min, 1998)? What inspired the making of this movie?

HT: It was made with Pauline Park, a transgendered Korean adoptee I met while living in New York. *Pocahontas* was originally a Disney cartoon, and I used the different language soundtracks (of the theme song) to create the music. Pauline wanders through Central Park in Native costume. It was my first attempt at 'directing,' so a lot of movements were improvised by her. I told Pauline what I was looking for so that she could explore with her character. Pauline is not a professional actor so I ended up letting her be herself.

We first see her wandering in what looks like a natural forest but slowly discover that it is only a park. I really had to thank her for performing in cold fall weather in a skimpy costume. I wanted Pocahontas to end up 'returning' to the American Museum of Natural History, which is just across Central Park, but this was a scene we never got to record. When we worked together, Pauline was only beginning to explore gender roles, and now she has become an activist for the transgendered in New York City. I would like to think that *Pocahontas* has been somewhat instrumental in her transformation.

I lived in the Washington Heights area of New York. There are almost no other Asians living in that area. If someone sent me a letter, even if they didn't have the correct address, somehow the letter would

Hair Cuts

get to me. I enjoyed my experiences there. I went to this wild party, and *Miracles on 163rd Street* (25 min, 2001) was made in that neighbourhood. I took an ethnographic approach. I let the subjects express themselves with minimal editing: what you see, going in and out of the rooms, talking to different people, or waiting as they have their conversations, is a record of the evening.

Why did I leave New York? There was so much to do and no time to do it, and I wasn't going out anymore. Mostly I stayed inside my apartment and worked all the time. I came back to live in Toronto, and also returned to Hong Kong to make a few works as well, for instance *Cop Strings* (6 min, 1999). It's about the different personas of an individual, and the identification with work as identity. I was picked up by this guy in the Vancouver airport when I was going back to Hong Kong and found out he was a very talented musician. The video is a personal portrait. Raymond learned to play the guzheng, a 16-to-26-stringed zither with movable bridges, when he was a kid. He was actually a child performer and competed in musical events around the world. I asked if I could record *Battle with Typhoon*, which was shot in his apartment in one take. As you can see in this recording, he is definitely a showman.

Later on, he let me follow him around town wearing his auxiliary police uniform. He had this fantasy of uniforms and guns and being in the forces. The actual filming was supposed to be a secret – he could get into trouble if found out. He would never really address the camera, and I was always at a distance (and therefore I never got into the police station). But the exhibitionist in him was excited. I don't know if he had much idea of what I was doing but we had established a trust. I think it was a bold decision for him. Later on, the Hong Kong queer film festival asked to screen it, but I declined.

The idea behind this filming of the cop, which I have almost forgotten myself, is that my father was a policeman! When I lived in Hong Kong as a kid I sometimes hung out at the police station. By filming Raymond, I was recalling my own childhood memories.

MH: In *99 Men* (3 min, 1998), you present headshots of 99 men in suit and tie, all a bit softfocused, with musical accompaniment. The pictures are mysterious: who are these men and why have they been collected like this? They make me think of information gathered in official files, data waiting to be put to use. It seems also a reflection on how most pictures, even narratives, bend pictures toward an idea of 'use.'

HT: The interest in showing Asian men has been an ongoing interest for more than ten years, both in my painting and media work. In *99 Men*, I decided to go back to my reference materials, picture clippings of Asian businessmen from the community newspapers. They are in fact drawn from some sort of a file, although not an official one. These men are realtors, car salesmen and insurance agents, their photographs taken from advertisements. From my point of view, all these portraits are both individual and indifferent. I am intrigued by the grouping and I think of the salesman in all of us. Years ago I wrote an ironic article called 'Confessions of a Salesman':

In time, I also learned to make use of my sexual identity. You see, I had gone out with girls before. But I found that being a straight Asian man was not half as much fun as being a queer Oriental boy. Although we are not as desirable as the All-American types in the gay culture, we do have our share of clientele because the market is very diverse. I began to learn to accentuate my exotic look, to sell my youngish features and to master my slim and compact body. ['Confessions of a Salesman' by Ho Tam]

MH: You have made a number of movies where you collect pictures on a theme and present them as a catalogue succession, without comment. In *99 Men* and *Hair Cuts*, for instance, but also *Matinee Idol* (16:30 min, 1999), which shows clips from some of Ng Cho Fan's 250 films, while *In the Dark* (6 min, 2004) presents a series of grainy, high-contrast pictures made in Toronto during the SARS epidemic. Why this strategy of collecting, gathering and presentation?

HT: My German friend Lothar Albrecht once told me that photographers are collectors and archivers of images. This is obvious in many photographers' works which are about the same subject matter year after year. My work is definitely in that vein. Maybe I just couldn't think of anything better to do. It is only through study of the multiple that similarities and differences emerge. This interests me tremendously. Sometimes I wish I could take pictures of everything simply to document its existence. No other motives. Perhaps I am afraid of letting go? I often wish that I had filmed every building, storefront or site that no longer stands so I could remember what it used to look like. Tape is cheap and takes less space than photographs, so why not? But I am a bit tired now. Some want pristine pictures, but that's not so important for me – videotape suits me fine.

MH: In *Ave Maria* (7:20 min, 2000), you return to the New York subway and film through glass, watching commuters eat French fries, or wait anxiously, or sit with their mothers or fathers, producing a picture of family life in transit. Everything has a gloriously ravaged, hazy look; it feels like a movie made 'by hand,' that you have run these pictures through your fingers. Or is all the tactility the result of video post-production magic? Why was this quality important to you? Why the musical hymn on the soundtrack? You look at people unaware of their recording: is this voyeurism, are you stealing these moments? Are they giving consent because they are in a public space? (If I can see them I can shoot them: they are fair game.)

HT: The technique is not post-production, it was actually shot with a camcorder using a slow shutter speed. It was the only way to capture reflections from windows, because I did not point directly toward the subjects. But the camera was not hidden either. I played on my assumed position as a Japanese tourist with a camera on the subway! I often sat on the subway watching cars passing on the next track, which created beautiful reflections. I am really happy that the video captures that experience and heightens it. The hymn was recorded in Spain, in a sacred place called Montserrat, where a church was dedicated to the Black Madonna. Regarding the permission issue, I know that they are unaware of being filmed, but

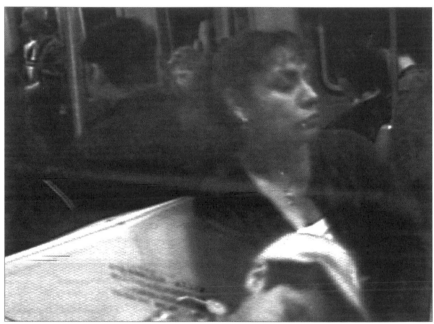

Ave Maria

they could tell I was taping. You have seen the film, so you know I have total respect for my subjects. Yes, I was stealing those moments. But I remember when I was a child my mother took me on a trip, and that day has stayed with me all these years. Nothing special happened, nothing important occurred. I can't recreate this time, which is more of a feeling, after all. This video is a commemoration of that particular moment.

MH: *She Was Cuba* (16:25 min, 2003) feels like a signal departure in your work, a watershed of sorts, where the highly structured conceptual underpinnings of your earlier work give way to something more narrative, more like 'a movie.' Can you talk about how it began?

HT: Well, it is a long story. After working on a series of non-narratives, I was ready to reintroduce a voice. I haven't thought about incorporating writing into my work for a long time, but that

doesn't mean I'm not interested in it. I was also trying to find a way to reinsert myself into my work, so to speak. The project arose from a conversation with a Cuban friend of mine, Alfredo Gonzalez. He described the reasons he moved to Canada, and talked about his friend Ada, the 'she' in *She Was Cuba*. Ada was already dead, and I was living in New York City, so we never met. The story of her defection may not be unique, but the theme of beginning again is universal.

I wondered how to create a piece around Ada. I thought of the way one talks about a place or person that is no longer there, how one is always outside of absence and how we fill that gap with our imagination and constructions. I was interested in exploring or constructing narrative through some kind of recollection. This led me eventually to use found footage. I juxtaposed her story with mine. I was searching for her, but there is also an implied search for someone else, my deceased partner, Kirby. In a sense, Ada and Cuba become one, both inaccessible to me. The memories of Ada are told in reverse, from her last days to her first arrival in Canada, while my own travelogue moves forward in time.

MH: This double quest-narrative set in Cuba lets his story and hers proceed in alternating scenes, cast over 'found' or 'stolen' pictures. How would you feel if someone took pictures from one of your movies and reused them for their own ends? Would that be okay? Does the author no longer exist, only contexts, temporary frames and arrangements?

HT: It is an interesting question that I think about a lot these days. It also has to do with how one treats materials. In *She Was Cuba*, I studied the materials in terms of their contexts before deciding to use them. It is basically a film about films. My friend Alfredo gave some history on Cuban cinema, and I also went on my own to look for materials. I quoted certain movies from this research.

She Was Cuba can be seen as an anthology of movies made in and about Cuba, and how Cubans are portrayed in the cinema. By introducing these clips, I am looking for layers of meanings within them.

The last scene with the woman walking in the street is from *Portrait of Teresa* by Pastor Vega. It relates the struggle of a female character who carries the burden of being a mother, wife, daughter, worker and artist. It reflects the roles that Ada plays both in Cuba and Canada, and conjures the space between expectations placed on her and who she wants to be. In both stories, women have to make a choice between starting a new life or following their heart.

Earlier we see a woman carried out on a stretcher, the actress Mirta Ibarra in *Fresa y Chocolate* (*Strawberry and Chocolate*) by Tomás Gutiérrez Alea. It is a film about a gay subject, and the woman pictured is a fag hag, so to speak. The Ibarra character's accident obviously mirrors Ada's death, and both incidents occur in a public space. Ada suffered an aneurysm on the Ottawa River during a kayaking trip. Her portrait emerges as a composite, working with many different images of women in Cuban films. I think Ada tried to recreate her own identity in a new environment (Canada), but I don't know if she was actually freed from her past.

If someone wants to use my work in their work, I think I would be flattered, but maybe there is a difference between borrowing and stealing?

MH: Could you tell me about the title *She Was Cuba*, which implies that she used to be Cuba, but is no longer. Why is the movie made in memory of Ada Pérez Esquivel (1967–1999)?

HT: Yes, that is my intention, to say she is no longer 'here' (in this world) and 'there' (in Cuba once she left). It is also a play on the film title *I Am Cuba*. *She Was Cuba* is about memories. I guess memory doesn't exist if the actual event/person has not already gone! I interviewed many of Ada's Canadian friends and they sometimes think of her as a representation of Cuba, since this is the only connection they have. I put her acknowledgment in the credits to make the film's inspiration and sourcings clear. Though the work also draws much from my friendship and conversations with Alfredo. Without him this work could not exist.

MH: The writing, as usual, is very beautiful. The closing passage is narrated in her voice and goes like this: 'She wondered what could possibly be on their minds when they first landed. Was it to seek, to explore, to conquer, to live, to let live, to be free or to submit? She realized that she was in a similar position, and on that particular day the world was filled with possibilities.' Does she occupy, here at the end of the movie, and at the beginning of her journey (which proceeds in reverse as you've mentioned, from her death, to her

arrival in Cuba), a place where she is able to embody all of the hopes of this island? And does she then 'fall' into experience, having to choose one particular lover, one particular occupation, moving all the while toward an early death? His journey seems complementary somehow; he has lost someone who he seeks again, impossibly, here in Cuba. He is at the end of his hopes – Cuba is an escape, a last moment to dream, perhaps, though death haunts him everywhere. Both figures are moving around death, the fated sense of their own endings. Can you comment?

HT: This work is about death, dying, separation and memory. It is a heavy piece, but in the end I'm looking for resolution or hope. Art imitating life and vice versa? Does being an artist make one more sensitive? Or is art another kind of therapy? I have been dealing with these questions for the past ten years and this work is a summarization or conclusion. Recreating a person I never met was a challenge; I decided to speak of her in very general terms – there is an interior, but no details. The path-crossing of the two characters describes an ellipse. The female character is never in Cuba but is caught up in her Cuban past, despite attempting to move forward. And of course, for others she 'was/is' Cuba. The movie ends with the scene you describe, as she arrives in Canada for the first time. She is neither here nor there, no longer in Cuba, not quite in Canada. The male character is her counterpart, her unconscious perhaps, who arrives at some kind of reconciliation with his past at the end of his search. He has been projecting his own loss onto someone else, living his life through another.

MH: Your new installation, *Romances*, takes you in a different direction, with footage drawn from a very different place. Can you talk about how that came about? Why did you refuse the image of sailors in this video? Why is there no conversation, no language used at all? How do the shots of the ocean, often digitally manipulated (using superimposition or speed changes), evoke

She Was Cuba

She Was Cuba

the presence of the military (as a force that dominates and controls nature)?

HT: I was accepted in the Canadian Forces Artists Program, which invites artists to travel with one of the three branches of the Canadian Forces. For a long time I heard nothing, but after I'd moved to Victoria two years ago, they contacted me, and thought that Victoria is an ideal place to be connected to the Canadian navy. I was flown to Hawaii and sailed back on the frigate HMCS Calgary from Pearl Harbor to Victoria. I brought still cameras and sketch pads and video cameras, and this is the piece I've recently finished. I hope to maintain contact with them so I can keep developing the work. *Romances* has a very sensitive soundtrack by American electroacoustic composer S. Lyn Goeringer. The romance of the sea has given rise to plenty of myths and imaginings. In bringing together the rich symbolism and reference about the sea and the voyage, I seek to construct a complex, yet open-ended, larger narrative. The video moves between attraction and repulsion.

In *Romances*, I attempt to use a number of mediums (paintings, video, photo and text) to reconstruct the experience. I think in the end the video piece will change, becoming more of a screening version than a one-monitor installation. The decision to show only the sea and the interior/exterior of the ship without the sailors is mostly because of the limited footage I collected. The trip was only ten days from beginning to end. I didn't have a concept and was just thinking on my feet. But the ship's motion left me off guard, and mostly I was trying to stay well without getting a headache. I would like to make some on-camera interviews, and film the crew in a certain way, but all this takes time, which I didn't have. I was in the company of 200 people with hardly a quiet moment. It took over a year to process the collected materials. I have

lots of snapshots that were used in the paintings, for instance. But I am thinking of fictionalizing the experience – hence the title *Romances*. So much of my past work is based on the real, and has a singular narrative, and I see this as a departure, weaving fact and fiction together. I would like to recreate the division between the claustrophobic space of the ship and the sea outside.

MH: One of the many things you're doing in Toronto is showing your new feature, *Books of James* (74 min, 2006). Can you talk about how that began?

HT: *Books of James* is a tape about a friend of mine, James Wentzy, a video activist in New York City. I met him ten years ago and became interested in his work when he shared his journals with me. They are filled with drawings and writing. As soon as I saw them, I felt someone had to do something with this material, but who? I wanted to take on the job of showing the world these intimate, tactile pages. I made a short piece, also called *Books of James* (16:30 min, 2002), based on the books as objects, as a way of presenting the diary pages. This movie stops at the moment Wentzy is diagnosed HIV-positive.

In the feature-length version, excerpts from his journals are shown onscreen in an extended passage accompanied by a piano piece by Wang Yemeng. This music is based on a folk song from Taiwan. The original song is a cautionary tale that contains moral advice and warnings, appropriate for the display of James's diaries.

I showed the short version to many people (some knew James, many did not) and received a lot of questions about where James was at. I came to the conclusion that in order to appreciate the diaries, one has to know James better. So the narrative portion came as a second thought. I decided to continue working on the

Books of James

video, since I had already collected so much material and knew that there was a lot of archival footage in James's video library as well. I thought I would work like Hollywood – if I didn't have a good idea I would simply replicate myself. I started remaking *Books of James* as a feature-length movie. This longer work uncovers his AIDS-activist years in the 1980s and 1990s and then moves into the present, post-9/11 New York.

It was hard to know what to do with the new materials, because James had stopped writing in his diaries, so there was no personal voice anymore (in *Part Two*). During this period he became a video activist, shooting demonstrations and conferences, and eventually he produced a community cable TV show. I decided to let his footage speak for itself. But I encountered a problem of explaining the footage, since I did not want to have a narrator. I had to carefully sort out his activist footage, then put them into three segments: interviews, protests and TV shows. I hoped this would sum up his work. They also provide the background of the social climate at the time.

In Part Three, the final section, I try to collapse the two previous sections, Private and Public, and make a conclusion and another update of James's life. I show him taking his first AIDS medication (the cocktail) and walking around New York City, and then finally out in the woods again. He had started writing in his diary once more, and out of these moments I was able to construct a glimpse into his personal world again.

MH: How did James's family react to the movie?

HT: James's parents passed away quite some time ago, so they didn't get to see the movie. His mother passed away in his college years, and his father passed away shortly after James told him he was HIV-positive. He also has a brother. James was very proud of the movie, so he sent it to his brother's family, but he got a note back from his sister-in-law saying she wouldn't appear in any more of his videos. They are fundamentalist Christians and objected to some of the content.

MH: Your tape is divided into three named sections: Private, Political and Postscript. Can you talk about why you have made this strict line between private and public?

HT: James is a very private, self-contained person, but after the diagnosis he turned outward. He remained behind the camera; however, he wasn't the one chasing down the police or shouting out at demonstrations – he kept his own sort of distance. He became an archivist.

His diagnosis changed so much of his point of view, he poured himself into video-making, which became a way to engage with

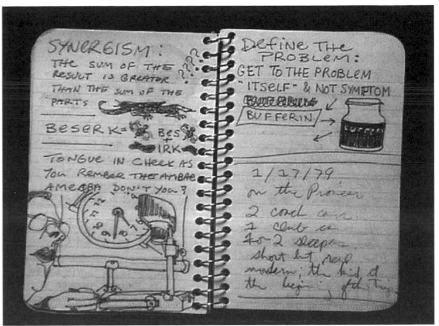

Books of James

a new community. He stopped everything else to attend ACT UP meetings and find out about treatments and to travel to AIDS conferences and demonstrations. He lost the urge to write in his diaries and found meaning by using art in another context.

Yes, the personal is the political. Even in his most straightforward political reporting, James spoke through the words and actions of others. Naming each segment separately and enumerating them parts One, Two and Three grants the viewer more to think about. My work is always (too much!) about structure (and literacy). I don't prefer it, but it's the way I work. I've tried to leave that tendency behind, but no luck so far.

With *Books of James* I wanted to open a dialogue, revisiting the history of AIDS activism, making people aware of what has been done and the possibilities of what remained to be done, as a motivator for new ideas. The climate around activism has changed a lot in the last 15 years. Today, for instance, an ACT UP meeting would be lucky to draw five people, whereas 20 years ago community centres gave way to large auditoriums to hold the hundreds who would attend. James is disillusioned by this situation and shuts himself away, though he does manage an ACT UP website that constantly updates news and events.

Showing work about AIDS is totally unfashionable; I'm lucky that any festival would accept the work. Who wants to see it? When I was making this piece I read a book about documentary filmmaking, and in the introduction it said there are some subjects you shouldn't take on because they're overdone – AIDS, for instance. You shouldn't make films about AIDS anymore.

Ho Tam's Videos

The Yellow Pages   7:45 min 1994
Season of the Boys   3:30 min 1997
La Salle Primary   5 min 1998
Pocahontas: TransWorld Remix   4:20 min 1998
99 Men   3 min 1998
Dear Sis   4:20 min 1998
Matinee Idol   16:30 min 1999
Washington Heights Untitled   4 min 1999
dos cartas/two letters   4 min 1999
Cop Strings   6 min 1999
Hair Cuts   8 min 1999
Fine China   8:30 min 2000
Ave Maria   7:20 min 2000
The Loop   18 min 2001
Miracles on 163rd St.   25 min 2001
My Memories of me   3 min 2001
Bus No. 7   3 min 2001
The Books of James   16:30 min 2002
She Was Cuba   16:25 min 2003
Still Lives (In the Americas)   20 min 2003
In the Dark   6 min 2004
Discopedia   8 min 2005
Books of James   74 min 2006

Distributed by Vtape, Video Out, Video Data Bank, Frameline.

Ho Tam was born in Hong Kong and educated in Toronto, Canada. He has produced over 20 shorts and two feature-length works. In addition to time-based mediums, Tam's art practice also includes painting, drawing, print work and photography. www.ho-tam.com; www.bookofjames.com

CHRISTINA BATTLE
COLOUR PROCESSING

When I was still young enough to believe in youth, I thought it was just a question of time before people got tired of the same formula stories. I trudged off to weekly screenings of obscure movies, often silent, scratched and flickering looks at landscape, or cameras that moved in unusual ways, or home movies, all the while thinking that soon this theatre would be crammed with folks wanting more. The theatre closed long before that impossibility became clear.

Twenty years on, it seems a miracle that young folks with smarts would trouble themselves by bucking the riptide of the media. We are shown how to live and how to make pictures of how to live. Isn't everyone busy seizing a moment with a handy cellphone, uploading those *in utero* scans to the website, sharing their vacation snaps on Flickr or YouTube? But along comes Christina Battle with her emulsion-heady 'experiments,' getting her hands all up into the chemical processes of film – yes, just like the old days. And when she talks about movies, she keeps on about things like colour, not even the wall, or what is behind the wall, but the damn colour of the wall. What are we without our restrictions, our narrow frames of looking? Christina is part of a final bouquet of film as film artistry, crafted by hand in the artist's bathtub and kitchen. In a few years the last lab will close and chemistry will no longer be available, and every motion picture will be digital. What will have passed is not only a technology but a way of working and seeing, a way of understanding the world, and those understandings are never clearer than today, when they have been summoned for a last stand. Small cells of artists around the world have returned to their basement labs, mixing up powders and solutions, running water over lengths of plastic in order to fix and bleach and tone film that has been run carefully through their cameras. A new generation of artists, young and traditional, not trying to hold on but to exclaim, indulge, celebrate.

MH: You are working in a field that is dominated by men, now and then and (say it ain't so) forever. The histories of 'experimental,' 'avant-garde' cinema feature few women and almost all the past heroes are white. Do you have any ideas about why mainstream norms have been reproduced on the margins?

CB: A history made of male white heroes stems more from those who have exhibited, documented and written about the practice. The less women are written about, the less impact their presence makes historically. There seem to be more women and people of colour making experimental works now, but maybe this is because the world is seemingly getting smaller, not because the art world is becoming more open. Why isn't experimental film or the art world itself more diverse? I think it is related to the lack of diversity in other areas of society. Artmaking is still a practice of privilege – if not economically, then ideologically.

MH: In *nostalgia (april 2001 to present)* (3:30 min, 2005), you present a series of perfect human drawings from the 1950s,

showing moms waving goodbye from their suburban habitats, boys and girls on bikes. The crisp, comic-book lines of these model lives have been torn up in your hands, their new emulsion transport mutilated, sometimes beyond recognition. Can you describe the material process and the original source material? Did you grow up in places like this, surrounded by these impossible, everyday utopias?

CB: Although I grew up in the suburbs, *nostalgia (april 2001 to present)* is more about America and ideas surrounding the American dream. In April 2001 I officially became an American citizen and soon after moved to California. I suddenly found myself confused. Growing up in Canada, I had travelled to America throughout my childhood, and felt it was familiar. My dad (a U.S. citizen) always talked about its strength and opportunities. But after moving, I became acutely aware of how much of an outsider I was. To me, America remains steeped in issues of civil rights (racial equality) and a history that they have neglected to deal with. I felt the resultant tensions everywhere; ideas of 'race' seemed to be very much on the surface, as if it was always on people's minds whether they directly referenced it or not. (I view the term *race* solely as a social construct.). It's a hard thing to explain unless you've experienced it. I felt I was seen first by my skin colour and second as me. Presumptions were made about how I thought and what I did because of what I looked like, not because of who I was. I don't feel that so much here in Canada – not that it doesn't exist here, it does, but it's not so obvious, it's not so much a part of the everyday. Maybe Canadians are more polite about it, I don't know. Imagine a world where you are acutely aware that the way you look affects the way everyone sees you. It can make you paranoid ... and make even a simple exercise like taking the bus about something much bigger.

Do I think skin colour itself is a kind of picture? I suppose, in the same way that a picture tells only part of the story ... left to be contextualized by the viewer, who may have no idea of the true context held within the picture itself.

When I began thinking about making *nostalgia (april 2001 to present)*, I was trying to understand where my place was in this new environment. Where did I fit in as a citizen of this country, with its flawed history and loathsome politics? I turned to the 1950s as a point of study because it was an era that defined issues that are still relevant – specifically, the ongoing promise of opportunity that is afforded to only a few.

Long before I had the film in mind, I came across a book called *The Good Citizen's Handbook: A Guide to Proper Behavior*. It was a collection of 1940s–1950s texts and pictures describing ideal ways of life. Many images were dedicated to community-based issues: how to be a good neighbour, what you owe your community, that sort of thing. This focus on neighbourhood and community prompted me to further research the rise of the suburbs, and I came across *Growing Up with Dick and Jane: Learning and Living the American Dream*. Here are two quotes that stuck with me: 'A 1954 Supreme Court decision barring segregation in public schools exposed widespread racial bias in America. It triggered fears among white Americans who didn't want to share access to the American dream.' 'The sense of suburban well-being filled advertisements, dreams and everyday life in the 1950s, but underneath the surface some leftover fears and some new anxieties were eating away at traditional values.'

Reflecting on the American Dream, the book spoke not only about the tensions and contradictions of the ideal, but also the role that images and advertising played in its proliferation. The nostalgic quality of these pictures raised further questions. Who had nostalgia for the period and why? At a time when a large part of society was struggling for rights, I had trouble believing anyone would ever want to go back to that time. These cheerful, optimistic images needed to be injected with a dose of reality; the conditions that eventually led to the uprisings in the 1960s were missing and needed to be included. I wanted to re-present these images so they would no longer keep their contradictions secret. I attacked them, stripped them of their nostalgia, in order to provide a new context that would allow them to be seen anew.

At the time I had started doing my own colour printing and processing, and worked to recreate the palette of the time. I shot a number of still images on an animation stand that had the saturated look I was interested in exploring. My primary method of working was with emulsion lifts – literally peeling away the emulsion from the surface of the film and reapplying it onto pieces of clear leader. Since the images were still, I wanted to give them a sense of turbulence, as if they were struggling to coexist on the film strip. In the end, the boy on the bike became my main character and I shaped a narrative around him. This ideal child from the 1950s chances upon an ongoing struggle and is forced to contend with it, whether he wants to or not. In the end he makes it through, but with a new understanding.

MH: In *migration* (5:30 min, 2005), a scarred emulsion provides the mauled and flickering ground against which a number of painted birds fly while a summer thunderstorm rages on the soundtrack. It possesses its own kind of beauty, but I need to ask you: is beauty enough? I mean, is it necessary? Does it have to exist? Or is that too much for any work of art to answer to? Are we that bird, subject to the random flickerings of accidental meetings and love?

CB: Before heading to California, I started hanging around Niagara Custom Lab. Until then I had been processing black and white and a bit of colour negative by hand, but always sent my negatives to the lab for printing. I wanted to know more about what happened behind the lab's doors. That's where I discovered contact printing and learned how to colour-time film. In colour timing, one adjusts the amount of red, green and blue light added to the film when making a print. It's an important stage, and colour is such a subjective thing – what does red look like? Printing on my own and selecting my own colour balance allowed me more control over how my works looked.

When I moved to California in 2003, I had to adapt to a different set of resources. I worked in Studio X at the San Francisco Art Institute, which had an old, one-light contact printer intended for printing black-and-white film. I started working with the printer to make colour prints, adding colour and neutral-density filters in front of the light source to affect overall colour and exposure. The prints needed to be processed, so I bought a bunch of print chemistry from Kodak and basically set up my own lab. I had to be quite methodical in my testing to make any progress. I printed and then hand-processed what felt like endless amounts of film. Since I was responsible for every stage in the process, I was able to have a high level of control over what my films looked like. *nostalgia (april 2001 to present)*, *buffalo lifts*, *migration*, *map (august 1 to 10, 2003)* and *the distance between here and there* all came out of this investigation of colour printing and processing.

migration came out of an interest in biological systems and thinking about things like chaos theory (which led more specifically to considering ideas surrounding the 'butterfly effect,' where a small change in the initial condition of a system can result in a chain of events leading to large-scale phenomena). I started reading more about the migratory paths of butterflies themselves, like the monarch butterfly, which migrates over 4,800 kilometres each year. *migration* imagines the path of migrating butterflies as they fly above a brewing storm. I gathered images of butterflies from library videos and found one that visually moved along a path I felt I could work with. The video footage was isolated and then printed onto sheets of paper and reanimated onto 16mm via an animation stand. Basically, I worked with loops made out of the same piece of footage, which were then painted, colour-toned, scratched and contact-printed. The entire film shows only one butterfly recreated in a number of ways. Since I was doing my own colour timing, I could

nostalgia (april 2001 to present)

print one loop in a variety of colours. Since I was doing my own lab work, the film took on some of the qualities inherent to hand-processing, with its scratches, undeveloped regions, strange red dots. These became both chance events encountered along the monarch's journey and the beginnings of potential changes influenced by the migrating insects themselves.

The soundtrack is made up of field-recording fragments gathered during travels to and from California: a rainstorm captured just outside of Edmonton, a storm recorded from inside my apartment in San Francisco and various bits and pieces culled from travels here and there ...

Is beauty enough? I think that something more than beauty is usually my goal. What seems beautiful on the surface carries rumblings of something more underneath. This 'more' tends to manifest as an unknown darkness – not threatening necessarily, but curious, unknown and unpredictable.

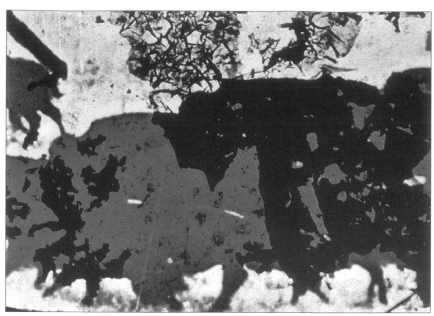

buffalo lifts

MH: Your description of *buffalo lifts* (3 min, silent, 2004) reads, 'A herd of buffalo desperately try to hold on as they cross the film frame.' These herds used to roam freely across North America, but were hunted into near-extinction. With its shuddering, scratched-up, yellow-and-black momentums, it is difficult not to read your movie as an elegy for film itself, hurtling toward its own demise. Because there are mountains of footage available, it can be difficult to narrow the field, to apply a frame of looking that persuades you to choose this and not that. What led you to buffalo? How did you achieve this sterling effect?

CB: Although I can see how it can be read as an elegy for film itself, for me this is an elegy for the buffalo. While gathering footage for *paradise falls, new mexico*, I came across a documentary with early black-and-white footage of a herd of buffalo running across the plains of the U.S. I knew it needed to be worked on its own. I researched the demise of the buffalo and was struck by the numbers. Here in Canada we still have discreet populations of buffalo, but in the U.S. they are virtually extinct. Sitting Bull put it into context: 'A cold wind blew across the prairie when the last buffalo fell ... a death-wind for my people.'

I began by rephotographing the video footage onto black-and-white 16mm film and held on to it for a year or so, not quite sure what to do with it. When I started colour-printing in San Francisco, I needed footage to work with for tests and looked more closely at the black-and-white film I had shot. I knew I wanted it to be reproduced in colour in order to bring it into the present; I didn't want it to be viewed only in historical terms, because the politics behind the extinctions are very much alive today. I colour-toned the footage and then began making prints. I loved the smoothness of the original footage and the way the buffalo seamlessly ran across the field, but it seemed too romantic. In an attempt to inject the scene with a sense of urgency and trauma, I worked directly with the emulsion. Using hot water to soften the surface of the film, individual frames are peeled away with a razor blade and then placed onto strips of clear leader. Once the film had been transplanted, I re-photographed it onto colour film, then began printing and hand-processing to find the 'right' colour palette. Each final print was individually processed, so no two are identical.

MH: The past few seasons have seen the fashion industry turn toward 'distressed' clothing. Brand-new jeans arrive with holes and patches, shirts come pre-frayed and torn in just the right way. Aren't these analog simulacrums partner and kin to your enterprise, which similarly looks to a physical re-engagement with the image? What does it mean that your gestures, small and at home, can be recuperated by multinational giants and turned into yet another marketing strategy? Does that lessen the kick, deflate the politics?

CB: I don't quite know what to think about that yet. I definitely see an interest, especially amongst younger generations, in working with film. I suppose this stems from a desire to move against the familiar. I taught an experimental film class to a group of 13- to 15-year-olds and they were completely mesmerized with film. They had never seen it before and, despite encouragements, had minimal interest in working with video. They had grown up with video, it was too familiar. Film, on the other hand, was something they spoke about with a sense of nostalgia, although they had never previously encountered it. Where does this nostalgia come from?

I see more artists working with materials in various disciplines and some are quite political. For many (including me), this stems more from a desire to create by hand as opposed to a desire to explore the chosen medium/material itself. It's part of a do-it-yourself reaction against mass production that is only too common now.

MH: *fall storm (california, 2003)* (3 min, 2004) is a minimalist's storm portrait, the mostly dark screen occasionally punctuated by flashes of lightning. By withdrawing pictures, you offer us a chance to listen to the beauty of the storm, but why isn't it longer? Why not grant us an hour in this almost-darkness, or the length of the original storm? Why do you record storms? Isn't the soundtrack as important as the picture? Why then do we say we're going to 'see' the movies, never to hear them? And why the precise placement of the storm in the title – what if the storm had been recorded somewhere else, would that matter? Do you feel this work is documentary?

CB: *fall storm* began as a sound piece, and I definitely see the images accompanying the track, not the reverse. Considering and capturing storms is an ongoing interest and pops up in my work frequently. I'm fascinated by the power and unpredictable nature of storms and see them as one of the few forces powerful enough to exert change regardless of societal constructs. I think weather will ultimately be responsible for evening the playing field and altering the world as we know it … most probably in my lifetime.

One night, when I had first moved to San Francisco, I was watching a news report warning of a potential earthquake that was being monitored in the area. I hadn't really considered the threat of earthquakes until that moment and realized I had no idea what I was supposed to do when faced with one. I had a strange moment of complete uncertainty. I searched for more information, but only one news report on a channel out of Oakland was broadcasting any information about it. I looked out my window expecting people to be preparing for the quake and saw nothing unusual. people were hanging out, unaware of the warnings. Time seemed to stand still. I sat and waited, and ultimately nothing happened. I realized that even though the sense of urgency lasted only a few minutes, the potential devastation could have been everlasting.

I wanted to recreate this sense of being powerless while observing a storm unfold outside the window, and *fall storm (california 2003)* came out of this consideration. The soundtrack is composed of storms gathered from many places, some field recordings (a few captured at the time I experienced the broadcast warning of the earthquake, a few bits and pieces from storms I recorded in various places), some gathered from nature videos. The footage comes from storms culled from science videos and documentaries. I rephotographed the imagery onto 16mm high-contrast colour film, transferred it back to video and worked with it in After Effects on my computer. Although both the image and soundtrack are completely sculpted, I wanted to root them in a particular time and place, which is where the title comes from. I wanted viewers to consider the piece as a document, to personalize it … to have it recall that moment when I began considering the power and possibilities storms hold – but

also to consider how we document and look back upon such cataclysmic events. If this storm had long-lasting effects, would we look back to the moment itself or its effects afterwards?

MH: *hysteria* (4 min, 2006) offers a series of schoolbook drawings that depict the Salem witch trials. These began in 1692 in Salem Village and Salem Town, Massachusetts, and resulted in the imprisonment of 200 and the public executions of 20. It began because both the daughter and niece of a Puritan reverend began exhibiting aberrant behaviour (a broad measure – Puritan strictures maintained that women were lesser than men and should serve them), and a widening circle of the accused were held responsible – they were 'witches' who had cast a spell on these children. Why is it important to look again at these pictures now? Where did you find them and what did you do to them (in a material sense)? How are they ordered and arranged?

CB: One amazing thing about San Francisco is its many used bookstores; one of my favourites was right around the corner from where I lived in the Mission, and I spent a lot of time in there. I came across two volumes of a New England historical series documenting the trials, each for a dollar – *The Witchcraft Hysteria of 1692* (Volumes I and II), by Leo Bonfanti. I picked them up out of interest; I was familiar with the Salem witch trials, but wanted to know more about the specifics.

Then Michael Moore's *Fahrenheit 9/11* came out and I was drawn by his comparisons of the Bush administration's actions to those of the witch hunts. This quote by Bernard de Voto from 1949 was inspirational: 'I say it has gone too far. We are dividing into the hunted and the hunters. There is loose in the United States today the same evil that once split Salem Village between the bewitched and the accused and stole men's reason quite away. We are informers to the secret police. Honest men are spying on their neighbors for patriotism's sake. We may be sure that for every honest man two dishonest ones are spying

hysteria

paradise falls, new mexico

for personal advancement today and ten will be spying for pay next year.'

Around the same time I was reading more about Steve Kurtz's arrest, and Michael Moore's comparison seemed even more relevant. Steve Kurtz is a member of Critical Art Ensemble – an art collective dedicated to exploring the intersections between art, technology, radical politics and critical theory. In May 2004 police entered Steve Kurtz's house in Buffalo, N.Y., after his wife had died of heart failure in the middle of the night. Searching through the house, police became alarmed by art materials present in the house (which had been exhibited in galleries and museums throughout Europe and North America) and contacted the FBI. Under the expanded U.S. Patriot Act, the FBI initially sought charges of bio-terrorism against Kurtz, even though the items seized were found to be non-threatening. Although charges of bio-terrorism are still a risk, Kurtz currently faces up to 20 years in prison for mail and wire fraud. Kurtz's lawyers have found that government agents misled judges when seeking a search warrant against Kurtz, and they, as well as many scientists and artists, consider the charges against Kurtz to be politically motivated. (For more info see www.caedefensefund.org.)

I wanted to revisit the trials because it was obvious that lessons remained to be learned, that we hadn't yet evolved beyond them. I gathered imagery mainly from library books and shot them in the basement of SFAI on a 35mm animation stand that had hardly been used. I quickly discovered that the camera's registration was severely misaligned. I knew I wanted to work with the frames individually by hand anyway, but the improper alignment forced me to think of a creative way to make the footage work. I emulsion-lifted each frame and reframed it onto strips of clear leader. Since I wanted the footage to remain recognizable and wasn't interested in agitating the image to the same degree I had with previous emulsion-lifted works, this was a detailed and lengthy task. Some of the footage was also created using photogram techniques; I printed the imagery onto clear acetate sheets on my computer and exposed them directly onto strips of film. I was interested in the images as documents of this past –

as line drawings, they are quite stark – so I worked to enhance these lines and texture through printing and hand-processing, which created a silver-heavy tone. With minimal resources, I printed the negatives by hand, using a motorized synchronizer I jerry-rigged into a contact printer, which pushed the film further into darkness. Then I sat on the footage until I moved back to Toronto in 2005. I shot some remaining images on LIFT's animation stand (with proper registration!), and finished the film as part of the co-op's *New Directions in Cinema* project in January 2006.

When editing the imagery, I wanted the structure to follow the history itself, moving from accusation to trial to hanging. The soundtrack needed to be minimal and dark; I used a field recording of wind recorded from inside a glass bottle on a beach in San Francisco that was then processed using a computer.

MH: Roberto Ariganello was the dynamic, in-your-face, beloved director of LIFT, a local film co-op that provided cameras and gear for the forever-young-at-heart. One afternoon last summer he had just finished delivering a motorized editing machine to the film co-op in Halifax when he was invited out for a swim. It was hot, it was a long trek to the swimming hole, and when he got into the middle of the water he had a heart attack and drowned. I can't help thinking of him on that walk to the water, with the sun bearing down on him, every step taking him closer to the end. You must have worked with Roberto at the co-op. Is there some moment you could share, some story that will bring him from the grave to breathe again?

CB: Roberto's spirit will forever be present in my work. He had a huge impact on me and how I viewed film as an art form. He provided my first introduction into experimental cinema and (most importantly to me) to the Toronto film community. He was a good friend and I think of him often ... always will. When we worked together at LIFT I was continually amazed, not only by his dedication, but by his openness – he was forever welcoming new members into the community. I'm fortunate to have many personal stories that include Roberto – most of them hilarious.

Everyone who knew him will remember his amazingly sarcastic sense of humour.

I don't think I can relate a story. The memories I've held on to surrounding Roberto are personal ones that I wouldn't feel comfortable sharing in this context. I know the role Roberto played in the community, I witnessed it and will never forget it, but the strongest memories I have are of him as a friend, and are not really associated with LIFTness or film. Maybe that will change over time ...

MH: Yes, I can imagine the difficulty of speaking or writing about Roberto, especially because you were friends, which I didn't know. I had hoped this would be a place, in a book, which remains rare in this micro-field, that he could be remembered, that some offering might be made that could honour his indomitable spirit. But I can imagine this an especially steep request for someone who is not a storyteller. Your movies work outside the conventions of storytelling – the way they convey meaning relies on texture and colour and material applications and a juxtaposition of elements. Why then expect a story about Roberto? But how else to allow strangers the chance to glimpse him, even as a mirage, even if only for a moment, in an anecdote only you can breathe warmth into?

Each movie offers a mark and a record: someone came here once and made this mark (which could be talking, or waving goodbye or a kiss), and here is the record, the film, of that mark. In this sense, movies are funerary monuments, they memorialize something past, leading Cocteau to remark that in the cinema, we watch death at work. Could you make a movie about Roberto's passing? Or about the way he lives inside you as friend and colleague, to show something of his Roberto-ness?

CB: Although my works are quite personal and often stem directly from particular experiences, I'm much more interested in creating things that are more universal. I try to look toward histories and events that have shaped my perspectives. I'm interested in how historical ways of thinking manifest themselves in the personal and how we all have these events in common.

I'm predominantly interested in working with material, because it allows me to work with my hands. I need to touch, to engage with the process in order to express my views. For me, it's not necessarily an exploration of the medium of film itself. I'm interested in working with time-based media, and, at least for now, film is the only medium that allows me to work so directly with the material. I work with photography and objects very much in the same way. If I were a painter, I'd expect a similar approach. Working directly with film as a material injects 'me' into my works: my perspectives, my emotions, my reactions.

Hmm ... I suppose if I did make a film about Roberto, he would be more present in the overall shape, tone, colour, rhythm of the work than in the image itself.

MH: Both *paradise falls, new mexico* (5 min, dual projection, 2004) and *Cooper/Bridges Fight* (3 min, 2002) are Westerns, a genre I'm not so familiar with, but which I understand provides necessary myth camouflage for the genocide of Native Americans. The armies that slaughtered the First Nations peoples were then used to dismantle the Spanish Empire, so that the American empire could take its place. In *paradise falls*, you replay a Western (what is it?) on one screen, while the other shows us a series of emptied or abandoned landscapes, forlorn houses, deserts. Why this double-vision approach, and where did you go to shoot this desolate footage? In *Cooper/Bridges Fight*, you emulsify a fight between Gary Cooper and Lloyd Bridges in *High Noon*, looping moments via re-photography, scratching into the surface of these fighters, accentuating their brawl by physically attacking the surface of the film. Cooper plays a sheriff in the film's original, while Bridges is his deputy, and their struggle gives a nod to cold-war tensions. Can you elaborate? How did this movie refigure the cold war, and why did you want to bring this fragment back to life?

CB: In 2001, a friend and I planned a road trip to the southwestern U.S. in search of ghost towns. At first my interest was solely in viewing the landscape and the surviving structures. I was researching the histories of these towns, which were often what one would expect from places quickly erected during the western expansion of North America, with its dependence on gold and silver mining. But I wanted to have a better sense of what the towns looked like in order to compare them to the present. The Western movie genre recreated these towns, and our ideas of what they were like are often shaped by Hollywood's betrayal.

It's funny – I grew up thinking I always hated Westerns. I remember my dad watching *Gunsmoke* on TV and I just didn't get it. But once I revisited the genre, I fell in love. Western movies follow quite an interesting formula, often blurring the boundaries between good and evil, legal and illegal. After shooting the imagery that became the right screen of *paradise falls*, I wanted to contrast these remnants of the past with an idealized view of what they looked like before abandonment. I gathered as many Westerns as I could and rephotographed key images onto 16mm stock. The left-hand side, made up of the Westerns, is structured to follow the movement westward, as well as to create a story similar to that found in these films. Groups of covered bandwagons cross the land, towns are developed, outlaws arrive, struggles for independence and/or control ensue and, in the end, a reflection back on the land. The role of the railroad was also integral to the rise and fall of many of these towns; hence, the appearance of the train in the film stimulates the breaking apart of the film frame itself.

The ghost towns documented in the piece are: Tumco, California (1880 to 1909); Vulture, Arizona (1880–1897); Fort Bowie, Arizona (1862–1894); Ruby, Arizona (1912–1941); Arivaca, Arizona (1812–present); and Riely, New Mexico (1880–1931).

While gathering Westerns, I came across *High Noon*, which is one of the best-known of the genre. The story is about a sheriff abandoned by his townsmen, who is then forced to stand up against a gang of cowboys approaching the town in search of revenge. The screenplay was written by Carl Foreman and was considered thoroughly un-American (despite its being a hit!). He was blacklisted in Hollywood and ultimately left the U.S. because of it. I found the relationship between the sheriff (Gary Cooper) and his deputy (Lloyd Bridges) to be most interesting. Except for the approaching gang, the film deals with good versus evil in a very subtle way. Cooper is about to marry a Quaker who is opposed to war and violence. He is the ultimate good guy, dedicating his life to serving a town that turns its back on him when his life may be in danger. (It was Cooper who had put the gang in prison, ironically in order to protect the town.)

He tries to rally men to help fight with him but they refuse. Bridges' character (Cooper's deputy and metaphorical son) also shies away out of jealousy. He figures he'll become sheriff after the gang takes Cooper out. He's a bad guy, but not bad in the same way as the gang. Bridges and his fellow townsfolk are more apathetic than evil, similar to U.S. society during the time of the cold war, when the film was made. The fight poses a good guy against a not-so-terrible guy. It forces an audience to consider what they truly deem to be good and evil. Behind the scenes, similar challenges were unfolding amongst the cast and crew; most were questioned by the House of Un-American Activities Committee about Foreman and the film. This committee started in 1937, its chief goal the investigation of un-American and subversive activities. Ten years later, they began an investigation into Hollywood. As a result, more than 300 people were banned from working in the industry; some were tried and jailed.

MH: Some artists imagine specific audiences for their work, others don't. Are you concerned about who sees your work, that because of the difficult rhetorics and encodings, it may be truly visible only to an audience already in the know? While the work ranges across many issues, is it only speaking to the converted?

CB: I hope people can see my work without feeling the need to read it in an art-speak sort of context. Reactions that come from experiencing experimental works without this context are important. I'm interested in site-specific presentations as well – mainly as a way to engage with an audience that may not get to the gallery or cinema to view artworks. I pull from the world around me to create and shape works and hope that this allows for an entry point into understanding.

With a B.Sc. in Environmental Biology from the University of Alberta and an MFA from the San Francisco Art Institute, Christina currently lives and works in Toronto, Canada. Working with film, video and installation, her internationally exhibited works often investigate the intersection of natural and industrialized environments and violent weather phenomena. www.cbattle.com

Christina Battle's Films

Cooper/Bridges Fight   3 min 2002
oil wells: sturgeon road & 97th street   3 min 2002
paradise falls, new mexico   5 min 2004 (dual projection)
fall storm (california, 2003)   3 min 2004
buffalo lifts   3 min 2004
following the line of the web   4 min 2004
the distance between here and there   7.5 min 2005
nostalgia (april 2001 to present)   3:30 min 2005
migration   5:30 min 2005
Behind the Walls and Under the Stairs   3 min 2006
three hours, fifteen minutes before the hurricane struck
   5 min 2006
hysteria   4 min 2006
traveling thru with eyes closed tight (map #2 – january 03
   thru january 06)   4 min 2006

Distributed by Canadian Filmmakers Distribution Centre.

ALEX MACKENZIE

BLINDING LIGHT

He looks at it and says *no, that won't do*. The first reaction, the one he can feel coming up from the guts, always says *sorry, not that*. These are the famed negations of the avant world (no more paintings, no more kings, or wars, or subjects) – they are his home, or perhaps his bone structure, the place he looks out from, the way he makes contact with the world. I keep feeling I will never see him again – he will begin living off the grid, and then leave the systems of signing and communication behind. But before that, there are questions to be asked, and work must be produced in order to pose them. He is working with an inheritance of pictures (and aren't we all? don't I have memories of decades when I wasn't yet alive, aren't there pictures of love and hate and beauty that have schooled me only too well?), and while these pictures are usually busy rushing past us, he likes to hold them up, and live with them, and watch until they begin to watch back. This is what he offers us, in his ragged, smeared junkyard treasure trove, a place where we can look and understand. It's so very rare.

But why put more stuff in a world already too full of it? Even short fringe movies were a little too attached to the buying and selling of experience for Alex, and turning yourself into a self-made office machine in order to get them shown just didn't seem worth the trouble. So he decided he would present his work only if he were there (it's integrated, it's part of my life), massaging the flow of pictures, performing in the dark with his machine accompaniments. On some days, the company of machines is preferable to that of humanoid hosts, and he has spent many hours breathing new life into forgotten formats, allowing them to speak to us again from the ghost world, another place he calls home. There will come a day, very soon, when no one will have ever heard of things like automobiles or telephones – capitalism is always producing the brand-new thing, and along with it, the desire to have it. Already I have nostalgia for what hasn't yet been invented. Alex can be found in the junkyard, rescuing forgotten moments of marginal media history, threading up old movies inside left-behind machines. He shows us another kind of beauty, and through it, a way to pause beside something in our too-busy hours that might have brought an angry hurt, only now we have to greet it with a smile. At last we know what it is, and instead of wounding us, we know how to receive it – it is also welcome, we will make a home for it. What used to wound us brings us pleasure. That's how far he takes us.

MH: Some artists who work with ready-made pictures (made by strangers, already in circulation) feel that there are already too many images in the world, and their work functions as recycling. Others have more political agendas and aim to point the mainstream back at itself. Why do you use found footage?

AM: Years ago, I began to see work that uses found footage and, over time, came to understand the emotions and false nostalgia they evoked. By slowly, unconsciously and quite serendipitously building a collection of these films so often sourced for this retrofitted practice, I think I began to care almost more for the unadulterated industrial and educational films themselves. They possessed a touching utility and helped fine-tune interests in moviemaking that were not based on drama or storytelling. No attempt was made to seduce or convince. These films assumed there were things I needed to know and were bent on demonstrating them: drilling techniques in coal mines, clearing the lungs of newborn infants, systems for closing a deal.

MH: Every movie is a marker in time, evidence that someone passed this way once, as well as a superego doggie biscuit, career stepladder, capitalist object of transmission. You don't produce these objects much, preferring performance. Can you explain why?

AM: The present is all that we have. Psychically, I can't afford to believe anything else. Legacy has never much interested me, and I suspect that I fear investing these objects with too much power, power that could move me in directions I may not want to go or that could bind me in some way. And if I am honest with myself, it is most definitely induced by fear more than by some grand statement. When I was making 'finished' work, I would send it out to festivals and get no feedback besides form letters, thanks or rejection. I realized that this part of the making was uninteresting and, at its core, meaningless. A by-product of process. Creating a store of work was sucking me into 'body of work'–think (How many have I got now? What is this arc looking like?), which I felt was limiting my ability to move past and forward. So I wondered how I could keep the development of the work alive. Performance seemed the obvious way. As a bonus, it also required my presence at screenings and enforced communication with audiences.

I struggle with trust. I have seen so many 'movements,' and the judgments for and against are interpreted in a manner that best suits the needs of those doing the interpreting. History has a way of lying to cushion the blow of truth for the latest reader. Still, I am glad for traces of the past that help to build strategies for managing my world. That said, I am insecure with my work, and I enjoy the idea that it exists only in the moment of its presentation. Maybe memory is kinder than document.

MH: The avant world is a place of refusal (of audience, venue, narrative conventions). Can you discuss this in terms of your work?

AM: The work that has moved me the most has at its core a kind of beauty and imperfection of form that is consistent with the world it inhabits, and this kind of beauty – with all its sadness, wonder and impurity – keeps me making things. What the avant world does with it, be it refusal or acceptance, is largely secondary. We can't escape the narrative imperative – it seems we need to attach it to most anything we see or experience. Pursuing it in a conscious way seems an obvious and uninspired strategy.

I am not naturally driven at all times to make work. Most of the time, I worry I should be doing more, but then see that I can only do as much as I do, and that is my lot. I distrust the institutions that rally around art and artmaking. It may be that my view is less than charitable, but I often see personal agendas and a lack of genuine selflessness, which makes me feel cautiously doubtful and at odds with the economy of art. The avant world, as you call it, is a place where the rules of economy (of money) play a much less central role. A reasonable living cannot be made in this zone without doing a whole lot of grotesque self-aggrandizing, running around and pushing your 'thing' on the current tastes. This strategy doesn't seem to bring a lot of pleasure or satisfaction. And given that my ideas and message are humble and very personal, it doesn't make much sense either. Why attempt to throw these things at everyone? Seeking approval and dollars from a system I have little regard for seems a little bit pointless and self-defeating.

This Fleeting

MH: Do you feel that you are part of an avant-garde? What about other people?

AM: I really don't think about it much. I know there are a handful of folks on the planet pursuing like-minded ideas and forms (projector performance, film manipulation, etc.), but I never feel the need or pressure to fit into a grouping or system. Maybe by situating myself where I have, I can avoid that. Is it an avant-garde? I imagine so, as it sits on the edge of a cliff with an ocean far below, always ready to topple over, risking failure, error, missteps and death. As difficult and scary as it is, the edge can offer a view I can't find anywhere else.

Mostly I feel quite alone in my practice. Certainly I can relate to others, enjoy and discuss their works, but more often than not, I create in a vacuum of my own design. The majority of those I'm close to either don't get my work or don't take an interest in it. Rather, they take an interest in me, and I in them. The work is secondary at best, sometimes a way in that takes a backseat, finally.

MH: Could you talk about your lovely movie theatres?

AM: I started the Edison Electric Gallery of Moving Images in 1995 after returning to Vancouver from a year in Montreal. I was becoming more and more interested in uncovering old ephemeral films. I was in touch with Rick Prelinger at that time, and visited his huge archive of works down in New York City's Meatpacking district. I had also been trying to correspond with Amos Vogel about the works he discussed in his book *Film as a Subversive Art*, trying to locate some of these prints. I thought that programming the so-called avant in concert with entirely obscure, ephemeral works that had the potential of 'fun' might draw more folks out to discover both of these invisible cinemas.

These were my two primary interests at the time: films once made for industries that no longer held any value and were now living very far from their intended forum if at all, and films made for personal reasons that had a very small (if any) audience. When you read the history books on the avant-garde, you quickly recognize that these films never had significant audiences. Even in the heyday of the American 'Sitney' period in the centre of New York City, audiences were usually made up of a few dozen at most. Have you ever read Mekas's old *Village Voice* columns? He was ranting and raving at how crucial and potent and life-altering this stuff was, all the while acknowledging that five people showed up. So, for me, arriving at a moment when interest was clearly waning, I was trying to create a space and atmosphere that felt inclusive, unpretentious, non-academic, but took the work seriously (ephemeral, avant and otherwise).

Why start a space in Vancouver? It had potential at the time, very much the untamed west, without a lot of cultural competition. I also didn't know what else to do with myself. I was making the occasional film, doing graphic design to get by and trying to imagine *what next?* A new space seemed like a good idea. So I programmed this stuff along with a mix of other live shows, performance work, retrospectives, etc.

It was at this time I met Owen O'Toole, who came up to do a show. He definitely planted the seeds of inspiration for pursuing projector performance, as well as hand-processing. I ran shows mostly on weekends, barely getting by, living in the back room in less-than-desirable conditions: no heat, rotting floorboards, etc. I did this for two years and considered the experiment a success. When the lease was up, the landlord wanted way more money and I was getting tired of the living conditions. I closed up shop and put the seats in storage. I don't know that I really thought about reopening with a new plan at that time, but I didn't sell the seats, so it must have occurred to me.

I worked on films and continued with the graphic design for a while, then happened upon a space in Chinatown that looked promising. There was a grouping of studios surrounding a large central room on the second floor of a two-floor building. Next door was a booze can and, downstairs, a Chinese grocery store. I decided to dive in headfirst. A few friends and I cleared the place out (it was filled with junk from past storage, artists, etc.) and started painting and planning the space. I rented out the studios that surrounded the 'theatre' to artists with the understanding that the central room would be used for screenings and events half the week, that they were welcome to attend and participate, but that noise levels had to be nil during shows. A few artists rented the first couple of studios with a promise of others to come. By opening day I had a schedule printed for the coming months and fully distributed, and a big opening night party planned (Halloween) with a haunted maze, bands, films and more, with lots of publicity to boot. That afternoon, as I was wiring something under a platform, I saw these two sets of feet approach me from across the room. It was the city engineering department and the fire marshal, come to close me down before I even opened. The space was not zoned for assembly, and if I dared to go ahead with the opening they would lock the doors and slap me with a heavy fine, so they strongly recommended I don't have the opening party, or anything else! My heart sunk lower than low (though I have to admit to a simultaneous and strange lifting of my spirits too – all the weight of the project was suddenly gone and I was free of this monstrous responsibility of my own making).

Heather, my girlfriend at the time, and I spent the next week at City Hall with planners, the cultural sector and the building-code people, learning a huge amount about the rise and run of stairs, heritage building status, selling off building height to developers – a load of things I didn't care to know and that, finally, didn't help me an ounce. After much anxiety and soul-searching, I decided (or finally initiated) the inevitable fate of the space – pull out, cut my losses and regroup. The experience left me extremely gun-shy about trying the 'illegal space' idea again, and what little funds I had to spare were gone. My memories of that space now are the smell of the Chinese grocery store, the low ceilings that nagged me from the start, and the piles of programs I left in the middle of the room for the next tenant to deal with. (I know one of the folks who ended up renting the space, and he complained of the mess when he moved in. Had he only seen it before we cleaned up. He didn't last long there. I think the booze can is still next door, untouched.)

Half a year later, a friend of Heather's mentioned an empty theatre space in Gastown I might want to have a look at. I had never set foot in Gastown except for the occasional live music show at what was then the Town Pump. The theatre stood on the very edge of Gastown. It was really a part of the downtown eastside – a rough area full of homeless people, junkies, prostitutes, old men, ex-fishermen and

loggers, many living in rooming houses and cheap hotels. Of course, there were also housing co-operatives, low-rent apartments and a community of people interested in addressing the atrocious state of this neighbourhood, which remains the poorest postal code in Canada. A handful of artists' studios nested nearby, along with a strange oil-and-water mix of condo owners who never left their lofts, ordering takeout and watching their big TVs while the living dead roamed the streets below.

The space itself was perfect for what I had in mind: a black box with risers, a front-end area that could act as a café during the day and a concession at night, and an office area in the basement for film storage, computers and dry goods. Some paint, a few fridges, coolers, a coffee machine and the construction of a booth were the primary concerns. Relatively speaking, not that big a deal. The rent was very high for me but cheap for the area – with the strata fees and property taxes it came to about $3,000 a month. Looking back now, it made absolutely no sense to move forward given where I sat financially, but I had some kind of blind faith that this would work out. I signed a five-year lease and made myself a promise: that if I was still around in five years I would decide if it was something I wanted to pursue beyond the lease. And if, on the other hand, I sank ... then I sank. Well, we – and that 'we' includes a list of about fifty volunteers, to say nothing of the moral support of friends – managed to sustain it for the whole five years, sometimes running credit cards to their max as we awaited funding or prayed the weekend shows would do well enough to make the rent. Those who came to the popular shows saw a place that was wildly successful, while those who came to the more rigorous, 'difficult' and unknown films and videos or live presentations saw just a handful of people, scratching their heads at how we could possibly keep things afloat. We also ran the Vancouver Underground Film Festival out of this space for five years with tremendous success, garnering a reputation all around for uncompromising programming, an absolute lack of pretension, and a spirit of will and refusal to falter (even with numerous thefts

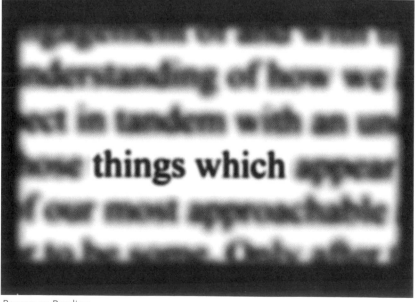

Barzon on Reading

– a few with bricks through the window, a few more by infected needle-point). The only folks getting paid were the café day staff. I never pulled a salary in the entire five years, except for a small symbolic stipend for running the film festival four days a year. Somehow, I managed to find space for a few design contracts, lucked into a few personal art grants, and actually squeaked by while running the cinema seven days a week. The website for the space, www.blindinglight.com, still stands as an archive for film reference and as a testament to a very intense five years.

And then it was over. Contrary to popular mythmaking, it wasn't burnout that stopped me, though I did worry it was coming. Better to stop while I still liked the place, I figured. And enough with all this administration, I needed to get back to my work and see what it felt like to make it without this weight over my head every day. A few folks came forward with a desire to keep the place going, wanting to take over. But after explaining the finances involved and the massive workload, it became clear that the task was far too overwhelming and financially daunting. The smart people I approached with the idea of taking over at the outset of my decision to close shop didn't need to be convinced of anything – they knew the job was too much and wisely refused my 'generous' offer outright.

I ran the place in a fairly unconventional way, in that I managed the bulk, if not all, of the creative and primary administrative tasks myself: programming, design, advertising, marketing, projection, café management and ordering, accounting, etc. Had I tried to hand it off to someone else, they would likely and sensibly wanted to piece this work out. But the place was so tightly run that handing tasks around to volunteers would have meant a major restructuring and a heck of a time commitment on each of their parts – all for no pay, of course. Finally, with two major problems haunting us endlessly – the extremely high rent and noise issues with upstairs neighbours – the space itself was starting to feel less and less viable. I recommended that those interested in pursuing something like it do so in a cheaper space where noise levels would not interfere with shows. A few places have come up since, but finding good space in Vancouver has always been a trial.

MH: Did you notice overarching trends or themes in the work you were seeing while you were programming the Blinding Light?

AM: As far as the moving image is concerned, there seems to have been a move away from new ideas and 'ways of seeing,' and a move toward revisiting ideas we have already seen or felt. Maybe a period of clarification or confirmation? Work has become more overtly political, and personal politics seem less central. Gender and body politics still hold sway, but are of less interest to larger audiences. There is so much material out there, and so little manages to make it to our eyes that any kind of generalization about trends is precisely that. There was a brief period when it seemed handmade, hand-processed movies were having a resurgence, but that seems to have subsided, looking more like a

sub-trend in retrospect. I still believe that older technologies and mechanical apparati will come into their own eventually as artists' tools, but again, this may sound very quiet in the larger halls ...

MH: Didn't having to watch too many movies (mostly bad ones) provoke a terrifying anxiety of influence when it came time to making your own? How did you find your own voice after being so attentive to others' needs?

AM: Making didn't precede or follow the job of programming, it occurred simultaneously. So as I saw these works, good and bad, I was also working on my own materials, projecting ideas and ideals. The primary impacts this simultaneity had were time constraints and focus. As ever, though, I find it difficult to get started at all. The lure of soaking up information and literature and the catatonic state I manage to get into regarding self-expression may keep me from producing much. But then I remind myself that if pace is forced, it usually shows.

MH: Why did you first get interested in movies?

AM: I took a college English course called Short Story/Short Film, where the two forms were compared. *An Occurrence at Owl Creek Bridge* was the first film I saw that dreamed out loud, showing another way of seeing and thinking through film. This course piqued my interest enough that when I went to university I registered in a first-year film course, and as luck would have it, Peter Harcourt was the professor. I followed that course with another in Canadian avant-garde cinema with Peter, and declared my major in film studies. The degree was, as it turned out, more of a course in cultural and political studies: semiotics, Marxism, Heath, Bellour, Durgnat, etc. This left me both filled up and drained. I moved back to Montreal and looked for work while getting involved at the local film co-op and eventually landed a job there creating a tour of independent short works around the province.

MH: Why is a smart guy like you still living in Vancouver? As a cultural anthropologist, how would you describe Vancouver?

AM: *What is a smart guy like you still doing living in Toronto?* might be a better question, but the answers to these kinds of inquiries are generally dull: economics, familiarity, friends – and by the way, there are plenty of people smarter than me living here! I am held here by relationships and cheap rent, mountains and ready access to nature, a buffer from the centre of the universe. I don't think too much about Vancouver's cultural qualities; it is getting more and more expensive here, but I continue to manage my way on the cheap. I don't consume much besides food and am always working toward getting rid of 'stuff.' It is a good and bad place to make work for me, far from any sense of pressure, but also lacking in any real dialogue around this sort of work. I can count Vancouver's experimental filmmakers and fans on one hand, though the number would be even smaller if I lived in the woods, which feels more and more appealing. I also travel, and as much as I am not a big internet flag waver, it certainly opens up windows.

MH: Do you worry about getting older, money and savings, the ability to work, losing your hair, illness and death?

AM: I suspect that I am ready to die right now, so anything beyond today seems like a gift, though I may not always manage it well. As for future fiscal planning, something generally comes along. I could always get a job.

MH: Could you talk about how your two-projector performance *Parallax* (50–65 min, 2004–5) was developed?

AM: *Parallax* began with a daily ritual of hauling four or five reels up from the basement and throwing them on the Steenbeck to see what they were, sometimes fast-forwarding, sometimes getting completely wrapped up in the subject matter. It has been a curious education, to say the least. I now feel equally confident about delivering a baby at home, managing sales employees and knowing what to do in case of hypothermia on the trail. I was looking for images that moved me in some way, often completely divorced from their content. Turning the sound off helps. Over time, I compiled lists of images I wanted to work with, not knowing how they might sit together.

Then I began working with the images via rephotography and optical printing (partly at a residency in Grenoble, France, with the group Atelier MTK), trying different film stocks and multiple rephotography to kick up the contrast, varying techniques of hand-processing (all the material in *Parallax* is hand-processed at home, and the originals are projected). Then I began the ordering and assembly of images. All of this happened in fits and starts, between long periods of navel-gazing and distractions. As I assembled the piece, I was looking for variable-speed projectors I could control on the fly. With this I could create a kind of spontaneous optical printing effect, allowing me to layer negative and positive images with a range of light 'interference': gels, hand-masking, lens manipulation, etc. These projectors were designed for use in laboratories to study micro-organisms, for sports teams to analyze football plays, and by the military to study future targets. I spent a lot of time on eBay searching out auctions, as well as asking around at university audiovisual cages to see if they might have a few kicking around. Finally, I managed to cobble together a set that worked fairly well and needed only a little coaxing and fixing. The next stage was running through the images and testing and retesting timing, speed and effects.

Once I felt comfortable with the estimated length of each segment, I began the soundtrack. In the recent past, I have used a sampler I play live using prerecorded samples mixed with a CD burn. In this instance, I realized that my attention would need to be so focused on image management that handling a sampler would be out of the question. I decided to create a number of distinct 'tracks' that would be played with each segment and would act as my guide for the images. If the sound was finishing and I was behind on the image work, I would need to speed up, if the images were nearing their end, I would need to slow down to allow the music to catch up. With many rehearsals and shows behind me now, I have managed to find a pacing and strategy that works. Every time the piece is performed, the material slowly degrades – an erosion I take pleasure in, both aesthetically and conceptually. Eventually it won't be possible to perform this piece any longer.

There's a man who appears two-thirds of the way into *Parallax* who sits at a desk and seems to speak from a position of authority – he gesticulates with precision and speaks with confidence – but his words are muddied and indecipherable. Is he a sage or a snake-oil salesman? Should we trust him, or do we need to find a way to make our own decisions? He appears both in negative and positive, and the two projectors move him in and out of phase and focus. The appearance and disappearance of his face into his own shadow speaks to an alternating sense of trust and fear that we place in authority. The ghosting of this figure foregrounds his illusory nature; he appears as an invention of our own making, a spirit presence.

While working on this film, I was reading a bit about Buckminster Fuller, and was struck by a pact he made with himself after his daughter died at a very young age. He promised to better the world with the tools he had, which meant architecture mostly, new spaces for living that would be lightweight and simple to build and available to all. It was a promise of utopian ideals, but a genuine gesture nonetheless. I found a documentary where he discusses this at length – and I have always liked his voice, which has an almost Burroughs-like mumbled quality. It was this explanation of his paradigm shift, his vision, that I use over the image of the man behind the desk – this figure also physically resembles Bucky Fuller, so it fell together quite nicely.

This segment was originally four times the length, and even now it's quite long. It was actually the one area I worried about because of its clear sourcing from educational films and its potential for falling into humour. But its length and the time I am given to develop its sculptural shape in the performance helps move it away from that potential pitfall. I really didn't want to fall into the trap of easy and familiar uses of found footage. Conversely, there are other moments, in the nature footage, for example, where I wanted to embrace those clichés precisely because of their beauty and familiarity. To see a single water droplet or a flower opening, these are moments for me that deserve returning to.

MH: How do you get through the cliché?

AM: By spending time with the material and remaining open to it beyond standard impressions. Things become clichés precisely because they are effective. If I am trying to express some moment of wonder or beauty, then they can be recalled. In their original settings, these pictures function according to familiar strategies, whereas in my work these moments are redisplayed within a new context. It's simpler than it sounds. For example, I have a film about life in the woodlot, which explains why farmers preserve a chunk of forest in otherwise razed prairie areas – the wildlife and plant varieties that occur, and how these are both useful and necessary to the maintenance of such a property. The movie has a very functional purpose, but the person who made these images seeks out beauty because they have an eye for it. The subject falls away, and the beauty or truth of these images becomes the focus.

When a baby is first born, it is brought into a room where every orifice in its body is penetrated by a tube to make sure all passages are clear: that it can shit, piss, hear, breathe. These pictures occur in an educational film made for doctors and nurses, demonstrating the standard process that takes place in the first five minutes of life when child gets pulled away from Mother to make sure everything works. In some ways it's a horrifying procedure, but it is deemed a necessity, and as aggressive

Parallax

as it is, there is still a beauty to be found in it. These pictures appear at the beginning and end of my film. They run in metaphoric parallel with a CPR segment where there is an attempt to resuscitate a woman – yet another medical procedure that looks absolutely violent. These particular film segments were shot in actual hospitals and were originally shown to demonstrate a failure of technique – in the case of the CPR, the woman dies. This made me very tentative about using this footage, especially because it looks like the doctors are pressing life out of her, even though they're trying to save her. *Parallax*, for me, is about this clash between life-giving and life-taking. My intention is never violent, though there is most definitely a violence in the imagery.

MH: Can you talk to me about the salamanders?

AM: A salamander is an amphibian that is poorly adapted to both land and water. It doesn't swim well because it lacks fins, but it needs to be in the water in order to breathe and maintain its moisture. On land, its body is too long – its stomach drags and it doesn't move very efficiently. And so it finds itself caught between these two spaces and has to bridge them constantly with no one place it can settle. The newborn and the CPR patient each perform a similar bridging, which is returned to and developed in much of the imagery throughout.

In nature, places that offer safety may be quickly interrupted by risk and danger. This is what *Parallax* finds in the natural world. The struggles of a bird feeding its young and abandoning them while it searches for food. A lone squirrel hiding below ground, a scattering of insects moving across space, another cluster of bugs taking apart their prey. Then there is a shift into so-called civilization, with the movement of a car heading directly toward us, filling the screen with its grill. Cars are emblematic of our culture, creating new spaces and pictures of the space we inhabit – the so-called 'grid.' Following the baby at the film's beginning, the next human we see (much later) is heralded by a car – a startled young girl turning to look. It is this look that brings us into the city. At this point there is a long shot of the skyline glimpsed across the water, a bridge, and then the city itself, its characters in motion, surrounded but alone, trying to make their way. Nature and civilization each have a necessary brutality. When a robin comes to its young and drops a worm into their mouths, those babies are fed but unsafe, and they are left exposed and crying out.

MH: Your use of two projectors suggests a duality that is echoed in the title.

AM: The physical displacement of the image plays off one of the meanings of parallax, that a subtle shift of perspective can change everything. If I close one eye, that painting on the opposite wall shifts; if I close the other eye, again it shifts. This perspective shifts with only inches of adjustment from the viewer's perspective. The greater the distance away, the larger that angle reaches; in this way, there is something of the butterfly effect here too. I also want to play with the tension between identical images, their movements toward and away from each other, and our innate desire for things to come together. I show paired 16mm reels, one negative, the other positive, and when these images meet in sync there is a containment, but it is fleeting and mostly they remain apart, and it is that tension that drives the piece. The containment, the labelling, the knowing, is always temporary. The answer we're looking for is difficult to grasp and we can't maintain it. In theory, the perfect superimposition of negative and positive would produce an image of nothing. This relates to the performative aspect as well; the moment I decide to make *Parallax* a

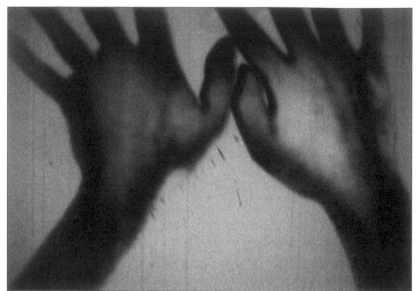

Parallax

single-channel work, it would be contained and repeatable, and that cuts completely against the theme of the piece.

There's something similar at work in *Nightsky*. The projection materials are taken out of their original context and rebuilt to celebrate the potential never manifested in the original. *Nightsky* is a film performance for three Super 8 cartridge projectors, which were invented and marketed to encourage the use of Super 8. These units are about the size of a slide projector, and load from the rear with an endless loop cartridge of Super 8 film potentially running anywhere from a few seconds to about three minutes. The idea was that teachers could more efficiently load and unload the projector 'instantly' for classroom use. This simplification and the looping format is precisely what appealed to me. I took these cartridges, cracked them open, removed the original film and reloaded them with my own hand-processed black-and-white Super 8. For *Nightsky*, there are about 25 cartridges loaded and unloaded throughout the piece. There were a lot of different projectors marketed in Super 8's heyday – slow-motion and high-speed, bookcase style, rear screen, portable, multi-format, cartridge, etc. – all intended to guarantee and enforce the economics of the medium. The more the merrier, not unlike the range of video cameras and monitors available today. To make these mechanisms useful in a new way was very much a part of both *Nightsky* and *Parallax*. The irony is that they're in direct opposition to their original economic imperatives. I'm using these projectors because they're cheap and available, not because they're the cutting edge of technology, which they once were. The reinvention of these tools finds a thematic parallel in the use of found footage. In both the mechanics and the material, there is a hijacking of their originally intended uses.

MH: But you're reacting to footage you find?

AM: I've seen about two percent of the material in my basement. The selection process comes initially from what the canister reads and what I think I might find in there. It arrives through

curiosity. Then the process takes on a shape familiar to me from more traditionally experimental approaches. You go out and shoot a bunch of film over an extended period, then months pass during which you review footage and try to uncover common threads. The common thread is your own living: you shot it, and that provides a continuity of attention or concern. With the basement footage, I choose images I am drawn to, catalogue them, then set them aside and continue looking. I'm not thinking of how they move together at all, not until months later.

MH: *Nightsky* (25 min, 2002) is a film performance for three Super 8 cartridge projectors that narrates a lost utopia of science. Can you describe it?

AM: I can at least describe one version. We open with a centre-screen title credit: *Nightsky*. The left screen shows the blowing branch of a tree tinted with a green filter; on the right screen is a homemade wind chime made of forks and knives, sepia-filtered. The centre screen switches to a candle blowing in the darkness, the side screens go dark, then there's a number of variations. In one version the card *Close Your Eyes* appears on the left, and on the right a shot of churning whitewater. In the centre screen, the title gives way to a close-up of eyes, looking. These three images merge to the centre, and we spend time on the churning water and the eyes with some hand-manipulated filtering bringing the water and eyes in and out of sight and in combination with one another.

The water disappears, and we're presented with the first of a series of loops depicting space technology: satellites spinning in orbit (in negative) and then a pan across dozens of radio telescopes, remarking the play between the earth and space. Then the second layering begins, containing clusters of meteorites, close-ups of artist renditions of Saturn's rings, sometimes in negative, sometimes positive; images from left and right projectors are both layered onto the eyes. Then they pull apart, one to the left, the other one to the right, and the centre eyes are replaced with slow-motion phases of the moon in black and white. The two outside screens switch to very short loops of a close-up face of an astronaut with a coloured gel laid on top of each projector lens. The centre image shifts to a positive image of the astronaut with a blue filter, then these three images (all showing the astronaut) slowly merge, achieved by my moving the projectors together to create a pseudo-three-dimensional version of the astronaut moving in and out of sync with his shadow-self.

On the soundtrack, we've moved from sparse wind sounds to technological blips and radio frequencies, looping radio tones and a short sampling of the well-known space radio broadcast, 'One small step for man ... ' which loops incompletely until all three images merge one on top of another.

Then the screens pull apart once again, each picture appearing separately as the imagery shifts toward a study of sunlight, the impact of solar radiation, the deflection of heat off the earth. The material becomes less about wonder and more about information – the science of the universe. Then we return to material from the original mechanisms of space (satellite dishes and telescopes) and more natural materials: rock formations, planetary surfaces and meteorites. The centre image shifts into an extreme close-up of a television screen that reads as abstract video noise, the right screen shifts to a close-up of a radio telescope with raked shadows, while on the left the eyes from the beginning return. These three images merge, the visual noise disappears, and we end with a play between the radio telescope and the two eyes, and then back to the *Nightsky* title-card loop. The end.

MH: Were you concerned working with this material that it would be overtaken by nostalgia? That there is already too much meaning attached to some of these moments?

AM: I wonder about this fear of nostalgia. How do you see it as problematic?

MH: Nostalgia can provoke an easy sentimentality, a glaze of received associations that prevents thinking or seeing. Nostalgia can short-circuit attention, and part of your project requires opening the material on display for new arrangements and new meanings. There are certain pop songs, for instance, that are already my songs, attached to moments of my life, so when I encounter them in a movie the song never makes its way all the way over from the speakers.

AM: But the fact is, I need it to be your song if I'm going to do anything with it, as nostalgia is a prerequisite for meaning to shift. I want to maintain the wonder these images once evoked, but also question meanings that we may have missed the first time around. *Nightsky* brings back a subject that we haven't looked at for a while, asking questions about the loss of that wonder, those frontiers, those hopes. Where are they now? Today's images of space exploration – transmissions from the surface of Mars, for instance – don't carry the same potency because they're less aesthetically rendered, they're videotaped surfaces of a dull red planet, so the magic is also lost. What we are seeing, in fact, is more true and less an attempt to capitalize on our imaginations. There will be a generation of children who carry no fascination with space (or at least a different kind) because of these kinds of images.

MH: Does your project want to redress the inadequacy of the image around us?

AM: Not redress, but to pose a question: What did those images finally do for us? Or were they empty promises? Like a lot of things that carry nostalgia, there's a melancholic aspect to it. We miss the things we never had in the first place.

Part of the appeal of space is that there is nobody out there; it's unspoiled. *Nightsky* uses images from a period of history when space was treated with wonder and awe. These pictures also depict a frontier of knowledge and human potential, hope and other-worldliness. Conversely, the images that historically followed the ones I chose show us utopian ideals of cityscapes and new social orders that don't have the same appeal: television shows like *Battlestar Galactica* and *Space 1999* presented us with familiar earthly situations transplanted into space stations. To boldly go where every man has been before.

MH: You have produced performances that are played and played again, but others that have a much shorter life.

AM: Most of the one-night stands are inspired by events or collaborations. In 1999, Western Front had a year dedicated to the experimental film image as a thematic, called ~scope, and they invited me to do an installation as well as a live performance. I collaborated with two other filmmakers (Brad Poulsen and Brian Johnson) and a musician (Claudio Cacciotti) to create a six-projector, three-screen piece entitled *Solar Radiation*, which inspired *Nightsky*.

Strand was made for a regular monthly event organized by the now-defunct Vancouver-based collective Multiplex Grand. It was built around found-footage animation of a DNA strand on a black background. This was run through the projector, then reintroduced into the same projector, bi-packing the material.

In a related work, I ran one film through a projector, then instead of taking it up on a reel, ran it into a second projector. So the viewer is presented with a comparable image on both projectors with a delay of three feet of film, about seven seconds. I played with focus and the colouring of the images while they ran together.

Some one-offs are more playful and precisely about taking the opportunity to experiment with an audience's expectations, as well as developing new ideas and techniques. With *The Wallpaper Horizons* I discovered a perfect matchpoint between an instructional film on hanging wallpaper and Norman McLaren's *Lines Horizontal*. About five minutes into the film, a string is tautly stretched to level the wallpaper, and all that appears on screen is a red string on a white background. At this moment, McLaren's film is cut in on the same shot, albeit animated. The soundtracks are combined as we get inextricably lost in some alternate reality well outside our aspirations to redecorate ...

Another experiment I returned to many times was a visual exercise I would play with as audience members entered the cinema prior to a screening (at the Blinding Light). I would layer a found-footage 16mm film with a simple digital painting toy (My First Sony Electronic Sketchpad) run into the video projector so that the frame of the video projector matched that of the film. In this manner I could 'draw' over the 16mm images as they appeared, marking off and surrounding characters with Haring-esque thick lines, interrupting the images with drawn text and dropping symbol stamps into the scenes.

At the invitation of Maija Martin, for her project entitled *The 100 Greatest Books of All Time*, I used a film that was originally intended to teach speed-reading. She asked twenty participants – filmers, videomakers, friends, performers – to each make a thirty-second video representing their five favourite books. In my portion, a cluster of words appears on an otherwise blurred screen. The selected portion of the text references cinema, and the frame was videotaped smaller and centred, but at 24 frames per second instead of 18, it all moves too quickly even for speed-readers, playing on Maija's theme of 'exploring the impossibility of creating cohesive superlatives at the end of the 20th century.' The project was created for Pleasure Dome's *Blueprint* project, a post-millennial touring collection of commissioned works.

MH: Was *I Am Watched While Paranoia Follows* (1998) your last 'single-channel' movie? The quality of attention is very familiar from your performances, so this movie appears as a bridge of sorts between two kinds of practice. Is it a bridge?

AM: *I Am Watched* isn't single-channel: it is two cartridge projectors, performed with lots of tricky masking. Also, it is now titled simply *I Am Watched*.

I have made few single-channel films since beginning projector-performance works, and if there is a switchover point it is likely *A Current Fear of Light*, which was made by videotaping a performance (albeit one I performed in a dark room by myself). This piece was created entirely of scratched, scraped and punctured black leader which was then looped in a projector and videotaped while altering the framing (zooming in and out) as well as the shutter speed – a sort of instant optical printing.

I Am Watched begins in the dark with an alarm that never quite stops ringing throughout the film and low, slowed tones. A found-footage woman approaches and gently touches a door, over and over, in stunned recognition. Slowly, from the right, a new picture wipes in, showing clouds running past a tower that holds the letter W. All the refilmed footage is hand-processed, so uneven development, dirt, scratches and cinch marks are very much in evidence. The mysterious W wipes into an aerial view of a sidewalk where people walk, as if they are being seen by the sign. A found-footage policeman (Keystone Kops?) scampers down an alley fourteen times, caught in a loop that searches for meaning perhaps, some order in these proceedings. Then a projector lens appears in close-up with a dark disc sliding over it (almost like an eclipse) and inside the lens an aging Super 8 porn film appears. The motion is so repetitive it's hard to know if this is also a loop, but at last she takes out his cock and jerks him off on her chest. These images blend back into the first pictures of the woman by the wall, recoiling from the primal scene.

MH: You make a new narrative from these looped picture fragments – is the aim to show that the tyranny of one-way mainstream flow can be reimagined via reordering? Is it an examination of sexual hysteria?

AM: There is something of sexual hysteria here, and also a fear of the gaze – both in its ownership and its reception. The woman is actually tentatively looking into the next room through the door she is approaching, only she never reaches that door, while the imposing and brittle, aging W (a well-known landmark here in Vancouver) seems to speak of an ever-watchful Orwellian state control, observing all actions on the street below. The looping of our Keystone Kop effectively renders any potency he may have had to nothing, and yet his presence is constant. The porn element comes as a shock to most audiences and is unexpected, but in fact it plays right into this self-conscious paranoia that has rendered even the most intimate act into clichéd re-enactment. The performance is built from loops, and is the one piece I thought about reworking for galleries with this looping in mind.

MH: Is there a relationship between your work and DJ culture?

AM: I just read somewhere that the turntable now outsells the electric guitar in the U.K., and so the turntable as instrument has most definitely hit the mainstream, and the economic potential rolls on as kids continue to buy new records (at least with a guitar there were only so many effects pedals you could care about). But the relationship to my work is tenuous. The crucial difference is that the material I'm working with isn't available, nor marketed. If DJs took their source material from music no one listened to anymore, made their own recordings and pressed the results on their own vinyl, then put these records out on relic turntables and accompanied them with contemporary visual material, we'd be more eye to eye.

MH: You are very sensitive to small details in the picture world, like a lover who comes to know every moment of a body, every possible response. This sensitivity requires a mutual openness, which leads, inevitably – not all the time, but sometimes – to heartbreak, new forms of pain. Could you speak about this wounding in terms of the pictures you see? Or the pictures you form of those around you?

AM: While working, I develop a deepening relationship with pictures, much like time spent with another human being. We learn to separate the impossible from what can reasonably be hoped for, to recognize the fault lines. How do we manage the impossible? The limit. A delicate step and loving respect is requisite if we hope to maintain mutual growth. This is the hardest thing about any relationship. The pain comes when we don't have the tools or understanding to recognize the change that is always happening. The same can be said for my relationship to moving pictures – how best to cradle these images without sheltering them too much, how to draw them together without sacrificing autonomy, how best to create true relationships that allow weakness, fragility, strength and beauty, all at the same time.

MH: I remember seeing Abigail Child's work for the first time at the Collective in N.Y. She showed, among other things, *Covert Action*, a movie that beautifully and disturbingly reworks home-movie footage to underline shifting relations of power. Jonas Mekas castigated her for not preserving the original footage. In his eyes, all movies are an important part of a vanishing past. How would you respond to this?

AM: As dramatic as this may sound, it actually pains me to cut up films. I tend to agree with Mekas, that each of these films, regardless of intent or content, deserves to retain its integrity. But for me that doesn't mean we can't use these images in new contexts – we just have to respect their first version. While the film is inanimate, our relationship to it brings it to life.

MH: There is a marked disparity between the solitariness of your making and the collectivity of presentation (people gathering to watch), unlike a book, for instance, which is written and read alone. Does this disparity trouble you?

AM: No matter how many come to the theatre, I'm always alone when I watch a film, and I believe the rest of the audience feels this way too. It is a way of gathering with others yet maintaining a solitary position, in the dark, preoccupied with your own emotional reactions. This is why we all find it so troubling when that focus is broken by someone's phone going off or incessant whispering – the tacit agreement of aloneness in a group of people has been broken and threatens the magic of a very fragile relationship. When the lights come up, there is a sense of loss, but also a quick (but still gradual) reintegration into the room, and the world. This format – this way of seeing and being – is very specific to the presentation of film. It doesn't strike me as a disparity at all, but rather a way of presenting a solitary and personal expression to a group that remain individuals.

MH: Do you feel (via Freud) that something is missing in most artists, and art is the means to fill the hole? If there was/is something missing in you, what would it be?

AM: I wouldn't dare to speak for most artists – everybody has their own reasons or inevitable struggles that are wholly specific. I have looked at prolific or focused artists in the past with envy, wishing that my muse visited with more frequency. Now I see more clearly that for every apparent edge or plus, there are as many minuses, and we all manage our output and creativity in the best way we know how. Asking for more, or whining with less, seems only to augment what can already feel like a burden if not carefully managed and fairly treated.

MH: If you were happier, would you stop making movies?

AM: They would be different. My discomfort with the world plays a major role in artistic output, and if I were more comfortable with it, I would be less inclined to look inward so much for some kind of spiritual peace. I am beginning to become more interested in drawing and writing lately, so who knows where things may lead ...

MH: How has the fringe managed to respond to the politics of empire? How does your work respond to it?

AM: I think the more personal a work can be, the more universal it becomes. By not bogging down in fashion and current politics, a work can speak more clearly, unfettered by a reactionary methodology. We cannot help but respond to the politics of empire. We sit inside it, and blood is on our hands from the moment we are born. How we choose to respond – by finding beauty in our midst, for example, or granting value to a different path – is the best any of us can hope for. In my work, I feel that looking into the past, the way we have imagined ourselves and our world, reflects upon other ways to live. It might provide tools to rise out of traps that are entirely personal.

I sometimes distrust the romantic cliché that equates solitude with beauty, but there is a reason the cliché exists. When I am alone, I feel most capable of understanding myself and the world around me. The balancing act of the world outside ('civilization') and inside is what occupies my life.

MH: Do you ever fly in your dreams?

AM: I've had only one dream about cinema, which I remember vividly. I am standing on loose grey rock creating a shoreline that falls off in the distance, and beyond is forest on all sides. On my right stands a new shed or large boathouse with oversize windows in front. A number of people – maybe thirty in all – start to file out of it, solemn and naked. They seem healthy and attractive, but normal-bodied as well, not generically good-looking at all. Confused, I realize that a few hundred more people are emerging from the woods and converging in one area. Suddenly the ritual/movement ends and they all break from their focused activity, loosening up and talking among themselves.

Two women are walking back from the proceedings. I casually ask what's going on, trying to be confident and relaxed with everyone's nudity, especially theirs, as they are very close to me now. They tell me they are shooting a movie. I say something like 'So, looks like maybe a B-movie, something low-budget?' Trying to make them feel comfortable with the fact that it isn't anything special and hey, ya gotta work, right? They stop and say quite directly that no, it is a very important film. The fact that these aren't trained actors is somehow central.

I turn away and head up the hill from the water, arriving at my granny's house. I come around to the front and see that a new scene is being set up. More naked people at one end of the lawn (toward the garage) are mixed in with others in maid/servant clothing. Someone says *Okay*, and they all start to move across the lawn toward the woodshed at the other end. I notice the director for the first time, an older Ingmar Bergman–looking guy, a woman with a clipboard and three or four middle-aged others surround him, all looking serious.

The camera is a relic from past camera ideals, beautiful and stylish like a big old American car. I study the director as the dolly glides toward me, filming in the direction of the garage. A women in a dark blue denim dress with a pen strung around her neck walks across the action, very close to the camera. The woman with the clipboard breathes in sharply, obviously upset this has happened. She says to turn the camera off, but the director quickly interjects, asking that the lens cap be put on slowly, and only then to turn the camera off. It seems this woman was not part of the scene and they are concerned they will now have to get permission. This has been difficult in the past. It turns out that the director has a policy of using everything he shoots. If the stranger does not agree to participate for whatever reason, the entire film will be lost.

Alex MacKenzie's Media Work

Still Life   3 min 1991
In Security   3 min 1992
Blind Light   8 min 1993
Watching you ... on the late show   3 min 1995
A Current Fear of Light   7 min 1996
Home Safety   8 min 1997
X-Ray Pi   3 min 1997
I am Watched/Horizontal Fix   1998 (Super-8 cartridge performance)
I, Endemic   1999 (commissioned interactive
    web-based installation)
Somber   1999 (gallery installation)
Solar Radiation   25 min 1999
Barzon on Reading   30 sec 2000
Escape Velocity   20–30 min 2000 (Super-8 cartridge
    projector performance)
Strand 2   10 min 2001 (2-projector performance)
Nightsky   25 min 2002 (Super-8 cartridge projector
    performance)
Onlooking   7 min 2002
Medi(cine)   20 min 2003 (2-projector performance)
This Fleeting   45 min 2003
Parallax   50–65 min 2004 (2-projector performance)
Possible Model for a Microcinema   2005 (gallery installation)
Antidote   2005 (LED light projection installation)
Underfoot   5 min 2006
Goldenleaf   6 min 2006 (2-projector performance)
Loom   23 min 2006 (2-projector performance)
The Wooden Lightbox: The Secret Act of Seeing   45 min 2007
    (handmade emulsion/projector installation/performance)

Distributed by the artist. See www.alexmackenzie.ca.

Alex MacKenzie's live media works are presented at festivals and underground screening spaces throughout Europe and North America, most recently at the Rotterdam International Film Festival, Scratch Projections in Paris and the K-raa-k Festival in Brussels. He is currently designing handmade film emulsions and manually powered projection devices for installation and live performance. www.alexmackenzie.ca

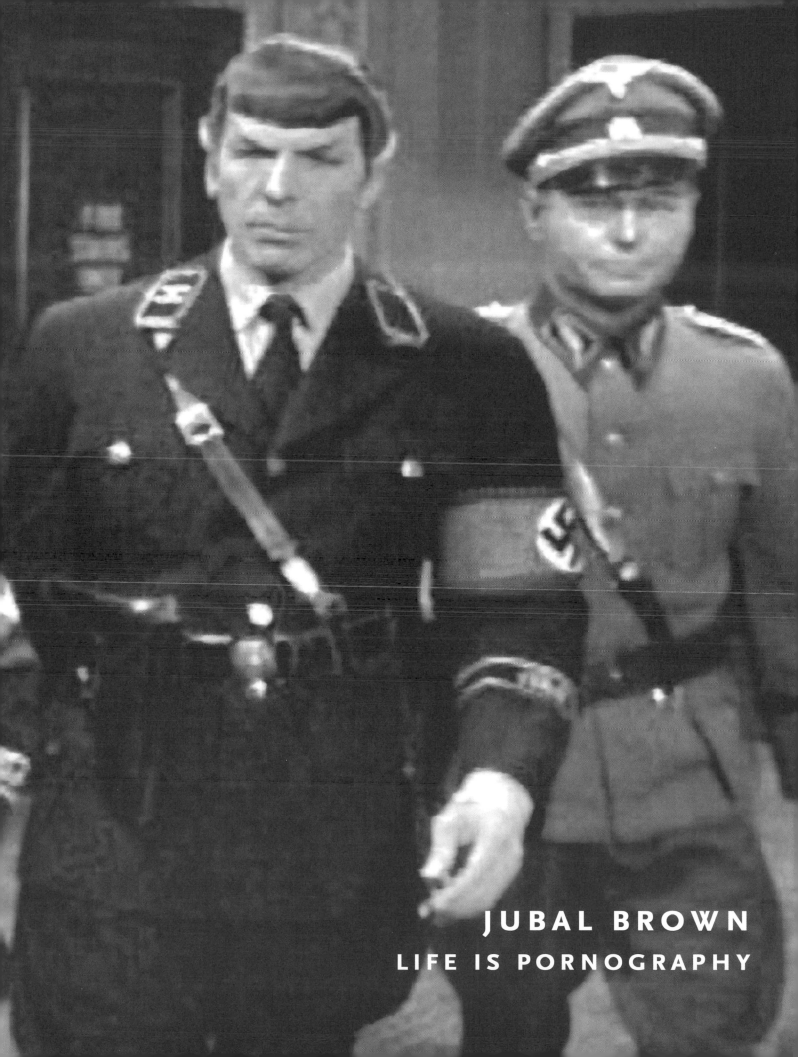

JUBAL BROWN

LIFE IS PORNOGRAPHY

Canadian video art had its founding mothers and fathers, a generation of pioneers who performed themselves in front of lo-fi mono cams. There was Colin and Lisa and Rodney and Paul and Vera and how many others? Not so many, as it turns out. And then there was the second generation of folks, the silent ones, the ones who arrived 'too late' somehow. Now that we're in the grip of '70s nostalgia, the efforts of the first generation are hot all over again, busy moving off the shelves while the second keeps its silence. And then there is the third generation, filled with art-school brats and talkaholics and urban primitives. First among equals is Jubal Brown.

I guess someone had to be Jubal, waving dark flags at the rally, spitting up paint at masterpieces in the museum – ten years after punk rock, he kept it alive. Snow-white tan, skater scars and needle misses, with the kind of charisma that doesn't come in a bottle yet. He started making videos in art school, fast cut-ups of revolutionary moments or sci-fi dreams (someone else's future) or TV clips. Fast, faster, fastest. Watching his work was like walking into a scene, young and pale and going very fast nowhere at all. It was beautiful and heady and heartfelt, but what did it mean? Hip to the body-art mutilations of the Viennese school, he took a pocket knife to his side and took out some fat. That was almost real. Replayed his teacher's vid-art classic that showed off her soft-focus scars and named his *Deathday Suit*. Ran a gallery and tore it all down when the lease ran out. Organized a copy-wrong clusterfuck around an Arnold Schwarzenegger movie about cloning, inviting a dozen artists to join him in remixing it for a late-night show. All that energy and nerve and time spent working and reworking the same rhythms on the machine. A computer kid, grown up bad on video.

And then came a summation of sorts, *Life Is Pornography*, where he showed he can talk and shoot and steal at the same time, he's not dead yet, he's survived his worst intentions and lived to tell about it. His tribe, the ones he runs with when he's not at home interfacing with his machine, is called famefame. Romantic malcontents. Almost glamorous, almost young, almost dark movement fodder.

MH: Steve Reinke once wondered aloud why he made videos. He's ambitious and intelligent, so why this interest in a medium that is so sub-visible, relegated to specialist houses and in-crowd affairs. Why do you make videos?

JB: Because I'm stupid. For all practical applications, it's one of the stupidest things to devote time to. But it's also the only relevant medium: television. Brian Oblivion: 'The battle for the mind of North America will be fought in the video arena, the video drome ... '

MH: You begin *Life Is Pornography* (23 min, 2005) with a signed foreword, a cautionary note that sprawls across the opening image: 'All this is stolen and fake you should go away and not watch any of it.' Why the warning? (Is it intended only to parody the copyright warnings on mainstream videos, or the ratings-board provisos?) And why did you sign it?

JB: That intro was stolen, or 'quoted,' as they say, from Kathy Acker's intro to *My Mother: Demonology*. Yes, I'm a big fan of Kathy Acker, one of the living saints, although she's dead now – aren't we all? I guess my use of it was intended as a bit of a disclaimer, and a slight parody of that FBI warning garbage, but a preparation for the video-art audience who might be offended by the use of appropriated 'video art' clips. My general position on that is that anything we see or hear enters through our senses, into our brains, and if what's in my brain isn't mine to use as I like then: fuck!?! Anything you can see or hear, you can steal (Mark Schubin). One could spend ten years developing a program to replicate audiovisual memory onto video tape; I don't write software, so I just press Record. Why did I sign it? Maybe I'm an arrogant prick or just a fraud ready to confess.

MH: Your critique of video art begins with a computer voice saying, 'I am video art,' while a Pac-Man game plays, one of the most elementary and simplistic forms of electronic gaming. Is this what you feel the present-and-always state of video art is? Has it changed? Was there a historical moment when video art was relevant? Has it been overtaken now? Has video art become, like Pac-Man, a once-amusement, anachronistic, necessary for some further stage of corporate development of spectacle but no more than that? And finally, how do you view your own past video work in relation to this statement?

JB: The negativity toward video art wholeheartedly includes myself, though I am nowhere near the icon of video art as the people I take a friendly poke at in this video. My feeling about video art and experimental film is that their aims were very noble and worthy. It's reductive to say this, but the point was to create alternatives to mainstream uses of the mediums and primarily to oppose spectacle, to not entertain and sometimes to create a voice for the marginalized individual. But the result was failure, or at least not very interesting; because it was so good at not entertaining, too good at remaining marginal, in the end it's very boring.

My generation, and the ones that have come after, have accepted the mediums into their lives as a part of us; they are like new organs, not an exterior technology anymore, so there's no point being critical of something you can't fight. 'The television screen is part of the physical structure of the brain,' says Brian Oblivion, 'therefore television is reality.'

My dismissive summation of video art in *Life Is Pornography* is that it's either joke – cheap laughs, one-liner ideas designed to amuse and endear, to suck up to an audience – or porn – seductive, image-based wank, even if – especially if – the images are intellectualized or politicized, which only provides more levels of fetishization.

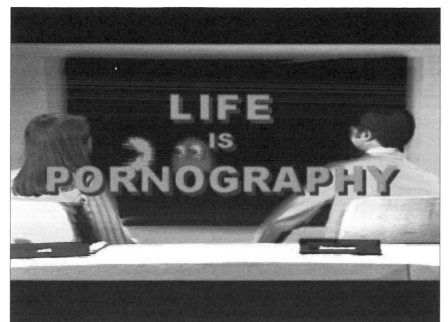

Life Is Pornography

Pac-Man calls up a nostalgia for a primitive video interaction beyond which video art has barely evolved. Because video art is basically unexploitable – i.e., no one wants to see it, so it can't be sold, therefore it doesn't exist. We at famefame are evolving the medium of video, bringing it up to speed with the contemporary mind. Long live the new flesh!

MH: Could you tell me something about famefame? Is it part of 'the death of the author,' a new subjectivity conceived in group form (yet its members seem to sign their videos individually), or does it represent an ethos, a way of working and living held in common?

JB: famefame is our little make-believe secret society. It may be seen as an arts collective, but it is really more of a cult. The public persona of famefame is that of an arts entity through which we are able to manifest various projects, art events, screenings, performances, concerts, release records, DVDs, CDs, hopefully eventually publish books, etc.; to produce and promote all manner of culture that gives form to the collective desires of the famefame/jawa militia, which is basically the 'production and promotion of the aggressive, intense and volatile. Our aim is to promote an immediacy that transcends the physical means of the work itself, threatening the boundaries of video, sculpture, performance and event arts, audio and music ... Our work is the residual iconography of the new ethos condensed into a singular gesture. We give form to the wall of history as it crashes into itself, obliterating the lines of demarcation, to break out of time into the experience of the perpetual present ... ' [famefame Manifesto 2003]

MH: Returning to your fringe film and video summation, your primary critique (certainly the taste they've left behind for you)

is boredom. But doesn't the rapid-fire editing you deploy also take part in a temporal politics that bends to the corporate masters? Does art also have to be entertainment? At what point does this stance mean giving up on art altogether, or simply declaring whatever's No. 1 on TV 'the best art' because it's watched by the most people? Isn't the art you're proposing simply another way of giving in to the rapid proliferation of media globalization?

JB: I have given up on art altogether. Duchamp and Beuys gave us freedom from art: everything's art or nothing is art, it doesn't matter anymore, the world is just a bunch of shit and no one really cares whether it's art or not, only whether or not it's interesting or useful. Once in a while entertainment is very interesting. The 'best art' is one that gives form to the urgency of a contemporary ethos, grants form to the collective dreams and nightmares of the contemporary mind, and sometimes Paris Hilton does that better than Tom Sherman.

About the 'rapid proliferation of media globalization,' at this point it's just a given, it's not something we have any control over, it is happening, like the weather, and the weather isn't evil or good. If it rains, you get an umbrella or become waterproof. The evolution of the world can't be avoided – one can choose to adapt or die.

It is important for the media artist to speak in contemporary language – that language is evolving, fast, there is no time to judge. By that language we may be indoctrinated into our own enslavement, or we may be freed into an ecstatic manifestation of the contemporary; we must act fearlessly and venture into the future.

After the loss of the real, we can still access the stuff of life; the simulacra, or crumbs or whatever, can be temporarily broken open, and in that rupture it is possible to live for a moment or two. That alone is desirable.

Ultimately, I am more interested in breaking things than making things. At this point in human evolution, we have made enough shit – it's time to start breaking shit. 'We been lying down for much too long, now it's time to dance to a different song ... ' The Damned. Smash everything.

MH: In *Life Is Pornography*, your voice-over says, 'The nude: the ideal image of the human form,' but you show only young white women, which I assume is your ideal. Your use of absolutes, of inclusiveness when saying *I* (meaning *we, everyone, always*), is a typical power imperative for the white male, used successfully to justify genocide and murder for centuries now. Why all this work to make the colour white – and the male gender – transparent again?

JB: Come on, white girls are people too! I am white, more or less, I guess, or non-cultured you could call it (non-ethnic?) and predominantly het and male these days, but I don't define myself by these physiological incidents. Besides, identity politics is over – race, gender, fat rights, whatever, it's just not interesting. I've sucked enough dicks in my lifetime as a boy whore and I'm marginalized enough as a poor mental patient, but it just doesn't interest me to whine about it. There's no such thing as being fair; if it's not my 'issue,' I would be a poseur to try to speak genuinely to it. I can only speak with the voice I have. We grey people from the future consider ourselves a part of the human race, we're all the same – that's what the 'organ bar' is about, the fragmentation of the whole body of the human species is what permits us to justify killing 'others,' but we're all the same. All people are abominable monsters, and their continued existence cannot be justified, even if they did start being nice to each other. Whites – if there really could be a category called 'white' – would have no monopoly on murder; in the 'genocide's greatest hits' segment of the vid, the clear winner, with the highest score of 40 million!, is Mao: Chinese killing Chinese. People can come up with any excuse to kill each other, excuses are just lip service; when there's no good or evil, there's no reason to make excuses or place blame, and there is no good or evil! People just have a tendency to hate, it's in our nature, and killing is a natural solution. In nature, when a species overruns a territory, it develops ways to thin itself out and return the balance, and we've gone so far that 40 million doesn't even put a dent in it. There are too many people, some definitely have to die – why stop at some, why not kill them all? If we got rid of the white man, there would just be some other jerk to blame for everything.

MH: I'm not calling down some political-correctness tribunal to squeeze you into place, but to remark on the pictures that you show that aren't random assemblages but exact and exacting. These pictures 'speak' and make meaning and feeling, and, of course, they demonstrate a point of view, a way of looking. Let me return again to your voice-over, which states, 'The nude: the ideal image of the human form,' but you show only young white women. Isn't this the old objectification returning again? You present these looks as hot little glimpses: even Manet's model looks dirty with the look you press her into, not at all as this nude appears in the original: as a subject who looks back! Why do you rob her of the subjectivity the painter granted? You show these art nudes like someone flipping through *Playboy*, impatient for the next thrill. In other words, it's all about the one who looks (the maker, the author, the invisible hand, you) and not at all about who – or more aptly what – is being looked at. And haven't we seen this all before, in fringe forms and mainstream, this tired misogyny, over and again,

woman's body as truth or whatever the excuse is to get her to take her clothes off in front of the camera? As usual, she is – they are – lying naked while he is (you are) telling us the story of her body. I guess these bodies don't have voices. Can't they speak for themselves? Or is this another silence the viewer is expected to view as 'normal'?

JB: The piece is called *Life Is Pornography*. It is about pornography; pornography is mainly a white heterosexual male institution, as was nude painting, and the whole of institutionalized looking. To avoid acknowledging that would be naive, to oppose it would be futile – it is part of the contemporary condition. My crop of the Manet says in six seconds that this token subjectivity of the returned gaze has long since been reassimilated; the gaze is returned, if it matters, by the woman deep-throating, accompanied by Bowie's 'Heroes.'

This video is also admittedly about me and my relationship with pornography: yes, I like skinny white girls. I also like Asians, Europeans, latinas, blacks, etc. (whose images, for what it's worth, are represented in the video). I beat my meat indiscriminately. I'm also hot for the olds: 'I love Joan Rivers' is a central theme that is partly about the transcendence of body through image, but also about its failure. Anything can be fetishized, from Joan's scars to Nazi death camps. No one is safe, desire will eat us all, especially the desire to look. All images are pornographic.

The intention was indeed to 'demonstrate a way of looking,' and to consider the fact that there is something corrupt and sinister about the whole experience of looking at, seeing and making pictures; it is a perverted, corrupt, twisted and – according to the Muslims – blasphemous practice. Blasphemous against reality, truth, maybe even beauty. Personally I am not going to poke out my eyes (or stop watching television) anytime soon, so until reality can give us something better, that's all we have: an image world that is perverse, wrong, twisted, fucked-up, oppressive, whatever – those are the eyes we have.

Life Is Pornography

'The nude: the ideal image of the human form' was changed from earlier drafts. I intentionally took out all direct verbal gender references so as not to confuse the issue. I am not concerned with gender; people objectify women, men objectify women, women objectify women, the whole of human civilization objectifies and subjugates women, even nature sticks it to the woman. I am not interested in complaining about that. The feminists tried and failed; it wouldn't make any difference if they had succeeded – objectification and subjugation is part of all of our experiences of image, and probably of all human existence.

There is no expectation of the viewer other than they are morons and not worth making anything for. The viewer can fuck off – that whole relationship was ruined decades ago, it is a lost cause. The viewer is garbage, the artist is garbage. We can still try to make something or do something today, but if we do it for anyone but ourselves we are already lost. Any anticipated exchange is tainted to death by mediation after mediation.

I am not telling the story of anyone's body; pornography is not people, it's images. Images are not neutral representations of the people they came from – they are image and image is the enemy. It is my voice I speak with, who I am is another question, am I just another cheap fifth-cut jib dealer, pusher of images? I am doing my best. 'I am.' (Gowan)

MH: Desire, beauty, virtue and truth are the four values projected onto nude females, and your movie suggests that these romantic ideals contain the roots of misogyny, which finds its fullest declarative expression in pornography. Yes/no?

JB: I think I identify, and reflect critically on the fact that those values are, and have been, projected onto the female by centuries of traditions of image-making. The nude, pornography, etc. – I don't think I project those virtues onto the female, I reflect on our imagization of the human, female or otherwise. Our problem is what we idealize; the misplacement of value, the attachment of sexual desirability to the female body, is now totally ridiculous (for the male). We don't need to breed anymore, to make any more people – we need to kill more and make less. 'Love thyself': a lot of schmucks say it. I'll attribute it to A. O. Spare. Pornography is made for masturbation.

I refuse to acknowledge misogyny – it's misanthropy, we are all the same, women are not that special, they are a part of the human race like the rest of us. All of this idolization of the image of the female is a foolish distraction; they are basically men with long hair and a hole in the bottom. Not ideal at all. Just another humanoid. If anyone tries to hate women (misogyny), usually what they really hate is themselves; ultimately they hate the human (misanthropy), and in that respect they are right.

MH: 'Video art is jokes,' you say in voice-over, serving Steve Reinke up as example. Video art is a joke, or the joke is on video art. And besides, no one cares. Is it because only mediocrities and people without imagination have been drawn to this medium?

JB: I don't know why video art is so bad, but I really think it should be better. Steve Reinke is not that bad; he is funny, and smart and clever, it was just a friendly little poke, like 'Come on, is that all you got?' The rest of the artists in that segment, I just selected work that was archetypal of video art. The whole of 'video art' is a bit of a joke, a depressing joke; the most depressing part is that this is what I do too, and I'm even less successful than those guys. It may be impossible for video artists to compete with the expectations that mainstream media culture has created in viewers – the *Sesame Street* attention span, the MTV-addicted eye – but we can't go back. We have to take attention deficit disorder, or whatever they're calling it these days, to the next level, push it till it breaks.

MH: When you remark about video art that 'no one cares,' who are you speaking about? Who is 'no one'? Who should video art be talking to or reaching, that it isn't? Are these failures of exhibition also failures of production and distribution? Do you see video art as a resistance to mainstream production, or a subset of it? Is resistance possible, and how can this be enacted in exhibition?

JB: The failures are in production, distribution, exhibition and viewing. Like the parallel gallery system, video has become a little sister of its mainstream predecessor, which it originally set out to oppose. It became not oppositional but parallel, yet another restrictive system on a smaller scale. Like the use of the word *experimental* to describe a genre of music or film, it doesn't actually mean experimental anymore, if it ever did; it now simply describes another very strict traditional genre. About the possibility of resistance, I don't know. I do think it's essential to try to do what is 'right' or appropriate in any given situation – to me that generally means not to resist but to revolt in the most beautiful way imaginable. Whether it's possible requires further research. Do you think resistance is possible, Mike?

MH: Re: sistance. I don't believe only in the negative. (Not not. Who isn't there?) Not only to define motion-picture art as non-narrative, non-pleasure machines, but to say yes.

I have a friend who appears, at first glance, to be leading the most conventional life imaginable. Married with children, home-owner, car driver, the list goes on. But he is in the middle of a catastrophe and continues to behave with grace, refusing to take his revenge, to blame others; he remains a model for what humans might one day become. Is resistance possible? My friend is living it every day.

Or my friend Tom, struck low with Parkinson's and AIDS. Some days he doesn't manage to get out of bed, his muscles paralyzed by the illness, or else he shakes uncontrollably. Tom never complains, never imagines another life (if only …). Instead, he reinvents himself, he finds new friends (even though he can't leave the apartment without assistance), develops new sexual practices, new kinds of pleasure. Is resistance possible? It's necessary.

What continues to strike me in the field of video art is just how low the bar is. Anything goes, oh it's all right, it's only a video, right? No one is held accountable, no standards (but what do I imagine, a censorious quality board, helmed by who?), and tapes that are either about so very little, or else tapes that desperately need to be made, only they're produced by people who have no inkling how to make them. This isn't resistance – it's the playground.

But let's return to your tape. You remark (am I remembering this wrong?) that German folk in the '30s resemble contemporary audiences. What do the German people in the 1930s have to do with the people who watch or don't watch video art here in Toronto in 2005? Or is it more widespread than that? Should I ask instead: what does a population that permits the Nazis to come to power have in common with contemporary Canadian society?

JB: Yeah, I use the quote from some 1970s video artist who says, 'So video allows me to play in my playpen.' This is quickly followed by, 'That's why genocide is great.'

The examples you offer (not to dis your friends) demonstrate only survival, a resistance of physical death in the second example and avoidance of crisis in the first. Some call it a coping mechanism, some call it denial. Resistance is more proactive counterattack than mere damage control. In *The Revolution of Everyday Life*, Raoul Vaneigem calls it 'survival sickness' to just go on eating, shitting and using air, or having sex, etc., and to feel accomplished in achieving mere avoidance of literal death is the most counterrevolutionary behaviour of all. Survival is submission. 'Happiness exists only at the price of revolt' (says Kristeva), as if happiness were enough!

The onset of Nazism was normal. The people of Germany were not monsters, yet they pretty much put up with, welcomed or participated in actions that later became perceived as the most horrific in the century. I say or Raoul says, 'We're all looking for

a laugh, just like the good people of Germany in the '30s' – like we don't care, we have no values, just give us something! I speak of a complacency, and a desperate mediocrity that is as wrong or more wrong than genocide.

MH: In your tape you announce that pornography is the 'imagined fulfillment of desire.' Is the same true of art? What desire does video art fulfill, or does it fail entirely?

JB: Yeah, that's a good question. If we continue to do it, it must fulfill some sort of desire or some need, but generally I can't imagine what that would be. I think Bruce Mau said '"cool" is conservative fear dressed in black' – something like that is probably true of most art. Fear is the same thing as hope, the other side of the same coin. Hope is a weaker form of desire. The desire my work attempts to fulfill is to make dreams reality, to access a contemporary manifestation of the real in which the individual imagination reigns and destroys every limit to the flight of the spirit. I fail constantly, unwaveringly, eternally.

MH: Part of your critique about video art is that there is so much talking. Do you feel that art shouldn't speak, or that some primary experience is being dodged because talking is getting in the way?

JB: I can't remember who said it, but 'That which can be put into language can be commodified.' Talk is cheap; talk without action is worse. Put up or shut up. I will accept that in order to be social and interact with other people we do have to talk a little, but from what I can see, most people do little else (not just in video, but in life). There are sacred forms of experience that are beyond words; most of my other work is an attempt to access that more primal direct experience. This piece was me doing one of those talky videos. I think Joan is really hot; the final version of this vid will have Joan in Frankenstein porno collages where her head is attached to dirty sex parts, like in *Frankenhooker*. Also she is good at talking, I could listen to her all night; she's vicious, funny, dangerous, sexy, Jewish and totally out of this world.

Life Is Pornography

MH: You replay various genocides as video-game scores, presumably to show the cheapening of life via the gaming industry. This seems a rather obvious point, bluntly made. What is your juxtaposition adding to the debate exactly?

JB: I've never claimed for a second that this was a smart video. I don't think I have anything to contribute or would even want to contribute to any debate on that subject. Are you saying that the military's solution was the proliferation of first-person shooter games? Conspiracy theories are useful as dark movement fodder.

I'm definitely not complaining about the gaming industry, though it is one of the most vacuous wastes of time available right now. I like Pac-Man okay and I think comparing the scores of mass murderers is really funny. The only thing I take a real stance on in this video is that 'I love pornography' and the human race is generally pretty crappy.

MH: You segue into a science rap about the lizard brain, suggesting it is the root of the nervous system (all desire and action) and that it extends throughout the body, an invisible hand guiding our actions 'from long ago.' Murder and desire, love and death, you suggest, are the primary, motivating emotional elements of personality and are framed before language, before birth perhaps, already hard-wired. Do you agree? How do pictures (clearly a second tier of experience) affect the lizard brain?

Life Is Pornography

JB: I don't know officially how images are supposed to affect the lizard brain, but I posit that there is some evil conspiratorial relationship at work. The voice of the video is a somewhat stupid, schizophrenic voice that speculates about elements of science without fully understanding them. It trusts an intuitive paranoia beyond empirical logic or knowledge. Supposedly there are three distinct parts to the brain – the reptilian brain at the centre that controls instincts and drives and primal needs, another one I forget, and the mammalian brain that we generally use to think with. They are each distinct, and the communication between lizard and mammal is virtually non-existent. As human animals, we are functionally divorced from any application of instinct. So how do those primal drives apply today? Without a natural course to follow, it adapts to its situation; its nature twists and perverts into an unknowable monstrosity. I think images have something to do with this.

MH: You segue from 'I am the lizard king' to a Bee Gees (?) song: 'Why do you have to be a heartbreaker? Is it a lesson that I never knew? ... my love for you.' Sorry, I'm missing the connection here. What's this all about? And what singer are we watching in her papery, reanimated kitsch beauty?

JB: It's Dionne Warwick, not the Bee Gees, and the accompanying image is another distorted porno clip. The lamenting 'Heartbreaker' expresses disappointment in the pornographic image, which is all promise and no consummation, because the relationship to pornography (and all image) (and life) is a strict one of image and viewer, spectacle and spectator. A love of image will always be unrequited, unconsummated, because there is no exchange, only observance. But even with all its faults, shortcomings and lies, we love our pornographies.

MH: You offer this critique (via voice-over) of pornography: 'The reduction of human culture into exploitable parts.' But you never tell us why you like porn, are fascinated by it, returning to it over and over in this tape. You're not alone in this, of course – porn is a word that is often followed by the word *industry*, suggesting its part in the globalization of pictures. Do you feel your relation to porn is different than most because you also produce pictures in video? How is it different?

JB: 'Why do we love porn?' is another good question. I think it's part of a rabid overabundance of desire – impossible, incredible, unquenchable desire. Of course it's not a desire to look at naked pictures or sex pictures – porn is a surrogate desire object. It's not even sexual desire necessarily; society's cult of appearances, of show and spectacle, attempt to turn every desire into one that can be bought and sold. The porn industry makes more money than the Hollywood film industry, no joke. Desire has been tamed and colonized in every way possible; desire is constantly transferred onto commodity products. Porn is just the most obvious example. Our culture seduces us, constantly teasing, tempting, eliciting more and more desire so that we will be better consumers, but never allowing us fulfillment of any kind.

I don't think my relation to porn is different than most people's. I watch it both critically and non-critically. Most people probably do that. I may have a higher level of tolerance for the vile and disgusting. Ultimately porn is about degradation; since the advent of video, a certain segment of porn has incrementally investigated the limits of the disgusting, the medical prying speculum, the shit-eating, golden showers, the deep-throating to cause vomiting, the pull-my-hair-and-call-me-stupid trend, the ass to mouth, the gaper-capers, cum-swapping, etc. I am very interested in the human capacity for horror and degradation. How bad can it get and what effect does that horror have, and what is it that makes it horrific? I think the 'little white chicks and big black dicks' is an attempt at a kind of degradation that reveals taboos and discriminations that remain strong in our society. By looking at the worst, at what we most fear, we can learn a lot about ourselves. These degradations and horrors degrade both the objectified and the viewer, the way a sadomasochistic relationship is much more revealing of the dominant than the submissive.

Because I don't really produce pictures, I just rearrange them, recontextualize and reproduce, my relation to porn is that of a watcher, an active consumer, a digester. My work is a glimpse into my brain and the way I watch.

MH: You show many pictures that are difficult to watch, like the montage of eye injuries, the photograph of someone with a nail driven through his eye. Can you talk about collecting pictures for this sequence? Do you feel that exposure to these pictures sensitizes us to the pain of others, making us more empathetic, or is it the reverse? Are they part of the numbing spectacle that causes each of us to withdraw? These pictures are part of an essayistic polemic in your video. You are not producing subjects here – the person with the nail through his eye does not speak to us, we know nothing of him, he is a blip in the image flow, that's all. How does your use of his picture differ from the shock tactics used by neocons (who enjoy decrying the 'filth' made in the name of art)? Isn't your tape also a kind of pornographic propaganda?

JB: Most of the stills are found on the internet. I spent several months trying to find the most horrible images I could. If we consider the possibility that images are evil, then the images that are literally horrible and have an unpleasant effect on the viewer are the most true or honest. I treat them as 'images,' not as 'images of.' They are raw material and no longer refer to their subject. The same is true of pornography. A masturbator has no real interest in the people they watch fucking – the subjects are iconic. They are not people fucking, they are fuck; the bodies are not the bodies of people, they are flesh itself.

These horrible images definitely desensitize. De Sade's idea of the libertine was someone who indulged his worst fears and repulsions, who performed the most horrible deeds imaginable in order to become desensitized and thus freed from his apprehensions and inhibitions. To him this was a desirable effect. They were then free to act however they desired. Like Nietzsche's Superman, beyond good and evil.

I don't think these grotesque images can be part of the spectacle at large. They are too poisonous to be assimilated into commodity culture, too poisonous even to be incorporated into any viewing experience. When one sees these images, there is a basic physical response that is automatic, maybe instinctual. I'd like to think this knee-jerk response may have a chance of operating outside of the viewer/art, artist/audience relationship.

I don't think of myself as left-wing, so I don't feel any need to avoid the traits of the conservative. I feel no connection to any dualist politic. I like to think I can act independently of those categories and avoid being reactionary. 'Shock tactics' is a dismissal of intention and meaning. I don't think I'm using shock tactics – I purposefully use these images to contribute to my argument. Shock may be a part of the viewing process, but it's not the point.

'Pornographic propaganda': is that a bad thing?

MH: Not only genocides 'over there' or in some other time, but in our lifetime, in the global village. My genocide and yours. Will you play Croatian to my Serb? Acts of unspeakable horror have occurred, and continue to occur (Guantánamo Bay, in secret CIA prisons across Afghanistan, in the occupied territories of

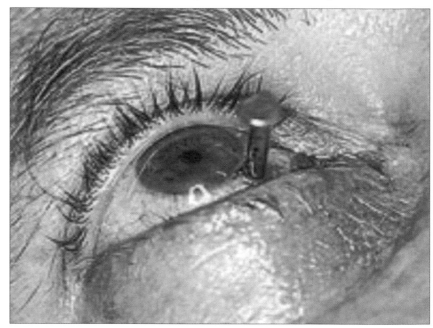

Life Is Pornography

Palestine, in Chechnya), all around us. What is the relation between the images produced in the First World that grant permission for these atrocities? Your tape calls for further slaughters, further deaths, and many around the world are already fully committed – the soldiers of multinational companies and petty tyrants are busy plying their grim trade. How does your tape respond to these events (and why this reaching back to 'the Nazis' to provide pictures of fascism – why not John F. Kennedy or Ariel Sharon or Vladimir Putin)? Isn't abstraction, of the sort you practice here, another kind of totalitarianism – as Heidegger put it, the beginnings of fascism?

JB: The simple and honest answer is I don't really care. The only good one is a dead one (people), regardless of race, class, religion. Sure the whites and the rich and the Christians deserve it best, but that is value judgment. Judgment is unbalanced and unnatural; nature doesn't judge, it just kills – some slowly, some fast – without prejudice. I jokingly suggest that any genocide is a good thing regardless of how imperfect or incomplete.

I know there's tons of other genocides; in the genocide segment of my video, the Nazis score only fifth and they are way behind the top four. Nazis are just the coolest, they had a really great aesthetic that history has turned into the very image of death and genocide. This is more stuff about image and perception, and projection of meaning onto an image. Again, I'm concerned with icons more than statistics or current events.

The piece isn't really about fascism. I'm not specifically against fascism – even we in North America basically live under fascist rule. It's not nice, but it's unavoidable for the moment. Like those horrible images, fascism is the same as the rest, just more honest and therefore better, more pure and true and more desirable.

MH: *Life Is Pornography* is a deeply wounded, romantic and despairing tape that seems also a call to action. It is often polemical, but aimed at who, I wonder. Who is the tape for and what kind of action is required?

JB: The obliquely called-for action is the annihilation of the human race. How to do that? I don't know, it seems impossible, like finding fulfillment in pornography. Who the tape is for is a good question. I don't know. I'd like to say I don't care about the audience and it's made for myself, but if there were no other people on the world I wouldn't make this, I wouldn't make this crap for myself. Maybe it's made for me to talk to other videomakers, to respond to the work of other experimental film and videomakers, a sort of confession of my position and a mild attack on the positions of others. Or maybe it's directed bitterly at a lack of audience.

MH: Why do you rework stammered moments of Britney Spears' *Toxic* video into *Life Is Pornography*?

JB: Britney is used to represent the happy, party-positive attitude of the mainstream vacuous cunt as a counterpoint to the misanthropic assertions of the robot and me. The whole 'life goes on,' 'let's have a good time' bullshit. As if by partying enough, the human could avoid its own shittiness in the bleak horror of existence. I cut it up to make it mine and to make it more exciting.

MH: 'The nude is the roadway to Auschwitz,' says Derrida, and to make sure we don't miss the point, you scroll it in yellow across the death camps. Can you elaborate? Is this how you understand your own body, when you step into the shower to clean yourself, for example? Is the act of showing a nude body in a painting or drawing, is undressing in front of someone else (giving them the power to look at you), part of the same gesture as the death camps?

JB: My understanding of the Derrida point is that the idea of the nude relies on the creation of a false ideal, which then allows everything else to be judged against that ideal, and anything that doesn't measure up may be exterminated. Judgment is the main problem; that may be another point relating to pornography, which is the most judged, the most maligned form of image-making. Manson says, 'You have no right to judge me, you can do anything, you can kill me, but you have no right to judge me.' And he was right.

MH: You are a computer artist, at the vanguard of computer-usage hours, allowing the machine-human interface maximum time to seep in, but no different than millions of other workers, cultural or not, in North America. How has the computer changed your sense of morality, self, emotions? If 'the medium is the message,' what is the message of computers?

JB: I don't think the medium is the message anymore. That may be true of new technologies, when they are raw and undirected, uncontrolled, but new technologies become colonized more and more quickly these days, and they have a prescribed purpose before they are even available. Now the message is the same as the rest of consumer-oriented society: capital and death.

The purpose of a lot of the work of the famefamers is to access aesthesis of the media we cut and of the computer itself. Aesthesis is the aesthetic truths inherent to a structure. The computer has tendencies indigenous to itself, primarily random access memory, which frees us from chronology. The computer is also a natural system in and of itself that handles data indiscriminately; all is fair, there is no morality, no judgment, anything

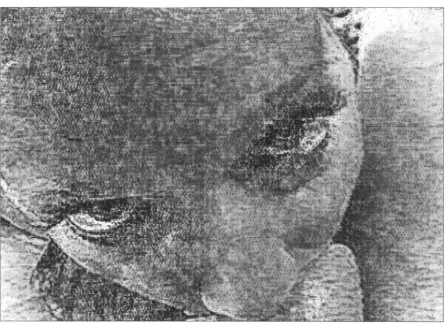

Life Is Pornography

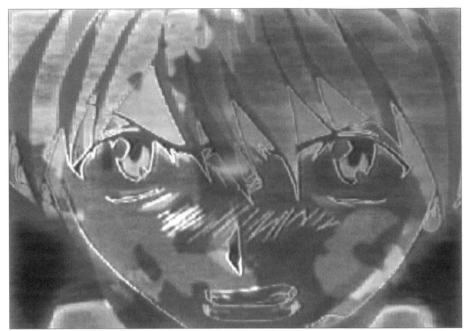

Glut

that is possible may be done, your only limits are the programs you choose to work in.

Some physicist said about freedom, 'We are free to do anything we want, but I can say I want to run up that wall, but the laws of gravity prevent me from running up that wall.' But kung fu masters can run up walls. Laws are made to be broken.

MH: It's someone else's frat party and someone else's holocaust. Doesn't the refusal to introduce pictures of yourself, and your own life, help create the tautology your video decries? The world is pictures. The pictures are bad. The world is bad. Or: all my pictures are stolen. All stolen pictures are morally equivalent. The world is a picture. The world is comprised of exactly interchangeable events that carry the same moral weight (blowing my nose or blowing someone's face off with a gun is the same thing).

JB: Yes, I agree. Everything is morally equivalent. Images are just images; they replace reality, but they are not real and in their falsehood they are all equal, equal in their failure to be real. Therefore napalmed babies = Hamburger Helper ads, skinny Jews = Paris Hilton, Hutus and Tutsis = the NBA game. I watch television and partake in the televisionary communion, so it is my holocaust, as much as anyone else who wasn't there. As a cultureless white person, I am free to choose, to take what I will from these lies; my culture, which I make for myself, is selected from an endless bounty of stolen souls, a pirate's booty of histories, legacies, etc. I don't think I 'refuse to include pictures of myself.' It is just not pertinent – the work is my digest and regurgitation of the things I see. I am an eye, not a subject.

MH: Can you describe your *Wasteland* project? How did it come about? Can you talk about who was involved and what they did? How did this project impact on your future doings?

JB: The entirety of the realm of art and culture is corrupted and destroyed by the structures under which it is forced to exist. Any and all exchange is mediated by commerce, cliques, stultifying expectations, safety, complacency and banal submission to the norm. One of the primary targets of the *Wasteland* project was to eliminate the relationship of audience/performer, artist/viewer. It was a beautifully naive attempt to give something real, and to be alive and engage with others in an environment free of any of those stigmas associated with art or culture or any of that bullshit. We took people back to the cave, and together we burned, we bled, we feasted, we indulged in pleasures and pains, we were alive for a moment or two. It was the only good thing I've ever done. It was initiated by an amorphous group of individuals acting out of frustration and boredom with existing avenues of expression. Originally it was myself and Steve Rife, an American fire artist; eventually a group built itself under the name the Cult of Po-Po, which was short for 'post post-modern, modernist, neo-romantic contemporary.' We also did numerous intervention-type performance stuff – pamphlets, a magazine, postering, graffiti, etc. I was the main catalyst of the cult, but not a leader, the membership was totally anarchic and we welcomed even the worst artists and gave their ideas consideration. That was the ultimate downfall of the group, and then *Fight Club* came out and nailed most of our clichés quite well in a mainstream Hollywood movie. You know you're redundant when ...

MH: You began Art System, a small gallery on Spadina Avenue, along with Daniel Borins. Can you talk about why you became involved in this project, what you hoped to accomplish, what difference you feel the gallery made? Can you talk about closing the gallery, what happened that night and why you decided to shut it down?

JB: Daniel Borins became involved at the end of the *Wasteland* project, and soon after we started Art System together. It was funded by the student union of the Ontario College of Art and Design, but aside from that everything about the gallery was Daniel and I. Anyone who says different is a liar. It was started because we were finishing school and looking at the options available to young artists or curators, and there were little or no avenues open to us and even fewer that were attractive to us at the time. Our intention was to create an environment both physically and socially that catered to our needs and the needs of our contemporaries. We wanted a whole new art scene that was fun and exciting and accessible, one that was relevant to people we knew without being limited to a local, Queen West sort of curse, of the narrow Toronto 'arts community' of 50 'art' people who go to every lame show. We were the blood transfusion that the Toronto scene needed. We raised the bar a few notches. Or brought it down a few, depending on how you look at it.

The gallery closed because of problems with funding. The closing night was wonderful; there was a spontaneous eruption of chaos. We had a giant trough of wine that was part of an installation by Josh Avery, and a few patrons took off their clothes and began writhing in it, people started smashing the shit out of everything, the walls were literally torn down while people freaked out on the dance floor; other naked people swung from the rafters, there were some small electrical fires from smashing lights, a parking meter was used to destroy a wall, a guy I know rounded a corner and realized he had just passed through the piss stream of one of the artists' fathers, people were bleeding, being hit by flying debris or crushed under a falling wall and they loved it; a ball-peen hammer came through the drywall and missed my head by inches, it was truly beautiful, a work of art.

MH: Do you believe in the notion of an avant-garde, a small elite pushing boundaries of aesthetics, of living, of moral codes, of social organizations that offer possible futures? Is there an avant-garde at work today? Do you feel yourself to be part of it?

JB: I believe absolutely in that fantasy. Unfortunately there is no real cultural avant-garde in terms of community or scene or movement. But there are those who fight in isolation, those who strive to give form to the urgently burning spirit of the contemporary and to make advances on the front lines of cultural evolution. I place myself and my famefame brothers and sisters on that front line.

Jubal Brown's Videos

Ad Death   1 min 1997
Fuck the Black Hole   5 min 1997
Fuck Jawa   2 min 1997
High Priced Spread   1 min 1997
The Star Wars   1 min 1997
O Huge Vault of Vaseline?   3:30 min 1997
Musick of the Spheres   1998
Riot 98   3 min 1998
Teletubbies Rising   2:15 min 1999
Still Walking   3 min 1999
Dead Museum   10 min 1999
Little Girls   2:30 min 1999
Anal Jupiter   2:10 min 1999
In My Room   3:07 min 1999
Intimate Moment   5 min 1999
The End (Millennium Project)   3 min 1999
Operation   10 min 1999
Children of the Grave   3 min 2000
Complicity   2 min 2000
The Blob   9 min 2000
Leibensraum   3 min 2001 (w. Tasman Richardson & Robin Simpson)
WAR   3 min 2001
Apollo Shrapnel: Part 5   2 min 2001
Screaming Head in Space   1.5 min 2001
See   1 min 2001
The Greatest Story Ever Told   2:40 min 2002
The Horror   2:50 min 2002
Deathday Suit   8:41 min 2002
Speed   11 min 2002
Generation   2.5 min 2003
Glut   1 min 2003
Satanism, Just Be Yourself   6 min 2003
The Worst Ever   7 min 2003
Runway   4 min 2003
The 6th Day   9:25 min 2004
The Blackness   15 sec 2004
In Bloom   15 min 2004
Life Is Pornography   23 min 2005
We're in Heaven   33 min 2005
Party Tape #52   6 min 2006

Distributed by Vtape.

Jubal Brown is a Toronto-based media artist and founding member of the famefame collective. He is a graduate from the Ontario College of Art and Design, and co-organized the Art System gallery. Working largely with reused video materials, his high-velocity reconstructions celebrate post-romantic nihilism.

PAULETTE PHILLIPS
MONSTER

aulette is a filmmaker who makes videos, a performance artist who directed theatre, a fine-art detective who spent a decade writing feature films. She has reinvented herself over the course of two and half decades of prolific media art practice, shifting her attentions while holding her audience front and centre. Her multiplying practice stages the eye of its beholder,

It is personal work, bubbling up out of the mysteries of personal choice (Why always him? Why always that way? Why now?) but strained through a reflexive frame. Yes, yes, it's a love story, but at the same time, and more importantly: you're looking at me looking at you. The methods of showing are on display here; she activates her viewers, surrounding us with a whirlpool of sound that drowns us like the sad dollhouse onscreen, or getting us to bend into the fur-lined trunk that holds her paddling-down-the-river-with-magic-animals video. Or else we become the frank object of attention as her characters, the ones we're supposed to be watching perform a simulacrum of the artist life (or ours), simply stare back at us. The look between people is her material (the exchange of magnetism, of science, of a measurable energy unit that is also emotion). She takes this look into her hands and bends and moulds and pushes at it. She allows us to see ourselves looking, caught in the act, and instead of making us shrink back into shame and cowardice, these encounters are designed to empower flights of imaginative fancy. There is a luxury of time in this work, time enough to drift and rethink the name we were born with and to unname every object in the room and the meaning of love besides, before settling back down inside the screen. Now that we have welcomed the time bomb of the personal computer into the home, we need these pictures more than ever.

MH: In 1983, you performed a suite of ambient street actions, which paired posters of yourself in various personas with live appearances where you waited at street corners, also 'in costume.' These were actions without an audience exactly, at least not in the traditional sense. Most performances strive for a very controlled display (of words or pictures or gestures), while this work hovers between the visible and the invisible.

PP: Yeah, that piece, *Find the Performer*, could be considered a relational work. The action was comprised of a series of four posters and four performances. The work was anonymous; no one knew who was responsible for covering the city with confrontational posters of a nude woman captioned FIND THE PERFORMER. (The images showing me in 'art historical' poses were meant to challenge the viewer to think about the subject turned into object within the image.) The performances took place over a four-month period between May and August; each month a new poster would cover the previous one. The posters would stay up for a month, and then I'd do it again a month later. The posters were printed oversized with blueprint ink that fades in sunlight. This fading reinforced the ephemeral nature of the action. I rented a van to facilitate the nighttime intervention of me postering the city of Toronto from the Lakeshore to York University, from Scarborough to Mississauga, so when the city woke up there would mysteriously be a new poster.

After a night of postering I would do performance. Each performance occurred at a street intersection chosen for its character, each place recognized as a hub for specific activities. For example, the corner of Yonge and Bloor is the centre of the shopping neighbourhood in the heart of the city; Sherbourne and Queen East is a meeting place for transient men; King and Bay is a centre for banking and commerce; Bathurst and Queen West was bohemian then, a neighbourhood that included artists and war vets, loners and flâneurs, outsiders.

The use of a camera was central – it functioned as a framing device, as a declaration of the event and as a mirror. I stood at each corner, dressed as if to mirror the people around me, taking on the character of the neighbourhood. The camera, set up across the street, suggested an event was taking place. Passersby would look back at the camera and wonder what's going on. The camera framed me, but it was far enough away to introduce doubt. They look at me, waiting for me to do something, only to find me looking back at them, also waiting. It was like a game of tag: you're it. You're the agent. And I'm you, I'm exactly you, don't you see? We're it.

Each performance lasted the length of a two-hour vHs videotape, and they were exhausting to perform. Most unnerving for me was the performance at Sherbourne and Queen Street, for I was truly an imposter there. The dynamics shifted because of the class and gender impersonation. But the guys on the corner were really cool with what I was doing. The documentation is extraordinary, although I have never shown it in public. It is amazing to watch the way people react to me and to the camera.

The first public performance I did was called *Days of Discovery* (90 min, 1982), which used film and video as a kind of expanded cinema. Twin video screens implied the domain of the left and right hemispheres of the brain, the logical and irrational. A film was projected behind a live performer showing cityscapes, locations I inserted myself into. It was about the formation of fantasy, fear and sexuality. One aspect of the performance had me physically touch everyone present to directly address our presence and complicity.

I consider the viewers, their participation, physical engagement and role in producing meaning to be central to my work. *It Depends* (video, 30 min, 1984) was for me an important work very influenced by Roland Barthes' *The Death of the Author* ('We know that in order to restore writing to its future, we must reverse the myth: the birth of the reader must be requited by the death of the Author.') *It Depends* was a fragmented narrative constructed out of units of observation taken from the street. I am a voyeur and some of my work is constructed out of observations of people and events that occur in the public arena. The piece was concerned with how stories get made, how meaning gets produced and how we form opinions based on the appearance of something.

Find the Performer

My ongoing concern is to question the role of the viewers in relationship to their responsibility to complete the work.

MH: Do you feel this is a utopian hope, that each of your audience members could be empowered through viewing and become an artist?

PP: No, I don't wish everyone was an artist, I wish everyone appreciated art. In North America, art is viewed as an incomprehensible elitist activity. There is a dumbing down in media, and artists are the brunt of a joke. In Europe, going to galleries is something that people do regardless of their profession; in North America (excepting New York and maybe Montreal), the general public is not interested in art, it isn't valued, it is seen as superfluous and unnecessary. This country is very conservative – funding exists but few look at work except artists. It's depressing. Imagine being a soccer player and playing only to an audience of other soccer players.

MH: *Sink or Swim* (7 min, 1981, co-made with Geoffrey Shea) shows a pair of bodies underwater strapping themselves together, intercut with the same couple sitting at a table. The two spoken

words, *gravity* and *buoyancy*, reflect a relationship's ups and downs. You and Geoffrey made a suite of movies together: can you talk about your collaborations?

PP: *Sink or Swim* was our first official collaboration. There are two visual elements; one is shot underwater through a handmade periscope, revealing a naked couple attempting to strap themselves together. The couple walk toward each other, and due to the resistance of the water, it appears as if they are moving in slow motion. We only see bodies, not heads. Movement is difficult underwater; there is this struggle and tension set against the luminosity of the bodies and the blueness of the pool. This is intercut with slow-motion footage of the couple engaged in conversation. This tape, like my later piece *Under the Influence*, is about negotiating intimacy amidst external influences.

Collaboration is the dialectic in action. It requires negotiation to clarify and justify ideas. Geoffrey and I were always working on the front end of what video could do technically. It doesn't appear like that now, because the technology has changed so much. But the way our work looked was always very important to us – we wanted our work to look professional. We were interested in producing broadcast quality and we wanted to influence television, we wanted to see art on television, to work in television as artists, to reach people through broadcast.

But it is kind of by default that I worked in video, because I started shooting Super 8 in the early 1980s and hoped to become part of the film community. I remember going to the Funnel, the experimental film theatre and co-op, and asking director Anna Gronau if I could join, but she said I couldn't because I wasn't a member. I signed up with Trinity Square Video, a video equipment access centre, because it was accessible. But I approached video as if it was film, with an emphasis on high production standards. That may be why I was never embraced by either the video or film community. I have always been outside both of those worlds.

MH: Portable video in the 1960s permitted an unprecedented accessibility of production, and the next step was to revolutionize access to exhibition outlets, the most obvious one being television. There were various forays made in this direction.

PP: These ideals of networking and dissemination are now embedded in the internet, but I still think television has enormous potential. It comes into our homes, but we can access or influence its content – it is potentially a more powerful site.

Early on we were very serious about getting work on television. We formed an artist collective, United Media Art Studies, with Christian Morrison, Edward Lam and Dimitrijre Martinovic, Geoffrey Shea and myself. In those days we had some success. We received a commission from Radio Canada (the French CBC) and made *Salomé* (5 min, 1987). We condensed the Richard Strauss opera into five minutes and staged it in the back of a stretch limousine.

We produced a video magazine called *Diderot*, named after the French philosopher who wrote the first encyclopedia. Like in his book, we wanted to posit a description of the universe and to catalogue experience. We commissioned five artists per issue to produce a new work in video and we facilitated the production, offering equipment and our technical expertise as crew and producers. We distributed the magazine internationally through bookstores and galleries. We commissioned local artists like Andrew Paterson and Fast Wurms, critic Jeanne Randolph, and also Laura Mulvey, Krzysztof Wodiczko, Victor Burgin and Jacques Derrida. It was ahead of its time; VHS distribution and video stores were just beginning. It didn't take off, no one bought the videos then. So you keep reincarnating yourself.

We were part of the lost generation of Canadian video art. The first wave of media artists got attention, and then – and this relates back to how art is not valued in this culture – the only video that got exposure or distribution was work that dealt directly with issues. Video was seen as an instrumentalized tool. If you weren't directly addressing a post-colonial or queer critique then the work was not picked up, did not get exposure, at least in English Canada. That changed for a younger generation of artists like Jubal Brown, Leslie Peters and Robert Lee, but it felt to us that we fell through a crack. I see the parallel in the art world as well. The institutions did not respond to a generation of artists who are now in their 40s. Only recently has there been an upswing in opportunities here in English-speaking Canada to get our work seen. Anyway, I don't consider myself a 'media' artist. I am on the periphery watching from the sidelines. I think of myself as an artist who works in film, as a gallery artist.

MH: Unlike much of your other work, *Work* (35 min, 1989, co-made with Geoffrey Shea) is really a drama, a story movie, though for the most part it doesn't admit actors, but artists playing roles. Why not actors? And why the turn toward 'full-fledged' narrative? There are two interwoven threads: a woman announcer and her religiously obsessed and disturbed brother live in one apartment, while a very quiet man looking for work lives next door. What is the relation between these two? There is a confluence of work and identity throughout. *Work* admits one into a social class, a societal role, and provides the means to achieve a particular lifestyle. The tape asks, 'How can you think of who you are if you're unemployed?' Why this equation between work and identity?

PP: It was an attempt to look, as comprehensively as possible, at what work means. The piece began with the idea that 'we are defined and judged by what we do.' John Porter, the main character (a well-known Super 8 filmmaker), plays an unemployed man who is looking for work. We contemporized Descartes'

'Cogito ergo sum' into 'I work therefore I am.' But our main character is unemployed – he watches events, but doesn't exist in a real sense. He even phones Studs Terkel, the popular sociologist, and asks him about invisibility. He goes to a job-training centre and watches tapes of people describing their work (a scientist, a navy officer, a businessman, a nun). *Work* tackles the idea of identity through complexity.

The religiously obsessed brother character, though not explicitly identified as such, is schizophrenic. His character poses this question to the viewer: what if your brain doesn't work like that of others? What if you don't work? This character throws into relief a rationalist perspective: I don't exist because I don't work, because I live in a society that only values success as capital gain and commerce. *Work* was a fragmented narrative – no one relates to each other, nobody's 'working,' on every level it's about being broken. It was a great time making the piece. Greg Woodbury played the brother and did an amazing job, and John Porter was

Work

a real sport, though he didn't understand why anyone would make drama. You know how straightforward he can be. He would say, 'This is just a big lie, this isn't really my apartment. As soon as you say this is supposed to be someplace, you spend the whole time lying.'

MH: Why do you play a radio announcer?

PP: She is the narrator, the glue, the conduit between public and private, she is public and she is private. But there's an implication that something is missing in her life, that she's not working either. Her relation with her brother is strained, for one thing. He doesn't speak to her, he rants, and the boundary of where he ends and the television begins isn't clear to him. The information is a river that flows through him. He feels he causes wars to happen; for instance, he is part of whatever he sees.

MH: The video was obviously made with great care and attention to detail.

PP: The professional quality of the work was extraordinary for the time, the lighting and tracking shots. I'm a real tech nerd when it comes to that stuff; I loved the idea of creating an illusion and pulling it off with video. We were committed to using video as a primary tool and not as a second-rate version of film. We wanted to prove that video could be aesthetically beautiful. We really pushed, through lighting and camera movement, what video was capable of at that time.

MH: That's a quality you share with Dennis Day and Su Rynard, to name only a couple.

PP: That's us, the lost generation. We were interested in making meaningful and beautiful, well-crafted work, extending ourselves narratively, and technically.

Work is about invisible people. You're valued in this society because of what you do. This question comes out of being an artist in a society that does not value art, where value is measured only in monetary terms. The Conservative government has just recalled curators from our embassies around the world. There is a reassignment – these international cultural centres are being reassigned as trade initiatives, as if culture and cultural production is a waste of time. Why? Art is where we contemplate as a society who we are and why we are. During the last election I asked my students: why is health care more important than art? They all repeated what the media reinforced without thinking about it. Of course health care is important, but here they are in art school and they still can't conceive of art as a priority. It's a received idea; they aren't thinking for themselves.

MH: *Under the Influence* (60 min, 1991) is a theatrical two-hander about a dysfunctional relationship framed by your address. Why this triangle? Figure and ground are in a constant state of collapse and upheaval, the set is a 12 x 12 teeter-totter that occasions regular pratfalls and stumbles. In the him-and-her relation, both are caught in mirrors of themselves, repeating shared monologues, stuck in their patterns, condemned to meta-commentaries. Both are drowning and hope to be saved by the other. How do the loops of language and gesture conjure subjectivity?

PP: *Under the Influence* was conceptualized to take place on a giant teeter-tottered stage that pivoted in the centre, so any movement one performer took threw the other performer off balance. It required coordinating every movement, or you fell down; it was a metaphor for negotiating an intimate relationship, where every action causes a reaction in the other person. When the audience entered the unfamiliar warehouse space, they saw what they

Under the Influence

believed was a solid stage – they thought the actors were on solid ground. Once the actors fall in love and onto the stage, the audience sees that what they assumed was solid and stable was a giant movable thing of causality and reaction.

I appear at the beginning and the end of the piece and speak directly to the audience. I come out, circle in front of the stage and then trip and fall to the floor. It was shocking to the audience and made everyone uncomfortable, it felt like a terrible mistake. And then I did it again, and then again, and eventually the audience has permission to laugh as it becomes slapstick. I introduce the love story by speaking at a microphone, but also to confuse matters: who are we, why do we fall in love, is this fact or fiction? What does it mean to witness these things?

The characters are articulate and both conscious and unconscious of their desire, alternately in and out of control. They are animals busy scratching, lusting, laughing and farting. They analyze and debate, enacting a ritual of falling in and out of love. It's an hour-long deconstruction of a marriage. It shows how we act out our passions, as if it were an experiment, using the theatre as a laboratory. I am asking: why can't we decide to be happy, what is the connection between will and action, what is outside of our control, what will we allow to happen to ourselves? I was looking at the end of a relationship that I had been in and wrote two unnamed characters (he and she). What does the impulse of attraction mean inside the dynamic of a long-standing relationship? The play doesn't reside in a zone of personality and character, but looked at a set of behaviours. The actors play generic he/she roles; they are blank entities who meet and dance in a choreography without personalities. They will want to have sex, eat, sleep, and the movement is up when they fall in love, or down if they fall out of love. From this simple trajectory we get a sense of what our relationships look like. The play represented an event where the audience could project their own experiences. It's formalized. It's as if you could say this experience is a triangle and this one is a circle and this is what those geometries look like together. Much to my surprise, it was nominated that year for three Dora Mavor Moore Awards, for best new play, best production and best direction. I was up against Shakespeare's *As You Like It*.

MH: Did it play as a regular theatrical production?

PP: It began as a performance in an unleased commercial space at Adelaide and Spadina. We rehearsed in the space and built the set (Danny Bowden built the set) for a month then it played to the public for three nights, then it was torn down and hauled away. Louise Garfield, of Clichette fame, and Triptych Media saw it and took it to Factory Theatre Lab where it ran for a month. When that happened I was up at the Canadian Film Centre as a resident director. I decided to make feature films since narrative had always informed my work and I was interested to reach a broader audience. But the moment I decided to work in the feature film world was the moment the provincial funding for film evaporated. The golden era of the independent film as art, which I grew up with, was over, and by 1990 it was becoming apparent that art films would no longer be supported. I don't think the film industry is very interesting now, it's been dismantled. I unfortunately spent the 1990s working on feature film scripts that could not be produced.

MH: It was a shared illusion in the artists' world that if you built it, they would come. If small movies would lean a little more toward the kind of thing already showing in movie theatres, people would check it out. But many were already making that work and it was hardly visible. There were a few exceptions endlessly discussed, and these, of course, became the rallying points for another cruel hope.

PP: I wrote and directed one other play in 1995 at Theatre Passe Muraille called *Controlling Interest*. It featured Tracy Wright as a feminist film director who hires a beautiful young actress, Sigrid Johnson, to play the femme fatale in her movie. The play is about how difficult it is for women to develop support structures, how jealous and competitive we are, and how complicated it is to work within constructions of power and hierarchy. It is the avant-garde's version of *The Devil Wears Prada*. The film Tracy is making is projected onscreen in fragments throughout the theatrical production, where her voyeurism is on display. The filmmaker Phillip Barker designed the set, which we worked on really hard to get right. I remember that Kate Taylor reviewed the piece and called it 'Atom Egoyan on a bad day.' But, funny to mention, two years later Atom directed an opera that Phillip

Lockjaw

Barker designed and the set was very similar to the one we used in *Controlling Interest*.

I ultimately found working in theatre disappointing. The work was reasonably well-received; probably 2,000 people came to see it, but I did not find it was a sophisticated arena where meaningful discourse with audience occurs. It's an engine of entertainment. The actor is more important than the play or the ideas here, which is fine, but not so interesting to me.

MH: Unlike some fringe media artists who continue to produce single-channel things for micro-fests and occasional in-person appearances, you have taken a forthright step into the art world, producing one installation after another, often with sculptural components. Can you talk about why you wanted to leave the thankless, unpaid and unseen world of single-channel movies behind in pursuit of a lucrative and glamorous career in galleries? What is the biggest difference for you in conceiving work for a white cube as opposed to the theatre's black box?

PP: I have always aligned myself with the art world. I have been teaching in an art college for 20 years. And my very first work was performed at Mercer Union back in 1982. Sculpture is what I look at, as much as anything else, music, literature, film – you can see through all my work that installation has been there from the beginning. But the shift or kick in the pants to get out of my office and move away from the black hole of feature film production came in 1999, when Deirdre Logue, then executive director at the Images Festival, invited me to produce an installation using a 2.5-inch flat screen. I had been knocking my head against the wall for eight years trying to make films for the big screen, writing feature scripts and talking to producers. It clicked and I was able to shift my thinking from the big screen to 2.5 inches and make *The Secret Life of Criminals*.

I was reading about the morphology of the criminal face through Cesare Lombroso who, in the early science of criminology, studied mug shots and wrote scientific texts that identified and categorized the physiology of the criminal. I had been working on a story that involved questions that surrounded the death of a woman: was she murdered or had she taken her own life? Was she a victim or a perpetrator of her own demise? You know that famous phrase of Edgar Allan Poe, 'the death of a beautiful woman is, unquestionably, the most poetic subject ... ' I was working with the irony of the death of an old whore. I couldn't write it as a movie of the week and was having a hard time because the film industry is conservative. So when Deirdre invited me to produce an installation I jumped on the impulse to make something spontaneously. *The Secret Life of Criminals* provided a new start.

I constructed a steel cone, which hovered above a small screen that displayed a female contortionist. The monocular field of the cone applies the scientific gaze, taking events out of context, examining things in isolation, but this gaze is met with shape-shifting gestures. The contortionist is Jenny Jacinto, who has worked with Cirque de Soleil and Robert Lepage, and can turn her body into a pretzel – she's constantly in motion. Her body mutations suggest the unknowable presented under a scientific gaze – Heisenberg's Uncertainty Principle at play, suggesting that the observer affects the observed. A critique of how we judge appearance is central to my work.

The elements that determine the difference between cinema and installation could be identified through the social space, the physical experience and the conventions of duration. The cinema is a form of shared social space, mentally stimulating but physically passive. You remain seated while your mind travels. With installations, the gallery site offers the viewer an energized encounter with the work. Scale and duration become factors that inform the work; the ability to embed the experience within an apparatus is another factor; reflective surfaces, matte-ness, the dampening of space, the social interaction, the agency of the viewer to move away from and toward the object/experience are all factors that enhance the receptive experience of the work. I like the fact that as a viewer I determine the duration of my encounter. It's a generous dialogue and form of commitment.

It's interesting to think about how I migrated the script I wrote for *Lockjaw* (1992) from a performance for two performers to a film. A real transformation occurred. The performance included a performance area that was covered in metallic detritus, two performers and an LED board with a constant stream of questions and statements. One performer wore a wireless microphone, street clothes and magnetic shoes, and when she walked, the metal bits of nails and chains clung to her shoes. The other performer stood silent, staring confrontationally at the audience as if she was waiting to speak. The performer with the magnetic shoes was the only one talking, and she talked non-stop for 25 minutes. Halfway through the performance, the non-speaking woman starts to take off her clothes and eventually stands naked in front of the audience. The piece is an examination of power and is a summation of 1980s feminist discourse, which positioned women as a site of meaning (as the muse or origin) but outside of language (not a participant or agent).

Lockjaw is a funny, ironic, 'post-feminist' critique of feminism, full of puns and playful language. I turned it into a film because I thought it was worth preserving, and as it turns out it is a part of many media libraries in this country and was broadcast many times. As a film, the work was constructed within a self-contained room where the woman talking is locked inside the transitional space of a hotel room. There is a couple in the corner who are there as figments of her imagination. She is enacting a talking cure, speaking directly to the audience as if they were the therapist. She speaks about temporomandibular joint dysfunction – common to women – which I relate to as a form of hysteria. TMJ is a pain in the jaw joint, hence the title *Lockjaw*. The film is a constructed space where the space is explored through the subject's intimacy with the camera, the confessional genre.

And getting back to the sexy, lucrative world you describe as the gallery world ... very funny. The gallery work involves materiality, physicality and the articulation of the framing apparatus. In my piece *'It's about how people judge appearance'* (2001), an attractive, well-dressed woman walks along the street, then wilfully smashes her head into a wall, and then repeats in it in the form of a jump cut over and over again. It is a work about hysteria or the illogical, the relocation or migration of one pain into another. It is presented on a flat-screen monitor embedded in a frame. The frame is made from pink leather (skin), the same colour that Prada used that year in their collection. The frame is cushioned and invites you to touch it, offering a stark contrast to

Crosstalk

The Floating House

what is happening inside the frame. You can't do that in the cinema.

MH: *Crosstalk* (6 min, 2004) features a cadre of art-world familiars staring back into the camera as they cross an intersection. This looks like a major logistical strike, as well as a comment on the circularity of the look. You confront us with ourselves, our own need to stop and stare, our need for accident, spectacle and distraction.

PP: There are two versions of *Crosstalk* – one version is five minutes and was made for television; the other is a seven-minute loop for installation. The television version depicts a particular urban trauma. A woman, Veronica Hurnik, crosses a busy street, causing a streetcar to come to a halt. Then she refuses to move and play-fights with the vehicle, causing a city-wide traffic jam. In the filming, which was done on 35mm, I hired a streetcar, stopped traffic and had a woman freeze in front of the car. I constructed the shooting, and due to financial constraints I had my friends form the backdrop of bystanders. They looked on as she enacts this moment of transgression. I wanted a disconnection between location and event to show the performativity of hysteria, so I shot them separately. I filmed part of her performance in front of a blue screen, and then brought them together as a composite picture.

When the footage came back, the background struck me as powerful; it showed people staring at something as they crossed the street. I knew I had a second piece, a more interesting proposition than what I had set out to shoot. This filmed background of onlookers is shown full figure, and when presented in the gallery the viewers are the same scale, a democratization, which located the viewers in the gallery as the 'site of trauma.' The freak of what they are staring at has been removed, but we can

imagine it more powerfully as a result. The audience is engaged and implicated through the look, and physically involved in the viewing experience, forced to stand and stare. It's a seven-minute loop, although most stay longer. The elaborate technical set-up involved a circular track, and the camera movement, nearly invisible, encircles the viewer like trapped prey.

MH: Can you talk to me about *The Floating House* (5-min loop, 2002)?

PP: There is a series of works that make up *The Secret Life of Criminals*, which includes *Crosstalk*, *Homewrecker #1 & #2* and *The Floating House*. They relate to a memory from my childhood of a woman who died in the woods behind my house in Halifax. Through research I discovered her name was Joyce Belliveau. She was a war bride from England who, as I was told by a police officer who investigated the case, became known for taking off her clothes. She lived on Gottigen Street, a neighbourhood marked by the social upheaval and dislocation associated with Africville. She froze to death and her naked body was found in the woods in March 1965. All I knew when I was young was that a woman's naked body was found frozen. Years later I uncovered as much information as I could about her, though her death is cloaked in mystery.

The Floating House developed from the idea of dislocation. 1965 marks a transition period where urban renewal eradicated the traces of rural migration within the city. Having grown up in Nova Scotia, affected by the power and vastness of the ocean, I wanted to work with the force of that body of water. The ocean represents a force that can both sustain and subsume life. A floating house became a way to show her experience, but it's not only about her, it's about the paradoxical, the dark and light at the same time. The house, like us, could collapse or keep floating. The house performs an irrational or hysterical act. It's doing what it shouldn't do.

MH: You present it as a looping catastrophe.

PP: But it always comes up again. It's comi-tragic, and we're all going to die. When I previewed it for a gallery owner, she said, 'I don't think the house should sink.' But it does.

MH: Sound is very important in this work.

PP: The soundtrack was made by Richard Ferrin in 5.1 Surround Sound. I invited a number of friends over for a dinner party and recorded it, so the house has the sound of life and sharing food, and as the house moves from one side of the screen to the other, the sound moves as well. There are five speakers around the gallery, though the sound of the house is located frontally. Behind you a vortex of audio moves through all five speakers, creating a sink pool where you're pulled under by synthesized ocean sounds mixed with foghorns and many other real sounds that Richard recorded in Halifax. I believe that our sense of space is apprehended through sound even more than picture. We understand the quality of space through our ears. How big is a space, is it safe or threatening? The way sound moves through the gallery is very physical, like the way the camera moves in *Crosstalk*. The camera in my work is often moving; perhaps that's why it can't be reduced to a single iconic image. In *The Floating House*, sound is mobilized as well.

We shot in Sambro Cove, off the coast of Nova Scotia, on the Atlantic Ocean. I found a cove I wanted to work with, and in the next cove there were 15 identical houses, all 150 years old. They were the kind of houses a kid would draw, with a door, two windows, a slanted roof and chimney. The idea of house, the Ur, a typical house. These houses were built in Mahone Bay and put on a barge and shipped to their present site, as there were few roads back then. The idea of moving houses on the ocean was more prevalent than it is now. A friend of mine who lived in Newfoundland talked about seeing her house cut at the foundation, floated out to the ocean and relocated to another village. She described the horror and the fear that everything she had would be lost. I felt the power of this story and thought I could shoot that. I drove to Nova Scotia, found a recent art school grad, Jamie Clarke, who designed and built the house over the next month and a half in the art college's woodworking shop. Then we went out with Christopher Ball, the cameraperson, and Skipper Dave and his fishermen friends, to make the piece. The shoot was so hard I couldn't look at the footage for eight months. To build something and then destroy it was emotionally draining and disturbing.

MH: Your installation *Homewrecker #1 & #2* (2004) features a white cloth (can I call it a handkerchief?) suspended magically in air, hovering beneath some kind of magnet mechanism, which is bracketed into the wall. It evokes a primitive sort of wonder, like the kind my cat had when I would turn the water tap on. Why do you call it *Homewrecker*? And why have you produced an object at this scale, with its delicate, small-scale intimacy? It requires the viewer to get right on up to it, and produces an overwhelming urge to touch.

PP: Isn't that interesting that everybody wants to touch it, although the work is so fragile that when touched the magic is broken and the small ghost falls to the floor. It is a kind of metaphor for infatuation, which is the homewrecker I refer to. It is about the electromagnetic impulse that we act upon when we want to touch and shouldn't. Everything is electrically charged; love and attraction form a part of that.

There's also a film component to the installation. Walking into the gallery, viewers encounter a woman, played by the artist Janet Bellotto, in a Victorian-style nightdress with four feet of hair billowing around her. She locks her gaze upon you and draws you in, holding you electromagnetically with her powerful presence. The space of the film contracts and expands (the camera zooms and dollies at the same time), creating an uncanny effect. This image is shot on 16mm black-and-white-film, then projected onto a screen held invisibly by wires, so it looks as if the image is floating in space with her mesmerizing hair, and small electric bolts running across her face. She appears like someone called up from a séance, like the Bride of Dracula. She and the film are mesmerizing, a word coined by Franz Anton Mesmer, who employed electromagnetic currents to 'heal' or correct the body.

I have a long-standing interest in the relation between science and art, especially before they divided into separate disciplines. The harnessing and utilization of electricity coincides with the rise of spiritualism, a pseudo-science promising contact with outer space and the dead. As radio and wireless communication is developed, narratives were created that involved the spirit world. There was a need to understand the materiality of electromagnetic phenomena, to embody it in stories. This history is invoked in *Homewrecker*. In the gallery installation, the viewer encounters the film first and then, when you disengage with her gaze and turn to leave, you realize she wasn't staring at you but at a ghost, the small, hovering, white chiffon held in space by an invisible electromagnetic field. Ghosts, electricity, home wrecker: can you work with that? *Homewrecker* was a way of talking about an act of passion that ruined a domestic situation. What is love if not a minefield of ghosts? It was made for a show dedicated to Nicola Tesla, called *Electromagnetic Bodies*, and that led to the Niagara Falls piece. I have lots of video sketches related to electricity and the metaphors of science.

Homewrecker #1 & #2

MH: In *Monster Tree* (2006), you visit Niagara Falls with a smoothly moving 16mm camera. There are occasional tourist glimpses, but for the most part this is a landscape study; the usual figure-ground relation seems reversed here. The ground, in this case a gnarled tree, has a pair of eyes briefly superimposed into it, and the laboured breathing on the soundtrack leaves the impression that we are hearing this tree giving air to these views of the waterfall. How did you arrive at the idea for this strange movie?

PP: While in Niagara Falls researching *Homewrecker*, and Nicola Tesla, who along with the Westinghouse Company built the first alternating-current generator there, I found a tree that has a face growing out of it. It looked like a little monster and I thought of this abnormal cell growth as a kind of hysteria that the tree was performing. I studied it for years and finally worked up the nerve to shoot it. In *Monster Tree*, the face appears in a tree as a hysterical growth crying, 'Help me, I'm dying here.' Hysteria is about the displacement of a trauma that erupts somewhere else. It could occur as laughter, or a monologue, or a burl on a tree. I wanted to emphasize that this little wonder sits beside the most powerful natural wonder in the world. People come great distances to gaze at the spectacular falls, but no one notices this remarkable beech tree. I wanted to place these two events beside each other and used the zoom lens to suggest an expansion and contraction of focal planes.

The tree only appears twice, though there is a pronounced sound of breathing throughout. It's a laboured breath, nearly a death rattle, and connects with your own breathing. It locates the subjectivity in the piece, but you don't know that until you see the tree.

In Paris I visited the Musée Fragonard, which is a kind of cabinet of curiosity, featuring a collection of animal anomalies like Cyclopes and strange 'freaks' of nature: glass cabinet after glass cabinet of two-headed lambs and eight-footed dogs and critters born with one eye. I had one of those eureka moments when I noticed beneath each display a small card with the word monstre written on it. *Monstre – Monster*: 'to show, to demonstrate.' What is a monster showing us? Why do we need to look and what does this mean in a greater context? What about the criminal, the abhorrent, the surreal, the abnormal ... ?

Before the movies there was the insane asylum. In what we call the Victorian period, asylums were opened up for public viewing. People came to look at the exception and the exceptional. The exhibited ones who drew particular interest were the hysterics – they expressed trauma through performative gestural tics. The most famous 'hysteric' was Augustine, who was a patient of Dr. Charcot, whose photographic studio was devoted to 'studying' the physical traits of the hysteric. That Augustine was photogenic is probably not coincidental. Her hysterical presentations read like passion tableaux and presented a very camera-ready subject. These hysterical demonstrations of compulsive eye twitches, unusual gaits and limbs frozen in twisted forms were adopted as comic gestures in vaudeville and cabaret routines. The tics became part of the early vocabulary of slapstick comedy. This idea is put forward in Rae Beth Gordon's book *Why the French Love Jerry Lewis*. It is an acting out of hysteria as a form of entertainment. Chaplin and Keaton emerge from this tradition. In the later part of the 19th century there was wide-scale migration from the countryside to the city. This trauma is relocated within the body in the form of a tic. Slapstick reproduces the tic, and offers humour as a way of dealing with pain.

On another level I am interested in monsters as examples of the hybrid. My dog is a hybrid, genetically manufactured. I think of her as a little monster. She has been bred as a gun dog, a German wire-haired pointer. She is an amazing hunter with remarkable endurance, but her genetic makeup includes an enormous need for physical touch and companionship. She has been bred with an incompatibility; she is not a kennel dog, you can't leave her alone outside, which is what a hunter does with his dog. So you have a monster – she can't live the life she has been bred to live. You see this kind of dog in animal rescue centres because they are abandoned by hunters who can't stand their clinging needs.

MH: Does the tree express a trauma related to the Falls?

PP: The trauma of the tree is more emblematic. Niagara Falls was raped almost instantly after it was 'discovered' by Europeans. The American side soon became littered with highly polluting factories like Nabisco, which flooded the Niagara River with effluents. There's been a lot of natural tragedy and disaster and mass commercialization, and a long history of 'punks' on display. The word *punk*

Dogwood Pond

Smut

monitor embedded inside a beaver-fur-lined box made out of pine. This cabinet sits on top of the shipping crate for viewing. The seven-minute looping video shows a moving image shot from the bow of a canoe traversing a marsh in southern Ontario. Hybridic critters come to life in this swamp. It's a bit like a chimera – you'll be looking at a stump that turns into a horse, then a spider appears on a lily pad that turns into cat's tails, or you see a flower and inside is the face of a monkey, and then the flower floats through the air. It's a very whimsical and poetic work about transposing natural species from one environment to another, and the way our imagination acts on the landscape. It's a subtle, circular piece – mostly you're in a canoe looking at the shoreline and every so often a critter arrives.

Dogwood Pond returns to a moment of newly gained mobility, and the wonder attached to collecting things from all over the world: gems, shells, alligators, dodo eggs, pelts. It's the beginning of natural-science collections as we know them today. Historically, the nobility had curiosity cabinets, which contained a collection of diversity in the world. The Tradescants are the first to make this available to the general public. Between 1350 and the beginning of museums in the 1800s, private collections held sway. A woodworker would make a cabinet for your collection, which might be as large as a room or just a small jewellery box with drawers containing artifacts.

I am questioning the idea of received knowledge as wholesale truth; I want to encourage curiosity, especially within the natural world. I'm interested in uncomfortable knowledge, in states of unknowing. I think art plays a role in celebrating this territory.

comes from the Barnum and Bailey days when objects (of the two-headed kind) in formaldehyde in glass jars were put on display as entertainment. Again, people wanted to see 'freaks.' There were many punk shows around the Falls. The trauma implied by my *Monster Tree* incorporates this history without being explicit or didactic.

Monster Tree was made for a show in the Museum of Garden History in London called *Repatriating the Ark*. The museum is dedicated to the John Tradescants, father and son, who were amongst the first explorers in North America. They were gardeners to King Charles I and introduced hybridity into the English landscape, collecting and planting non-indigenous species, and monkeying with nature. They travelled to several continents collecting plant specimens and rarities. In the 1620s they placed their rarities on display in the first public museum, which they called the Ark. They showed necklaces and beads, the mantle of Pocahontas, and the Tartar Lamb, a funny little creature considered at the time to be both animal and plant, which is still on display in the museum today. I made *Monster Tree* to commemorate the 500th anniversary of the museum and I brought a monster tree (the face of a man in a tree is a hybrid) from Niagara Falls to England.

I made an earlier piece for the museum called *Dogwood Pond* (2003). My interest in the ethos prior to Enlightenment began here. Again it was the Tradescants and their marvellous collection that predates Linnaeus and scientific classification that caught my curiosity.

I was asked by the Museum of Garden History to choose an historic person who was buried on the grounds of their deconsecrated gravesite, and that's when I discovered the Tradescants. My partner, Michael Buchanan, and I made this piece together. We built a shipping crate to facilitate and house a handmade cabinet. *Dogwood Pond* is a curiosity cabinet with a flat-screen

Paulette Phillips' Film, Video and Performance

Sink or Swim   7 min 1981 (with Geoffrey Shea)
Edie   4 min 1981 (with Geoffrey Shea)
Still Here, Still There   25 min 1982
Days of Discovery   1982 (film/video/performance)
Garbage   11 min 1982 (with Geoffrey Shea)
Find the Performer   1983 (performance, poster series)
K Is for Chicken   7 min 1983 (with Geoffrey Shea)
Re-enactment of an Event Which May Have Happened   12 min 1983
It Depends   30 min 1984
The Cadence of Insanity   25 min 1985 (performance)
How I Am Abused   10 min 1985
Yell, Hell and Pages   4:30 min 1987
Salomé   7:30 min 1989
Work   35 min 1989
Under the Influence   1991 (theatre)
Fear of Lying   1991 (theatre)
Lockjaw   22 min 1992
The Lorca Play   1993 (theatre)
When I Fall in Love   4 min 1993
The Chocolate Bath   1994 (director)
Controlling Interest   1995 (multimedia theatre)
Memo:Re:Joyce   1995 (theatre)
The Secret Life of Criminals 1 & 2   2000, 2004 (video, shelf,
   cone, 2 sculpture pieces viewed through cones)
'It's about how people judge appearance'   2001 (1-min 16mm DVD
   loop on flatscreen, framed in padded pink leather frame)
Ecstasy   2002 (2-channel video projected onto glass shelf)
The Floating House   2002 (5-min 16mm film loop projected
   with 5.1 Surround Sound)
Dogwood Pond   2003 (video loop, 7 min, within a curiosity cabinet)
Who Is Sky Gilbert?   60 min 2003
Crosstalk   2004 (7-min DVD loop, with stereo sound)
Smut   2004 (9 digital backlit photographs, DVD on flatscreen)
Homewrecker #1 & #2   2004 (1-min loop with magnetic sugar
   and film projector)
Bubbalova   2006 (video of a temporary sculpture, 30-foot replica
   of the Bulova Tower)
Monster Tree   2006 (5-min DVD loop, flatscreen)
Touche   2007–08 (installation)
The Open, 1–13   2007 (digital animations)

Distributed by Vtape and the Canadian Filmmakers Distribution
Centre.

Paulette Phillips is an artist who works with film, sculpture and photography. She is based in Toronto and and teaches installation art and film at the Ontario College of Art and Design. Her work is represented by Danielle Arnaud Contemporary Art, London, and Diaz Contemporary, Toronto. www.paulette-phillips.ca

RICHARD FUNG
THINKING PICTURES

When he tells me the story of how he got his start in fringe media, I have to sit back in my chair for a moment. Wait, wait. There was a time when Richard wasn't making videos? It's hard for me to grasp exactly, just as it's hard to imagine what the Canadian media-art scene would look like if it had not grown up with Richard's accompanying text missiles, which have blown apart commonly held wisdoms again and again. His justly anthologized essay, 'Looking for My Penis: The Eroticized Asian in Gay Video Porn,' took on stereotypes of gay desire. His 'Programming the Public' missive looks at the way queer fests help shape the identity of their audience (who is looking in the mirror now?). It begins with this line: 'Whenever I go to a gay bathhouse, I'm struck by the ordinariness of so many of the men, who seem to evade all recognizable gay styles of masculinity and femininity ... '

One things is for sure: Richard always knows how to lead, though his characteristic modesty keeps him from standing at the front of the theatre and hectoring us with his keen intelligence. For 20 years he has reworked the documentary, leavening it with personal insights, bringing his camera inside the home, settling it beside his mother, then his father and, most memorably, his sister Nan. In his brilliant summary work, *Sea in the Blood*, he lays down a duet of his sister's fatal illness and his own lifelong romance with Tim, an AIDS activist with an illness of his own to contend with. The personal is always and necessarily political in these mosaic recountings, which never shirk from the task of unsettling received wisdoms. How warming to imagine that we live in a post-identity culture, that we're all just getting along, that the glass ceilings and racial profilings and hate crimes are relics of a bygone time. And how much rarer, and how much more urgent, is the need to continue to point out the inequities that continue to exist in a North American art world that is primarily white (from consumers to producers), and where power brokers in the off-off-off-off-Broadway world of fringe productions are still similarly monochrome. Richard's work (as teacher, mentor, programmer, artist, writer) stands in the face of this backward tide, quietly persistent, bristling with intelligence, ravelling out the effects of global empires in local details.

MH: Pictures from your childhood have appeared occasionally in your work, which leads me to wonder if there are early encounters with picture-making that were 'formative.' It is by now commonplace to state that pictures take the place of memory, but are there memories that continue to follow you around – and are these memories pictures most of all? Or is it a smell, the touch of someone, that insistently recurs? Sometimes my memory dreams are nothing but text scrolls, elaborate title sequences that admonish the guilty (moi), offering remedies and reflexive treatments (Keep reading! Never stop reading me!), as if the future/past existed only as a book. Do you feel that your work, which spools out the same ordered picture sequence again and again, is an image not of memory but of time travel?

RF: I grew up in Trinidad. I was the youngest child in the family, and by the time I hit puberty all of my siblings except one had moved away to study. My mother was the second-youngest in her family, so I never knew my grandparents or any of their generation. And my father, having emigrated alone from China, had no close relatives around. So from very early on, photographs were these little bridges across time and distance. There were the tiny sepia prints of my grandparents and the great aunts I heard stories about; the photo of my father's fortress-like house in China; the images of the siblings who had died before my birth, three by that time; later there were the snapshots and graduation portraits my brothers and sisters sent home from Ireland and Canada. Photographs were about death or absence. As I grew up, photographs also came to represent holidays and special occasions. These were different, always in colour.

Regarding the apparatus, *Brownie* is the word I recall first hearing, but I don't have a strong image of the camera. I think it was the colour of milk chocolate, but then I'm also getting a flash of yellow, which makes me wonder if I'm not thinking of my teddy bear. In my teenage years, my sister and I shared a Kodak Instamatic, where little cartridges replaced spools of film – very modern. I took many pictures with this camera. In my last years at home I did a series with my sister Nan as model and me as fashion photographer. She struck Twiggy poses and I shot in canted angles. Whether it was the Instamatic or the home-movie camera my mother used, the film always had to be sent to America for processing, so the photographic image necessarily carried the glamour of 'away.'

Funny you should mention the feeling of being implicated by the photograph. Here is a story I don't think I've ever told. From the time I was really young I used to like to dress up. My sister and I used to raid my mother's closet, she picking the lock. We would find things like my grandmother's jewellery, my mother's dressy dresses (she had a whole funeral collection in black, white and violet, the Trinidadian mourning colours), my cousin's wedding dress. We tried them all. In my teenage years, I remember finding a black-and-white picture of me dressed in one of my older sister's dresses, sitting on the floor with the wide skirt spread out around me in the classic pose of the late '50s. I was mortified and I think I destroyed it. I looked for it years later and was relieved not to find it in the family album. I assumed the empty rectangles on the pages marked off by the little gold sticky corners indicated the success of my censorship. Now I'm not so sure the photo was actually destroyed, and perhaps one of my siblings or someone else has it. It's so long ago that I'm wondering if that photo and its demise wasn't an anxious fantasy in the first place. So yes, photography also contained the threat of evidence that could be used against me.

As for dreams, they are primarily visual. They are almost always set in the childhood house I left for good 35 years ago, which has been sold and completely remodelled. The atmosphere is always tropical and I don't think I have ever dreamt of snow. I don't recall smells in my dreams, nor text.

MH: Did you feel that motion pictures were waiting for you, all along, to pick up a camera and begin? I wonder what kind of movies you grew up with in Trinidad? Did they sow the seeds of what was to come, or does your practice emerge from a place completely removed from the burnished starlight of the big screen or the melodramas of the small one?

RF: I grew up on Hollywood films served up in art deco confections around Port of Spain. The theatres had names like Deluxe, Globe and Roxy, and were divided into balcony (the most expensive), house (where we sat mostly) and pit (the cheapest section, just in front of the screen). People spoke back to the movies then, especially from the pit, shouting advice to the 'star boy' and 'star girl,' or making witty commentary, so much so that at times you couldn't hear what the actors were saying.

Movies were not an obsession, but an enjoyable treat, like hamburgers – they were things I did with my sister and her friends. My parents rarely went to the cinema, and my mother didn't approve of snack food. As a child I watched cowboy-and-Indian movies and war films. Later I marvelled over *Mary Poppins* and *The Sound of Music*, and could sing all the songs from both. At 12, the catechism class at my Catholic high school went to see *The Greatest Story Ever Told*. At 14, the English class went to see Franco Zefirelli's *Romeo and Juliet* and I couldn't take my eyes off the codpieces. Now as I'm thinking about it, I also remember nights at the drive-in watching movies like *Blue Hawaii* with Elvis and the beach-party series with Frankie Avalon and Annette Funicello. And how could I forget Shirley MacLaine in *What a Way to Go!*? I loved the glamour of that movie. I think the last film I saw in Trinidad was *Dr. Zhivago*.

Then I went away to finish high school in Ireland and started thinking of myself as grown up. With this hip new identity, movies seemed frivolous – until I saw *Claire's Knee* by Eric Rohmer. That film put me into a delicious, rapturous yearning for weeks, so much so that I haven't dared see it since. (I had a similar reaction to *Brokeback Mountain*.) In Ireland I also saw *The*

Ruling Class with Peter O'Toole and I began to see that cinema could make you think. When I came to Toronto I happened in on a double bill of *Women in Love* and *Sunday Bloody Sunday*. I had a huge crush on Alan Bates and the male kiss in *Sunday Bloody Sunday* came as a complete shock; I thought it was going to be a war movie. But it was during Andy Warhol's *Lonesome Cowboys* at Cinecity, the now-defunct rep cinema on Yonge Street, that I held hands with the straight guy I was in love with. Afterwards we made love for the first and only time.

With all this cinema in my life, I still never thought of taking up a movie camera, and when I entered art school it was to study industrial design. Later I majored in cinema studies at university, but it was only by chance that coming out of art school I got a job at a community TV station. My advisor at the Ontario College of Art, the journalist Morris Wolfe, was extremely supportive, and after I graduated he set up an interview with the editor of *Saturday Night* magazine. I was so out of it I had no idea what I might do there, so it was an awkward meeting. If I'd been more sure of myself, perhaps I could have ended up as a journalist. Instead I auditioned for a community TV animator job in Lawrence Heights, and that's how I learned to make video.

MH: Godard has often stated that watching a movie, writing about it or making one are the same for him, that the cinema is an extension of critical faculties. As someone who is constantly on the road delivering state-of-the-cinema addresses, do you feel the same?

RF: I do occasionally give talks, but the topics are much more defined and modest than 'The State of Cinema.' I was reminded of the dangers of such a project just last night at the Toronto International Film Festival, when I saw *The Pervert's Guide to Cinema* by Sophie Fiennes, a three-part documentary featuring Slavoj Žižek. Over the course of two and a half hours, the philosopher and psychoanalyst reads specific films and ponders the meaning of cinema in general. Žižek has an uncanny and fascinating screen presence, and Fiennes employs a clever device of seemingly dropping him into the films he is talking about, using recreated sets and intercutting. However, I found myself in equal parts seduced and distanced from the interpretations as I began to conduct my own meta-analysis about Žižek 's discourse, which is unselfconsciously asocial, apolitical and Eurocentric, even as he universalizes subjectivity and sexuality. His selection consisted of Hollywood movies, not surprisingly heavy on Hitchcock and Lynch, with a nod here or there to a handful of European directors: Bergman, Tarkovsky, Eisenstein. There were, as far as I remember, no Asian, Latin American or African films discussed. Yet he talks about how 'we' think and how 'we' invest in 'cinema.' At the start he shows a clip from an American film whose name slips me. In the scene a train

Orientations: Lesbian and Gay Asians

My Mother's Place

cuts across the path of a woman walking down a street. As she waits for it to pass, she looks into the windows of the train, which show first a couple of black cooks, a black bartender, a black maid ironing, then a white woman dressing, the silhouette of a man shaving, then an elegantly dressed white couple in a spacious compartment, and finally a well-dressed white man with a martini. My memory may deceive me, but this is how I remember it unfolding. In talking about the scene, Žižek entirely overlooks the astounding display of racialized class structure. This film underlines for me the limitations of close reading as a strategy for understanding films.

Now, as for Godard's provocation, he is obviously talking about his own engagement with thinking through cinema, which he does as a viewer, critic and maker. He incorporates and implements in his films and videos observations and analysis, as few others are able to do. I have a dual practice as a writer and a maker, and I watch a lot of work – though it does involve a degree of hubris talking about what I do in the same paragraph as Godard. It seems to me, however, that the phenomenological dimension of a film or video – single-channel, installation or on the web – is quite distinct from that of text on a page. So even though they involve a critical faculty, I couldn't say that the activities of writing and making videos, far less viewing, are the same for me. There are some videos of mine that have a kind of 'tightness,' closer to that of a written essay – *Dirty Laundry*, for example. Nevertheless, even here there are purely audiovisual metaphors whose presence hits at an altogether different register than the dry reasoning of writing allows. One cannot control the interpretation of the timbre of voice, the personal resonance of a soundscape, the idiosyncratic associations of colour. This holds true for even the most conventional documentary. Think what it would be like if laws were not written with black ink on paper, but held as videos or films, voiced and imaged.

MH: In *My Mother's Place* (49 min, 1990), you don't deliver your mother to us right away; the voice-over states that you wanted to show a picture of her emerging on a snowy morning from her suburban house, but because the weather was uncooperative you shot the scene later, sans mother. And before she appears as a speaking subject, you show a succession of women who narrate questions of representation: what to frame and why. Why this deferral and delay of your mother – and why did you choose to frame her through women closer to your life than to her own?

RF: I knew that my mother could be easily consumed as a classic ethnographic subject, a native informant. Though not so in a cosmopolitan city like Toronto, in many places people find the combination of Chinese and Trinidadian heritages surprising. By deferring her appearance, I wanted to foreground these issues and the stakes of representation to create a more critical and self-aware context before you actually see her.

Regarding the other women, I wanted to situate her story in a broader historical and global context, but I didn't want experts interpreting her story. I wanted to juxtapose these other stories so they would sit next to hers. That was the strategy.

MH: Why did you decide to begin this project?

RF: There were two reasons. I began making independent video by accident. It's partly John Greyson's fault. After returning from living in New York, he offered me the use of his camera and his services as cameraman. What we shot became *Orientations: Lesbian and Gay Asians* (56 min, 1985). It was my first independent production. I didn't expect it to go anywhere, but it was programmed at the Flaherty Seminar and the Grierson Seminar, and all of a sudden I was a video artist. In the mid-1980s there was growing interest in a politics of identity, gay/lesbian imagery and questions of sexuality, and my work was taken up in a surprising way. My second video, *Chinese Characters* (20:30 min, 1986), was an examination of gay Asian porn and owed its circulation to Colin Campbell, Gary Kibbins and John. I was increasingly situated as the gay-Chinese-Canadian filmmaker. There was a lot of interest, which was great, but I also became concerned about being trapped as a maker. There is a developed infrastructure of gay and lesbian audiences, festivals and critics. It's very tempting to produce something suitable for this ready-made platform. But I began to feel the need to address my other interests.

I'd been long fascinated by my parents, and made a tape about my father, who was born in China, but came to Trinidad at a young age. After my father died, I finally went to his village in southern Guangdong in the fall of 1986 and made *The Way to My Father's Village* (38 min, 1988). This experimental documentary examines the way children of immigrants relate to the land of their parents. It is about the construction of history and memory, the experience of colonialism and about Westerners looking at China. I didn't know China at all, but felt related to it in a passive sense, because others connected me with it. The tape is constructed of discrete segments, each representing different kinds of knowledge about China. Interspersed are different Western versions of China, from the quasi-historical account of Marco Polo to the organ of the Communist Party of Canada Marxist-Leninist. I situated my video as yet another Western description.

Then I made *My Mother's Place*, a companion piece about my mother, which is about the dynamics of race and gender in Trinidad. As opposed to my feeling of distance from the supposed Chinese fatherland, this tape is about my roots in the Caribbean motherland.

My mother was born in 1909 and grew up in a village in one of the most remote places in that small country. I was interested in her consciousness as a British colonial subject, and my own formation as a child of independence, which came in 1962, when I was eight. The social and racial hierarchies my mother had been brought up with were already crumbling, in a formal sense, by the time I came of age. These hierarchies of race and class, though not so fixed or monolithic, persist today. The tape looks at the two of us; it's about place, people's place in society.

MH: The normative shaping modes of biography are absent in this tape. Instead we receive her scattered recountings, which speak of episodes but not stories. Was this resistance to 'full disclosure,' or even closure, a conscious strategy on your part?

RF: Definitely. I've done autobiographical work, but it wasn't until *Sea in the Blood* that I became interested in my own story as narrative. In *My Mother's Place*, I was interested in the relationship between colonialism and post-independence in Trinidad and Tobago. I was using my family to look at the way those changes played out in people's lives. I was much less interested in an assessment of individuals for their own story. That's why it functions differently than *Sea in the Blood*, which culminates in a confessional moment. And there were things that couldn't be spoken of. My mother is part of a large family on a small island and the level of gossip is amazing. The tape says, 'I'm not telling you the whole story. Details have been held back to protect the guilty.'

Family stories there have such large arcs, they're all epics. If you look at the post-colonial literature that comes out of Canada, from writers like Shani Mootoo or Shyam Selvadurai, Rohinton Mistry or even Ann Marie MacDonald, you see epic family histories. When I first arrived here, stories from the East Coast felt familiar to me because they were filled with ghosts. I grew up in a place that was overwhelmed by supernatural figures, some of which are mentioned in the tape, like the soucouyant who sucks your blood at night. She flies through the air like a ball of fire, and if you find her skin you have to put salt on it so she won't be able to put it on again. To protect yourself, you have to put rice in front of your house because she has to count the rice, and by the time she's finished counting, the sun will come up and she has to leave. I grew up in a place haunted by spirits. Even though I

grew up in a middle-class suburb built in the '50s, most of our neighbours – the parents, that is – came from the country. It didn't help that when they dug up the street to put in a sewer system they discovered a slave cemetery.

MH: It's strange and wonderful to see home movies of you and your mother, which, as you tell us in voice-over, have more to do with the fantasy of your lives than its reality. Are home movies always staged? Who were these screen moments for? Were they an externalization of the same *Good Housekeeping* norms that led your mother to describe herself as a housewife on your school forms, even while she was busy managing a store?

RF: There may be moments where people sneak cameras and the subject is unaware – baby footage, perhaps – but mostly home movies are staged moving picture albums. Trips, opening birthday presents, Christmas and sports events all stage the family. My mother would bring out the projector and we'd watch the movies as a family. It was never a production for others. It was about seeing ourselves.

Patricia R. Zimmermann, for one, has talked about the ways in which home-movie technology occurred at the same time as the growth of suburbs and the nuclear family. Home-movie instruction manuals constructed gender in a particular way. They insisted that the technology was so simple even a woman could use the camera. As a genre, home movies are about the growth of leisure time, celebrating freedom and the goods of capitalism. It isn't about production, but the benefits garnered from production. So our home movies never showed my mother at work – the workplace is what home movies were explicitly not about.

My mother suffered from an ongoing desire for legitimacy, in class terms. She was raised poor and worked with my father to pull themselves into the middle classes. But by way of context, her first cousins were absolutely wealthy and she came from the poor branch. She was very earthy and proud of it. She couldn't abide pretension. On the other hand, there was a lot of pressure for her children to succeed, particularly through education. I'm the youngest by far and they had eased up by the time I came around. My parents made their money through an old-fashioned style of business, putting in long hours at a grocery store, and my father had a farm. But he didn't want that for us, which was quite different from the Chinese business milieu in the Caribbean where fathers expect their family to keep their business.

My mother, being third-generation, came from a group of Chinese who were very Westernized, creolized. Some had taken European last names, and many of my mother's cousins couldn't use chopsticks.

On a school form my mother didn't note her occupation as shopkeeper, but as a housewife. To construct herself as a housewife in 1960s Trinidad had a racial as well as class component, I think. White women might have described themselves as housewives. Similarly, we moved to a 'residential' area when I was four. The quotation marks signify that the word is a new one; the idea that a neighbourhood would be classed as residential was fresh and modern.

MH: Here's my favourite line of the movie: 'I look at her and I know who I am.' What a beautiful sentiment this is. But perhaps there is a shadow falling over this beauty as well?

RF: When I go back to Trinidad, I feel like Spiderman, trapped in a web of social relations. When I was growing up, I felt watched all the time. I felt that my place was fixed. After learning someone's last name, my mother could tell which part of the island their family was from and what their parents did. Social hierarchies were so stratified and clear-cut, it was difficult to move out of your class. Coming to Canada was liberating for me, because in a city like Toronto you can create yourself and form fresh relationships. It's a much more fluid society. When I had my first job, my boss was from Northern Ireland. He was Catholic and his wife was Protestant, and he said they could never have married in Ireland. It was Canada that allowed them to do this. At the same time, that fluidity could sometimes make me feel disconnected and alienated. But when I saw my mother, I was very aware of my genealogy, my roots, that social web.

When I go back to Trinidad, I am aware of the ways my physical movement is subtly controlled, more so than in Toronto. Because I'm Chinese and middle-class, I am unmarked in a suburban shopping mall, for instance. But in a working-class context my presence stands out. For instance, if I go to the market people might call out to me as Chinese and I become self-aware of my difference in class and race terms.

MH: In *Islands* (8:45 min, 2002), you reconvene John Huston's *Heaven Knows, Mr. Allison* (1957), which narrates the unfulfilled hopes of a marooned marine (Robert Mitchum) and an Irish nun (Deborah Kerr). The movie is set in the Pacific during World War II, but is filmed in Tobago more than a decade later. As your uncle was one of the extras hired to play a Japanese soldier, you foreground his part in a series of overlaid titles that makes the background visible and pushes the exertions of the film's stars into the background. Why did you begin this project? What is National Sex? Did your uncle Clive, your movie's main character, often speak of his experiences during the Huston movie?

RF: Actually, two of my maternal uncles were extras in that film. It was part of the family mythology growing up, as well as a glamorous moment in the history of the islands. *Fire Down Below* (1957), directed by Robert Parrish and also starring Mitchum, together with Rita Hayworth and Jack Lemmon, was shot in Trinidad around the same time. I imagine it had to do with the presence of the American bases during that period. I had long mulled over a larger project about my family's enlistment as

movie extras because they were Chinese in funny places – my brother was an extra in a Fu Manchu film when he was a university student in Ireland in the 1960s. But like many of my concepts, the idea mulled too long. My uncle Cecil died in Trinidad, and later my uncle Clive in Toronto. I had helped care for Clive when he got sick and I became fascinated by his life. Part of the narrative in *Islands* is the way the awkward masculinity of the Mitchum character paralleled my uncle's. He was a very manly man and his passion was hunting. He had his buddies, but to my knowledge, and according to my mother, he never had a romantic relationship – with either gender. He last worked on the offshore oil rigs in Trinidad and he had a car accident where I shot the blurry coconut trees that bookend the video. He stayed in a ditch overnight and was later put in traction for almost a year, but the hip had not been properly set, and after many operations he failed to heal. The real trigger for *Islands*, though, was the fact that the Huston film finally came out on video and I was able to see it for the first time. I found myself in the act of trying to recognize my uncles and the landscape of Tobago.

Islands

MH: When Huston's film is finished, your uncle sees it, though the filmed drama is undermined by the incongruity of animals appearing that have never been seen on the island, or nocturnal creatures appearing in daylight. Why were the islanders' reactions important to include in your movie?

RF: Actually, the animals are typically Trinbagonian and shouldn't be in the Pacific. This is a reference to the way so many Hollywood films featured the sound of the kookaburra, an Australian bird, to signal the African jungle – in Tarzan films, for example. But as an aside, I actually misidentified the bird in *Islands*. I don't think it is in fact a kookaburra, but something local that the sound recordist must have gathered. Interestingly, at a recent screening there was an Australian outside the theatre where *Islands* was playing and she said, 'That's an Australian bird.'

As for the cinema dynamics, in the Trinidad of my youth, cinemagoers spoke back to the films, made comments on the plot or actors, gave them advice, created their own humorous dialogue. I wanted to show that people were not passive viewers but actively reinterpreting and subverting the text right there in the act of consumption. There is a particular strategy of resistance in Trinidad that manifests itself in a kaiso aesthetic, a way of representing the world with a cutting, subversive wit.

MH: *Islands* ends with a tantalizing openness. Your closing two titles remark on the screening of *Heaven Knows*: 'Uncle Clive sees the stars close-up for the first time. He strains to see himself.' What follows is a montage of blurry, rescanned crowd scenes filled with indistinguishable figures. Are these hazy pictures the best Hollywood can do?

RF: Thus far, I'm afraid. This montage is composed of all the scenes in the films featuring the Japanese soldier extras. There are many Hollywood films I like, don't get me wrong, but they are still subject to overwhelming systemic pressures. For instance, for a film to get production money in Hollywood, you need stars – usually American stars – and the characters they portray become the moral and emotional centre of the film, no matter where it is set. Whether the location of the story is the Caribbean, Africa or the South Pacific, whether the film is socially or politically astute, it almost always ends up being about the American and from an American perspective. Even when the film criticizes the Americans, it's still about them. How can it be otherwise? The solution is to have more films made in places like Trinidad – which, by the way, had its first feature at the Toronto Film Festival this year: *Sistagod* by Yao Ramesar – and to give them proper distribution. Just like we want for Canadian films.

In the last while, there have been a couple of films that suggest a new trend, that is, using African-American actors to play African protagonists in American and/or British features. Prime examples are Forest Whitaker as Idi Amin in *The Last King of Scotland* (2006) and Don Cheadle as Paul Rusesabagina in *Hotel Rwanda* (2004). Cheadle will also portray Haitian revolutionary leader Toussaint L'Ouverture in an upcoming production. In the context of Hollywood film and American race relations, it's a positive development that black actors can get head billing. It's a long step ahead of white actors doing blackface in early cinema, or the long-standing practice in liberal films where racism or oppression is confronted by a white protagonist. An example would be *Cry Freedom* (1987), ostensibly about murdered black South African activist Steve Biko, but from the perspective of his white friend Donald Woods, played by Kevin Kline. But this new trend in casting doesn't necessarily move us beyond the Western standpoint on Africa or the Caribbean.

MH: *Sea in the Blood* (26 min, 2000) is a stunning work, deeply personal, wounded and lyrical. It narrates the story of your sister Nan who has a fatal blood disease, and marries this with the story of your lover Tim, who is HIV positive. This familial tragedy is filled with tenderness without ever becoming sentimental, and touches on difficult questions, allowing old hurts to be aired out with an inspired equanimity. How did you begin to structure this work? Was it difficult to speak to your mother about these past events? When did you know Tim would be part of the mix?

RF: It was awkward speaking to my mother about my missing my sister's death, as I knew it would take us back to a difficult place, one that neither of us really wanted to revisit. In the end I think it was cathartic: for her, in getting things off her chest, and for me, in hearing what she had to say and putting that pent-up conversation behind us.

Tim was always going to part of that mix, because it was through AIDS and the theoretical and political reflections and activism that it engendered that I began to rethink thalassemia and my family's history with illness and medicine. I always thought my father's pressuring all of us to study medicine had to do with a drive for upward mobility from his peasant background, but seeing four of his children die must surely have played into the mix. I was also interested in putting those two strands of my life together, as I set myself the challenge of intertwining – or colliding – established film genres, including the Asian family drama, the AIDS narrative, the gay memoir. On the concept side I was influenced by writing and activism about AIDS, particularly Douglas Crimp's essay 'Mourning and Militancy' (in *Out There: Marginalization and Contemporary Cultures*, ed. Russell Ferguson et al., 1990). Crimp was heavily involved in ACT UP New York, and when he talks about activists needing to also deal with loss and mourning, to confront emotions and not just political agendas, it struck a note. I lived in a communal house that was a centre of AIDS activism in Toronto. My partner

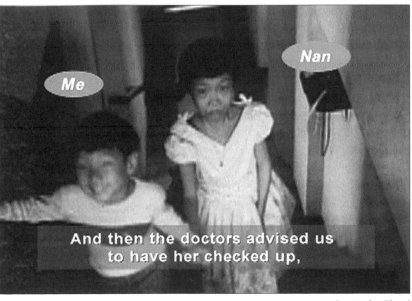

And then the doctors advised us to have her checked up,

Sea in the Blood

Tim and our housemate George Smith were founding members of AIDS *Action Now!* Everyone was involved to some extent. It was true that in the '80s and '90s so many people died and there was so much work to do to pressure governments for treatments, to demand rights for people living with HIV and AIDS, to fight for safer sex education and so on, that mourning was indeed less of a priority. Crimp uses psychoanalytic theory to talk about the consequences of neglecting to deal with the emotional fallout.

MH: Did you feel an overwhelming pressure during this pre-cocktail period to produce useful work, work that could be deployed in the struggle? What good could beauty bring when people were dying in such numbers and so near?

RF: I have never really made work directly tied to issues, that's something I admire in the work of someone like John Greyson. John is able to take up current issues and turn it into art, but I'm not able to respond so quickly. I did do some work on AIDS in that period, though, like *Fighting Chance* (32 min, 1990), a documentary on gay Asians and HIV done for a series produced by John and Michael Balser. I was doing AIDS work with the Gay Asian AIDS Project and was struck that the educational material that went out to gay men constructed gay men as white. The material made for Asian communities constructed Asians as heterosexual. Gay Asian men fell out of both paradigms. I was in workshops with other gay Asian men who felt that AIDS was something that couldn't happen to us. I attended one workshop with a man I knew to be positive, and who had come to the group seeking support, but the idea of being positive was so repressed he never disclosed. That was the reason I made *Fighting Chance*. It was filled with talking heads, because it was important to show gay Asian men who would appear onscreen and talk about being positive.

I don't recall thinking of *Sea in the Blood* as strategic; it was just a story I had sat on for a long time and finally wanted to get out of my system. I was nervous that anyone would want to see it, though, since as a programmer I knew that by that time audiences already tended to shun AIDS programs.

MH: *Steam Clean* (3:30 min, 1990) is a safe-sex bathhouse romp that follows an Asian male cruiser to his white-towelled consort. They kiss and jerk each other off, then one puts on a condom and fucks his new love. The titles 'Fuck safely use a condom' appear as overlaid titles in a variety of languages. Who was this tape made for? What was the response at the time, and what is the response to the tape now? I was going to ask, is it still 'effective,' does it still work, and then had to catch myself. Would the same questions be asked of a painting or sculpture? Most art doesn't carry the burden of eternity, and that's a good thing, right?

RF: The question of efficacy is quite appropriate in this case, actually, as this was a commission by Gay Men's Health Crisis in New York as one of their 'safer sex shorts.' These PSAs were meant to play in clubs and other gay venues to eroticize and therefore naturalize the idea of safer sex. They were 'community-specific,' and I was asked to do the Asian one. I addressed some of the conceptual and theoretical questions that arose for me in an article titled 'Shortcomings: Questions about Pornography as Pedagogy' (in Queer Looks, ed. Martha Gever, John Greyson, Pratibha Parmar, 1993). In this essay I tried to pull apart and examine the assumed relationships between subjects and objects of desire in a racialized context, and the (mal)functioning of sexually explicit images harnessed to an educational agenda. In the end, I have no idea how effective it was at accomplishing its various intended goals, but it did receive quite a bit a play, including most recently at the Guggenheim in their retrospective of AIDS media.

MH: In your 'Shortcomings' essay you write: 'I met Jean Carlomusto and Gregg Bordowitz, video production coordinators for GMHC, in 1989, at a conference on gay and lesbian representation. Although I am based in Canada, they approached me to produce the 'short' for Asians, presumably because they knew and liked my work, but also because they could not locate an openly gay Asian videomaker in the United States who would undertake such a project.' This comes as some surprise to me. While I don't imagine there are cities packed to the brim with videomakers of any stripe, the fact that not one openly gay, American Asian media artist came to mind seems strange.

In the same 'Shortcomings' essay, you go on to write:

I already knew that in depictions of sex between East Asian and white men, the Asian man was almost invariably the 'bottom.' I knew that this reproduced a stereotype that Asian men resented. I could not, therefore, portray the Chinese man as the 'passive' partner in anal intercourse if I wanted East and Southeast Asian men – the target group – to get pleasure in the tape. But what about the other man? Was it less problematic to show a South Asian getting fucked because, as a group, they are rarely represented sexually in North America? And how did all of this relate to the privileging of penile pleasure and patriarchal assumptions about the superiority of penetration? In the end, I had the Chinese man penetrate, though I attempted to 'equalize' the situation by having the Indian man sit on him, thereby asserting the pleasure of the anus.

I'm wondering if you would make the same choices today? You didn't go on to make more art porn – why is that?

RF: I'm not sure I would make the same choice today, because the context has changed and other video artists have taken on the question. There are some great subversive rejoinders to the whole thing. These include Wayne Yung's *Peter Fucking Wayne Fucking Peter* (1994) and Nguyen Tan Hoang's *Forever Bottom!* (1999). Both these tapes foreground anal pleasure in an erotic and a humorous way, respectively. Ming Yuen S. Ma also takes on these issues in several works.

Uncomfortable: The Art of Christopher Cozier

As for art porn, it never interested me as a consumer or as a producer. I don't find most attempts at the domestication of the porn genre successful – in fact, for the most part I do not find straight-up porn that interesting either.

MH: Why did you make *Uncomfortable: The Art of Christopher Cozier* (47:38 min, 2005)?

RF: It wasn't planned; I had a research production grant from the Canada Council for which I'd proposed a series of short works around sexuality and the nation state, looking at Canada and Trinidad and Tobago. I was interested in the fact that when Trinidad outlawed lesbian sex in the 1980s, it was a part of a larger set of legal changes in the Caribbean that brought lesbian sex under the law. Gay male sex, on the other hand, had been criminalized since the 1880s, when Britain introduced laws against sodomy. But Queen Victoria couldn't imagine women having sex together, so lesbian sex remained uncriminalized.

MH: Why were lesbians criminalized in the 1980s?

RF: In Trinidad it was related to feminist-inspired legal changes, which, for instance, allowed a man to be charged with the sexual assault of his wife. M. Jacqui Alexander, a Trinidad-born theorist who is now teaching at the University of Toronto did a lot of theoretical work around this question, which is how it came to my attention. At around the same period, Canada began accepting refugee claims based on gay/lesbian discrimination. I had been approached by a lawyer to write an affidavit for someone trying to move to Canada, and had to write convincingly about Caribbean homophobia. At the same time I was weary about rehashing old tropes of Third World backwardness. Besides, both Canada and Trinidad are more complicated when it comes to how queer people live their lives.

Anyway, I was in Trinidad doing research, talking to gay activists, but wasn't satisfied with how the project was going. I

didn't want to do a documentary about gays and lesbians in Trinidad and Tobago but something more essay-like. Then I was introduced to Christopher Cozier by a mutual friend and saw his blackboard piece, which looked at a certain construction of a Trinidadian national identity and its relation to xenophobia and homophobia.

He uses an old-fashioned blackboard, divided into two columns beneath the headings 'Us' and 'Them.' 'Us' lists supposed national characteristics: people who work hard, love their leaders and so on. On the other side is 'Them': white people, rich people, bullers (Trinidad slang for *sodomite*; it's connected to the word *bull*, which means *to sodomize*). I was struck that an artist I knew to be heterosexual would take this on, and so we began different sorts of exchanges.

What fascinated me about Christopher's work is the way he deploys that kaiso aesthetic I spoke about earlier in contemporary art. For instance, the way he deconstructs the use of wrought-iron grating on windows. These can be found not only in Trinidad and Tobago, but also anywhere that social disparity leads to burglary. In Trinidad, Chris noticed how people began to treat them as decoration and compete for original patterns. He responded by making eyeglasses with the wrought-iron pattern where the lenses should be, and two-sided cards with an identical image of a grille pattern on each side, but one says 'inside' and the other 'outside.'

Bars came onto our house only after I left in the 1970s. My sister became scared after a burglary, so my father barred the windows. When I was young, people were just beginning to put them up, so it's a relatively recent phenomenon. By now it's become so naturalized people don't see them anymore.

MH: How does Cozier's work relate to larger currents of dissent in Trinidad?

RF: Christopher's slyly critical stance is closely related to the quintessential Trinidadian art form: calypso. Non-Caribbean listeners may have only experienced calypso through its more recent manifestations like soca, or soul calypso, which is more pop-oriented and sometimes devoid of content. But calypso is a critical art form. The calypso singer often uses very crude sexual metaphors or makes dangerous commentary on local politics or world events, but escapes censure and censors through his or her verbal dexterity.

When the Americans established a military base during the World War II, traditional mores were upset. My aunt married an American soldier, for instance. And, as you would expect, there was a lot of prostitution. In his famous calypso 'Jean and Dinah,' the Mighty Sparrow sings that these prostitutes would never give him a second look, but now that the Americans are gone he claims he can have any of them. 'The Yankees gone, Sparrow take over now' is one of the refrains in the chorus. Even the well-known 'Rum and Coca Cola' talks about mother and daughter working for the American dollar. I don't remember if the Andrews Sisters cleaned it up when they turned it into an American hit.

Christopher's artworks are very much in this Trinidadian tradition. He nevertheless complains that at times he's dismissed as having too much foreign influence, because he has a Master of Fine Arts from Rutgers University, and because he often shows abroad. In both Trinidad and Canada there's an obsession with claiming and rejecting. I'm always struck when I open the papers and read that Keanu Reeves spent three years in Toronto as a teenager, or that Paul Haggis was born in London, Ontario. Trinidadians similarly claim but they also reject people much more often and fiercely than Canadians do – though remember how Ben Johnson suddenly became more Jamaican after the drugging scandal? Charges of foreignness are common. But if cultural and intellectual purity holds anywhere, it certainly doesn't in Trinidad and Tobago, since, as Christopher points out in *Uncomfortable*, the Caribbean was born in globalization as offshore production sites for Europe. Trinidad and Tobago has a population mostly brought in from Africa, Asia, Europe and the Middle East. The ways that people see themselves are in constant flux with transnational currents, so for instance even the Amerindian community has re-envisioned itself in recent years through contact with North American First Nations. This phenomenon isn't just a matter of one-way passive reception either. For example, international figures in black consciousness like C. L. R. James, Stokely Carmichael/Kwame Ture and Michael X came from Trinidad.

For me, what is going on in these debates about the local and the foreign is really different and competing visions for the direction of the country. So, for example, someone like Christopher would want to resist what he would see as the Miamification of Port of Spain in the development of shopping malls and gated communities. Yet someone who lives in a gated community might well reject the criticality and the contemporary forms in Christopher's work as 'imported.' This person might instead

champion one of the many painters of local flora and fauna and quaint village scenes as representing true Trinidadian art and values. I've noticed that the wealthier the household, the more ubiquitous are pictures of ramshackle houses and half-naked children. He or she may not know – or may ignore – the roots of their cherished local artworks in French and German painting of the 19th and early 20th centuries.

MH: You've shown work in Trinidad – are you a foreign currency?

RF: My work has screened there, but there aren't a lot of venues for the kind of work I do. Trinidad is a relatively wealthy society. It has a petroleum-based economy and one of the highest per-capita incomes in the Latin American region. But although there are several artists making interesting interventions, the art market is rather conservative and there is not a lot of backing for contemporary practice – no real grants, for example. The most exciting thing is CCA7, a contemporary art centre that houses a Canada Council residency and acts as a staging ground for interesting projects.

MH: Cozier's political engagements seem to flow directly into and out of his art practice; everything around him seems charged with a post-colonial current he is busy rerouting into his work. His personal identity and his identity as a citizen seem very close, at least in part because he has lived through the departure of the English empire and the establishment of a Trinidadian government. Is that part of what drew you to him?

RF: One of the questions I asked Christopher was: do you feel like an activist? He said no, he is an artist. But his work features an ongoing aesthetic and political critique. He remains socially engaged: the tape shows him doing documentation in a neighbourhood colonized from the swamp by squatters, hoping that by bringing witnesses there and working with people in the community he can weigh in against the eventual destruction of this

Dirty Laundry

place. But he is not an artist whose work is about slogans; instead he tries to spark epiphanies.

Christopher is a bit younger than me, but we both came of age during the fervour of independence, with a new flag and the inauguration of television (given as an independence gift). When I saw his blackboard piece, I recognized it immediately. It was installed in a large gallery before a flotilla of white-bread sandwiches wrapped in wax paper. Each bore a tiny national flag hoisted on a toothpick. I had taken similarly wrapped sandwiches to school. I grew up singing 'God Save the Queen' and then had to learn a new anthem when I was 10 or 11. Christopher and I share this moment of formation. His situation was different because his parents are both from the Barbados and came to work in the government, so there's a way in which the nation was the bread and butter of his family. He also lived in a quintessentially new middle-class suburb. Everything about his life is tied to a narrative of independence. A younger artist doing work about contemporary Trinidad wouldn't have such an obsession with the formation of the nation and citizenship and the promises of that moment.

MH: In *Dirty Laundry* (30:30 min, 1992), the remarks of historians, archival footage and onscreen text are woven into a present-day 'narrative' that takes place on a cross-Canada train. Researcher 'Roger Kwong's' great-grandfather was one of the thousands of immigrant Chinese workers hired to lay track. History, as you point out in the tape, consists largely of documents produced by those in power. Your project works the other side. Why did you reconvene history with these unusual layerings and why did you decide to tell these stories?

Dirty Laundry

RF: I became fascinated with Chinese-Canadian history because I came from another Chinese new-world context and was inserted into this one. The first Chinese came in small numbers as part of the gold rush, mostly from California. When the building of the national railway commenced, the Chinese were encouraged to immigrate. They worked longer hours and were paid less than other workers. They sent money back home to China, usually assuming they would return to China. When the railroad was finished, there was a head tax imposed on Chinese immigration. Then a Chinese exclusion act was introduced, barring all immigration, except for merchants, students and diplomats. It was very much a class imperative: if you were wealthy enough you could come; the law was designed to keep workers out. The class dimension to the immigration laws in the succeeding period has fallen out of the retelling of how restriction took place. I was interested in the way class played such a strong role in Chinese-Canadian history, and how that has been evacuated from the telling of that history, whether in government commissions or advocacy documents. Those were the triggers for my work.

The founding image for Chinese-Canadians is the building of the Canadian Pacific Railway, and around that the growth of bachelor societies on the West Coast attached to mining or the railroad. Only after World War II were Chinese women able to immigrate in large numbers and families could take root. Before that, Chinese communities were mostly comprised of single men, which made Chinatowns such interesting spaces. In Trinidad there was never a bachelor society. Men came to work first as indentured labourers, but because of different racial hierarchies, Chinese men intermarried with African women and later with Indian women. Most of the Chinese community in Trinidad is mixed-race. But because of the racial hierarchies in North America, the men remained bachelors, or married Native or Irish women. The Irish in that period weren't considered white.

I was interested in the way that in the current period the Chinese are thought of as a model minority – industrious, hard-working, high-achieving, accommodating to the system – and used against other minoritized communities. This is so different from the dominant image of the Chinese in the 19th century, associated with gambling, prostitution and crime. These two opposing stereotypes have actually competed for a long time, and if you look at the report of the Royal Commission on Chinese Immigration from 1885, you see both the positive and negative versions of the Chinese. I was interested in the importance of sexuality in these images – female prostitutes and male sodomites, or virtuous celibates. The negative images were pretty successfully cleaned up and repressed, though they surface every so often in stories about triads or massage parlours.

MH: Why did you reconvene history as a story?

RF: I've been long interested in the way that different forms have different abilities to communicate. Documentary relates certain kinds of truth, but fiction can communicate nuanced emotions. This arrived with the epiphany that what is considered avant-garde work is a fairly closed lexicon of gestures. It's codified in the same way as a documentary interview. In my work, I've moved between these different traditions. With *Sea in the Blood*, for example, I hired Carole Larson because of her experience editing fiction. I needed the technical construction of fiction to make the tape work.

Dirty Laundry has three layers: the proto-narrative (someone described it as the kind of narrative you see in a porn film, which is a good assessment) about a man riding cross-country on a train, interviews with historians and the historical documents brought to life as tableaux. I wanted each layer to undermine the other. Like many of my projects, it's an itch I'm scratching, an attempt to come to terms with something that's bothering me. I wanted to undermine a variety of forms while allowing them to speak.

MH: Whiteness was a term reserved for Anglo-Germanic countries, but broadened to include all of Europe in light of Asian immigrations. Pardon my naiveté, but why did so many public officials here in Canada (a nation of immigrants, after all, usurpers of Native land every one) make so many unapologetically racist statements for the public record?

RF: Well, racism was official ideology at the time. Remember that slavery was only abolished in the United States a mere 20 years before. So they did it because they could, and they hoped the constituencies they were speaking for would agree. There's a shifting bar of propriety determining which groups can be disparaged. We've seen this bar shift greatly in our own lifetime. In the 1970s, people said the most outrageous things about homosexuals in public discourse without shame or embarrassment. Now even right-wing politicians like Stephen Harper have to code their homophobia.

   Below today's bar are terrorists and pedophiles. One can say anything about them and few would come to their defence. Today it's hard to imagine the bar shifting to grant pedophiles more protection, but in ancient Greek societies certain kinds of pedophilia were the norm.

MH: You trace an early 'gay' Asian presence in the multiracial, largely male worker settlements attached to the railway. Bed-sharing was a common practice, though most men wouldn't openly identify as being gay. Historian Nayan Shah says the idea that sexuality is an integral part of identity is brand-new. Could you elaborate on this?

RF: Well, that was Michel Foucault's discovery, right? He looked at the way in Western society that sexuality is seen to hold the 'truth' about an individual. In earlier European societies, church laws inveigh against certain sexual practices, but those acts don't constitute an individual identity. There's a difference between what one does and who one is. When I came out to my mother, one of her responses was: why can't you get married and have a family? In traditional Confucian society, so long as men fulfilled their filial duties and produced offspring to worship their ancestors, no one cared about what they did outside their obligations. Don't ask, don't tell.

   This is different from the idea that you are what you desire. And that inner being matters to you and to society. This, though, is at the core of gay liberation: the task is to liberate the truth, the gayness inside, to bring it out of the closet. With the shift from gay and lesbian to queer in the last decade or so, this notion is slowly but surely being modified to accommodate a more fluid understanding of how sexuality works. In *Dirty Laundry*, the question for me remained: to what extent can one regard same-sex sexual activity in working-class Chinese communities of the 19th century as an ancestor to present-day Asian gays? The tape poses this question but avoids answering it. The audience is enticed to draw their own conclusions.

Richard Fung's Videos

Orientations: Lesbian and Gay Asians   56 min 1985
Chinese Characters   20:30 min 1986
The Way to My Father's Village   38 min 1988
Safe Place: A Videotape for Refugee Rights in Canada   32 min 1989
Fighting Chance   31 min 1990
Steam Clean   3:30 min 1990
My Mother's Place   49 min 1990
Out of the Blue   28 min 1991
Dirty Laundry   30:30 min 1996
School Fag   16:35 min 1998
Sea in the Blood   26 min 2000
Islands   8:45 min 2002
Uncomfortable: The Art of Christopher Crozier   47:38 min 2005

Distributed by Vtape.

Richard Fung is video artist, cultural critic and educator. His video narratives move through individual lives to explore the fateful repercussions of culture and history. The politics of race, sexual orientation and colonialism are central themes in his work. His lectures and writings are at the forefront of arts and cultural activism. He teaches at the Ontario College of Art and Design.

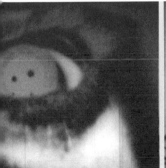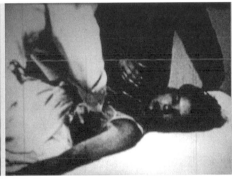

DISTRIBUTORS

Canada

Canadian Filmmakers Distribution Centre
401 Richmond St. W., Suite 119
Toronto, Ontario M5V 3A8
416.588.0725   fax 416.588.7956
cfmdc@cfmdc.org
www.cfmdc.org

Domino Film and Television International Limited
4002 Grey Avenue
Montreal, Quebec H4A 3P1
514.484.0446   fax 514.484.0468
www.dominofilm.ca

Jessica Bradley Art and Projects
1450 Dundas Street West
Toronto, Ontario M6J 1Y6
416.537.3125
info@jessicabradleyartprojects.com
www.jessicabradleyartprojects.com

Moving Images Distribution
402 West Pender Street, Suite 606
Vancouver, B.C. V6B 1T6
604.684.3014   fax 604.684.7165
mailbox@movingimages.ca
www.movingimages.ca

Tiny Sumo Entertainment
161 Bay Street, 27th Floor
Toronto, Ontario M5J 2S1
416.572.2590   fax 416.572.2201
www.tinysumo.com

Video Out International Distribution
1965 Main Street
Vancouver B.C. V5T 3C1
604.872.8449   fax 604.876.1185
www.videout.ca

Vidéographe
6560, Avenue de l'Esplanade, Suite 305
Montreal, Québec H2V 4L5
514.866.4720   fax 514.866.4725
info@videographe.qc.ca
www.videographe.qc.ca

Vtape
401 Richmond Street West, Suite 452
Toronto, Ontario M5V 3A8
416.351.1317   fax 416.351.1509
info@vtape.org
www.vtape.org

USA

Frameline
145 Ninth St., #300
San Francisco, California 94130
415.703.8650   fax 415 861 1404
info@frameline.org
www.frameline.org

Video Data Bank
The School/The Art Institute of Chicago
112 South Michigan Ave.
Chicago, IL 60603
312.345.3550   fax 312.541.8073
info@vdb.org
www.vdb.org

Women Make Movies
462 Broadway, Suite 500WS
New York, NY 10013
212.925.0606   fax 212.925.2052
info@wmm.com
www.wmm.com

Overseas

argos
Werfstraat 13 rue du Chantier
B-1000 Brussels, Belgium
+32 2 229 00 03   fax +32 2 223 73 31
info@argosarts.org
www.argosarts.org

Collectif Jeune Cinéma
Mains d'Oeuvres (atelier 11)
1 rue Charles Garnier 93 400 Saint Ouen, France
tél/fax : +33 (0)1 40 11 84 47
cjcinema@wanadoo.fr
www.cjcinema.org

LUX
18 Shacklewell Lane
London E8 2EZ
UK
www.lux.org.uk

Heure Exquise!
B. P. 113
Le Fort, avenue de Normandie
F-59370 Mons-en-Baroeul, France
+33 (0) 320 432 432   fax +22 (0) 320 432 433
contact@exquise.org
www.exquise.org

NMI/Netherlands Media Art Institute
Montevideo/Time Based Arts
Keizersgracht 264
1016 EV Amsterdam, The Netherlands
020 6237101   fax 020 6244423
info@nimk.nl
www.nimk.nl

MIKE HOOLBOOM

Mike Hoolboom is a Canadian artist working in film and video. He has made twenty films and videos, which have appeared in over 400 festivals, garnering 30 awards, including four in Oberhausen, a Golden Leopard at Locarno, and he has twice won the award for the best Canadian short at the Toronto International Film Festival. He has been granted two lifetime achievement awards, the first from the city of Toronto, and the second from the Mediawave Festival in Hungary. He has enjoyed retrospectives of his work at the Images Festival (Toronto), Visions du Reel (Switzerland), Cork International Festival (Ireland), Cinema de Balie (Amsterdam), Mediawave Festival (Hungary), Impakt Festival (Holland), Vila do Conde Festival (Portugal), Jihlava Documentary Festival (Czech Republic), Stuttgarter Filmwinter (Germany), Musée des Beaux-Arts de Caen (France) and the Buenos Aires International Festival (Argentina).

He is a founding member of the Pleasure Dome screening collective, and has worked as the artistic director of the Images Festival and as the experimental film co-ordinator at Canadian Filmmakers Distribution Centre. Since 2004, he has been working on Fringe Online (www.fringeonline.ca), a web project that makes available the archives of a number of Canadian media artists. This ongoing project currently consists of hundreds of pages of transcripts, reviews, interviews and scripts, and remains the largest publishing project in the Canadian fringe media sector.

He is the author of *Plague Years* and *Inside the Pleasure Dome: Fringe Film in Canada*. A novel, *The Steve Machine*, will be published in fall 2008 by Coach House Books.

Typeset in Scala and Scala Sans
Printed and bound at the Coach House on bpNichol Lane, 2008

Edited and designed by Alana Wilcox
Front cover image by Steve Reinke, from *Anthology of American Folk Song*, courtesy of the artist
Back cover image (repeated on pages 1 and 317) by Alex MacKenzie, from *Parallax*, courtesy of the artist

All images are stills from the artists' film and video works; the titles of the works from which they were taken appear in the caption below each still. Stills appear courtesy of the artists.

Coach House Books
401 Huron Street on bpNichol Lane
Toronto, Ontario M5S 2G5

800 367 6360
416 979 2217

mail@chbooks.com
www.chbooks.com